IMPORTANT

HERE IS YOUR REGISTRATION CODE TO ACCESS MCGRAW-HILL PREMIUM CONTENT AND MCGRAW-HILL ONLINE RESOURCES

For key premium online resources you need THIS CODE to gain access. Once the code is entered, you will be able to use the web resources for the length of your course.

Access is provided only if you have purchased a new book.

If the registration code is missing from this book, the registration screen on our website, and within your WebCT or Blackboard course will tell you how to obtain your new code. Your registration code can be used only once to establish access. It is not transferable.

To gain access to these online resources

1. **USE** your web browser to go to: **www.mhhe.com/dietsch**

2. **CLICK** on "First Time User"

3. **ENTER** the Registration Code printed on the tear-off bookmark on the right

4. After you have entered your registration code, click on "Register"

5. **FOLLOW** the instructions to setup your personal UserID and Password

6. **WRITE** your UserID and Password down for future reference. Keep it in a safe place.

If your course is using WebCT or Blackboard, you'll be able to use this code to access the McGraw-Hill content within your instructor's online course.

To gain access to the McGraw-Hill content in your instructor's WebCT or Blackboard course simply log into the course with the user ID and Password provided by your instructor. Enter the registration code exactly as it appears to the right when prompted by the system. You will only need to use this code the first time you click on McGraw-Hill content.

These instructions are specifically for student access. Instructors are not required to register via the above instructions.

The McGraw·Hill Companies

Mc Graw Hill **Higher Education**

0-07-319578-2 T/A DIETSCH: REASONING & WRITING WELL,
A RHETORIC, RESEARCH GUIDE, READER, AND HANDBOOK 4E

Thank you, and welcome to your McGraw-Hill Online Resources.

REGISTRATION CODE

G8JR-Y9P7-TTEH-9487-THW4

REGISTRATION CODE

The McGraw-Hill Companies

Mc Graw Hill **Higher Education**

REASONING & WRITING WELL

FOURTH EDITION

A Rhetoric, Research Guide, Reader, and Handbook

Betty Mattix Dietsch

Marion Technical College
Marion, Ohio

Boston   Burr Ridge, IL   Dubuque, IA   Madison, WI   New York   San Francisco   St. Louis
Bangkok   Bogotá   Caracas   Kuala Lumpur   Lisbon   London   Madrid   Mexico City
Milan   Montreal   New Delhi   Santiago   Seoul   Singapore   Sydney   Taipei   Toronto

Higher Education

REASONING AND WRITING WELL: A RHETORIC, RESEARCH GUIDE, READER, AND HANDBOOK
Published by McGraw-Hill, a business unit of The McGraw-Hill Companies, Inc., 1221 Avenue of the Americas,
New York, NY, 10020. Copyright © 2006, 2003, 2000, 1998 by Betty Mattix Dietsch. All rights reserved. No part of this
publication may be reproduced or distributed in any form or by any means, or stored in a database or retrieval system,
without the prior written consent of The McGraw-Hill Companies, Inc., including, but not limited to, in any network
or other electronic storage or transmission, or broadcast for distance learning.

Some ancillaries, including electronic and print components, may not be available to customers outside the United
States.

This book is printed on acid-free paper.

2 3 4 5 6 7 8 9 0 DOC/DOC 0 9 8 7

Student ISBN: 978-0-07-296297-0
Student MHID: 0-07-296297-6

Instructor ISBN: 978-0-07-321722-2
Instructor MHID: 0-07-321722-0

Editor in Chief: *Emily Barrosse*	Cover Designer: *Gino Cieslik*
Publisher: *Lisa Moore*	Manager, Photo Research: *Brian J. Pecko*
Sponsoring Editor: *Christopher Bennem*	Art Editor: *Katherine McNab*
Developmental Editor: *Joshua Feldman*	Cover Credit: © *2005 Getty Images*
Marketing Manager: *Lori DeShazo*	Senior Media Project Manager: *Todd Vaccaro*
Managing Editor: *Jean Dal Porto*	Senior Production Supervisor: *Carol A. Bielski*
Project Manager: *Becky Komro*	Permissions Coordinator: *Marty Granahan*
Art Director: *Jeanne Schreiber*	Composition: *G & S Typesetters*
Lead Designer: *Gino Cieslik*	Printing: *45 # New Era Matte, R. R. Donnelley*
Text Designer: *Maureen McCutcheon*	*and Sons, Inc./Crawfordsville, IN.*

Credits: The credits section for this book begins on page C-1 and is considered an extension of the copyright page.

Library of Congress Cataloging-in-Publication Data

Dietsch, Betty M.
    Reasoning and writing well : a rhetoric, research guide, reader, and handbook / Betty Mattix Dietsch.
        p. cm.
    Includes indexes.
    ISBN 0-07-296297-6 (softcover : alk. paper)
    1. English language—Rhetoric.   2. English language—Grammar—Handbooks, manuals, etc.   3. College
readers.   4. Report writing.   5. Reasoning.   I. Title.
PE1408.D5437 2006
808'.0427—dc22   2005041553

The Internet addresses listed in the text were accurate at the time of publication. The inclusion of a Web site does not
indicate an endorsement by the authors of McGraw-Hill, and McGraw-Hill does not guarantee the accuracy of the
information presented at these sites.

www.mhhe.com

This book is dedicated to my students, as well as the rhetoricians, composition theorists, and linguists upon whose work I build. To name them all would be impossible, but a few outstanding and influential names are in order, beginning with Aristotle (384–322 BC), who formulated rhetorical principles that are still widely used today. For his work in *Poetics,* Aristotle has been called the founder of literary criticism. Later Cicero (106–43 BC) and Quintilian (AD 40?–95?) developed and refined the process of argument.

I am also indebted to many twentieth-century critical thinkers and advocates of "plain writing," including John Dewey, Albert North Whitehead, E. B. White, William Strunk, William K. Zinsser, Jacques Barzun, Henry F. Graff, Edwin H. Newman, John Ciardi, Theodore M. Bernstein, Edward P. J. Corbett, John Langan, Judith Nadell, and Donald Murray. I appreciate, too, the work of Linda Flower, John Hayes, and Peter Elbow in formulating the basic steps of the writing process and that of Carl Rogers in argument.

CONTENTS

RHETORIC AND RESEARCH WRITING GUIDE   1

PART 1   The Context of Writing   2

PART 2   Revision Workshop: Rethinking the Draft   58

How Does the Rhetorical Situation Affect Information Design?   60

PART 4   Strategies for Critical Thinking, Evaluation, and Argument   224

PART 7   A Research Guide for Writers   420

THE READER: A Reader for Writers   541

THE HANDBOOK: A Guide to Grammar, Punctuation, Mechanics, and Usage   725

LIST OF FIGURES

A Note to Instructors

Reading, critical thinking, and writing are essential elements of an education. Recently, public speaking and oral presentations have been added to graduation requirements by many colleges and universities. These elements, cemented by a concern for ethics, serve as a solid foundation not only to higher education but also to a successful career.

To gain credibility in the workplace, employees must be able to present their ideas cogently, convincingly, and ethically, both in writing and in speaking. Yet in a recent survey, the National Association of Colleges and Employers found that the number one lack in "college job candidates [was] good communication skills." Debra Vargulish, college recruiter for Kennametal, Inc., said, "A lot of them don't know what to say at all." Although these applicants are skilled in technology, they tend to be "inarticulate," "shy," and unskilled in standard English (*Pittsburgh Post-Gazette* 6 Feb. 2005).

To help students meet and exceed requirements of their schools and employers, *Reasoning and Writing Well* demystifies the art of writing. Students learn to analyze the rhetorical situation and apply the four steps of the writing process. Succinct explanations and a wealth of student examples, as well as professional, show students how to sharpen their thinking and improve their writing. Workplace case studies and case problems present actual situations to consider and react to. Numerous opportunities for practice appear throughout the book. The central aims of *Reasoning and Writing Well* are to enable students to:

- Write with a purpose according to the rhetorical situation
- Consider the audience, topic, and occasion for writing
- Develop an awareness of the voice of the writer
- Read and think critically
- Interpret, evaluate, and react logically, objectively, and ethically
- Write clearly, concisely, and accurately
- Use language correctly and appropriately
- Understand and apply punctuation according to the context of a sentence
- Research a topic using a variety of print and electronic sources
- Document sources correctly and avoid plagiarism
- Improve time management skills, doing more in less time
- Give a presentation before an audience
- Prepare effective documents for a job search
- Appreciate the value of effective writing and speaking

The philosophy of *Reasoning and Writing Well*, fourth edition, is based on the belief that students at all levels of preparedness can be motivated to do their best through encouragement and clear, logical instruction in plain English. My philosophy has been shaped by experience in the workplace, graduate education at Ohio State University, over twenty-five years of teaching and curriculum development, participation in Toastmasters International, research, and professional writing. Employers, editors, reviewers, librarians, and students have all influenced the content of this book.

PROVEN FEATURES

Four books in one, *Reasoning and Writing Well*, fourth edition, provides not only convenience and value but also comprehensive coverage and abundant learning resources. Instructors have remarked that the "author demonstrates the principles advocated," and the text is "almost self-teaching." Proven features include the following:

Student Friendly

Students consistently comment that the tone of the book is friendly, respectful, and encouraging and that explanations are clear and examples helpful.

Career Focus

Timely and relevant, *Reasoning and Writing Well* provides practical reasons and examples, showing why writing and speaking skills are essential to succeed in college and the workplace. In addition, thirteen case studies, based on actual incidents in the workplace, offer insight into rhetorical situations and provide topics for writing. Related activities and case problems also offer opportunities for discussion and writing. Chapters 23, 24, and 25 are presented as a "Survival Guide: Preparing for Exams, Oral Presentations, and Employment."

In-depth Coverage of Rhetorical Strategies

The rhetorical situation is introduced in chapter 1 as integral to the writing process and is reinforced throughout the book. Students are asked to consider elements of the rhetorical situation and how the elements influence writing and speaking. Separate chapters cover each major rhetorical mode, including numerous student papers.

The Writing Process

In parts 1 and 2, step-by-step instructions explain the four stages of the writing process. These early chapters include clear, specific help for focusing ideas with topic sentences, thesis statements, purpose statements, working outlines, controlling questions, and examples.

A Unique Revision Workshop

Four chapters are devoted to the stages of revision, editing, and proofreading. Chapter 6 explains elements of effective paragraphs, including topic sentences, and shows various options for organization. An entire chapter, "Restyling Sentences," explains the voice of verbs, phrases and clauses, conjunctions, parallelism, eliminating wordiness, and using punctuation in five basic sentence structures. Positions of emphasis and the effects of various sentence lengths are also discussed. Chapter 8, "Selecting Effective Words," covers negative and positive words, trite phrases, jargon, abstract and concrete words, as well as sexism, racism, and ageism.

Critical Thinking, Problem Solving, and Argument Coverage

Five chapters focus on critical thinking, including the related skills of evaluation, problem solving, and argument—the most comprehensive coverage of these important academic and workplace skills available in a four-in-one composition text. Chapter 3, "Beginning to Think Critically: Accuracy and Ethics," opens with three reasons why accuracy and truth are important. Criteria are provided for evaluating so-called facts, distinguishing inferences and value judgments from fact, and avoiding hasty generalizations. Chapter 16, "Investigating Cause and Effect," continues this emphasis.

Chapter 17 explains Dewey's version of the scientific method and applies problem solving to report writing and research papers. Chapter 18 shows how the classic appeals of logos, ethos, and pathos can be combined in an effective argument. Chapter 19 explains how to recognize common logical and emotional fallacies.

Critical Reading Strategies

Students are taught how to read critically, take notes, interpret, defend a position on a literary work, and write papers that react and respond to literature. The three-chapter literature unit is unusually complete. Chapters 20, 21, and 22 focus on essays, short stories, drama, and poetry. The elements of each major genre and common literary devices are explained. This unit plus the Reader with its numerous essays and short stories, along with a novel, can be used for an entire literature course. (See sample syllabi in *The Idea Book: An Orientation and Resource Manual*.)

Comprehensive Research and Documentation Coverage

The five-chapter research guide provides thorough support for students writing research-based papers or reports. Chapter 26 explains three kinds of research papers and offers help in planning. Chapter 27 affords extensive help for conducting research both in the library and on the Internet. Chapter 28 presents separate sections on the latest Modern Language Association (MLA) and American Psychological Association (APA) formatting guidelines and documentation models. Chapter 29 explains and shows how to use sources to write research-based papers.

Included are a student outline and research paper in MLA style. Step-by-step instructions and numerous examples will help students through every stage of writing a research paper. Chapter 30 covers observation, interviews, and surveys, including a sample questionnaire, a student report of findings, and a student paper, based on observation.

Integrated Coverage of Writing and Researching on a Computer

Reasoning and Writing Well offers numerous tips and precautions to give students helpful "insider" information and alert them to possible pitfalls in writing and researching on a computer. Three Internet directories list reliable Web sites. Criteria are also provided for evaluating the reliability of Web sites.

Plentiful Student Models

Exemplary but realistic models of student writing appear throughout the book. Dozens of introductions, conclusions, outlines, and complete papers illustrate various rhetorical strategies and techniques for writing from sources.

Exceptional Learning Resources and Study Aids

In addition to the many essay assignments, *Reasoning and Writing Well* includes a wealth of resources for individual and collaborative learning: numerous guides to generating topic ideas, and abundant practice activities. Colorful study aids—checklists, guidelines, and boxes—appear throughout the text. Role plays, case studies, peer review exercises, and small group discussion guides help students strengthen their understanding of concepts and processes, analyze situations, and explore other points of view. Figures, tables, and other illustrations also help students to deepen their understanding while strengthening skills. More practice exercises and ready-to-use materials are provided in *The Idea Book: An Orientation and Resource Manual.*

Convenience and Flexibility

Chapters are arranged incrementally, yet this arrangement is flexible. Instructors can easily assign chapters in tandem with readings. Some instructors also combine composition and oral presentations (chapter 24). Others include résumé writing and letter writing (chapter 25). This book works particularly well for a two-course sequence of freshman composition and research writing. The five-chapter research guide is exceptionally complete.

Easy Access

For quick access to related readings and study skills, reference boxes appear at the ends of chapters. Colored cross-references abound in the margins. Cross-references in the Handbook will help students quickly find related examples and explanations in the rhetoric. To avoid confusion, the MLA and APA sections are separate and easily located by contrasting color strips. Directories are included in several chapters.

All-purpose Handbook

The Handbook contains all the references most first-year students will need: parts of speech, including gerunds, infinitives, participles, and misplaced modifiers; punctuation rules; capitalization; abbreviations; numbers; spelling tips; and glossary. In addition to providing numerous examples, the Handbook cites related *chapters in the rhetoric that explain punctuation in the context of sentence structure.* (To supplement the Handbook, grammar and usage worksheets are provided in *The Idea Book: An Orientation and Resource Manual.*)

Reader, Organized by Rhetorical Modes

Convenient reference boxes at the end of each rhetoric chapter cite page numbers of related readings in the Reader. A thematic table of contents is also included. This flexible structure suggests several groupings according to theme and avoids needless leafing through unused readings.

Famous Authors, as Well as Newer Ones

Forty-four engaging essays and short stories, representing diverse authors and points of view, compose the Reader. Maya Angelou, Amy Tan, C. S. Lewis, John Ciardi, Eudora Welty, Deborah Tannen, Elisabeth Kübler-Ross, John Updike, Kate Chopin, William Raspberry, Dan Greenburg, Andrew Sullivan, Stephen L. Carter, Judith Ortiz Cofer, Dan Henninger, and Nancy Masterson Sakamoto are among the authors.

NEW TO THE FOURTH EDITION

The fourth edition of *Reasoning and Writing Well* has been revised from cover to cover. The overall result is a keenly focused text that offers the latest coverage of such evolving topics as ethics, documentation styles, résumés, and Internet research. Among the many improvements are the following highlights:

Expanded Coverage of the Rhetorical Situation

Chapter 1 explains the rhetorical situation and the writing process. Chapter 2, "Thinking Rhetorically," shows how the rhetorical situation influences the writer's voice and includes coverage of levels of usage. Chapter 3 explains how accuracy and ethics build trust and influence readers' perception of the writer's voice. Chapter 24 explains how the rhetorical situation of writing differs from that of speaking. In fact, the rhetorical situation is referred to throughout the book.

Increased Emphasis on Critical Thinking and Reading

There is new in-depth analysis of the rhetorical situation and the benefits of reading widely. The introduction to critical thinking has been moved up to chapter 3. New material in part 2, "Revision Workshop: Rethinking the Draft," supplies criteria for evaluating a draft and strategies for reworking it. A new part 3 overview, "Mixing Writing Strategies for a Purpose," and other new material, including new professional examples, emphasize the rhetorical situation.

Parts 5, 6, and 7 continue this analytical approach, explaining criteria for evaluation and strategies to apply. Chapter 20, "Reading Critically and Responding to Essays," supplies a step-by-step reading strategy to increase comprehension. Part 7, "A Research Guide for Writers," provides step-by-step help for planning, using sources, and writing a research paper. In the Reader, three new introductions to pairs of arguments demonstrate objectivity by providing an overview of the issue.

New Sections on Ethics

In chapter 1, the reader is introduced to "Writing and Ethics." Chapter 3, "Beginning to Think Critically: Accuracy and Ethics," and chapter 13 continue this emphasis. Chapters 17, 18, and 19 link ethics to evaluation, argument, and fallacies. Chapter 24 discusses ethics and speaker credibility; chapter 25, ethics and accuracy of résumés. Several essays in the Reader discuss ethical concerns.

Hooks to Motivate Reluctant Readers

New openings for several chapters spell out benefits for readers. For example, chapter 1 begins with five important reasons why students should learn to reason and write well. Chapter 3 cites three practical reasons for achieving accuracy. Chapter 8, "Selecting Effective Words," discusses the advantages of reading widely, choosing words carefully, and cultivating civility. Chapter 25 opens with ten reasons résumés are discarded. These and other hooks should motivate students to learn.

Strategies for Writing Thesis Statements, Making Outlines, Taking Notes, and Reading Critically

Part 1 offers detailed explanations and examples to help students draft thesis sentences and expand scratch outlines into working outlines. Parts 3, 4, 5, and 7 show numerous examples. Chapters 20, 21, and 23 provide strategies for critical reading, taking notes, and analyzing content.

New Sections on Courtesy Words, Tact, Diplomacy, and Message Privacy

Unusual for a rhetoric, Chapter 8, "Selecting Effective Words," presents communication strategies to help students improve the tone of their messages and develop better pubic relation skills. Chapter 25 contains additional help, including "Ten Common Mistakes in Letters." Precautions for writing e-mail and posting résumés online are also provided.

Survival Guide

Three chapters have been revised and grouped as a "Survival Guide" to promote students' success not only in college but also in preparation for employment. The overview, "Fending Off the Wolves," points out the practical value of the guide for both college classes and a job search. Chapter 23 contains new sections on taking objective exams and on time management. Chapter 24 has more on incorporating visuals into presentations. Chapter 25 provides the latest help with résumés and other employment documents as well as new Internet directories of career Web sites. New features also include "Ten Reasons Résumés Are Discarded," "Writing a Summary of Qualifications," and "Handling Gaps in Work Experience."

Expanded and Updated Coverage of the Internet

The fourth edition contains timely tips and instruction for students who conduct Internet research. There are detailed criteria for evaluating both research material and Web sites, new directories of reliable Web sites, and new documentation models for online sources in the MLA and APA style sections. APA coverage has been thoroughly revised, according to the fifth edition of the *APA Publication Manual.* New MLA coverage is based on the sixth edition of the *MLA Handbook.*

Increased Help in Summarizing, Paraphrasing, and Quoting

Explanations and examples will help students distinguish the copied words that need to be enclosed in quotation marks from those that can be reused without quotation marks. A new section on *major* and *minor words* and *generic nouns* clarifies distinctions that often baffle students.

Annotated Research Paper

An exemplary student research paper (MLA style) on workers' compensation in chapter 29 has been annotated. This paper models research skills—summarizing, paraphrasing, integrating short and long quotations, and preparing an extensive works-cited list of both print and electronic sources.

Prevention of Plagiarism

Increased emphasis and help has been added to avoid this ogre. Chapters 26, 27, and 28 not only warn against plagiarism but also show how to prevent it. A new box, "How Easily Is Plagiarism Detected?" should convince most students that they cannot outwit a shrewd instructor.

Improved Organization and Access

Due to requests, critical thinking is introduced early in chapter 3. Since many high schools now teach prewriting and drafting, those topics have been condensed and combined in chapter 4. The research guide has been moved to the end of the rhetoric because research is generally taught in a second course. The subject index has been expanded and more cross-references have been added.

More Quick Reference Boxes

To spur students to start good study habits, a chapter 1 reference box, "Reading, Summarizing, and Other Study Skills," lists six skills sections. New boxes of checklists, tips, and guidelines have been added to other chapters and the Handbook. Updated reference boxes in chapters 9 to 18, 20, and 21 direct students to corresponding essays and stories in the Reader.

Fifteen New Readings

Fresh new topics will hook readers' interest. Three sets of arguments have been added on Wal-Mart, the "pursuit of happiness," and flag burning, along with introductions that provide overviews of these issues. The thematic table of contents groups multiple readings on similar themes for easy access.

Expanded Handbook

The Handbook now includes nouns, adjectives, and adverbs, as well as the other parts of speech. There is also new coverage of relative pronouns, gerunds, gerund phrases, participial phrases, infinitives, and misplaced modifiers. Examples show common errors and corrections. The section on arabic numbers has been expanded, and a new section on roman numerals has been added.

Marginal Catalyst 2.0 Icons

Icons have been added throughout the text, pointing students to further coverage of the subject at hand on Catalyst 2.0, McGraw-Hill's award-winning online reading, research, and writing resource. Catalyst 2.0 provides exercises, tutorials, reference material, and more, giving students the opportunity for further practice in strengthening the skills introduced in *Reasoning and Writing Well*. This coverage is located at www.mhhe.com/dietsch.

New Photos and Related Exercises

To make the book more visually appealing and practical, the fourth edition offers an updated interior design that includes new part-opening photos with practice writing exercises.

Revised and Expanded *Idea Book*

This unusually robust instructor's orientation and resource manual has been revised and enhanced to reflect all of the changes in the textbook. New elements also include several quizzes and four model syllabi.

PRINT AND ELECTRONIC SUPPLEMENTS

The Idea Book: An Orientation and Resource Manual

Designed for instructors with varying levels of experience, this manual to accompany *Reasoning and Writing Well* contains a wealth of materials. Included are sample syllabi, lesson plans, teaching objectives, supplemental assignments, answers to exercises, grammar worksheets, transparency masters, guides to selections in the Reader, a bank of quizzes, and activity worksheets. The *Idea Book* is available for download at www.mhhe.com/dietsch.

Online Learning Center Powered by Catalyst 2.0

The premier online tool for writing and research, Catalyst 2.0 features hundreds of interactive exercises, tutorials, reference materials, electronic bibliomakers for APA and MLA styles, and much more for both students and instructors. The *Reasoning and Writing Well* Web site <www.mhhe.com/dietsch> is compatible with most online course management systems, such as WebCT and BlackBoard.

For students the site provides 500 interactive grammar, punctuation, and editing exercises, as well as interactive activities focused on skills such as critical reading and evaluating Web sites. Chapter-by-chapter links in *Reasoning and Writing Well* offer easy access to Web sites. Marginal notes point students to specific sections of Catalyst 2.0 that extend coverage of the topic at hand into the online realm.

For instructors the Online Learning Center provides *The Idea Book: An Orientation and Resource Manual.* This unusual book includes answers to exercises, quizzes, and tests—which are password-protected for instructor use only. A wide array of other online resources are also provided for composition and speech instructors.

A NOTE OF GRATITUDE

This book could not have been written without the generosity of the many students who have contributed their work. Heartfelt gratitude is also extended to my Marion Technical Community College colleagues Professors Nancy Gilson and Leslie Weichenthal, as well as librarians David Evans, Nanette White, and Eden Wirth Allison. Also lending expertise, as well as encouragement, were family members George, Neil, Scott, Jeanne, Julie, and Christine.

My thanks also go to the reviewers who helped us develop this new edition of *Reasoning and Writing Well:* Harryette Brown, Eastfield College; Anita Bryan,

Northeast Mississippi Community College; Alisa Cooper, South Mountain Community College; Allisson Cummings, Southern New Hampshire University; Carl C. Curtis III, Liberty University; Arnold R. Girdharry, Bridgewater State College; Kimberly Harrison, Florida International University; Richard Randolph, Kauai Community College, Linda Rose, Cerritos College; Leslie Vitale, Mott Community College; and Michelle W. Zollars, Patrick Henry Community College.

Still deeply appreciated are the contributions of reviewers who helped guide the development of this text's first, second, and third editions: Robert Barnett, University of Michigan–Flint; Joyce Cherry, Albany State University; Gay Church, Northern Virginia Community College–Manassas; Barbara Cruz, San Antonio College; Michel A. de Benedictis, Miami Dade Community College; Gretchen E. DiGeronimo, Becker College; Helen Groves, University of Louisiana at Monroe; Tracy Haney, Walla Walla Community College; Sarah Harrison, Tyler Junior College; Michael J. Hricik, Westmoreland County Community College; Glenn D. Klopfenstein, Passaic County Community College; Michael Mackey, Community College of Denver; Miles S. McCrimmon, J. Sargeant Reynolds Community College; Shirley Nelson, Chattanooga State Technical Community College; Dr. Jeanie Page Randall, Austin Peay State University; Mary H. Sims, Ball State University; Ron Sudol, Oakland University; Martin T. Baum, Jamestown Community College; Patricia Blaine, Paducah Community College; Brian Cotter, Chattanooga State Technical Community College; Julie Ann Doty, Southeastern Illinois College; Joel B. Henderson, Chattanooga State Technical Community College; Linda Jarvis, Kilgore College; Dorothy Lockridge, Chattanooga State Technical Community College; Bill H. Lamb, Johnson County Community College; Robert Lesman, Northern Virginia Community College; Sharon Poat, Paducah Community College; Bonnie C. Plummer, Eastern Kentucky University; Jonah Rice, Southeastern Illinois College; Lana Richardson, Northeast Mississippi Community College; Deneen M. Shepherd, St. Louis, Community College at Forest Park; Phillip Sipiora, University of South Florida; and Marilyn Terrault, Macomb Community College.

Betty Mattix Dietsch
Marion, OH

WRITING GUIDE

RHETORIC AND RESEARCH

RHETORIC AND RESEARCH

The Context of Writing

© David Aubrey / CORBIS

The hatching of a chrysalis into a butterfly is rather like the hatching of an idea into an essay. Like a butterfly, an essay undergoes a process of growth that has four stages. Before an idea becomes an effective essay, it develops as the writer rethinks and revises. Then the full-fledged essay emerges, lovely to the eye and satisfying to the ear. Part 1 explains the rhetorical situation and the writing process to help you better understand the factors that influence writing.

1. How would you describe the writing process from your point of view?

2. Have you ever felt as if you were passing through various stages of social, intellectual, or spiritual growth? Describe your thoughts and feelings.

The Rhetorical Situation and the Writing Process

CHAPTER 1

> Freedom to be your best means nothing unless you're willing to do your best.
>
> —Colin Powell, *Priorities*

Rhetoric, the art of writing or speaking effectively, implies study and practice. But in this age of remote controls, fast food, and instant messaging, many Americans have come to expect instant results by expending little effort. Learning to write well, however, is neither quick nor effortless. Assessing a rhetorical situation, prewriting, drafting, revising, and proofreading take considerable time and energy. For students who have become used to learning just enough to pass a multiple-choice test, college and workplace writing will pose quite a challenge.

That's the bad news. Read on for the good news—the benefits for you.

WHY LEARN TO REASON AND WRITE WELL?

Possibly you take your ability to write for granted without much thought to improvement or the results that quality writing can yield. Perhaps you are unaware of the complex thinking skills that polished writing requires and the long-term advantages it provides. Here are five excellent reasons to exert the effort necessary to reason and write well.

Writing Sharpens Thinking Skills

Learning to write well will improve your thinking skills—your ability to question, analyze, evaluate, and make decisions. You will become not only more efficient in defining and sorting information but also more alert to possible cause-and-effect relationships. Your organizational skills will improve, enabling you to select writing strategies best suited to a particular rhetorical situation. By applying these strategies, you can pin down wayward thoughts, draft more quickly, and develop ideas more effectively.

Learning to write well will improve your ability to analyze a piece of literature or a situation. You'll learn up-to-date research strategies, how to digest and summarize information, and how to prepare an effective argument. As you improve your thinking skills, you can improve the quality of your life.

Writing Opens Opportunities to Learn

Writing is a process of discovery. As you write, you will discover thoughts and ideas that lie beneath the surface of your mind. You will become more aware of your own beliefs and values—what is important to you. Your curiosity may sprout and spur you to read and research new avenues. Writing assignments will challenge you to expand your knowledge, to become more aware of the forces that influence the way you think. You will be more alert to hasty generalizations, slick phrases, and common fallacies that often deter logical thinking.

Writing Nurtures Personal Development

As you deepen your awareness and improve your ability to put your thoughts on paper, your self-confidence will rise. The sound of your written voice and your spoken voice will become stronger and more confident. Learning to write and speak well fosters not only self-confidence but also a sense of control over your own affairs. The ability to communicate well gives you power to direct your life into channels you may have once thought impossible. Keeping a personal journal will help you track your progress, as well as provide ideas for essays. By recording significant events and impressions and thinking about them, you can identify your views and the reasoning behind them. You can set objectives, specify concerns, and rate your success. As you gain insights, you will grow and mature.

Writing Helps to Establish Relationships

The ability to write well and cultivate a friendly written voice will help you establish and maintain relationships with friends, family, coworkers, and clients. As you learn to select positive words, de-emphasize negative ideas, and style sentences effectively, the tone of your e-mails, letters, and other writing will improve. You will learn strategies to present negative news in ways that soften the tone and blunt the impact. Considering a rhetorical situation will give you insight into ways to make your writing effective while building relationships.

Writing Fosters Success in College and the Workplace

Skill in writing is crucial to succeed in college and to advance a career. Good writing skills can help land a job and single you out for promotion. As you learn to think and write well, your written work and your ability to present your thoughts orally in class and in employment interviews will improve. You will learn to tailor your résumé to highlight your skills and achievements. On the job you will be better prepared to think and write about real concerns and problems, whether in e-mail, memos, letters, reports, grants, or proposals.

Whether you relish or dread writing or range somewhere in between, *Reasoning and Writing Well* will guide and encourage you to do your best. As you expand your writing repertoire, you will learn how to assess the context of a piece of writing and respond appropriately.

WHAT IS THE RHETORICAL SITUATION?

Every piece of writing has a context or circumstance surrounding it—called the *rhetorical situation.* A rhetorical situation has five elements: the *occasion, purpose, topic, audience,* and *voice.* All five influence the effectiveness of writing. If a writer or speaker neglects any element, the message may ramble, go astray, or miss the mark. If the rhetorical situation is neglected, the primary goal of writing— to communicate—may not be attained.

Occasion for Writing

The *occasion* is the event, condition, or need that causes you to write. On the job your writing may spring from a client's need, a problem with a supplier, or another complication that requires a written response. Thinking about the nature of the occasion that prompts writing or speaking will help you determine your writing purpose, audience, topic, and voice. Various occasions with different audiences call for different writing strategies. For example, the occasion of writ-

ing an e-mail to a friend is quite unlike that of sending a cover letter to a prospective employer. And the occasion of giving an after-dinner speech is quite
different from that of paying tribute to the deceased at a funeral.

The occasion for classroom writing has certain implications, depending
upon the assignment. For example, in-class writing is not expected to be as polished as out-of-class papers, where several revisions are expected. Usually, your
instructor will give you a general purpose for a paper or presentation, but you
will choose the topic and the specific purpose. Often your classmates are the
audience.

CHECKLIST   ASSESSING AN OCCASION FOR WRITING

To assess an occasion for writing, ask yourself these four questions:

1. Why is there a need to write or speak?

2. What is required or expected?

3. What will be suitable for this situation?

4. What strategy will be effective?

Purpose for Writing

Purpose refers to a writer's reason for writing, which can be stated or implied. To
be clear, expository writing should have both a general purpose and a specific
purpose. Identifying your purpose early can help you keep your draft on track
and select organizational strategies to fit ideas.

The General Purpose   Writing has four general purposes: *to inform, to persuade, to express,* or *to entertain.* Often these general purposes are combined in
various ways. For example, most writing is intended to inform, but it also has
a secondary persuasive element: to convince the reader that it is factual and
reliable. Other writing is primarily persuasive, designed to argue a point and
secure agreement, yet it is also informative. The degree of persuasion varies according to the occasion, purpose, audience, and voice.

Some writing is primarily expressive, allowing the writer to reveal feelings
and opinions, often by recalling experience. Expressive writing may take the
form of personal essays, journal writing, diaries, poetry, fiction, or plays. Yet
you may also be expressive to a lesser extent in a business letter, report, or proposal, depending upon the rhetorical situation.

Although some humorous writing seems intended merely to entertain, it
may also make a serious point. The clever use of humor can advance a point, as
in the writing of Mark Twain. Former president Ronald Reagan used humor
in his speeches to sway the audience to his way of thinking. A lighthearted approach captures the attention of readers and makes them more willing to listen.
To be successful, humor must not be heavy-handed or derisive—otherwise, it
may backfire. See page 365.

The Specific Purpose   The specific purpose may be implied or stated. In literature the purpose is invariably implied in a theme that permeates the piece. In expository writing the purpose is usually stated directly for clarity, either in a topic sentence or in the thesis. In the introduction to *Watch Your Language*, Theodore M. Bernstein explains the specific purpose that directed the *New York Times* during his seven years as the assistant managing editor.

The first sentence below states Bernstein's specific purpose: to inform readers of the guiding editorial philosophy of the newspaper. The second sentence gives a valuable tip for assessing the audience.

> Today we think it well to make each issue as nearly self-sufficing as is reasonable so that the reader does not feel the need for a research staff to help him understand the day's news. Perhaps the best slogan a newspaper could post in its city room would be this: "Keep two readers always in mind: the high school sophomore and the man who has been marooned on a desert island for three months." Both of them, for different reasons, have to be told what it is all about.

Writing a Purpose Statement   A purpose statement is a helpful tool to explain the specific purpose, whether you are planning an essay, a research paper, or a report. To focus your thoughts and direct the flow of ideas while drafting, try writing a purpose statement. It can serve as a preliminary step to writing a topic sentence or a thesis statement. In the first example below, the general purpose is "to inform." The rest of the statement is the specific purpose.

- **Purpose:** To inform the reader of the advantages and disadvantages of TaxCut as opposed to Quicken.
- **Purpose:** To inform and entertain the reader by comparing the behavior of the male praying mantis to that of the female.
- **Purpose:** To convince the reader that the way medical personnel are portrayed on television is often unrealistic.

Topic

Writing topics spring from real situations in the workplace and in daily life. Perhaps there is an incorrect shipment, an overdue payment, or a progress report for a contractor. Then you have a specific rhetorical situation to respond to and little need to narrow the topic. Ordinary situations, injected with a bit of humor, can serve as the subjects of essays. Coping with contrary toddlers, mischievous pets, or disgruntled customers may provide interesting material. Or you might draw from other experience, such as travel, hobbies, vacations, unusual events, or interesting people you have met.

Whether you write from experience or from research, this book will show you how to proceed. Chapter 27 explains Internet opportunities at length because the Internet has greatly affected research and writing. Suggestions for topics appear at the ends of many chapters, which should stimulate your own ideas.

The first guideline for successful college writing is to *select a topic you care about.* The second is to *narrow the topic* so that you can focus the paper on one main idea and develop it well for your audience.

WRITING SUCCESS TIP: SELECTING AND NARROWING A TOPIC

Audience

The writer's *audience* is the reader. To accomplish your purpose, you should recognize, respect, and respond to your readers' needs. Knowing characteristics of their backgrounds, interests, and viewpoints will help you to choose a suitable topic and devise an appropriate writing strategy. The more you can learn about the person or group who will be reading your writing, the more effective you can make it. *Writing that is addressed to no one in particular will lack a sense of purpose.*

Before starting to write, you would do well to assess your audience: Who will be reading your writing or listening to your presentation? In the workplace your readers are probably people you have met or talked to on the telephone or communicated with via e-mail, teleconferencing, or videoconferencing. They may be coworkers, clients, wholesalers, service personnel, or others. In the classroom your instructor may assign an audience or suggest you write for your classmates. Or you might visualize a typical reader and write directly to him or her. If puzzled, ask yourself, "Who would be likely to read this writing or attend this presentation?"

1. **To whom am I writing?** What do I know about the age, gender, education, social class, economic status, interests, and attitudes of the readers? How will these characteristics influence my writing?

2. **Why will they read this piece of writing?** How can they benefit? Will they gain information? Be entertained? What else? (Predicting these answers will help you to capture the attention of the audience and maintain their interest.)

3. **How might they feel about the subject?** How will their feelings affect my word choice and writing strategy?

4. **How will they react to my point of view?** How should I approach the topic (based on their probable reaction)?

5. **How much do they need or want to know?** How much can I assume they already know about the subject? What terms should I define? How much should I say? (These questions will help to limit the topic and the amount of information.)

QUESTIONS TO ASSESS AN AUDIENCE

A helpful tactic in assessing your writing audience is to deliberately shift your perspective from writer to reader. Try to put yourself into the reader's role—to feel and think as the reader might. In "Don't Blame the Editors," Sloan Wilson explains this dual role of writer/reader:

Each of us is both writer and reader, and no reader has mercy for dullness. My editor, who as politely as possible had told me that my work was boring, had learned to speak for millions of readers, and I was grateful to him for making me clean up my act before putting it before the world's sleepy eyes. . . . Those listeners would start getting restless if I confused them; they demanded clarity above all else.

If a writer ignores readers and neglects their needs, they will respond by ignoring the writing. A keen awareness of how readers think and feel will assist you in shaping your writing purpose and in finding an appropriate voice.

The Voice of the Writer

The *voice* of writing is the presence of the writer as perceived by the reader. A writer has many voices, and the voice selected for a rhetorical situation will affect how the audience responds. The writer's voice shapes the sound and the effect of the words. Writers' voices are influenced not only by their knowledge, experience, and beliefs but also by their biases or impartiality—how they *feel* about the act of writing, the reader, and the topic. To listen to the sound of your written voice, read the piece aloud. How do you sound? Confident? Knowledgeable? Encouraging? Amused? Critical? Chapter 2 explains how the level of usage and degree of formality you choose affect the sound of your written voice.

To help you lessen frustration and start drafting easily, this book explains the writing process and provides numerous tips, checklists, and activities. To start, here is an overview of the writing process.

WHAT IS THE WRITING PROCESS?

> www.mhhe.com/dietsch
>
> For general information related to the writing process, visit:
> Writing

Assessing the rhetorical situation could be considered the preliminary stage of the writing process. This invisible stage requires thinking about why you are writing and how you can shape ideas appropriately for the rhetorical situation. Traditionally, the process has been divided into four stages that can be observed. Yet writing is rarely neat and linear, even though it may seem so if you have thought long about a subject. Most writers shuttle back and forth between stages.

Part 1 of this book focuses on the early stages of writing—considering the rhetorical situation, prewriting, and drafting. Critical thinking is also introduced, for the sooner you begin to focus on accuracy and logic, the fewer revisions you will need later. Part 2 focuses on concerns that arise during revision and editing. Although there is no one way to write, there are ways to make writing easier, faster, and more effective, which you will find as you traverse this book.

An excellent way to gain confidence is to dispel any myths you may have heard about writing. Then you will be less likely to become entangled in the "perfect draft" approach, expecting to perfect each sentence the first time. This

- **Prewriting.** The first stage of writing is simply setting forth ideas in whatever shape or form that is handy for you—fragments, lists, sentences, or clusters. The purpose of prewriting is to capture and preserve ideas.
- **Drafting.** While drafting, you transform ideas into sentences in a semiorganized manner. Here the purpose is to let your ideas develop, expand, and form connections. Drafting is primarily a stage of discovery and exploration.
- **Revision.** Although revision is classified as the third stage of writing, it is ongoing—recurring whenever needed. During revision your goal is to rethink ideas, refine them, and develop them. You may drastically reorganize the draft. During this time, you reshape ideas—expanding, deleting, and clarifying.
- **Editing/proofreading.** This final stage requires examining ideas, details, words, grammar, and punctuation—attending to matters *within each sentence.* Here the emphasis is on accuracy, correctness, and clarity.

FOUR STAGES OF THE WRITING PROCESS

method is tedious and exasperating. Those who use it proceed at a snail's pace. Nor will you be lulled by the false belief that inspiration alone can transform a first draft into a final draft without several revisions. High-quality papers require much more than an hour or two of effort. They require considerable thought and multiple revisions.

WRITING AND ETHICS

When writing poetry or fiction, authors create imaginary scenarios, characters, and events. But in expository writing, responsible writers present the whole truth: they do not fudge facts, misrepresent, mislead, or omit significant details. *Their purpose is to inform accurately, to express honestly, or to persuade ethically.* If they exaggerate to entertain or make a point, they do it in such a way that the exaggeration is apparent to the reader.

Responsible writers write about a topic they know, either from experience or from research. When citing the work of another, they give credit to the author and list the source of the material. They look at both sides of an issue and appraise it accurately and fairly. They clearly tell the reader what he or she needs to know. Writers who follow these ethical practices respect not only the rights of authors but also the right of readers to know the truth.

Throughout this book, you will find guidelines to help you write ethically. As you progress, you will become more aware of the risks of using unethical shortcuts such as unqualified generalizations, stereotypes, derogatory words, fallacies, and plagiarism. You will learn to read critically—to question and

See chapters 3, 18, 19.

analyze, to search for the real truth. You will also find tips and guidelines to help you write diplomatically. Reading and study tips, guidelines, checklists, and other study aids are placed strategically in various chapters.

FOR YOUR REFERENCE
Reading, Summarizing, and Other Study Skills

- **"Critical Reading."** Explains a strategy to increase reading comprehension and notetaking skills. See pages 292–294.
- **"Reading and Taking Notes."** Explains a strategy for taking notes on a literary work. See page 310.
- **"Research Reading."** Explains summarizing, paraphrasing, and quoting research. Includes examples. See pages 488–497.
- **"Making the Message Appropriate."** Provides valuable help with word choice. Covers triteness, clichés, denotation and connotation, negative and positive words, and courtesy words. See pages 112–117.
- **"Strategies to Prepare for Exams."** Includes reading tips, time management, reviewing, predicting exam questions, taking objective exams, and writing complete essay answers. See chapter 23.
- **Handbook Directory.** For quick answers to grammar, punctuation, and usage questions, turn to the directory on page 726.

THINKING ABOUT WHAT YOU HAVE LEARNED

Unless we think about what we learn and link it to our own lives, the learning can disappear as fast as snowflakes in May. Which points do you consider the most important in chapter 1? How can they benefit you? When can you begin to use them? Asking yourself such questions is an excellent way not only to recall knowledge but also to discover ideas.

PRACTICE

CASE PROBLEM: Responding to a Rhetorical Situation

Directions: Last night you went to a keg party just off campus. Three students spray-painted parked cars, but you just watched. Soon the police arrived, sirens screaming. The culprits threw down their paint cans and blended into the crowd. One can rolled near your feet, so you tossed it into the nearest trash can. Police questioned bystanders and noticed an orange smudge on your index finger. They handcuffed you and three guys, whose faces were misted with orange spray, and took you to the station. The three confessed; you were released. In a letter how would you tell the following people about the incident?

1.   Your guidance counselor
2.   Your best friend, who is doing her student teaching in a nearby town
3.   Your parents

Thinking Rhetorically

CHAPTER 2

> True ease in writing comes
>   from art, not chance,
> As those move easiest who
>   have learn'd to dance.
> 'Tis not enough no harshness
>   gives offence—
> The sound must seem an echo
>   to the sense.
>
> —Alexander Pope (1688–1744),
> *Essay on Criticism*, part ii, line 162

Alexander Pope knew that for writing to be effective, a writer must think about the sound of the written voice and the other rhetorical elements that influence it. The writer's voice must be consistent with the writer's purpose and appropriate for the occasion and the audience.* This guideline applies not only to poetry and other literature but also to college papers, workplace writing, and writing in daily life.

---

*I am indebted to Dona J. Hickey for her definitive work in *Developing a Written Voice* (1993), Mayfield Publishing Company.

THINKING ABOUT THE WRITER'S VOICE

The written voice is the sense of the writer's presence as perceived by the reader. The voice is like a mirror that reflects not only authority on a topic but also mind-set and personality. Beneath the words is the distinctive sound of the writer's voice, which radiates from word choice, phrasing, and sentence style. This voice reveals an attitude—positive, negative, or indifferent—toward the reader and toward the topic. The writer's voice may involve readers or irritate or offend.

As writers develop proficiency, they listen to the voice of their writing. They consider not only literal meanings of the words but also shadowy nuances—the subtle shades of meaning and feeling that accompany words. Some words are as soft and soothing as a lullaby. Some sound prickly; others crack like a whip. A writer's choice of words greatly influences how the audience perceives the message.

A writer has many voices that vary according to the rhetorical situation. In between the *conversational voice* and the *academic voice,* there is a range of voices that differ in the degree of formality. For college essays, you will be expected to have a clear, knowledgeable voice, perhaps informal but not overly so. For research papers, most teachers expect an academic voice with a confident, objective tone, written in third person. Now let's listen to the three different voices in this series of collection letters.

See page H-3 for *person of* pronouns.

A SERIES OF COLLECTION LETTERS

Just as the occasion and status of the reader change in each stage of the collection process, so too the writer's voice changes. As the urgency for payment escalates, the concern for the customer's feelings lessens. (Company policies vary.)

Stage 1: Cheery Reminder
(Assumption: Customer overlooked and will pay.)

Are you enjoying that lovely cherry desk you purchased on April 12? Will you please look around on it for your bill—which seems to have been overlooked.

Your payment is now five weeks overdue. If payment has already been mailed, please disregard this reminder. If not, take a minute to write a check for $55, the amount of your first month's payment.

Stage 2: Firm Request for Payment
(Assumption: Pressure needed to collect.)

For many years, you have been one of our preferred customers. We appreciate your patronage and your promptness in sending past payments. You have been fair and responsible; you have kept your credit in mint condition.

continued

WORKPLACE CASE STUDY

But now that A-1 rating has begun to slip away. You are two months behind on the cherry desk, purchased April 12. To protect your credit rating, stop by and pay the $115 (two payments plus interest) this week.

Stage 3: Demand
(Assumption: Warning needed to motivate payment.)

Your credit rating is in serious danger! Your payments on the desk, bought April 12, are three months overdue. To clear this obligation and avoid dealing with a collection agency, send $175 today.

If you are unable to clear the entire obligation, we would like to help you. To discuss an alternative payment plan, call us at (800) 555-9891.

Stage 4: Ultimatum
(Assumption: Customer may not pay.)

Unless payment is made within TEN DAYS of the above date, your bill will be turned over to a collection agency. A payment of $220 will clear your obligation for the desk, purchased April 12.

YOU CAN STOP THIS ACTION! Call us now at (800) 555-9891.

How Should a Writer's Voice Sound?

Readers expect a writer to be knowledgeable and reliable, to explain the topic clearly and accurately. Usually, they are quick to sense incompetence, insincerity, arrogance, or dishonesty. To be respected and believed, your written voice should reflect authority, sincerity, integrity, and (at the right times) empathy for the audience. Warm, understanding words help readers relax and accept the message. Most readers want a receptive, understanding voice, one that does not talk down or sound smug or superior. Most importantly, they want a voice they can trust.

Word Choice Influences Voice

www.mhhe.com/dietsch

For online resources related to word choice, check out:
Editing>Usage

See chapters 8, 10, 22.

Seasoned writers select words that are suitable for the occasion, purpose, and audience. They not only think about the meaning but also listen to the sound of the words. Precise nouns and vivid verbs specify exactly what the writer intends. Little surprises of sound, such as assonance and alliteration, dispel dullness and delight the ear. Using devices such as simile and metaphor can add depth of thought as well as interest.

To better understand voice in writing, think about what you do when chatting with a friend face to face. You automatically adapt your voice to the occasion and the listener. Your tone is pleasant and friendly. You welcome your friend by your words and manner. When writing informally, you might think of the reader as a friend and use a similar tone.

CONSIDERING HOW CASUAL CONVERSATION DIFFERS FROM FOCUSED WRITING

In casual conversation the spoken voice tends to be more friendly and less purposeful than the written voice. Casual conversation ambles along at a leisurely pace, often wordy and repetitive, perhaps punctuated by witticisms. Often fragmented and abbreviated, it may become sidetracked and never get to the point. The speaker may omit transitions and significant information. When this happens, the listener may frown, raise an eyebrow, or ask a question. Then the speaker has the opportunity to backtrack and explain.

In contrast, focused writing has a logical order—steadily advancing toward the point to be made. Since few writers have the chance to observe nonverbal feedback or to answer questions of the reader, they must exert more effort than conversationalists to be clear and diplomatic. To be effective, writing must be more specific, concise, and complete than casual conversation. The writer must also monitor the words more carefully to avoid offending. A keen ear for distinctions in usage and levels of formality is invaluable.

In college and on the job, you will be writing for different readers of e-mail, letters, reports, papers, and other documents. These pieces will require different voices, adapted to each occasion, purpose, topic, and audience. To achieve an appropriate voice, ask yourself three crucial questions:

- **Who will be reading this writing?** The motivation, interests, and values of the audience will influence how you shape your purpose. Think in terms of advantages: How can readers benefit? What approach will be effective and appropriate for the occasion?
- **What level of formality is appropriate?** Adapt your written voice to the occasion and the audience. Consider their expectations, culture, education, occupation, and gender.
- **Can I write reasonably about this topic?** Read your writing aloud. Does it sound fair, unbiased, and reasonable? Do the words say what you intend? Is the tone suitable? When you take a position or a particular point of view, do you present enough logical evidence to support your point and convince?

WRITING SUCCESS TIP: ASK THREE CRUCIAL QUESTIONS

THINKING ABOUT USAGE: STANDARD AND NONSTANDARD

With each technological advance, new generation, and fad, newborn words fly over the airwaves and into cyberspace. Dictionary publishers scramble to keep up by bringing out revised editions every few years. All dictionaries have two broad categories of usage: standard and nonstandard. For most audiences you will need standard usage for your writing. To determine the status of a word, consult a recent collegiate dictionary.

Standard Usage

To sound knowledgeable, a writer needs a command of standard usage. Most English words are standard usage, meaning they are widely accepted by educated speakers and writers. These words follow conventional spellings and rules of grammar. Standard usage varies widely, ranging from informal to formal words.

If a word in the dictionary has no usage label, then it is standard. Note, however, that some words have several meanings—both standard and nonstandard. So if you use the word, be sure to apply it in the context you intend. Some dictionaries provide examples showing usage. If a word is used primarily in conversation, it will be labeled *colloq.* or *colloquial, slang,* or *dialect.*

Sometimes the status of words changes. A word can also gain or lose acceptance as it acquires new meanings. For example, the word *punk* has several colloquial or slang meanings, but after *punk* was applied to a style of dress and music, that meaning became standard English. Often language is a mixture of the informal and formal, technical and nontechnical.

Nonstandard Usage

See chapter 25 for e-mail.

Although nonstandard words are sometimes used to lend a sense of realism to poetry and fiction, they are generally inappropriate in college and workplace writing. In fact, Bloomberg, the financial news and data company, filters electronic messages not only of its staff but also of traders and subscribers who use Bloomberg's desktop terminals. When profanity or ethnic, racial, or gender slurs are typed, a warning appears, and the user must reword the message before it can be sent.

Dialect and Regionalism   Words that are limited to a geographic area are identified as *dialect* or *regional.* Dialect is the natural way some folks talk, using colloquialisms such as "hit the road," regionalisms such as "down the road a piece," and fractured grammar such as "didn't never" or "them books." Such nonstandard usage can be difficult to understand. Although dialect is incorporated into some writing to suggest regional or informal speech, it should be avoided in academic papers and business writing.

Where Are Keys to Usage Labels and Abbreviations Found?

The keys to usage and abbreviations are usually located in the introduction of a dictionary. Here are nonstandard usage labels and their common abbreviations:

- N.S. or nonstd. = nonstandard
- substand.   = substandard
- dial.   = dialect
- vul.   = vulgar (common)

What If Dictionaries Disagree?   Since the spelling and the status of a word can change in a relatively short time, consult an up-to-date dictionary. Even then dictionary makers may not agree on the status of a word. For example, *complected* is listed as "regional dialect" or "substandard" in several dictionaries whereas *Merriam Webster's Collegiate Dictionary,* eleventh edition (2003) states, "Not an error, nor a dialectal term, nor nonstandard—all of which it has been labeled—*complected* still manages to raise hackles."*

If you are trying to decide whether or not to use a word of dubious status, it is safer to be conservative. Avoid the word lest the reader, unaware of the diversity in opinion, regard the word as an error.

Three Vocabularies: Speaking, Writing, and Reading

A factor that complicates word choice for beginning writers is that most of us have three distinct vocabularies—one for speaking, one for writing, and one for reading. The spoken vocabulary is the smallest and least formal; rough drafts are often written at this level. The vocabulary for writing lies somewhere in between those for speaking and reading. Your final draft, after being revised several times, should contain this middle level, which uses standard words and grammar.

The reading vocabulary is the largest, most specific, and most formal. Sometimes students pull words from this vocabulary or use a word found during research but do not look up the meaning. This practice can result in confusion and error. Awareness of the different levels of formality and your own three vocabularies can help you select an appropriate voice for each rhetorical situation.

THINKING ABOUT LEVELS OF FORMALITY

In college and workplace writing, three levels of formality—Informal English, Professional English, and Formal English—are used. All three levels follow the conventional rules of grammar. The level you select will depend on the rhetorical situation. The level of formality you choose will influence the sound of your written voice and how you are perceived by the reader. Normally, a writer's voice should sound knowledgeable, trustworthy, and kind.

www.mhhe.com/dietsch
For further work on levels of formality, visit:
Editing>Word Choice

Nonstandard	Informal English	Professional English	Formal English
Least _ _ _ _ _ _ _ _			*Most*
Formal			*Formal*
(nonstandard		Standard grammar	
grammar)			

LEVELS OF FORMALITY

---

*By permission from *Merriam-Webster's Collegiate® Dictionary,* Eleventh Edition. Copyright © 2004 by Merriam-Webster, Incorporated (www.merriam-webster.com).

Informal Standard English

Most of your writing in college and on the job will require complete sentences. Although Informal Standard English may include a well-placed fragment, the verb forms, pronoun agreement, and other grammatical structures are always standard. Dictionary entries usually label informal words, but not always in the same way; you may find either of two labels to denote *informal* usage:

- inf. = informal
- colloq. = colloquial (conversational or casual)

Informal Standard English is a language of conversation. You read Informal Standard English in many popular magazines, novels, short stories, poems, comics, ads, newspaper articles, and other writing. A *Wall Street Journal* article entitled "In 24-Hour Workplace, Day Care Is Moving to the Night Shift" uses Informal Standard English in the opening paragraphs:

> There are plenty of places to sleep at the Children's Choice Learning Center here, but nine-year-old Najah Finch isn't napping. Wearing a pink "I am Boy Crazy" T-shirt, she cartwheels around the floor, breaks for juice and popcorn, then settles down at the TV for a Muppet video. Najah's mom isn't due to pick her up for another three hours.
> At 3:30 a.m.

> —Barbara Carton

Did you note the conversational voice and the fragment "At 3:30 a.m."? Other clues to informality include the contraction *isn't* and the colloquial use of *mom* (mother). There are different varieties of Informal Standard English. Many business letters and printed materials require all sentences to be complete. The voice may be a bit more formal, as in Stuart M. Berger's *What Your Doctor Didn't Learn in Medical School:*

> The word *hypoglycemia* is the kind of six-syllable medicalese word that my patients hear and tell me: "That's Greek to me, doctor." Well, in the case of this word, it really is Greek! But just in case your ancient Greek is a tad rusty, let's review: *hypo* means "too little"; *gly* is the Greek root for "sugar"; and the suffix *-emia* means "of the blood." String them together, and you have "too little sugar in the blood." (The disease is the polar opposite of diabetes, which creates too much sugar in the blood.)

See page H-3 in the Handbook.

Watch the Pronouns   Did you notice Dr. Berger's use of the first person (*me*) and second person (*your*)? This usage is typical of Informal Standard English. Although Professional English and Formal English sometimes include the first person (*I, me, mine, we, our, us*), it is used only for a good reason. As a rule, these two levels do not include second person when written. In an oral presentation, second person is desirable since you will be talking directly to an audience—and you will probably mix levels of formality.

Mixing Levels of Formality   Once in a while, a writer may mix levels of formality for a special effect, but only for a purpose. Making a switch *between* paragraphs, as Barbara Carton did, is easier than doing so within a paragraph, which requires more transition. As a rule, it is better (and certainly easier) to use just one level of formality in business writing and academic papers.

Professional English

Professional English marks a writer as well-educated and knowledgeable. Certain audiences in the professional world (of business, higher education, and literature, for example) expect a more serious, reserved, and authoritative voice than that found at the informal level. Some writers call this level Edited American English. Actually, the term *level of formality* is somewhat misleading. *Range of formality* would be more accurate, but no one calls it that. Professional English contains the most words, so it goes *unlabeled* in all dictionaries.

The hallmarks of Professional English are complete sentences, correct grammar, and standard word choice. This level of usage is found in many newspaper articles, textbooks, business reports, annual reports to stockholders, and much academic writing, including research papers. In the article on twenty-four-hour day care, Barbara Carton's voice changes in the fourth paragraph, where she switches to Professional English. (Note that there are no contractions or informal words.)

> As more single parents and working couples cope with a 24-hour economy, day care is making an uneasy transition to night care. Employers are building round-the-clock centers to attract and keep employees. State and local governments are also supporting extended-hour and night-care initiatives, partly because they feel obliged to help the single mothers they sent to work under welfare reform.

Informal Standard	Professional English	Formal English
memos	memos, e-mail	legal notices, letters
customer letters	bulletins	proposals
newsletters	newsletters, letters	laws, statutes
sales talks	bids, proposals	legal documents
letter reports	professional reports	technical reports
informal speeches	presentations	formal speeches
conversation	policies	policies
newspaper articles	contracts, forms	contracts, forms
e-mail	manuals	technical documents

THREE LEVELS OF FORMALITY IN THE WORKPLACE

Formal English

You may be familiar with Formal English. If enrolled in prelaw, paralegal, education, premed, nursing, data processing, engineering, or other such programs, you may read Formal Technical English in your textbooks. Or you may work in a profession where it is spoken and written daily.

Formal English may include foreign phrases, literary allusions, and specialized or technical terms unknown to the average reader. The sentence structure tends to be long and complex, written in third person. All of these characteristics tend to make the voice of the writer impersonal.

Formal English usually goes unmarked in dictionaries, but archaic words and foreign phrases are labeled. If you find the following labels, you will know the words are formal:

- arch.   = archaic (antiquated or rarely used)
- obs.   = obsolete (used chiefly before 1775)
- poetic (found in poetry)

Formal English is primarily written. It is the language of technical manuals, some college textbooks, professional journals, formal reports, many insurance policies, and legal and government documents. The following passage from a legal decision written by former U.S. Supreme Court chief justice Earl Warren is easier to understand than many other legal documents:

> The plaintiffs contend that segregated public schools are not "equal" and cannot be made "equal," and that hence they are deprived of the equal protection of the laws. Because of the obvious importance of the question presented, the Court took jurisdiction. Argument was heard in the 1952 Term, and reargument was heard this Term on certain questions propounded by the Court.
>
> The School Segregation Decision of 1954
> *Brown versus Board of Education of Topeka, Kansas*
> 347 U.S. 487–496 (May 17, 1954)

CONSIDERING FOUR COMMON CONCERNS

Just as the level of formality should be appropriate for each occasion and audience, so too should the writer's voice. Students who have been exposed to informal talk on television and elsewhere may select an overly casual written voice. Although slang, informal abbreviations, and colloquialisms give an air of casual friendliness, they may cause problems in clarity. For much college writing, they are inappropriate. Switching pronouns in midsentence can cause confusion and disrupt the flow of the sentence. Knowing when to use prescriptive tone can help to avoid wordiness and achieve a confident voice.

Slang and Abbreviations

Slang is a quick, cool way to show that you belong to a group. In writing, however, don't assume that all readers will understand such words. Since slang tends to be ethnic, occupational, generational, or other group–centered, chances are that some readers may be baffled by it. For example, not all of you will perceive *cool* in the first sentence to mean *hip* as I intended. In this context, *cool* and *hip* mean *excellent, stylish, or fashionable.* Similarly, some informal abbreviations are indecipherable to many readers. For example, they may not have seen the abbreviations used in singles columns (SWF) or in instant messaging (lol) or heard them in teen talk.

www.mhhe.com/dietsch

For more help with slang and colloquialisms, go to: Editing>Clichés, Slang, Jargon, Colloquialism

Since many standard abbreviations are not widely used, they may also be unfamiliar. Guidelines for using abbreviations vary according to the purpose and style manual used. For example, abbreviations in a table differ from those used in a research paper. Another puzzling question is whether or not to use periods after abbreviations (not all require periods). For help with standard abbreviations, Modern Language Association (MLA) style, see page H-41 in the Handbook.

Misused Colloquialisms

Colloquialisms can add extra words and abruptly change the tone of writing. A sudden, unnecessary downshift to informality is jarring for the unsuspecting reader. Such shifts need to be made carefully and only for a sound reason. As you edit your college essays, watch for colloquialisms that differ in the level of formality from the rest of your writing. If you find one, check to see that it serves a purpose. Otherwise, substitute a standard synonym. To help you avoid some common colloquialisms, consider the following lists:

COLLOQUIAL	STANDARD
Steve downloaded *a lot* of songs.	Steve downloaded *many* songs.
She cleared the *stuff* out of her desk.	She cleared out her desk.
The client *really wants* to sell.	The client *is eager* to sell.
She got a *good deal* on her car.	Her Ford Escort was a *bargain*.
I'd hate to see her do that.	*I would prefer* she not do that.
Erin is an *awfully* good friend.	Erin is a *very* good friend.
Jason added his *two cents' worth*.	Jason added his *opinion*.
When did Sue *get married?*	When *was* Sue *married?*
He takes his *kids* to the office.	He takes his *children* to the office.
Bret is *looking to find* work.	Bret is *looking for* work (or a job).
"Toyota Is *Looking to* Build Hybrid in U.S. Plant" (headline)	Toyota Is *Planning to* Build. . .

Other colloquial expressions to avoid in expository writing are listed below, along with standard alternatives:

COLLOQUIAL	STANDARD
got shut down	was closed
seeing as	since, because
sort of	rather, somewhat
headache	problem, concern

a couple of	two
fight (verbal)	argument, quarrel, spat
really good	very good, excellent
mad	angry, irate, upset
ballpark figure	estimate
stuff	items, articles, supplies

Switching Pronouns in Midsentence

www.mhhe.com/dietsch

For help with pronouns, visit:
Editing>Pronouns

When students write the way they talk, they may suddenly switch from first-person to second-person pronouns unnecessarily. An abrupt shift in person changes the point of view and misdirects the flow of the sentence. Consider this student's rough draft:

> Years ago *I* would start my vegetable plants from seed because it was much cheaper, and *you* could get a jump on the season. But as *I* expanded my garden, more and more plants were needed, too many to grow from seed. So *I* would go to garden centers, which is exciting. *You* can select from dozens of kinds and dream of big, red, ripe tomatoes.

See page H-5 in the Handbook.

These unneeded shifts in person could be easily remedied by deleting each *you* and replacing it with an *I*. If you have this habit, beware of using *you* in academic writing except in process papers and business letters. Then use *you* correctly for a purpose.

Using Prescriptive Tone Appropriately

Just as a doctor prescribes medicine, a prescriptive writer offers advice, makes suggestions or requests, or issues a directive. Used appropriately, according to the rhetorical situation, prescriptive tone lends authority to a statement. Some prescriptive language is easily identified by the words *must, should, ought,* or *need,* as in the first example below. More often such statements begin with an action verb because the subject is implied (*understood you*), as shown in the other three examples.

APPROPRIATE:

- **Business etiquette manual:** The boss, not the employee, *should* issue the first invitation to a lunch, dinner, or party.
- **Emergency:** [You] Call 911 now! (The subject is implied.)
- **Process paper:** First, *detach* all the parts from their plastic frames.
- **Persuasive speech:** On the eve of the November election, *set* your alarm clock so that you can cast your ballot and fulfill your civic duty.

Yet prescription is sometimes unnecessary and undiplomatic. Inappropriate prescription can intrude, irritate, or inflame. As you read the examples below, think about each rhetorical situation and why prescription is inappropriate.

INAPPROPRIATE:

- **Order to friend:** Set the lawn mower up a notch. It's too low!
- **Order to roommate:** Call the phone company today and get this bill corrected!
- **Absolute generalization in a paper:** Setting goals *should* be a person's most important task in life.

In college papers you may be expected to use prescription to explain a process or argue a belief. For a report or actual situation, you may be expected to write a recommendation. Any prescriptive or descriptive language should be worded appropriately according to the occasion, purpose, topic, and audience.

Diplomatic Strategies

The most diplomatic director I have known kindly shared three "magic" phrases to precede suggestions and advice: "I wonder if," "It might," or "You might try." These tentative words soften the impact of statements in touchy situations. Another effective tact is to phrase a statement as a question and add a courtesy word. You might read the the following examples aloud and listen to how they differ in tone from the inappropriate examples above.

- *I wonder* if the lawn mower would work better if it were raised a notch?
- *Might* the blade need sharpening?
- It *might* be best to buy a new blade for the mower.
- Will you *please* call the phone company and have this bill corrected?
- Setting goals *is an* important objective for me.

Note that four of the five statements above do not include *you*. Using second person in ticklish situations can be unwise. If a person is testy or short-fused, you might try phrasing a suggestion or advice in third person with no reference to the individual. Or it might be wiser to say nothing at all.

THINKING ABOUT WHAT YOU HAVE LEARNED

How does casual conversation differ from focused writing? How can listening to your written voice help improve your writing? What other points in this chapter do you consider especially helpful? How can you apply them? When do you plan to start?

PRACTICE

REWRITING SLANG, COLLOQUIALISMS, AND CONTRACTIONS

Directions: When you find slang, colloquialisms, or contractions below, rephrase the sentence into Professional English. If the sentence is already Professional English, mark with a C.

1. Tasha is looking to buy a riding horse.
2. Seeing as Milo has the lead in the senior play, he'll miss basketball tryouts.
3. Jaden's new car is really sweet.
4. Tara and Grace had a fun time at the flea market.
5. Yesterday Lance had a client who was a big headache.
6. In the employees' lounge are some awfully good cinnamon rolls.
7. That's a ballpark figure.
8. Connor made a lot of money on eBay selling flea market stuff.
9. I heard Owen and Faith got married last week.
10. Caleb was really mad when Maya started dating Liam.

LEVELS OF FORMALITY FOR DIFFERENT AUDIENCES (FOR GROUPS)

Directions: Read the case problems below. Then discuss which level of formality would be best for each audience. Cite reasons.

1. You are a newspaper reporter interviewing Colin Powell for a feature in the Sunday paper about his career. Which level of formality will you use?
2. You are a systems analyst, and your boss has assigned a systems project. He has asked for weekly memo reports. What level of formality will you use?
3. You are writing a cover letter to mail with your résumé. What level of formality will you use?
4. You are writing a television commercial for antifreeze. You want to appeal to everyone who drives a car, so you are featuring a mechanic at a local garage. Which level of formality will you use?
5. Imagine you are a physician writing an article that describes a new treatment for cancer. The article will appear in a medical journal that is read primarily by other doctors. What level of formality will you use?

Beginning to Think Critically
Accuracy and Ethics

We live in an era when propaganda, myth, and other misinformation masquerade as truth. Unproven items are often repeated and widely believed before being discredited. When the star reporter of a major newspaper fabricates front-page stories, when bogus news and scams flood the Internet, when CEOs of major corporations plead guilty to fraud, and when well-known historians admit to plagiarism, one wonders what to believe.

> Whatever is only almost true is quite false, and among the most dangerous of errors, because being so near truth, it is the more likely to lead astray.
>
> —Henry Ward Beecher (1813–1887)

This climate of information confusion and moral relativism has influenced the programs and policies of our top business schools. Many now offer courses in ethics; for instance, Harvard has a course entitled "Leadership, Governance, and Accountability." The Columbia University Business School requires that all students take an ethics core curriculum. At the Mendoza College of Business at Notre Dame, long noted for its ethics research and education, Dean Carolyn Woo said: "We must challenge students about how much their values are worth and develop an awareness in them of the ethical implications of business decisions (*Wall Street Journal* 17 Sept. 2003: R9)."

The Kelley School of Business at Indiana University created a twenty-page conduct code that follows corporate models, covering topics such as "cheating, fabrication, plagiarism, professional behavior with recruiters, and proper classroom manners." The Fisher College of Business at Ohio State University originated a code that MBAs sign: "Honesty and integrity are the foundation from which I will measure my actions. I will hold myself accountable to adhere to these standards" (*Wall Street Journal* 17 Sept. 2003: R9).

WHY ARE ACCURACY AND TRUTH IMPORTANT?

Chapter 3 explores the answer to this question and lays the framework for critical thinking from an ethical perspective. You will find guidelines and examples to help detect any overstatement or half-truths in your own writing, as well as in research material. But first, here are three excellent reasons for making the effort to be accurate and for maintaining high ethical standards.

Employers Expect the Truth

When you apply for your next job, you may be surprised by the number of questions aimed at evaluating your character—your values, principles, and ethics. In all likelihood, your résumé and references will be closely checked to uncover possible padding, exaggerations, or fabrications. Fingerprinting may be required and a thorough background check made. The current climate of misinformation has led numerous companies to change their methods of evaluating prospective employees. If any deviation from the truth is found, that is a prime reason for rejection.

The *Wall Street Journal*/Harris Interactive survey (2003) revealed that 84 percent of the recruiters stated that "personal ethics and integrity are very important attributes in job candidates." Peter W. Schutz, former president and CEO of Porsche AG, agrees. Schutz advises: "Hire character. Train skill." Schutz is convinced that an employee's character greatly influences his or her work habits, reliability, and productivity (*Reader's Digest* May 2003).

Regardless of your future occupation, you need to know how to determine the truth and present yourself accurately on the job. You need to know the difference between fact, inference, and value judgment so that you do not confuse them. If you will be working with patients, accuracy may mean the difference between life and death. Inaccuracy and unethical conduct pose risks not only to reputations but also to patient health.

An Audience Expects the Truth

Readers expect expository writing to be factual and reliable. *As writers, we are ethically obligated to check our facts and examine our claims critically so that we provide the most accurate and up-to-date information possible.* But not all newspapers fulfill this obligation. The *Wall Street Journal* was so concerned with the public's perception of the media that it printed a groundbreaking letter from the publisher (3 Jan. 2001). Reprinted here are the first two points of "What We Value":

- **Fairness and accuracy.** There is no substitute in our business for getting the story right, and for putting it in context, for being both accurate and fair.
- **A clear distinction between news and views.** There are places in most any publication, and certainly in every newspaper, for both news and views, for reporting on and analyzing events and trends and for expressing opinions about those events and trends. . . . But we pursue these two missions separately. Our opinions are clearly labeled; our news judgments are arrived at independently.

Whether you write papers, reports, or letters, the two guidelines above can assist you in finding facts and presenting them to your audience.

Truth Is the Cornerstone of Trust

When someone lies and those lies come to light, doubt and skepticism shatter trust. Throughout the ages, civilizations have accepted the basic premise that truth is the cornerstone of trust. Truth undergirds trust in business as well as social relationships. The handshake after a business transaction is a symbol of that trust.

Businesses, partnerships, friendships, and marriages are built on truth and trust. Broken promises and contracts lead not only to ruptured relationships but also to legal problems and financial loss. Our courts take a firm stand on the need for truth in business and trade: Fraud, forgery, copyright infringement, slander, and other violations of truth are punishable by law.

EVALUATING: SEARCHING FOR TRUTH

www.mhhe.com/dietsch
For more help evaluating sources, go to:
Research>Source Evaluation Tutor (CARS)

To present information accurately, a writer must distinguish between facts that have been established and various forms of opinion. This is not always simple, for a statement may be a mixture of fact, theory, or faulty opinion. What is true in one instance may not be true in another.

What Is an "Established Fact"?

An *established fact* is one that is observable or one that has been rigorously tested and finally accepted by most authorities in the field. We can observe firsthand and verify that certain conditions, creatures, or objects exist. Scientists in a laboratory can test to compare blood types, DNA, and other materials; they can repeat experiments by others to verify the results. Surveys and polls, however, cannot be regarded as true for an entire population. They merely reveal what is true for the segment surveyed. Their results may represent trends in the entire population, depending on the reliability and validity of the survey.

See "Surveys" in chapter 30.

When you think something is probably true, consider whether or not it is an established fact. Can you find reliable research or other evidence to *prove* it? If not, then it is still in the realm of theory or opinion. (A *theory* is an inference that may or may not be true; it has not been proved.)

Evidence Accepted as Fact in Court

In court, sworn evidence and the risk of perjury should keep witnesses truthful. Yet there can still be problems in accuracy. Two eyewitnesses can disagree about the same event. Perhaps one did not see the entire event, or each interpreted it differently. Then too, recollections fade with time. Expert opinion seems to be reliable most of the time, but even experts disagree. Legally, fact is based on three types of evidence, sworn under oath:

1. Eyewitness reports
2. Expert opinion by an authority in the field
3. Material evidence (physical items that can be tested)

Without a doubt, material evidence is the most reliable of all. Hair, body fluids, DNA, fingerprints, voice prints, tire casts, and other materials can be carefully analyzed. Usually, the results are accurate, but once in a while human error does intrude. Even electronic devices are not foolproof. Temperature and other factors can hinder the performance of equipment, or someone may tamper with photographs, tapes, or other evidence. Determining what is true can be difficult.

Inferences Are Unproven

An *inference* is an assumption—an opinion—that is thought to be true but has not yet been proved. On a subzero morning, for example, a neighbor's car fails to start. This is the first time the engine has refused to budge. Since the gas gauge registers half full, he *infers* that the battery is weak. He calls a local service station for a quick charge. After that, the motor starts. A battery check reveals a faulty cell. Thus the inference has been proved to be a fact. Other inferences are tested and discredited.

As long as inferences are reasonable and not presented as facts, they seldom cause problems in writing. But sometimes beginning writers confuse inferences and facts, as in the following example about a hunting dog:

> When his owner's red pickup truck approaches his pen, Buck, realizes raccoon season must be here. During hunting season, his mind is strictly on tracking coon, but at other times his chief pleasure is chasing cats.

What are the problems here? First, dogs cannot understand the concept of "raccoon season" (although they might associate a truck with hunting). Second, the word *strictly* means 100 percent of the time, and it is doubtful that Buck thought about only one thing. Dogs are easily distracted by noises, other animals, and hunger pangs. The final statement—"his chief pleasure is chasing cats"—it is not an established fact but a value judgment. His chief pleasure might be eating.

Value Judgments and Point of View

Lew Wallace's familiar words, "Beauty is altogether in the eye of the beholder," point out the illusive nature of value judgments. Too often we regard our opinions as fact. Actually, they are perceptions, which can be illogical and unpredictable. Often we assume other people have (or should have) the same values we cherish. The problem is that value judgments are opinions that often masquerade as fact.

Value Judgment   A *value judgment* is an opinion, a subjective evaluation. We often hear value judgments in the form of ratings of worth or beauty or skill. Something or someone is labeled as bad or good, cheap or expensive, ugly or beautiful, poor or excellent. Actions are said to be crude or refined, foolish or wise, wrong or right, immoral or moral, according to one's value system and experience. Value judgments are imprecise and variable. They vary from person to person and change with the times. For instance, baseball cards were originally just prizes collected by schoolchildren from packs of bubble gum. Now the cards are considered valuable and sought by adult collectors.

Point of View   The way someone perceives something is referred to as *point of view* or *perspective*. Both terms can refer to either a way of thinking or the physical angle from which an object is seen. Our value judgments are based on our differing points of view. Sinclair Lewis, in his early novel *Main Street*, describes two young women who see the town of Gopher Prairie through very different eyes. The impressions of Carol Kennicott, a city girl from Minneapolis, reveal her point of view:

> She glanced through the fly-specked windows of the most pretentious building in sight, the one place which welcomed strangers and determined their opinion of the charm and luxury of Gopher Prairie—the Minniemashie

House. It was a tall lean shabby structure, three stories of yellow-streaked wood. . . . In the hotel office she could see a stretch of bare unclean floor, a line of rickety chairs with brass cuspidors. . . . The dining room beyond was a jungle of stained tablecloths and catsup bottles.

At the same time Bea Sorenson, "bored by farm work," walked along the other side of Main Street, thinking about the "excitements of city life" and the Minniemashie House. Her impression reveals very different judgments and a very different point of view:

A hotel, awful high, higher than Oscar Tollefson's new red barn; three storied, one right on top of another; you had to stick your head back to look clear up to the top. There was a swell traveling man in there—probably been to Chicago lots of times.

Carol and Bea, coming from varying backgrounds, view the town differently. Later they make value judgments about Gopher Prairie, based on their points of view. Carol thinks: "I must be wrong. People do live here. It can't be as ugly as—as I know it is! I must be wrong." But Bea reasoned that even if she didn't receive a salary of six dollars every week, she would work for much less "to be allowed to stay here."

CHARACTERISTICS OF FACTS, INFERENCES, AND VALUE JUDGMENTS

Fact	Inference	Value Judgment
Act, deed, event, state or condition of reality	Assumption, generalization, or decision derived from evidence	Opinion or estimate of worth, an evaluation or rating
Objectively proved by observation, experiment, eyewitness, or expert opinion	Has not been proved; has possibility of being proved or discredited	Cannot be proved; will always be an opinion

Evaluating the Writer's Voice

Depending upon the rhetorical situation, the tone of a writer's voice may range from essentially *objective* to highly *subjective*. Some writing requires an impersonal voice that presents the facts squarely. The front pages of many U.S. newspapers, for example, carry factual reports in which writers attempt to relay news stories objectively. The purpose is to report what happened—not to push a particular view. The voice of objective writing is impartial—unslanted and unbiased. Readers seldom get a sense of the writer's opinion or personality.

In contrast, the purpose of editorial pages is to allow writers to express their individual points of view and opinions. In editorials, columns, and letters to the editor, writers interpret facts subjectively, based on their own political, ethical, and economic values. They offer opinions and judgments; they praise and criticize; they urge specific courses of action. Their written voices may carry conviction, indignation, anger, amusement, or appreciation.

A degree of subjectivity is inevitable in almost any writing, but it should be controlled and appropriate. Reading your draft aloud will help you to listen to your written voice and judge its impartiality.

FOUR WAYS MISINFORMATION ARISES

As we grow up, we hear folk wisdom, propaganda, myths, superstitions, and other inaccuracies presented as fact. Steeped in these beliefs, we tend not to question them, and so we accumulate much misinformation without realizing it. Here are four ways misinformation commonly comes to be accepted as fact.

Expert Opinion Occasionally Changes

We all know that one should not swim for an hour after eating—or do we? This bit of advice was published by the American Red Cross over fifty years ago. A lifesaving manual claimed that a swimmer who ate immediately before a dip risked stomach cramps or even death. Now the *Journal of Health, Physical Education, and Recreation* disputes the idea of "stomach cramps." A prominent physical educator was quoted as saying that he had never seen a case of such stomach cramps, although he had seen thousands of persons swimming soon after meals. Medical opinions as well as other expert opinions sometimes change over the years.

A Small Survey Is Inadequate Proof

Sometimes we hear someone generalize after surveying a few friends or considering a few unusual incidents. It's the old story of "everyone else is getting a new prom dress but me." But a small sample is hardly a reliable survey (see chapter 30).

Overstatement, stereotypic thinking, and generalizing from an unrepresentative sample can lead to the fallacy of hasty generalization. A *hasty generalization* is a broad statement, an inference, that lacks sufficient proof. A hasty generalization can occur when a *trend* or a *tendency* is overstated as if it were true for an entire group or population. Although assumed to be true, a hasty generalization is not an established fact. (This fallacy and others are explained in chapter 19.)

Facts Are Misstated or Overstated

Unintentional misstatement or overstatement sometimes occurs. We may not recall exactly what we read or heard. Or we may paraphrase, using synonyms that give an impression different from the one we intended. And some people exaggerate without being aware of it. For example, the student who wrote the following paragraph was convinced it was absolutely true:

▶   Lack of participation by the American people in their government is the
number one cause for their loss of control over their own affairs. They say: "I
don't care." "My vote doesn't matter." "I didn't have time to vote." These are
some of the excuses given for not carrying out one of the most important
rights given to the people, the right to vote.

Here a partial truth has been stretched ("number one cause"). This so-called
statistic is not an established fact. The writer could have made the statement acceptable by adding one word, *possibly.*

Stereotyping Shuts Out Fact

A writer must be on guard against stereotypes based on gender, race/ethnicity,
sexual orientation, age, religion, and the like. Stereotyping is pigeonholing, classifying someone or something, into a tight little box. A stereotypic belief supposedly typifies a group, place, issue, or event. Although the characteristic attributed to the group may be true for some individuals, it is not true for all.
Consider the following statements carefully. Then mark each one true or false.

_____   1. Redheads have quick tempers.

_____   2. Men are stronger than women.

_____   3. Politicians can't be trusted.

If you marked all of the statements true, you have probably grown up hearing these stereotypes presented as fact. If you marked some false, you are to be
congratulated on your growing skepticism. If you marked all false, you rate an
A. Why are all three statements false? None allows for an exception. These statements are *absolute* or all-inclusive: they claim to apply 100 percent of the time.
Think about it. Do *all* redheads in the world have quick tempers? Are *all* men
stronger than *all* women? Isn't there even one politician who can be trusted? To
further complicate matters, item 2 contains an *undefined term.* What kind of
strength are we talking about—physical, emotional, intellectual, or spiritual?

Experienced speakers and writers avoid stereotypic thinking, for it is not
only unfair and undiplomatic but also inaccurate. Stereotypes shut out new information that conflicts with old, embedded beliefs. Stereotypic thinking is a
quagmire that can lead to charges of sexism and discrimination as well as hurt
feelings.

ETHICAL CONSIDERATIONS: WRITING RESPONSIBLY

Responsible writing presents the truth, and responsible claims are backed by
adequate evidence. Readers should not have to grope through a fog of unsupported statements to determine the facts. Once you become aware of the slip-
periness of fact, you can take three precautions to avoid misstatement: Limit
your generalizations, use absolute terms accurately, and identify inferences and
opinion.

Limiting Unsound Generalizations

To be accurate and useful in writing, generalizations must be factual. If they are overstated and too broad, they undermine your credibility. Thus you need to limit, or "qualify." *Qualifiers* are words or phrases that modify meanings and allow for exceptions. Qualified generalizations often serve as topic sentences and thesis statements. The generalizations below were used successfully as thesis sentences in student essays. (Qualifiers are italicized.)

- *Some* outstanding women have graced history with their heroic feats during battle.
- In today's hurried pace, the giving and receiving of love is *often* overlooked.
- Crash dieting *seems* to be the surefire approach to coping with obesity.

To limit an overly broad generalization for which you lack evidence, you may need a verb that indicates flexibility, such as *may, might, tend, seem,* or *appear.* Other qualifiers refer to indefinite numbers, such as a majority or a minority. Consider which one you are referring to, and state the indefinite number in an acceptable manner without overstatement.

WORDS TO INDICATE A MAJORITY OR A MINORITY

Without thinking, it is easy to overstate. If in doubt, check a dictionary for fine distinctions in meaning. To indicate a *majority,* select a term that means *over 50 percent,* similar to those listed below:

most	largely	routinely	as a rule	principally
mostly	primarily	typically	generally	essentially
chiefly	mainly	usually	normally	ordinarily

To indicate a *minority* (less than 50 percent), use words that are less specific than those referring to a majority. Note, too, that the size of a minority can vary and influence word choice. For example, there is a big difference between *a few* and *many.*

Small Minority		**Large Minority**	
rarely	relatively few	many	often
few	seldom	frequently	numerous
some	sometimes	oftentimes	countless
occasionally	several	profusion	plentiful

Using Absolute Terms Accurately

Absolute terms are inflexible words that state or imply *none* or *all.* These words mean zero or 100 percent. When you revise, examine every statement that contains an absolute term. Be sure you consider what the word means, not just what you intend. If you overstate a case by misusing an absolute, the reader will be apt to take the literal meaning unless you plant a clue that the statement is ironic or joking. The list below will help you recognize absolute terms:

all	always	everyone	no one
none	never	only	same
every	completely	exact	anything

Some verbs and adjectives are also precise and all-inclusive. Unless you have the evidence to support a hard-and-fast statement, look for an accurate alternative wording. When using the following words, think carefully, for they can lead to overstatement and misstatement:

DEFINITE	IDENTICAL	ONE OF A KIND	
is	exact	unique*	greatest
are	same	biggest	smallest
was	perfect*	worst	best

*There are no degrees of uniqueness or perfection. Something is either unique or not unique; perfect or imperfect. Phrases such as *very unique* or *very perfect* are incorrect. If in doubt about such usage, check a dictionary or style guide.

Can you find Peppermint Patty's absolute term?

PEANUTS reprinted by permission of United Feature Syndicate, Inc.

Identifying Inferences and Other Opinions

In workplace writing and college assignments, you may be asked to "draw a conclusion" (an inference) from a set of facts, to "write a reaction" (see chapter 20), or to "interpret facts." To complete such assignments successfully, you need to know how to identify inferences and other types of opinion. Qualifiers like those below indicate inferences:

theory	seems	probably	apparently
conjecture	imply	possibly	suggests
indicate	infer	evidently	it appears

As you revise, check to see that no opinions are presented as facts. For example, a widely held belief that is unproved should be identified as opinion. Phrases such as "a common belief" or "the conventional wisdom" indicate the tentative nature of such statements. Other terms that identify opinion include the following:

current thinking	viewpoint	reaction	perception
appraisal	impression	feeling	folk wisdom
point of view	estimate	prediction	view

REVISING FOR ACCURACY

Whether you write a report, an essay, a research paper, or some other document, double-check every item to be sure it is logical and accurate. In the flurry of pinning down ideas during prewriting and drafting, it is easy to leave out a word, transpose a number, overstate a generalization, or commit some other blunder. Develop the habit of being thorough, of questioning information that doesn't quite ring true or seems suspicious. The following checklist should be helpful.

CHECKLIST   REVISING FOR ACCURACY

1. Are all data established facts?

2. Have inferences, value judgments, and other opinions been qualified?

3. Do any generalizations need to be limited?

4. Are all words accurate?

5. Does the tone sound appropriate?

6. Have any significant facts been omitted? Are any more needed?

Only when we learn to think logically and critically—to analyze carefully our own ideas as well as the ideas of other speakers and writers—can we begin to approach "the whole truth." That is what the writing process is all about.

THINKING ABOUT WHAT YOU HAVE LEARNED

Why should you, as a writer, be concerned about accuracy and ethics? What points in this chapter did you find most interesting? Most helpful? What information can you begin to use? This chapter is the first of several that explain critical thinking. Below is a reference box, in case you wish to read on ahead about this subject.

FOR YOUR REFERENCE:
Accuracy, Ethics, and Guidelines

- "Investigating Cause and Effect," chapter 16
- "Shaping an Effective Argument," chapter 18
- "Detecting Fallacies," chapter 19
- Compiling a résumé: see chapter 25
- Criteria for evaluating sources and Web sites: see chapter 28
- Plagiarism: see chapter 29

PRACTICE

COLLABORATIVE LEARNING: Fact, Inference, or Value Judgment?

Directions: Mark each item as fact (F), inference (I), or value judgment (VJ). If both fact and inference, mark I; if both fact and value judgment, mark VJ. Discuss any disagreement.

_____ 1. Great Britain is an island, not a continent.

_____ 2. Many exquisite bays line Britain's coast.

_____ 3. The beautiful white cliffs of Dover, overlooking the English Channel, are composed of chalk.

_____ 4. The Isle of Man lies in the Irish Sea.

_____ 5. If you mention hunting to a Brit, he or she will immediately think of fox hunting.

_____ 6. Most Americans are surprised to learn that a subway in London is an underground passageway for pedestrians.

_____ 7. If you want a delicious meal in London, order fish, not steak.

_____ 8. The Tower of London is the most fabulous sight in the city.

_____ 9. In the spring after a rain, Paris has a delicate, shimmering beauty.

_____ 10. The Louvre, the largest art museum and palace in the world, is located on the north bank of the River Seine in Paris.

Prewriting and Drafting
Discovering and Developing Ideas

CHAPTER 4

I. STRATEGIES FOR PREWRITING

The first stage of the writing process is a time of discovery—you unearth raw material to shape and polish later. Prewriting can condense swirling thoughts into words. Prewriting can help you find a topic for your purpose and audience or enable you to narrow a broad topic. There is no need to think about order or correctness in the prewriting stage—*the objective is to produce as many ideas as possible.* You can prewrite however you like—on paper, at a keyboard, or with a tape recorder. Mystery novelist Agatha Christie often paused while washing dishes to jot down notes. Just pin down your ideas before they flit away. By trying all five prewriting strategies, you can find out which one works best for you.

> Most productive writers share the feeling that the first draft (and most . . . that follow) is an opportunity to discover what they have to say and how they can best say it.
>
> —**Donald Murray, "The Maker's Eye: Revising Your Own Manuscript"**

www.mhhe.com/dietsch

For online information about prewriting, visit:
Writing>Prewriting

FREEWRITING

Freewriting, uncensored writing in fragments or sentences, is a good way to find a topic and details. Just turn off your internal editor and jot down ideas. To save time, set a timer for ten minutes. When it rings, stop, examine your catch, and develop whatever seems promising. Here is an example:

> What to write? There's so much debris in my mind. Clutter. What is significant? Let's see. Life is significant—very much so. Yet some individuals toss it away so lightly. Just last week two young guys carried out a suicide pact. They were drinking and doing drugs. A bartender heard them planning but didn't tell anyone. Thought they were just talking—old saying, you know, those who talk won't. But they often do. How sad. They jump into eternity without a parachute, not knowing where they will land.

This freewriting sample has unearthed three general topics: the value of life, suicide, and the possibility of life after death. The writer might take one of these topics as the subject for a second round of freewriting or *focused freewriting*. During a second round, the writer freewrites about one topic.

BRAINSTORMING

Brainstorming is often used to create new products, improve existing products, or solve problems. You can brainstorm to find a topic for a paper, to narrow a topic, and to find supporting details. In a group, one person can record responses while others contribute. *The secret of success in brainstorming is to think fast and forgo criticism.* All ideas are respected, no matter how wild. Remarks such as "That won't work" dampen enthusiasm and dam the stream of ideas. A chalkboard is helpful for recording ideas because looking at them may trigger more.

Alone you can talk into a tape recorder without the distraction of making notes. Or you can write a general topic at the top of a sheet of paper and start jotting down possible ways to narrow it, as in this example:

WATER GARDENS

half barrels	landscaping a small pond	choosing fish and snails
molded ponds	selecting water plants	preventing algae
dig your own	building a waterfall	cost of materials
amount of labor	installing a fountain	legal liability

After you narrow your topic down to one aspect of water gardens, you can start listing possible supporting details.

CLUSTERING

Clustering, devised by Gabriele Rico, is uncensored brainstorming combined with doodling. To begin, take a fresh sheet of paper and write a general subject in the center. Then circle the word. As each new thought bursts forth, jot it near the word that prompted it. Circle the new word. Next, draw a line between the

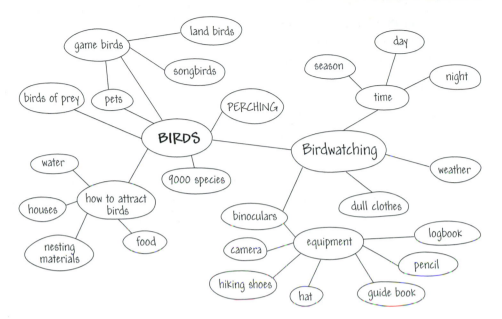

FIGURE 4.1 Clustering.

two. Repeat the procedure. The sample cluster (fig. 4.1) began with the subject of birds. The central idea branched out, leading to the specific topic of bird-watching.

QUESTIONING

By questioning and thoughtful reflection, you can take notes on a significant incident or event and transform them into an essay. You might try projecting yourself into the role of a reporter. What questions could you ask other people? Or you might ask yourself: "How did this event influence me? What did I learn?" Questions like these can prod your thinking toward a meaningful conclusion. Whenever your writing stalls, ask more questions to restart the flow of details. The traditional "five Ws and an H" (who? what? when? where? why? how?) can be expanded to full-fledged questions:

- Who was involved?
- What happened?
- When did it happen?
- Where did it happen?
- Why did it happen?
- How did it happen?
- What will its probable effect be?

- What can be learned?
- What is the subject like or unlike?
- How has it changed over time?

KEEPING A JOURNAL

Some instructors require that students keep journals to store ideas for writing. When you conduct firsthand research, a journal is useful for recording observations, impressions, reactions to a piece of literature, or incidents. For example, a student who worked in a restaurant researched nonverbal communication in her workplace. By smiling and lightly touching patrons as she served them, she found that her tips nearly doubled. The daily notes she kept in her journal provided the material for her report.

In some ways a journal is similar to a diary, but journals often include a wider range of material. A journal can be a private account of conversations, events, perceptions, reactions, or anything else you care to record. Some writers save quotations, funny stories, or poems. Any of these items may jump-start ideas for writing.

II. STRATEGIES FOR DRAFTING

www.mhhe.com/dietsch

For more coverage of drafting, go to: Writing>Drafting and Revising

The second stage of the writing process, drafting, is the time to develop ideas and start thinking about focus and order. With each new draft, you will discover more details the reader might desire to know. You can begin by scanning your prewriting notes and selecting core ideas.

FLESHING OUT PREWRITING NOTES

Start writing wherever you wish—beginning, middle, or end of your draft. There is no need to worry about a thesis statement, transitions, or other concerns just now. Don't stop to correct errors or do anything that will disrupt your concentration. Just keep writing!

Turn Off Your Internal Censor

Let ideas sprawl over the page in any fashion that seems comfortable to you. Don't worry if your first draft wanders into byways. Unnecessary details and mistakes may litter the path of your main idea. That's fine, since this draft is for your eyes only. You can rearrange and delete later. If your inner censor will not allow you free rein, then circle suspicious spellings or mark questionable words. If a word or idea eludes you, just draw a short line and keep on writing. Carefree, you will be more apt to experience the fun of discovering what you know as you write.

When Ideas Disappear

As you roam the hills and valleys of your memory, collecting bits of experience (incidents, anecdotes, examples, and other specific details) for your exploratory draft, sometimes there is little to find. That may be the time to stop and take a short exercise break. Refreshed, you can return and restart. To refocus and find more material, try asking yourself:

- What might readers like to know?
- How might readers feel about the topic?
- How do I feel about the topic? Why?
- What else needs to be said?

FOCUSING AN EXPLORATORY DRAFT

Some writers do much of their prewriting and drafting mentally before they ever start to write. They have a distinct sense of purpose and audience, which enables them to focus their exploratory draft surprisingly well. A clear central idea unifies the material so that it progresses in a logical way and fulfills the purpose. Other writers know the general topic but circle aimlessly around it, unsure of the central point they will make. Pausing to limit the topic and write a thesis statement, however, can establish a direction for writing.

Narrowing a Topic

When you narrow a topic, focus on a segment that you can develop well. Write more about less. If you find yourself rambling or lost while exploring your topic, stop and consider the range you are covering. Is the topic too broad? Can it be covered adequately in the required number of words? To be manageable, a topic should be whittled down to fit the assignment and the rhetorical situation. The pyramid below shows how a very broad topic (top of the pyramid) can be narrowed.

Ohio

touring Ohio

touring the Ohio River

steamboats on the Ohio River

my steamboat ride on the Ohio River

Identifying the Audience and Writing a Purpose Statement

If you have your topic clearly in mind and can state your purpose, that will save time in drafting. A purpose statement directs the flow of thought; it will provide the foundation for your thesis statement (which can be written later). First, jot down a brief description of your readers. This step will help to clarify your approach to the topic and the perspective you will take, as in these examples:

- **Audience for a letter to the editor:** Readers of the local paper who have never ridden a steamboat on the Ohio River.
- **Audience for a paper on litter control:** Voters who are concerned about the numerous cans and bottles littering city streets, roads, and highways.

See also page 124.

Next start writing a purpose statement. There are just two basic parts—the general purpose (italicized) and the specific purpose:

- **Purpose:** To *inform* readers about the scenic beauty of the Ohio River, the convenience of a steamboat trip, and the reasonable cost.
- **Purpose:** To *persuade* readers to vote for a bill requiring deposits on and recycling of all beverage cans and glass bottles.

WORKPLACE CASE STUDY

NITA NARROWS HER TOPIC

Over the years Nita Jones has read about solar energy, but she wonders about recent discoveries. She suspects that her general readers are also hazy about the topic and may not care. She asks several classmates and verifies both inferences. How can she interest them? How might they benefit from reading about solar energy? She writes her questions and starts a list to narrow the topic.

Question: How might readers benefit by learning more about solar energy?
Narrowing: general to specific

solar energy
practical applications for solar energy
solar heating for homes
solar heating during construction of new homes
solar heating for existing homes

As Nita reviews her list, she realizes that every reader is a potential home owner. At first she considers discussing applications for new home construction, but then she thinks about budget constraints. Few of her readers will be building their first home. Most will buy older homes and repair or remodel them. At this point, she briefly describes her audience and writes a purpose statement. Later she converts it into a thesis statement.

continued

- **Audience:** College students who are potential buyers of existing homes and who are interested in comfort at a reasonable cost
- **Purpose:** To inform the reader of solar heating applications for existing homes and to evaluate practicality
- **Thesis statement:** Solar heating installations can reduce fuel bills and improve the value of an older home. [states two advantages]

Drafting a Thesis Statement

Just as a topic sentence states the main idea of a paragraph, so too the *thesis statement* states the main idea of a paper. Both the topic sentence and the thesis statement act as a contract—a promise the writer makes to the reader. A thesis can be stated in just one sentence, or it may extend over several sentences. A thesis statement performs four specific functions:

FOUR FUNCTIONS OF A THESIS STATEMENT

1. Identify the subject.
2. State a claim, an approach, or an attitude.
3. Suggest the direction of the writing.
4. Set the tone.

Thesis statements come in all shapes and sizes. Throughout this book you will find various kinds and lengths in the professional examples and in the student papers. In the case study above, Nita cites two benefits. Michele Flahive's thesis below contains three parts. Her thesis demonstrates the four tasks of a thesis statement:

> **Thesis:** For the dedicated player, the challenge, the enjoyment, and the camaraderie make softball a game worth playing.
>
> > *Topic:* Playing softball
> >
> > *Claim:* For the dedicated player, softball is worth playing.
> >
> > *Direction:* The focus is on three main points—challenge, enjoyment, and camaraderie—in that order.
> >
> > *Tone:* Middle level of formality

The sooner you can write a tentative thesis statement, the fewer drafts you are likely to need.

Where Should the Thesis Statement Go?   Usually, the thesis statement is placed in the introduction, often in the opening paragraph of short papers. Sometimes it appears in the first sentence, but more often it is at the end of the opening paragraph. There it can forge a tight link to later paragraphs. In re-

www.mhhe.com/dietsch

For additional help writing your thesis statement, visit:

Writing>Thesis

search or other long papers, the introduction may contain two or more paragraphs. In that case, the thesis sentence generally appears at the end of the introduction.

Omitting a Thesis Statement   Some kinds of writing have a thesis that is never specified but is clearly implied. The omission is not a lapse. Careful planning and considerable skill are required to keep the controlling idea apparent without stating it openly. Omission of a thesis sentence is hazardous for a budding writer, especially for the kinds of writing often done in college. Most instructors expect an explicit thesis.

Dozens of different kinds of thesis statements appear in parts 2, 3, 4, and 5 of this book. You can find examples and explanations within the chapters as well as in the sample student papers.

DRAFTING A BASIC THESIS STATEMENT

The three-part thesis statement is an easy way for inexperienced writers to start drafting. Then it can be revised as desired. This basic thesis states the main points (usually three but adaptable for more) in the order they will be discussed—setting up the bare structure of the paper. To start, just make a list and fill in the blanks below:

Topic: _____

Main points: _____

_____

_____

Thesis statement: _____

_____

FOR PRACTICE

Choose a topic that can be divided into parts. For example, "Three reasons I chose _____ college/university." First, write the topic in the top blank. Second, think of reasons (main points) and list them in least- to most-important order. Third, condense and combine the items to make a complete sentence. Even if this tentative thesis doesn't seem quite right, it can act as a controlling idea and help you organize an exploratory draft.

Starting a Scratch Outline

www.mhhe.com/dietsch

For more coverage of outlines and outlining, go to:
Writing>Outlines

A brief outline will help you focus your essay and save time in organizing your paper. To start a scratch outline, place your thesis statement or your introduction at the top of your screen (or paper). Then examine your draft for clues to the order needed. For example, if you have main points, use an order of importance (see the outline on page 176). Or if you are describing a procedure or process, list the steps in chronological order, as you normally do them.

> **Introduction:** Present your thesis statement. Consider the reader. Do you need a definition or brief explanation of the topic? Is a warning necessary to forestall possible danger?
>
> **Body:** List steps of the procedure or process in chronological order.
>
> 1.
> 2.
> 3.
> 4.
> 5.
>
> **Conclusion:** Mention benefits or make another appropriate comment.

SCRATCH OUTLINE FOR A PROCEDURE OR PROCESS

Selecting a Title

If the muse smiles, you'll easily devise a clever title that is just right for your essay. But many of us have to wait until a draft is finished and we start revising before settling on a title. Even then we may be vaguely dissatisfied and ponder before finding an appropriate one.

The primary requirement for a title is relevance to the central idea. A title should give at least a hint of what is to come. If the title can also arouse the curiosity of the reader, so much the better. Some titles are specific, such as "The Myth of the Latin Woman." Others are more elusive and tantalizing, as are "Caterpillar Afternoon" and "When the Lullaby Ends." Still others appeal to a need for information, as does "Write Your Own Success Story." These and titles of other essays in the Reader (page 541) present a range of interesting approaches. To gain ideas, you might scan these essays.

DRAFTING AN INTRODUCTION

An effective introduction affords a graceful entry into the topic. Whether you draft your introduction first or last, keep your audience in mind. Make the first sentence notable. You might dangle an intriguing quotation, a striking statistic, or some other novelty to arouse curiosity and lure the reader on. Although a wide array of introductions appear throughout the book, here is a preview of five basic types.

www.mhhe.com/dietsch

For online help writing introductions, go to: Writing>Introductions

Begin with an Anecdote That Sets the Scene

An *anecdote,* or a brief narrative, can capture a reader's attention. You can begin by setting the scene. To orient readers and forestall puzzlement, state *when* and *where* the experience happened. Even a few carefully chosen details can give a sense of time and place:

My Worst Job

When I was sixteen, my cousin suggested I take a job where she worked. Because she liked the people and the wages, I hired on. The sight and sound were overwhelming. Rows and rows of sewing machines whirred while hundreds of women worked at a furious pace. Finding an empty chair, the trainer demonstrated how to operate the machine and sew a facing on the bodice of a cotton dress. Since I had made my own clothes for years, the task was simple. Outwardly, the power sewing machines resembled the old Singer at home. But the motor was as much like my old machine's as a Mercedes' is like a Model T's. Careening around the curves, I hung onto the cloth and somehow guided it under the presser foot. By lunch time, however, I had mastered the machine and the two-minute task. Day after day for an interminable week, I repeated that mind-numbing procedure.

www.mhhe.com/dietsch

For more work with pronouns, go to: Editing>Pronouns

Overuse of the Pronoun *I*   A successful narrative opening not only provides interest but also aids in avoiding *I* as the first word in a paper or paragraph. If your draft starts with *I*, you might move a prepositional phrase up front. Or you might invert the sentence, placing a subordinate clause first, as in the example above. Even one word, such as *yesterday, although,* or *while,* will provide a smoother opening than a reference to self.

To begin a first-person narrative, briefly tell when and where the action took place. Often a phrase of just three words or so will do. To help you start, here are some ideas.

OPENING WORDS TO SET THE SCENE

References to Time	References to Place
Five years ago I . . .	From my front window, I . . .
In 1999, I . . .	While working as assistant manager, I . . .
After I graduated	On Kelly's Island

WRITING SUCCESS TIP: THINK TWICE BEFORE OPENING WITH "I"

Using *I* as the first word focuses on the writer, not the reader, and makes writing sound amateurish. For example, a well-planned application letter for employment focuses unobtrusively on what the writer can do for the company. If, however, most sentences start with *I*, the interviewer may conclude that a supersize ego is not what the company needs.

Begin with a Description

A few words of artful description at the beginning of a paper can explain, illustrate, or provide a bit of background. In the following introduction, Kenny

Patrick sets the scene and informs his classmates about fly fishing, using vivid words to explain his fascination with the sport:

Hooked on a Tradition

Icy water swirls around the wading fly fisherman. With experience gained from thousands of casts, he deposits the tiny brown deer hair fly directly beneath an overhanging branch at the water's edge. His pulse quickens as he gently twitches the tip of the rod. Like a living being, the tiny fly dances across the surface.

Begin by Stating a Problem

Stating a problem can be a practical way to open. The purpose of Janet Edington's paper was to inform pet owners of ways to enhance the safety of animals when transporting them to the vet:

Safety First!

Pet owners are frequently faced with the challenge of transporting their animal friends to the veterinarian. This task can be not only nerve-wracking, but also hazardous, particularly if they are transporting a nervous cat or a large animal. In an automobile, an even-tempered pet can swiftly turn into a frightened, hostile enemy. The following suggestions are offered to spare anyone the battle scars I carry today.

Begin with a Surprising Statistic or Striking Bit of History

You may be able to spur a reader's curiosity with a surprising statistic or striking bit of history. The purpose of Kathy Cordle's paper was to inform classmates of a way, which worked for her, to stop smoking:

Kicking the Habit

Concern about the hazards of tobacco is not new. In 1604 King James I of England officially condemned the use of tobacco. An 1859 report about the dangers of tobacco stated that of the sixty-eight persons suffering from cancer of the mouth and throat in a hospital in Montpelier, France, all were tobacco users. In the United States during the early 1900s, admonitions such as "Don't smoke, or it will stunt your growth" and "Now that you are expecting, you'll have to lay off smoking" were common.

Begin by Disputing a Common Belief or Defying a Stereotype

The writer who surprises readers with a statement that disputes a common belief or an example that defies a stereotype will grab their attention. In the next paragraph, Paul Giacalone's purpose was to entertain his classmates. He begins by expressing a view that runs counter to the conventional notion that everyone should love the family dog. His offbeat perspective and critically amused tone surprises readers and hooks their curiosity.

▶ **The Trials of Tia**

Recently my father brought home a very small and very ignorant animal. My parents named it Tia, and they have tried to convince me that it is a dog— I swear it is a rat. Actually, Tia is half rat terrier and half poodle—a strange-looking animal that has not been easy to train. Therein lies the nub of the problem.

SEVEN BASIC WAYS TO ORGANIZE A DRAFT

To be clear and readable, every completed manuscript should have a logical order. As you sort through your prewriting notes and write your first draft, watch for a dominant order to emerge. Look closely at the transitions you have included. Do they refer to time? To location? To cause and effect? Are some points more important than others? Or does your thesis statement contain a clue to a suitable order? Seven basic orders are commonly used, and combined, to organize writing.

THE SEVEN BASIC ORDERS

1. **Chronological order** (time): chronological/reverse chronological
2. **Spatial order** (space): organized by layout, design, direction, or location
3. **Order of importance:** least to most/most to least
4. **Order of generality:** general to specific/specific to general
5. **Order of formation:** whole to parts/parts to whole
6. **Order of complexity:** simple to complex/familiar to unfamiliar
7. **Order of materiality:** concrete to abstract/abstract to concrete

Chronological Order

When dates or events are placed in a natural sequence according to *time,* this arrangement is known as *chronological order.* In process analysis you arrange the steps or stages chronologically (1, 2, 3, etc.). In a research paper, you may combine chronological order with other orders. Narratives usually move forward in chronological order, but not always. A sidewise shift in time may be indicated by transitions such as "meanwhile" or "at the same time."

Résumés are usually organized in *reverse chronological order.* This arrangement presents the most recent experience first, then goes backward, ending with the earliest.

Spatial Order

Organizing details according to location, layout, design, or direction is referred to as *spatial* order. For example, property descriptions use spatial order. In the essay "Through a Child's Eyes," the student writer describes her father, beginning with his head and moving down to his lap (see pages 80–81). Any of the following spatial orders (or their reverse) might be used in description:

head to toe	outside to inside	clockwise
bottom to top	north to south	circular
left to right	up and down	horizontal

Order of Importance

Newspaper articles typically use *most- to least-important* order, beginning with the most important information and leaving the least important details until last. Editors know that readers often read only the first few paragraphs of an article or only the front page section. For other writing, *least- to most-important* order is often used. This order places the emphasis on the final point. You might use least- to most-important order in essays of division, classification, illustration, or argument.

See "Buckeye Fever," pages 180–181.

Order of Generality

The order of generality is effective to inform or to convince. You can begin or end with an observation, generalization, or basic principle, depending on the rhetorical situation. To use the *general-to-specific* (deductive) order, you begin with the (general) basic premise, then supply enough specific details to support it. For example, a student wrote, "The magic of a carousel has a way of turning men and women into children again." Then she presented specific details to support her observation.

If the reader will need to be convinced, you can reverse the order to *specific to general*. This *inductive* order is often used in argument; the evidence is presented before the conclusion.

Order of Formation

The order of formation may be used in two ways: *whole to parts* or *parts to whole*. In problem solving, the whole-to-parts arrangement works well. You can present an overview of the topic before covering all significant alternatives, angles, or parts. You begin with a summary of a problem or an issue, then move on to look at the individual factors or aspects. In a basic argument, the whole-to-parts order is often used to describe the issue, followed by inductive reasoning (see chapter 18).

The whole-to-parts order can also be used to explain less complicated topics. For example, a student described an old rocking chair, starting with the overall appearance of the rocker and then going to its parts. He created an image of the old chair before explaining how it functioned in the life of his family. In some writing situations, this order can be reversed to move from the parts to the whole.

See page 86.

Order of Complexity

Often an effective way to explain an unusual topic is according to its complexity. Going from *the simple to the complex* or *familiar to unfamiliar* will help to clarify the topic. By starting with what readers already know and accept, you can orient them and establish rapport. Then they will be more comfortable and willing to explore the complex or the unfamiliar. If you were to begin with a difficult concept or highly technical material, some readers might refuse to read further.

Order of Materiality

Using an order of materiality, you can arrange details by going from *the concrete to the abstract* or from *the abstract to the concrete*. Concrete words refer to actual physical data about a condition, event, experience, object, animal, or person. Through our five senses, we can perceive evidence of these elements. Most of us are able to see, hear, touch, taste, and smell to obtain firsthand proof that concrete items exist. For example, tears are concrete—we can see them, feel them, even taste them. Sometimes tears indicate sadness, but sadness is an abstraction.

Abstract refers to ideas that have no physical referent; nothing material can prove they exist. We can think and talk about abstractions, but we *cannot* see, hear, taste, touch, or smell them. For example, patriotism, love, and integrity are all abstractions. The only way that we can infer they exist is to look for *concrete* evidence that *implies* their existence. Jeannine Caudill uses *abstract-to-concrete* order in "Mother Love."

See page 208.

Writers of description often move from the concrete to the abstract, presenting physical details about a subject before the symbolism. For example, you might briefly describe the Statue of Liberty before explaining its symbolic significance. For an essay of definition, you might use the reverse order, abstract to concrete. Then you would introduce an abstract concept, such as friendship or bravery, followed by concrete instances and examples.

WRITING AN EFFECTIVE CONCLUSION

www.mhhe.com/dietsch

For online help writing conclusions, go to: Writing>Conclusions

An effective ending flows logically and smoothly from the body, giving a sense of completeness or *closure*. Such an ending seems appropriate for the purpose, the reader, and the topic. It does not rehash opinions or recite the obvious. No new material intrudes. Personal essays often end by sharing how the experience or event influenced the writer—the effect it had upon the inner self. Five basic ways to conclude are described here.

End by Referring to the Thesis

To provide a sense of completeness, writers often refer briefly to the thesis. Notice that this device is an allusion, *not* a repetition of the entire thesis. By reworking an old cliché and repeating key points, Nora Lee Corbett establishes *closure:*

- **Thesis:** We raise leghorn laying hens for their hardiness, longevity, and egg production.
- **Conclusion:** On our farm the chicken comes before the egg. And we have learned over the years that the best chicken according to hardiness, longevity, and egg production is the leghorn.

End with a Personal Response

Sometimes writers explain how an event affected them and confide in the reader. They may share feelings of sadness, embarrassment, satisfaction, elation, or another response, especially at the end of the piece. The student who described her "worst job" concluded this way:

> After a week of repeating the same deadly dull, two-minute procedure, my hands guided the cloth under the pressure foot automatically. But my mind was in limbo—I knew I could not continue unless I underwent a lobotomy. So at quitting time on Friday evening, I picked up my paycheck, inhaled the fresh air of freedom, and left with a light heart, knowing I would never go back.

End on a Note of Optimism

Adding a note of optimism can create a satisfying conclusion. The note might be one of encouragement to yourself or to the reader, or it might be a look toward the future. Kathy Cordle concluded "Kicking the Habit" with a congratulatory note to herself:

> Since November 7, I have not had one cigarette. Yes, there are times when I still want one, and I am struggling to drop those extra pounds, accumulated from eating all that candy, but I feel really good about myself. I am a winner!

End with a Reference to a Benefit

Sales letters cite the benefits, advantages, and value of a product or a plan. A college paper may conclude in a similar way. In ending her paper, Diane Zachman pointed out the benefits of a good manicure:

> The process of manicuring, when done correctly, gives your nails a vibrant, healthy appearance and keeps them from becoming weak and brittle.

End with an Unexpected Twist

A conclusion that creeps up on readers, catching them off guard, can surprise and delight. When well done, such an ending seems spontaneous and appropriate. A brief comment or fact can pose an absurdity or profundity that causes the reader to smile or think. Paul Giacalone ended with a twist in his paper about his parents' dog Tia:

> I feel the only solution to this problem is either I go or the dog goes. After I discussed this with my parents, they went out and bought me a set of luggage for Christmas.

Although a twist may be appropriate for personal writing, it is rarely appropriate for business writing. Customers, employees, and managers need to know what to expect and need to understand the writer's purpose early.

DRAFTING ON A COMPUTER

Although we all know that simple precautions can prevent lost text, some writers still take risky shortcuts. Overconfidence can lead to predicaments, so even if you are an experienced computer user, read on. When copying, cutting, and moving entries in a works-cited or reference list for a research paper, be especially careful. With any text, it is wise to take the following precautions:

- Check to make sure you have the entire section, and only that section, highlighted.
- Paste in the excised material *immediately* and *save.* If you stop to do something else, there is the risk of forgetting and losing the material.
- Back up your document on a floppy disk, CD, or other means during the drafting session and again at the end (power failures may occur).
- Print out an early copy of the draft to be safe. Then too, if there is a question about originality, you have your prewriting notes and early draft to prove that the work is yours.

SUCCESS TIPS FOR PREWRITING AND DRAFTING

1. **Print out your prewriting notes to use while drafting.** That way you can see the entire list at once.

2. **Study your prewriting to see whether or not the topic is adequate for the assignment:**
   - Is the topic significant?
   - Is the topic suitable for your audience?
   - Has the topic been narrowed to fit the assignment?
   - Are there ample facts, examples, and details for support? If not, can you think of other related material to add?
   - How can the topic be presented in an interesting way?

3. **Schedule a block of time for writing your exploratory draft.** Start early so that you will have plenty of time to revise, edit, and proofread.

4. **Begin composing anywhere in an exploratory draft.** If you have an idea for the ending, draft that first. Write in a way that is comfortable for you.

5. **Double-space and leave wide margins.** Allow room to mark your draft. Most instructors prefer double-spacing and 1-inch margins.

6. **Think about your written voice.** How do you want the tone of your paper to sound? Amused? Serious? Outraged? Your attitude toward the topic (and the assignment), as well as your knowledge of the

topic, will influence your written voice. To check the tone, read your draft aloud, listening attentively (see chapter 2).

7. **Make an outline.** Some writers use an outline to prewrite. Others make an outline to check the organization of their rough drafts.

8. **After finishing a rough draft, leave it for a while.** You need time to distance yourself intellectually and emotionally, preferably a full day, before revising.

9. **Before starting to revise on-screen, relabel the draft and save a copy under a new file name.** That will allow you to go back to the original if you lose material or impulsively delete it. (For tips on revising, editing, and proofreading, see chapter 5.)

THINKING ABOUT WHAT YOU HAVE LEARNED

Which strategy of prewriting works best for you? Which tips for drafting were especially helpful? What can you do to increase your efficiency in composing a first draft? You might make a list of your answers so that you can refer to them before starting your next paper. Placing a paper clip on the chart of seven organizational strategies will provide a handy reference tool.

PRACTICE

FREEWRITING TO FIND TOPICS

Directions: You might freewrite by beginning with one of the following phrases, or you might draft an essay based on item 8, 9, or 10:

1. I wish . . .
2. I wonder . . .
3. Tomorrow . . .
4. I can't . . . but I can . . .
5. Once I . . . but now . . .
6. When I see . . . , I remember . . .
7. My job is . . .
8. Describe your worst mistake. What have you learned from it?
9. What would you most like to do? How might you do it?
10. Sketch a career plan. What training or education will you need?

Revision Workshop: Rethinking the Draft

To coax the seed of an idea to flower into an essay takes time and effort. Like a floral designer who snips stems, repositions flowers, and fills in empty spots with greenery to create a graceful arrangement, so too a writer snips and rearranges sentences and paragraphs, filling gaps with transitions to create an effective essay. Although a first draft may seem perfect, most writers later find flaws. They rethink, revise, edit, and proofread until the final draft is clear and complete. Part 2 explains these vital steps.

WRITING EXERCISE

Describe the writing you do—journal, e-mail, letters, reports, essays, or others. For which pieces of your writing are revision, editing, and proofreading an absolute necessity?

HOW DOES THE RHETORICAL SITUATION AFFECT INFORMATION DESIGN?

During the Iraq war, the release of a three-year-old presidential daily brief entitled "Bin Ladin Determined to Strike in U.S."—written before September 11, 2001—sparked a political explosion. Accusations of blame for not taking proper action flew in various directions. Amidst the hue and cry, reporter Jessica Mintz pinpointed a possible cause: the design of the brief (*Wall Street Journal* 4 May 2004).

Mintz interviewed information architects whose ideas are more widely used on the Internet than in print. *They said the design of the brief hindered readability and emphasis, for "significant details" were buried in the text*. They suggested placing these points at the top in boxes, shortening paragraphs, color coding, and other highlighting. Yet a benefit of the original design is that "Information . . . presented as a narrative, [lets] the reader make judgments."

Mintz mentions just some of the stylistic guidelines and tips discussed and demonstrated in this textbook. Parts 1–4 and 7 explain important factors that influence clarity, ease of reading, and writing effectiveness:

- **The rhetorical situation:** Why are you writing? Consider the occasion, purpose, topic, audience, and voice of the writer (chapters 1 and 2).

- **Positioning:** Place ideas strategically, according to the purpose. Significant details should not be placed in the middle of sentences and paragraphs. The beginning and end positions carry more emphasis (chapters 6 and 7).

- **Formatting:** Use headings, subheadings, bullets, boxes, and graphics for emphasis, according to the rhetorical situation (graphics: see chapters 2, 3, 9, 12, 13, 16, and 25–30).

- **Length of sentences and paragraphs:** Long blocks of print slow the reader and increase the difficulty of comprehension (chapters 6 and 7).

- **Level of language:** The words you choose should be appropriate for the occasion and the audience. Assess your audience beforehand, especially when using technical or formal language (chapter 2).

- **Word choice:** Concrete nouns, active verbs, and other precise words distinguish and clarify (chapters 3 and 8).

- **Tone:** As you revise and edit, listen to the sound of your written voice. Is it suitable? Does it sound knowledgeable and trustworthy? (chapter 2)

Applying these guidelines as you revise will increase your writing effectiveness.

Considering Revision, Editing, and Proofreading

Although most instructors do not expect Donald Murray's level of dedication, they do expect several revisions of papers. Yet too many students skip or skimp on revision, editing, and proofreading—turning in rough drafts instead of polished papers. A good way to start revising your rough draft is to assume the role of an editor.

> A piece of writing is never finished. It is delivered to a deadline, torn out of the typewriter on demand, sent off with a sense of accomplishment and shame and pride and frustration. If only there were a couple more days, time for just another run at it, perhaps then . . .
>
> —Donald Murray,
> "The Maker's Eye: Revising
> Your Own Manuscript"

www.mhhe.com/dietsch

For a wealth of revision resources, check out:
Editing

HOW DO YOU BECOME YOUR OWN EDITOR?

Someone once said that a writer must eventually become his or her own editor. This is even more true today when employees work alone at a computer. They are unlikely to have someone to mark errors and make suggestions. To become your own editor, evaluate not only the effectiveness of word choice and grammar but also the effectiveness of structure, logic, and development. As you revise, edit, and proofread, you might ask yourself five critical questions:

- Is the entire piece focused on one main idea?
- Is the level of language suitable for the purpose, occasion, and audience?
- Does the written voice sound appropriate?
- Are there any unsupported inferences or other errors in reasoning?
- Have I fulfilled the purpose? Should anything else be said?

REVISION: STAGE THREE OF THE WRITING PROCESS

The goal of revision is to rethink and reshape your writing so that it effectively reaches your audience and accomplishes your purpose. Revision involves the larger aspects of the draft: the organization and presentation of ideas. The smaller items within the sentences—word choice, grammar, spelling, and punctuation—are treated in the final stage of the writing process, editing and proofreading. Yet you can skip back and forth between stages, working any way you wish. Many writers, however, find it easier and more effective to consider one aspect at a time.

FIVE MAJOR STEPS OF REVISION

Perhaps you revise in a hit-or-miss fashion that, more or less, works for you. In this chapter you may find a more efficient way to achieve your purpose. The tips should save you time and improve the quality of your writing. The secret of successful revision is this: just keep repeating the process as often as needed.

Step 1. Acknowledge the Need for Revision

Some inexperienced writers seem to think they have hit the jackpot on their first draft. They evade the fact that every exploratory draft needs more work. Others think they can merely change a word here and there. But revision is not that quick or easy. No matter how pleased you are with early drafts, keep looking for ways to improve them. After your euphoria wears off, you will find many imperfections.

Judy DeGregario confides, "Anger erupted in me like hot lava when an editor met with me to critique. . . . I wanted to be petted and stroked like my calico cat. . . . Instead, the editor had informed me, in effect, that my writing had fleas. . . . After I cooled down, however, I realized the suggestions he offered me were invaluable. They were specific. They were accurate. They were true. I needed to hear them" (*The Writer* Apr. 2003).

Step 2. Look at the Big Picture

Print out your draft and read it quickly to determine the direction of your controlling idea. (It is difficult to do this on-screen, one frame at a time.) Then ask yourself questions: Is there just one main idea? Does it keep advancing steadily toward the final point? Is there a final point? Place a check mark wherever you have doubts or wherever the main idea goes astray. If you are unsure about the effectiveness of the ending, write "What is my point?" "Do I allude to it?" Then come back later.

Step 3. Reread and Mark the Draft

Reread your printed draft silently and carefully. Mark it as you go but hold off on any drastic action. Just place parentheses around surplus or doubtful material. In the margins pencil notes, questions, and possible restatements. If your draft has extra-long paragraphs, use brackets to divide logical units of thought into shorter paragraphs. Recheck and number any changes in their order. Then mark the changes on your working outline to see how the new order looks. When you are sure about the changes, mark them on-screen.

See "A Strategy for Critical Reading," page 293.

Risky shortcuts while using a computer can devour time and elevate blood pressure. The following advice is based on hard-won wisdom:

1. **Print out copies to work from periodically.** Do not try to do all your revision on-screen. On a printed page, you will notice peculiarities that you may well miss on-screen. Marking your draft is an essential step in revision.

2. **Save drafts periodically.** Why risk losing text when your screen freezes or a power failure occurs? Save your work at least every half hour.

3. **Move text without losing it.** To be safe, insert the copied portion right away and save.

4. **Place drafts in a folder.** Saving early drafts under different file names, such as "Research 1" and "Research 2," allows you to retrieve deleted items if needed. To avoid confusion, place the drafts together in one folder.

5. **Back up your data.** If your computer were to die suddenly, would you be lost without your hard drive? Prevent data loss by using back-up software—CDs, floppies, or other means of storage—at the end of each writing session.

6. **Submit your latest draft.** It sounds so simple—but one student submitted a six-page formal report with misplaced graphics. After receiving a C−, he realized he had not submitted the final draft, which had ten pages.

WRITING SUCCESS TIPS: REVISING WITH A COMPUTER

Step 4. Revise, Refine, and Question

Before you start to revise, rename and save your new draft—just in case you should have second thoughts and want to retrieve items. Revise from your marked copy, making changes on-screen. Be prepared to define, slice, splice, condense, or summarize any wordiness. If you need more details, review your prewriting notes and outline or do online research. To evaluate writing, ask questions such as these:

- What else needs to be said?
- What else might the audience like to know?
- Do any parts need to be trimmed?
- Are any details insignificant or irrelevant?

Step 5. Let the Draft Cool, Then Check the Focus

See chapter 2.

After the first revision, let your draft cool for half a day or more, if possible. Your thoughts need to settle so that new ideas can sprout. At least take a break and do something that requires you to move around. But be sure to set a time to return. Then, without looking at your paper or outline, jot down your audience and specific purpose. Has the purpose changed? Continue to ask questions to assess your draft:

- Is there one clear central idea throughout the paper?
- Are paragraphs arranged in a logical order?
- Does each paragraph have a transition to link back to the thesis statement?
- Are paragraphs well developed and interesting?
- Does the conclusion flow logically from the body?

The topics that follow are based on common problems encountered by student writers. If they don't apply to you, skip to the next section.

REFOCUSING A DRAFT

As you revise, you may decide to narrow your topic or refocus it. You might try the pyramid method, shown on page 43, or you might refocus the title, create a new title, look for a fresh perspective, or revise your outline.

Focusing the Title

A focused title for expository writing not only sharpens the topic but also suggests the approach the writer will take. A focused title specifies and limits the topic, particularly for serious writing. Let's consider some examples of titles for research papers:

UNFOCUSED	FOCUSED
• Age Discrimination	• Forestalling Age Discrimination When Applying for a Job
• The Internet and Education	• Using the Internet in a Writing Class

The unfocused titles are so broad that the topics could not be covered adequately in a paper. But the focused titles offer a feasible scope and a direction for the main idea. For lighter topics, you may want to consider an amusing or playful title.

Creating an Intriguing Title

For personal essays and short stories, you may prefer an engaging title that provides just a hint of what is to come. Alliteration, assonance, and word play are often used to spice up titles, as in "States of Stupidity" and "Every Breath He Takes," articles in *Reader's Digest* (Dec. 2003). Writer Doug McPherson suggests using rhyming with clichés as a way to come up with an amusing title:

See chapter 22.

> Look through a book of clichés. . . . Turn "All's well that ends well" into "All's well that bends well" and you have a story [title] on yoga. . . . "Two heads are better than one" could become "Two beds are better than one." The story? How couples have trouble sleeping together because of snoring, nightmares, twitching, or other bedtime ailments. (*The Writer* May 2003)

Finding a Fresh Perspective

If your draft is just not going the way you intend, you might look for a different point of view, a fresh perspective on the topic. For example, P. M. Brady, in his comic strip "Rose Is Rose," shows Pasquale, tired of his toys, pleading for a new one. His father listens, then opens the door, hinting there is a big toy outside. Wading through newly fallen snow, Pasquale looks around and asks where the toy is. His father replies that Pasquale is standing in it.

We are all standing knee-deep in ideas for invigorating our writing. And like Pasquale, we often overlook them. Creativity involves taking everyday experience and transforming it. As writers we can benefit by stepping back to get an offbeat view of our lives. Sometimes an ordinary topic can be enlivened by looking at it from an angle the reader does not expect. John Yeoman gave an imaginative spin to an experience by writing from the perspective of his two-year-old self:

Babysitting for Grandfather

Everyone except me was getting ready to go somewhere. Being the youngest of the family and a member in good standing of the club known as "the terrible twos," I was used to receiving a lot of attention. But that night my four-year-old sister, dressed in a lacy white dress and black patent leather slippers, was the center of attention. In her hands, she carried a beautiful bouquet of fresh flowers for her role in a wedding.

www.mhhe.com/dietsch

For an electronic outlining tutorial, visit:

Writing>Outlining Tutor

Outlining

Rather than committing mayhem on a draft, you can save time and effort by testing changes on an outline. Expand your scratch outline into a working outline on-screen. Then save and adapt as needed. Print out a copy to keep track of changes as you revise. This outline can be developed as needed. Some instructors require a formal outline, particularly for research papers. (See the model below.)

FORMAL OUTLINES

> Formal outlines may be written in fragments or sentences. How detailed an outline is depends on the writer and the assignment, but here's a word of warning: Shy away from elaborate outlines. You can invest so much time and energy that you may be reluctant to revise. (For examples of outlines, turn to chapters 17, 18, and 29.) Both topic outlines and sentence outlines use the following format, with numerals and letters to distinguish parts and subparts:
>
> I.
>   A.
>   1.
>   a.
>   b.
>   2.
>   a.
>   b.
>   c.
>   B.
>   1.
>   a.
>   b.
>   2.
>   a.
>   b.
> II. (Repeat as needed)
> III. (Repeat as needed)
>
> **POINTERS FOR MAKING OUTLINES**
> - Begin with a large Roman numeral. Follow with a capital letter, then an arabic number.
> - For subtopics, use small letters
> - Use periods after each of the above.
> - If you have an A, then you need a B. If you have a 1, then you need a 2. Otherwise, the section does not need a letter or number.

CLARIFYING THE DRAFT

After you are satisfied with the focus of the draft and the external order of paragraphs, it is a good idea to check the sound. Read the draft aloud and listen as a reader might. Be critical. How might some readers regard your point of view? How might they perceive your purpose? Is the main point clear, or might they misconstrue something? The following checklist will help you assess your written voice.

See chapter 2.

www.mhhe.com/dietsch
For further help moving through your drafts, check out: Writing>Drafting and Revising

CHECKLIST: LISTENING TO YOUR WRITTEN VOICE

1.   Is your written voice appropriate for the occasion, purpose, and audience?

2.   Does your written voice sound knowledgeable?

3.   Might the reader misunderstand some of the words?

4.   Will a synonym improve the sound without changing the meaning?

Revising Sluggish Openings

Does your first sentence beguile readers, tempting them to read on? If not, take a look at the sample openings in chapter 4 to stimulate ideas. Does your thesis statement need a little tinkering? Do readers have to stumble through unnecessary words, vague generalities, or other nuisances? To focus a thesis, try writing a purpose statement, as shown in chapter 1. Or you might leaf through part 3 and look at student papers at the ends of chapters. There you will see various openings and thesis statements.

Revising the Body

As you check the internal order within each paragraph, consider that all details should connect to one central idea. Usually, one sentence—the topic sentence—announces the subject of the paragraph and makes a claim. Supporting sentences provide evidence for the claim. They undergird the topic sentence with explanations, examples, anecdotes, reasons, and facts. If you should find more than one subject to a paragraph, you can either split it into two paragraphs or discard the less important idea.

See chapter 6.

Skinny paragraphs may need to be fleshed out with more details. Or you may spot gaps in thought. A transitional phrase, sentence or even a paragraph may be needed to bridge ideas. (To find what you need, turn to the index in the back of this book and look up *transition*.)

CHECKLIST: REVISING PARAGRAPHS

1.   Is each paragraph organized around *one* central idea?

2.   Does each supporting sentence closely relate to the topic sentence?

3. Do the sentences flow in a logical sequence?

4. Is a transition needed to connect any sentences?

5. Does any paragraph need more explanation, examples, or details?

www.mhhe.com/dietsch
For online help with your
conclusions, go to:
Writing>Conclusions

Revising the Conclusion

An effective conclusion gives a sense of completeness and leaves the audience with something to think about. The ending should flow logically and smoothly from the body and be consistent with the opening. An effective ending does not rehash opinions or belabor the obvious. No new material pops in unannounced. To see examples of conclusions, turn to chapter 4 or to the student papers at the ends of chapters 9–16.

WORKPLACE CASE STUDY

A SERIES OF STUDENT OUTLINES AND DRAFTS

Roger Moore's draft was revised eight times. The four examples here show key points of his progress. Roger wrote a first draft from his prewriting list, revised it, and decided it was still vague. To focus, he expanded the prewriting list to a scratch outline, listing the audience, purpose, and thesis statement. Note how he refined his thesis from a basic three-part version to a more subtle final version.

Scratch Outline   (Order of importance)

Audience: classmates
Purpose: to inform the class about swap meets and the people who attend
Title: Kinds of People Who Attend Swap Meets
Thesis statement: Jack and I have found that three general types of people come to swap meets to buy auto parts.
Body:
   Type A. Arrive in late afternoon and up till closing time. Nonbuyers.
   Type B. Are there at 4 a.m. Dealers. Get in the way.
   Type C. Come at 8 a.m. Family folks.
Conclusion

Using his scratch outline, Roger wrote drafts three and four. Dissatisfied, he revised the outline, switching the main points to chronological order. To refocus the internal order of each body paragraph, he renamed attendees and classified them according to "arrival, purpose, and behavior." With the structure of his paper firmly in mind, he wrote draft five, which follows the working outline.

continued

WORKPLACE CASE STUDY

Revision: A Working Outline   (Chronological order)

Title: Swap Meets

Thesis statement: My son and I have met three types of people who attend swap meets: early birds, buyers, and sightseers.

Body:

1. Early Birds
   Arrival: 4 a.m.
   Purpose: Buy cheap for resale
   Behavior: Buy little. Give us a hard time
2. Buyers
   Arrival: 8 a.m.
   Purpose: Find parts they need themselves
   Behavior: Pleasant, polite
3. Sightseers
   Arrival: Late afternoon till closing time
   Purpose: Look around
   Behavior: Complaining, demanding

Conclusion: Swap meets are fun with Jack along. We make a little money and meet some interesting people.

Fifth Draft

Swap Meets

Jack, my son, and I have decided there are three types of people who attend swap meets—the early birds, the buyers, and the sightseers. Swap meets are like flea markets, except these swap meets are for car parts only. Set-up times usually start at 4 a.m. This is the time when the early birds try to buy our car parts. They hope to run across a good deal. They don't buy much.

The buyers don't arrive until 8 o'clock or thereafter. They usually look for hard-to-find parts to fix up an old vehicle they are working on. They take their time and hunt carefully through the boxes and piles of parts. They are serious buyers and do not give us a hard time. Some are almost like old friends—we see them regularly.

Sightseers generally come late in the afternoon, often at closing time. They are always complaining about something. Years ago we used to unload parts so they could see them, but then we noticed they would not buy anything anyway.

Swap meets are enjoyable because Jack and I get together, make a little money, and meet some interesting people.

continued

WORKPLACE CASE STUDY

Although Roger's fifth draft was focused and clear, it still needed additional details to provoke interest and provide support. Three more revisions yielded his final draft.

Final Draft

People Who Flock to Swap Meets

In the summertime my son and I load my panel truck with used auto parts and head for a swap meet every Saturday. Swap meets are like flea markets, except swap meets are for used car parts only. There Jack and I not only make a little money and enjoy our time together but also meet some friendly people and hear some fascinating stories.

As soon as we drive in at 4 a.m, before daybreak, the early birds begin flocking around the truck, often getting in the way as we unload and set up. They crowd around, hoping to find something and strike a good bargain. They are usually dealers, out for a fast buck. A few may offer to help unload, but most stand around, drinking coffee and giving us a hard time, joking and razzing us. They don't buy much.

The buyers arrive later, eight o'clock or so. They often look for difficult-to-find parts to repair a vintage vehicle. Working in their spare time, many are restoring a classic car in their garage. They like to tell us about it—how much it cost, how far along the project is, how it looked originally, and its history. We've heard some surprising stories about thousands of dollars being made from restoring an old, rusty junked car. One fellow claimed his 1946 Ford was once owned by a notorious bank robber, who used it in several getaways.

Some of the buyers return regularly; they are almost like old friends. Sometimes they bring their families along. They take their time, hunting carefully through boxes and piles of parts. They are serious buyers who ask how much a part costs. If they don't want it, they go on to the next display. Otherwise, they buy.

Sightseers usually come late in the afternoon, often near closing time. It seems they can always find something to complain about. Seldom do they find what they want, and they often become irritated when we are too busy loading the truck to help them. Some even ask us to unload so that they can look over the rest of the parts! Years ago we tried unloading the parts for them to see, but we noticed they would not buy anything anyway. They just wanted to sightsee.

Despite the little irritations, swap meets are still a good place to spend a leisurely Saturday, visiting with my son, meeting friendly people, and hearing interesting yarns.

EDITING AND PROOFREADING: STAGE FOUR OF THE WRITING PROCESS

During editing and proofreading, you attend to matters within the sentence. *Editing* refers to correcting the sentence structure and improving the word choice. *Proofreading* means examining grammar and punctuation. The goal in stage 4 is to clarify meaning and eliminate grammatical distractions so that the writing purpose can be achieved.

MAJOR TASKS IN EDITING AND PROOFREADING

An essential part of editing is looking closely at the meaning of each sentence as well as its structure. Proofreading requires a scrutiny of grammar, punctuation, and keyboarding errors. For more intense concentration, many writers separate editing and proofreading. Regardless, there is one guideline that is certain to be fruitful: Go through your revised printed draft three or more times. Editing and proofreading just once will not catch all the errors.

> **www.mhhe.com/dietsch**
> You'll find numerous electronic tools to assist you in editing at:
> Editing

Marking the Revised Draft

After you have added all your revisions on-screen, save them, then run a spelling check. Next print out a clean, double-spaced copy to edit. Off-screen, you will be apt to notice more problems than on-screen. In the first round of editing, do not disrupt your concentration by consulting a thesaurus, dictionary, or handbook—that can come later. Just mark the spot and go on. Your first task is to find and mark items that interfere with clarity, completeness, and accuracy.

PROCEDURE FOR EFFECTIVE EDITING AND PROOFREADING

1. **Read every word.** After your second silent reading, read aloud to spot omissions, errors, and undue repetition. Listen carefully to the sound of the words. Are they pleasing, accurate, and appropriate?

2. **Mark the draft.** Use brackets to set off wordiness. If you notice an error in spelling or grammar, circle it. Place a check mark by any word or sentence you want to return to. Or devise your own system of marking.

3. **Revise sentences and improve wording.** Write changes on your hard copy. In the margins, list possible synonyms for dubious words. To select the best words, look up the meanings.

4. **Add changes on-screen.** After you finish marking your hard copy, make each change on screen.

5. **Print out a copy.** If your printed draft is quite messy, make a clean copy. Repeat the editing process as needed.

Making Sentences Clear and Concise

Reading sentences aloud will also help you to evaluate word choice and positioning of ideas. Important words should be placed in positions of emphasis—at the beginning or end of a sentence. To edit, underline the important words in your draft, then rearrange the sentence. Simply inverting the sentence and adding a comma will often improve the emphasis, as in this opening of a résumé cover letter:

> **DRAFT:**   I have developed a keen eye for detail, line, and color as an artist.
>
> **REVISED:**   As an artist, I have developed a keen eye for detail, line, and color.

If ideas are vague and lightweight, rethink them and restate in more specific words. You might ask yourself, "What do I really intend?" Shorten long rambling sentences by omitting unnecessary phrases: *sort of, color of, kind of, number of, in view of, type of,* and other wordiness. Watch, too, for passive voice of verbs, which adds extra words and numbs ideas. Try rewriting the sentence so that the subject is doing the action. Another way to clear out wordiness is to combine short related sentences:

> **DRAFT:**   Do you have short, choppy sentences? Are they related? Can they be combined into one sentence?
>
> See chapter 7.   **REVISED:**   If you find too many short, choppy sentences, try combining related ideas into one sentence.

WRITING SUCCESS TIP: PRUNE EXTRA WORDS

Keep sentences clear and vigorous by pruning unnecessary words. Consider these redundancies and their edited counterparts:

Redundant	Edited
absolutely essential	essential
actual truth of the matter	truth
advance warning	warning
cancel out	cancel
getting educated	learning
free gifts	gifts
past history	history

---

www.mhhe.com/dietsch

For more coverage of redundancies, and how to avoid them, visit: Editing>Eliminating Redundancies

Finding Fresh Language

Specific words, fresh language, and comparison enliven humdrum sentences. By choosing precise nouns and action verbs, you can create vivid images. Instead of using a general word such as *bee* or *roll*, you might say, "A large *bum-*

blebee lit on my blueberry muffin." Add power to verbs by making them specific. Instead of *went* through a red light, say *sped;* instead of *walked* down the street, say *strolled, ambled,* or *hurried.* Avoid overused words. And don't try to sneak slang or a pet colloquialism such as *mess up* or *stuff* past the reader by wrapping it in a set of quotation marks. Find a better way to say what you mean.

Create a Simile or Metaphor   Business and technical writing, as well as literature, employ similes and metaphors. These unusual comparisons use familiar images to lead readers to understand less familiar images. A *simile* is an explicit (or stated) comparison of two unlike items or ideas, using *like* or *as.* Let's take a look at these student similes:

- "My tires, *smooth as the soles of worn-out tennis shoes,* have tiny cracks in the sidewalls." (Kim Coffey)
- "Spade, whose pedigree was a mystery, had a tail eighteen inches long that *he could use like a whip.*" (John Spillman)

A *metaphor* is a figure of speech that contains an implicit (or suggested) contrast, such as "His last car *was a lemon.*" Notice that such metaphors contain *is* or *was;* they have no other signal words to announce them. Verbs, too, can act as metaphors: the motor *purred;* employees *support* their manager's decisions.

Experiment with Alliteration and Rhyme   *Alliteration* is the repetition of the initial (first) consonant sound. In a speech titled "Run-of-the-Mill Miracle," Gary Fenton used alliteration in the title (two m's). Later he commented on his daughter's birth: "No doubt about it. Having a baby is not easy. If it were, we would refer to it as leisure, not labor (two l's)."

Note too, that *leisure* and *labor* also rhyme, as does "No doubt about it." Alliteration and rhyme can be pleasing and emphatic as long as they are not overdone. Alliteration is easy to use; anyone can use it in titles or phrases.

---

1. **After adding your major revisions, print out a clean copy.** On-screen editing and proofreading carry the risk of overlooking errors you would normally notice on a printed page. Even after you think your text is error-free, print out a copy and proofread it carefully several times.

2. **As you make each change on-screen, check it off on your hard copy.** This way you will be less likely to omit corrections.

3. **After you make a change on-screen, read the sentence aloud.** This habit will help to ensure no words have been omitted and no extra ones have been left when text was moved.

4. **Before printing out your last draft, run a final spelling check.** Last-minute changes can cause errors. If you are not the world's best typist, typos could be lurking in your text.

EDITING AND PROOFREADING ON-SCREEN

PROOFREADING EFFECTIVELY

No significant piece of writing—whether a college paper, a report to a boss, or a business letter—can be considered complete until it has been carefully proofread at least twice for errors. Three times is better. Lapses in grammatical usage, punctuation, and spelling undercut your credibility as a writer and call into question your commitment to your work. In college these errors can lower your grade; at work they may damage your career prospects. We recommend that you:

- **Correct your graded papers soon after their return.** Look up words and errors. Correct every error. Look up misspelled words and write each one ten times to rivet the correct spelling in your mind.
- **Keep a list of errors pointed out in your graded papers.** Make a list of common errors you need to work on. Once you become aware of specific errors, you will be better prepared to avoid them.
- **Review the word pairs in the Glossary of Usage (page H-50).** These words are commonly confused because they look or sound alike. Examples: effect/affect, ensure/insure, all ready/already.
- **Learn the basic rules of grammar, punctuation, and spelling.** Don't ask someone else; you may get bad advice. Check your own work carefully. On the job you will be glad you did. You can start by memorizing the eight basic rules for using commas (pages H-24 to H-26).
- **Use a thesaurus and dictionary** to help in refining word choice.

PEER REVIEW: HELPING TO IMPROVE EACH OTHER'S WRITING

Published writers often receive input from writing groups, agents, editors, or reviewers. Peer review in a classroom provides similar help. These reviews not only enable class members to help each other with early drafts but also to sharpen their skill at identifying rough spots in their own writing.

The job of a peer reviewer is to pinpoint problems, not solve them. Revision, editing, and proofreading are the responsibility of the writer. When giving feedback, the reviewer should be tactful. Comments that are overly blunt, unduly critical, or vague can be worse than none at all. Before critiquing, you might ask yourself, "How would I feel if I received this feedback?"

The difference between callousness and tact often lies in the phrasing. Vague reactions such as "I don't like the opening" or "Confusing" or "Dull" are not very helpful. Responses should be fairly specific so that the writer understands where and what the problem is. Responses can be softened in three ways:

1. **Begin with a positive comment about the draft:**
   - This is an interesting topic.
   - That example is well developed (or funny or unusual).

- The anecdote is delightful (or amusing or charming).
- The spelling is correct.

2. **Be tentative.** Offer comments as opinion, not a final decree:
   - This sentence *appears* negative. Is that what you intend?
   - This passage *seems* unclear. What do you mean? (If the person clarifies, say, "That's a good start. Why don't you write it down so you'll have it?")
   - I *wonder* if this part might work better if moved over here? (Not "You ramble.")

3. **Ask polite questions:**
   - Where is the thesis? (Not "You don't have a thesis statement.")
   - Have you thought about the ending yet? (Not "There isn't any conclusion.")

Writers who are mentally prepared to accept constructive criticism can learn much from peer review. Still, peer responses should not be taken as gospel. As you start to revise, evaluate the quality of each response and extract what is useful.

REVIEWERS: Consider one aspect of the writing at a time. Word your comments and suggestions thoughtfully and carefully. Identify concerns tactfully, but don't whitewash.

REVIEWEES: Keep an open mind. Be willing to consider suggestions. Ask about comments that seem unclear. Evaluate each suggestion thoughtfully. If in doubt, make an appointment with your instructor or the campus writing center.

SUGGESTIONS FOR PEER REVIEW

THINKING ABOUT WHAT YOU HAVE LEARNED

How can you become your own editor? Why is this important? Which steps of revision do you need to spend more time on? Which tips about titles, perspective, openings, and endings seem especially helpful? What do you plan to do to improve your editing and proofreading skills?

PRACTICE

IDEAS TO START WRITING

Directions: You might describe an incident, experience, or tradition, or try one of these options:

1. The job you would like to have in five years
2. Broken promises
3. An anecdote about a family holiday or vacation
4. An incident at summer camp, school, or work
5. The earliest childhood scene or event that you can recall

Revising Paragraphs

CHAPTER 6

> There is a poignancy in all
> things clear,
> In the stare of a deer, in the
> ring of a hammer
> in the morning. Seeing a bucket
> of perfectly lucid water
> we fall to imagining prodigious
> honesties.
>
> —Richard Wilbur, "Clearness," *Ceremony*

Clarity is the heart of effective writing, and well-crafted paragraphs are essential to achieve this quality. Opening and concluding paragraphs, discussed in chapter 4, act as a frame for an essay, paper, or report. Body paragraphs focus on making specific points and presenting information in a complete and coherent way. Transitional paragraphs provide connections between ideas. A single well-developed paragraph by itself can form a complete brief essay, exam answer, or business communication.

This chapter discusses the qualities and elements of successful single paragraphs, as well as body paragraphs within essays. It covers not only strategies for organization and development of paragraphs but also prewriting and drafting of a topic sentence.

See chapter 4 for seven basic orders.

QUALITIES OF EFFECTIVE PARAGRAPHS

Effective paragraphs have four distinctive features: interest, unity, completeness, and coherence. These four factors contribute to clarity. As you revise, check to see that your draft has all of these features.

Interest

To write an effective paragraph that is worth reading, choose a topic you know and care about. Consider how you might arouse interest. Scan your prewriting; you may find an overlooked gem that will be just the hook for your opening. Can you approach the topic in an unusual way? What might readers like to know? A secret of good essay writing is to remember that readers like to be entertained; include anecdotes and offbeat examples. Supply action verbs and concrete nouns that enable the reader to share your vivid impression (see chapter 10).

Unity

www.mhhe.com/dietsch

For more help writing unified paragraphs, check out: Editing>Unity

To unify a paragraph, focus on one major idea in the topic sentence. *Then relate all of the support sentences in the paragraph to the topic sentence.* Support sentences may amplify the major idea with examples, facts, statistics, opinions, or reasons. If a sentence lacks a connection to the topic sentence, either establish one or discard the sentence. During the drafting stage, don't worry unduly about unity. At that stage your goal is to expand ideas on paper. But when you start to revise, unity becomes a priority. To check the unity of a paragraph, ask four questions:

- What is the purpose (main idea) of the paragraph?
- Does each support sentence supply specific details?
- Does each support sentence help to explain the topic sentence?
- If not, what needs to be deleted or added?

Completeness

To be complete, a paragraph must supply adequate and appropriate information. But how much is enough? What is suitable? You, the writer, must decide according to each rhetorical situation. Whether your professor assigns a single paragraph or a lengthy paper, think about the purpose and the audience:

- How much are readers likely to know?
- How much more do they need to know?
- Why? How will the information be used?
- Are there enough examples, reasons, or anecdotes to be interesting?
- Is there enough specific support to make my point?

Coherence

You might think of a paragraph as a jigsaw puzzle—each piece must fit. If not, the paragraph lacks *coherence;* it does not flow smoothly. During revision, you rearrange any words, phrases, or sentences that are in the wrong places. If there are still gaps between details, you can add transitions, either signpost or embedded, to bridge the gaps, or you might devise parallel structures. Transitions and parallelism show relationships.

www.mhhe.com/dietsch
For additional coverage of coherence, go to:
Writing>Coherence

Signpost Transitions   Like highway signs, signpost transitions direct the reader. Usually, these signal words and phrases appear at the beginning of sentences to indicate how the material fits with the preceding sentence. Just adding a word, phrase, or clause to indicate how the material relates to the preceding sentence often makes a paragraph clearer and easier to read.

COMMON SIGNPOST TRANSITIONS

- **To show time:** once, years ago, later, soon, now, today, then, before, when, while, after, meanwhile, as, next, first, second, and so forth
- **To add:** too, also, and, another, besides, in addition, furthermore
- **To show difference:** but, yet, however, still, otherwise, even so, although
- **To show similarity:** like, likewise, similarly, both, resemble, identical
- **To show effects or results:** because, for, therefore, as a result, since, thus
- **To emphasize:** in fact, indeed, above all, again, regardless, nonetheless
- **To point out examples:** for example, for instance

In the following student essay by Sonny Dyer, the italicized transitions show the passing of time:

Playing Possum

While defending an ambush position in Vietnam, I was run over by a tank. Hurt and bleeding, I was left lying in a rice paddy. My buddy, *after* routing the ambush against "Charlie" (the enemy), took off in pursuit, believing I was dead. *After an hour,* which seemed like an eternity, night fell. *A few hours later* the sky was pitch black. There was no moon or stars, just blackness. Suddenly I heard someone sloshing through the paddy. It was "Charlie." *As I lay there motionless,* I heard the Viet soldier rummaging through my Jeep. *After he finished with the Jeep,* he started to strip the dead. *Before I knew it,* he was standing over me. *While* lying there playing dead, trying not to breathe, I was sure he could hear the blood rushing from my wounds. Luckily for me, he was in a hurry and just stripped off my watch, flak jacket, lighter, and cigarettes. *After he left,* I took a big breath and let out a sigh of relief.

Hours later, as dawn broke, a patrol finally happened across my Jeep and discovered the bodies lying around. Tears came to my eyes as I heard a U.S. soldier call, "Medic, this one is still alive!"

Embedded Transition   Transition within a sentence is said to be "embedded." Four types of embedded transition are repetition of *key words, synonyms, pronouns,* and *natural relationships.* By repeating key words, substituting synonyms, using pronouns that refer to key words, and establishing natural links (spring/ fall, in/out, farm/crops, etc.), you can knit sentences smoothly into a paragraph. Note how the four types of embedded transition make the following paragraph coherent:

> *My mother* was the eldest of *her* generation—of nine children—and came from a slightly more elevated social station in Jamaica. *She* had a high school education, which *my father* lacked. . . . Before emigrating, *Mom* had worked as a stenographer in a lawyer's office. *Her* mother, Gram McKoy, was a small, lovely woman whose English wedded African cadence to British inflection, the sound of which is still music to my soul. The McKoys and the Powells both had *bloodlines* common among *Jamaicans,* including *African, English, Irish, Scotch,* and probably *Arawak Indian.* My father's side even added a *Jewish strain* from a Broomfield ancestor.
>
> —Colin Powell, *My American Journey*

See chapter 7.   **Parallelism**   Parallel structures provide balance in writing and contribute to coherence. Undoubtedly, you already use parallelism in several ways: to balance items in a series, compoun79d sentences, and pairs of related sentences, as well as to coordinate phrases and clauses. You may sense that parallelism smooths sentence structure and gives equal emphasis to coordinate ideas. To check the coherence and parallelism of paragraphs, read them aloud. The ear is often a better detector of imbalance and other irregularity than the eye. Note the parallelism in the following descriptive paragraph by student Nancy Smathers:

▶

Through a Child's Eyes

> A tall, husky man has long been a very special person in my life. *His hair is the color of bricks in a schoolhouse,* while *his eyes are the color of hickory nut shells. Above his eyes* he wears a permanent frown, but *in his smile* I can see his inner warmth peeking through. *When he speaks,* his voice sounds like a semi-truck going through a tunnel at a high rate of speed. The low, gravelly tones echo like a bouncing tennis ball in an empty room. *When he enters a room,* he re-

sembles a bear just waking from its winter slumber. But *when he sits,* a lap appears that would never turn away a child who wished to crawl upon it. When sitting there, I can detect the faint scent of Old Spice. *His big, muscular arms* make me feel safe from any possible harm. *His huge, powerful hands* are *like vice grips,* but when wiping tears away, they are *like soft cotton.* As rough as this man appears *on the outside, on the inside* he is soft and gentle, just like a newborn kitten. . . . This very dear person is my dad.

Clarity

For writing to be effective, readers must be able to determine the meaning upon the first reading. True, they may need to reread for specific details, but the main idea should be clear the first time. Clarity is the end result of knowing your purpose, correctly assessing the audience and occasion, selecting appropriate words, being complete, and connecting details to a central idea. Important influences on clarity are the level of formality, the voice of verbs, sentence structure, the length of sentences and paragraphs, and positions of emphasis (see chapter 7). Careful revision and editing will help to make your paragraphs clear.

ELEMENTS OF AN EFFECTIVE PARAGRAPH

To be effective, a paragraph must be centered on one idea, and the sentences must flow in a logical sequence. Regardless of whether the paragraph stands alone or comes in the body of an essay (or other piece of writing), it contains certain elements. For clarity, most paragraphs have a topic sentence.

The Topic Sentence

The *topic sentence* contains the main idea of a paragraph. This sentence tells the reader *what* will be covered and *why.* Some topic sentences also tell *where* or *when.* A basic topic sentence has two essential functions:

> **www.mhhe.com/dietsch**
> For more help creating topic sentences, check out: Writing>Thesis

1. *To limit the subject to one main idea* that can be developed in the paragraph.
2. *To make a claim, assertion, or statement of opinion.* This part of the topic sentence may be a belief, impression, generalization, or recommendation.

Let's consider a topic sentence that performs both these functions:

Uncle Jake, who came uninvited, was a difficult house guest.

The subject of the sentence is "Uncle Jake," and the claim is that he was "a difficult house guest." This topic sentence sets up the expectation that the writer will describe Uncle Jake's behavior. In the body of the paragraph, readers will expect support—examples of what he said and anecdotes of what he did—so that they can see for themselves how difficult Uncle Jake was.

Support Sentences

Support sentences explain the main idea of the topic sentence. They supply *evidence* to convince the reader of the soundness of the claim, assertion, or opinion. You might regard the topic sentence as an argument (view) to be proved. The support sentences supply evidence in the form of facts, definitions, reasons, examples, or illustrations to back up the claim in the topic sentence.

The minimum number of support sentences is generally three or four; often there are more. As you search for support, keep in mind that *quality* is more important than quantity. A few excellent examples are worth more than a dozen mediocre ones. Established facts, definitions, and valid reasons provide credible evidence. Appropriate illustrations and anecdotes increase readers' interest, understanding, and conviction.

A Concluding Sentence

Besides the topic sentence and support sentences, some paragraphs have a third part: a *concluding sentence.* This final sentence may be a summary of the points made in the support sentences. It can also serve as a *clincher,* providing the paragraph with a sense of completeness by commenting on the subject in an interesting, surprising, or humorous way. In the following student paragraph by Bonita M. Goings, the concluding sentence serves as a clincher: First, it alludes to the topic sentence; then it makes a point.

Climb Aboard!

The magic of a carousel has a way of turning men and women into children again. As they approach the carousel house, their steps and their hearts suddenly become lighter. Tots tug at adult hands, eager to climb aboard this remnant from a fairy tale. The magnificent carousel stands with hundreds of lights reflected in mirrors on the brightly painted rounding boards. Adventurous riders select mounts from rows of prancing horses or from the menagerie of bears, big cats, goats, ostriches, rabbits, a zebra, a giraffe, or a hippopotamus. The timid and the elderly seem to prefer the sedate pace of the two chariots. When all riders are seated, the calliope signals the ride is about to begin. As the carousel gains speed, whirling faster and faster, the riders' faces are transformed by smiles. Their cares seem to disappear as they are charmed by the magic of the carousel.

PREWRITING AND DRAFTING PARAGRAPHS

www.mhhe.com/dietsch

For online help drafting, visit:
Writing>Drafting and Revising

Beginning writers frequently struggle to whittle down a general topic and then find details to develop it. This section explains the basics of paragraph writing. As you revise, check to see that you have completed all these tasks successfully.

Narrowing a Topic Sentence

Narrowing a topic requires selecting one significant aspect. The problem may be that you know so much that you can't decide where to start. For example, a first attempt might read: "I like horses." But you realize the sentence is boring and too broad. Your mind spins with ideas, and you prewrite. Soon you have a list that yields a suitable topic:

- Horses
- Riding horses
- Riding horses I have owned
- My first riding horse

Topic sentence draft: I'll never forget my first horse.

First revision: Pinto was my first riding horse; actually, he was a pony.

Second revision: My first riding horse was actually a pony, but to my five-year-old eyes, Pinto was the finest of horses.

Positioning the Topic Sentence

Once you draft a topic sentence, your next concern is where to place it in the paragraph. Before positioning the topic sentence, consider its function and the effect you want to obtain. Will you place it at the beginning, the middle, or the end?

The Topic Sentence at the Beginning   Most expository paragraphs follow the direct approach: the topic sentence is placed at the beginning. There the topic receives more emphasis than it would in the middle, and the reader knows immediately what the writer will explain. Yet topic sentences sometimes wander into odd places. While revising this book, I was surprised now and then to find a topic sentence huddled in the middle of a paragraph for no apparent reason. Unless I found a reason to leave it there, I yanked it back to the beginning. Check your drafts to see that your topic sentences are in the most effective position for the purpose and audience.

The Topic Sentence in the Middle   Sometimes a writer may wish to take a leisurely path to the main idea. Then the topic sentence may appear in the middle of a paragraph. Placed there, the major idea receives less emphasis than it would at the beginning or end. In a paragraph of comparison, for instance, a topic sentence may be located midway between the two subjects. There it can identify the purpose and connect the items being compared. Or the topic sentence may be in the middle for other reasons, as in the following paragraph, which describes nonverbal communication:

> Mrs. Clark, who teaches math, is explaining an essential aspect of the subject. She notices that Fred is staring at her with unblinking eyes, his body taut

and erect, his feet flat on the floor. She discerns no motion whatever from Fred. Do you think that Fred is listening to the lecture, evaluating what Mrs. Clark is saying? *If you think he is interested, you are wrong.* A young teacher unaccustomed to this posture might fall for it, but a more experienced educator would not. Fred has turned his teacher off and is using a cover-up technique to convince her that he is "all ears."

—Gerard I. Nierenberg and Henry H. Calero,
How To Read a Person Like A Book

Placing a topic sentence in the middle of a paragraph does carry a risk, however. The danger is that if readers are impatient or in a hurry, they may skim over the middle and miss the key idea. If the idea is important, place it at the beginning or end.

The Topic Sentence at the End   At the end of an expository paragraph, the topic sentence acts as a summary, spelling out the controlling idea that is implicit in the sentences that precede it. The following paragraph, for example, builds up to a concluding topic sentence that offers a startling and bleak statistic:

Many illiterates cannot read the admonition on a pack of cigarettes. Neither the Surgeon General's warning nor its reproduction on the package can alert them to the risks. Although most people learn by word of mouth that smoking is related to a number of grave physical disorders, they do not get the chance to read the detailed stories which can document this danger with the vividness that turns concern into determination to resist. They can see the handsome cowboy or the slim Virginia lady lighting up a filter cigarette; they cannot heed the words that tell them that this product is (not "may be") dangerous to their health. *Sixty million men and women are condemned to be the unalerted, high-risk candidates for cancer.*

—Jonathan Kozol, "The Human Cost of an Illiterate Society"

A topic sentence at the end of a paragraph requires the reader to look at the support before the main idea. Since the writer takes time to explain the reasons before making the claim, the readers are less likely to reject it. A topic sentence at the end can also let readers know how and why you arrived at a decision. (In the paragraphs above, the topic sentences have been italicized for emphasis.)

Unifying a Paragraph without a Topic Sentence

Not all paragraphs have a topic sentence. Nonetheless, the main idea must be clear. In narrative writing a topic sentence is often lacking, but a general point (or theme) is implied, as in the following paragraph:

In the spring of 1948, in the first softball game during the afternoon hour of physical education in the dusty schoolyard, the two captains chose teams and, as always, they chose other boys until only two of us remained. I batted last, and first came to the plate with two or three runners on base, and while my teammates urged me to try for a walk, and the players on the field called, "Easy

out, Easy out," I watched the softball coming in waist-high and stepped and
swung, and hit it over the right fielder's head for a double. My next time at bat
I tripled to center. From then on I brought my glove to school, hanging from
a handlebar.

—Andre Dubus, "Under the Lights"

The paragraph has no topic sentence, but its point is clearly implied and
might be stated as "Without warning, I had become a good softball player." Using this inductive order (supportive details before the main point) provides interest by building to a climax. Another excellent reason for omitting a topic sentence is diplomacy. Some business letters, such as credit refusals, may not state
the main idea directly. Instead, the refusal is *implied* in a subordinate clause. Unless there is a good reason to omit a topic sentence, however, include one.

Adjusting Paragraph Length

Reportedly, when Abraham Lincoln was once asked "How long should a man's
legs be?" he answered, "Long enough to reach the ground." A similar answer
comes to mind when students ask "How long should a paragraph be?" A paragraph should be long enough to cover the central idea well according to the
needs of readers and their purpose in reading. As a general rule, avoid one- and
two-sentence paragraphs as well as a series of short paragraphs. These will give
your writing a choppy, careless appearance.

Introductory paragraphs of short papers (500 words or less) usually range
from three to five sentences; introductions for research papers tend to be longer.
Body paragraphs often range from five to eight sentences. Conclusions tend to
be rather brief, perhaps three to five sentences. A one-paragraph essay may
range from seven to twelve or more sentences.

Complexity of the subject also influences length; difficult subjects tend to
require more explanation than easy ones. If a paragraph becomes quite long,
consider the needs of the reader, the purpose of the writing, and the coverage
required for clarity. If division is needed, look for a shift from one aspect of an
idea to another.

1. Divide when a paragraph has more than one main idea. Divide
   where the second idea or a shift to another facet of the major idea
   begins.
2. Divide where there is a lapse in time. Time provides a natural
   break. *Tip:* Look for transitions of time or a shift in verb tense.
3. Divide if there is a shift in person. First, check to see that the shift
   is necessary. If it is, that may be an excellent spot to divide. If the
   shift is unnecessary, revise the sentence. (See "Case of Pronouns,"
   page H-3 and item 4, page H-5.)
4. In dialogue, start a new paragraph for each speaker.

**GUIDELINES:
DIVIDING LONG
PARAGRAPHS**

STRATEGIES TO ORGANIZE AND DEVELOP PARAGRAPHS

You can organize a paragraph by any strategy that is clear and suitable for the purpose. Narrative and process paragraphs generally present events and steps in *chronological* order, in the sequence they naturally occur. *Spatial* order locates parts or physical features. For example, to describe objects, animals, or people, you might go from head to toe, left to right, or outside to inside or in another direction. (See "Through a Child's Eyes," earlier in this chapter.) For other orders to organize paragraphs, see pages 50–52. The student paragraphs that follow use strategies of narration, description, process analysis, illustration, and comparison/contrast.

Narrative Paragraphs

Narrative paragraphs tell a story or relate an event or anecdote. The writer often sets the scene first, telling *who* or *what, when,* and *where.* Description, dialogue, or illustrations may be included to kindle interest and to clarify. Action verbs keep the story moving. Narratives often build suspense, reserving a surprise for the end. They may reveal rather than explain, letting the reader interpret the meaning, or they may direct attention to a social or political concern that has universal relevance (see chapter 9). The following student narrative by Suzanne Omaits suggests a fear we all might experience:

Home Alone

Quiet holds many eerie sounds. I never knew how many until I found myself alone one Friday night. Was that the wind rubbing a bare branch against the house, or was the front step groaning under someone's weight? To blot out the sounds, I turned on the television. But something compelled me to turn around. Dreading what I might see, yet afraid not to look, I slowly turned. For a moment I froze! Through the fogged glass, I saw a man's face pressed against the window pane, staring at me! Leaping to my feet, I flipped off the lights and TV. He began to pound on the window. Realizing he could still see me dimly, I ran to the back room and hid. After a moment I knew I had to get help. Shaking, I crawled back to the living room. My hands trembled so I could hardly dial the phone. Anxiously, I waited for the familiar voice of my neighbor. Suddenly the pounding stopped. Minutes dragged by until my neighbor arrived. After checking, he assured me the intruder was gone. Just then a car drove up. Never was I so glad to hear my parents call, "We're home!"

Descriptive Paragraphs

An effective description has a specific purpose; details are not just a pleasant filler. Significant physical details can capture the essence of a person, place, or object. Concrete words reveal perceptions obtained through the five senses: seeing, hearing, touching, tasting, and smelling. A single dominant impression can unify the details. In the next student paragraph, by Michael Schnitzler, the physical details about a chair and how it has been used down through the years yield a dominant impression of an affectionate family.

See chapter 10.

The Old Rocking Chair

In the corner of our living room sits an old wooden rocking chair. The chair is made of solid maple, varnished and trimmed in gold. The arms are worn smooth, as if someone had used the finest of sandpaper on the wood. On the edges of its arms, I can see indentations in the wood where little tykes did their teething. As I rock back and forth, the old chair squeaks and creaks; but the sounds are soothing. This rocking chair has served several purposes. It has helped to console our three children, countless nieces, nephews, and children of friends. It has rocked babies to sleep for naps and at bedtime. With its soothing rhythm, it has comforted and quieted them when they were restless or sick. Now that the children have grown older, the old chair is seldom used. Yet it sits patiently, awaiting the years when it will hold our grandchildren.

Process Analysis Paragraphs

Process analysis explains how to do something or how something happens. Chronological order is the clearest way to organize process analysis. Just list steps or actions in sequence as they normally occur. Include enough details for the reader to understand. *If there is a risk during any part of the procedure, give a precaution early.* For conciseness and clarity, use second person (mainly the understood *you*). In the following example, which is directed to someone who has never used a coin-operated car wash, notice how student writer Kristi Gruber takes an ordinary topic and transforms it into an interesting paragraph:

See chapter 11.

How to Get the Best Shine from a Coin-Operated Car Wash

Whether your car is a prized possession or a necessary nuisance, it deserves an occasional wash. By following five simple steps, you can make your vehicle sparkling clean in just five minutes. First, vacuum the interior with the hose located outside the entrance of the car wash. Be sure the hose inhales every crumb, pebble, and gum wrapper. Second, drive into the wash cage. Third, before you add coins, read the directions for the wand. Then turn the dial to "Prewash." Add the coins and be ready to work fast. Fourth, spray all the exterior once to break up grime. Fifth, switch to "High Pressure Soap" and grip the wand tightly. As you move around the car, spray the top, hood, sides, wheels, and trunk. Sixth, change the mode to "High Pressure Rinse." To prevent streaking, rinse all suds off. Next, switch to "Spot-Free Final Rinse." This final step will prevent water spots and ensure a brilliant shine. If you are very dedicated to your four-wheeled friend, take time to wipe her off with the old bath towel you brought along. After that you will probably head down the highway only to be greeted with a gift from a passing bird!

Illustration Paragraphs

Illustration paragraphs—also called paragraphs of exemplification—present a *series* of examples to support the topic sentence. To maintain unity, every example is closely linked to the controlling idea. As you read the next student paragraph, notice the order Sharon K. Cleveland used for the examples:

The Fearsome Rabbit

Bathsheba was not the typical Easter bunny. Sheba was a Newfoundland flop-eared rabbit. Soon she grew into a fat fur ball. At maturity, she weighed 35 pounds—more than my two-year-old nephew! Our guests loved to watch her hop down the hall, then stand on her hind legs while she washed her face. With her long floppy ears hanging down, she had a sad, gentle look, which was deceiving. One day we came home to find her chewing on a camera bag that belonged to my husband. He yelled, "If I didn't love that rabbit so much, she would be dinner tonight!" Soon electrical cords, woodwork, wooden chairs, books, and other objects also bore the marks of her sharp teeth. As Sheba grew older, she developed a mean streak. One day our son, who was six, went near her litter box and came running—Sheba hopping close behind. As she nipped his bare heel, he screamed, "HELP!" After this incident she would hop toward him, and he would leap onto the couch. He had become afraid of her. Soon we took her to a farm that raises rabbits, where she seems fat and happy.

Comparison or Contrast Paragraphs

See chapter 14 for outlines.

Comparison includes both similarities and differences, while *contrast* refers to differences only. The key to writing a good comparison or contrast paragraph is first to select two subjects that might make an interesting pair. Then list specific, significant features of each, matching every detail you list for one subject with a corresponding detail for the other as student Peggy Walker did:

The Eye of the Beholder

This year when the first warm days of April began, I overflowed with energy. I wanted to make our family room as fresh as the spring buds outside. In a frenzy, I started to throw out one piece of junk after another, but each time Jerry would intervene to save a "treasure." First, I discarded a faded, cracked plate; but he rescued his family heirloom. Then I seized the tattered quilt; he returned his comforter for cold nights to its rightful place on the couch. Next I tossed out the stack of old *Time* and *Newsweek* magazines from the coffee table; he retrieved them because he might need a reference for a "current" event. And so it went. Finally, I said, "That sagging old couch we bought at a garage sale simply has to go!" But he objected sharply, "That's my favorite spot to watch football!" Refusing to argue, I stopped. But the first day he goes golfing, I'm calling Goodwill for an immediate pickup. . . . I may keep the plate.

Paragraphs of Definition

Sometimes a paragraph of definition is needed to explain the meaning and context of a word. A technical definition may specify the purpose and the function of a part or appliance. A literary definition may specify the root or origin of the word, the part of speech, and the standard meaning—or several meanings in different contexts. During practice writing, student Mark Jones speculated about the meaning and uses of the word *shaft:*

Words are fun to play with and think about. For example, *shaft* as a noun is a pole or long handle of a spear or other weapon. By that definition, an arrow could be considered a shaft, although it would seem strange to say we shafted a deer. The space shuttle might also be called a shaft. A pretty girl can wear a short dress and show a little shaft. The White House has many shafts; there are pillars at the entrance. *Shaft* is also used as a verb, but only in slang. If Bill shafted Al, then Bill did a wrong or injustice to Al. Bill did not hurl an arrow, spear, or space shuttle at Al, although Al has been hurt by Bill's action. *Shaft* is also the name of an old movie featuring a super-cool, super-bad bald man named John Shaft. If violent movies about super-cool, bad, bald men are not appealing, then paying five dollars to rent the film and not liking it would be getting the shaft.

Transitional Paragraphs

In the middle of an essay or paper, you may need more than just a signpost transition or embedded transition to bridge a gap—directing the reader to a shift in thought. A special paragraph of transition serves to connect two major ideas in a logical sequence. For example, Patty Seigneur wrote a brief transitional paragraph for a paper contrasting two good friends. Below is the paragraph she placed between her descriptions of Sue and June:

> Sue is a wonderful person and friend, but I found myself wanting a friend more like myself. Then I met June. Quickly, she and I became good friends. We both realized how alike we are and how much we enjoy each other's company.

Notice that only one signpost transition, *then,* is used in this transitional paragraph. But the writer repeats key terms and uses pronouns to establish clear *embedded* transition.

THINKING ABOUT WHAT YOU HAVE LEARNED

What did you learn about paragraphs that you did not already know? What information will be the most useful in the future? Which student paragraph did you enjoy most? Why?

PRACTICE

SMALL GROUPS: Evaluating Topic Sentences

Directions: Which sentences would make *good* topic sentences? Why?

_____   1. My motto "play before work" received a severe blow this week.

_____   2. The leftover macaroni and cheese in my refrigerator was covered with green mold.

_____   3. Mary Todd married Abe Lincoln.

_____   4. The older I become, the more I appreciate. . .

_____   5. Overnight the amaryllis opened one large red trumpet.

_____   6. Mr. Inskeep is my favorite teacher.

_____   7. Computers are necessary for most workplaces.

_____   8. A roommate who is a musician can be exasperating.

_____   9. Cutting the Brazilian rain forest is causing weather problems.

_____ 10. Every Thursday night I watch my favorite TV program.

IDEAS FOR PARAGRAPHS

1. Describe a small object you own and its meaning to you.
2. Share a bit of advice given by a parent, grandparent, or other significant person. How did it influence you?
3. Describe a pet you once owned.
4. A book you read in your early years. How did it influence you?
5. The day I almost . . .

Restyling Sentences

CHAPTER 7

> What is conceived well is expressed clearly.
>
> —Nicholas Boileau, *L'Art Poétique* (1674)

In the workplace, you may be expected to write strong, clear sentences at a moment's notice. You may have to dash off an e-mail, a memo, a letter to a customer, or a short report. Regardless of the time crunch, rereading and revising are imperative. Otherwise, your message may be unclear, ungrammatical, inaccurate, or offensive. The clarity of a message depends not only on sentence style and word choice but also on correct punctuation.

In this chapter, punctuation is explained in the context of each sentence type. The chapter also covers five ways to clarify, unify, and spark vigor into sentences of a rough draft by—

1. Replacing verbs in the passive voice and forms of *be* with verbs in the active voice.
2. Adapting sentence structure to the purpose, occasion, topic, and reader.
3. Positioning ideas at strategic points for emphasis.
4. Creating parallel forms for similar ideas.
5. Eliminating wordiness and unwieldiness.

STRATEGIES FOR EFFECTIVE SENTENCES

Styling sentences is a challenging task, but it is the mark of a proficient writer. Effective sentences can be short or long, simple or complex, plain or ornate, depending on the purpose. The design and strength of sentences also depend on the occasion, the topic, the audience, and the voice of the writer. Although some sentences can do without certain parts of speech, a verb is always required.

www.mhhe.com/dietsch

For more work with verb voice, go to:

Editing>Verbs

CHOOSING AN EFFECTIVE VOICE FOR VERBS

Strong action verbs energize writing by showing movement, enabling readers to visualize an activity. For example, *ski, swim,* and *skate* evoke images of physical activity; *think, puzzle,* and *dream* indicate mental activity. Action verbs can be written in either the active or passive voice.

Favoring the Active Voice

See page H-9.

Active voice simply means that the subject of the sentence is *performing the action.* A verb is in the *passive voice* when the subject *receives the action.* Something or someone else is performing the act or deed, not the subject. Compare the two examples below:

ACTIVE VOICE: Johnny *shot* the huge bear.

PASSIVE VOICE: The huge bear *was shot* by Johnny.

Which sentence do you prefer? Why? You probably noticed that the sentence in active voice gives the sharpest image of the event. And perhaps you noted that the sentence in active voice has just five words whereas the one in passive voice contains seven words. Note, too, that the passive voice consists of a helping verb and a past participle (*was + shot*). Although passive voice is useful at times, it lessens the impact of a sentence. To make writing clear and direct, experienced writers prefer the active voice in most situations.

1. **The person responsible wishes to remain unknown.**
   Example: The new rule *was enacted* to tighten security.
2. **The one who performs the action is unknown.**
   Example: The oriental rug *was made* in China.
3. **To place emphasis on an important word.** Passive voice allows the important word to become the subject of a sentence.
   Example: The *needs* of the student *should be considered.*

GUIDELINES: WHEN SHOULD YOU USE THE PASSIVE VOICE?

Using Understood *You*

Sometimes nouns and other words are omitted—leaving a verb in the active voice to stand alone as a one-word sentence. For example, "Go!" "Heel!" and "March!" are each a complete sentence. In these brief sentences, the subject is implicit—understood to be *you*. Omitting this implicit subject and using active voice make the sentence more concise and to the point. Therefore understood *you* is often used in giving directions and orders, or in explaining a procedure or process (chapter 11). In the following examples, the understood subject is marked by brackets:

See pages H-4 to H-5.

- [You] Turn left at the third stoplight.
- [You] Throw me the ball!
- To make excellent tea, [you] first heat the water to a rolling boil.

Replacing Forms of *Be*

Be verbs do not show action. *Be,* in all its forms, indicates a state of being, living, or existing. Although *be* verbs are sometimes necessary, too many of them dilute writing, weakening the effect. The main forms of the verb *be* are *is, am, are, was, were, be, been,* and *being.* For quick recall, you might practice saying them aloud.

With a little thought, you can often replace a *be* verb with an action verb. This editing shortens and strengthens the sentence. The following examples illustrate why action verbs are generally preferred:

BE VERB: Sammy Davis, Jr., *was* a famous entertainer who entertained millions with his singing and comedy. (14 words)

ACTION VERB: Sammy Davis, Jr., *entertained* millions with his singing and comedy. (9 words)

CRAFTING SENTENCES AND PUNCTUATING

For most of your college writing, you will be relying on three basic sentence types: the *simple* sentence, *complex* sentence, and *compound* sentence. Used less often are the *compound-complex* sentence and the *periodic* sentence. All have a different purpose and function. A simple sentence highlights *one* idea.

SIMPLE:	Interviewers may ask about weaknesses. (one independent clause)
COMPOUND:	Interviewers may ask about weaknesses, but savvy applicants prepare for this question. (two independent clauses)
COMPLEX:	Since interviewers may ask about weaknesses, savvy applicants prepare for this question. (dependent clause + independent clause)

By mixing and varying these three basic sentence structures according to the rhetorical situation, you not only add interest and emphasize major points but also clarify relationships between ideas.

The Simple Sentence

www.mhhe.com/dietsch

For additional coverage of sentence types, go to: Editing>Sentence Types

The research of Rudolph Flesch revealed that simple sentences compose about 70 percent of most expository writing. A *simple sentence* contains a subject (which may consist of more than one noun) and one or more verbs. The simple sentence is an *independent* clause—one complete thought that can stand alone. At its simplest, such a sentence may consist of just a subject and verb:

- Eagles soar.

More often though, simple sentences contain other sentence parts, including objects, prepositional phrases and other modifiers, and perhaps additional verbs:

- Eagles build *large nests.* (subject + verb + direct object)
- Eagles build large nests *in isolated places.* (+ prepositional phrase)
- *Most commonly,* eagles build large nests in isolated places. (+ adverbs)
- Most commonly, eagles build large nests in isolated places and *lay two or three eggs.* (+ second verb and object)

If only simple sentences are used, however, writing can sound choppy and dull. Every now and then, as you revise your drafts, look for ways to expand simple sentences into complex sentences. Or if two simple sentences are of equal importance, combine them into a compound sentence.

The Compound Sentence

A *compound sentence* emphasizes *two ideas of equal rank or importance.* Two related simple sentences can be joined to form a compound sentence. The compound sentence gives the clauses *equal* rank because both clauses contain important ideas. This means that a compound sentence has two main subjects and two main verbs. If a transition is needed, the two clauses are connected by a *comma* and a *coordinating conjunction,* as italicized in the following examples:

- Geraniums are easy to grow, *for* they are quite hardy.
- Mammoth Cave is the largest cave in the United States, *but* Carlsbad Caverns are the most colorful.

But careless compound sentences can add unnecessary words. In the second example below, the simple sentence is just as clear yet more concise:

- Minarsi entered the Maine Turnpike at Falmouth, *and* she followed it to Augusta.
- **Edited:** Minarsi entered the Maine Turnpike at Falmouth and followed it to Augusta.

Coordinating Conjunctions   These special words connect (or coordinate) elements of equal rank, such as parallel clauses, phrases, or nouns. Since there are just seven coordinating conjunctions, you can soon memorize them. An acronym that will jog your memory is *fanboys:* for, and, nor, but, or, yet, so.

To choose a suitable conjunction for a compound sentence, look at the relationship of the ideas in the two clauses. If the second clause provides additional information, use *and*. If the second clause contrasts with the first, use *but* or *yet*. Or if the second clause has a cause-and-effect relationship with the first clause, use *for* or *so*.

If *both* clauses in a compound sentence are *four words or less,* you may join them with a comma. If one clause or both have *five words or more,* you have three options—according to the relationship:

1. **Comma and Conjunction.** Connect two related independent clauses with a *coordinate conjunction* preceded by a comma when transition is needed.
   - The hidden job market consists of an estimated eighty percent of available jobs, *but* most job seekers seem unaware that it exists.
2. **Semicolon.** When the connection between the ideas is so close that no transition is needed, use a *semicolon* between the independent clauses.
   - The hidden job market consists of an estimated eighty percent of available jobs; only twenty percent or so of the available jobs are ever advertised.
3. **Colon.** When the second clause of the compound sentence explains the first, join with a *colon*.
   - The astute job seeker compiles a packet of employment search documents: the packet can contain an up-to-date résumé, cover letter, thank-you letter, and sheet of references.

PUNCTUATING COMPOUND SENTENCES

Avoiding Comma Splices and Fused Sentences   Long independent clauses (five words or more) cannot be linked with just a comma. The resulting error is called a *comma splice*. When punctuation is omitted between two independent clauses in a compound sentence, the error is called a *fused sentence*.

www.mhhe.com/dietsch
For further coverage of comma use, visit:
Editing>Commas

COMMA SPLICE:	Terrariums are costly at a flower shop, they are inexpensive to make at home.
CORRECT:	Terrariums are costly at a flower shop, *but* they are inexpensive to make at home. (comma and conjunction)
COMMA SPLICE:	Weather bulletins warned of ice-glazed roads, however, some drivers ignored the warning.
CORRECT:	Weather bulletins warned of ice-glazed roads; however, some drivers ignored the warning. (semicolon)
FUSED SENTENCE:	The ordinance won wide support it was passed by a two-thirds vote.
CORRECT:	The ordinance won wide support; it was passed by a two-thirds vote. (semicolon)

To select a suitable sentence type, consider the importance of the idea or ideas. When one idea is more important than the other, subordinate the minor idea in a complex sentence.

The Complex Sentence

A *complex sentence* consists of an independent clause and one or more dependent clauses. The complex sentence ranks a major idea and a minor idea. The major idea appears in the independent clause; the minor idea appears in the dependent clause. To the untrained eye, a dependent clause may look like a complete sentence because both have a subject and a verb. But the dependent clause has a word at the beginning that makes the (minor) idea incomplete. Thus *a dependent clause is always a fragment and cannot stand alone.*

FRAGMENTS (INCOMPLETE IDEAS)

That has white forepaws

When the doorbell rings

Because McDaniel Motors gives dependable service

SENTENCES (COMPLETE IDEAS)

- The black cat that has white forepaws is Jeff's.
- When the doorbell rings, my sheltie barks.
- Because McDaniel Motors gives dependable service, Jason has his car serviced there.

Adjective Clauses   *Adjective clauses* are dependent clauses that refer to nouns or pronouns. These clauses are easy to identify because they always start with one of five relative pronouns: *who, whom, whose, which,* or *that* (or a variation such as *whoever* or *whomever*). To remember the five relative pronouns, think: four *w*'s and a *t*.

See "Relative Pronouns," page H-8.

ESSENTIAL: The car *that he prefers* has bucket seats.
                    The young woman *who is wearing blue jeans* is Jay's sister.

NONESSENTIAL: Terry, *who is my brother,* is an avid photographer.
                    The yellow truck, *which is a Dodge,* represents her life
                    savings.

Did you notice that the sentences with *essential* clauses need no commas? But *the sentences with nonessential clauses require a pair of commas.* These commas act like tiny parentheses to set off extra material, which could be removed. To test whether or not a clause is essential, try covering it with your hand and reading the rest of the sentence. Does the basic meaning of the sentence change? If so, no commas are needed; the clause is essential. If the meaning does not change, set off the extra material (the nonessential clause) with commas.

1. *That* is always used to indicate essential information. Sometimes *that* is omitted for the sake of conciseness if the meaning is clear. *That* can refer to people, animals, or things.

2. *Who* and *whom* refer only to people. *Which* can refer to animals or things. *Who, whom,* and *which* can introduce essential or nonessential clauses.

DISTINGUISHING WHO, WHOM, WHICH, AND THAT

Adverb Clauses   *Adverb clauses,* like adverbs, tell *when, where, why, how,* or *under what conditions.* Adverb clauses begin with *subordinating conjunctions.* Some introduce reasons or explanations (*because, since, whereas, although*). After you learn to recognize the common subordinating conjunctions, you will be able to identify adverb clauses easily.

COMMON SUBORDINATING CONJUNCTIONS

when	although	if	as	whether
while	even though	until	as long as	before
where	so that	unless	as though	than
since	because	as if	after	whenever

The adverb clause may come before or after the independent clause in a complex sentence. Let's look at two versions of a sentence with the dependent clause italicized:

- *When the big Doberman snarled,* I slammed the door.
- I slammed the door *when the big Doberman snarled.*

Which sentence do you prefer? Actually, the first sentence has two advantages: (1) the ideas appear in chronological order; (2) the word *I* appears in the middle of the sentence, where emphasis is minimized.

**PUNCTUATING
SENTENCES WITH
ADVERB CLAUSES**

1. **Introductory adverb clause.** When a long adverb clause (five words or more) appears at the beginning of a sentence, *place a comma after the clause.* If a misreading is possible, use a comma after a short clause.
2. **Concluding adverb clause.** When an adverb clause appears at the end, in a sequence of two events, no comma is needed.

The Compound-Complex Sentence

An expanded version of the complex sentence, the *compound-complex sentence* contains *two or more* independent clauses and *one or more* dependent clauses. Since compound-complex sentences tend to be long and complicated, they slow down reading and understanding. Therefore, they are used less often than other sentence styles in ordinary writing. But in some cases, a compound-complex sentence may be necessary.

If you construct a compound-complex sentence and find that it is cumbersome, you might consider two options: dividing the sentence into two sentences or creating a complex sentence (subordinate one idea into a dependent clause). Both options allow for condensing, as shown here:

COMPOUND-COMPLEX: Mark disagreed with the other board members who wanted to raise the CEO's salary from $350,000 to $500,000 per year; nevertheless, he said nothing and raised his hand to vote for the huge raise. (independent clause + adjective clause + independent clause = 34 words)

- **DIVIDED:** Mark disagreed when other board members wanted to raise the CEO's salary from $350,000 to $500,000 per year. (complex sentence = 18 words) But he said nothing and raised his hand to vote for the raise. (simple sentence = 13 words)

- **COMPLEX SENTENCE:** Although Mark disagreed about raising the CEO's salary from $350,000 to $500,000 per year, he said nothing and raised his hand to vote for the raise. (adverb clause + independent clause = 26 words)

The option you choose will depend on the rhetorical situation and how much emphasis you need to place on each idea. To hear the differences in emphasis in the examples above, read them aloud.

The Periodic Sentence

A *periodic sentence* affords an opportunity to combine several related ideas into one grand sentence. This sentence pattern builds anticipation and suspense by presenting less important details before the major idea. This means that the major idea always appears just before the period. Although the subject may be placed early in the sentence, *the verb is always delayed*. Periodic sentences provide a refreshing change of pace, as well as emphasis. Sometimes they are the ideal structure for a concluding sentence. James Herriot uses a periodic sentence at the end of his story "The Strychnine Episode at Darrowby":

> To me, the outbreak is a sad memory of failure and frustration. Fergus was my only cure. But over the years, when I saw the big dog striding majestically in his harness, leading his master unerringly around the streets of Darrowby, I always had one good feeling.

In the final sentence, Herriot builds to a climax, saying in one sentence what someone else might have said in three. Yet the periodic sentence is not an everyday sentence—it should be used for a significant idea. The next two examples of periodic sentences are taken from James Kelly's article "Rocky Mountain High":

- In Sandpoint, Idaho, a favorite refuge of disillusioned Californians, boutiques and craft shops flourish and stores sell wooden tubs for outdoor bathing.
- Of the eight states, Montana, Idaho, Wyoming, Nevada, Utah, Colorado, New Mexico and Arizona, which occupy 863,524 sq. mi., an area considerably bigger than all of Western Europe, Washington [the U.S. government] owns about 80% of the resources and nearly one-half of the land.

Sentence Length

Since Elizabethan times, sentences have been shrinking. In the 1600s the average sentence had about 45 words. One early English writer named Hakluyt actually wrote sentences that averaged 90.5 words. By Victorian times, the average sentence was down to 29 words. Now the average sentence length, according to Rudolph Flesch, is 17 words. ("Average" does not mean you should make every sentence the same length. Vary your sentences to produce variety and a change of pace.)

The length of a sentence is influenced by the kind of idea it houses. Brief sentences emphasize key ideas. Long sentences are like baskets, collecting several less important details. Each type has its place, but neither should be overused. Too many short sentences can cause choppiness whereas too many long sentences interfere with clarity.

POSITIONING ELEMENTS WITHIN THE SENTENCE

To emphasize an important word, phrase, or clause, place it in a *position of emphasis*—at either the beginning or the end of the sentence. If you place important material in the middle, the reader may skim or skip it. If you are unsure about the best way to position elements, rewrite the sentence in two or three different ways, examine the differences, and read the sentences aloud.

Moving Elements in Independent Clauses

Normally, independent clauses follow the subject and verb, plus any other elements in the message. To emphasize an element, move it to the head or end of the sentence. Which of these three versions seems best? Why?

- My neighbor worries about her son's lack of progress in English. (original)
- My neighbor worries about the lack of progress in English by her son.
- Her son's lack of progress in English worries my neighbor.

In the third sentence, the greatest emphasis is on the child's lack of progress, which is the most significant element.

Moving Modifiers and Adding Commas

When you invert material in a sentence or change its normal order in some other way, this move often causes an interruption that requires commas. All of the changes below necessitate commas.

NORMAL ORDER:

- The unshaven and unwashed homeless man slept on a piece of pasteboard. (no commas needed)

CHANGED ORDER, REQUIRING COMMAS:

- Unshaven and unwashed, the homeless man slept on a piece of pasteboard.
- The homeless man slept, unshaven and unwashed, on a piece of pasteboard.
- The homeless man slept on a piece of pasteboard, unshaven and unwashed.

See pages H-19 to H-21.

Note, too, the difference in emphasis that each change makes. The first example places too much emphasis on less important details. The second sentence emphasizes the important details. In the third sentence the modifier is misplaced and dangling.

Using Expletives

The English language includes two common expletives, *there* and *it*.* Expletives occupy space in the sentence, adding extra words but not contributing to the meaning. As an expletive, *there* or *it* often appears at the beginning of a sentence. If you use either one, check the sentence carefully; expletives are rarely needed.

REGULAR ORDER:

- A bee is on your pumpkin pie.
- In preschool most boys lag behind most girls in verbal proficiency.

---

*In other contexts *there* can function as an adverb and *it* as a pronoun.

EXPLETIVE ADDED:

- *There* is a bee on your pumpkin pie.
- *It* is a fact that in preschool most boys lag behind most girls in verbal proficiency.

Yet an expletive sometimes adds zest to a sentence:

- *There* are no words to convey the depth of my appreciation.
- *It* is wonderful to see sunshine in November!

CREATING PARALLEL STRUCTURES

www.mhhe.com/dietsch
Further coverage of parallelism can be found at:
Editing>Parallelism

Parallelism is a balancing act, easily accomplished, yet one that improves the grace and style of sentences. You may have used parallelism in your writing without realizing it. You may have chosen parallel forms because they sounded clear or right. Experienced writers use parallelism not only for clarity but also for emphasis and style. Martin Luther King, John F. Kennedy, and other great speakers used parallelism often in their formal speeches. Kennedy's most famous words, "Ask not what your country can do for you; ask what you can do for your country," serve as a prime example.

When you write compound sentences, the two independent clauses are parallel. In other words, the elements of equal rank balance because they have the same grammatical form (subject + verb; subject + verb). To create parallelism, you pair or match similar structures, just as you do with items in a series. Nouns are matched with nouns, active verbs with active verbs, passive verbs with passive verbs, and *be* verbs with *be* verbs. As you edit, be alert for instances of faulty parallelism.

Parallel Items in a Series

To read smoothly, items in a series require balance. Regardless of whether the items are single words, phrases, or clauses, all must be parallel: Every item in the series must match according to grammatical form.

Parallel Adjectives   In the following example, the final three adjectives are not only parallel but also alliterative (all start with the same consonant sound of the letter *p*):

> Three factors in the Complainers' view of the world combine to convert useful problem solving into complaining: They find themselves *powerless, prescriptive,* and *perfect.*
>
> —Robert M. Bramson, *Coping with Difficult People*

A writer who was not paying attention to parallelism might have written "without power, prescriptive, and perfect."

Parallel Phrases   Among the most famous examples of parallelism in the English language is Abraham Lincoln's statement in the Gettysburg Address that "... government *of the people, by the people,* and *for the people* shall not perish from the earth." Although Lincoln began all three phrases with different prepositions, they are still parallel. When the same preposition applies to all phrases in the series, it may be stated before every item or stated once at the beginning of the first phrase:

- I spend most of my time *at* work, *at* school, or *at* home.
- I spend most of my time *at* work, school, or home.

The final item in the series of gerund phrases below is not parallel. Yet it can be corrected easily:

NOT PARALLEL:	I enjoy listening to music, taking long walks, and *also like to work crossword puzzles.*
PARALLEL:	I enjoy listening to music, taking long walks, and *working crossword puzzles.*

Parallel Clauses   A famous sentence from the Declaration of Independence contains three parallel clauses: "We hold these truths to be self-evident, *that all men are created equal, that they are endowed by the Creator with certain unalienable Rights, that among these are Life, Liberty, and the pursuit of Happiness.*" (All the parallel clauses start with *that* and all contain the verb *are.*)

As you edit, make sure that all items in a series are parallel. Reading your writing aloud can help you to detect nonparallel structures.

Parallel Items in Pairs

When a coordinating conjunction is used, the structures on each side should be balanced, although the degree of parallelism can vary. In *Coping with Difficult People,* Bramson often uses pairs of parallel nouns and verbs, as in the following examples.

Parallel Nouns   There are different degrees of parallelism. Note that in the second example, the slight variations make it less parallel than the first example:

- "It pays to follow up any *complaint* or *suggestion* with an inquiry about what's happened."
- "Your coping reply should be to ask, 'Is that a *decision* or just your *opinion* at this stage?'"

Parallel Verbs   Notice that to be parallel, verbs *must be the same tense, the same form, and the same voice.* Different tenses should not be mixed. One-word verbs should not be mixed with verb phrases. Passive voice should not be mixed with active voice. The italicized verbs below are parallel:

- The students *are protesting* parking fees and *are requesting* free parking. (Both verbs are present tense and active voice.)

- The student *protested* campus parking fees and *requested* free parking. (Both verbs are past tense, active voice.)

Parallel Phrases   Pairs of phrases in the same sentence should be balanced:

- *For richer* or *for poorer, in sickness* and *in health* (prepositional phrases)
- *To run a company profitably* and *to treat the environment responsibly* need not be conflicting goals. (infinitive phrases)

Parallel Comparisons

Comparisons formed by using *as* or *than* should be parallel. To balance, the two subjects being compared must have the same grammatical form:

- A *spelling check* (noun) is not as accurate as *careful proofreading* (noun).
- For most interviews, *wearing a suit* (gerund phrase) is safer than *wearing casual attire* (gerund phrase).

As you check your comparisons, look for faulty parallelism. Note how the imbalance in the first sentence below can be rectified in two ways:

NOT PARALLEL:	It is better *to do* (infinitive phrase) schoolwork throughout a semester than *cramming* (gerund) the night before an exam.
EDITED:	It is better *to do* schoolwork throughout a semester than *to cram* the night before an exam. (two infinitive phrases)
EDITED:	*Doing* schoolwork throughout a semester is better than *cramming* the night before an exam. (two gerunds)

Parallel Correlative Conjunctions

Correlative conjunctions work in pairs to link words, phrases, or clauses. These conjunctions add style and emphasis to a sentence by requiring parallel structure. Common correlative conjunctions include these five pairs:

either . . . or

not . . . but

both . . . and

neither . . . nor

not only . . . but also

Correlatives need to be in the correct place in a sentence to be logical and balanced. Place the correlative right *before* the word or phrase that it modifies:

NOT PARALLEL:	*Either* you pay the fee for parking *or* a penalty.
PARALLEL:	You pay *either* the parking fee *or* a penalty. (Each correlative precedes an article and a noun.)

NOT PARALLEL: *Not only* was the defendant charged with breaking and entering *but also* with resisting arrest.

PARALLEL: The defendant was charged *not only* with breaking and entering *but also* with resisting arrest. (Both of the correlatives precede a prepositional phrases.)

PUNCTUATING SENTENCES WITH PARALLEL STRUCTURES

SIMPLE SENTENCES

Unless a simple sentence contains items in a series, there is *no comma* before the final conjunction. In the first set of examples, the parallel structures are italicized:

- The talk was both *interesting* and *inspirational*. (two adjectives)
- The talk was interesting, insightful, and inspirational. (items in a series)
- David has been outstanding not only *in football* but also *in academic work*. (two prepositional phrases)

COMPOUND SENTENCES

The main subjects and verbs in a compound sentence should be parallel. Note that the final correlative conjunction is preceded by a *comma*.

- *Not* everyone received a bonus, *but* everyone received a raise.
- *Either* he would pay the 96 parking tickets, *or* he would go to jail.

STRATEGIES FOR CHOPPING OUT DEADWOOD

Although Ernest Hemingway's finished writing is sparse and clean, he worked long and hard to bring it to that state. Once Hemingway was questioned about how often he had revised the ending of his novel *A Farewell to Arms.* He said it had taken thirty-nine revisions. As you revise, don't hesitate to chop out the deadwood—the surplus words that litter sentences. Among the most common are unnecessary references to self.

OMITTING UNNECESSARY REFERENCES TO SELF

Self-confident persons sometimes refer to themselves often during conversation. In writing, however, this tendency should be monitored, lest it give the impression of an oversized ego. If *I* appears at the beginning of a sentence, the writer may be able to invert the sentence. Placing *I* in the middle of a sentence makes the reference to self less noticeable. Delete unnecessary words as long as there is no change in meaning:

DRAFT: I will graduate on June 12 and will be available for employment after that. (14 words)

EDITED: After graduation, June 12, I will be available for employment. (10 words)

When a rough draft has two sequential sentences that begin with *I*, try to combine the sentences and delete one of the *I*'s as well as extra words. Then check the edited sentence to be sure it is clear and complete.

DRAFT: I use Microsoft Word daily to write letters. I also use Quicken for other tasks. (15 words)

EDITED: Daily I use Microsoft Word and Quicken. (7 words)

Still another way to bypass *I* is to substitute *me* or *my* when a reference to self seems necessary.

DRAFT: I can type accurately, answer the telephone courteously, and perform basic accounting functions, as you requested in your ad for a receptionist. (22 words)

EDITED: My keyboarding skills, telephone etiquette training, and experience with accounts payable/receivable should qualify me for your position of receptionist. (20 words)

Sometimes a writer will go to another extreme: completely avoiding *I, me, my,* or *mine*. Some writers resort to stilted phrases such as "the writer" or "the author of this paper." Experienced writers use *I* sensibly and sparingly.

DELETING USELESS PREPOSITIONAL PHRASES

A string of unnecessary prepositional phrases may be another source of wordiness. If you find more than two prepositional phrases close together, check for wordiness. Although a string of these phrases may not affect clarity, there may be a more concise way to make your point. Consider the following examples:

See pages H-16 to H-17.

DRAFT: A new type of compact, the Stallion II by CMG, was rated the safest in recent collision tests of compacts. (19 words)

EDITED: CMG's new Stallion II was rated safest in recent collision tests of compacts. (12 words)

Common phrases such as "this *type of* car" or "this *kind of* oven" or "*in the amount of $10*" may be shortened to "this car" or "this oven" or "$10."

CONDENSING ADJECTIVE CLAUSES

Sometimes there is little justification for an adjective clause, and the sentence can be made more effective by trimming the clause down to an appositive. Or you might substitute an adjective for an adjective clause. Consider the following examples:

DRAFT: Dr. Goldberg, *who has been our physician since I was a child,* is going to retire. (adjective clause)

EDITED: Dr. Goldberg, *our long-time family physician,* is going to retire. (appositive)

DRAFT: My Appaloosa mare, *which is only two years old,* placed first in the "Best-Trained Horse" trials. (adjective clause)

EDITED: My *two-year-old* Appaloosa mare placed first in the "Best-Trained Horse" trials. (adjective)

THINKING ABOUT WHAT YOU HAVE LEARNED

How many of the five sentence structures featured in this chapter do you normally use? Which ones do you plan to try? What have you learned about verbs that you didn't already know? Conjunctions? Have you become more aware of parallelism? What do you consider the most useful point you have learned about editing?

PRACTICE

Parallelism

Directions: Make the italicized segments parallel.

1. Peach orchards dot the south-central shore of Lake Erie in Ohio, but *grapes are grown* along the eastern shore in New York.
2. Ohio's principal crops are corn, soybeans, and *sometimes wheat is also grown.*
3. Raising soybeans is much more profitable than *to raise corn.*
4. Canola, which yields an edible oil, is grown more often than ordinary rape, *yielding a similar oil.*
5. Many farmers who live near large cities have switched from planting grain crops *to vegetables.*
6. To produce a pound of meat on chickens costs much less than *producing* a pound of meat on beef cattle.
7. Collies are a favorite farm dog because they are intelligent, suited to herding, and *they are gentle with children.*
8. A well-trained collie can round up a herd of cows and see *that they go into the barn.*
9. Border collies range from 25 to 65 pounds whereas *Scotch collies range from 45–70 pounds.*
10. Border collie puppies often sell for $300 *and up to $600 each.*

Selecting Effective Words

> Words play an enormous part in our lives. . . . Words have power to [mold] . . . thinking. . . . Conduct and character are largely determined by the nature of the words we currently use to discuss ourselves and the world around us.
>
> —**Aldous Huxley**

Have you ever thought about the power that words wield? Words can encourage or discourage, gladden or sadden, attract or repulse, soothe or incense, strengthen or weaken a relationship, win or lose an election. Words color our perception of situations, events, actions, and the world around us. The words of parents, teachers, and others help to shape our attitudes, values, and beliefs. The words we hear on television and see in print affect us in a myriad of ways.

The words we choose influence the tone of our speech and writing—and how the listener or reader perceives them. Regardless of what we may intend, if the words are inappropriate for the subject, audience, and occasion, they can create a negative impression and distort the intended message. Through study and reading aloud, you can increase your awareness of your written voice.

ADVANTAGES OF READING

Reading widely and often will help you acquire not only more knowledge and a larger vocabulary but also a deeper awareness of the nuances and subtle meanings of words. Through challenging reading, you can confront new words and become more alert to variations in a writer's voice. As you peruse this chapter, your awareness of delicate distinctions in word meanings will surge, and your knowledge of positive communication strategies will increase. Your skill in detecting inappropriate words and in selecting words appropriate to the rhetorical situation will be honed. With careful editing, your writing will have more depth, diplomacy, and clarity.

I. IMPROVING WORD CHOICE

Selecting words is rather like shopping in an enormous supermarket. But instead of roaming the aisles for groceries, a writer thumbs through the pages of a dictionary or thesaurus, or goes online to search for the right words. The supply is plentiful, for the English language has more words than any other language. Whether a writer wants plain bread-and-butter words, sweet words, tart words, tasteless words, kosher words, gourmet words, or playful words—they are all there for the taking, free of charge.

The problem is this: Which words will best suit your audience and fulfill your purpose? How do you choose words to increase the power and effectiveness of your written voice? How can you be sure that your words are clear and appropriate?

MAKING THE MESSAGE CLEAR

Make sure you say what you mean. In expository writing, words should be clear and precise so that they can be easily understood. Too many unexplained abstractions can cause confusion. A key to clarity is to use concrete words—to be specific.

Using Abstract Words

An *abstraction* is an intangible concept that lacks a physical existence. Abstract words identify ideas, theoretical terms, or qualities, such as *honesty, patriotism, fear,* and *courage.* When you use abstractions, be prepared to provide concrete examples—specific instances with details. Otherwise, your audience will interpret your words in their own individual ways. Unexplained abstractions can make language vague and unclear.

You can start by avoiding the use of *thing*, a shapeless blob of a word, the most abstract of all. *Thing* can refer to a monster or a gnat, a flask of poison or a glass of buttermilk, a viper or a star. *Thing* can mean a condition, quality, vegetable, animal, mineral—or any bit of matter on or off this planet. Another vague word is *stuff*. *Stuff* is an elastic word that can refer to objects, talk, or actions: "I picked up some stuff"; "Don't give me that stuff about being too busy."

Thing and *stuff* often serve as substitutes for thinking. As you revise, watch for other abstract nouns and adjectives (*beautiful, terrible, great*, and the like) that are overused and vague. With thought, and perhaps a thesaurus, you can replace them with concrete words.

Choosing Concrete Words

Concrete words describe actual details that can be perceived through one or more of the five senses. You can *see* a purple crocus, the rings of a lunar eclipse, and the muted hues of a rainbow. You can *hear* the whir of a hummingbird's wings or the thump of a human heart. You can *smell* the fragrance of honeysuckle or the pungent odor of an annoyed skunk. You can *touch* the fur of a baby rabbit or the grit of sandpaper. You can *taste* the sweetness of raspberry jam or the piquancy of horseradish. Concrete words stimulate the imagination and evoke vivid images, allowing the listener or reader to quickly understand what you mean.

QUESTIONS TO FIND CONCRETE WORDS

1. How did *X* look? Size? Shape? Color? Length of hair/coat?
2. Does *X* make a sound? Volume? Rate? Pitch?
3. How does *X* feel? Texture?
4. Does *X* have a fragrance or odor? Fresh? Faint? Pleasant? Perfumed?
5. If *X* is edible, how does it taste? Sweet? Sour? Tangy? Acid? How does it feel on the tongue? Smooth? Satiny? Lumpy? Coarse?

Moving from General to Specific

Depending on the purpose, much writing can be made clearer and more interesting by editing general terms, such as *cat, dog*, or *horse*, and replacing them with specific terms, such as *black kitten, border collie pup*, or *sorrel stallion*. In the sentences below, note the differences in the effects of general words and specific words:

GENERAL: A *frog was in my garden.*

SPECIFIC: A *large leopard* frog *sat under a fringed canopy of parsley in my garden.*

GENERAL:	Bicycling is a good way to see fall leaves.
SPECIFIC:	Bicycling on country roads allows me to *savor the brilliance of an Indiana autumn.*

Although specific words create interest and imagery, don't drench the reader with details unrelated to the purpose. In some situations, a general word or a less specific word may be the better choice. Consider how specific you want to be. For example, *unclean* and specific degrees of uncleanliness vary greatly in meaning: *slightly soiled, soiled, stained, grubby, dusty, dingy, dirty, murky, mucky, foul, filthy,* and *squalid.* Think carefully about how your words will affect the audience.

Scholarly or Simple Words?

A woman went up to Adlai Stevenson after a speech. Enthusiastically, she said, "Oh, Mr. Stevenson, I think your speech was absolutely superfluous!" He replied, "Thank you. I think I shall have it published—posthumously." "Fine!" she said. "The sooner, the better."

Leafing through a thesaurus, some students select scholarly or other unfamiliar words without consulting a dictionary. The results may be disastrous or unintentionally amusing. Even if used correctly, words may be inappropriate for a piece of writing. Novelist Kurt Vonnegut says: "Simplicity of language is not only reputable but perhaps even sacred. The Bible opens with a sentence well within the writing skills of a lively fourteen-year-old: 'In the beginning God created the heavens and the earth.'" Vonnegut recommends simplicity for most writing.

Lewis Thomas, an editor, physician, and contributor to the *New England Journal of Medicine,* used simple language to explain a complicated process in his book *The Lives of a Cell:*

Everything in the world dies, but we know about it [only] as a kind of abstraction. If you stand in a meadow, at the edge of a hillside, and look around carefully, almost everything you can catch sight of is in the process of dying, and most things will be dead long before you are. . . .

There are some creatures that do not seem to die at all; they simply vanish totally into their own progeny. Single cells do this. The cell becomes two, then four, and so on, and after a while the last trace is gone. It cannot be seen as death; barring mutation, the descendants are simply the first cell, living all over again.

Since Thomas is writing for a lay audience, he selects words they will understand. He begins with a statement about death and relates it to his readers. Then he compares the familiar process of death to that of cell division, which is unfamiliar. Because he supports the abstractions with concrete examples, the result is beautifully clear.

Considering Technical Jargon

Technical jargon is the professional or formal language of a trade, profession, or similar group. For example, medical jargon is used daily by pharmacists, physicians, nurses, and technicians. Technical jargon among peers rarely causes problems. But when a message is intended for a layperson, unfamiliar jargon may make the message unclear. At times the resulting confusion could be dangerous. If you are wondering when technical jargon is appropriate, the answer seems to hinge upon two questions:

- Can the language be understood by the intended audience?
- Does the language serve a technical purpose?

If the answer to both questions is yes, then use technical jargon. If the language is too technical for many readers, reword it. For example, the box of an over-the-counter hydrocortisone cream, sold to the general public, carried an unclear direction that could have been revised as follows:

"Warning: For dermatological use only. Not for ophthalmic use."

Revision: Warning: Apply to the skin only. Do not use near or in the eyes.

MAKING THE MESSAGE APPROPRIATE

To receive the attention it deserves, a serious message should be worded appropriately. Grammatical errors, trite language, and clichés can distract the reader and interfere with the writer's purpose. Two commonly overused and misused words are *a lot* and *get*.

Although *a lot* is frequently heard, it is informal. "Alot" is a common misspelling. Instead, you can use a synonym such as *many, much, several, various, some,* or *considerable*. The word *get* has numerous informal meanings that are unsuitable for college writing, for example, "got married." *Were married* is standard English.

Another misused and overused word is *like* in phrases such as "She, like, uses it in almost every sentence" and "He is, like, so hot." In present-day slang, *like* often functions as a filler for gaps of thought, much as *um* does. This usage can be jarring in writing. (For questions of usage, see the glossary in the back of this book or a good dictionary.)

Weeding Out Trite Language and Clichés

www.mhhe.com/dietsch

For more help avoiding clichés, go to:
Editing>Clichés, Slang, Jargon, Colloquialism

Like favorite recordings, clichés become worn from overuse. Although they were once fresh and original, clichés have become familiar, ingrained in our daily language. Avoid common phrases that echo in your ears during casual greetings and small talk, such as—

richly rewarding	last but not least	never meets a stranger
each and every	tip of the iceberg	enclosed please find
to the tune of	ballpark figure	in this day and age

Many of William Shakespeare's brilliantly descriptive lines, written four hundred years ago, are now clichés. How many of the following have you used?

FAMOUS LINES	SOURCE
The naked truth	*Love's Labour's Lost*, V, ii, 715
Out of the jaws of death	*All's Well That Ends Well*, III, i, 396
A dish fit for the gods	*Julius Caesar*, I, i, 173
Parting is such sweet sorrow	*Romeo and Juliet*, II, ii, 184

Perhaps you are familiar with other timeworn phrases such as "fresh as a daisy," "happy as a lark," "solid as a rock," or "His bark is worse than his bite." For most conversations and some informal writing, a cliché now and then may be acceptable. In academic and professional writing, however, clichés do not belong except when used creatively for a reason.

Distinguishing Denotation from Connotation

For years you have been looking up *denotations* in dictionaries. Denotations are the specific, literal meanings of words. If you look up *horsecar* in *Merriam-Webster's Collegiate Dictionary,* you will find two precise denotations: "1: a streetcar drawn by horses [1833] 2: a car fitted for transporting horses."* Denotations seldom cause confusion when writers know a language well and take time to edit carefully. Denotations seldom change. When they do, the changes often take place over a century or more, as in the example above.

Connotations are the imprecise impressions or emotional overtones we bring to words—the fuzzy associations beyond the denotation. Connotations are suggested meanings that vary by culture, occupation, education, region, generation, and gender. For example, men tend to use some words differently than most women, yet dictionaries do not make this distinction.

Connotative meanings can be illusive and difficult to pinpoint when they are not in dictionaries. Another complication is that some connotations change rapidly whereas others remain steady over the years. Connotations may also vary according to individual perceptions, which are shaped by experience and education. As you read the lists of unfavorable and more favorable words, think how they sound to you. Do you agree with the labels?

---

*By permission from *Merriam-Webster's Collegiate® Dictionary,* Eleventh Edition. Copyright © 2004 by Merriam-Webster, Incorporated (www.merriam-webster.com).

CONSIDERING HOW WORDS SOUND

Unfavorable	More Favorable
wrong	incorrect, inaccurate
omitted, forgot	overlooked
failed	missed
mistake	error
advice	suggestion, recommendation
complained	reported, informed
claimed	stated
problem	concern, challenge
deal	bargain, offer, opportunity

Considering Euphemisms

Euphemisms are words with overly favorable connotations. For politeness or to avoid confrontation, they may be substituted for direct words that might annoy. For example, the manager who bluntly evaluates work as "poor" or "sloppy" will undermine morale and productivity. But the manager who allows an employee to save face with euphemisms such as "needs to improve" or "can do better" and who encourages with constructive suggestions will have a better chance of motivating.

If a euphemism is needed in a touchy situation, that is fine—as long as there is no deception. There is a big difference between tact and deceit. Much academic writing is direct and factual. Since euphemisms obscure reality, they are seldom advisable in student essays.

Thinking about Negative and Positive Words

A negative word or an inappropriate word can contaminate an entire message, causing readers to misunderstand or become so irritated they stop reading. By including positive words, courtesy words, gender-free terms, and inoffensive phrasing, you can improve your writing—making it tactful and diplomatic for sensitive rhetorical situations.

Focusing on the Positive   During revision, the old adage "Tell them what you can do, not what you can't" is invaluable. Often an idea can be restated indirectly in positive words to soften unpleasant news, as in the examples below:

NEGATIVE: We are *out* of the HP Cwi23T tricolor inkjet print cartridges. They will *not* be available for three days.

POSITIVE: The HP Cwi23T tricolor inkjet print cartridges *will* be here in three days.

NEGATIVE: I *don't* have my paper finished. I had to work seven days last week.

POSITIVE: Professor James, although I worked seven days last week, I *do* have a typed draft. *May* I have another day to *revise?* Or would you *prefer* the rough draft now?

A strategy that will promote harmony in sensitive situations, along with positive words, is to ask suitable questions. Carefully worded questions tend to elicit pleasant responses. When struggling to find a positive word, look up the negative word in a thesaurus and check antonyms. Sometimes we simply overlook positive words, such as the ones below, that could greatly improve the tone of our messages:

advantage	courtesy	help	save
assistance	encourage	invite	succeed
benefit	enjoy	pleasure	success
cooperation	glad	prompt	win

WRITING SUCCESS TIPS: TACT AND DIPLOMACY

1. **Think about the rhetorical situation.** Will the reader be apt to disagree? Is the topic a sore point and apt to pose a risk? How will you proceed?

2. **Begin on a positive note.** Before discussing a negative item, you might thank the person for a previous favor or find an *area of agreement.* (See chapter 18.) If you offer a proposal, consider the benefits to the individual and to the company. Focus on long-term advantages that outweigh any short-term disadvantages.

3. **Choose words carefully.** Consider connotations. Might any words irritate or offend? Can you find a more positive word that has the same denotative meaning? (Consult a thesaurus.)

4. **Offer suggestions softly.** In some situations, consider prefacing a suggestion with a tentative phrase, such as *I wonder* or *You might.* These terms soften the impact of giving advice.

5. **Let your draft cool.** For touchy situations, wait twenty-four hours. Revise and edit before sending. If rushed, have a trusted friend or coworker react to the draft.

6. **Read/listen carefully to the receiver's response.** Do not argue. If you disagree, you might say, "Let me think about it" or "That's an interesting (or different) perspective." You could plan a logical and diplomatic reply, or you might decide to let the matter drop.

Using Negative Prefixes   If you can't find a positive word and there is a reason to state a negative idea directly, then soften the impact with a negative prefix.

There are nine common negative prefixes: *non-, un-, im-, in-, dis-, il-, ir-, a-, ab-.* All enable a writer to delete *not.* For example, instead of *not perfect*, you might say *imperfect* or *irregular.*

Using Courtesy Words   Words such as *please, may I, thanks, thank you, appreciate, appreciation, gratitude, your thoughtfulness, your generosity,* or *your effort* rally a positive response in the reader or listener. Conveying civility will enhance the tone and effectiveness of employment cover letters, other business letters, thank-you notes, e-mail, and other written or oral messages.

For best advantage, place courtesy words at the beginning and end (the positions of emphasis) of the document. As a safeguard, never send an e-mail, note, memo, or letter without rereading and reconsidering your word choice, as well as the spelling, grammar, and punctuation. When a situation is sensitive, take a day to mull over the best way to word the message. If you are applying for a job, make sure the letter is 100 percent error-free.

II. USING INCLUSIVE LANGUAGE IN THE WORKPLACE

Just as society and culture change, so too does language. The Civil Rights Act of 1964 forced the U.S. Department of Labor to revise its *Dictionary of Occupational Titles* to eliminate sexist and ageist terms. Likewise, the Bureau of the Census modified 52 of the 442 categories of work. Newspapers have even changed their former two columns "Help Wanted—Male" and "Help Wanted—Female" to one column titled "Help Wanted." With this legislation has come the idea that language should reflect equality by being gender-free or gender-neutral.

Other important changes that also affect language in the workplace have occurred. To prevent lawsuits and other problems, many companies have enacted policies that forbid sexism, abusive language, and various forms of discrimination. Regardless of where you work, an understanding of inclusive language will enable you to interact and to write more effectively.

REPLACING SEXIST TERMS
WITH GENDER-FREE TERMS

Some words carry sexist overtones because they contain the root *man: fireman, policeman, mailman.* But these forms are gradually being dropped in favor of gender-free counterparts such as firefighter, police officer, and mail carrier. Although masculine nouns and pronouns (*he, his, him*) were used for centuries to include women, this usage is also outmoded. One way to avoid this faux pas is by writing in the plural, for example, "players . . . they." But the plural is not always possible. Then one "he or she," or one "his or her," is relatively unobtrusive. Often the best and simplest way is to use gender-free words, omitting any reference to gender.

PLURAL:	The *deans* are to bring *their* projected department budgets.
GENDER SPECIFIC:	Every dean should bring *his* projected department budget. (Correct only if all deans are male.)
GENDER FREE:	Every dean should bring *a* projected department budget.

Sexist	Nonsexist
man, men (if applied to both sexes)	person, people
chairman	chair, chairperson
male nurse	nurse
girl, gal, my woman	woman (adult)
man and wife	husband and wife

REPLACING SEXIST TERMS

REPLACING OFFENSIVE TERMS WITH RESPECTFUL TERMS

In some high-stress jobs, crude and disrespectful language is not uncommon. As a result, many companies have created language codes of ethics. One policy forbids "unwanted, deliberate, repeated, unsolicited profanity, cussing, swearing, insulting, abusive or crude language." Penalties may include counseling or firing, depending on the case.* Definitions of verbal harassment and policies vary.

Although some words may not seem discriminatory, they may be unwise in regard to politeness and the law. The general advice is to avoid mentioning personal attributes, such as size, body parts, attractiveness, or age—even when joking. Careless jokes about absentmindedness, memory loss, or Alzheimer's are best avoided. Although such remarks may be made in a playful way, they can undercut image and irritate, especially when the teasing continues. Still other words clearly discriminate and disrespect on the basis of ethnicity, religion, race, or color.

HOW, WHEN, AND WHERE WILL YOU DELIVER THE MESSAGE?

Not only is the choice of words in a message significant but also the method of delivery and timing. Whether you have an important business message or a lesser personal one to deliver, consider the rhetorical situation carefully. Think about the occasion, the nature of the subject, and how the audience will be likely

---

*Rachel Emma Silverman, "On-the-Job Cursing: Obscene Talk Is Latest Target of Workplace Ban," *Wall Street Journal* 8 May 2001: B14.

to perceive the message. Does it concern a sensitive issue? Should it be delivered in private? Should it be said face-to-face or written? When would be the best time to deliver the message? Poor timing and lack of privacy can affect reception. Some messages should be conveyed where they cannot be heard over cubicle walls or in public places.

Sometimes the rhetorical situation is best served by a prudent memo or letter. In some cases, a written message has three advantages:

- **Privacy.** (Do not send sensitive messages by e-mail; see chapter 25.)
- **Opportunity to revise.** You have more time to consider your words.
- **Record.** You can retain a copy for reference.

Wherever you communicate—in the workplace, in social settings, or at home—the suggestions in this chapter can help you improve the tone and effectiveness of your messages, as well as the impression you make.

CHECKLIST   EDITING FOR CLARITY AND APPROPRIATENESS

The clarity and effectiveness of your message depend on how well you fulfill the purpose and tailor your writing to the audience. To be convincing, your written voice should sound knowledgeable, trustworthy, and appropriate.

1. Are the words clear, specific, and suitable for the audience? (See chapter 2.)

2. If you use abstractions, do you define or give examples or other support?

3. Do any words have negative connotations? Might they offend? (Read your message aloud and think about how it might sound to someone else.)

4. Do any words seem trite?

5. Are any words repeated unnecessarily? If so, can you condense or find an accurate synonym?

THINKING ABOUT WHAT YOU HAVE LEARNED

As you become more aware of subtle word meanings and the expectations implicit in certain rhetorical situations, you can enhance your ability to communicate. Tact and diplomacy are significant not only in interaction with clients, patients, customers, coworkers, and employers but also in written messages. Below are four questions to think about:

1. Why do we say that words have power?
2. Can you think of other ways that words influence us?
3. Which suggestions in this chapter are the most helpful?
4. What points do you plan to apply in your daily interaction and/or in your writing?

PRACTICE

COLLABORATIVE LEARNING: Negative Connotations

Directions: Pretend you have had a mild disagreement with a family member. Later you overhear the person describing the exchange. Which terms below would you dislike hearing? Which would be acceptable? Do your group members agree or disagree? If so, why? (Consult a dictionary if you wish.)

dispute	quarrel	spat	scrap
conflict	disagreement	fight	row
hassle	difficulty	argument	brawl
tiff	altercation	fracas	confrontation

WRITE A DESCRIPTION USING CONCRETE WORDS

Directions: In one paragraph, write a description. Give concrete details and examples. If you wish, describe one of the following topics.

1. An unusual pet
2. A family heirloom
3. A vehicle you use or have used
4. Your favorite footwear
5. Your favorite place when you were a child

Options for Organization

A well-planned garden is a delight to the eye. The symmetry of shrubs and trees, textures of bark and leaves, and multicolored hues creates a sense of harmony. Usually, there is a focal point—perhaps a fountain, pond, or courtyard. This garden has a bridge that not only spans the stream but also unites elements. Similarly, a well-planned essay is pleasing to the ear. Apt words and smooth phrases enhance the balance and flow of sentences. The thesis sentence is the focal point that unites details, anecdotes, and examples. The writer, like a landscape designer, organizes and develops a harmonious pattern for a purpose. Part 3 explains options for organization and their purpose.

1. Do you have a garden, window boxes, or patio pots? Describe your gardening.

2. If you do not, describe the garden of your dreams.

WRITING EXERCISE

MIXING WRITING STRATEGIES FOR A PURPOSE

It was the best of times, it was the worst of times,
it was the age of wisdom, it was the age of foolishness . . .
it was the spring of hope, it was the winter of despair,
we had everything before us, we had nothing before us,
we were all going to Heaven, we were all going direct the other way—

Charles Dickens (1812–1870), *A Tale of Two Cities*

With these immortal words, Dickens opened his epic novel of the French Revolution. In each line he posed a paradox, mixing description and comparison. Dickens' rhetorical purpose was to inform, as well as to entertain, by exposing the evils of the times. Yet his novels also carried an implicit element of persuasion. As a result, they led to many reforms. In all fifteen of his novels, Dickens deftly combined various writing strategies.

Seldom is one writing strategy adequate for any writer. Although you undoubtedly combine various writing strategies, too, you can improve your organization and style by studying part 3. Each chapter focuses on one major strategy of exposition, its chief purpose, and the opportunities it opens to writers. The student examples, as well as those of professionals, should spark your interest and creativity.

You have many rhetorical options. Your purpose may be expressive, to describe a memorable moment and preserve it in a journal. Or the purpose may be to inform by recording family narratives. To entertain your classmates or another group, you might recount an amusing anecdote. Or your purpose might be to persuade readers to vote for a certain candidate. Regardless, if your rhetorical purpose is genuine, it is a valid reason for writing.

Think long and deep—you have a wellspring of experience to draw upon and diverse thoughts to share. The more you write, read, and think, the more polished your writing will become. Writing is a process of discovery—with each revision more ideas arise. Keep writing and surprise yourself!

Narrating Memorable Events

Daily we use narration to relay news of a neighborhood or news of a nation, to share research data, to write reports and other documents. Histories, biographies, journals, magazines, advertisements, and college essays employ narration. Stories impart information in an appealing way—stirring the imagination, eliciting empathy, and lending support to opinion. This chapter explains techniques of narration that have a wide range of practical uses.

> Tell me a fact and I'll learn. Tell me a truth and I'll believe. But tell me a story and it will live in my heart forever.
>
> —**Native American proverb**

PURPOSE OF NARRATION

You can use narration as a major or minor writing strategy. For example, medical personnel write reports of patients' conditions and progress. Managers keep brief histories of employees' performance. Law enforcement officers record the events that precede a crime and occur during an arrest. In college, you may write narratives not only in English, business, and technical writing classes but also in anthropology, psychology, prelaw, engineering, and other classes. Although these narratives invariably include description, narration is the major strategy.

General Purpose

An effective narrative recounts action for a purpose, according to the rhetorical situation. If the *general purpose* is to entertain and establish camaraderie, then it may not matter whether the account is fiction or fact. But when the purpose is serious—primarily to reflect, inform, or persuade—then the audience expects facts and should receive them. *Then the writer is obligated to put forth the unvarnished truth.*

Specific Purpose

To be worthwhile, every narrative must have a *point*—a valid reason to be told or written. Whether the point is stated or unstated, it always shapes the narrative. If the purpose is to inform, the main idea, fact, or event is often stated first. When writers probe into causes or motives underlying an event or experience, they may place the point at the end. There they provide an observation, insight, or lesson learned.

In "The Death of the Moth," Virginia Woolf begins by giving facts about moths, then narrates the brief experience of one moth. She compares the moth's struggle for life with that of all living things: "One could only watch the extraordinary efforts made by those tiny legs against an oncoming doom which could, had it chosen, have submerged an entire city, not merely a city, but masses of human beings . . ." As the moth struggles to live, Woolf is reminded of her own mortality and concludes with this insight:

> The struggle was over. . . . As I looked at the dead moth, this minute wayside triumph of so great a force over so mean an antagonist filled me with wonder. Just as life had been strange a few minutes before, so death was now as strange. The moth . . . now lay most decently and uncomplainingly composed. O yes, he seemed to say, death is stronger than I am.

Woolf's specific purpose is to share her wonder that so small a creature as a moth would struggle so hard to live—just as humans usually do.

ELEMENTS OF NARRATION

Every narrative has six basic elements: the *where, when, who, what, how,* and *why* of an event. Where did the action take place? What era and time? Who was involved? What happened? How did it happen? Why did it happen? Who is the narrator? The answers to these questions and the narrator's point of view influence the effect of the story. The first four questions are usually answered early and easily when the writer sets the scene, giving the necessary background details. After that the telling or writing becomes more difficult.

Where and When

Early in the narrative, the writer sets the scene of the action, event, or conflict that will take place. Readers need to know basic facts about the place, era, culture, and conditions that prevail. They do not need long, involved descriptions. In fact, certain details of the setting can be imparted gradually as the narrative unfolds.

Who

A narrative usually revolves around people, although an animal may take the central role. The writer discloses significant characteristics and qualities of the participants, either explicitly or implicitly, often showing rather than telling. Dialogue can reveal a person's inner life, values, and insights. Personality and character are revealed by the way the person responds to challenges and interacts with others.

What

Whether one event or a series occur, action, conflict, and change are essential to the story. Often the action hinges upon a physical conflict such as person against person (war), person against nature (tornado), or person against animal (attack by a mountain lion). Sometimes the conflict is internal. The individual must make a decision or solve a problem when information is incomplete, or there is no ideal solution.

How

The *how* of a narrative often involves cause and effect. To trace a cause, you might look at the effect and trace it backward. Then your first step is to describe the effect. Consider the short-term effect and any long-term effects (chapter 16). The second step is to look for possible causes. To start, you might ask yourself these questions:

- What exactly was the effect? Was it short term, long term, or both?
- Who or what started the action that caused the effect?

- Could there have been more than one cause?
- Did a series of events result in the effect?
- How did the central participant respond?

Why

The *why* of a narrative is the reasoning or motivation, usually of the central character, that propels the action. The factor(s) or influence(s) behind the action may seem hazy until you are heavily into revising and reexamining the facts. To explore why an event happened, you might ask yourself these questions:

- Why did the central character (or another influential character) act as he or she did?
- Was there a change in attitude or a shift in values that directed the behavior?
- Did relationships, connections, and character influence the outcome?
- What motivated the person?

Point of View in Narration

The way the narrator tells a story influences its credibility. Is the narrator giving an eyewitness account or passing on something heard from someone else? How reliable is the narrator? How objective? How does the narrator regard the subject? From which angle or attitude? Depending on your role in the story, the rhetorical situation, and the purpose, you can use either a first-person or a third-person point of view.

First-Person Narration   First-person narration lends a sense of immediacy, giving the reader a front-row seat on the action. This account, told by an observer or participant in the story, is often written in a conversational tone. Whether you choose first person (*I, me, my, mine, we,* or *ours*) or another perspective will depend upon your role. Is it your story or someone else's? Barb Bronson uses first person in her essay. The first three paragraphs appear here:

Clipper Ship Mom

Unique and truly American, the clipper ship is a fast-sailing cargo ship whose shipmaster's talents have never been surpassed. My mother reminds me of those early ships and courageous sailors. Whenever the open sea of marriage gave warning of an approaching storm, Clipper Ship Mom would batten down the hatches and set her course in preparation for the rough voyage ahead. As a child, I watched helplessly as Clipper Ship Mom sailed to a hell where my father resided as gatekeeper.

Even when my father was sober, his behavior was unpredictable. Petty, trivial incidents would arouse his raging temper. But whenever he had too many drinks, it was like coming face to face with Satan himself. So many times I wished Mom would take us away to some safe place where we could hide.

I also knew Mom had been taught to honor her marriage vows—for better or worse.

   When I was fourteen I awoke to an argument which led to my father's yanking my mother to the front yard in her nightclothes and placing a gun to her temple as her five children watched. He told us to say goodbye to our mother; she was going to "meet her maker." Frozen with fear, we clung to each other as tears streamed down our faces. Looking to the heavens above, I whispered a prayer for God to spare her life. He must have heard the prayer, for after a while Dad calmed down, and we all went back to bed.

Mixing Writing Strategies   In this excerpt from "Clipper Ship Mom," Barb Bronson mixes writing strategies. She supports her thesis with comparison, description, and narration. Comparison begins in the title, "Clipper Ship Mom," and continues through the first paragraph. The second paragraph describes and summarizes the problem. The third paragraph narrates an episode. Comparison then reappears in the conclusion (page 166).

Third-Person Narration   Writers or narrators who are not involved in a story adopt a third-person point of view. They restrict pronouns to words such as *he, she, it, they,* and *them.* Third-person narration puts distance between the reader and the topic, producing a more detached voice than first person provides. A professional response, such as those found in many business and technical reports or research papers, usually requires third-person point of view. There the goal is to focus on facts and results, not on feelings or opinions. Reporters, biographers, and historians use third person in an objective way for various reasons.

   The following third-person narrative recounts a disastrous 1981 accident at the Hyatt Regency Hotel in Kansas City. Think how differently a narrative of the accident by a first-person survivor would have sounded.

   At 7:05 p.m. on Friday, July 17, 1981, the atrium was filled with more than sixteen hundred people, most of them dancing to the music of a well-known band for a tea dance competition, when suddenly a frightening, sharp sound like a thunderbolt was heard, stopping the dancers in mid-step. Looking up toward the source of the sound, they saw two groups of people on the second- and fourth-floor walkways, observing the festivities and stomping in rhythm with the music. As the two walkways began to fall, the observers were seen holding on to the railing with terrified expressions on their faces. The fourth-floor walkway dropped from the hangers holding it to the roof structure, leaving the hangers dangling like impotent stalactites. Since the second-floor walkway hung from the fourth-floor walkway, the two began to fall together. There was a large roar as the concrete decks of the steel-framed walkways cracked and crashed down, in a billowing cloud of dust, on the crowd gathered around the bar below the second-floor walkway. People were screaming; the west glass wall adjacent to the walkways shattered, sending shards flying over 100 ft.(30 m); pipes broken by the falling walkways sent jets of water spraying the atrium floor. It was a nightmare the survivors would never forget.

   —Matthys Levy and Mario Salvadori, *Why Buildings Fall Down*

There may be a time when you decide to write in third person about your experience. Perhaps the topic is still hurtful, even heartrending. To gain distance and objectivity, you might write in third person about yourself, perhaps using a pseudonym. But first consider the nature of the experience. If a recent event has been traumatic, beware. You can become so entangled in emotion that you hit a writing block and lose the point.

WRITING A NARRATIVE PAPER

www.mhhe.com/dietsch

For online help writing narrative essays, visit: Writing>Writing Tutors> Narration

You have a treasure trove of stories just waiting to be told, some sad, some happy. Perhaps they are family stories, passed down from generation to generation. Prewriting will help you find them. Mull over the episode and consider:

- How did the experience influence me? Am I happier? Wiser? How so?
- What did I gain or learn? Can I find a lesson or moral?
- How might the narrative affect the audience?

Prewriting

www.mhhe.com/dietsch

For further coverage of prewriting, check out: Writing>Prewriting

The simplest way to start prewriting is to list key events in the order they occurred. Leave an inch or so of space between items to insert related details. After listing key events, jot down significant details about each one. Asking questions can guide you:

- What is the point of the narrative?
- Who are the readers? How much do they need to know?
- Does the experience remind me of an event in the public eye? How?
- Is the comparison relevant to my purpose?
- What is the source of tension or conflict? (barrier, problem, decision)

The diagram below depicts how movement might flow from the beginning to the end of a narrative. The central character's motivation and reactions to events, as well as other factors, influence the pace and resolution at the end.

MOVEMENT IN A NARRATIVE

FIGURE 9.1

Drafting an Introduction

Lately some editors have advised writers that they have just five to ten seconds to hook most readers. As you prewrite, watch for a hook that will lure readers on. To begin an introduction to a narrative, you might ask yourself these questions:

www.mhhe.com/dietsch

Want more help with introductions? Go to: Writing>Introductions

- How should the story start? How can I grab the reader's attention?
- What is unusual, amusing, or ironic?
- Should I use first person or third person?
- Is the opening related to the point of the story?

The purpose of the narrative will guide you in deciding whether to place the thesis at the beginning or end. Does the reader need to know immediately where the main idea is headed? For reasons of clarity and practicality, some rhetorical situations call for an early thesis. Other times the writer may delay the thesis, *laying a foundation to support the point of the narrative* and building to the peak of the action. Then the thesis comes at the end, where it can be stated or implied, depending upon the purpose.

Opening with Action   An *action opening* plunges the reader into the story with no unnecessary details or explanations. Right away the main participant is faced with a decision or immersed in a predicament that must somehow be resolved. At the same time, the writer sets the scene, identifying the person, place, time, and conditions. As the action starts rolling, description is usually sparse. Only essential details are shown. Gradually, necessary bits of background appear as the conflict continues and the suspense heightens. (See "Just a Walk" at the end of the chapter.) Other types of openings reveal the action, problem, or conflict gradually.

Opening with a Quotation   If you find an appropriate quotation that *specifically* relates to your main idea, then you can easily tie it to the beginning of a narrative, using embedded transition. Be sure that any explanation does not delay the action unduly. Do not belabor the point of the quotation lest the reader perceive it as talking down. If you want to use a quotation that relates in a *general* way to your main point, then you may have to look long and hard to connect it adequately.

See chapter 15.

Opening with a Comparison   An unusual comparison in the title or first paragraph can hook the reader and serve as a unifying thread throughout the narrative. An effective comparison is introduced early and alluded to periodically. Sometimes a comparison may involve a symbol rich in connotations, as in "Clipper Ship Mom," earlier in this chapter. Note that along with this striking symbol, the writer used water imagery: matrimonial seas, rough seas, tears, and similar images in developing her paper.

Organizing a Narrative Paper

Narratives need a clear progression. Each event, detail, and section of dialogue should advance the narrative point and contribute to the unity. If you can limit the focus early, then it will be easier to decide what to include—and what to omit. Or if the white heat of inspiration seizes you, write down everything, then go back and delete extra details, no matter how interesting. Make sure that every detail helps to establish a coherent design.

In most narratives the action is presented in the order that it occurs. Sometimes, however, a writer may disrupt the chronology by a sudden shift to the past, or *flashback*. For example, you might begin a narrative at a dramatic moment near its chronological conclusion, then flash back to events leading up to this point. Keep in mind, though, that flashbacks are tricky to manage effectively because of the special transition and plotting required. As a novice writer of narrative, you may want to stick to chronological order.

Developing the Narrative Paper

As you develop a narrative, keep in mind the nature of the central character. It is usually advisable to look at people and events from a positive perspective but to be realistic. Human beings are a mix of negative and positive traits, and life is a blend of potholes, porcupines, and poppies. The following questions may be helpful to consider:

- Does the main character have a need or compulsion to reach a goal?
- Does the person have an internal or external conflict? A barrier to face?
- What will the person do?
- What is the darkest moment—the crisis? (It usually occurs about halfway.)
- How does the person react?
- What is the high point of the action—the climax?
- Does the person change or learn?

Dialogue   Selected dialogue can enliven a narrative, advance the action, and give clues to the personality of the speaker. It should have the ring of real conversation but move more quickly. Including the actual words of participants can make the story come alive and ring true. The writer may edit the dialogue to make it more direct and to the point, compressing, leaving those words that convey information and lend flavor to the narrative. Note, however, that it would be unethical to twist the words out of context and distort the intended meaning. Diane P. includes just one line of dialogue in the opening of her narrative:

> My first night in Houston, Texas, while visiting a friend, a hurricane hit. I slept through most of it. But when her brother yelled, "It's going to take the roof!" I awoke. As I sat up in bed, half awake, he dashed down the hall in his

underwear, headed for the front door. Then both doors of the house blasted open—even though they were dead bolted.

When writing dialogue, minimize the use of "he said" and "she said." As long as the identity of the person who is talking is clear, no other identification is needed. Just indent for a new paragraph with each new speaker, no matter how short the exchange. Set off the dialogue with quotation marks. (Also see "The Mulberry Tree," later in this chapter.)

Concrete Details and Action Verbs   The trick to writing an effective narrative is to nab the reader's attention and retain it by keeping the flow of details interesting. Include just enough *concrete details* of the setting and action to enable readers to visualize events and feel as if they know the people involved. Use vivid verbs, specific nouns, and modifiers that will appeal to your readers' senses not only through sight but also through hearing, touch, taste, and smell. Beware of including unnecessary description that slows the pace and distracts from the point of the narrative.

Building Suspense   Another way to keep readers interested is to build *suspense*. You can do this by hinting at something but withholding crucial details in order to reveal them at a strategic moment. You can also build tension by pacing your narrative so that readers are kept wondering what will happen next. By the end, however, all loose threads should be clearly connected and the conflict or problem resolved. This technique is not applicable to most workplace writing.

Writing a Conclusion

Although endings of narratives vary widely, every ending should have a sense of completeness. It should leave readers satisfied, convinced, empathetic, hopeful, amused, thoughtful, or wiser. Usually, the complication, problem, or conflict is resolved or alleviated at the end. To resolve matters successfully, the writer must tell enough but not too much. If an ending is too long and wordy, it may become tiresome or confusing. Underdeveloped endings may leave readers feeling disappointed or cheated. They should not be left hanging without a clue to the outcome.

www.mhhe.com/dietsch
If you want to learn more about conclusions, go to: Writing>Conclusions

Writing the ending of a narrative may be painstaking. In fact, you may attempt more than one before finally being satisfied. If in doubt about your ending, try asking these questions:

- What is my narrative point?
- Was there an unexpected result?
- Are there any loose ends to resolve?
- Does the ending seem complete?
- Does the voice of the narrator sound appropriate?

Ending with a Hint or a Hope   Even if the full story remains untold or the conflict is not resolved, there should be a clue so that readers can draw their own inferences. For example, in *Gone with the Wind*, Rhett is leaving Scarlett, and she is agonizing over his departure. Yet the reader is offered a hint and a hope that life will get better. The novel closes with these words:

> She could get Rhett back. She knew she could. There had never been a man she couldn't get, once she set her mind upon him.
> "I'll think of it all tomorrow, at Tara. I can stand it then. Tomorrow I'll think of some way to get him back. After all, tomorrow is another day."
>
> —Margaret Mitchell

Ending with a Surprise   An unusual incident or twist may bring a story to a satisfying close. The surprise ending contains something the reader does not expect. The surprise may be amusing, embarrassing, enlightening, romantic, or dramatic as long as it is appropriate. To be effective, the unexpected event should grow out of the action, problem, or conflict. For example, Shasta Scharf used a surprise ending that sprang from a key event in "Just a Walk" (at the end of the chapter).

See chapter 20.   **Ending with a Reaction**   Sometimes a narrative ends with a brief *reaction*, a focused response or thoughtful commentary. The reaction may mention influences, implications, or consequences of the action. There may be an attempt to explain an underlying motive. Columnists, biographers, historians, novelists, and other writers often explore motives that may have precipitated an event. Or the reaction ending may connect a personal experience to one with universal implications, as in "The Mulberry Tree," later in this chapter.

WRITING A NARRATIVE REPORT

A *narrative report* is written in response to the need for a record of a real situation or event. Before starting to write any report, consider the *purpose* and the *audience.* Why is the report needed? To whom is it directed? Will one person or several read the report? Might it become a public record? Considering these questions will help you judge the amount of detail needed, the level of language expected, and the degree of privacy involved.

Unlike personal narratives and fiction, a narrative report always has *a thesis at the beginning.* Reports do not withhold information to build suspense. In the workplace, the reader immediately needs to know the *purpose and scope,* which is the usual heading of the first section. This section tells why the report is being written and the range it will cover.

The body of a report also has a suitable heading. This major section explains the topic. The conclusion (use a heading) may summarize, recommend, or look to the future. For instance, research reports sometimes mention a need for future research. (See "How Research Papers and Research Reports Differ" in chapter 30. An example of a report appears at the end of that chapter.)

REVISING A NARRATIVE

When revising a narrative, look at the larger items first. Check the shape of the story. Is the setting clear? Does the action flow well, or should some events be rearranged? Is the sequence of events clear, or are more transitions of time and place needed?

Watch for complicated sentences or cumbersome words that slow the pace unnecessarily. When the action is fast-paced, use short sentences. When movement slows, use longer sentences, combining ideas, to reflect the pace (like this one). The checklist that follows will also help you revise.

www.mhhe.com/dietsch

For general help with revision, check out: Writing>Drafting and Revising

CHECKLIST   **REVISING A NARRATIVE**

1.   Does the narrative begin at a significant spot?

2.   Is the complication, conflict, or problem clear?

3.   Is the action arranged in the most effective order?

4.   Do major details advance the point of the narrative? Do minor details clearly relate?

5.   Does the pace of sentences reflect what is happening?

6.   Does the ending give a sense of completion?

TWO STUDENT PAPERS: NARRATION

The student writers of these two personal essays show unusual skill in their use of concrete detail, strong verbs, and dialogue. Betty Russell briefly sets the scene before the action begins. The point of her story appears at the end.

The Mulberry Tree

Mr. Grump's mulberries were big, plump, and tempting. At the edge of his yard stood two large trees, loaded with luscious blue-black mulberries. Although I would not have dreamed of stealing, I picked a few off the grass, and ate them; the other kids followed. The berries tasted so good.

There were eight of us—me, Alice, Dorothy, and Shirley, my sisters, and our friends, the four Smith sisters. I was ten years old and they were all younger. We often played at a vacant lot near our homes. There we would fill our cans at the "red haw" (hawthorn) tree. We used the red haws to string for necklaces or for pretend food when we played house.

That afternoon, however, we had taken a different way to the red haw tree, past Mr. Grump's house. When we saw all those big dark berries going to waste underneath the trees, we decided to fill our cans. Then we thanked "Mr. Mulberry Tree" and ran home. Our mother washed the berries and put them in a big bowl for supper. That evening we piled whipped cream on the berries for dessert. We felt so proud because there were enough to treat the whole family.

Two days later all eight girls agreed it was time for more berries and cream. Our parents, thinking the trees were in the empty lot with the red haws, gave permission to go. To our dismay, when we reached the tree, there were no berries on the ground. Even the lower halves of the trees were bare of fruit. Lucy Smith and my sister Alice, tomboys of the group, climbed a tree, and started jumping and shaking the branches. Mulberries fell like black rain.

We had started to fill our cans, when suddenly a voice thundered, "What are you kids doing? I'm going to call the police. You are on MY property STEALING my mulberries!"

Within seconds Lucy and Alice slid down from the tree. The other kids were running in different directions. Alice grabbed five-year-old Shirley by the hand, and they ran toward home. I turned to pick up my can and, to my horror, saw Mr. Grump holding my seven-year-old sister, Dorothy, up by the back of her neck. Her feet dangled in the air.

"Let her go!" I shrieked.

"I'm going to hand you both over to the police," he yelled. He held her with one hand and tried to reach me with the other. We circled—he, trying to reach me and I, trying to reach Dorothy. But I could not get close enough to grab her without his grabbing me. So I ran up and threw the berries, can and all, in his face. He released his grip on Dorothy, and I snatched her hand.

As we cut across yards and down an alley, we could still hear Mr. Grump yelling. When we reached our yard, we slumped against the back of the garage to catch our breath. Our hearts seemed ready to leap out of our chests. How long we leaned there, I don't know.

Then we sneaked in the house. I hid in the closet under the stairs. Dorothy ran upstairs and hid with Alice under their bed. Shirley ran to the kitchen and clung to Mom like a second skin. When dinner was ready, Mom made us come out of our hiding places and demanded to know what we had done. No one said a word.

For two days we stayed in the house, expecting the police to come any moment and take us away. Our fear and guilt stayed with us for a long time. "Thou shalt not steal" was a commandment we never forgot.

QUESTIONS FOR DISCUSSION

1. What do you learn about the narrator in the first paragraph?
2. What strategy supplements narration?
3. What is the effect of including dialogue?
4. What is the effect of having the commandment in the last line?
5. Does this story remind you of another about a tree with forbidden fruit? What similarities do you see?

The second paper, by Shasta Scharf, is written in the third person. For the concluding paragraph, she shifts to first person for a reason.

Just a Walk

Jimmy was seventeen the day he joined the armed forces. Fresh from the coal mines of West Virginia, with only a sixth-grade education and six weeks' survival training in Massachusetts, he was flown over 9,000 miles to Corregidor. Suddenly, his life became a battleground for survival. The day that General MacArthur left the Philippines, Jimmy shot his first enemy warrior. "This," he said, "was the first time I walked through Hell."

As the Japanese took possession of the Philippines, Jimmy was captured and the Bataan Death March began. Jimmy was near the head of the line. For over ninety days, he and the other U.S. soldiers suffered severe malnutrition, dysentery, malaria, and abuse as they walked to a prison camp. That was another walk through Hell. For three years, Jimmy was the camp interpreter. Being the interpreter gave him the chance to send messages to and receive them from the United States Army covertly. The Japanese never knew that "Jimpie," as they called him, was using their equipment for spying.

In 1945 Jimmy and the others left the Philippines via three "Hell Ships." Each ship was designed to hold 200 passengers. Over 1,700 men were crowded into quarters intended for 600. Only 482 men walked off the ships in Osaka, Japan. Poor ventilation, no food, no water, and no place to lie down had taken a heavy toll.

When Jimmy reached the United States, he was decorated for bravery and given a six-day pass to see California. He and three friends drove up to Mt. Shasta to ski. There he beheld "a sight that restored [his] sanity." With seven years of hell behind him, Lake Shasta and the snow-capped mountain in front of him, Jimmy came face to face with a young deer. Only five feet away, the fawn stared straight into Jimmy's eyes. Tears flowed down his cheeks as he gazed at the most beautiful scene he had encountered in his twenty-four years of life.

After his experience at Mt. Shasta, Jimmy's life became less chaotic. He went back to the dark, damp coal mines with his father and brothers. Since mining coal is a "filthy, unsafe job and most people do not live to regret their old age in the mines," Jimmy soon headed north to Ohio and the steel mills. . . .

Jimmy's dream included having a home, a wife, and a daughter, but after marrying "Kat," two sons were born within three years. He loved his sons, yet his heart yearned for a daughter, one who would never engage in combat or shoot another human being. One evening two years later, a girl was born to him and his wife.

The birth certificate was not signed until Jimmy got home from work after midnight, eight hours after the birth. As he stared at his newborn daughter in amazement, he whispered, "She is the most beautiful sight I have ever seen." Recalling that earlier moment of overwhelming joy and peace, my father named me Shasta.

QUESTIONS FOR DISCUSSION

1. Evaluate the effectiveness of Shasta's title. Give a reason for your opinion.

2. Contrast the death march and the drive up Mt. Shasta. Consider what awaited Jimmy at each place.

3. How are a new baby and a fawn similar? How are these two moments connected in the story?

4. Discuss the switch from third person to first person in the last line. Do you think third person throughout would have been more or less effective? Why?

5. Shasta could have ended with her father's death from black lung disease as his final walk through hell. Would this ending have been more or less effective? Why do you think so?

| FOR YOUR REFERENCE Narrative Essays in the Reader | • "Sound and Fury," Dan Greenburg, page 548
• "Momma's Encounter," Maya Angelou, page 550
• "The Art of Acknowledgement," Jean Houston, page 555
• "How to Get Out of a Locked Trunk," Philip Weiss, page 558 |

WRITE A NEWS STORY

Directions: Assume you are a reporter for your campus or hometown newspaper. Write a news story, using the five *w*'s (pages 125–126). You may want to conduct interviews to gain specific details. The following suggestions may stimulate an idea you can use:

1. New construction, new business, or restaurant
2. Historical highlight: A story from the city's history
3. Profile of the president of the university or college
4. Student interviews about campus concerns
5. Plans for an activity such as May Day, a concert, or a pig roast

WRITE A FIRST-PERSON NARRATIVE

Directions: Select an incident from your experience that may have caused you to laugh, to cry, to run, to show courage, or to learn. Then do some prewriting about the key events, including your reactions. After that, write a unified paragraph or short narrative. Perhaps one of the suggestions below will help you to find a suitable topic:

1. A learning experience—gulp!
2. Your dog's list of New Year's resolutions for you
3. Finding a . . .
4. A wonderful day
5. Your cat's proposal for reorganizing the family household

TWENTY IDEAS FOR NARRATIVE PAPERS

1   An incident on the job (a narrative report)

2   A narrow escape

3   A new wife's (or husband's) first home-cooked dinner

4   Civility pays off!

5   My first day on the job

6   A strange or unusual experience

7   Learning how to drive

8   Fatherhood/motherhood is . . .

9   One evening as . . .

10   My most embarrassing experience

11   My first taste of defeat

12   A prank that backfired

13   The first time I rode a . . .

14   How I met my husband/wife

15   My experience with . . .

16   My first encounter with a . . .

17   The secret in . . .

18   My favorite one-day trip

19   Sadder, but wiser

20   _____ weren't meant for . . .

Describing Significant Impressions

Reporter Monica Torline has captured the essence of Tammy Taylor-Wells' personality in a feature-length description of the diver's duties at the Columbus Zoo and Aquarium. Torline chooses sensory words that encourage readers to visualize the experience and accompany the diver in this underwater world by sharing her impressions vicariously.

> While volunteering at the Discovery Reef exhibit, Tammy has discovered an oceanic passion for a world of quiet beauty. She doesn't need a degree in marine biology to know that a stingray feels like "a soft, wet, velvet blanket," and she has seen the peaceful grace that exists in a sea turtle's eyes.
>
> —Monica Torline, "Under the Sea,"
> *The Marion Star*

PURPOSE OF DESCRIPTION

Successful description has a rhetorical purpose; it is not just a meandering by an author. Description usually serves as a minor writing strategy, supplementing a major strategy, such as narration, process analysis, or comparison. This chapter, however, explains how description of concrete details can serve as a major writing strategy for various rhetorical situations. Description has three general purposes:

1. To create imagery, a mood, or an aura of a place
2. To stimulate understanding and convince
3. To urge the listener to action

In expressive writing such as personal essays, narratives, autobiographies, and poems, you can guide the emotional responses of readers by describing physical details that create a *dominant impression of your main idea.* Then description becomes the major writing strategy.

WHAT EXACTLY IS DESCRIPTION?

Description has been defined by philosophers as "a mode of perception," a means of knowing. It is a way to impose order upon the confusing complexity of the real world and to understand it, at least partially. *Description* is a recording of concrete details that you see, hear, smell, taste, or touch. To provide depth and understanding, authors often include an impression of an experience and its significance. For example, the beauty of a spectacular sunset, the delicate mist of a rainbow, or the thundering magnificence of Niagara Falls can be overwhelming, creating a silent awe in the beholder.

See "Caterpillar Afternoon," page 564.

In field research we *observe, describe, interpret,* and *write* our impressions of concrete details that we perceive firsthand. This four-stage process enables us to relate the physical parts of what we observe to the whole subject or unit. Then we can contemplate its meaning, whether it be a caterpillar or the earth's crust.

In research and technical writing, writers use description to help readers understand the qualities and structure of physical objects, organisms, and phenomena. In an argument a writer may describe a shocking or heartrending incident in order to move listeners to action. Then description reinforces the thesis; factual details provide support for the major idea.

CREATING A DOMINANT IMPRESSION

When description is the chief writing strategy, it conveys a prevailing impression, a mood that remains throughout the piece for a purpose. Sensory details unite to produce the mood, such as delight, fear, or curiosity—adding interest as well as evidence. The mood may be implied or expressed directly. In *Gift from the Sea,* Anne Morrow Lindbergh creates an implicit impression as she describes a shell, found on the beach:

> The shell in my hand is deserted. It once housed a whelk, a snail-like crea-ture, and then temporarily, after the death of the first occupant, a little hermit crab. . . . Did he hope to find a better home, a better mode of living? I too have run away, I realize, I have shed the shell of my life, for these few weeks of vacation.
>
> But his shell—it is simple; it is bare, it is beautiful. Small, only the size of my thumb, its architecture is perfect, down to the finest detail. Its shape, swelling like a pear in the center, winds in a gentle spiral to the pointed apex. Its color, dull gold, is whitened by a wash of salt from the sea. Each whorl, each faint knob, each crisscross vein in its egg-shell texture, is as clearly de-fined as on the day of creation. . . .
>
> My shell is not like this, I think. How untidy it has become! Blurred with moss, knobby with barnacles, its shape is hardly recognizable any more. Surely, it had a shape once. It has a shape still in my mind. What is the shape of my life?

As Lindbergh describes the shell, it becomes a symbol of her life—an *anal-ogy* that extends throughout the book. As she reflects, the images establish a thread of continuity, allowing the reader to sense her inner peace amid the prob-lems of life. There is a tranquility, an acceptance of change, as she collects in-sights along with shells.

Subjective and Objective Description

When writing, you can use subjective or objective description or combine them as Lindbergh did. Her description is primarily *subjective.* Although it includes facts about the shell, the focus is upon her emotions and thoughts—her inner life. The purpose of a subjective description is to share feelings and ideas with the reader. But feelings must be kept within bounds so that they do not get out of control. Too much emotion can backfire.

In contrast, the tone of an *objective* description is literal, factual, and fair—impartial and impersonal. In scientific and business writing, much description is based on unbiased, objective observation. Its aim is to reproduce for the reader exactly what the writer observed without reference to the writer's feel-ings about the subject.

See chapters 26 and 30.

PLANNING A PAPER OF DESCRIPTION

Whether you have toured Ravenna, Italy, looking at mosaics, or never ventured beyond your city's limits, you have stored numerous sensory impressions. Per-haps you recall a lovely moment, painting, or place that was significant to you, one that might serve as a topic for an essay. Or perhaps you own an unusual ob-ject that has a story behind it. Think about the memory or object and its value or meaning to you.

www.mhhe.com/dietsch

For online help writing description essays, visit: Writing>Writing Tutors> Description

Or you might write about a person you admire. In "Aunt Ruthie Shows the Way," published in the *New York Times Magazine*, Patricia Volk describes her unusual aunt, primarily through dialogue that reveals her aunt's spritely spirit. Here is an excerpt:

> "Your Uncle Al and I had a whirlpool romance," Aunt Ruthie tells me. Then she pauses. "Is that the word I mean?" We're having lunch to celebrate her 89th birthday. She dabs a little applesauce on her blintzes.
> . . . .
> Maybe you've heard about Aunt Ruthie. She was the woman taken hostage in her Bronx apartment four years ago. An ex-paratrooper, Jose Cruz, climbed in her window and held Aunt Ruthie hostage for five hours before the police exchanged her for two cigarettes. "When you go to prison," she counseled him, "take out some books. Learn a different profession. It's important in life to get hold of yourself."

In just three pages, Volk relates incidents that reveal how her aunt is enjoying life and taking old age in stride. If you were to describe someone, you might begin by jotting down any interesting or amusing memories that come to mind. You might include favorite sayings, reactions to responsibilities, hardships, dilemmas, or anything else that conveys a dominant impression of the person.

Prewriting

www.mhhe.com/dietsch

For further coverage of prewriting, check out: Writing>Prewriting

After you select a topic, think about who might like to read about it. At the top of your paper, jot down "Audience" and "Purpose" so that you can begin to focus your thoughts. Then mine your memory by prewriting details about your topic. When writing from experience, try asking yourself these questions:

- **AUDIENCE.** Who might be interested?
- **PURPOSE.** What is the point of the description?
- **Sight.** What specifically did I notice?
- **Sound.** What exactly did I hear?
- **Smell.** What did I smell? Did it remind me of anything?
- **Touch.** How did the item or object feel?
- **Taste.** Was taste involved? Could I compare the taste to something else?

Determining the Dominant Impression

A hodgepodge of details without a central point will lack unity. Consider their overall meaning. Why is this topic significant to you? What is the overriding impression, the main idea that links the details? The idea need not be dramatic or earthshaking; it need only be important to you for a specific reason.

As you draft, you may uncover the wisp of a story. At first it may appear unimportant, or it may make you uncomfortable. But before tossing it away, take a second look. Paul Allen Dotson, Jr., drafted a description of a dining room light fixture. As he revised, he speculated about its meaning to him and realized it was more than just a beautiful object. There was a memory, an untold story behind it—one he did not want to tell. But by referring to the story, he enriched the dominant impression.

The Crystal Chandelier

In the dining room of a house where I once lived hung a crystal chandelier. It was a gorgeous old-fashioned fixture with eight lights and numerous dangling crystals that sparkled with the colors of the rainbow. The chandelier had three settings: high, medium, and low. When it was set on high, my wife and I would entertain friends and relatives, balance our accounts, and write letters. When the chandelier was on medium, I would often lounge in a chair next to the stereo and listen to soft music while staring at the colors emanating from the crystals. Yet my favorite setting was low. There were nights I would arrive home before my wife and would prepare dinner for the two of us. When she would walk into the dining room, the colors from the crystals would shine on her hair; she would smile, and I would see the most beautiful woman in the world. Though we are no longer together, those moments under the crystal chandelier are among my fondest memories.

Although Paul merely hinted at the story in the last line, he enriched the description. Rarely is an entire story told. Someone once said that a story is like an iceberg: seven-eighths of it stays beneath the surface. The writer must decide how much to reveal. If you think there might be a story lurking in your prewriting notes, ask yourself these questions:

- Why do I have a special fondness for the object or impression?
- Did something happen that cast a shadow on or changed my life?
- How much do I want to say?
- Will that be enough? Will the ending seem complete?

Selecting a Vantage Point and Transition

You might think of a writer as holding a camera, aiming the lens in a certain direction to record an impression or a story. Wherever the writer is viewing the scene from is the *vantage point.* The writer may remain fixed in one spot or move around. A *fixed observer* describes only what can be seen from one position. A *moving observer* describes from more than one position. With each movement, the writer keeps the reader informed with transitional phrases such as "turning at the first country road," "reaching the summit," or "descending a narrow, crooked stairway."

Imagine in your mind's eye the position from which you will view your topic. Will you remain in one spot or will you move? Will you be close or distant? Will you be observing for a few moments or over a span of time? What would be the most interesting vantage point for the reader? What transitions will you need to keep readers informed of your movements?

See chapter 4.

www.mhhe.com/dietsch

For general drafting help, visit:
Writing>Drafting and Revision

DRAFTING A PAPER OF DESCRIPTION

Before you begin to draft, review your prewriting notes. Consider each item and whether or not it will contribute to the mood you aim to create. Mark only the details that will effectively convey the impression you have in mind.

Drafting an Introduction

www.mhhe.com/dietsch

Want more help writing introductions? Go to:
Writing>Introductions

A good introduction raises questions in the reader's mind: "What happened?" "Why is it significant?" "What kind of person is this?" "What sort of place?" Some openings create an image, taking readers directly to a scene with a short transitional phrase, such as "*In 1890 Central City* had dusty unpaved streets and 132 inhabitants, not counting 56 horses, 63 dogs, and 75 cats." Or a descriptive phrase may focus on a current scene: "*Nestled in a valley* . . . is a small village that still has a general store and a post office where patrons pick up their mail."

Sometimes a description opens with a specific thesis, perhaps a striking comparison that makes a claim. Jennifer Ramey begins her paper, "Maintaining a Marriage," with an analogy (a comparison that extends throughout her essay): "A good marriage is like a fine-tuned car. Care for it, work on it, and treasure it; and it will run well."

Developing a Description

An unusual viewpoint or perspective of an ordinary topic can arouse interest. In the body of her paper "Maintaining a Marriage," Jennifer develops her comparison:

> Communication is the engine of a marriage. Effective communication cannot be left to chance or the marriage may run out of gas. Real communication requires effort; and it goes beyond knowing a partner's favorite foods, television programs, clothes, and activities. Heartfelt communication requires sensitivity—an ability to tune into the other person's moods, feelings, and embarrassments without hearing a lot of explanation.
>
> Quality communication requires listening with empathy, trying to understand what the other person is experiencing without voicing criticism. Refraining from interrupting is essential. Words of appreciation are also vital, for they are the oil that keeps a marriage running smoothly.

A comparison of two views of a seldom seen object can provide a fresh slant. For example, a pair of swords used by an ancestor in the Civil War and the tarnished belt buckle from his uniform might be viewed as worthless by one cousin. But to another, the items might be priceless family heirlooms.

Organizing a Description

The organization of a description often arises naturally from a particular topic. If you describe an object, a place, an animal, or a person, then *spatial order* usually works well. In spatial order details are arranged according to space or location. For instance, to describe an Irish Setter, you might go from the head to the tip of the tail.

Chronological order, a sequence of time, may be used to describe the changes in a neighborhood or a person. Another possible order for description is from *abstract to concrete* or from *general to specific* (or vice versa). Or if a topic requires emphasis, you might go from *least-to-most important* or *most-to-least important.* For more about the seven basic orders, see chapter 4.

Writing a Conclusion

Successful endings give a sense of completion and satisfaction. In description, as in narration, the major point often appears at the end. The ending may be a brief summary that explains the point in an interesting way. Or the ending may sound an optimistic note as it looks to the future. A philosophical ending may relate physical details to an abstract thought. Anne Morrow Lindbergh is both optimistic and philosophical at the close of *Gift from the Sea:*

> The waves echo behind me. Patience—Faith—Openness, is what the sea has to teach. Simplify—Solitude—Intermittency. . . . But there are other beaches to explore. There are more shells to find. This is only the beginning.

Sometimes a surprise or twist ending is effective. Such endings require preparation. You cannot simply swoop down and attach an ending that is foreign to the description or story. You need to prepare the reader in small ways. Note that Paul mentions his wife early in "The Crystal Chandelier." He does not suddenly introduce her at the end. Effective endings are smooth; they grow out of whatever has preceded them.

REVISING A DESCRIPTION

When revising a description, choose words that convey sharp, clear images— vibrant verbs, specific nouns, and modifiers that crackle with meaning. The audience should be able to visualize the spot, object, or person and savor the other sensory details. The aim is not only to increase interest but also to enhance the dominant impression.

In *The Elements of Style,* E. B. White warns against the use of meaningless modifiers. He calls *very, rather, little,* and *pretty* "the leeches that infest the pond of prose, sucking the blood of words." Beware, too, of stacking adjectives in a series; use one if needed, seldom two, rarely three.

Although the right adjective can convey an idea, an action verb can often convey it better. For example, the two sentences below carry the same idea, but the first slows the pace with a weak *(be)* verb, the adverb *very,* and two vague adjectives. The second version deletes the adverb and adjectives. A strong action verb and a specific noun replace them:

- The tomcat *was* very upset and vocal.
- The tomcat *hissed* his displeasure.

www.mhhe.com/dietsch

For online guidance on writing your conclusions, check out:
Writing>Conclusions

www.mhhe.com/dietsch

For general help with revision, check out:
Writing>Drafting and Revising

In the previous example, note the repetition of the *s* in the second sentence—the sound echoes the meaning. Such subtle surprises work well in prose if not overdone. As you revise, you may want to consult the following checklist.

CHECKLIST   REVISING A DESCRIPTION

1. Does the opening line arouse interest for this audience?

2. Is the vantage point suitable? Is any transition needed?

3. Is the written voice appropriate? Should it be more personal or friendly?

4. Is the imagery sharp and clear? Have I involved at least three senses?

5. Are all details effective? Could their order be improved?

6. Are most verbs in the active voice? Are nouns and adjectives specific?

7. Is the dominant impression clear and effective?

8. Does the ending seem complete?

TWO STUDENT PAPERS: DESCRIPTION

In the first paper, Jean Ice pays tribute to a favorite aunt. Her purpose is to inform, to preserve for her children this memory of an earlier family member whom they did not know. Jean uses the concrete-to-abstract strategy, describing appearance before personality.

Aunt Marzia

Marzia was an elegant lady. Even as a young girl, she exhibited unusual characteristics for a country lass. Her coal black hair glistened from regimental brushing and frequent shampooing. Her hair was a halo for a lovely face with arched eyebrows and curling lashes. Her eyes were light green or gray, depending upon the color of her apparel. Her high cheekbones gave her a slight resemblance to a Native American. Her mother was said to be of Indian ancestry.

Marzia was taller than most other women of this generation. She carried her height proudly. Her erect posture and uplifted chin gave her a regal air. Somewhat out of sync with her physical perfection was her quirky little walk. She turned each foot slightly to the side as she strolled the country lanes.

Marzia was different from other members of her family and from her classmates. The other schoolchildren wore plain homemade garments, but Marzia used her sewing skill to put tucks in her waists. She also put flounces in her skirts and attached lace or embroidery to her collars. Few people would have guessed her wardrobe was made from feed sacks.

Marzia adored her first name, but she abhorred the way it was pronounced "Marzie" by others. Even her older sisters Clara and Ara did not follow her wishes and mispronounced her name. This elegant lady was a perfectionist in many other ways. She seemed to believe it was her responsibility to reform others to her way of thinking. This was especially true of her nieces. There were only five of us, compared to many more nephews. She expected us girls to speak correctly, dress attractively, and excel in good manners. She tried to accomplish these objectives by correcting us whenever we made an error. Often I, the youngest niece, was overwhelmed by a miscue. Once I pronounced *chic* as "chick," confident that I was right. Consulting a dictionary, after she corrected me, proved how little I knew.

Marzia was well educated for her time and situation. She was graduated from high school when most students were satisfied to complete the eighth grade. She went to normal school and became a teacher in a one-room school. The school was on the outskirts of a very small town, composed mostly of people of color. Marzia prized her students, and they were very fond of her.

When Marzia decided to marry, she was forced to give up teaching; for years ago only single women were allowed to teach. Unlike her sisters, who married for security and a home of their own, Marzia married because of her love for a ne'er-do-well. Although he was short, unattractive, uneducated, and rough of manner and speech, he had a jolly personality, which attracted the young ladies. But even Marzia could not contend with the old demon—liquor. After three years of silent grief, she divorced this man. She was the only member of her family to be divorced.

Marzia lived a long and productive life in spite of the divorce. She was greatly loved by all her younger kin, who were so different from her. When Aunt Marzia died, we all missed her so much. Nobody ever took her place in my life; no one else reminded me that I could do better.

QUESTIONS FOR DISCUSSION

1. Is Jean's dominant impression implicit or explicit?
2. How is the claim that Marzia is different and "elegant" supported?
3. Jean mixes writing strategies. How? What order is used in her last three paragraphs?
4. What type of ending does she use?

In the second paper, student writer C. J. Banning creates an unusual analogy to inform readers about the effects of severe depression upon personality and behavior. Implicit in the essay is a plea for understanding of this illness and for help from family members and friends. C. J. shows unusual insight into this condition and presents an array of concrete details to support her thesis.

Please, Do Not Forget Me

In England, on a barren hillside, stands a long-forgotten castle that has given way to centuries of neglect. Fragments of its once stately gray stone walls litter the courtyard. A spire that once stood tall atop a tower now lies upon a heap of rubble. Windows that once gleamed in the sun are darkened with grime. Winged creatures of the night fly through broken windowpanes. The storeroom is dank and musty; gone are the fine foods and wines. Gone are the people who danced in the ballroom; gone is the grandeur of former years.

So too, can be the life of a person suffering from severe depression. Often the person will go into seclusion, letting time and the world pass. Hiding in the dark recesses of the mind, the victim of depression cringes, hoping others will pass on by, paying no heed to the one that dwells within. Little by little, parts of the person are lost in the rubble of distress. Slowly, bit by bit, the self seems to be less and less. No longer does it feel that anyone might want anything it might be able to give. There is no room left for the food of good thoughts or warm feelings. The dark coldness of lost hope and worthlessness permeates the empty storage room. Unkempt thoughts weaken the body as well as the mind.

One summer day someone wonders how the old castle used to be. How had it looked with sturdy walls, clean windows, and polished floors? Had the steeple, standing tall and straight against the blue sky, seemed inviting to all who passed? Was the storeroom full, waiting for the banquets that were to come? Finally, someone decides to do something about the neglect. He picks up a stone and places it back into the wall, then another and another. He washes windows and the sunlight once again streams through. He sweeps the dusty floor and dreams of the day the castle can be restored.

Despite protests, the victims of depression, too, need help and caring commitment to pick up the pieces of their lives, to wash their eyes and let in the light. They need help to discard the dark thoughts that flit about their minds, help to air the dark musty places that need a caring touch, help to let in a fresh dream of what they might be. Then one piece at a time, their lives can be restored to become a little better day after day.

Not all the castle walls and floors that are polished will shine as brightly as before. The storeroom will still have a faint mustiness, and a few stray creatures may venture in. But the castle can be a wonderful, grand place of peace.

QUESTIONS FOR DISCUSSION

1. What is the impression in paragraph one? What words contribute heavily?
2. What specific details in the second paragraph link it to the first?
3. What do you notice in the third paragraph?
4. What advice does the writer give in paragraph four?
5. Does the writer seem to have firsthand or secondhand knowledge of the topic? Why do you think so?

FOR YOUR REFERENCE
Descriptive Essays in the Reader

- "Caterpillar Afternoon," Sue Hubbell, page 564
- "One Writer's Beginnings," Eudora Welty, page 567
- "Dawn Watch," John Ciardi, page 569
- "Pedestrian Students and High-Flying Squirrels," Liane Ellison Norman, page 573

IDEAS FOR WRITING A PARAGRAPH

Directions: Be specific, using concrete words and vivid verbs. End with a thoughtful comment, perhaps about the function, meaning, or qualities of the object or person, *so that your paragraph has a point.*

1. Describe the vehicle you are driving or riding. What is the dominant impression of you in or on this vehicle?
2. Describe a prized object. Why is it special?
3. Describe the contents of your purse (if you have one). What is the dominant impression to a casual spectator?
4. Describe someone you know. What predominant qualities does he or she have?
5. Describe your favorite piece of old clothing. Why is it special?

TWENTY IDEAS FOR DESCRIPTIVE PAPERS

1. A special moment
2. A family of bald eagles (or rabbits, ducks, etc.)
3. My first job
4. A shop in Chinatown
5. A flower garden to attract butterflies
6. Riding a cable car in San Francisco
7. A favorite place to be alone
8. My father's toolbox
9. The most courageous (or some other quality) person I know
10. A favorite hangout
11. Riding the rapids in Colorado
12. My neighborhood

13 A ride on the Staten Island ferry

14 The first time I . . .

15 A kind teacher

16 An incident in . . .

17 Earliest childhood memory

18 My high school reunion

19 My _____ heritage

20 The best dog I ever had

Analyzing a Process

Writing clear, concise directions is not always easy even for the professional. Perhaps you have worked with inadequate or nonexistent instructions and know how frustrating that can be. One young man, lacking any instruction, began a welding job only to find the equipment was different from that used on his previous job. He ruined $400 worth of equipment the first night. To write clear directions, you need to analyze the process.

> It is far easier to discuss Hamlet's complexes than to write orders which ensure that five working parties from five different units arrive at the right time equipped with proper tools for the job.
>
> —G. B. Harrison

WHAT IS PROCESS ANALYSIS?

Regular occurrences in the natural world—such as digestion, icicles, and hurricanes—involve processes. A *process* is a series of steps, stages, phases, or natural changes that lead to a result. You engage in a process whether taking a shower, brewing coffee, or driving a car. On the job you may explain a procedure to a new worker, show someone how to operate a machine, or write instructions for operating software.

In *process analysis* you describe or explain a series of actions, operations, or changes that occur. A paper of process analysis may explain how to do something, how a condition develops, how an organism grows, or how a phenomenon evolves. For clarity, explain the process in the order that changes/events normally occur. Some processes require one certain order; others can be done in more than one way.

Directions for Procedures

The simple experiments you conducted in high school science and chemistry labs were procedures. When you assemble shelving or pour a concrete patio, you also perform a procedure. To ensure good results, you follow the instructions carefully. If any steps are omitted or the order is reversed, the deviation may mar the final result. Some procedures, such as operating a chain saw, require warnings so that users take precautions. *Include a reason for each precaution so that users will take heed.*

Other kinds of processes require multiple sets of directions, all of which have phases, steps, or stages. For instance, the production of steel and the publication of a book involve many processes and people. The *audience* for directions consists of the people who will be performing the procedure.

WORKPLACE CASE STUDY

ETHAN SOLVES THE OFFICE LOUNGE PROBLEM

The sink of the employee lounge is usually stacked full of dirty dishes. The room smells of stale coffee grounds. Green mold grows on uneaten lunches in the refrigerator. Although employees are assigned days to tidy the room, they often forget. Those who remember may wash only the dishes. Ethan has been asked to devise a new system.

After careful thought, Ethan gives each office employee a copy of a quarterly assignment sheet with his or her day marked in red and tacks a copy in the lounge. In a memo he asks the employees to add this date to their calendars. On the refrigerator, he posts a sign that reads: "On Fridays all lunch containers and open soda will be discarded." On a cupboard, he posts the following notice:

continued

Daily Cleaning Procedure

On your assigned day, please clean between 3 and 5 p.m. Then no one will be using the lounge. The following procedure will save time. (It should take 10–12 minutes.)

1. Close the drain and fill the sink with hot water.
2. Add detergent and let dishes soak.
3. Clear the table and counter of debris. Wash them off.
4. Wipe the microwave inside and out.
5. Wash dishes, rinse, and stack on drainboard.
6. To prevent fire, unplug coffeemaker. Dispose of grounds.
7. Wash and rinse coffeemaker.
8. Dry dishes and put in cupboard.
9. FRIDAY: Throw out all lunch containers and open soda cans in the refrigerator. Wipe up crumbs and spills in the refrigerator.

The system has worked well. Grumbling about clutter and odor has stopped. The lounge is a much more pleasant place to sit and relax.

Use Second Person for Clarity   Directions for a procedure should be clear and concise. Therefore, they are usually written in second person with *understood you*. Each step begins with an active verb: "*Insert* the tab . . . ," "*Open* the chamber . . . ," "*Lift* the switch. . . ." Most instructions should be more than a brief list, unless there is a sound reason to limit. They should explain according to readers' general level of knowledge. On the job, steps of a procedure are often simplified and numbered.

Process Descriptions

Students in all academic disciplines analyze processes and write *process descriptions*. For example, you might interview a patient, write a case history, and describe the onset of a health problem. Or you might explain how a hobby grew into a successful business or explain a process to a group touring a factory.

   The purpose of a process description is to describe a procedure, natural phenomenon, or other process for an audience who would like to know more about it. They will *not* be performing the process. First, you supply enough details to provide an overview. Then you state the function of each step or stage and explain how each fits into the process. Process descriptions are often written in narrative form, using either first- or third-person pronouns.

See page H-3.

Using First Person   Student writer Janice D. uses first person and past tense to begin the story of how her rock garden evolved:

▶ **Gardening with Rocks**

Rock gardening wasn't something I gave much thought to until a few years after we bought a house. I can remember the seller pointing out an overgrown bush in the front of the weedy yard, trying to use that as a selling point. Later my husband and I agreed "that will have to be the first thing to go." The first year we were so busy inside we didn't do much outside except to mow the lawn and kill the weeds. But over the next few years, we began to beautify the outside as well. We started small with a tree here, a few flowers and a rock there, which led to our lovely rock garden of today.

See "Caterpillar Afternoon," page 564.

Using Third Person   Process descriptions that are not drawn from a writer's personal experience are usually written in the third person. Present tense verbs in *active* voice are used for actions that recur: "The mollusk *opens* its shell . . . ," "Each year the tree *grows* new rings," "The furnace *melts* the glass. . . ."

TRANSITION IN PROCESS ANALYSIS

A *transition* is a word, phrase, sentence, or paragraph that connects ideas or informs the reader of what is ahead. Transitions indicate shifts of meaning and relationships of time, location, sequence, similarity or difference, certainty or uncertainty. *Signpost transitions* appear at the beginning of sentences. This method is generally used in procedures. *Embedded transitions* appear at other places in a sentence, as explained in chapter 13.

For process analysis, use transitions that indicate *chronological* order. Distinguish between major and minor steps. For major steps, use *numerical* transitions (*first, second, third,* and so forth). For substeps, use other transitions of time, such as *then* or *next.* (Two or three *first*'s and *second*'s would be confusing.)

TRANSITIONS TO CLARIFY A PROCESS

To Emphasize Major Steps or Stages		To Indicate Substeps	
first	(begin)	next	then
second		after that	later
third		while	when
fourth		meanwhile	as soon as
fifth	(finally)	during	after one hour

WRITING A PROCESS PAPER

www.mhhe.com/dietsch
For online insight into process papers, visit: Writing>Writing Tutors> Process Analysis

The purpose of a process paper can be to provide directions for a procedure or to describe a process, according to the assignment. To fulfill either purpose, you first need to estimate how much readers know about the topic and whether they are likely to have performed or witnessed the procedure or process.

This estimate is particularly important when writing directions. It will help you gauge not only the amount of explanation needed but also the need for *pre-*

cautions and reasons at strategic points. At tricky or risky points, include a reason for the step. For example, "Follow directions carefully *to obtain a smooth finish."* Otherwise, some users may take unwise shortcuts.

Selecting a Topic and Prewriting

The topic for a process paper should be based on your personal experience or observation unless you plan to do research. The topic should be complex enough that readers won't find it obvious. You may find that narrowing the topic is essential: even a fairly simple process paper can become surprisingly lengthy. To develop your thinking skills, avoid a recipe or any other process you have learned from printed instructions.

The quickest way to start is to make a scratch outline, listing the steps or stages in chronological order. Leave spaces to jot in brief explanations and insert necessary precautions or warnings at the beginning and at strategic points—not the end. *Many readers will not read the entire set of directions before they start.*

www.mhhe.com/dietsch

For more coverage of prewriting, go to:
Writing>Prewriting

Drafting an Introduction

The length of an introduction to a process paper may vary, depending on the purpose for writing and the assignment. Particularly for directions, state the finished product or result of the process in the introduction. If you dive into the first step with no thesis statement, readers may become confused. The thesis should identify the process, make a claim, and specify the result, product, or benefit for the reader:

www.mhhe.com/dietsch

For general help writing introductions, check out:
Writing>Introductions

- White-water rafting can be an enjoyable experience for the beginner who is well prepared. (Claim/result: enjoyable experience)
- Setting up a backpacking tent correctly can net a good night's sleep. (Claim/result: good night's sleep)

The following student introductions illustrate just two of many options for an introduction.

Generalization Followed by Restriction   An accurate generalization may be used for the beginning of a process analysis. Patricia Jones Black opens with a generalization followed by a restriction. Safety is her key idea. Since Patricia's introduction is only two sentences long, she chooses to combine it with the first point.

How to Process Green Beans

Home-grown green beans can be served year round when they are properly processed and stored. By following the twelve steps listed here, you can safely take green beans from the garden to the table several months later. First, pick beans that are plump and tender. Three to five pounds of beans will be needed for each quart to be processed.

Historical Opening   Melinda Ham selected an unusual topic that carries a hint of nostalgia. She begins by describing the slow-paced life of pioneer days (a life without television, computers, or expensive toys).

▶ **Apple-Head Dolls: A Remnant of Yesteryear**

Years ago when life was less complicated and most families lived miles away from their nearest neighbors, family entertainment was more often homespun than manufactured. Children had to invent their own games. Parents frequently made toys for their children out of natural materials because cash was scarce. One popular homemade toy was the apple-head doll. These dolls had wizened faces, like very wrinkled old people, with a variety of expressions. By following these simple instructions, you, too, can make an unusual doll for a child in your family.

Combining Second Person with Third Person   Note that Melinda begins the introduction by using third person. Then she skillfully switches to *second person in the middle of the final sentence* of the paragraph. This way she makes the pronoun shift smoothly.

Developing a Process Paper

As you draft, keep a specific audience in mind so that you will know how much explanation is needed. If you are writing directions, ask yourself, What points might be difficult, unclear, or risky? Present the steps in an orderly sequence so that the reader can understand and possibly duplicate the procedure. At the beginning, specify the equipment and material necessary to complete the process. In her paper on making apple-head dolls, Melinda Ham explains the process clearly, using numerical transitions and active verbs to indicate major steps. Her transitions are italicized here:

▶ *First,* gather the necessary materials. An apple and cotton balls are needed for the face, hair, and beard of a male doll. Or you may wish to make a pair of dolls, male and female. The apple should be large because the head will shrink later. The body consists of a fine-gauge wire coat hanger, a large paper clip, clean cotton rags (an old sheet, pillowcase, or shirt), varnish or shellac, and scraps of fabric for clothing. Other items needed are a sharp paring knife, pliers, a small bowl, a bottle of pure lemon juice, plain table salt (not iodized), and about eighteen inches of heavy thread or fine cord.

Second, make the face of the doll. With the paring knife, thinly peel the apple. *Then* carve out the tiny eye sockets, nose, mouth, and ears. *After the head is carved,* place it in a small bowl. Pour one-fourth cup of lemon juice over the apple. Let set for thirty seconds, *then* rotate so that all sides are covered with juice. Wait one minute. To make the eyes, press two apple seeds horizontally into the carved sockets.

Aging is the *third* step. Unbend the paper clip, leaving the smallest "hook." Push the straight end of the clip into the top of the core down through the apple. *When the wire emerges,* bend it about an inch to make a right angle to support the apple. Loop a length of heavy thread over the top hook and tie a knot. *Next* suspend the thread from a window catch, away from direct sunlight, where the apple can hang for two to four weeks. *When the desired "wrinkling" occurs,* apply a thin coat of clear shellac or varnish to prevent further deterioration. Let dry overnight.

Fourth, add "hair" to the head. For a male, pull apart a cotton ball to form a beard. Glue around the jawline. A narrow strip of cotton around the back will form a fringe of hair around a bald spot. For a female doll, a large cotton ball (or two) will be needed for her hair, which can be arranged as desired.

Making the body is the *fifth* step. Use pliers to twist a thin wire coat hanger into a simple stick figure. Wrap strips of rags around arms and legs to give a rounded effect. Secure the rag strips with rubber bands or adhesive tape or both.

Creating clothing is the *sixth* step. Design simple clothes for the dolls. The male doll might wear a simple dark suit with a white shirt and perhaps a cap or hat. The female doll might wear a tiny apron, shawl or cape, sunbonnet, and long dress.

The final step is attaching the head. Attach the apple head firmly to the neck wire. Twist the clip wire tightly around the body wire so that the apple head will remain upright. If wire shows, cover with a necktie, shawl, or scarf.

Writing a Conclusion

An effective conclusion to a process analysis provides a sense of completion, often by referring specifically to the result of the process. If possible, end on a positive note. Even if the results of a procedure are negative, you might summarize what was learned, refer to a benefit or emotion, or add a bit of humor. Melinda ends by pointing out what makes apple-head dolls special:

> Apple-head dolls are not only easy to make, but unusual. The face and expression of each doll will vary somewhat. The clothing can vary greatly. Apple-head dolls make attractive and distinctive gifts.

> www.mhhe.com/dietsch
> For online guidance on writing your conclusions, check out:
> Writing>Conclusions

Revising a Process Paper

Clarity and completeness are the main qualities to check for as you revise your process paper. The following questions should be helpful.

> www.mhhe.com/dietsch
> For general help with revision, visit:
> Writing>Drafting and Revising

CHECKLIST: REVISING A PROCESS PAPER

1. Who is the audience? (*Tip:* On your outline list age, experience, and any other relevant characteristics of the audience. Refer to the list as you revise your paper.)

2. Does the introduction establish the purpose and point out the product or result of the process?

3. Are necessary precautions included at appropriate spots?

4. Are reasons included at strategic points?

5. Do transitions clearly distinguish major steps as well as substeps?

6.   Is each step or stage of the process discussed in sufficient detail?

7.   Does the conclusion complete the paper in a satisfying way?

A STUDENT PAPER: PROCESS ANALYSIS

The purpose of Keith Witzel's paper is to explain how to replace a defective electrical outlet safely. He directs the paper to the average homeowner with relatively little experience in home repairs.

▶   **Replacing an Electrical Outlet Safely**

Many people refuse to replace defective electrical connections in the home, either because of a lack of knowledge concerning the proper procedure or from fear of creating a fire hazard. By following a few simple guidelines, however, almost anyone can make minor repairs safely.

Most electrical circuits in the home are made up of general lighting circuits of either 15- or 20-amp circuits. These are the circuits used for small appliances, lamps, television, and others. These items are connected into the general lighting circuits by plugging into the wall outlet receptacles. If one of these receptacles becomes defective, it is a safe and simple process to replace it by following five main steps: First, assemble the necessary materials; second, shut off the house current; third, remove the receptacle; fourth, install the new receptacle; fifth, restore power and check the operation of the new receptacle.

First, assemble the necessary materials. These include a pair of needle-nosed pliers with a jaw approximately two inches long, tapering to a pointed end; a slotted screwdriver; a utility knife; and a new receptacle rated at 15 amps or 20 amps as required.

Second, shut off the power to the circuit that contains the defective receptacle. This is done by turning the main switch (marked on handle) to the "off" position on the circuit breaker or fuse box. Check to make certain that the electricity is off by trying to operate appliances in various locations of the house. They should not function.

Third, remove the cover plate from the defective receptacle by turning the screw in a counterclockwise direction. Remove the two screws that hold the receptacle outlet to the utility box (the small metal box mounted in the wall), and pull the receptacle from this box. There will be a white insulated wire, a black insulated wire, and possibly an uninsulated ground wire (depending on the age of the structure) attached to the receptacle. Remove these wires and discard the used receptacle.

Fourth, install the new receptacle and replace the cover. Before installation, inspect the black and white wires to ensure that each end is free of insulation for approximately five-eighths inch and the ends are formed into loops. These loops should be made in a clockwise direction. The purpose is to ensure that the wire is secured around the screw as the screw is tightened.

After that, install the wires to the new receptacle. The white wire is connected to the silver-colored side of the receptacle and the black wire to the brass-colored side. Tighten each screw firmly. Next, connect the uninsulated wire (if used) to the green screw on the bottom of the receptacle. Push the receptacle into the utility box and tighten, using the screws supplied with the new receptacle. Remount the receptacle cover, being careful not to overtighten this screw, which could cause the cover to crack.

Finally, restore power to the house and check the receptacle to see that it is functioning properly. If not, check to see that you have flipped all breaker switches.

If each of these steps is followed closely, you will have not only the satisfaction of doing the job yourself but also the satisfaction of saving the cost of an electrician.

QUESTIONS FOR DISCUSSION

1. Is Keith's paper a set of directions for a procedure or a process description? How do you know?
2. What transition does he use to indicate the substep of step four?
3. Does he provide any precautions or warnings? Where?
4. What type of ending does he use?
5. How clear do you find Keith's analysis? Is any step or substep unclear? If so, how might it be clarified?

• "Fast Track to Perfection," Ian Dunbar, page 577 • "How to Cook a Carp," Euell Gibbons page 581 • "Write Your Own Success Story," Carol Carter, page 585 • "How Do You Know It's Good?" Marya Mannes, page 590	**FOR YOUR REFERENCE** **Process Analysis** **Essays in the Reader**

PRACTICE

WRITING IDEAS FOR PARAGRAPHS

1. How to prune a shrub neatly and safely
2. Making homemade ice cream
3. How to bathe a dog with little fuss
4. How to make a paper airplane that will fly
5. How to tie a shoe (as explained to a five-year-old child)

TWENTY IDEAS FOR PROCESS PAPERS

Describe or explain:

1   How to start a chess club for schoolchildren

2   A natural process you have observed (butterfly hatching, erosion of a beach, aging of an oak tree, or other)

3   A procedure that you perform at work

4   How to preserve flowers for dried arrangements

5   How to install landscaping logs for a flower garden

6   How to water-ski

7   How to bathe a bedridden patient (or an infant)

8   How to give a shot with minimum discomfort

9   How to construct a concrete patio

10   How to make a minor household repair

11   Burglar-proofing your home

12   Grooming a horse for show

13   How to have a successful garage sale

14   How to pack a suitcase efficiently

15   Weight lifting for beginners

16   Touching up paint on a car

17   How to refinish furniture

18   Organizing a Neighborhood Watch program

19   How to preserve the natural beauty of a wood deck

20   Fireproofing a home

Illustrating with Effective Examples

CHAPTER 12

> Example moves the
> world more than
> doctrine.
>
> —Henry Miller

For nearly fifty years Charles Schulz entertained Americans with the exploits of Charlie Brown, Snoopy, Lucy, Linus, and other characters in *Peanuts*. Schulz based many of his daily comic strips on examples taken from his own experience. He said, "If you were to read the strip, oh, for just a few months, you would know me because everything that I am goes into the strip." For instance, Charlie Brown's fear of rejection from the little

PEANUTS reprinted by permission of United Feature Syndicate, Inc.

red-haired girl originated from a refusal to a marriage proposal that Schulz once endured.*

In the comic strip reprinted above, Charles Schulz depicted an incident from his boyhood. Then he reacted, and explained what friendship meant to him. You might say that he derived a statement of his philosophy of life.

PURPOSE OF EXAMPLES

An effective example can explain, convince, or lure a reader on. The right selection of examples can help you demonstrate your knowledge—whether in an employment application letter, a technical report, an essay exam, or a paper. Examples are valuable for explaining a concept, illustrating a problem, or supporting a reaction for papers in psychology, law enforcement, business management, literature, composition, philosophy, and other fields.

See chapter 20.

ELEMENTS OF ILLUSTRATION

To illustrate or to exemplify simply means to clarify through example. You include impressions, facts, statistics, or expert opinion to lend substance to your writing, according to the rhetorical situation. The key is to choose examples that count, that enable your audience to understand what you mean and to see that you know what you are talking about. On the job you might use illustration to persuade, as in a proposal or grant application. In an academic paper or a personal essay, you might use illustration to explain (see "Envy" at the end of this chapter).

———

*Brendan I. Koerner, "Good Grief! Charlie Brown Says, So Long," *U.S. News & World Report* 27 Dec. 1999: 28.

Various examples may relate an incident, compare, describe, or explain for a purpose: *Anecdotes* are brief stories, often humorous. An *analogy* is an extended comparison. *Historical examples* usually describe people or events. *Literary allusions* are examples taken from literature. *Hypothetical examples* are conjectures—supposedly true. However, real examples drawn from life are the most interesting and convincing illustrations.

WRITING A PAPER OF ILLUSTRATION

For a paper of illustration, you have a wide range of topic choices and organizational strategies. Select a topic you can develop with interesting examples. Then arrange the examples in an order that reflects your purpose.

> www.mhhe.com/dietsch
> For further information about illustration, go to:
> Writing>Writing Tutors>Exemplification

Prewriting

The topic may be concrete or abstract, according to the assignment. When something is concrete, it is detectable through at least one of the five senses, often more. You can see, hear, feel, smell, or taste it. If you write about an abstract principle, you can clarify it with concrete examples familiar to the reader. You can cite a variety of examples as long as they all have a central thread.

> www.mhhe.com/dietsch
> For more coverage of prewriting, go to:
> Writing>Prewriting

Excellent illustrations can often be lifted from everyday life. For instance, if you have a family heirloom, memento, or special gift (possibly a music box), you might find a topic there. Perhaps your great uncle has a collection of old coins. What do these objects represent to your family? Or perhaps your home has an unusual feature: a tower room, a secret room or stairway, or something else. Perhaps the house was once a one-room school, barn, or stop on the Underground Railroad. What is the story behind it?

Once you have chosen a topic, prewrite to form a pool of details. To start your creative juices flowing, write your topic at the top of a clean sheet of paper. Then jot down every idea that dives into your mind—anything that might be used as support. If you know the topic well, you will soon have a page of examples and details. To start prewriting, the following questions will be helpful:

- Why am I interested in the topic?
- What examples can I recall?
- Who is connected with the topic?
- Did he or she have a favorite saying, mannerism, or habit?
- How has he or she influenced me? Can I give an example?
- What changes have occurred; how do I feel about the changes?
- What is my main point?

Finally, draft a thesis that makes a point about your topic, ideally one that is unfamiliar to your readers.

Organizing and Developing a Paper of Illustration

See chapter 4.
To organize and develop your paper, choose an order, select examples, and weave explanation with examples, all the while focusing on your purpose and considering your audience.

Order   To organize a paper of illustration, select an order that suits your purpose and topic. You might organize examples chronologically or according to importance or in any other way that will advance your point. As you read the student papers in this chapter, notice the organizational strategies. Dixie O'Rourke combines chronological order and contrast:

Envy

I. *Introduction.* Age ten: Staring through window. Envy, resentment, and fear influence Dixie's childhood.

II. *Body*

   A. Junior high: Was learning to control feelings of envy.

   B. Age thirteen: Sudden change in perspective.

   C. Today: Envy seldom occurs.

III. *Conclusion.* Focusing energy in a positive way.

Other topics can be organized according to an order of importance. For a paper about exotic pets, you might move from familiar examples to surprising ones. For a paper on natural cures for common ailments, you might move from cures for minor ailments to cures for life-threatening ones. This way the examples increase in interest.

Relevant, Accurate, and Sufficient Examples   Every example you include should be *relevant* to your thesis, illustrating your main point in some way. Resist the temptation to include an example just because it is odd or funny. Illustrations should illuminate a point. Irrelevant examples distract from the thesis.

Check to see that examples are *accurate.* In attempting to be humorous or to dramatize a point, writers sometimes embellish examples, but extravagance can sabotage logic. An example may be dramatic, but it should not be too far-fetched or unusual—the one-in-a-million variety. To palm off an atypical example as typical is unethical. If you generalize from an example, it should be *typical of its class.* When researching, consider the source of your statistics. Is it reliable? Is the information up-to-date?

How many examples will be sufficient? The answer depends on the nature of your thesis and the weight of the examples. The sheer number of examples is less important than their quality. Select impressive examples that will provide strong support for your thesis. A controversial or debatable thesis will require several high-quality examples to convince a skeptical audience. As a rule, when examples are brief, you need more than when they can be developed in detail.

In a paper entitled "The Talent Within," Nicole Vanderkooi cites several brief examples in each paragraph. Each example is clearly relevant. Her third paragraph appears here:

> Possessing a natural skill can be overpowering, a constant pressure. Children with such talent have expectations already set for them. At age six, Sarah Wells was told she had a promising future in gymnastics and was enrolled in nightly classes. Despite many strained muscles, injured ankles, and missed slumber parties, she persevered and gained confidence. Yet she endured many lows as well as highs; she became critical of herself. Constant pressure from her parents and coaches and a desire to win made her dream a reality. At thirteen, Sarah began her powerful run to the vault. To keep her lead in the meet, she had to score at least a 9.5. As her hands hit the leather, she felt the adrenaline pump, and she scored a perfect 10. A spectator cheered, "That's awesome!" Sarah Wells won the meet. By now her childhood was gone, but in its place was a confidence powered by success. To some people, that is robbery; to Sarah it is a rewarding way of life.

Weaving Examples with Explanation   As you draft, try to find an interesting approach to your topic. You might start with a series of short examples, eye-catching details drawn from everyday life. To connect the examples to your thesis, you will need to interlace them with explanation. Bryan Vaughn weaves example with explanation as he describes his perceptions of happiness:

> During my childhood, happiness meant anything from having waffles for breakfast to being able to stay outside after the streetlights came on, catching lightning bugs and playing tag. Early in my adolescence, happiness seemed to take on another meaning. Driving fast was my new source of happiness. I discovered that a motor could be affixed to just about anything. My first few inventions were just this side of lethal. When I consider these vehicles, it's a wonder I'm still alive today. I rode go-carts, three-wheelers, snowmobiles, motorcycles—anything I could put gas in, I drove.
>
> During mid-adolescence, my perception of happiness changed again. Sports became my passion. For me, nothing could compare with the exhilaration of being part of a winning team. Our football team was the defending state champion. Our basketball team finished third in the state, and our baseball team was the conference champion. Happiness was being one of the main players on every team and having the potential to play college sports and possibly having a career in professional sports.
>
> But those dreams ended during a football game when I received a severe spinal injury. After two months in the hospital, I was sent home—handicapped, but thankful. At this time happiness took on yet a new meaning: I was just glad to be alive and able to walk. . . .
>
> As my life began to return to normal, I saw a new source of happiness. One day I saw, parked in front of a Sunoco station, a red 1969 Pontiac GTO Judge. That same day I bought "The Judge" and spent every spare minute working on it. . . . But later an old man drove out in front of me without warning and wrecked my happiness. . . . Although I bought another car, it was not the same as the Judge.

Now that I have matured to a ripe old twenty-two, the word *happiness* means much more than ever before. . . .

Writing a Conclusion

www.mhhe.com/dietsch

For general coverage of writing conclusions, visit: Writing>Conclusions

The conclusion for a paper of illustration, as with any essay, should provide a satisfying close. Ending on a positive note, especially after the recounting of a painful experience, is gratifying for the reader. Barb Bronson ends "Clipper Ship Mom" (see chapter 9) by continuing the comparison and expressing gratitude:

My clipper ship, my mom, has endured many rough storms. Every day I thank God that my mother stood fast. Words can never express how lucky I feel to have her. At the present Clipper Ship Mom and crew continue to sail steadfastly on course, but on different seas.

In a paper about a series of failures she faced, Phyllis Parks ends on an optimistic note, providing some specific examples of current successes:

Despite the failures I have experienced, all phases of my life have not been grim. My daughter from my first marriage has grown into a beautiful, healthy young lady. Fifteen months ago my new husband and I were married. I am also enrolled in college classes. Now I truly feel successful.

Sometimes writers tend to repeat their introductions in slightly different words or to summarize their body paragraphs. Try to find a more satisfying conclusion. Consider explaining a particular insight, noting an advantage, offering a suggestion, or expressing an opinion that is supported by your examples. Leave readers feeling they have learned something from the examples.

Revising a Paper of Illustration

www.mhhe.com/dietsch

For online revision guidance, check out: Writing>Drafting and Revising

After your first draft has cooled a bit, go back and read through the examples carefully. Try to distance yourself from each one so that you can evaluate it impartially. As you make revisions, consider the principles you have learned so far. The following checklist will help you revise.

CHECKLIST: REVISING A PAPER OF ILLUSTRATION

1. What is the main point of the paper? Is the point clear?

2. Is each example relevant, accurate, and valid?

3. Does each example add substance to my claim?

4. Do the examples create interest?

5. Are there enough examples?

6. Are examples arranged in a clear, logical order? Or could the order be improved?

TWO STUDENT PAPERS: ILLUSTRATION

In the first paper, Anita Ketcham describes her hobby in an unusual way, blending explanation with example. Her purpose is to entertain as well as to inform.

Bathtub Solitude

An avid tennis player can be found lobbing away on the court; a woodworker may enjoy crafting furniture in a workshop; a gardener may relax by tending flower beds. I, too, have an enjoyable hobby—one that is not only relaxing and challenging but also educational. Like tennis, woodworking, and gardening, my hobby is done in the best possible place. That is why I do crossword puzzles in the bathtub.

As a mother of four young children, I rarely find time to sit down. Any time I do take for myself is soon interrupted. Mom sitting down is like a red flag waving, signaling a parade of little feet. This is why the bathtub is the perfect place to relax while working puzzles. There I cannot answer the telephone or pour a glass of milk or dress a Barbie doll. Those tasks have to wait. For a half hour, I escape to my own private retreat. Although it's not like Hawaii or the Bahamas, yet I am totally alone with my book and my bubbles, and it seems like heaven. The toughest problem I have to face is a six-letter word for supplication.

Working crossword puzzles is challenging. My favorites are the large "challenger" puzzles because the clues are difficult, requiring considerable thought. Still, I enjoy matching wits with the puzzlemaker. Some words can have several meanings and the clues can be ambiguous. A good puzzle solver learns to look at clues from different angles. For example, a five-letter word for the clue "drop a line" could be *write* or *angle,* but the answer the puzzlemaker wanted was *erase.* "Iron clothes" could be a clue for *press;* however, *armor* was the answer. A very difficult clue can be frustrating, especially for a puzzle printed in a newspaper because answers are not available until the next day. Although I rarely complete a difficult puzzle, I always try to improve my skills in order to do better with the next one.

Working crossword puzzles is educational. By using a dictionary often, I have expanded my vocabulary. Words such as *hirsute* and *litigious* have been added to my lexicon—as well as the word *lexicon.* And where else but in crossword puzzles could one find such a plethora of insignificant information? I know that Guido's note is an *ela,* but I do not know who Guido is. I know that the answer to "Roman bronze" is *aes* and that Caesar's road is an *iter,* should anyone ask. Not all of the knowledge I have gleaned from crossword puzzles is this trivial; some I have even found useful. Knowing that Siam is the former name of Thailand and that Istanbul was once Constantinople has helped me to defeat my husband during heated games of *Jeopardy.* He thinks he is married to a genius! I will never tell him my secret.

For my soon-to-be birthday, my husband will probably give me a bottle of bubble bath, the latest copy of *Dell Championship Crosswords,* and an hour to myself. Then I can enjoy some peace and quiet, sharpen my wits, and discover words new to me. All knocks on the door will be ignored. I will come out only when my toes are too wrinkled to stay longer.

QUESTIONS FOR DISCUSSION

1. Look at Anita's opening. What expectation does she set up with the first three brief examples?

2. What comparisons do you see in paragraph two?

3. What is the purpose of examples in paragraphs three and four?

4. Look at Anita's ending. How do the examples function there?

Next, Dixie O'Rourke offers a series of extended personal examples to show how she learned to control her emotions.

Envy

One evening without warning, envy crept into my young heart. The year was 1967. The place was a backyard ice rink at the home of my best friend, Sylvia. Although the time was only 5 p.m., dusk had already settled. Sylvia had just gone inside to eat dinner with her family in their comfortable brick home in a pleasant neighborhood.

Outside I continued to cut figure eights and spin on the ice while Sylvia ate dinner. As I paused to catch my breath, I found myself staring through the dining room window. Inside, the brightly lit room appeared warm and friendly as the family gathered around the table. Sylvia's father stood at the head, reading from the family Bible.

As I continued to window peek, I felt an overwhelming surge of envy and ill will. Suddenly, I was resentful not only of Sylvia's many possessions but also of her intact family. I longed to live like Sylvia. This flood of painful feelings changed not only how I felt toward her but also how I felt toward myself. The contentment of my childhood had shattered: I was ashamed of my house, my family, and myself.

Only ten years old, I was unable to deal with these new feelings of inferiority and kept them locked tightly within. I feared losing my best friend; I was afraid that if I told Sylvia how I felt, she might not like me anymore. I also feared telling my grandparents (with whom I resided); they might feel hurt and angry. So I told no one.

By junior high school, the feelings of shame and resentment had begun to diminish. Although I still felt pangs of envy when my friends flaunted their possessions, I had learned to control the envy so that it did not overwhelm me. The technique was simple—nothing new. I would count my blessings and thank God for each and every one of them. My grandparents had set a good example for me.

When I was thirteen, a sobering experience brought my perspective into a more realistic focus. During the school lunch hour, a group of students, whom I envied, gathered in front of the malt shop across from the school. This particular day the group welcomed and invited me to go with them to a carnival at a shopping center across town. The plan was to meet after school the next day and walk to the carnival. Knowing my grandfather's second job took him near the area, I offered the group a ride.

When school let out that afternoon, I ran home to plead for a ride and money for the carnival. Smiling, my grandmother lifted the lid of an old blue sugar bowl and gave me several silver coins. The next day grandpa drove his old Chevrolet, freckled with rust, to the school; and five of us piled in. When we reached a large parking lot, my friends hurried off toward the carnival without a word or backward glance to either of us.

Grandpa locked the car doors, bid me goodbye, and started toward the factory. As I watched him fade into the crowd, my eyes watered. Not one person had thanked him for the ride or waited for me. The envy I felt for that group fled. Suddenly, I felt proud of my grandfather even though he wore bib overalls and carried a lunch bucket. I felt fortunate to have both my grandparents.

Although I still feel a twinge of envy now and then, I no longer have the strong feelings of my youth. As my values have changed, I have focused my energies in a positive direction; presently, I'm working full time and attending classes for a nursing degree. Over the years, I have learned to subdue envy and to make the most of what I have.

QUESTIONS FOR DISCUSSION

1. What do you notice about Dixie's opening?

2. How does she set the scene for the reader?

3. What do you notice about Dixie's vantage point? (See the second paragraph: "outside," "inside.")

4. What incident causes a sharp shift in Dixie's perspective?

5. Examine her conclusion. What do you notice?

- "Mothers of Invention," Ethlie Ann Vare & Greg Ptacek, page 597
- "Road Rage," Vest, Cohen, & Tharp, page 600
- "Black and Well-to-Do," Andrea Lee, page 605
- "Going for Broke," Matea Gold & David Ferrell, page 607

FOR YOUR REFERENCE
Illustration Essays in the Reader

PRACTICE

IDEAS FOR WRITING

1. A pet food company is seeking winsome cats and dogs to be featured in television commercials. Write a letter explaining why your pet should be featured. Include examples of behavior and training.

2. Recently you purchased a home. Near the back fence, on a neighbor's property, stands an apple tree. Several limbs extend over the fence. Rotten apples, covered with insects, dot your lawn. Bees have stung your children twice. Legally, you can cut the tree back to the fence line, but for the sake of diplomacy, you prefer to talk to the neighbor. Map out your strategy by prewriting.

3. Describe a seemingly small incident such as a chance meeting or a sudden impulse that influenced your life.

4. Describe your first ride on a roller coaster.

5. Write an article for your campus newspaper using humorous examples to spoof a campus condition or a consumer product.

TWENTY IDEAS FOR PAPERS OF ILLUSTRATION

1   Optimism pays

2   How my view of work has changed

3   Soothing upset restaurant patrons is an art

4   Beware of bargains in flea markets

5   How my parents' divorce affected me

6   Learning from hardship

7   Aggressive drivers

8   What are good manners?

9   Easy ways to save money

10 Being a latchkey kid is not for the timid

11 Adversity can be an asset

12 A wonderful friend

13 The most frugal person I know

14 Perils of baby-sitting

15 Common gardening mistakes

16 My Achilles heel

17 Ways to attract hummingbirds

18 View the wonders of West Virginia (or another state)

19 My grandmother's perseverance

20 My father's gift: persistence

Classifying: Sorting into Groups

CHAPTER 13

> Out of clutter, find simplicity.
>
> —Albert Einstein

PURPOSE OF CLASSIFICATION

Classification allows us to establish order in our lives and to function effectively. In daily living we classify, selecting categories according to our needs in various situations, rhetorical or otherwise. Perhaps as you clean out the attic, you find an old stack of comic books, long forgotten, handed down through the family. You are surprised to see that all the covers are still intact. "Hmm—maybe they are valuable," you murmur. You sort them into piles, grouping according to the title: *Batman, Superman, Flash, Green Hornet, Justice League, Donald Duck, Uncle Scrooge, Scamp, Mickey Mouse, Smokey Bear, Woodsy Owl, Junior Woodchucks,* and *Metal Men.*

Whether you look for a job by scanning the classified ads, file documents on your computer, sort your laundry, stock shelves in a store, or consider investments according to risk, you classify.

WHAT IS THE BASIS OF CLASSIFICATION?

Classification is a method of sorting—grouping and dividing—items or ideas logically. To classify various pieces of information, you look for a common feature that certain items have—a shared *principle of selection*—that marks them as

Unclassified Buckeye Fans

■■❚❚○○❚❚❚○❚❚○❚○○❚❚❚○❚❚❚❚

Classified Buckeye Fans

Casual Fans	Concerned Fans	Ardent Fans
○○○○○○	❚❚❚❚❚❚❚❚❚❚❚	❚❚❚❚❚❚❚

FIGURE 13.1 Classification of Buckeye fans.

belonging to a group. To fit into the group, each item must have this similarity. Then, if needed, you can subdivide the group, making finer distinctions as to relationship.

Everything on this planet can be classified in some way. The millions of species are divided into five formal classifications or kingdoms: animals, plants, fungi, bacteria, and algae/molds. And each one is subdivided into categories. For example, one category is *felines*—big and little cats, both wild and domesticated. Felines can be subdivided according to species: tigers, lions, panthers, and others. Each species can be further subdivided into kinds, such as albino tigers, Bengal tigers, and Siberian tigers.

Student writer Jane Tinker humorously classifies Ohio State Buckeye football fans, dividing them into three groups, according to their degree of "Buckeye Fever" (later in this chapter). Her principles of selection are "casual fans," "concerned fans," and "ardent fans" (see fig. 13.1).

WRITING A PAPER OF CLASSIFICATION

A paper of classification not only groups and divides but also analyzes, describes, and explains. The purpose and the way the topic is approached determine the order. As you choose a topic, consider the rhetorical situation, especially the way you will treat the topic. Regardless of whether you adopt a serious or light tone, your written voice should be appropriate and the development should be ethical.

www.mhhe.com/dietsch

For online help writing classification essays, visit: Writing>Writing Tutors>Classification

Ethical Concerns

As you prewrite and draft, think about your written voice and how it may sound to readers. Beware of applying negative labels—such as ageist, sexist, racist, or ethnic stereotypes—that might be hurtful to any particular group. Be creative and original, if you wish; but strive for objectivity and fairness. As you classify, you might ask yourself these questions:

- Are the categories suitable for the purpose, audience, and assignment?
- Is the word choice appropriate?
- Have I avoided stereotyping and other unsound generalizations?
- Is the main idea of my paper presented ethically?

See chapter 3.

For example, a nursing student writes a research paper that classifies certain illegal drugs; the purpose is to warn readers of dangers in usage. She consults numerous sources written by authorities in the field. Then she summarizes the evidence, describing the effects of the drugs in an objective tone and warning of possible side effects. Thus written, her development of the topic would be balanced and ethical.

But if another student were to write an essay on a similar topic without doing valid research, then the topic would be inappropriate and the development unethical. Although the student might interview several friends, then classify the various recreational drugs they use and describe the euphoria-inducing effects they experience, apparently with no negative side effects, the survey would be unreliable. It would be merely the opinion of a small group, not necessarily fact or representative of users as a whole. Effects of drugs can vary from person to person; and side effects can be incremental, perhaps not showing up until much later. And human memory is not always reliable.

Shaping a Topic to the Purpose and Audience

Chances are that you already have a lode of details to be mined and classified that you can use for an interesting informative essay. If you have a collection or hobby, you might classify the objects you have accumulated over the years, perhaps record albums, pedal cars, or video games, pointing out little-known facts, bits of history, and the value of the collection. Or perhaps you live near a scenic area with little-known features that might attract tourists (including the reader). If you were to write a brochure, what features would you describe and how would you classify them?

GUIDELINES: CLASSIFICATION

1. **Classify items according to the purpose and audience.** Have a reason.
2. **Avoid overlapping parts or categories.** Be clear-cut.
3. **Make each part or category large enough to contain a significant number.** Have a minimum of three items or details in each category.
4. **Make all parts parallel.** All items in a category should be similar, having a common principle of selection. Then they will be parallel.
5. **Organize all parts or categories to fit into one logical system.** All the parts should fit together into one organized whole.
6. **Arrange in a logical order.** See "Seven Basic Orders," page 50.

Student writer Patricia Rush described her observations of a restaurant buffet. Her writing purpose was to amuse; her audience was her classmates. She classified "Annoying Eaters of America" as "inspectors, critics, conversationalists, and gulpers." Here is how she described the fourth group:

Gulpers are the Indianapolis drivers of the table. To prepare for the race, they pile their platters high, thus cutting down on stops for refueling. They are determined to finish the meal first, even at the cost of indigestion. Stuffing their mouths and chomping, they shovel in the food and wash it down with great gulps of water. When every scrap is gone, they sometimes take a morsel of bread and swab their platters clean. Often their belches can be heard throughout the restaurant. Gulpers are usually males in ragged T-shirts and dingy jeans. For them, these garments may have more than one use; gulpers sometimes finish by wiping their hands across their chests or thighs.

With a topic in mind, you can use any of the prewriting and drafting techniques you learned in chapter 4. Still another way can be helpful: the "because" technique.

Prewriting with the "Because" Technique

www.mhhe.com/dietsch

For further coverage of prewriting, go to:
Writing>Prewriting

If your topic can be divided into advantages, benefits, or reasons, you might try the "because" technique to simplify your prewriting. Just ask a question about the topic, then answer "because. . . ." Jot down your answer and ask "What else?" Repeat the sequence until you have enough material. After that, group the details logically into main points.

Let's assume you have a fourteen-year-old daughter, Kim, who has been invited to go for a drive with Brad, the sixteen-year-old next door. But you are convinced Brad is a reckless and irresponsible driver. Simply stating your belief and forbidding Kim to go may not carry much weight with her. You need evidence to support the claim and reinforce your decision. Prior to your talk, you use the "because" technique to help you classify relevant facts into main points:

QUESTIONS	ANSWERS
1. Why does Brad seem rude and immature?	*Because* he insulted a neighbor who reprimanded him for backing into her driveway and almost hitting her cat. He has yelled crude comments to neighborhood children on bikes and scared them by coming too close.
2. Why does Brad seem irresponsible?	*Because* I have seen him speed on city streets, run stop signs and red lights. He brakes sharply, squealing his tires.
3. Are there any other reasons?	*Because* he has put several dents in his car although he's had it only three months. He backed into his mother's car last week.
4. What else?	*Because* he has been cited for speeding twice.

Your prewriting could continue until everything you know about Brad's driving has been listed. Then you could analyze the details and divide them into categories such as *rudeness, carelessness, speeding, ignoring traffic rules,* or in other ways.

Organizing a Classification Paper

Perhaps the most common order for a paper of classification is some order of degree: simple to complex, least to most important, easy to difficult, and so forth. To make a case against Brad as a driver, you might organize points from the least to most dangerous aspects of his driving.

BRAD IS A RECKLESS AND IRRESPONSIBLE DRIVER:

1. *Because he is careless.*
   He almost hit the neighbor's cat in her driveway.
   Last week he backed into his mother's car.
   His car has several dents in it after only three months.

2. *Because he is rude and immature.*
   He told old Mrs. Smith to shut up when she reprimanded him.
   He yells crude comments at children on bikes and drives too close to
   them.

3. *Because he speeds.*
   He has had two speeding tickets.
   He drove 50 mph on a street posted at 35 mph.
   He turns corners too fast, squealing his tires.

4. *Because he often ignores traffic signs and signals.*
   He turns quickly without signaling to other drivers.
   He drove through a stop sign last week.
   He sometimes drives through red lights.

Drafting a Thesis Statement

www.mhhe.com/dietsch

For online help with your thesis statement, check out:

Writing>Thesis

The next step is to draft a tentative thesis. A first draft might be a brief claim: "You can't go out with Brad for four reasons." But the tone is inappropriate and specifying all the reasons in the thesis would prove unwieldy. A second stronger draft might read: "Brad is an immature driver who lacks consideration and judgment." Then you could make an outline listing the main points you intend to make.

Developing Main Points and Embedding Transition

As you draft, develop your main points with specific evidence—facts, reasons, and examples. Each paragraph should support the claim made in the thesis. And each paragraph should have a clear link to the thesis, either through signpost or embedded transition. Subtle transition is the mark of a proficient writer.

In the following example, Mark Brady begins by stating an opinion. In the second sentence he gives facts. Next he cites three reasons (italicized) to support the claim made in the first sentence:

> Upland bird hunting in Ohio is in a sad condition. Populations of three
> game birds—the ring-necked pheasant, the blue grouse, and the bobwhite

quail—have dwindled. Three main factors for this decline are *the kind of hunters, increased pollution,* and *clearing of woods and underbrush for farming.*

Note how Mark creates a direct link from each of his body paragraphs back to the thesis. In other words, he embeds his transition:

> Along with the good *hunters* in the fields are a number of ignorant *hunters* who shoot every bird they can, despite the fact that they are exceeding the daily bag limit. . . .
>
> The second reason for the dwindling bird population is the *increased pollution* in our environment. . . .
>
> The *farmer* is probably the biggest reason for declining bird populations. . . .

Again, in his conclusion, Mark reinforces each of his initial main points by alluding to the thesis:

> Frankly, most of those concerned seem to contribute to poor hunting conditions. The *nonsportsman hunter* takes home more birds than allowed. The *manufacturers who make pesticides and weed sprays* sometimes fail to adequately check the long-term effects of products upon birds and their eggs. Many *farmers* clear their land and plow in the fall, not leaving cover or grain for the game birds. Surely we must work to solve this problem before it is too late.

Mark does an excellent job of connecting his thesis to the main points of his paper, using all four kinds of embedded transition: repetition of key terms, synonyms, pronoun and antecedent, and natural relationships.

1. **Repetition of key terms:** hunters, increased pollution
2. **Synonyms:** ignorant hunters, nonsportsman hunters
3. **Pronoun and antecedent:** hunters/they
4. **Natural relationships:** pollution/manufacturers/pesticides/sprays, nonsportsman/bag limit, farming/farmers

FOUR KINDS OF EMBEDDED TRANSITION

STUDENT ESSAY STATING MAIN POINTS IN THE THESIS

Michele Flahive briefly states three main points in the thesis. She uses embedded transition to establish clear links from the thesis to body paragraphs. These links mark the path of the main idea and provide unity. Note how she repeats a key term (italicized) in the first sentence of each body paragraph:

Diamonds: A Girl's Summer Friend

As the batter walks up to the dusty plate on the diamond, she scans the outfield. Spying a vacancy between left and left center, she knows this is the best area to hit the ball. While the pitcher gets ready, the batter stands in position, watching every move. In a slow pitch, the ball sails off in a perfect arc, dropping right where the batter wants it. With heart pounding, she swings the aluminum bat and cracks the ball. Quickly, she runs three bases, listening to the cheers of teammates and hoping to reach home plate before the ball. For her the *challenge*, the *enjoyment*, and the *camaraderie* make softball a game worth playing.

The first game of the season seems always to pose a special *challenge*. The players often feel a bit rusty and nervous. Just walking onto the field and up to bat that first time takes strength of will. But once the umpire yells, "Play ball," the nervousness melts away and determination flows in. Enthusiasm for the game takes over.

Enjoyment of softball is the heart of the game. After a long day of work or school, it is a pleasure to leave the stress behind and walk out onto the diamond. Since both teammates and crowd are just out for an evening of recreation, there is no great pressure to win. The fun and action provide a refreshing reward at the end of a day.

The challenge and enjoyment would be incomplete without the *camaraderie* of teammates who share the same passion for a rousing game of softball. And when a member is feeling down for missing a ball or for striking out, words of encouragement flow from other members. Then too, there is a sense of unity as everyone plays together in the infield and outfield, backing each other up as needed.

As August slowly winds to an end, so must the summer softball season. It can be a sad time for many die-hard ball players who must leave the diamond and put away their gloves. Yet some players take heart, for not only does autumn bring bright foliage and cool evenings, but it also heralds the fall softball season!

Did you notice how Michele sets the scene and pulls the reader right into the action at the very beginning? With just a few concrete details, she creates an image of the dusty plate, batter with pounding heart, aluminum bat, sound of the bat hitting the ball, perfect arc, and cheers. This vivid description helps the reader to relive what she feels and sees as she walks up to the batter's box. Examples also help readers share the emotions that pervade the game.

Making Main Points Parallel

See chapter 7.

When main points are parallel, the resulting balance strengthens transition, sentence structure, and unity. In the example below, note how Joanne M. Pohlman begins each main point with the same type of structure, a gerund phrase (italicized). Each main point in the body explains the matching point in her thesis:

THESIS: As a volunteer member of the National Ski Patrol, I earn the opportunity to meet many interesting people, learn challenging skills, and spend time with my family.

PARALLEL POINTS:
1. *Joining the Central Division of the Patrol* has acquainted me with approximately eighty other patrollers. . . .

2. *Becoming a member of this national organization* takes more than being a proficient skier. My training. . . .

3. *Being able to ski with my family* is the main reason I chose to become a patroller.

Writing a Conclusion

www.mhhe.com/dietsch

For online help with your conclusions, visit: Writing>Conclusions

A conclusion should flow logically and smoothly from the main idea. As a result, the reader should gain a sense of completeness or closure. To provide a satisfying ending, writers often allude to the thesis, as Joanne Pohlman does. At the end of the paper about skiing, she repeats the name of the organization and expresses appreciation:

> Finally, I feel fortunate to belong to the National Ski Patrol. Although I receive no wages, I do gain new friends, invaluable skills, and a closeness with my family that is priceless.

Revising the Paper

www.mhhe.com/dietsch

For general help with revising, check out: Writing>Drafting and Revising

A paper of classification is more complex than those discussed in earlier chapters. The checklist below should help you to revise your paper successfully:

CHECKLIST: REVISING CLASSIFICATION PAPERS

1. Has the topic been narrowed to one item?

2. Is the introduction focused and interesting?

3. Do the main points follow the order set up in the thesis statement?

4. Are the main points linked with the thesis?

5. Are the main points parallel?

6. Are the main points well supported with specific details and examples?

7. Does the internal order of each paragraph flow well?

8. Can clarity be improved? Is more transition needed?

TWO STUDENT PAPERS: CLASSIFICATION

In the first paper, Nicole Vanderkooi's purpose is to inform, and her classmates are her audience. Her thesis (fourth sentence) is much different from the previous ones; it is all-encompassing. Although Nicole makes several generalizations, notice that she qualifies them.

The Melting Pot of New Orleans

The sweet voice of jazz and spicy smell of Cajun cuisine capture Nicole's senses as she strolls through the French Quarter of New Orleans in the bright sunshine. On the corner of Bourbon Street sits a homeless man, cross-legged, playing his harmonica. Occasionally, a passerby drops a few coins or a dollar bill in his soiled cap. People from every walk of life seem to wander these cobblestone streets.

Tourists dot the avenues of New Orleans. At daybreak they begin to roam the high-priced novelty shops and spacious old plantations surrounding the area. Frequently, a woman is escorted by an overburdened man and a trusty guidebook. Often dressed in walking shorts, they sport "I survived New Orleans night life" T-shirts and sun visors or sunglasses. Before sundown nocturnal pleasures begin, enticing sightseers to partake in Cajun feasting and boisterous drinking.

In a horse-drawn carriage, a tourist reclines, listening to the gentle clip-clop of hooves and the driver's southern drawl. Carrying briefcases, three businesspeople stride past shops, apparently bent on another destination. In a jewelry store, a couple examine pendants, intent on a possible purchase. In an art gallery, a sightseer from New York purchases yet another work, possibly for his loft.

Draped with tattered overcoats and wearing tennis shoes, the homeless of this elusive city often wear weathered grins amid week-old whiskers. Many of their daily hours are spent collecting tips, as they stand on street corners, providing the pleasure of hearing their sultry saxophones. The night brings them home to humid, stagnant alleys and alcoves. These bumbling creatures usually walk alone, accompanied only by their instrument and a bottle, enclosed in a brown paper bag.

Yet another colorful feature of this Louisiana melting pot is the local businessman. Often attired in a single-breasted black suit, an ivory silk shirt, and a brilliant tie, this worldly person exudes professionalism and sophistication. Finding him in a trendy coffee shop, drinking a black brew from a small cup, is not unusual. At night he often dines at a specialty restaurant and listens to the rhythms of jazz. His companion may be a colleague or a breathtaking, well-dressed woman.

New Orleans graciously accepts the prize for the most captivating city in the U.S.A. There an array of sights and sounds—musical vagrants, inquisitive visitors, and local residents—catches the eye and captures the heart.

QUESTIONS FOR DISCUSSION

1. How many types of people does Nicole classify?
2. How does Nicole link body paragraphs to her thesis?
3. What kinds of specific details does she use to describe each of her categories?
4. How does Nicole establish closure in her ending?
5. How would you describe her tone?

In the next paper, Jane Tinker classifies Ohio State football fans into three categories. Her tongue-in-cheek tone and adroit use of concrete details enable readers to share her amusement.

Buckeye Fever

Every autumn for the past twelve years, I have witnessed an outbreak of "Buckeye Fever" in my neighborhood. The ailment seems to hit victims in varying intensities. They are the casual, the concerned, and the ardent fans of the Ohio State Buckeyes.

The mildest strain of Buckeye Fever is evident in the casual fans. When time permits, they enjoy watching the game on television or listening on radio. But if time is limited or the weather turns sunny and warm, they forsake the game without a second thought. If given tickets, they will go—they may even buy them occasionally. The casual fans usually know the names and numbers of a few star players. Some casual fans feel that if the Bucks lose the game, an afternoon's viewing time is wasted. Casual fans are not interested in watching the Saturday night replay, for they already know the result.

Buckeye Fever hits concerned fans with moderate severity. They watch or listen to every Buckeye game possible. With buddies they enjoy seeing the Bucks on television. Enthusiastic, the concerned fans enter into the game, yelling and screaming as excitement mounts. If they have to miss a game, they will tape it on the VCR to watch later. They will purchase tickets to a game if readily available, but they will not stand in line for hours. They know the names and numbers of all starting players and are also aware of the opponent's capabilities. If Ohio State loses, the concerned fans are very disappointed, but not upset if the game was well played.

The ardent fans have contracted a serious case of Buckeye Fever. This strain may be terminal to some relationships. On Friday nights, the ardent fans are planning and preparing their elaborate tailgate lunches for the next day's game. Saturday mornings they rise early to proudly display their scarlet and gray flags in a prominent place and to beat the traffic jam to home games or any other within driving distance. Their tickets have been purchased either by waiting long hours in line or by knuckling into scalpers.

Dressed in their red sweaters and gray pants, the ardent fans anticipate the glory of Buckeye victory. They know the names, numbers, and personal statistics of all fifty team players as well as the high school players being recruited for next season. Later the ardent fans watch the replay to relive moments of victory. Depending on the outcome of the game, the Buckeye coach is either a saint or a bum. When the Bucks lose, the ardent fans are furious; then they become depressed. The depression may last until the following Tuesday, when they begin to anticipate the upcoming game.

Despite the degree to which a fan catches the fever, they all agree that football can be a very exciting game to watch. And for them, no team is more exciting than the Ohio State Buckeyes.

QUESTIONS FOR DISCUSSION

1. How does Jane's introduction differ from Nicole's?

2. What principle of organization has Jane used for her paper?

3. Where has Jane used embedded transition to link body paragraphs back to her thesis?

4. Why do you think Jane devotes more attention to her final category than her first two?

5. How does Jane's ending differ from Nicole's?

PRACTICE

Classification

Directions: Analyze the statements below and classify them according to the listed categories.

cliché   common belief   myth
old saying   superstition   fad
stereotype   tradition   trend

_____ 1. "Punks" dye their hair unusual colors such as green, orange, or purple.

_____ 2. Groups of people who ride motorcycles and wear black leather jackets are dangerous.

_____ 3. Red sky at night; sailors' delight
                Red sky in morning; sailors take warning.

_____ 4. Down through the ages, our family has baked Christmas fruitcakes.

_____ 5. When a couple divorce, the mother should receive custody of very young children.

_____ 6. To win at bridge, select a seat that is parallel with the bathtub in the house.

_____ 7. Money is the root of all evil.

_____ 8. According to Greek legend, Cerberus guarded the underworld, the realm of Hades, devouring anyone who tried to leave.

_____ 9. Don't make mountains out of molehills.

_____ 10. The middle class is gradually disappearing.

COLLABORATIVE LEARNING: CLASSIFICATION

Directions: Select the word in each group that is not in the same category as the other three words. Then compare your selections with those of other group members. Discuss disagreement. You may use dictionaries.

1. orange   2. gannet   3. putter
    kiwi   petrel   baseball bat
    lemon   dodo   tennis racquet
    ugli   trogon   hockey stick

4. lace
   snowflake
   frost
   water

5. crocus
   daffodil
   zinnia
   tulip

6. lobo
   sheltie
   wolverine
   coyote

7. wombat
   kangaroo
   opossum
   aardvark

8. daisy
   violet
   chrysanthemum
   echinacea

9. arrowroot
   fennel
   holly berries
   juniper berries

TWENTY IDEAS FOR CLASSIFICATION PAPERS

When you develop your topic, you should have a definite audience in mind. In the suggestions that follow, some possible audiences are mentioned.

1 Classify the groups you belong to and explain why each is meaningful to you. *Audience:* Your parents who want you to study more.

2 Classify the voters in your town and discuss major characteristics of each group. *Audience:* Assume you are preparing a report for a politician who is planning to run for mayor.

3 Classify small cars (or some other vehicles) and evaluate them. *Audience:* Assume you are writing for readers of *Consumer Reports.*

4 For the home gardener, classify and describe hardy perennials that thrive in the sun, partial shade, or full shade.

5 Job considerations for an engineer (secretary or whom?)

6 Annoying drivers

7 Students in your classes

8 Interesting one-day trips within your state

9 Hazards in buying a used car (or anything else)

10 Caves in the United States

11   Relatives

12   Commercials that irritate

13   Types of homes available in the price range you can afford

14   Classify and evaluate sports news shows

15   Friends

16   Classify and evaluate local restaurants

17   Day care facilities in your area

18   Classify the major nonservice employers in your city

19   Kinds of patients/clients/customers

20   Kinds of teachers you have had

Comparing and Contrasting for a Purpose

CHAPTER 14

> Happiness is like a sunbeam, which the least shadow intercepts.
>
> —Chinese proverb

A striking comparison can capture the essence of an idea in a single sentence. Comparing an abstract idea with a concrete image, as in the proverb above, explains the resemblance in a delightful way. We smile or sigh and think "How true." *Comparison* includes both likeness and difference with an emphasis on likeness. A *contrast* shows or emphasizes differences.

In daily living you frequently use comparison and contrast in making purposeful choices. Whether you purchase a car, clothing, or cell phone, you undoubtedly compare and contrast the features of various brands before making your decision. On the job you may purchase supplies, screen applicants, preview software, or perform other tasks that require comparing prices, qualities, or features. Daily we weigh advantages against disadvantages, pros against cons, possibilities against difficulties in order to make wise decisions.

PURPOSE OF A COMPARISON OR CONTRAST PAPER

Every paper needs a specific purpose, a valid reason for a comparison or contrast, according to the rhetorical situation. The fact that an instructor assigns the paper is not a purpose. The comparison or contrast should illustrate a point the writer wishes to make. The point may be placed at the beginning or the end of the paper.

Determining a Purpose

To determine your specific purpose, try asking yourself, "Why might the audience like to read about this topic?" What is the point? When a topic is unfamiliar to readers, your purpose in comparing and contrasting may be to inform them of significant relationships and distinctions between the two subjects. When the topic is familiar, your general purpose may be informative; but to hold readers' attention, you need to present specific insights or a fresh perspective. You might entertain, as well as inform, by presenting the features of the two subjects in an amusing way.

See "Writing a Purpose Statement," chapter 1. When the general purpose of comparison or contrast is to persuade, you shape a specific strategy to influence readers toward a certain viewpoint. For example, an employee might write a proposal comparing a present procedure to a proposed new procedure, weighing advantages and disadvantages (if any). The specific purpose would be to convince readers that the new procedure would save time and money.

Selecting a Suitable Topic

Regardless of the subjects you choose to contrast or compare for this paper, they must have something in common. *They should be of the same species, class, or category.* For example, there would be no practical reason to compare hockey to stock car racing, for you would be unable to find opposing points to match for a logical purpose. But if you wanted to compare different kinds of race car designs, you could find logical points of comparison or contrast. To avoid boring the reader, steer away from predictable topics and stereotypes.

Predictable Topics   Beware of mundane topics, such as "winter versus summer" or "a ranch house versus a two-story," which can cause readers and instructors to wince. The old axiom "Don't tell readers what they already know" still applies. To move beyond trite generalities, ask yourself, "How much do readers already know?" "What are they unlikely to know?" You might refresh the topic by putting a new spin on an ordinary idea. Try looking at the topic from an unusual angle. For example, your title might be "What Kind of Bait Do Blue Gills Really Like?" Then you might compare the advantages and disadvantages of using night crawlers versus using your own special dough balls.

Stereotypes   Broad, general topics can lead to unsupported generalizations. For example, a student who selected the topic "city life versus country life" generalized from stereotypes. The result was a series of overstatements, such as this one: "City dwellers take little time to enjoy life and nature." Without thinking, writers may repeat misstatements they have heard or think are probably true—even though they have no evidence to substantiate the claims.

To sidestep unsound generalizations, first narrow your topic. Then check each claim carefully: Do you have adequate evidence to back it up? To be safe, avoid pronouncements about what a majority does or does not do. Writing about your own experience decreases the likelihood of blundering into unsupported generalizations.

ANALOGY: A SPECIAL KIND OF COMPARISON

Although the subjects of a comparison or contrast are usually of the same species, class, or category, a writer may choose to make an imaginative comparison—*finding unusual likenesses in things that are of completely different categories*. In "The Attic of the Brain," biologist and essayist Lewis Thomas compares the unconscious human mind to the attic of a house. In "Snapping the Leash," journalist Murray Kempton compares the darker forces of human nature to "a raging tiger" that each individual "spends [his or her] life building a cage to pen . . . in."

Such imaginative comparisons are similar to simile and metaphor. But when extended over the course of a paragraph or an essay, comparisons like these become *analogies*. To be effective, an analogy should be consistent, apt, and fresh. It should also help readers see the subject in a new light. Note how the analogy of "cowboying" is used to illuminate the work of a writer:

> Both jobs—writing and cowboying—take up the whole mind and heart. . . .
> A good hand on a ranch requires vigilance, acute powers of observation,
> readiness to anticipate what might go wrong or what's coming next, a taste for
> recklessness, intuitive skills, patience, and what cowboys look for when they
> buy a horse: a lot of heart. Aspiring to those qualities as a rancher, I can only
> hope my writing will benefit as well.
>
> —Gretel Ehrlich, "Life at Close Range"

Analogies are often used to help explain abstract ideas in scientific and technical writing. If you use an analogy, make sure that it has a clear explanatory purpose. Readers may not see the point of an analogy that is used primarily for decoration or entertainment.

www.mhhe.com/dietsch

For further guidance on writing comparison or contrast essays, visit: Writing>Writing Tutors> Comparison/Contrast

WRITING A PAPER OF COMPARISON OR CONTRAST

In composing a paper of comparison or contrast, you examine relationships between elements, distinguish their similarities and differences, and organize them in a logical order that reflects your purpose.

Gathering Information and Prewriting

If you were to compare two cars, the purpose might be to determine which one would better suit your needs and to inform an interested reader. To gather information, you might visit showrooms, talk to sales representatives, and drive the two cars. You could quote and identify the source in general terms such as "One salesperson said that. . . ." If, however, you were to read *Consumer Reports* or another publication, you would need to supply specific documentation, as explained in chapters 28 and 29.

To save time, prewrite details in parallel lists. Simply head two columns with the selected topics, then skip a space and start listing. Each time you write in a detail for one item, add a corresponding detail for the other. Placing the details side by side will make the lists parallel.

www.mhhe.com/dietsch

For additional information on prewriting, go to: Writing>Prewriting

	HONDA CIVIC HYBRID	TOYOTA PRIUS
Features:	————	————
	————	————
	————	————
Price:	————	————
mpg:	————	————
Warranty:	————	————
Styling:	————	————
Handling:	————	————
Comfort:	————	————
Maintenance:	————	————

Next, classify details into categories. These categories can act as main points in your paper. For example, the price, expected cost of maintenance, and cost of operation (mpg) could be grouped under the category of economy.

After prewriting and grouping details, focus your paper with a thesis statement. Check to see that it (1) identifies a specific topic, (2) indicates similarity and/or difference, and (3) sets up an order of main points. Although not all thesis statements are this explicit, many instructors prefer such a clear focus, as in the following examples:

- **THESIS:** Although the Chevrolet Lumina and the Ford Taurus are similar in several respects, they vary in comfort, performance, and cost.

- **THESIS:** Whether I am in the mood for an exhilarating challenge or a leisurely ride through the woods, I have horses for each mood. (Kathy Burton)
- **THESIS:** Despite obvious differences, the two series *Earth's Children* and *The Hitchhiker's Guide to the Galaxy* have much in common. (Melissa Baker)

Organizing a Paper of Comparison or Contrast

The *block* and *alternating* methods are two basic ways to organize parallel points of comparison or contrast. For an easily understood topic, the block method is simple and suitable. This order lists all the pertinent points about the first subject in one block of parallel details, then lists the points about the second subject in corresponding order. This balanced arrangement ensures that the details are easy to follow.

BLOCK OUTLINE OF CONTRAST

www.mhhe.com/dietsch
For help outlining, check out:
Writing>Outlining Tutor

   I. *Thesis statement:* Mr. Courtney and Mr. Graham, my former neighbors, contrasted greatly in appearance, demeanor, and friendliness.

  II. Mr. Courtney

     A. Appearance

       1. Meticulous. Clothes perfectly pressed.

       2. Clean-shaven. Hair neatly groomed.

       3. Short, trim, and muscular.

     B. Demeanor

       1. Solemn. Never seemed to smile. Eyes glared.

       2. Never out except to care for lawn. Swore and hurried.

       3. Children afraid of him. He scowled when greeted.

     C. Friendliness

       1. Unfriendly.

       2. Protected his privacy.

 III. Mr. Graham

     A. Appearance

       1. Clothes never hung quite right.

       2. Hint of a beard. Hair untidy.

       3. Tall and rather heavy.

     B. Demeanor

       1. Always smiling. Kind eyes.

       2. Often outside. Hummed, sang, worked in rose garden.

       3. Charmed children. Pitched ball, played hide and seek.

C. Friendliness

    1. Regarded as grandparent by children.

    2. Concerned, a real neighbor.

IV. Conclusion

For a complex comparison, the alternating method is an effective way to organize. You explain comparable points paired in parallel order. In other words, you alternate the subjects. Because of frequent shifts from subject to subject, the alternating method requires more transition than the block method.

OUTLINE OF CONTRAST (ALTERNATING SUBJECTS)

  I. Introduction

 II. Appearance

    A. Mr. Courtney

    B. Mr. Graham

III. Demeanor

    A. Mr. Courtney

    B. Mr. Graham

IV. Friendliness

    A. Mr. Courtney

    B. Mr. Graham

  V. Conclusion

When only similarities are discussed, the pattern can be similar to one of the preceding examples for contrast. When you include both similarities and dissimilarities, the structure of the comparison becomes more complicated. Usually, similarities are discussed first, unless there is a reason for reversal.

Drafting an Introduction

www.mhhe.com/dietsch

Want more coverage of introductions? Go to: Writing>Introductions

Introductions of comparison or contrast papers can set the scene for the two subjects by revealing what, where, how, and when. Chuck Chesnut gives these details as he wryly contrasts two neighborhood animals. (His thesis is italicized.)

The Pet and the Pest

In my neighborhood there are several animals, but none quite like "the pet" or "the pest." When I walk out my back door and see or hear the pet, as I call him, I smile. He is a friendly old basset hound that lives in the next yard behind our house. But when I walk out my front door and see or hear the pest, my hackles rise. She is the high-strung miniature poodle that resides across the street. Some days I mutter, "The dog from Hell!" or something unprintable. *These dogs vary greatly not only to the eye and the ear but also to my sense of values.*

A narrative opening is an easy and effective way to set the stage for a comparison or contrast. Terri Bloomfield uses narration by presenting a few graphic details to describe a sudden change in her life.

My Life After Dealing with Death

As I pushed my Fiero up to sixty-five miles an hour, the possibility of being killed in an automobile accident was miles of thoughts away. Being young, I felt invincible—why should I worry about an unpleasant subject like death? In a few days, however, I had to confront that topic in an instant. On August 18, 1993, my best friend and my cousin were killed in an automobile accident. The realization of how quickly life can be snatched away changed my life, starting the moment I met death face-to-face.

Developing a Comparison or Contrast Paper

The order in which you develop your parallel points in a comparison or contrast depends upon the purpose and the audience. One technique, order of familiarity, starting with the familiar and going to the unfamiliar, is quite effective, allowing less explanation than the reverse requires. You use analogies, anecdotes, or examples to flesh out ideas before moving to more complex points. A topic that involves physical description will need numerous concrete details to support the main points.

In the next example from "My Two Neighbors," Betty Fetters' precise descriptions enable the reader to visualize two individuals, see beyond outer appearances, and appreciate their own good neighbors.

> Mr. Courtney was a meticulous person who seemed to reflect this quality in every aspect of his life. His clothes were always perfectly pressed, his face clean-shaven, and his hair neatly groomed. His short frame was trim and muscular despite his age. He seemed always to wear a solemn expression; I never once saw him smile. His glaring eyes echoed his disgust with people and his contempt for life.
>
> Seldom did I see Mr. Courtney outdoors except to care for his lawn. Despite the swearing and hurrying to get the job done, his yard was the best tended in the neighborhood. Local children never went near his house because they knew that the slightest transgression would be met with angry retribution. Mr. Courtney was a private person, and everyone treated him and his property with the respect he so vehemently demanded.
>
> Many times a greeting to Mr. Courtney would be answered with an angry scowl. Mr. Courtney was indeed an island unto himself. Every encounter with him would remind me of another, much more gentle, man—a very dear friend who had taught me the value of friendship and the real definition of the word *neighbor.*

Note that after the first block of details, Betty smoothly introduces the second block with "would remind me of another, much more gentle man . . . ," leading into a description of Mr. Graham:

> If judged by first appearance, Mr. Graham would not have made a very good impression. His clothes, although neatly pressed, never hung quite right on his tall, rotund body. He seemed always to have a shadow of a beard, and his hair usually looked as if he had started to comb it but had been interrupted. He was, however, always smiling; and his love for people and life was reflected in his eyes.

Many times I would hear Mr. Graham singing or humming while he worked in his garden or trimmed his rosebushes. He always worked with the same patience and deliberation, nurturing and caring for each plant. With this same calm concern, he charmed the children of the neighborhood. It was common to see him pitching a ball, playing hide-and-seek, or sitting on his porch with a group of children at his feet. The children regarded him as a grandparent and treated him with great respect, as did everyone in the neighborhood. He was a real neighbor to all, friend or stranger.

Transition to Indicate Similarity or Dissimilarity

As you move from detail to detail while comparing or contrasting, you will need special transitions to indicate shifts in meaning. For your convenience, here are some transitions that point out likeness or difference:

SIMILARITY		DISSIMILARITY	
also	too	but	yet
and	both	in contrast	on the other hand
again	similarly	however	on the contrary
likewise	in addition	still	although
besides	then too	conversely	nevertheless

Now and then you may need a *transitional sentence* to bridge a gap in thought. For example, after discussing one horse, you might supply a sentence of transition to introduce another horse: "Whereas Rocket looked as if he had been groomed for the Kentucky Derby, Skip had the careless air of a beach-comber." Two other tips you may want to consider: (1) Place *also* or *however* within a sentence rather than at the beginning, where they may sound tacked on or out of place. (2) Substitute *too* or *then too* to avoid overuse of *also*.

www.mhhe.com/dietsch

If you want additional coverage of writing conclusions, go to:
Writing>Conclusions

Writing a Conclusion

When the purpose of a comparison is to inform, a brief summary may be in order. In her conclusion, Betty Fetters not only summarizes but also shares insights gained from experience:

Although Mr. Graham died a year ago, his memory will live in the hearts of the people who were lucky enough to have known him. For me, he made it easier to accept the Mr. Courtneys of the world. Mr. Graham knew the secret of happiness, and the values that he taught will remain a part of my life forever.

For a serious topic, a change of perspective can provide just the right note for ending. Terri Bloomfield concluded with this thought:

After witnessing the death of my cousin and best friend, I cherish life much more. I know firsthand that life is precious and fragile. Now I never take today or tomorrow for granted. I feel as if I must appreciate life not only for myself but for my cousin and my friend, too.

REVISING A PAPER OF COMPARISON OR CONTRAST

www.mhhe.com/dietsch
For general revision
resources, go to:
Writing>Drafting and
Revision

As you revise your paper, keep your outline handy and your audience in mind. The outline will help you to maintain the balanced order that comparison and contrast require. Thinking of the audience will help in selecting words and in knowing how much to explain. Strive for originality. Concrete nouns, vivid adjectives, and verbs in the active voice will invigorate your descriptions. Yet trite expressions sometimes infiltrate papers of comparison and contrast. Few readers enjoy frayed phrases like these:

different as day and night   a different story altogether

like two peas in a pod   are worlds apart

spitting image of his father   looked like twins

If you find common, overused expressions in your draft, get out a thesaurus and dictionary. Select a fitting synonym and rephrase the sentence. If needed, add examples of interest. Read your paper aloud so that you can hear the flow of sentences and check to see that transition is adequate. The checklist that follows will help you to find possible trouble spots.

CHECKLIST   **REVISING A PAPER OF COMPARISON OR CONTRAST**

1. Is the thesis clear and specific?

2. Is the order of points in the thesis the same as their order in the body?

3. Are main points and paragraph details arranged in parallel form?

4. Does every paragraph have a topic sentence?

5. Does every topic sentence have adequate support?

6. Does the conclusion seem complete?

7. Have I fulfilled the purpose of the comparison or contrast?

8. Does anything else need to be said for this audience?

TWO STUDENT PAPERS: COMPARISON

In the first paper, Jeff Patten contrasts two books by the same author. Jeff's purpose is to inform. His audience consists of readers who enjoy historical fiction.

I, Claudius and *Claudius the God*

In 1934 Robert Graves published a rather lengthy book of historical fiction entitled *I, Claudius*. The novel was written in such a manner as to have the reader believe it was an autobiography of the Roman emperor Tiberius Claudius Drusus Nero Germanicus. *I, Claudius* takes the reader from the emperor's earliest childhood remembrances up to the year 41 AD, when he became emperor of the Roman Empire. It is there, minutes after Claudius's ascent to the throne, that the book ends.

This abrupt ending seemed to demand a sequel, and in 1935 Graves published *Claudius the God*. This second "autobiographical novel" chronicled the life of Claudius from his ascent to the throne to his murder. Although each of the novels was written about the same person, by the same author, there are few similarities. *I, Claudius* and *Claudius the God* seem similar only in the basic form in which they are written. They differ in readability, style, and entertainment value.

The two books resemble each other only in narrative autobiographical form. The reader experiences the life of ancient Rome, narrated through the thoughts and words of the emperor Claudius. Graves has an almost mystical way of making the reader feel as if the emperor Claudius had penned the words himself. The novels provide accounts of the seedy, scandalous lives of the ruling Caesars. Greek and Latin phrases reveal careful research. The historical accuracy makes the novels seem authentic.

There the resemblance ends. *I, Claudius* is an easily read, thoroughly engrossing book. Readers receive the impression of a smooth, flowing manuscript. They are led chronologically, with a few pauses for reflection, through the turmoil and pageantry of the Roman Empire and its rulers. *Claudius the God,* however, is a rather choppy, disjointed work. Readers are required to leap from one story line to another with little or no hint of a chronological advance. One can only speculate as to the reason. Yet one thing is certain. The readability and style of *I, Claudius* are far superior to its sequel.

Style is a significant difference between the two novels. Although both manuscripts were thoroughly researched, the historical data are presented in two very different ways. In *I, Claudius* the facts are colorful; the pompous and elegant lives of the ruling class make for fascinating reading. In contrast, the facts presented in *Claudius the God* seem dry and mundane; furthermore, the story line makes for dull reading.

The net result of these differences makes the books unequal in entertainment value. *I, Claudius,* whatever its historical worth, is a very good story. Even readers who ordinarily do not enjoy histories or autobiographies will likely enjoy this novel because it is so entertaining. The sequel, however, is a chore to read—much like reading a history textbook.

If it were not for the many weaknesses of *Claudius the God,* the set would make worthwhile reading. Robert Graves's prowess as a poet and distinguished writer shines brightly in his first novel but fails miserably in the second.

QUESTIONS FOR DISCUSSION

1. What is the function of Jeff's first two paragraphs?
2. How are the two novels alike? How are they different?
3. What method of organization does Jeff use?
4. How would you characterize the tone of Jeff's essay?
5. Comment on the conclusion.

In the second paper, Rosy Erdy pays tribute to her parents. She looks at her parents' few similarities and many differences, then makes an important point at the end. Her purpose is to inform; she envisions an audience of descendants who will read this comparison in the family history.

Parents through a Child's Eyes

In this modern age when divorce is more common than not, my parents are in the minority. They have lived contentedly for nearly half a century despite distinctive differences in childhood backgrounds, political views, and personalities. Some folks might view them as ordinary, but to me they are very special, and I want my descendants to know more about them than their photos in the family album reveal.

The old axiom "opposites attract" certainly seems true in regard to Mom and Dad. Despite a physical resemblance, their differences far outnumber their likenesses. Born only a year apart and now in their middle seventies, my parents both have thinning, silver-colored hair. Both are less than average height: Mom refers to herself as "petite." Dad, with a smile, says he is "not tall."

The childhood backgrounds of my parents were certainly not alike. Growing up, Mom lived only in the city whereas Dad knew only the life on a farm in the 1920s and 1930s. Mom was the first of her family to graduate from high school; Dad went to work immediately after completing the eighth grade at a one-room school. A strong religious environment influenced Mom whereas no visible religious commitments existed in Dad's family. Shortly after their marriage, however, Dad adopted Mom's religion. He still attends church regularly with her, but only half-heartedly.

My parents' political differences became quite apparent when I was very young because Mom is a loyal Democrat and Dad is a proud Republican. Every four years after a presidential election, they return from the polls loudly declaring that it is fruitless to vote. They know that the vote of one cancels out the vote of the other, but still they vote each year.

My parents' greatest difference is in personality. Mom has always been more friendly and outgoing whereas Dad tends to be shy. Mom seems to be always laughing, even with tears in her eyes, but Dad is more serious. Mom demonstrates affection freely; Dad has difficulty in letting his emotions show. Years ago, Mom administered discipline, while Dad stayed in the background. Afterward he would give us hugs and smiles on the sly.

Mom is forthright and open, but Dad is soft-spoken and reserved. Mom seems to have a strong opinion on everything; Dad tends to be quiet and easily swayed. No one in the family needs to worry about anything because Mom does it for us. If Dad ever worries, he keeps it well hidden. Privacy is not a word in Mom's vocabulary; it seems to be her God-given right as a mother to know everything about her family. On the other hand, Dad quietly respects everyone's privacy.

Despite their many differences, my parents have been steadfast in their devotion to each other and to the family. As a result, my brother and I have been greatly influenced by the blending of their differences. From our wonderful parents, we have gained a balance and stability that has been transmitted to our own families' lives.

QUESTIONS FOR DISCUSSION

1. What is the effect of including similarities? What would be the effect if Rosy had included only differences?

2. Which method of organization does she use?

3. Notice that she mixes a few first-person references with the third person. Are these necessary and effective? Why or why not?

4. Are her examples convincing support for her claims?

5. How would you describe the tone of the essay?

6. Comment on her conclusion.

FOR YOUR REFERENCE Comparison and Contrast Essays in the Reader	• "Gender Gap in Cyberspace," Deborah Tannen, page 630 • "A Nonsmoker with a Smoker," Phillip Lopate, page 633 • "Mother Tongue," Amy Tan, page 637 • "Conversational Ballgames," Nancy Masterson Sakamoto, page 642

PRACTICE

GROUPS: Selecting a Topic for Comparison

Directions: Would the topics below be suitable for a 500-word paper of comparison? Mark them as suitable (S) or unsuitable (U). Compare your answers and discuss.

_____ 1. The courage of two United States presidents who faced monumental decisions.

_____ 2. Two pets I have owned

_____ 3. Before and after: stay-at-home mom, then career woman

_____ 4. Good and evil

_____ 5. Tipping versus nontipping

IDEAS FOR PRACTICE WRITING

Directions: Select a topic from the list below (or one of your own) to contrast in a paragraph. Prewrite by making parallel lists of details.

1. Two routes to a destination
2. Two methods of fishing
3. A date you enjoyed and one you did not enjoy
4. Two appliances you have owned
5. Two pets (same species) you have owned

TWENTY IDEAS FOR COMPARISON OR CONTRAST PAPERS

1 Profit: a garage sale or eBay?

2 Compare two Harry Potter films

3 Buy or lease a car?

4 Cost comparison of two landscaping designs

5 Two attitudes toward a family heirloom

6 Two views of family reunions

7 Your life and your grandmother's or grandfather's life

8   Life before attending college and after

9   An owner's view of a property and a bank appraiser's view

10   Life before and after losing weight

11   Two news commentators

12   Two versions of an accident

13   Expectations of an event as opposed to what actually happened

14   Two cars I have owned

15   Two unusual restaurants

16   Two athletes in the same sport

17   Two people who have influenced your life

18   Two opposing views of buying term papers

19   Two very different bosses

20   Attitudes before and after an unsettling experience

Defining: Identifying Basic Characteristics

CHAPTER 15

> ## The beginning of wisdom is the definition of terms.
>
> —Socrates (470–399 BC)

PURPOSE OF DEFINITION

Clarity is crucial in communication. Undefined terms can lead to confusion, error, and costly problems. Definition at the right time can dissolve misunderstanding, improve communication, cut costs, and promote safety. On the job you may write simple definitions or help write complex definitions in policies or reports—defining the background, objectives, criteria, and scope of a project. On exams you may write formal sentence definitions or longer extended definitions.

Learning to write clear, complete definitions will sharpen your thinking and enable you to be more precise and accurate in your speaking and writing.

FORMAL SENTENCE DEFINITION

A writing instructor had just explained formal sentence definition to his freshman composition class. Turning to a student who seemed half asleep, he said, "Nick, will you please define mammal for me?"

Suddenly awake, the student stammered, "Er . . . a mammal is hairy; uh . . . it has a hard skeleton and provides milk."

With a twinkle in his eye, the instructor replied, "So far, you have not ruled out the coconut."

A formal sentence definition is a complete sentence that classifies an item or an idea and differentiates it from other members of its class. More complete than a fragmented dictionary definition, a formal sentence definition has four parts:

1. The term to be defined
2. A *be* verb—usually *is* or *are*
3. The classification (genus, class, or species)
4. The distinguishing features or characteristics

Below are two illustrations of the parts of a formal sentence definition:

TERM	VERB	CLASSIFICATION	DISTINGUISHING FEATURES
A pelican	is	a large, web-footed water bird	with a distensible pouch hanging from its bill for catching and storing fish.
Lynxes	are	a species of wildcat in the Northern Hemisphere	which has a very short tail; tufted, tapering ears; and a ruff on each side of the face.

Note the distinguishing features of each animal. There are many water birds with webbed feet, but only the pelican has a distensible pouch hanging beneath its bill. There are several species of wildcat in the Northern Hemisphere, but only the lynx has the slender tufted ears, unusual ruff, and very short tail.

To write a formal sentence definition about any concrete term, you might find these questions helpful:

1. What distinguishing features do all items in the class have?
2. How can similar items be ruled out?
3. What purpose or function does the item serve?

WRITING A SENTENCE DEFINITION

Start with a familiar object such as an apple. Consider: Which classification does an apple belong to? How do apples differ from other members of the class, such as plums, pears, and peaches? What are the distinguishing features of apples? Write a complete sentence that includes all four parts of the formal definition:

Term	Verb	Classification	Distinguishing Features
An apple	is	a/an _____	_____

An apple is a fruit, of course, but you might be more precise by stating the purpose: edible fruit. You might be more specific by giving its taxonomic category, the rose family. At first you may jot down features such as red and round. (Are all apples red? Round?) After you finish, see the example at the end of the chapter.

Two precautions will help you to sidestep common errors when writing formal sentence definitions:

1. *Do not define a term by repeating the term or using a derivation.*
   Avoid: A keystone is the key stone in an arch.
   Instead: A keystone is the central wedge-shaped piece at the top of an arch that holds the other stones in place.
2. *Avoid the phrase "is when" or "is where."* This usage is ungrammatical.
   Avoid: A greenbelt *is where* a band of parks, farmland, or unused land surrounds a community.
   Instead: A greenbelt is a band of parks, farmland, or unused land surrounding a community.

EXTENDED DEFINITION

The purpose of a paper of extended definition is to explain a term or concept clearly in an *original* way, drawing material primarily from your own experience. Research is generally limited to dictionaries, thesauruses, and books of quotations.

Consulting Sources

To gather ideas about your topic, consult two or three very large dictionaries. Especially helpful is the unabridged *Oxford English Dictionary,* a set of several volumes, that traces the history of words introduced into the English language since AD 1150. In the OED you may find an unusual detail to serve as an attention-getter for your introduction or for an example in your paper. You might trace the history of a word whose meaning has changed during your lifetime, your parents', or your grandparents'.

Famous quotations can be found online or in the library. *Bartlett's Familiar Quotations, The Quotable Woman,* a Bible with a concordance, and similar references are quick and easy to use. Include the source, if provided, and the name of the author. If the quotation was written before the twentieth century, also cite the date. Or you might interview people of various ages to gain insights about a new word or the new slang meaning of an older word.

Documenting Sources

If you decide to copy any material, be sure to set it off properly in your notes so that there is no confusion later. Legally, you are required to provide the following documentation:

See chapters 28 and 29.

1. Enclose short quotations with quotation marks.
2. Indent long quotations of five lines or more.
3. Specify the name of the author, the source, and the page. (Check with your instructor for the preferred format.)

www.mhhe.com/dietsch
You will find a wealth of online documentation resources at:
Research

Guidelines for Using Extended Definition

Readers tend to like a quotation that is appropriate but dislike a patchwork of quotations. They become impatient with old information unless it is a favorite story that merits retelling or a universal truth skillfully presented. Here are three guidelines for a paper of extended definition:

- **Use quotations for a purpose.** Use them to clarify and advance your discussion. Limit the number of quotations.
- **Use dictionary definitions for a logical reason.** Have a purpose, such as to clarify further or to disagree.
- **Include stereotypes or overstatement only for a purpose.** Perhaps you intend to disagree with a stereotype or to overstate to provoke amusement. If so, be sure the exaggeration is so great that readers will understand its purpose.

You can freshen an old topic by presenting it from your own point of view:

STALE: Growing old is a fear of most people. Many people believe they are old when they turn fifty.

FRESH: One chilly October morning, my fiftieth birthday tiptoed in. Glancing in the bathroom mirror, I suddenly felt old.

Perceptive readers dismiss sweeping generalizations. They want the truth, not distortions. Careless use of stereotypes not only bores the audience but also injures a writer's credibility. In the student examples below, can you spot the faulty stereotypes and other problems in logic?

- The elderly lead lonely, secluded lives, crisscrossed with financial worries.
- A mother's desired end is handling her three jobs well: housewife, mother, and career.
- "Friends are forever."

All of these sentences exaggerate. Not all elderly people fit this pigeonhole, for many are busy, active, and prosperous. Not all mothers desire a career; nor do all friendships last a lifetime.

See chapter 3.   Writers need to qualify illogical all-or-none statements (absolute generalizations) by identifying them as opinions, perceptions, or inferences.

WRITING A PAPER OF EXTENDED DEFINITION

www.mhhe.com/dietsch

For further help writing definition essays, check out:
Writing>Writing Tutors>
Definition

To learn as much as possible from writing a definition paper, select an abstract term for the topic. What do you feel strongly about? How does this topic relate to you? How does it affect your principles and values? How much support can you provide for your thesis? You will be wise to sidestep Herculean topics such as "time," "democracy," and others that are very broad. If you choose a term you

have learned in another class, do not merely summarize other people's ideas—
develop your own.

Narrowing a Topic and Prewriting

www.mhhe.com/dietsch

For additional help on
prewriting, go to:
Writing>Prewriting

First, narrow the topic so that it can be covered adequately in the assignment.
For instance, "discrimination" would be too broad. One student limited this
topic to "prejudice against short men." He gave examples of how he copes with
shortness through elevator shoes, hairstyles, and dress. Then he explained how
these changes have improved his life and gained him respect.

Next, consult your dictionary notes and think about them. Then prewrite to
unearth examples, anecdotes, comparisons, cause-and-effect factors, or changes
in meaning. Clustering is particularly helpful for prewriting about an abstract
concept.

See chapter 4.

The two sample scratch outlines below are arranged according to order of
importance.

EXAMPLE I: PROFESSIONALISM AT A GOLF CLUB

a. Ethics = respect

b. Customer service

c. Accuracy of records

d. Dress of personnel

EXAMPLE II: MY PROCRASTINATION

a. Examples: Cause

b. Effects

c. How I am overcoming

Drafting a Special Kind of Introduction

Opening with a quotation is one of the easiest ways for a beginning writer to
achieve a polished introduction. A relevant quotation can set the tone and indicate the focus of the paper. The quotations that open the chapters of this book
show how to format and document a quotation that precedes your main text.
Notice that because the quotations are indented and set apart from the text, quotation marks are not needed. The author's name appears beneath the quotation.
Inclusion of the source is optional. Include dates of works written *before* the
twentieth century.

Establishing Transition   To forge a link from an introductory quotation to the
text of your paper, embed transition in your first sentence. You can repeat a key
term from the quotation or use a synonym or related word to establish a clear
link. Try to be subtle. A direct reference, unless cleverly done, can mar the opening and stamp the work as that of an amateur. With thought, you can avoid

weak transition, such as "In this quotation . . . ," "As stated in the quotation above, . . . ," or "I think the above quotation means. . . ."

In the following example, the student writer (who prefers to remain anonymous) uses an embedded transition in her first sentence. A related word *(alcoholism)* echoes a word in the quotation *(drunkenness)*. Note, too, that the first sentence here is a formal sentence definition.

Living with an Alcoholic

Drunkenness . . . spoils health,
dismounts the mind, and unmans men.
                    —WILLIAM PENN

Alcoholism is a disease caused by continual heavy drinking of alcoholic beverages. In the acute and chronic stages, alcoholism consists of symptoms ranging from the obvious to the obscure. Usually, it is not difficult to recognize a person who is inebriated; generally, staggering and slurring of speech are apparent. Accompanying neurological disorders such as tremors (shakes), hallucinations, and seizures are easily discerned. Hidden to the naked eye is the damage endured by the liver, stomach, and pancreas. Not only is excessive drinking devastating to the physical and mental health of the alcoholic, but it is also devastating to the alcoholic's family.

Living for eighteen years with my father, who was a severe alcoholic, was much like living with Dr. Jekyll and Mr. Hyde. The alcohol would turn my kind-hearted, loving father into a brutal, hateful monster. Because of my father's unpredictable behavior, high anxiety and fear were normal, everyday emotions for me.

Did you notice that the first paragraph is written in *third* person? The writer gives general background information before narrowing the topic to the alcoholic's family. In the second paragraph, she shifts to *first* person because it reveals specific details about her life. See how she eases the shift from third person to first with a gerund phrase ("Living . . . with my father").

Did you note the simile in the second paragraph? The phrase "like living with Dr. Jekyll and Mr. Hyde" not only sets up a striking comparison but also establishes a natural relationship with "unmans men" in the opening quotation.

Developing an Extended Definition

Depending on the subject and purpose, a paper of extended definition may be developed by almost any strategy or combination of strategies—description, process, comparison, examples, or explanation. To find details and develop your paper, consider these five basic techniques of extended definition.

Operational Definition   To define an operation, the writer tells (a) what the object being defined does, (b) how it works, and (c) the basic principle underlying its performance. For example, a one-sentence operational definition might state that a refrigerator is a mechanized box, powered by electricity or gas, that circulates coolant to a condenser to chill food, medicines, or other items. An expanded operational definition would explain in detail how a refrigerator works. Operational definitions are often used in technical writing.

Defining by Comparison   Comparison is useful for explaining abstractions, such as emotions. If you can find an object to compare an idea or emotion to, then this technique will help to clarify your definition. In the following example, Marjorie Holmes begins with concrete images before going to abstract feelings:

> What feeling is so nice as a child's hand in yours? [It is] so small, so soft and warm like a kitten huddling in the shelter of your clasp. A child's hand in yours—what tenderness it arouses, what power it conjures up. You are instantly the very touchstone of wisdom and strength.

Defining by Synonym   In defining by synonym, a writer provides another word or phrase that has the same meaning. The synonym can be included either in parentheses or as an appositive:

- Rocky Collins will fight F. G. Jones for the bantamweight (112 to 118 pounds) world title.
- At one time many people believed that human intelligence could be judged by phrenology, the study of the shape of the skull.

Defining by Negation   Another effective technique of definition is *negation* (denial). The writer begins by telling what the term is not. In a paper entitled "Fear of Failure," Phyllis Parks uses negation in her opening sentence:

> *Failure* is not a pretty word. The very mention of it creates images and feelings of someone who is inept and incompetent. The word itself strikes fear in my heart. Sometimes my life has seemed as though it has been one failure after another. But with time has come an appreciation for the value of failure.

In *Faith of My Fathers*, Senator John McCain begins his definition of *glory* by explaining what glory is not. Then he describes what glory means to him:

> Glory is not a conceit. It is not a decoration for valor. It is not a prize for being the most clever, the strongest, or the boldest. Glory belongs to the act of being constant to something greater than yourself, to a cause, to your principles, to the people on whom you rely, and who rely on you in return.

Weaving Example with Explanation   A lone example without interpretation may be of little use to readers. You cannot assume that every reader will see the connection you intend. You need to link the example to the main idea and comment appropriately. Chris Layman, a student writer, first uses negation. Then he weaves example with explanation in an extended definition of honesty:

> "Do as I say, not as I do," my parents would often say as I was growing up. However, admonitions such as this often fade from the mind whereas examples form lasting impressions. As children grow they need models to follow. They need to determine how they will live their lives, what their values will be, and how they will treat other people. A father is a model that his children

depend on to learn how to act within their society and to form their own set of values.

Recently, my young son and I were in a store when he noticed a $100 bill lying on the floor. I had always told my son to be honest; now I could show him what honesty meant. Together we went to the store manager and put the money in his care, hoping the rightful owner would return to claim it. This incident allowed me to act as a role model for my son, and it set an example I hope he will follow throughout his life.

Including a Dictionary Definition for a Purpose

Seldom is a dictionary definition needed in a paper of extended definition. If, however, you wish to elaborate on a dictionary definition (or someone else's definition)—going beyond that meaning—you would have a valid purpose. When citing a definition, enclose the copied words with quotation marks and state the source or author. You also need to weave the definition into the text by providing adequate transition. The basic examples that follow will not be suitable for every writing situation, but you may be able to adapt them to fit your paper.

- Although *Webster's Collegiate Dictionary* defines _____ as the "_____," this definition does not. . . .
- According to *Webster's New World Dictionary*, _____ is "_____," but that definition does not. . . .
- Meanings can change over time. The first edition of *The American Heritage Dictionary* defines _____ as "_____." The fourth edition, however, has added another meaning: "_____." We might go beyond these to say. . . .

To integrate other types of quotations into the text of your paper, see "Using Signal Phrases to Integrate Quotations into the Text," page 499.

www.mhhe.com/dietsch

For general conclusion resources, visit:
Writing>Conclusions

Writing a Conclusion

A conclusion for a paper of definition should be brief and appropriate. One way to end is with a formal sentence definition. Another is to allude to an opening quotation. A third way is to summarize changes and end on a positive note.

Closing with a Formal Sentence Definition   Debby Ketcham concludes her paper with a formal sentence definition. The definition is followed by a sentence of summary and another of comment:

> Finally, poise is an inner mental balance, the ability to face new situations calmly, to hold one's temper, to cope with stress, and to deal with embarrassment. All these situations require a control over emotion and the ability to present a calm, tactful, polite manner. Poise is truly a valuable trait.

Alluding to an Opening Quotation   A reference to the beginning creates an "echo ending" and establishes closure. Using this technique, Penny Amrine repeats parts of a quotation by Joseph Conrad in her conclusion. In the last sentence she provides a formal sentence definition:

> My loneliness did indeed wear a "mask." For months I had endured its "naked terror" without being able to identify its misleading appearance. Loneliness for me was life without intimate friends and relatives to lean on for love and companionship.

Ending with a Personal Lesson   Those of us who successfully survive a painful experience often extract a lesson, a bit of wisdom. The student who wrote "Living with an Alcoholic" summarized her insights:

> Over the years I have tried to educate myself on alcoholism. Counseling has helped me to understand how alcoholism victimizes the entire family. Now, at age 33, I realize that despite how it seemed at the time, my father was only a human being who was consumed by a dread disease.

The last line reveals the writer's compassion as well as her intellectual and emotional growth since those early years of torment. The implicit note of forgiveness and the gentle tone provide a positive ending to a wrenching topic.

Revising a Paper of Definition

To revise a paper of extended definition successfully, you need to examine its many facets. If you include a quotation, whether a dictionary definition, lines from a poem, or a bit of wisdom, check to see that the material *is copied exactly as written.* The checklist below will enable you to scrutinize other parts of your paper.

> www.mhhe.com/dietsch
>
> If you want general revision help, go to: Writing>Drafting and Revision

CHECKLIST   REVISING EXTENDED DEFINITIONS

1. Is the topic narrow enough to be defined in a short paper?

2. Will the introduction interest the audience?

3. Have important terms been defined if they are apt to be unfamiliar to the average reader? Have terms with more than one possible meaning been explained fully?

4. Are all definitions necessary?

5. Do formal sentence definitions (if any) conform to the standard four-part format?

6. Does every detail, definition, and quotation support the thesis?

7. Are quotations worked smoothly into the text so that their point is clear in the paper? Has proper credit been given to each original source?

8. Have stereotypes and overstatement been avoided?

9. Is the organization of the paper clear?

10. Is the closing effective?

TWO STUDENT PAPERS: DEFINITION

Jeannine Caudill talked to her friends before she wrote the following paper, which is based on their experience as well as hers. Her purpose is to explain a term not found in the dictionary. Skillfully, she states several axioms (universal truths). Three questions begin her introduction.

Mother Love

Love cannot be forced, love cannot be
coaxed and teased. It comes out of
Heaven, unasked and unsought.
                    —PEARL BUCK

What is mother love? Is it a feeling, an emotion, or the dedication of an entire lifetime? Is it bad or good, imaginary or genuine? One thing is certain; mother love is difficult to define, especially to those who have not experienced it. None of the dictionaries seem to think *mother* and *love* should be combined into the phrase *mother love*. Yet there is motherhood, mother lode, and mother-land. Could any of these words be more fitting to combine with *mother* than the word *love?*

Psychiatrists define mother love, doctors prescribe it, lawyers divide it, children bask or drown in it, and fathers observe it. Perhaps even a mother cannot define it, but some still try. Love as only a mother can feel begins for some women with the first knowledge of pregnancy. For others, it comes with beholding the charm of their own soft, sweet-smelling baby. The baby does not have to be beautiful to inspire great love. Perhaps mother love at this stage of life is a myriad of feelings: infant dependency, mother's pride of accomplishment, and primitive emotions that have been basic to the human race since its beginning. Whatever the reasons, loving a baby seems very easy.

The real growth of mother love begins later. Much of the time during a child's life, no one seems to love him or her except the mother. True mother love develops over many years and through many trials. When a toddler throws a fit in a store, shouts a loud "No," or dampens a neighbor's carpet, mother love is put to a test. But even in this stage, the child is very appealing to her. Here a new facet of love begins, pride in the child's independence.

The early school years strain the most patient mother. After the thumb-sucking, leg-hugging, insecure years come the years of grade cards, teacher conferences, show and tell, and four hundred papers to be praised and hung up.

Many older mothers say to younger mothers, "If you think things are bad now, just wait till he's a teenager!" But the young mothers often counter with "Nothing could be worse." This lack of foresight must be a tool of Mother Nature. Otherwise, only the very brave would dare to have a child.

Mother love seems never to end. It usually begins with the birth of a child and continues to encircle and entwine the mother's heart down through the years. Strangely enough, the only person who can appreciate the real meaning of mother love is a mother.

QUESTIONS FOR DISCUSSION

1. What do you notice about Jeannine's introduction?

2. Examine the first sentence of the second paragraph. What do you notice about the sentence structure?

3. Do Jeannine's examples ring true? Why or why not?

4. What does she do before she comments?

5. How would you describe the tone of the essay?

In the following paper, Ron Willetts opens with a quotation and provides not only the author but also the source. Then he cites a dictionary definition and the parts of speech for the word *work* for a significant reason: to expand upon its meaning as a noun and as a verb. In the first main point, he uses narration and explanation to illustrate his early view of work. He defines later views by explanation, associations, and examples.

Changes in My View of Work

My friend there is a Hell . . . when a man has a family to support, has his health, and is ready to work, and there is no work to do. When he stands with empty hands and sees his children going hungry, his wife without the things to do with. I hope you never have to try it.
—Louis L'Amour, *The Walking Drum*

The *Oxford American Dictionary* defines work as a noun that means "Use of bodily or mental power in order to do or make something, especially as contrasted with play or recreation." Work is also defined as a verb: "to perform work, to be engaged in bodily or mental activity."* Over the years I gradually learned to understand these concepts, but only when I became unemployed for an extended period did I understand L'Amour's definition.

When I was very young, work was not a verb, it was a noun, a place to go and a place to leave. My grandfather would come home from work in the evenings, and we would go through a ritual. As he drove his truck into the garage, I would be waiting. He would pick me up, and somewhere between the truck and the house, I would remove the hat from his head and transfer it to mine. Once inside, he would place his dinner bucket on a chair, and I would rummage through it for the leftover cookie, banana, or candy bar that was always there. At that time in my life, I did not have to worry; all my needs were taken care of.

When I became a young adult, the word *work* took on a new meaning. It was not only a noun, but suddenly a verb, a task to be performed for which one received some form of remuneration. This definition began to form when I was in the eleventh grade and began helping the janitors after school during basketball season. For sweeping the classrooms and dusting the teachers' desks, I received a modest sum and attended the home games at no cost. Thus work became associated with money. And money became closely associated with girls, cars, entertainment, and other necessities. At this time, work was a necessary evil, for it took time away from my social life.

---

*From *Oxford American Dictionary.* Copyright © 1980 by Oxford University Press, Inc. Used by permission of Oxford University Press, Inc.

When I became older, I found the word *work* had to be redefined once again. Along with being a place to go and an activity to perform, work became a goal. This new meaning became associated with other words such as wife, insurance, children, house, and friends. Between 1975 and 2000, work was no problem for me. If I changed jobs, the longest period of unemployment was two days. Once I quit one job on Friday and started a new one the following Monday.

In 2000, however, the story changed. Due to economic conditions, I became unemployed after working at a company for fifteen years. That company and my coworkers were as much a part of my life as my own family. I felt rejected and depressed. The severance pay ran out. The unemployment benefits were exhausted. The retirement fund vanished, and the bills began to pile up. I was no longer able to provide for my family. But then I thanked God we were living in modern times when it was acceptable for a married woman to work. Although my wife's income did not pay all the bills, it did allow us to feed the family and keep the electricity turned on.

Being unemployed for over two years creates a situation that at times is almost unbearable. Perhaps the worst part is being told that one cannot be hired because he is overqualified and undereducated. Being told that one could perform the task, but would not be satisfied with the job is enough to make a person ill. A man needs to be able to provide for his family.

Yes, my friend, there is a hell—I know, for I have been there. It is my sincere hope that I am the last person that has to define the lack of work as hell.

QUESTIONS FOR DISCUSSION

1. Discuss the use of the dictionary definition in the introduction. Would the paper have been as effective without it? Why or why not?

2. What do you notice about the examples? How would you rate their effectiveness?

3. Briefly summarize the changes in Ron's viewpoint.

4. What causes are specified?

5. Discuss the effectiveness of this ending. What device does he use?

FOR YOUR REFERENCE Definition Essays in the Reader	• "On Being 17," David Raymond, page 646
	• "The Handicap of Definition," William Raspberry, page 649
	• "Becoming Educated," Barbara Jordan, page 651
	• "The Insufficiency of Honesty," Stephen L. Carter, page 654

COLLABORATIVE EXERCISE: Discerning Genuine Definitions

Directions: Identify the satisfactory definitions in the list below and mark with an S. Mark the unsatisfactory ones with a U. Discuss why they are unsatisfactory. (You may consult a dictionary.)

1. A sprinkling can is a utensil that is not a bucket, dishpan, or bowl.
2. A cut is when you slash open the skin.
3. A book is like a little golden door to opportunity.
4. The gemsbok of southern Africa is a large antelope with long, sharp, straight horns and a tufted tail.
5. Honey is a sweet gooey substance that is delicious on breakfast cereal.
6. "Monopoly" is a table game that resembles life because you trade, buy, and sell.
7. *Morale* refers to the condition of the spirits of individuals or employees.
8. The ruffed grouse, sometimes called "partridge" or "pheasant," is a North American game bird with spotted brown feathers.
9. Gelatin is a clear quivery substance, made in various colors.
10. A dandelion is a small edible weed with fuzzy yellow flowers and saw-toothed leaves.
11. Dissatisfied means not content.
12. A suitcase has a handle and is used to carry clothing.
13. A vacation is where you tire yourself out having fun so that you are glad to go home and go to work.
14. Empathy is as refreshing as pure cold water from a spring.
15. A fruitcake is a cake that contains fruit.

COLLABORATIVE WRITING: Formal Sentence Definition

1. Appoint a recorder to jot down the comments of the group. Define one of the terms below in a formal sentence definition:

   dog   cow   cucumber   chair   couch
2. Ask each other questions to limit the term and identify the essential features. For example:
   a. How does a dog differ from a wolf or coyote?
   b. What kind of dog? Prairie dog? Wild dog? What?
   c. What is the purpose of the dog?
   (*Note:* You may want to limit the term to watch dog, police dog, Seeing Eye dog, hunting dog, or another kind of dog.)
3. Revise. Does the definition have all four parts? Does it read smoothly?
4. Repeat the procedure, using another term.

POSSIBLE ANSWER FOR WRITING A SENTENCE DEFINITION (PAGE 200)

An apple is an edible fruit of the rose family that can be red, yellow, green, or multicolored; the small seeds are encased in a core connected to a flexible stem at the top and at the blossom end.

TWENTY IDEAS FOR PAPERS OF DEFINITION

1 What is the "positive attitude" that employers seek?

2 Ethics for the nurse (or other professional)

3 What is customer service?

4 Freedom (What kind or kinds?)

5 What is integrity?

6 What does a college degree really mean?

7 What is professionalism?

8 What is maturity?

9 Procrastination

10 Optimism

11 Attitude: victim or winner?

12 A family value

13 Appreciation

14 Loyalty

15 What is an education?

16 Compassion

17 Trust

18 Discrimination (What kind?)

19 What is happiness?

20 Responsibility

Investigating Cause and Effect

Thoreau's observation reminds us that a single decision, action, or event can cause far-reaching effects. The relationship between cause and effect can be more intricate and extensive than

> Our least deed, like the young of the land crab, wends its way to the sea of cause and effect as soon as born, and makes a drop there to eternity.
>
> —Henry David Thoreau, *Journal*, March 14, 1838

we may imagine. Sometimes we lack complete information and see only part of an effect. Or we may assume a connection between two events where none exists. Or we glimpse only *short-term effects* while significant *long-term effects* remain hidden for years.

All the while there is the ever-present risk of blithely underestimating the repercussions of certain acts and of making unwise decisions based on unproved assumptions and ill-founded predictions.

PURPOSE OF CAUSAL ANALYSIS

The purpose of causal analysis is to determine whether or not a cause-and-effect relationship actually exists. If it does exist, precisely what is the connection between the cause and the effect? What happened to bring about the change?

Causal analysis allows you to reflect on an experience or event and to learn from the past. With study and practice, you can improve your ability to analyze cause-and-effect relationships. You can question doubtful information and withhold judgment until adequate proof of the final cause is available.

On the job you may analyze cause-and-effect relationships, then give input into decisions that will influence the profit or loss of your company. According to the rhetorical situation, you may write a recommendation, proposal, or report, based on your causal analysis. The greater your knowledge and insight, the more accurate the analysis will be.

WORKPLACE CASE STUDY

THE ACCIDENT

Lisa was walking within the pedestrian lane of the large plant warehouse where she worked. The warehouse seemed even more noisy than usual. She was unaware that behind her a tow-truck driver violated company rules when he failed to sound his horn before coming around a corner. The next moment she heard the roar of a motor and glanced back. The vehicle hit her. A searing pain darted down her right leg. She crumpled and fell to the floor.

Lisa was rushed to the hospital, where a leg fracture and several deep cuts were treated. She was kept overnight. The emergency room physician said she would be unable to work for eight weeks. A witness to the accident corroborated Lisa's report, saying she was in the safety lane. The driver did not sound his horn before coming around the corner very fast. Losing temporary control of the vehicle, he swerved into the safety lane and knocked her to one side.

Activity

Assume the role of the supervisor. Write a summary of the accident in your own words and recommend action. The tow-truck driver was newly hired; he has worked only three days. The plant provides no training for tow-truck drivers.

WHAT IS CAUSAL ANALYSIS?

A *cause* influences or changes something or someone. The resulting change is called the *effect*. *Causal analysis* is an examination of effects that have one or more causes (conditions that may have contributed to the effect). To resolve a question of cause and effect, explore all the conditions that might have caused the effect. Since you already know the effect (by observation), start by noting its significant features. Then work backward through the chain of cause and effect. Describe the related condition(s). Then list possible explanations. Next, test each explanation and eliminate as many as possible. That should lead you to the cause(s). If not, keep searching.

For example, the supervisor of a department that spray-paints washing machines notices that the finish is uneven. He wonders what condition could have caused this effect. Has an atmospheric change occurred? Is there a mechanical defect? Has human error interfered? Was the batch of paint too thin? Could multiple causes exist? Only after he has ruled out all other possibilities will he be able to pinpoint the cause(s).

1. Specify the effects. Separate from the presumed cause.
2. Examine the conditions that existed.
3. Ask whether or not these conditions could have caused the effect(s).
4. Think about possible explanations. What might have happened?
5. Test your theories. Did the presumed causes actually produce the effect?

STEPS IN CAUSAL ANALYSIS

A Reversed Chain of Cause and Effect

To trace a simple cause, start with the observed effect(s) and work *backward* through the chain until you find proof of the cause. In the example below, the gas hot water furnace requires electricity to operate the pump and thermostat.

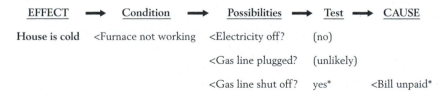

EFFECT	→	Condition	→	Possibilities	→	Test	→	CAUSE
House is cold		<Furnace not working		<Electricity off?		(no)		
				<Gas line plugged?		(unlikely)		
				<Gas line shut off?		yes*		<Bill unpaid*

———

*Since the pilot light cannot be lit, you assume that the gas has been shut off. Checking through old bills reveals three are unpaid. But until you check with the gas company, you do not have actual proof of the cause.

Logical Principles of Cause-and-Effect Relationships

As you explore possible cause-and-effect connections, examine the logic of your conclusion or inference. Is it reasonable, sensible, and sound? Or has an error occurred? To be valid, a claim of causal relationship must be based on two essential standards.

TWO PRINCIPLES OF LOGIC IN CAUSE AND EFFECT

- The cause is able to produce the effect.
- Other causes that might have produced the effect have been ruled out.

Two Fallacies to Avoid in Analyzing Cause and Effect

A systems analyst says that the most frequent mistake in logic that his team makes is to assume that because one event follows another, the first caused the second—even though there is no proof. This assumption is the *post hoc* fallacy; chronology is mistaken for causation. Events in a sequence do not always have a connection.

Another fallacy of cause and effect is the *non sequitur* (meaning *it is not necessarily true*). A non sequitur is also an assumption, but it does not involve the timing of events. Non sequiturs often occur in predictions. For example, it was once widely said that "a Catholic will never be elected president." Yet John F. Kennedy became the first Roman Catholic president of the United States. This common belief was disproved.

See chapter 19.

If we keep in mind that much of what we "know" is actually inference, theory, value judgment, or myth, we are more likely to pause and seek evidence before leaping to conclusions about why something happened.

www.mhhe.com/dietsch

If you want further guidance on writing cause-and-effect papers, check out:
Writing>Writing Tutors>
Causal Analysis

WRITING A PAPER ANALYZING CAUSE AND EFFECT

A paper of causal analysis allows for a wide range of topics to be organized and developed in various ways. Every time you inquire about *how* or *why* something happened, you begin causal analysis. To prewrite, you might sketch a reverse chain of cause and effect as shown in the earlier diagram. Keep in mind the following principle: *Complex events, conditions, or situations seldom stem from a single cause.* Therefore don't halt your search too soon. You may find more than one cause.

Planning a Cause-and-Effect Paper

After you have sketched a cause-and-effect chain, consider how to organize details. The big question is this: *"What does the audience need to know?"* Your answer will help you decide what to include and where to start. Then set up a scratch outline in a way that seems logical. To begin, consider the following questions:

- Was there a single cause and single effect? Or were several factors involved?
- Will the major emphasis be on the specific phenomenon (cause)? Or will it be on the consequence (effect)?
- What kind of order will work best?

Chronological order is often simplest and most efficient. This way you discuss the cause before the effect. Sometimes *reverse chronological order* is used with effect before cause. If you have multiple causes and/or multiple effects, you may need to organize your main points by order of importance. Several possible strategies are presented here. If one seems to fit your topic, adapt it as needed.

www.mhhe.com/dietsch

For help outlining, check out: Writing>Outlining Tutor

A. SINGLE CAUSE WITH MULTIPLE EFFECTS

I. Introduction (specifies the cause, then the effects)

   • *Claim:* High consumption of soft drinks containing sugar and caffeine contributes to overweight, other health problems, and mild addiction.

II. Body (most- to least-important order)

   A. Describes/explains effect no. 1: overweight

   B. Describes/explains effect no. 2: other health problems

   C. Describes/explains effect no. 3: mild addiction

III. Conclusion

B. SINGLE EFFECT PRODUCED BY MULTIPLE CAUSES

I. Introduction (specifies the effect, then the final cause)

   • *Claim:* Many farmers in the South are decreasing the acreage allotted to tobacco in favor of vegetable crops because fresh produce sold to urban markets yields more profit.

II. Body (chronological order: sequence of related events)

   A. Cause no. 1: Nicotine has been identified as a cause of cancer.

   B. Cause no. 2: Many people have ceased smoking because of possible health hazards.

   C. Cause no. 3: Prospects for future tobacco markets are dimming.

   D. Cause no. 4: High prices of fresh produce promise lucrative returns.

III. Conclusion

continued

STRATEGIES FOR CAUSE-AND-EFFECT PAPERS

STRATEGIES FOR
CAUSE-AND-
EFFECT PAPERS
(continued)

C. MULTIPLE CAUSES AND MULTIPLE EFFECTS (block method)

    I. Introduction: who, what, and where?

       • *Claim:* (state causes, then effects)

    II. Body (explanation of causes and effects)

      A. Causes

      B. Effects

    III. Conclusion (may be recommendations)

D. SERIES OF LINKED EVENTS (alternating method)

    I. Introduction (related events in a sequence)

       • *Claim:* During a heavy fog on . . . many drivers sped and failed to maintain a safe distance between cars, causing wrecks and a pile-up that blocked Interstate . . . for nineteen miles.

    II. Body (cause and effect alternated)

      A. Cause no. 1: heavy fog

      B. Effect no. 1: decreased visibility

      C. Cause no. 2: speeding too close to other cars

      D. Effect no. 2: drivers were unable to stop quickly (continue as needed)

    III. Conclusion

Drafting an Introduction

See chapter 4.

www.mhhe.com/dietsch
For general help writing introductions, check out:
Writing>Introductions

The introduction may take various forms, depending on the emphasis and kind of causal relationships. For example, you might begin with a *narrative,* possibly an eyewitness account of an accident, then go on to describe the cause and effect(s). Your thesis could then link the cause with the effects you will focus on.

Or you might open by describing a specific effect, showing why it is important or interesting to consider what caused it. You might explain the effect by classifying *examples* and presenting *illustrations.* Or you might provide an overview of the causal relationship or suggest that the causes or effects will be surprising. Watch for a hook that will make your analysis meaningful for your readers.

Developing a Paper Analyzing Cause and Effect

Your purpose will help you to devise a suitable writing strategy to develop your paper adequately. Most topics will require a thorough explanation with specific details and examples that reflect the purpose. Usually, the primary purpose of causal analysis is to inform or to persuade. Even when the purpose is informative, the paper will still have an *argumentative edge,* or element of persuasion. It may range from a hint to much more. In short, whether *implicitly* or *explicitly,* you will argue for your claim that a cause has led or will lead to an effect. (The difference between an informative and a persuasive paper of causal analysis is a matter of degree and strategy, not necessarily content.)

To support your claim, you need convincing proof. For example, you might contend that action should be taken to keep sixteen-year-olds from driving after midnight because of an extremely high rate of accidents for that age group. To make your claim plausible, you would have to produce valid research and possibly expert opinion to indicate that the hours after midnight are a dangerous time for sixteen-year-old drivers to be out on the roads.

Writing a Conclusion

The conclusion of a cause-and-effect paper summarizes the consequence or result. It may mention a repercussion, influence, benefit, or implication for the future. Or there may be an allusion to the title or opening that establishes closure, as in "Silver Lining," below. Regardless, the ending should flow from the description of cause and effect and give a sense of completeness.

See chapter 4.

Revising a Cause-and-Effect Paper

As you start to revise your cause-and-effect paper, look at the larger items first. Pay particular attention to the strategy, logic, and writer's voice. After you are satisfied with these aspects, check the smaller aspects, as explained in chapter 5.

The checklist below should be helpful.

www.mhhe.com/dietsch

For general revising help, visit:
Writing>Drafting and Revision

See "Editing," page 71.

CHECKLIST   **REVISING A CAUSE-AND-EFFECT PAPER**

1. Does the strategy emphasize the purpose?
2. Is the evidence adequate to support the claim?
3. If not, have I qualified my statements (with *seem* or *appear,* for example) to allow for chance?
4. Could another contributing cause exist?
5. Is the voice impartial and fair?
6. Is the connection clear? Have I explained enough?

TWO STUDENT PAPERS: CAUSE AND EFFECT

College students and others on tight budgets will empathize with Jo Rae Sloan. The purpose of her paper is to inform. She begins with the cause and explains the effects.

Silver Lining

To a nineteen-year-old girl, owning her own vehicle oftentimes seems alluring. But once the dream becomes a reality, the resulting responsibilities may seem overwhelming at times. Several months ago I had an opportunity to buy a pickup truck with help from my mother. Having my own transportation is convenient, and I do take pride in my Chevy pickup; yet the upkeep and expense can be exasperating.

Before I bought a truck, I had to schedule my activities around the other family members. I had to borrow my mother's car and worry about the possibility of putting a dent in the fender before I returned. Now I can hop in my Chevy and go whenever I need or wish without a care. I am a cautious driver and have insurance. Although I still park in a far row of parking lots, away from other vehicles, I no longer worry about possible dents.

When I drove someone else's car, I did not really care how it looked. Once I owned my own vehicle, however, my feelings changed. I take pride in my Chevy truck. When I first purchased it, I took it to a body shop for a new paint job with stripes and for window tinting. Now I vacuum my truck every week as well as wash and wax it regularly. All this takes time and effort. The work and expense are much more than I bargained for.

In the "good old days," all of my extra cash went for clothes, cosmetics, and anything else I wanted. Not now—every cent seems to go to my truck. The expected expense is bad enough, but the unexpected expense can be heartbreaking to a full-time student with a part-time job. Insurance takes a big chunk of my earnings. Filling the gas tank is another regular expense, along with the cost of oil and periodic maintenance. The unexpected expense of a new tire, a muffler system, and other repairs has been formidable. Thank goodness, I live at home and don't have to make payments to a car dealer. My mother is willing to wait for a payment when necessary.

As a result of buying my truck, I have been forced to budget—I haven't bought any new clothes since graduation last June. Although I seldom have more than a few dollar bills and some silver lining my pockets, I have a wonderful sense of independence. My Chevy truck has transported me from adolescence to adulthood.

QUESTIONS FOR DISCUSSION

1. What is the single cause of the effects Jo Rae describes?

2. How do her expectations compare with reality?

3. How does she feel about the effects at times? What is her overall feeling?

4. Does Jo Rae use the block or the alternating method of organization?

5. What is the effect of placing advantages before disadvantages?

6. What is the effect of the title? To what old saying does it allude?

In the next paper, Mary Ann Holvik also describes a single cause that produces multiple effects. Her purpose is to explain the difficulties of her job and the unexpected benefits she reaped.

Why Would Anyone Want to Be a School Bus Driver?

Often when two people are introduced, they initiate conversation by inquiring about each other's occupation. For six years my answer to that question produced raised eyebrows and caused my new acquaintances to exclaim, "You couldn't pay me enough to do that job!" Then I would explain that driving a school bus had rewards other than the usual monetary compensation: mastering a machine, enjoying nature, and participating in children's lives.

Achieving control of the school bus was an arduous task. I had to learn a maintenance routine which included checking all oil and fluid levels, inspecting all hoses and belts for signs of wear, and verifying that all lights and warning buzzers were functional. The most difficult aspect was backing the bus, 38 feet long, from a narrow country road into a still narrower driveway. Yet I derived great satisfaction from knowing the children on the bus were safe because it was in top running condition, and I was confidently in control.

Nature rewarded me for my early morning hours with a spectacular array of sunrises, which fired the deep-textured woods and fence rows with iridescent colors. Although I had grown up in the country, I never tired of watching the trees, wildflowers, and farm crops grow, blossom, and display the triumphant colors of a purpose fulfilled. Under the cover of vegetation, animals and birds carried on their daily lives, unabashed by the passing of so many curious eyes. The children and I enjoyed sights such as a buck deer bounding across an open field, a skunk hunting for his insect breakfast, a flock of Canadian geese flying in formation, and a hawk carrying away his prey with victorious cries.

The children, however, were my constant source of delight. The younger ones were always eager to share their concerns with me. I became a doll fashion adviser and new clothes admirer. I sympathized with the losing Little League team and empathized with the disappointed owners of bologna sandwich lunches. I patched dozens of scraped knees and critiqued hundreds of homework papers. Grade cards were presented for approval; and, occasionally, love notes were dropped surreptitiously into my lap by red-faced little boys.

Older students generally remained aloof until desperation brought them to me, seeking advice about dating or dealing with unreasonable parents. For homecoming queens I saved newspaper pictures, and I congratulated teams for their athletic feats and scholastic achievement. And I worried over their safety each weekend when carloads of teenagers jammed the downtown square. Although I do not have any children of my own, I have loved several hundred boys and girls who made me a part of their lives.

If, like my new acquaintances, I had considered only the hard work involved in my job, then I would not have been a school bus driver. Of course, I received a monetary reward, but my real rewards were the physical discipline of driving, intimacy with nature, and the trusting love of the children.

QUESTIONS FOR DISCUSSION

1. What is the cause in Mary Ann's paper?

2. What are the effects?

3. How does Mary Ann use description to convey her feelings about her job? Which examples do you find most vivid? Why?

4. What order is used to organize details relating to children? To organize main points?

5. How would you describe the voice of the paper?

PRACTICE

IDEAS FOR A CAUSE-AND-EFFECT PARAGRAPH

1. Haste makes waste
2. How learning to save (or not save) has affected my life
3. Honesty is the best policy
4. How an error in judgment caused . . .
5. How learning to _____ led to . . .

GROUP EXERCISE: Writing "If . . . Then" Statements

Directions: Discuss each claim and the implications that *logically* follow. Then write a series of inferences derived from each claim. (The hints will start your thinking.)

1. In 1998 a Canadian business group got a permit to export water from Lake Superior to Asia. After an outcry in Canada and the United States, Ontario canceled the permit in 1999. Now Global Water Corp. of Vancouver, British Columbia, has secured a permit to take water from a lake near Sitka, Alaska, to sell to China. Alaskans granted the permit because they regard water as a renewable resource.

   Claim: Alaska should not be allowed to export water to a foreign country. (How might it affect the local supply? Water table? Might depletion affect the rate of renewal? Why?)

   - If Alaska exports water, then there will be _____ water available to _____.
   - If a _____ should occur in the lower United States, then _____.
   - If Alaska continues to export water over the years, then _____.

2. *Claim:* Exercise is good for you; therefore, you should exercise regularly. (What conditions are implicit in this statement? Think about the exceptions and fill in the blanks with logical answers.)

   - If you have no _____ [what?], then you should exercise regularly.
   - If you have _____, then you should _____ [consult whom?] before exercising.
   - If your _____ recommends _____, then you should _____ regularly.
   - If _____ regularly, then _____.

TWENTY IDEAS FOR PAPERS OF CAUSE AND EFFECT

1. Good intentions—unexpected consequences

2. An act of kindness and its effect on me

3. The influence of my favorite teacher

4. Peer pressure in high school

5. The effects of fatherhood on a sports enthusiast

6. The effect of a telephone stalker on my life

7. How reading influenced my life

8. Influence of an alcoholic parent on a family

9. How my thinking has changed since attending college

10. Grandmother's favorite proverb and its influence on me

11. Effect of being the oldest of _____ children

12. How cancer changed my home

13. Thirty seconds of success and its effect

14. Influence of my stay-at-home mother

15. A father's example

16. Effects of losing a job

17. How my parents' divorce changed my life

18. A dream can generate power

19. The effects of being raised in a _____ neighborhood

20. How the events of September 11, 2001, have influenced my life

Strategies for Critical Thinking, Evaluation, and Argument

PART 4

On June 14, 1777, the Continental Congress adopted our first national flag. Thirteen red and white stripes represented the original thirteen states. A blue field with thirteen white stars symbolized their union. In 1794 when two new states entered the Union, two stripes and two stars were added. By 1817 the flag had twenty stars but just thirteen stripes to prevent clutter. Our present fifty-star flag evolved after Alaska and Hawaii were added in 1959.

Just as the flag has changed over the years, so too the pledge of allegiance has changed. In 1892 schoolchildren recited it to mark the discovery of America. In 1923 and 1924, the wording was expanded. In 1954 Congress added the words "under God," which has stirred heated controversy since 2000.

WRITING EXERCISE

1. Do you believe that our flag should hang in schoolrooms and students should recite the pledge of allegiance? Why or why not?

2. Do you think the words "under God" should remain in the pledge of allegiance? Why or why not?

Proposing a Solution

CHAPTER 17

> A problem well stated is a problem half solved.
>
> —Charles F. Kettering

Wherever you work, problems will arise—delays in deliveries, malfunctions of equipment, mistakes by personnel, customer complaints, missing inventory, or other snafus. How these problems are resolved can mean profit or loss—and even layoffs. Therefore, job applicants who have effective problem-solving skills, as well as good writing skills, have an edge in interviews.

This chapter shows you, step-by-step, how to mix various writing strategies into an effective format for problem solving. You can use this basic format in writing memos, e-mail, letters, reports, or research papers, according to the rhetorical situation.

DEWEY'S METHOD OF PROBLEM SOLVING

John Dewey, a twentieth-century educator, devised an effective problem-solving method, based on the scientific method (which has seven steps). Dewey omitted the step of formulating a hypothesis—which can hinder objectivity. The researcher who hypothesizes may find only support for the theory and halt the search too soon, thereby overlooking evidence against it.

Dewey's six-step procedure has been widely adopted and adapted by educators, business personnel, and others. The purpose is to describe the problem and inform the audience of possible alternatives for solving or alleviating it. A simplified version appears here:

1. **State the problem.** Identify it.
2. **Define the problem.** Limit its scope. Examine its history.
3. **Formulate criteria.** Devise standards to measure the problem.
4. **Propose alternatives.** Consider possible solutions.
5. **Evaluate alternatives.** Apply criteria to solution options.
6. **Recommend action.** Select the best possible solution(s).

Finding practical solutions was Dewey's chief concern. Dewey's primary criterion for evaluating an option was "Will it work?" He went to great lengths to be objective.

ETHICS: HOW CAN ONE BE OBJECTIVE?

To be objective, we must be willing to relinquish old biases, to question and seek the truth. Basically, there are two general ways to obtain information: firsthand and secondhand. Both ways can present problems in terms of objectivity. Although we observe something firsthand, we may see only part of it and think we saw 100 percent. Or we may misinterpret the meaning, make incorrect inferences, and treat them as fact. Information gained secondhand is also subject to error and distortion. So how can we become as objective as possible and minimize chances of error?

1. **Reserve judgment.** We can listen quietly to both sides of an issue and consider all facets of a problem before stating an opinion. We can look for facts and comprehensive coverage before making decisions.
2. **Strive to be impartial and fair.** We can remain open to new information, welcome different perspectives, and watch for errors in reasoning.
3. **Qualify generalizations and avoid overstatement.** We can distinguish inference and value judgment from fact. We can check our facts.   See chapter 3.

4. **Keep in mind that no one is immune to mistakes.** Although we think we understand something, our information may be only partial. Although we may tell what caused something, what affects it now and what may affect it in the future, or how it affects something else, vital information may be missing. This awareness should keep us not only humble but also alert.

WRITING A COMPANY POLICY

A marketing firm has recently installed software that allows executives to access and monitor electronic communication. This installation was made because several employees were playing games, gambling, job hunting, shopping, and watching porn online instead of working. (Each visit to a Web site drags along the company name.)

An attorney has advised the firm to write a policy covering e-mail and Web use. To balance company interests and employee privacy, the attorney advised appointing a committee that includes rank-and-file employees.

Activity

Meet with your group to draft specific guidelines for e-mail and Web use. Consider these issues: Should employees be allowed to use e-mail for personal messages? To trade stock during work hours? To grocery shop or engage in other leisure activities? If so, what kind of activities and for how long? Include penalties for policy violations. Should the number and severity of the offenses be factors?

WRITING A PROBLEM-SOLVING PAPER

A problem-solving paper combines various writing strategies into a basic format that is suitable not only for some short papers but also for some research papers. The outline on page 229 is based on Dewey's method of problem solving. Although you and your peers may use the same general pattern of organization, you will make individual decisions according to the rhetorical situation.

www.mhhe.com/dietsch

For more help choosing a topic, visit:
Writing>Prewriting

Selecting a Topic and Prewriting

To find a topic for a problem-solving paper, you might begin by considering your experiences, including work-related projects. Or perhaps you know of a family, a neighborhood, a community, or a city facing a problem. The problem should be significant, yet not too technical or complex. It should have at least three alternative solutions. That does not mean all alternatives must be feasible. Two or more can be ruled out, but one must provide a means to alleviate or to resolve the problem. Sometimes all alternatives may be needed. If the problem cannot be alleviated, look for another topic.

As you search for details to use in a problem-solving paper, watch for changes, cause and effect, side effects, risks, advantages and disadvantages. Note that changes may be negative or positive and their effects may be simple or complicated. Advantages and disadvantages may be short-term or long-term. Asking questions will speed your search.

QUESTIONS TO DISCOVER DETAILS FOR PROBLEM SOLVING

- What exactly is the problem?
- When was it first noticed?
- What or whom does it affect?
- What are its effects (Signs, symptoms, characteristics?)
- How far does it extend? (Scope?)
- What were the causes? (History?)
- What, if anything, has been done to alleviate the problem?
- What other alternatives exist?
- What are the advantages and disadvantages of each alternative?
- What is the best alternative? Or will a combination be needed?

Caution: Beware of oversimplification. Complex problems seldom have a single cause.

Organizing a Problem-Solving Paper

Dewey's method of problem solving furnishes an easy and effective way to organize information clearly for an audience. You can adapt this method to most problems. Using the six steps, you can start your scratch outline. Steps 1 and 2 form the introduction of the paper. Steps 3, 4, and 5, form the body. Step 6 forms the conclusion. Then you can convert your scratch outline into a working outline, as shown here.

WORKING OUTLINE

I. Introduction
   - A. Attention-getting detail
   - B. Summary of the current problem (description)
   - C. History of the problem (narration, using chronological order)
   - D. Identification of the causes (cause-and-effect order)

II. Body
   - A. Specific criteria to apply in evaluation (classification)
   - B. Alternative 1 and evaluation of effectiveness (order of importance)
   - C. Alternative 2 and evaluation of effectiveness (order of importance)
   - D. Alternative 3 and evaluation of effectiveness (order of importance)

III. Conclusion
   - A. Recommendation, citing best alternative (or combination)
   - B. Relevant comment

TRANSITION IN A PROBLEM-SOLVING PAPER

See chapter 16.

A problem-solving paper requires transitions to signal cause-and-effect relationships. To direct the reader, place appropriate transitions near reasons why an event happened or a description of how it affected another event or situation:

therefore	one difficulty	an offshoot	one part
thus	an outcome	a consequence	one complication
affected	one effect	a by-product	one influence
two factors	an outgrowth	as a result	one proposal
three aspects	influenced	contributed	changed

www.mhhe.com/dietsch

For general help writing introductory paragraphs, go to:

Writing>Introductions

Drafting an Introduction

Problem-solving papers can begin in several ways. You might open with an appropriate quotation or a brief dialogue that illustrates a vital aspect of the problem. Another way is to start with a narrative that describes the problem; then you might describe cause and effect. Keith Zuspan describes an incident that happened where he worked:

Preventing an Expensive Problem

One of the most recent crises at _____ State Headquarters in _____ occurred in the executive building. A twenty-five-year-old air-conditioning unit failed to maintain the required cooling level in this large complex. When such an event occurs, it is imperative that the Building Operations Supervisor take action immediately. The supervisor must be able not only to recognize the potential risks but also to correct the problem in the least amount of time and in the most efficient manner.

The introduction of a problem-solving paper sets the stage for the identification of criteria and a discussion of alternatives.

Identifying Criteria

To check decisions and to evaluate possible solutions to problems, we need to develop criteria. By identifying our own specific criteria, we can measure the existing alternatives and make more logical decisions than we might otherwise make.

What Are Criteria?   You may be used to terms such as "guidelines," "specifications," or "company policy," instead of criteria. Yet all those terms refer to criteria that are used to weigh decisions and evaluate alternatives. *Criteria* are simply the factors that influence decision making and problem solving.

Daily life offers many opportunities to apply criteria. For instance, when planning a major purchase, you use criteria to weigh the advantages and disadvantages of comparable products. Before buying a new television set, you might consider some, or perhaps all, of the following criteria:

- screen size
- brand name
- price
- warranty
- quality of sound
- high definition
- flat-screen options
- sharpness of details

A criterion (the singular of *criteria*) is *one* standard, rule, principle, or test used to evaluate a decision or proposal. For example, *Merriam-Webster's Collegiate Dictionary,* Eleventh Edition, defines *criterion* as "a standard on which a judgment or decision may be based."*

Dewey's first criterion—"Will it work?"—is a factor in solving any problem. Time is another important criterion to consider. Other common criteria are listed here:

- Is it cost-effective?
- Is it safe?
- Is it practical?
- Is it legal?
- Is it ethical?
- Is it fair?
- Is it appropriate?
- Is it beneficial in the short run? Long run?

Stating Criteria   To identify criteria, ask: "What factors will influence this decision?" Perhaps the simplest way to specify criteria is to pose each criterion as a question. In her paper Nancy Miller used that tactic:

> Making our house more energy-efficient required careful consideration. When the alternatives to this problem were evaluated, three main questions were asked. First, what is the cost? Second, how energy-efficient is the alternative? Third, will the alternative raise the equity in our home?

Another example was written by a mother who had recently lost her job through a layoff. Carol Walkins specified three concerns in her job search—day shift, pay scale, and location:

> A major problem that I faced was the possibility of having to work the evening or midnight shift if I found employment in another factory. With two elementary school children, I needed to be at home in the evenings in order to spend important time with them. Since my family depends on my income, I also had to find a job that would provide a pay scale similar to that of my former job. Location was another factor to be considered. My husband works locally, and we own our home. Therefore, moving was not an option.

For clarity in a problem-solving paper, some instructors prefer that students state criteria before alternatives. Regardless, do not confuse criteria with alternatives. *Criteria* are the factors or considerations that govern decisions. Alternatives are the options for action—possible solutions. In other words, criteria provide a means to weigh the benefits and risks of an alternative.

---

*By permission from *Merriam-Webster's Collegiate® Dictionary,* Eleventh Edition. Copyright © 2004 by Merriam-Webster, Incorporated (www.merriam-webster.com).

Proposing and Evaluating Alternatives

Usually, a problem-solving paper presents at least three alternatives. Perhaps two of the choices can be eliminated, leaving one that can best solve the problem. This does not mean that every problem can be solved with one alternative. Perhaps a combination will be needed. Or perhaps the best that can be done is to alleviate the problem.

After alternatives are determined, each possibility is evaluated according to criteria. In this fifth step, advantages and disadvantages become apparent. Upon a first glance, an alternative may seem to be a practical solution to a problem. After research and analysis, however, hidden disadvantages may emerge.

To evaluate alternatives for a paper, research the feasibility of each one. Do not assume there are no disadvantages. To be objective, a paper must specify disadvantages as well as advantages. (An omission of either would constitute card stacking. See chapter 19.) Then evaluate the alternatives according to the criteria. Note that a problem may have a short-term alternative and a long-term solution. When Carol analyzed her problem of unemployment, she found both:

> My first alternative was to collect the nine months of unemployment compensation that I qualified for. I could accomplish my household tasks during the day, leaving the evenings free for my children. Collecting unemployment and saving on sitter's fees would compensate for the weekly paycheck. Although the idea of staying home was appealing, collecting an unemployment check would be temporary and not a real solution to the problem.
>
> A second alternative was to go job hunting. Although it seemed like a logical solution, I knew that a good job would be difficult to find at this time. To secure factory work with daytime hours would be almost impossible. Daytime office jobs were available, but I lacked the training needed to qualify. I realized that it was unrealistic to expect to find a suitable, well-paying job locally.
>
> A third option was available, however. Because I had lost my job due to foreign trade, I was eligible for a new federal program under the Trade Readjustment Act. This program would pay for college tuition for two years as well as books and supplies. I could attend day classes while the children were in school. The plan would also pay a small allowance for living expenses for up to one year if grade and attendance requirements were maintained. Although this option would require a drastically revised family budget, I knew I could manage.

Carol combined steps 4 and 5 of the problem-solving method: she proposed an alternative, applied criteria, and evaluated. This order enabled her to avoid undue repetition. The parallelism of her points helped to make the paper clear and easy to read. The details prepared the audience for the conclusion.

Writing a Conclusion

www.mhhe.com/dietsch

For general assistance writing conclusions, check out:
Writing>Conclusions

The end of a problem-solving paper presents the recommendation the writer has prepared the reader to accept. In other words, the selected solution should flow logically from the discussion of alternatives. Some conclusions contain a call for action, perhaps pointing out the consequences of inaction. In his paper about the air-conditioning problem on the job, Keith Zuspan concluded by making a recommendation:

> Repairing the existing air-conditioning unit would, in fact, be the most efficient and economical method of regaining the desired environmental controls required for the complex. It is also the writer's opinion that by utilizing the in-house building mechanics to complete this project, additional money could be saved.

Other conclusions, like the ending of Nancy Miller's paper, summarize the action already taken and explain how a solution fits the criteria:

> After reviewing the three alternatives, we chose the third, which proved to be the most cost-effective as well as energy efficient. By purchasing the siding and windows together, we received a discount. The new furnace also proved to be energy-efficient, and we saw a sizable reduction in heating expense in the first year after installation. This third option has also increased the home's equity dramatically, although part of the increase is due to inflation. In 1972 we paid just over seven thousand dollars for the house; and now, three decades later, the house is worth over seventy-five thousand dollars.

Revising a Problem-Solving Paper

To produce your best work, allow plenty of time for revising, editing, and proofreading your problem-solving paper. Proofread for mechanical errors at least two or three times. After entering corrections on-screen, run a final spelling check—a vital step that will catch last-minute typos. The following checklist will help to ensure that you check strategic points:

www.mhhe.com/dietsch
For more help with revision, visit:
Writing>Drafting and Revising

See chapter 5.

CHECKLIST   **REVISING A PROBLEM-SOLVING PAPER**

1. Is the problem clearly defined in the introduction? Are the causes and pertinent history of the problem explained?

2. Are specific criteria for evaluating alternative solutions identified? Are these criteria reasonable and adequate?

3. Are different alternatives for solving the problem identified and described?

4. Is one alternative recommended? Is it clear why this solution is best?

5. Is the conclusion effective? Does it flow logically from the body?

6. Have transitions been used effectively?

TWO STUDENT PAPERS: PROBLEM SOLVING

In the first example, Rajini Maturu proposes a solution to a problem faced in her former workplace:

Unhappy Customers at the Bank of India

The Union Bank of India is a financial institution that has 1,000 branches all over India. In the city of Secunderabad, the Union Bank caters to the financial needs of local customers. There the branch manager has to tackle the problem of customer dissatisfaction toward the check-cashing procedure.

Presently, there are four staff members of the bank taking care of the four steps of the check-cashing routine. During the banking hours between 10 a.m. and 2:30 p.m., there are about seventy customers. The customer first presents the check to a clerk, who enters the check number and amount in a register. The clerk gives the customer a metallic coin, called a token, with a number.

Then the customer goes to another clerk, who debits the customer's account with the amount of the check. Next, an accountant verifies the customer's signature. Finally, the check is taken to the cashier, who identifies the customer by the token number and makes the payment. During this procedure each customer waits for at least thirty minutes to cash a check.

There are two important aspects to the problem of expediting the check-cashing procedure. One aspect is the cost involved in bringing about changes since the branch is allowed a budget of $2,000. The other aspect to be considered is the amount of time saved by introducing the changes.

A proposed solution is to increase the number of staff members. Three additional clerks could be appointed to handle the check cashing. The cost of this change would mean $500 per clerk. For three more clerks, the total cost would be $1,500, which is within the budget limit. The main drawback to this proposal is that the customers would still have to wait for at least fifteen minutes to cash their checks.

A second proposal is the opening of a teller counter. This would mean creation of a separate cubicle with ledgers containing customer information. The specimen signatures of the customers would be stored at the teller counter. Here the entire check-cashing procedure could be managed by one employee called the teller officer. When a check was presented for payment, the teller officer would scrutinize the customer's signature, enter the check amount in the cash register, and make payment to the customer. This proposal would cost $1,900; hence, the expenses would be within the budget. As all the operations would be managed by one employee, the check could be cashed in eight minutes. This would mean a considerable reduction in the customer's wait.

A third proposal is to computerize all the customer's records. With this method the check would be cashed in two minutes. This is the best proposal as far as the time element is concerned. The cost involved in purchasing the computers and training the clerks would be $4,000, however. The disadvantage to this proposal is that it does not meet the budget requirements.

The second proposal of creating a teller counter appears to be the most suitable action at this time. This proposal reduces the waiting period to cash a check from thirty minutes to eight minutes, and the expenses involved are within the budget specifications.

In the second example, Chris Hafley proposes a solution to a problem facing his community:

A Plan for Quality Emergency Care

In the small northwest Ohio city of _____ , the city fire department provides emergency medical care for its residents and township residents. In the past decade, a need for more advanced prehospital intervention has developed. To provide better medical care, the city council elected to send ten (of twenty)

Advanced Emergency Medical Technicians to paramedic school at Sandusky Providence Hospital.

Before these ten people graduate and begin to function as paramedics, a dilemma must be resolved as to how the rescue squad will respond to possible life-threatening medical and trauma emergencies. With only one paramedic on duty as part of a two-person team, it would be almost impossible for the squad to function properly and respond efficiently to all calls twenty-four hours a day. Therefore, a committee has been organized to investigate four possible solutions.

The criteria set up by the investigational committee for review of the recom-mendations were availability, training, and cost-effectiveness. The first solution suggested was to respond with an ambulance and two police officers. But the officers' level of medical training is limited to basic first aid and CPR training. They would not be much help with patients needing advanced life support. To upgrade all the officers' training to at least Basic Emergency Medical Techni-cian would involve considerable expense to the city. This method would be the most expensive option of the four, costing initially $30,000 to certify all eigh-teen officers. There are many times, however, when officers are out on call and thus are unavailable.

The second option would be to arrange for one additional paramedic to be on call at home for twenty-four hours a day. This plan would cost approxi-mately $27,000, but it would be the most effective as far as availability is concerned.

The third option would be to dispatch an additional ambulance as a backup system for the first ambulance. After researching this option, more people favored it than any of the others because of quality of assistance and cost-effectiveness. Personnel on the ambulance already have the necessary training. Availability, however, would be a problem at times since the ambulance per-sonnel make numerous out-of-town transfers.

The fourth option would provide for the fire department pumper to re-spond along with the ambulance. Research shows that this alternative would be the most cost-effective. The idea is to have two firefighters cross-trained as Basic Emergency Medical Technicians. There would be two firefighter EMTs on each shift. This option would cut down the number of personnel to be trained and would be the least expensive way for the city to provide the additional staff to assist in medical emergencies. The initial cost would be about $12,000 for training. An advantage to using the firefighters would be that they are usu-ally available to respond to medical emergencies with the ambulance.

After all the information was compiled and the alternatives were reviewed again and again, the review committee recommended both options three and four be implemented. Thus if the firefighters were unavailable, the second am-bulance might possibly provide a backup.

QUESTIONS FOR ANALYSIS

1. Does each paper provide a clear description of the problem?
2. Are the criteria clear?
3. Does the order of alternatives seem appropriate?
4. Are alternatives evaluated according to the criteria?

5. Does the conclusion seem logical and complete?

6. What are the chief differences in the way the two problems are solved?

FOR YOUR REFERENCE Problem-Solving Essays in the Reader	• "Sound and Fury," Dan Greenburg, page 548 • "Becoming Educated," Barbara Jordan, page 651 • "When the Lullaby Ends," Andrea Sachs, page 678 • "Why Marriages Fail," Ann Roiphe, page 665

PRACTICE

SMALL GROUPS: Identifying Criteria

After you read Patricia Davis's introduction below, brainstorm possible criteria that would influence the final decision. One group member should record them. Then examine your criteria and decide which are most important.

A Pet for Aunt Emily

My aunt, although eighty-three years old and rather frail, is still able to care for herself. Aunt Emily lives alone in her own home on a limited income. Ordinarily, she is quite independent and self-sufficient, but last week she surprised me. When I dropped by, she asked for advice. Confiding that she was lonely, she explained she needed companionship and was thinking about getting a pet. But she was unsure about what sort of animal would be best for her. She asked me to help in deciding what kind of pet would be the most enjoyable and suitable.

SMALL GROUPS: Case Problems

Directions: Select *one* of the authentic cases below. Steps 1 and 2 of Dewey's problem-solving method are given. Supply steps 3, 4, 5, and 6.

1. You are on the committee to plan the office Christmas party. You are instructed to eliminate past problems or cancel! In past years, employees have bought gifts for the owner of the firm. Some buy expensive gifts and appear to be currying favors, which causes grumbling. The owner gives everyone a small ham and provides a lunch of finger food and fruit punch. Someone always spikes the punch. Some employees have become rowdy and amorous. Devise a plan to prevent similar problems.

2. You are a software sales rep. While at a trade show, you meet a woman who asks if you still have the same sales manager, J. D. Smith. When you reply "Yes," she tells about her boyfriend buying software out of J. D.'s home. You mull over the pros and cons of telling the owner, whom you trust. You do not trust J. D. because of his office pranks and complaints behind the owner's back. What else should you consider? What do you decide?

3. Your neighbors often stay out until 2:30 a.m. on weekends. They leave their Doberman tied out in the backyard, where he howls—keeping you awake until they take him in. You do not know if he is hungry or lonely. The dog does not recognize you, but from a distance he seems fairly friendly. What are your alternatives? What risks are involved?

TWENTY IDEAS FOR PROBLEM-SOLVING PAPERS

1 Overreliance on credit cards

2 A problem on the job

3 Relocating to a new community

4 Coping with divorce

5 Security for twenty-four-hour businesses

6 Automobile security from theft

7 Mastering the fear of failure

8 How can we raise funds to replace playground equipment in the city park?

9 Staffing athletic programs on a low budget

10 Stress management for nurses, police officers, or . . .

11 Inadequate child-care facilities for working parents

12 Cutting expenses and living within a budget

13 Local litter control

14 Stray animal control

15 Financial problems for families when children are born

16 Investigating alternatives for elder care

17 Adjustment to college after _____ years

18 Good nutrition on a low budget

19 Breaking the nicotine habit

20 Maintaining an exercise plan

Shaping an Effective Argument

Hardly a day passes without your persuading someone of something. It may be as trivial as convincing a friend to try a new restaurant or as significant as convincing an interviewer you are qualified

> The best argument is that which seems merely an explanation.
>
> —Dale Carnegie

for a position. On the job you may write a proposal, a request for new software, a grant application, or other document. In a college class you may be asked to write a persuasive essay, a reaction paper, or a paper of argument. Skill in argument and persuasion will enable you to become a more effective writer and speaker, both in college and in the workplace.

239

PURPOSE OF ARGUMENT

Although there are many types of argument, the general purpose of any serious argument is to convince readers to accept a belief, adopt a policy, or enact a decision, proposal, or law. In the strictest sense, the term *argument* refers to an assertion that is based on logic and proof, a rational appeal to the intellect.

According to the rhetorical situation, however, many arguments contain not only rational appeals but also ethical and emotional appeals. This chapter explains a classic argument model that includes appeals to logic, ethics, and emotions. This model is flexible, effective, and practical. It can be adapted in various ways for general use.

THREE CLASSIC APPEALS USED IN ARGUMENT

More than two thousand years ago, the Greek philosopher Aristotle defined three kinds of appeals that make up an argument: *logos* (logic), *ethos* (moral character or ethics), and *pathos* (emotion). Aristotle realized that logic alone is not always sufficient to persuade an audience. To be convincing, you must also gain credibility—the trust of your listeners or readers. To do so, you must be perceived as honest, fair, and responsive to moral obligations. Aristotle called this the appeal to *ethos*. In *Nicomachean Ethics*, he explains:

> Virtue then is twofold, partly intellectual and partly moral, and intellectual virtue is originated and fostered mainly by teaching; it demands therefore experience and time. Moral virtue on the other hand is the outcome of habit, and accordingly its name *éthike*, is derived by a slight variation from *éthos*, habit.
>
> —from *On Man and the Universe: Metaphysics, Parts of Animals, Ethics, Politics, Poetics.* Louise R. Loomis, Editor

Logical and ethical appeals are often enough to convince on some issues, but unless emotion moves an audience to act on other issues, the argument will be in vain.

You can identify the three classic appeals by the questions they raise with readers:

- **Logical appeal.** Is the claim or petition factual and reasonable? True or false? Practical or impractical?
- **Ethical appeal.** Is the claim just or unjust? Honest or dishonest? Right or wrong?
- **Emotional appeal.** Do the words arouse such feelings as empathy and sympathy? Do they cause the reader to care about the subject?

The Logical Appeal

In most rhetorical situations, you will be expected to base your conclusions on sound reasoning and adequate proof. A logical argument appeals to the mind, using evidence, reasons, and examples to support a claim or proposition. Logical appeals are based on facts, sound inferences, and working theories. Reliable evidence may include established truths, primary sources, statistics, expert opinion, or personal experience.

"YOU GOT A TIGER BY THE TAIL!"

Matthew Resome was a programmer at XYZ Company. Matt was a quiet guy with an excellent work record who got along well with other employees. For three years he had tried to work through the right channels to improve wages and working conditions. But neither had changed despite the fact that the company's sales had increased 55 percent during those years.

When Matt contacted the National Labor Relations Board (NLRB), they said that if he could secure seventy-five signatures on a petition, then they could come in and conduct a vote to unionize the plant. The company would have to provide a room with a booth where employees could come during work hours. Matt secured the required signatures, and two NLRB representatives conducted the vote at the plant. The vote failed.

The next morning J. B. Smith, the plant manager, told his assistant to fire Matt. The assistant, who had attended law school, refused. Using a *logical* appeal, he warned, "You can't do this. Federal laws prohibit discrimination against peaceful and acceptable union activities. You got a tiger by the tail! Let it go."

But four days later, the irate plant manager called Matt in and stated: "Your job has been phased out. We don't need you any more. You can clear out your desk and leave right now." Matt contacted the NLRB.

Activity

Assume the role of the NLRB investigator. Examine Matt's work record and investigate the events preceding the firing. Summarize the situation and write a letter to J. B. Smith. Inform him that to prevent legal action, the company must reinstate and reimburse Matt for all lost wages. The company has thirty days to consider the offer.

WORKPLACE CASE STUDY

Established Truths   Some evidence is so solidly grounded that no reasonable person will seriously debate it. In the examples that follow, the first three are *established facts*, which have been conclusively proven. The fourth example has been accepted as fact, based on the existing evidence.

- **Historical fact.** Meriwether Lewis and William Clark explored the northwestern United States from St. Louis to the Pacific Ocean.

- **Geographical fact.** The Mississippi River is joined by the Missouri, Illinois, and Ohio Rivers before it flows down to the Gulf of Mexico.
- **Scientific fact.** When a heavy object is dropped, it falls to the ground.
- **Scientific theory regarded as fact.** The sun's gravitation attracts the planets and keeps them in their paths. Stars are held on course by the pull of heavenly bodies.

www.mhhe.com/dietsch

If you'd like more help gathering sources, check out: Research

Primary Sources   Research that is gathered firsthand carries more credibility than that filtered through secondary researchers. If you can obtain relevant documents, letters, autobiographies, or other primary source materials, these can lend strong support to your argument. Or you may choose to gather evidence firsthand yourself. For further explanation and suggestions, see chapter 30, "Field Research: Observation, Interviews, and Surveys."

Statistics   Reliable statistical findings from recognized and reputable authorities can strengthen your argument. To be reliable, the findings should be based on samples that are representative and random. Yet some widely quoted findings are neither random nor representative, as explained in chapter 30.

Another problem in reliability occurs when the researcher who is under extreme pressure, such as meeting a deadline, falsifies results. When you find unusual conclusions, check to see if the results are consistent with those of others in the field. Unless an experiment can be duplicated under controlled laboratory conditions by qualified researchers, it cannot be accepted as evidence.

Expert Opinion   The opinion of a recognized authority in a field generally conveys credibility and enhances an argument. If you decide to use expert opinion, check out the person's qualifications first. Here the Internet is an invaluable and speedy resource for checking on well-known authorities. Interviewing can also be helpful for local issues. For instance, if you were arguing for a proposal to thwart break-ins and burglary, then the chief of police, sheriff, or mayor could be credible sources.

See "Evaluating the Reliability of Internet Sources," chapter 27.

Personal Experience   The personal stories of people who have been involved in an accident, a tragedy, or a natural phenomenon such as a tornado can be powerful. A detailed description of such an event can have a strong emotional impact and buttress a logical argument. Personal experience stories should be used to supplement logical evidence, not supplant it. The experience should be significant and have a definite, relevant point.

Important Considerations   When you are presenting inconclusive evidence, avoid confusing theory with fact. Be accurate and precise so as not to overstate and weaken your case. For a reference list, see "Using Tentative Words to Discuss Findings and Theories," page 488.

Inferences are often confused with fact, and generalizations are often made from an invalid sample. For a further discussion of what constitutes reliable evidence, see chapters 3 and 19. To construct a flawless argument, you need to be able to recognize pitfalls in logic.

The Ethical Appeal

Ethical appeals are designed to strike a responsive chord in the minds of the readers, entreating them to do what is right, good, fair, and best. *Ethics* can be broadly defined as a set of moral values—principles of conduct for an individual, group, profession, or society. Sound ethics are essential for a well-constructed argument.

To be ethical, an argument must respect the rights and needs of the audience. In other words, deception to obtain a selfish aim is unethical—and often illegal. For example, a pastor of an Ohio church persuaded several elderly couples to donate their life savings to his church. However, he spent the money for expensive cars and other luxuries. Eventually, he was convicted of fraud and sent to prison.

An ethical appeal requires you to first demonstrate comprehensive knowledge of your subject. *You have an ethical obligation to give the reader the whole truth*, not just proof that will make your side of the argument *seem* convincing. In other words, if there are disadvantages to your proposal, you need to be honest about them. Second, you must approach the subject in an even-handed way, presenting differing viewpoints accurately and fairly. Your written voice must sound reasonable, controlled, and concerned.

The Emotional Appeal

Emotional appeals stir the feelings of readers with figurative language, connotation, and anecdote. Such appeals can be powerful, for they bypass the intellect. Emotional appeals work best, however, when used in moderation. They should also be ethical. Do not use an emotional appeal that gives you any misgivings or uneasiness.

Used wisely, emotion can motivate. For example, in the Workplace Case Study earlier, the assistant might have stressed his emotional appeal more. Instead of hinting with "You got a tiger by the tail!" he could have been more direct by saying, "You might lose your own job over this firing. Be careful." Perhaps the boss would have listened.

Using the Three Appeals

The bulk of your argument paper should be a logical appeal, based on sound logical proof. But keep in mind that credible persuasion rests on a blend of facts and ethical reasons, bonded with appropriate emotion. In other words, emotion usually plays a lesser role. To be effective, all three appeals must harmonize. An emotional appeal that conflicts with either a logical appeal or an ethical appeal is inappropriate and unethical.

As rhetoricians from Aristotle, Cicero, and Quintilian to those of today have indicated, ordinary propositions and assertions (unlike mathematical equations) are rarely clear-cut and undeniably certain. The conclusions of such arguments are probable, according to the weight of known or submitted evidence.

If significant evidence to the contrary is omitted or if the argument fails to rebut an opposing point, the argument is flawed. If the words disparage one opponent and favor the other, the argument is slanted and biased.

Dodging Fallacies   For an argument to be effective, the logic must be impeccable. A writer who misquotes, transposes statistics, misdiagnoses cause and effect, or lapses into hasty generalizations may be perceived as careless, uninformed, biased, or manipulative. Although name-calling, exaggeration, or other blunders may be discounted in conversation, readers are unlikely to be so patient or forgiving. Let's consider two fallacies from student papers:

- The most annoying thing in the world is to pick up the telephone after a long day at work and find a telemarketer at the other end of the line.
- A voluntary national service would solve the United States' problems.

Both assertions are hasty generalizations. Certainly there are greater annoyances than telephone interruption, and no one action could possibly solve the numerous problems faced by the United States. Another common fallacy is assuming that a complex problem results from a single cause. Rarely does a complex problem have only one cause. For example, presidents are often blamed for problems existing long before they took office. The truth is that many factors influence complicated problems.

A final precaution to keep in mind is that an analogy cannot constitute proof. *Although valid analogies are useful for explanation, they prove nothing.* For an explanation of common logical fallacies and propaganda appeals (emotional fallacies), see chapter 19, "Detecting Fallacies."

GUIDELINES FOR USING PERSUASIVE APPEALS

1. **Alert the audience to a problem by using suitable emotion.**
2. **Use restraint**. Do not overstate. Exaggerated appeals can backfire.
3. **Do not circumvent an issue**. Focus your argument on the issue. Answer all of the opposition's points with solid evidence and reasons.
4. **Do not oversimplify**. Guard against either/or alternatives.
5. **Avoid conflicting appeals**. Contradiction undermines arguments.
6. **Show and tell**. Use examples and anecdotes to illustrate and heighten interest.
7. **Read aloud to check for objectivity**. Evidence should be presented honestly without slanting or manipulation. The writer's voice should sound fair and trustworthy.

UNDERSTANDING OPPOSING VIEWS AND OVERCOMING OBJECTIONS

Two landowners were involved in a boundary dispute that dated back to their grandfathers' time. Years before, a rail fence had been erected by one grandparent and moved by the other. At last one man consulted a lawyer. Relating the history of the argument, the client presented one view of the dispute. The lawyer assured him that the law was on his side and asked when he wanted to sue. The client replied, "Never, I just gave you the other guy's version."

Researching both views of an issue provides an opportunity not only to weigh the facts but also to consider the priorities, values, and attitudes of readers who disagree. Sometimes readers may agree with a proposal but not act. Then your first task is to discover the *area of resistance* and determine why they are reluctant. The second task is to prepare a persuasive strategy to overcome their objections and resistance. Once you understand the opposing view, you can decide how to shape the argument to emphasize advantages and benefits.

For example, voters may agree that more money is needed to fund local schools, but they may resist voting for a bond levy. How do you convince them that the proposed benefits justify the expense? An appeal combining logic, ethics, and emotion might be the most effective:

> Several of our school buildings are over seventy-five years old. They are drafty and expensive to heat; those big windows have single panes. The frames rattle. The electrical wiring is inadequate; there is no way to plug in computers. Plaster has fallen from some ceilings. Building now will avoid expensive renovations and save money in the long run, for construction costs continue to climb.
>
> The buildings are also overcrowded. For instance, in one building a class meets on the auditorium stage, another in the lunchroom, and two meet at the ends of halls. The children are distracted by passersby, and the acoustics are poor. The children have no place to put their coats.
>
> Our children deserve better. They deserve a place where they can concentrate and do their best. Our children are the future leaders of this country. Surely, we need to give them a chance for optimum learning. Won't you dig down in your pocket to come up with the extra dollars to make this dream come true? Vote yes for the school bond levy!

1. How much does the audience know about the topic?
2. How strong is their disagreement or resistance?
3. If they agree on a proposal, why are they reluctant to act?
4. What is important to them?
5. What is important to me?
6. What change can I reasonably expect in my audience?

QUESTIONS TO ANALYZE AN AUDIENCE

WRITING A CLASSIC ARGUMENT PAPER

www.mhhe.com/dietsch

For electronic assistance writing an argument, go to: Writing>Writing Tutors> Argument

Long ago Aristotle conceptualized a basic argument structure that is still widely used today. This structure is practical and flexible; it can be varied in numerous ways. Aristotle's classic format can be adapted according to the purpose, the topic, and the amount of resistance to the proposition: Will the audience show reluctance, firm opposition, or downright hostility? By considering their views, you can focus your paper effectively. By using this classic format, you can simplify drafting and clarify your line of reasoning.

Many times it is not enough to research the facts on an issue, for facts alone may not convince. People often act on perceptions and instincts that are not always logical. When a problem arises, you may have a practical solution and all the relevant facts; but unless you can tap into your audience's priorities and needs, chances are your proposal will be rejected. *Careful audience analysis is essential to draft an effective strategy of argument.* (For explanations of audience analysis, see chapters 1 and 24.)

Selecting a Topic

The topic for an argument paper should be controversial and significant. A controversial topic has at least two points of view. To be significant, the disagreement would involve more than a definition of terms or a question of fact that could be easily checked. This means the topic would center on more than a simple question of truth or a matter of personal preference. For instance, to argue that computers can be fun would be unsuitable. Or to argue vaguely that U2 is better than the Beatles would be futile since this judgment hinges upon personal taste. But a paper that contains adequate support and criteria to evaluate the characteristics of both musical groups could yield a logical argument.

Claims of judgment involve an opinion or rating that is significant and logical, resting on facts and reasons. Aesthetic judgments evaluate the worth or value of music, art, and literature. Ethical judgments evaluate whether something is beneficial or harmful, humane or inhumane, moral or immoral, right or wrong. Functional judgments evaluate how well something or someone works. Arguments, including judgments, make five types of claims.

FIVE BASIC CLAIMS MADE IN ARGUMENTS

1. **Claim of judgment.** What is the writer's position on the issue? What are the criteria upon which the judgment is based?
2. **Claim of fact.** What is actually true? (Myth as opposed to fact or updates in scientific thinking might be typical examples.)
3. **Claim of interpretation.** What do the facts mean?
4. **Claim of cause.** Why did something happen? Why is it the way it is? (A valid hypothesis provides the simplest and best explanation.)
5. **Claim of policy.** What should be done? What is the best alternative to solve the problem? Or are there several acceptable alternatives?

Before an argument can be resolved, the participants must agree on a *basic premise* or *proposition* upon which the argument rests. For example, two students could agree on the basic premise that a college diploma should signify competency, although they disagree about how competency should be measured. Since they agree on the underlying belief, a logical argument could be constructed.

To write effectively about a value-laden topic, you must be open-minded, fair, and alert. Topics such as gun control, abortion, and religion carry emotional baggage that make them difficult to argue for three reasons: (1) rarely do the opposing views agree on a basic premise; (2) sources are often slanted toward one view; and (3) you must sift the evidence while keeping your own biases under control. Other topics for argument may have inherent hazards, too. For your consideration, some typical problems that students wade into are listed here:

COMMON HAZARDS IN SELECTING TOPICS FOR ARGUMENT

1. **The topic is too broad.** Subjects should be narrowed to a proposition that can be supported and discussed well in the allotted length.

2. **The topic is strictly informational.** A paper of argument does more than collect information. You strive to convince the reader of a proposition.

3. **The topic is hackneyed.** Sometimes students resurrect old papers or debate notes from high school. An important reason for assigning a paper of argument is to spur you to think and learn.

4. **Adequate support is unavailable.** If a topic is recent, you may find little data available. If a topic is heavily laden with emotion, you may find bias and fallacies in the sources.

Typically, instructors groan when they see old, overused topics such as capital punishment, legalizing illicit drugs, and the like. To be significant, a topic does not have to have worldwide or national implications—it may be a campus, community, or neighborhood issue. Such topics can yield fresh material.

1. Is there disagreement about the subject or an area of resistance?
2. Is the issue significant and challenging?
3. Can I obtain enough factual information?
4. After research, will I be able to thoroughly understand the issue?
5. Can I write about the topic in a fair, objective tone?

CRITERIA FOR SELECTING AN ARGUMENT TOPIC

Gathering Information and Prewriting

The more knowledgeable and sophisticated your readers, the more they will insist on adequate proof of a claim. Yet a writer seldom has all the facts needed to attain a comprehensive view of a controversial topic. To be knowledgeable and objective, you need information from a variety of sources and viewpoints. In the workplace, you may talk to personnel at other companies who have resolved a similar question or problem. You may also consult journals, trade magazines, or online services.

In a college class, you may be asked to take a position on a literary work and write a paper of argument. In that case, you examine the work closely, make notes, think, and write. Or you may be required to do a research paper with text

www.mhhe.com/dietsch
For general prewriting coverage, visit:
Writing>Prewriting

citations and a list of works cited. To focus a search for information, you might begin by posing a controlling question.

Drafting a Controlling Question

A controlling question narrows the search for information and establishes the focus of a paper. This question limits the topic and aids in finding suitable source materials. After you write your controlling question, check to see whether or not it performs these two vital functions:

1. Identifies the *specific* topic and scope.
2. Specifies the *direction* of the research.

For controversial topics, the wording of the question should receive special attention. The words should be fair and objective. Notice how a few words can change the tone of a question:

BIASED: Should students be *forced* to take achievement tests *every year?*

NEUTRAL: Should achievement tests *be given yearly?*

A neutral controlling question will help you to analyze a controversy fairly. Rereading the question from time to time will aid you in withholding judgment until key facts and implications are clear. The researcher who maintains an open mind is more likely to appraise an issue impartially than is one who leaps to a quick decision.

Searching for Reliable Sources

You need to gain an accurate overview of an issue, not just gather evidence to bolster one point of view. Understanding varying views is necessary to shape a convincing argument. To compare accounts and judge credibility, read from several sources. Not all sources are authoritative or reliable. Some may contain incorrect or outdated information, logical fallacies, or bias.

As you select books, look at the back cover, in the foreword, or in the introduction for the writer's credentials. Is he or she an authority in the field? Then scan a few pages and listen to the tone of the writing. Does it sound objective or biased? Does the coverage seem slanted? Do the significant points of the controversy seem to be covered? If you find inconsistencies or differing interpretations, jot down page numbers and authors. These discrepancies should be mentioned in your paper.

www.mhhe.com/dietsch

For electronic help evaluating sources, go to:
Research>Source Evaluation Tutor (CARS)

To research a local issue, you might interview the people involved and read newspaper accounts. To research a topic in a specialized field, consult journals or trade publications for technical information and opinions of authorities. Popular magazines may give brief factual overviews of issues, but the treatment may be incomplete. (Also see "Selecting Suitable Sources" and "Evaluating the Reliability of Internet Sources" in chapter 27.)

Note-Taking and Critical Reading

While interviewing and reading, gather facts, statistics, expert opinion, cause and effect, reasons, and examples that constitute support for *both* sides. You will need to know the points of the opposing side so that you can refute them effectively. If you cannot answer the opposition's points by citing stronger evidence and better reasons, then your argument will not be convincing.

Take care to represent differing views fairly. That does not mean you give them equal space; you condense their main points. Try to spot anything that seems illogical, biased, or irresponsible. Write your notes in the margins of a copy or on cards. For detailed suggestions for critical reading, see chapter 20.

Making Con/Pro Lists You can simplify the task of organizing the chief points of a controversy by listing pros and cons while reading. To separate evidence against and for the proposition, just write *con* and *pro* at the top of a sheet of paper. Then as you read, list proof in two vertical columns, placing parallel points side by side. Leave plenty of white space between items to add notes. Follow each item with the name of the author and page number. This identification will save time later. The lists will resemble those below except that actual points and answers will be listed:

CON	PRO
Main point (Barnes 140)	Agrees with facts, then disagrees about implications (Aker 39)
Main point (Barnes 141)	Objection and answer (Berry 149)
Main point (Smith 33)	Objection and answer (Conroy 12)

Stating a Position

After you list the significant points of disagreement for an argument, your next task is to select the viewpoint you think is soundest. Then write a proposition indicating your position on the issue.

Writing a Proposition The thesis statement of an argument is called the *proposition.* The tone of this statement is usually serious and much stronger than that of an ordinary thesis. To draft a proposition, you might start by rewriting your controlling question, then exploring its implications:

CONTROLLING QUESTION: Since privacy issues are involved, should telemarketing firms be subject to restrictions?

POSSIBLE THESIS: Telemarketing is an invasion of privacy that should not be permitted.

POSSIBLE THESIS: Telemarketing is a legal right that should not be abridged.

Taking a Position of Compromise Sometimes you may not agree wholeheartedly with either view; you see some validity in both views. If you reach an impasse, try a middle-of-the road approach. Can you think of a way to modify your stand with a compromise that is acceptable to you? The examples below may suggest some ideas:

COMPROMISE:	Telemarketing should not be permitted after 6 p.m.
COMPROMISE:	Telemarketing by computerized dialing should not be allowed.

Each time you revise your thesis, check it carefully. Does it say what you mean? Could the terminology be confusing to the reader? Does it need to be revised further? Creating a focused title may also be helpful at this point.

Writing a Focused Title   A focused title acts like a thesis statement, clearly stating the proposition. Focused titles can be quite beneficial. You can glance back at the title from time to time to ensure that the argument is staying on course. A focused title indicates a position:

FOCUSED TITLE:	English Should Be Declared the Official Language of the USA
FOCUSED TITLE:	The USA Does Not Need an Official Language

When an issue is heated, a writer may pose a question in the title to create a zone of neutrality. This zone allows the writer to present and evaluate the evidence before declaring a position in a *delayed thesis*. This *indirect approach* lowers the temperature of the argument and encourages consideration of differences. Although a neutral question title does not indicate a position, it does indicated a persuasive purpose:

NEUTRAL QUESTION TITLE:	Should English Be Declared Our Official Language?

Although the neutral question title can be quite effective, your instructor may specify a focused title to simplify the writing of your paper. When misused, the neutral question title can lead to vague, rambling papers. Regardless of which kind of title you use, understanding the opposing view will assist in focusing your persuasive strategy.

Planning the Shape of an Argument

There is no "one size fits all" strategy of argument. Arguments come in all shapes and sizes, depending on the rhetorical situation. Thus a writer is left to devise a strategy that will accommodate the situation in the best possible way. The structure of a logical argument consists of four basic parts: (1) making a claim (stating the purpose), (2) anticipating objections from readers, (3) countering objections by supporting the claim with solid evidence, and (4) submitting a conclusion derived from the evidence.

FOUR ELEMENTS OF A LOGICAL ARGUMENT

Claim. The specific proposition of a writer is the claim. A claim may be made directly or indirectly.

Objections. Knowing the main points of the opponents helps a writer to answer objections effectively.

Evidence. A writer supports a claim with facts, interprets the facts, and explains—giving statistics, reasons, examples, or other evidence. (The most effective arguments contain an appeal designed to satisfy or benefit the reader.)

Conclusion. The end of an argument is often a restatement of the claim. It may be a summary of main points or a logical generalization. It may attempt to motivate the reader to act.

To organize an effective argument, you first consider whether to use direct or indirect order. In other words, will an early or a delayed thesis be most persuasive? How the four parts of the argument are arranged and developed depends on the implications of the topic and the probable impact on the audience. Think: How will the proposition be received by readers?

Direct Approach   If your readers are likely to be well informed and only mildly opposed to a proposition, you may decide to be direct and bring out the proposal early. Then the thesis can be stated in the introduction. Here is an example of a proposition that would probably meet with little resistance from employees who will readily accept change:

> **Early thesis:** A new system of billing will speed up the collection process and save an estimated $50,000 annually in collection costs.

Indirect Approach   An indirect plan, on the other hand, allows you to delay your thesis until much later in the paper. A delayed thesis allows you to consider the main points of the other side before mentioning your points. This arrangement sets the stage for a congenial discussion. Often it is wise to treat an argument as a misunderstanding or as a difference in perception. This low-key approach is less likely to be perceived as threatening or combative. Any hint of antagonism, sarcasm, impatience, or superiority will undermine your stand. A reader who is patronized or derided may be offended. Negative undertones can sabotage the flawless logic of an argument.

Readers who are likely to be uninformed or hostile will require more facts and reasons than will readers who are well informed. You need to lay extra groundwork for your recommendation. The stronger the objection, the more time you will need to prepare them to accept the proposition. As long as the path of an argument is clear, the thesis statement may be postponed until the body or conclusion.

> **Delayed thesis:** Genetic engineering of food crops is beneficial and safe.

Sometimes, however, a thesis is implicit (unstated). Still, the argument is focused on one unmistakable conclusion. Since arguments with implicit theses require considerable skill, they are best left to experienced writers. Most instructors require an explicit thesis to aid in establishing the direction of an argument. Regardless of the type of argument you write, stress the benefits, advantages, and strengths of your proposal.

FACTORS TO CONSIDER IN PLANNING AN ARGUMENT	1. What does the audience believe about the issue? 2. How does the audience feel about the issue? 3. Which order will be most effective: direct or indirect? 4. What kind of title will be most effective? 5. How much transition will be needed to make points of view clear?

Presenting Opposing Viewpoints   To set the tone for a calm, courteous discussion, place the opposing view *before* your own. This method acknowledges the main points of the opposition and shows that you have considered the evidence. This arrangement is akin to listening, indicating a willingness to suspend judgment. This makes your argument stronger, for it emphasizes your answers to the opposing point of view.

When you are *for* an issue, the argument seems simpler to organize. *You take the pro side of the issue and place it second:*

(Opposing view) Opponents of gambling

(Pro view) Proponents of gambling

But when you are *against* an issue, setting up the terminology takes more thought. The order of the viewpoints is *reversed.* (Just remember that your view always comes second.) To prevent possible confusion in your notes, clearly label points of view and place them at the top of your lists of points:

(Other view) Proponents of gambling

(My view) Opponents of gambling

For help in keeping viewpoints clear, see "Labeling Points of View," page 254.

Block and Alternating Organization   After points of view are clearly identified, you consider whether to present the argument in block or alternating (point-by-point) form. An outline is essential to keep the argument on track. There are two basic ways to set up a controversial topic. The simplest is the block method. This way the main points of the opposing side appear in one chunk right after the introduction. One paragraph is usually adequate for this *summary of the opposing view.* Then in the next several paragraphs, you answer *all* the points raised and submit *evidence* to support your reasoning. The block method has an advantage in tone. Describing the opponent's view first not only conveys a sense of fairness but also postpones disagreement.

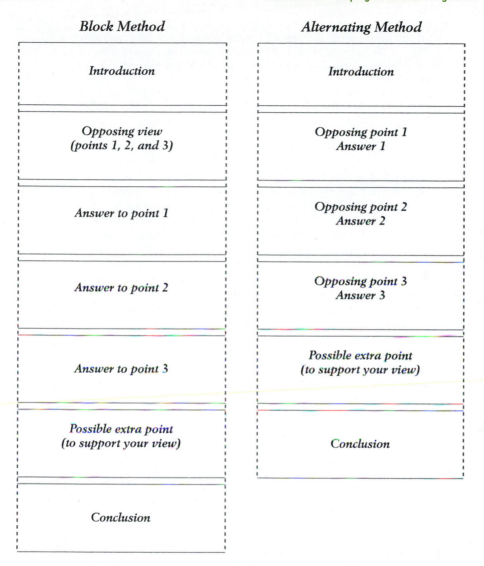

FIGURE 18.1 Ways to organize an argument.

When an issue is complex, the alternating method is clearer than the block method. The alternating pattern pairs one of the opposing points with one of yours, arguing back and forth, emphasizing your answers. (In fig. 18.1 each box represents a paragraph.) A possible disadvantage of alternating is that disagreement emerges earlier than in the block method. Then too, the alternating method requires extra transition.

An unanswered point would pose a serious flaw in any argument. If you cannot answer a point adequately and should decide to reverse your original

LABELING POINTS OF VIEW

If differing points of view go unlabeled, readers may become bewildered. To prevent confusion, identify each view *every time there is a shift from one side to the other.* Four pairs of transitions appear below:

| (con) adversaries | opponents | critics | opposition |
| (pro) advocates | proponents | supporters | sponsors |

Select either *one pair* of terms or *two closely related pairs* and repeat them throughout your paper for clarity. To provide variety, you might substitute *opponents* for *the opposition*. But abrupt shifts to dissimilar pairs would be distracting; the puzzled reader would have to stop and reread. Clarity is more important than variety.

When selecting labels for viewpoints, beware of slanting. For instance, a student writing about sex education called the opposition "right wingers" while labeling the other side "proponents." This mismatch of terms not only lacked parallelism but also revealed bias. Likewise, avoid the terms *liberals* and *conservatives.* These words have been bandied about so much their meanings have blurred. In some contexts, they have also taken on negative connotations.

To maintain an objective tone, try to avoid personal involvement in the argument. Two tips should be helpful: (1) Use third person, not first. (2) Try putting yourself in the role of a reporter writing a news item. This role should help you to distance yourself from the topic and avoid slanting.

position in the argument, it is fine to do so. It shows you have an open, logical mind.

Usually, main points are arranged in least- to most-important order so that the argument gradually builds. The best point is placed last, where it receives the most emphasis. To plan a paper on a controversy, you will find the following questions helpful:

QUESTIONS FOR SHAPING A CONTROVERSIAL TOPIC

1. What is at stake? Is there a hidden agenda?
2. Where is the best spot for the proposition? (Direct or indirect order?)
3. Is a definition needed?
4. How much background information will be needed?
5. Is there a common ground?
6. Can any concessions be made?
7. What are the advantages to accepting the proposition?
8. Are there disadvantages?
9. Will the block or alternating method be more suitable?
10. What is the best way to conclude the argument?

Drafting a Neutral Introduction

The purpose of an introduction is to present a factual overview of the argument. The introduction describes the issue and its origin, cause(s), and history. The introduction tells *when, who, what, how,* and perhaps *why,* defining the area of disagreement. The appeal is primarily logical: the tone is neutral. If readers are familiar with a topic, background information may be brief. If a topic is unfamiliar, the introduction should be more detailed. In the first example below, the writer describes a local problem that had been aired extensively by the media:

Curbing Overpopulation of Deer by "Harvesting"

The rapid growth of deer herds in Sharron Woods and Blacklick Park in Central Ohio poses problems. With no predators, the deer have multiplied to the point where they have stripped the woods and run out of food. Samuel B. Randall, attorney for Metro Parks, estimates that in the 700 acres of Sharron Woods, 375 deer live, which is "10 times the number the park can support." The controversy is over the means by which the deer herds will be decreased. One alternative is to let nature resolve the problem. Other alternatives are to use birth control or to move the deer. A fourth alternative, "harvesting," has led to requests for intervention. Recently, a Franklin Court judge declared he had no jurisdiction over the case (Candisky 1).

In the next student introduction, Pamela J. Van Camp begins with a definition, then gives logical reasons why so many people are turning to alternative medical treatments. At the end of the paragraph, she introduces the element of risk.

Alternative Medicine Has a Healthy Attraction

Alternative medicine is a term that describes nonconventional medical practices such as chiropractic, meditation, yoga, acupuncture, and herbal remedies. In the past two decades in the United States, more and more people are seeking alternative treatment. One reason for this growing trend is that people are looking for effective medical help without the side effects that often come with conventional medicine (Peeke 92). They are also attracted by the mind-body connection that alternative therapies claim to address for their total health (92). Many of the alternative medicine patients are well-educated people who pay for treatments out of pocket (Patel 49–50). Some are terminally ill and desperately seeking a cure even though it may carry a risk.

Finding Common Ground

Agreement sets the scene for mutual respect. A point of agreement or *common ground* increases the chances that a proposition will receive thoughtful consideration from readers who disagree. Common ground can be a shared interest, a belief, an understanding, or a goal. Psychologist Carl Rogers is generally credited with this form of argument, which aims to decrease hostility on a divisive question.

A common ground prepares the reader for a reasonable argument. In a paper about aspartame, Rita Fleming provides facts and advantages before presenting disadvantages:

▶ Nearly "180 times sweeter than sugar," aspartame is the most popular low-calorie sweetener available today. Each year over "100 million Americans consume carbonated beverages, iced tea, desserts, presweetened cold cereal and other products" sweetened with aspartame (Farber 52). NutraSweet has been referred to as a "dieter's dream" since it contains few calories, and many products containing aspartame have been labeled "low calorie" (*Sweeteners* 49).

To settle on a common ground, a writer not only presents facts but also listens to the connotations of words. Ill-chosen phrases can inflame feelings. But tactful words create an air of peaceful deliberation.

Acknowledging and Clarifying Points of Agreement

While analyzing the main points of the opposing view, watch for a way to grant a point or clarify what you mean. To show agreement with the opposition's point, acknowledge it with a word or phrase such as *certainly, granted, it is true, proponents agree,* or *advocates recognize.* Then present the related pro point. The following phrases or similar ones might be used according to the purpose:

- It is true that . . . but . . .
- Proponents realize that . . . , yet they believe . . .
- Supporters recognize . . . ; still they do not acknowledge . . .
- This is not to say that . . . but to . . .
- _____ argues that . . .
- _____ claims that . . . but [include evidence] reveals . . .
- In short, the opponents believe . . . because . . .

Agreeing before disagreeing is not only fair but also tactically sound. Rita Fleming extends the common ground of her argument by conceding a point (italicized):

▶ Many consumers assume that when the FDA approves a product, it is safe for them to use. *True, aspartame has been generally accepted as harmless, and many people use it with "no apparent ill effects,"* but others do "complain of side effects." According to Richard Wurtman, a neuroscientist at the Massachusetts Institute of Technology, aspartame has been linked to "numerous side effects." Some of the most common are "seizures, migraine headaches and mood swings" (*Macleans'* 31, 32).

Refuting Opposing Points

To refute means to show that the information of a claim is irrelevant or just partly true or completely false. In answering opposing points, avoid any hint of disrespect or antagonism; be respectful and friendly. When you show respect for the opponent's points, your chances for acceptance of the proposition will increase. To be convincing, a writer needs adequate evidence. The opinion of just one authority is inadequate; multiple sources are required. Opinion must be substantiated by facts, reasons, and examples. As a rule, the more evidence, the more convincing the argument, but do not oversell.

Select the most noteworthy points of the argument. Use quality evidence. Weak evidence will not support a claim for very long. Careful readers will be apt to spot distortions, omissions, quotations taken out of context, or other problems. There must be solid proof that the proposition is logical, beneficial, and ethical. Only a sound, ethical argument will stand up under intense scrutiny. Examining the two student papers at the end of the chapter will help you see how to refute points well.

Writing a Conclusion

A conclusion is the final nail in the building of an argument. The conclusion should be sound, appropriate, and complete. It should not stray into irrelevancies, fail to take a stand, or end abruptly. It should leave the reader persuaded that the reasoning is valid and worthy of consideration. If action is advocated, the tone should convey a sense of immediacy, a feeling that impels the reader to act. Rita Fleming closes with a reference to risk:

> Although the FDA has allowed aspartame to remain on the market, a look at the history of this chemical raises severe doubts about its long-term safety for everyone. The risks of using this product regularly far outweigh any advantages.

To be forceful and complete, most arguments need a restatement of the thesis. Restatement redirects the reader's attention to the proposition, as in the following example. Kathy Kerchner writes:

> Finally, the use of restraints is a prime concern in geriatric facilities. Research on physical or mechanical restraint use is vague, and more is needed. For many confused residents, restraints are harmful in the long run. If a restraint not only denies freedom and dignity for the aged but also leads to disorientation, then justification for use must outweigh possible consequences. Caregivers should exhaust all other alternatives before applying a restraint and continue to reevaluate its need from time to time.

Kathy's ending is one of compromise. She realizes that there is no one solution for all situations or all patients at all times. Still, she takes a firm stand, pointing out the dangers of long-term use of restraints.

Revising an Argument

Reviewing your outline will help you check the organization of your paper. Could the order be improved? Would any section or subsection fit better in another spot? Reread the paper and check it with the outline as you go. Do you see any discrepancies? This method forces you to look more closely at work that has become familiar. Using a checklist will help you guard against omissions.

CHECKLIST   REVISING AN ARGUMENT

1. Is the issue clearly defined?

2. Does the introduction have a neutral tone?

3. Has a common ground been established?

4. Are points of view clearly identified?

5. Are main points of the opposition presented fairly?

6. Is adequate evidence presented to refute each opposing point?

7. Is the logic sound and ethical?

8. Is the language calm and rational?

9. Does the conclusion restate the position?

10. Is the organization clear to the reader?

In summary, to build an effective argument about a controversial topic, you should (1) define the disagreement, (2) find the area of resistance or dissent, (3) respect the audience, and (4) ensure that evidence is logical and ethical.

TWO STUDENT PAPERS: CLASSIC ARGUMENT

See chapter 29.

Both papers are presented in the MLA format for research papers without a cover page. They are reduced to show proportional margins for an 8½- by 11-inch page. The first paper is by Bethany Shirk, who researched her questions on the legality of high-decibel noise and the effects of noise on human health. The second paper is by Cheryl Pickering, who discusses cockfighting, the legality of this "spectator sport," and the question of inhumane treatment of these roosters.

www.mhhe.com/dietsch

For other student-written arguments, go to:
Writing>Sample Argument Papers

Shirk 1

Bethany Shirk

Professor Nancy Gilson

Communications 112

1 February 2004

Automobile Stereo Speakers: Turn Them Down

The right of United States citizens to turn the volume of their automobile stereo speakers to any decibel level they choose is a controversial topic. Although the federal Noise Control Regulation of 1995 governs noise emitted from vehicles, including "amplified music," enforcement varies across the nation. The law states that "neighborhood noise" is left to local police and city councils ("Noise Control"). In many communities, police have been slow to enforce noise ordinances. Although they have the power to determine what noise is disruptive and to decide what penalty to administer, they often just issue a warning and tell the offender to turn down the music.

Still, some cities have drafted codes that specifically spell out violations and have begun to enforce them. For example, Cincinnati Municipal Code 910-7 states:

> No person, firm, or corporation shall operate . . . [a] radio or other sound-producing or sound-amplifying instrument so as to emit loud and raucous noises or . . . create noise or sound . . . as to disturb the peace and quiet of a neighborhood or as to interfere with the transaction of business or other ordinary pursuits.

Shirk 2

Pittsburgh, Buffalo, New York City, and Chicago have enacted much stricter laws against car stereo pollution. There police can impound offending vehicles and impose expensive fines ("Cut Volume").

Viewpoints of citizens generally fall into two directly opposed groups. Those who drive with high-powered stereos going full blast believe they have the right to play their music as loud as they like. Those outside the car often say the level of sound is rude, unsafe, and threatening to their health.

Those who believe they have the right to listen to their car stereo at any volume are critical of regulations that limit decibel levels. Marc Yarbrough, a twenty-year-old Aurora, Illinois, resident is quoted by the <u>Chicago Tribune:</u> "For police to be harassing people who spend time and money to make their cars sound better is senseless to me. There are much more important things that police should be worrying about."

For some drivers, pumping up the stereo is a form of entertainment. Dallas Wilson, who works in an electronics store and competes in car stereo sound competitions, said, "I will drop the windows, and I will crank my stereo to a point where I can enjoy my music at a loud volume" ("Aurora"). Although playing loud music is enjoyable for some people, many others believe the negative aspects outweigh the positive.

Those for stricter enforcement of laws limiting car stereo sound believe that it is not only inconsiderate but also unethical and

Shirk 3

unhealthy to pollute the environment with unnecessary noise. One group, the Noise Pollution Clearinghouse (NPC) is seeking to advance the "ethic of the commons." They think that noise polluters mistakenly extend "their own private property rights to that [air space] which is publicly owned or cared for." In other words, no one has the right to infringe on other people's rights by making loud noises that disrupt peace of mind and sleep ("Protecting").

Proponents of strict enforcement also point out that sound from car stereos can be dangerous not only to the offender but also to other drivers on the road. Excessively high volume prevents the driver from hearing horns of other cars or sirens of emergency vehicles such as fire trucks, police cars, and ambulances. Thus he or she may not move out of the way. Nor can the driver hear approaching trains over throbbing stereo speakers. Both situations can lead to tragic accidents.

The most common danger is to human health. Hearing is at risk when an individual is exposed to excessively loud noise over a length of time. Over twenty-eight million people in the United States already have impaired hearing, and more than a third of the cases are believed to have been partly caused by loud noise. Hearing loss is not limited to the elderly. Nancy Nadler, director of the noise center at the League for the Hard of Hearing in New York City, says that "Hearing loss is also affecting younger people" (Colino).

Shirk 4

Excessive noise contributes to many health problems other than hearing loss. According to the EPA, various research reveals that high noise levels in humans can increase headaches, "susceptibility to minor accidents," "reliance on sedatives and sleeping pills," and "mental hospital admission rates." Other associated conditions are "colds, changes in blood pressure, other cardiovascular changes," digestive problems, and fatigue ("Effects of Noise").

Many studies have linked noise pollution with hypertension, low birth weight, and impaired immune function (Colino). Arline Bronzaft, professor emerita of psychology at Lehman College, New York City, explains, "A person's pulse rate and blood pressure increase; adrenaline surges. Anything that puts added stress on the sympathetic nervous system . . . could lead to a breakdown of the body's systems (Colino). In addition, William Clark, PhD, reports there is medical evidence that excessive noise has caused heart attacks in individuals with existing cardiac injury (Wilson 77).

Excessive volume from car stereos is not just a breach of etiquette and ethics. It is much more serious. Excessive noise can damage hearing and health. High-decibel sound can also cause accidents involving other drivers on the road. Cities and communities without noise control ordinances should outlaw extremely loud sounds from car speakers. Then police should be advised to ticket those who violate the law and infringe upon the rights of other citizens.

Shirk 5

Works Cited

"Aurora Fighting Cars That Go Boom." <u>Chicago Tribune</u> 26 March

1996: 1.

Cincinnati, Ohio. "Cincinnati Municipal Code 910-7." <u>City Bulletin</u>

14 July 1995: 1.

Colino, Stacy. "Sounding Off about Noise." <u>American Health for</u>

<u>Women</u> Oct. 1997: 64.

"Cut Volume on Whining." <u>Chicago Sun Times</u> 30 Sept. 1998: 41.

"Effects of Noise." 1997. Environmental Protection Agency. 15 Jan.

2004 <http://www.epa.nsw.gov.au/soe/97/ch1/15_3.htm>.

"Noise Control Measures." 1997. Environmental Protection Agency.

15 Jan. 2004 <http://www.epa.nsw.gov.au/soe/97/ch1/

15_5.htm#0_15_5_6_0_0_0>.

"Protecting the Commons." n.d. Noise Pollution Clearinghouse.

15 Jan. 2004 <http://www.Nancy.or/commons.hum>.

Wilson. Brenda L. "All Quiet on the Noise Control Front." <u>Governing</u>

Sept. 1990: 77–78.

QUESTIONS FOR DISCUSSION

1. Where is Bethany's thesis statement located?
2. Is there a common ground in this argument?
3. Is the argument clear?
4. Does she use block or alternating order?
5. Would another order be more effective? Why or why not?
6. Examine the conclusion. What does she do here?
7. What types of appeals do you see?
8. The second entry of Bethany's works-cited list is for a government publication. How does this kind of entry differ from most?

Pickering 1

Cheryl Pickering

Professor Leslie Weichenthal

Communications 109

5 February 2004

Cockfighting Should Be Considered a Felony in Ohio

Cockfighting is a spectator sport that never appears on television. These contests generally take place in secluded spots at night, indoors or outdoors. In a pit or small arena, two roosters are turned loose to fight each other in a fierce conflict. Often the spectators place bets on the outcome of the struggle.

The legs of the roosters are fitted with "razor sharp steel blades from one to three inches long" or curved gaffs, metal devices as much as three inches long ("Facts"). When the roosters attack each other with their feet, the knives and gaffs cut the other rooster repeatedly. Sometimes the gaffs become stuck, and the handlers must pull the gaff out without damaging the injured rooster any further. The fight is then resumed. When one rooster stops fighting or dies, the match is over.

In "Feathers and Blood," Rob Simbeck describes an illegal cockfight that he attended in Kentucky. Not only is the actual fight gruesome but often the preparation and aftermath are, too. Simbeck reports, "Some cockfighters routinely drug their roosters, using everything from speed and steroids to strychnine." After a fight when a rooster is not quite dead, his head is whacked on the edge of the

Pickering 2

concrete stoop, and he is thrown "onto a pile of carcasses near the door" (Simbeck 4).

Cockfighting is illegal in forty-eight states and a felony in nineteen states (Animal Fighting Facts). Randall Edwards and Jim Woods, staff reporters for the <u>Columbus Dispatch,</u> state that cockfighting is only a "fourth degree misdemeanor in Ohio, with a maximum penalty of 30 days in jail and a $250 fine."

Yet Larry Cantrell, a cockfighting supporter, perceives the activity as "one of man's inherent rights." Cantrell was quoted in the <u>Columbus Dispatch</u> as saying, "I believe that man is a superior being. Everything put on earth is for man's use. . . ." Although Rev. David Couto, pastor of a Baptist church in Athens, Ohio, agrees with this basic premise, he disagrees with the interpretation of it. Rev. Couto points out, "Dominion doesn't mean being cruel. Dominion simply means reigning over. . . . Nowhere [in the Bible] can you find cruelty to animals sanctioned." Opponents generally agree that animal abuse should not be tolerated, regardless of who owns the roosters (Blackford and Edwards).

The owners of the gamecocks, however, say it is natural for roosters to fight. Clyde March, a veterinarian and retired professor of poultry science at The Ohio State University, says it is "natural for one chicken to fight another. I don't see cruelty in it" (Blackford and Edwards). To cockfighting supporters, this activity is perfectly normal and should be allowed.

Pickering 3

Opponents of this sport do not believe it is "natural" for roosters to fight with razor-sharp gaffs in a staged confrontation. Sandy Rowland, director of the Great Lakes office of the Humane Society of the United States, feels that "forcing roosters to cut and slash one another to death is cruel and barbaric" (Associated Press). They believe the fights are cruel and inhumane. They feel that cockfighting should be declared a felony, not just a minor offense, and that fines should be more severe than they are at present for people who engage in this activity.

When there is betting of large sums on a cockfight, a fine of $250 and a sentence of thirty days in jail are inadequate deterrents. According to Fred Bailey, director of the Ohio Department of Agriculture, "If you want to stop it [cockfighting], you're going to have to make it a felony" (Edwards). Rep. Dean Conley, D-Columbus, agrees and calls for "stricter penalties" for those convicted of participating of cockfighting (Edwards and Woods).

Animal abuse under the guise of recreation should not continue. Citizens should contact their state representatives and speak out. If cockfighting were declared a felony offense and if it carried higher fines and longer periods of incarceration, then more people would be deterred from watching, promoting, and betting on this inhumane and illegal sport.

Pickering 4

Works Cited

"Animal Fighting Facts." 19 January 2004. In Defense of Animals. 22

Jan. 2004 <http://www.idausa.org/facts/fighting.html>.

"Animal Fighting: The Final Round." n.d. Humane Society of the

United States. 14 Jan. 2004 <http://www.hsus.org/ace/

18708>.

Associated Press. "Over 300 Arrested in Southern Ohio Cockfighting

Raids." News Journal [Mansfield, Ohio] 13 May 1991: A3.

Blackford, Harris C., and Randall Edwards. "Supporters of Cockfight-

ing Say It's One of Man's Inherent Rights." Columbus Dispatch

15 May 1991: A1.

Edwards, Randall. "Raids Are Not Expected to End Cockfighting in

Ohio." Columbus Dispatch 19 May 1991: D2.

Edwards, Randall, and Jim Woods. "Lawmaker Seeks Stricter Penal-

ties for Cockfights." Columbus Dispatch 14 May 1991: B4.

"Facts about Cockfighting." n.d. Art of Cock. 14 Jan. 2004 <http://

www.artofcock.hypermart.net/>.

Simbeck, Rob. "Feathers and Blood." Weekly Wire 12 June 2000. 14

Jan. 2004 <http://www.weeklywire.com/ww/archives/authors/

nash_robsimbeck.html>.

"When Cockfighting Was First Banned in the United States." Jan.

2002. Oklahoma Coalition Against Cockfighting. 14 Jan. 2004

<http://www.bancockfighting.org/>.

QUESTIONS FOR DISCUSSION

1. Is a detailed description of cockfighting helpful? Why or why not?
2. Where is Cheryl's thesis located? Does this location affect the tone?
3. How would you describe the tone of her argument?
4. Where does she begin to answer the proponents?
5. Does she use the block or the alternating method?
6. Does the argument rely primarily on a logical, ethical, or emotional appeal?
7. Is the argument convincing? Why or why not?

FOR YOUR REFERENCE
Argument Essays in the Reader

- "When the Lullaby Ends," Andrea Sachs, page 678
- "Street-Fightin' Men Stomp the Quiet Virtues," Daniel Henninger, page 681
- "Wal-Mart's Big City Blues," Dan Levine, page 685
- "The War on Wal-Mart," Steven Malanga, page 687
- "Majority Opinion of the U.S. Supreme Court in Texas v. Johnson" (1989), William J. Brennan, page 701
- "Dissenting Opinion of the U.S. Supreme Court in Texas v. Johnson" (1989), William H. Rehnquist, page 706
- "We Have No 'Right to Happiness,'" C. S. Lewis, page 692
- "The Pursuit of Happiness: Four Revolutionary Words," Andrew Sullivan, page 696

PRACTICE

WRITING EXERCISE: Examining Opposing Points of View

Directions: Select a topic. Write two paragraphs from two *contrasting* points of view. Separate the paragraphs and indicate the person speaking. Be biased and emotional if the occasion calls for it.

1. *Animal control.* Your town council is considering hiring an animal control officer because of complaints about stray cats, bats, and raccoons. You are a citizen with high property taxes who thinks the officer is unnecessary. You have varmint-proofed your home yourself and cats are not a problem. Next, write the view of a citizen who has had flowers dug up, sleep disturbed, and a car scratched by cats. Raccoons have invaded his attic, and he is afraid they may have rabies.

2. *Deadline.* At 4:30 p.m. your boss hands you ten pages of a draft with numerous red-penciled changes. The typed project report is due at 8 a.m. tomorrow. He plans to revise the last six pages while you correct the first ten pages. You have a dinner date and know the job will take at least an hour. You normally work until 5 p.m. Write your boss's view and your view.

3. *Dental charge.* A busy dentist has a policy that if a patient misses an appointment without canceling, a minimum charge of $25 is added to the bill. A woman who missed her appointment because she took her injured child (who suffered a broken arm) to the emergency room is protesting the extra charge. Write the dentist's view, then her view.

4. *Broken window.* A ten-year-old has just batted a softball through the thermopane window of a neighbor's house. It landed on the dining room table while she was entertaining dinner guests. One guest received a nick on the face from flying glass. Write the batter's version of the event and then the neighbor's.

5. *Ball game.* Imagine you are two reporters writing accounts of the same game. One reporter favors the hometown team; the other does not.

WORKPLACE ISSUES FOR DISCUSSION

1. You do not have quite enough money to buy your lunch. Is it all right to borrow $5 from your cash register and return the money after you are paid that evening? (You will be returning after dinner to work overtime.) Why or why not?

2. Is it all right to use your company's computer to print ten posters for a garage sale you are planning? Why or why not?

3. Is it ethical to use the company computer during work time to send several e-mail messages to friends? To chat online? Give reasons for your answer.

4. Two office mates (one is married) are having a romance that has affected their productivity. Should the employer intervene?

5. In a foreign country where bribes are a part of the economic system, is it all right for an American factory owner to offer a bribe to a purchasing agent? Why or why not?

TWENTY IDEAS FOR PAPERS OF ARGUMENT

1 Should e-commerce be taxed?

2 Should cross-species cloning be banned?

3 Should schools score children on height and weight?

4 Nuclear power: revival or relapse?

5 Should perpetrators collect damages for injuries incurred during a crime?

6 Refusal of insurance: reasonable risk or genetic discrimination?

7 Should throwaway bottles be banned?

8 Should gender selection be outlawed?

9 Should classes for gifted students be required?

10 Should the growing of tobacco be subsidized?

11 Should athletic teams be suspended for repeated poor sportsmanship leading to violence?

12 Should lawmakers overrule courts in life-support cases?

13 Should the legal driving age be lowered or raised?

14 Should sex education begin in kindergarten?

15 Do we need stronger cybercrime laws?

16 Should search bots be restricted?

17 Should in-vitro fertilization be banned?

18 Should "great books" courses be revived in high schools?

19 Should power boats be permitted on environmentally threatened waters?

20 Should children under sixteen be sentenced as adults?

Detecting Fallacies

CHAPTER 19

> Doubt is often the beginning of wisdom.
>
> —M. Scott Peck,
> *The Road Less Traveled and Beyond*

You've probably seen dozens of astounding stories circulating on the Internet, but how many have you questioned? According to one e-mail, Microsoft had devised a new e-mail tracking system to keep Internet Explorer as the most popular browser on the market. The e-mail offered to compensate anyone who forwarded it—$5 for each copy sent on and $1 for each time it was further relayed in the next two weeks. The sender claimed to have collected $800 and wanted to share the good news. To read about such hoaxes, go to <www.urbanlegends.com> or <www.snopes.com>.

To protect yourself from propaganda, deceptive arguments, misinformation, and other fallacies, follow these three precautions:

1. **Develop a healthy sense of skepticism.** Don't believe everything you hear or read. The most convincing lies contain at least a few grains of truth.

2. **Consider the documentation or lack of it (author, place, date).** Lack of documentation should raise doubt about authenticity.

3. **Check out a claim before you accept it as fact.** Can you find the same information in a reputable source?

Studying the chief logical and emotional fallacies will help you to spot distortions in research, as well as daily life, and avoid them in your own writing. *Logical fallacies* often happen in three ways—through omission, oversimplification, and exaggeration. As we appraise an event or situation, we may overlook, ignore, or deemphasize a significant factor; or we may overemphasize another. Then we make incorrect assumptions. *Emotional fallacies* are more easily recognized by appeals to feelings. They contain a pitch designed to override logical judgment.

LOGICAL FALLACIES

Logical fallacies are false beliefs caused by errors in reasoning. Unless you stop to think and question, the errors may seem plausible and persuasive. Logical fallacies can be found in everyday conversation, talk shows, chat rooms, political speeches, advertising, published writing, and student papers. Histories, biographies, and other works may contain distortions, misinformation, or fabrications. There are eight common logical fallacies.

EIGHT COMMON LOGICAL FALLACIES

1. Card stacking
2. Either/or fallacy
3. False analogy
4. Red herring
5. Begging the question/circular argument
6. Hasty generalization
7. Non sequitur
8. Post hoc fallacy

Card Stacking

Card stacking (stacking the deck) is an act of slanting, distorting, or fabricating facts to suit the speaker's or writer's purpose. This fallacy involves misrepresentation, either intentional or unintentional. Although card stacking is unethical, scientific researchers have been known to fudge facts in order to support an illogical conclusion. To save time, they may take unethical shortcuts or falsify data. Or they may select only the facts that support a theory, omitting other evidence. Sooner or later, such practices are generally discovered and discredited.

But what are we to make of polls and studies from reputable sources that report widely varying results? As you gather data, be aware that research methods can be flawed in various ways. The way that questions are worded can influence the answers that are given. Then, too, if respondents are asked to recall data or events, their memories may falter. The size and kind of population samples may also vary, resulting in different responses. Keep in mind that the *sample must represent the general population to produce reliable results.* (See "Ethics: How Can One Be Objective?" in chapter 17 and "Observation" in chapter 30.)

Sometimes students unintentionally "stack the deck" while doing research for papers. They may have too few sources to provide objective coverage. Insignificant details may be exaggerated or significant details underemphasized. Important facts may be omitted through carelessness or insufficient research.

Either/Or Fallacy

The *either/or fallacy* occurs when we assume there are only two sides to an issue or two alternatives for a problem when there are actually more. Sometimes this fallacy is called the "fallacy of false alternatives." Basically, the either/or fallacy presents the writer's view as the only correct alternative. The either/or fallacy is a simplistic judgment that may occur from glancing at a problem and jumping to a conclusion. On bumper stickers you may have seen this fallacy in slogans such as "Make love, not war" and "America: Love it or leave it."

When speaking to voters, office seekers often oversimplify our country's policymaking process. For example, the either/or fallacy is apparent in this statement, voiced by a presidential candidate: "Either elect me and have a truly democratic government or elect one of my opponents and continue as we are." His either/or claim overlooks the possibility of change by other elected officials.

False Analogy

The fallacy of *false analogy* hinges upon an invalid comparison. Just as an invalid check will not clear a bank's requirements, neither will a false analogy clear a test of logic. In this fallacy two cases or items are compared and assumed to be similar although they are basically different. A conclusion that is true for one is assumed to be true for the other. You may have heard someone say, "We tried this before, and it didn't work." But conditions may have changed since the first attempt, or the way the alternative was applied may have counteracted its effectiveness. Two cases are seldom the same.

A false analogy exaggerates similarity, making the comparison illogical and unsound. The fundamental problem with a false analogy is that it ignores a basic difference in the two cases. For example, a few years ago a group of citizens who lived in an earthquake-prone state argued for underground rail systems, pointing out that such systems have worked well in other states. The analogy was false, however, since the successful systems were located in states with little earthquake activity. A false analogy can be revealed by pointing out a significant difference.

Red Herring

The fallacy called *red herring* drags in a side issue to distract the audience from the main issue. This fallacy is rather like the tactic that burglars in old movies often used, carrying steak along to throw to the watchdog before robbing the mansion. In the red herring fallacy, the writer suddenly tosses the reader a "bone," an irrelevant point, to avoid proving the original claim. In other words, the subject is abruptly changed in order to divert attention from the real issue.

Using the red herring fallacy, a speaker or writer attempts to prove a point by leapfrogging to an irrelevancy. For example, "The mayor is a man of integrity; he is a church member and a fine family man." But the discerning listener or reader knows the mayor's church membership and family status do not necessarily prove he has integrity. No real proof has been submitted.

Begging the Question/Circular Argument

In the fallacy of *begging the question,* or *circular argument,* the argument sidesteps the issue. Here the word *question* refers not to sentence structure, but to the subject under discussion. When a question is "begged," it is not discussed. To avoid giving a direct answer, people may hide their beliefs in a thicket of words. Begging the question in this case is simply empty talk that ducks the issue.

Statements that beg the question can be short or long. They may employ phrases such as "everyone knows," "the fact is," or "obviously" when the opposite is true. An example is "Everyone knows it is not safe to swim for an hour after eating." Students sometimes beg the question when writing essay answers on tests and exams. They pile up words in an attempt to disguise the fact they lack the answer—they neglect to provide support.

When an argument avoids confronting an issue by restating a premise, we call it a *circular argument.* For example, "Football is entertaining because it is such an enjoyable sport," or "Irrelevant courses such as ancient history are a waste of time." In neither case has proof been offered. The reader is asked to agree with the first part of each statement. The argument moves in a circle by repeating the claim in different words. The issue is dodged, and the proposition is assumed to be true.

Hasty Generalization

A *hasty generalization* is a broad general statement that lacks adequate support. The writer misstates, exaggerates, or minimizes the facts. Hasty generalizations are assumptions that occur in various ways. Three of the most common are (1) presenting inferences as fact, (2) stereotyping, (3) taking a small or atypical sample of a group and generalizing about a larger group or population.

Hasty generalization can be averted by careful, accurate word choice to reflect the facts. You can identify opinions and qualify generalizations so that they are accurate. You can avoid absolute terms unless adequate evidence is available. When conducting research, you can secure a representative sample.

A hasty generalization may resemble the non sequitur somewhat (both contain inferences), but the hasty generalization does not set up a false cause and effect as the non sequitur does. Nor does the hasty generalization refer to specific instances as the non sequitur does.

See "Ethical Considerations: Writing Responsibly," chapter 3.

Non Sequitur

Translated from Latin, the phrase *non sequitur* simply means "it does not follow." Such fallacies contain faulty assumptions about cause-and-effect relationships. In other words, a cause is asserted for an effect, but the effect "does not follow" logically from the cause. Non sequiturs may use words such as *because, therefore,* and *if . . . then,* and they may be attempts to persuade someone to do something. A student may claim, for example, "I should get an A on this paper because I spent thirty hours working on it and handed it in two days early." But the quality of the paper does not necessarily follow from either of the two reasons offered for a good grade.

Non sequiturs may appear in predictions: "Because Marilyn vos Savant is listed in the *Guinness Book of World Records* as having the highest IQ on record, she would make an excellent president." The fallacy here is in assuming that the chief requirement for the presidency is stellar intelligence. Jimmy Carter, for example, was highly intelligent, but many historians do not consider him to be among the better presidents.

Post Hoc Fallacy

One evening in New York City, so the story goes, a small boy kicked a lamppost. At that moment the lights went out all over the city; a power blackout had occurred. Yet the boy thought he had caused the power failure. This kind of thinking illustrates the *post hoc fallacy:* because one event follows another, the first is thought to have caused the second. But there is no evidence of a connection:

FACTS: Event A: Boy kicked lamppost.
                    Event B: Power blackout.

POST HOC FALLACY: A caused B. (Because event B followed event A,
                    A is assumed to have caused B.)

The full Latin name of this fallacy is *post hoc ergo propter hoc,* meaning "after this, therefore because of this." Although no proof is offered, this fallacy assumes that one event or condition was caused by another. The truth is that the two events or conditions only *correlate,* meaning they exist together but do not interact upon or influence one another.

We have all heard similar post hoc fallacies: Bad luck is often attributed to breaking a mirror, walking under a ladder, or stepping on a crack. And you probably know other fallacies based on superstitions. Hundreds, perhaps thousands, of years ago, these beliefs sprang up because two events happened one after the other. Perhaps someone broke a mirror and then cut a foot severely. Someone else may have walked under a ladder and broken a leg soon after. In each case, the first event was blamed for causing the second.

THE PATTERN OF SUPERSTITIOUS THINKING: A POST HOC FALLACY

Part 1. Superstition: Handling toads causes warts. (A causes B.)

Part 2. Because Shawn handled a toad and the following week a wart appeared on his thumb, the toad caused the wart. (Therefore, A caused B.)

A systems analyst says that his subordinates seldom have trouble with any fallacy except the post hoc. Once in a while a team member will seize on an obvious but incorrect cause for a problem. The member errs in assuming two factors have a cause-and-effect relationship when they merely correlate.

To avoid confusing the fallacies of cause and effect, notice that post hoc involves two events that occur in a sequence whereas the non sequitur has only one. If a statement contains both fallacies, label it post hoc. For your convenience, the following list summarizes the main distinctions between post hoc and non sequitur.

POST HOC	NON SEQUITUR
• Two sequential events or conditions (A apparently caused B)	• Only one fact or event plus an inference
• No proof that the first event caused (or will cause) the second	• Only an opinion, often a prediction

EMOTIONAL FALLACIES

Americans are bombarded with emotional fallacies every day. When we drive past a billboard, open a magazine, or turn on a television set, we are exposed to cleverly planned propaganda. Usually, the propaganda contains emotional fallacies designed to arouse strong feelings and impel us to buy products, donate money, or accept ideas. The propagandists know that if they can trigger strong feelings, then logic may be dethroned and emotion may rule. *Emotional fallacies not only conflict with logical thinking but also interfere with fairness and objectivity.*

Understanding these fallacies can help you to resist them and detect them in your research and writing. This is not to say that all emotional appeals are to be avoided. Some emotional appeals attempt to persuade honestly and fairly.

An emotional appeal may be warranted in an argument, but the emotion should be controlled and ethical. A modicum of emotion may also be appropriate in other kinds of writing. To decide, you need an alert eye and a sensitive ear. Deceit is never acceptable.

In most emotional fallacies, *transfer* plays an important role. Transfer is a device of association that uses the connotations of words and pictures to manipulate our responses. The idea is to carry positive connotations over to products, ideas, or people. Positive transfer presents products in the most attractive way possible with appealing names and surroundings. Commercials for some products, for instance, portray endearing family scenes—perhaps of children, puppies, or kittens. On the other hand, negative transfer is often used in political campaigns to disparage opponents, as in name-calling. Eight common emotional fallacies are discussed here.

EIGHT COMMON EMOTIONAL FALLACIES

1. *Argumentum ad hominem*/straw man
2. Bandwagon
3. Plain folk appeal *(ad populum)*
4. Status appeal
5. Scare tactics
6. Testimonial
7. Improper appeal to authority
8. Glittering generality

Argumentum ad Hominem/Straw Man

In an *ad hominem* argument, a person's character or appearance is assaulted. Name-calling, mudslinging, and smear tactics are all forms of *argumentum ad hominem* ("against the man"). A sly variation of ad hominem uses derisive humor to discredit. A personal characteristic that is irrelevant to performance becomes the subject of joking. Former president Gerald Ford was ridiculed for his lack of physical coordination and former vice president Dan Quayle for his misspelling of *potato*. Neither characteristic pertained to the ability to perform in office.

The *straw man* fallacy, a similar assault, is as flimsy as it sounds—lacking weight or evidence. The argument attacks an opponent or a group with a trumped-up charge or issue that is easily defeated or refuted. A classic example occurred back in the 1950s in a small city in the Midwest. A man who was running for mayor, a retired bank president, was the victim of a whispered attack. His opponents circulated a story that he was an active communist. It was said that he held "weekend 'Red' meetings in a party house beside his pond." When citizens demanded the sheriff investigate, he discovered that the so-called communist meeting was merely a bunch of buddies playing their weekly poker game.

Both *ad hominem* and straw man fallacies are unethical and impractical. The persons who indulge in name-calling, backbiting, and false charges endanger their own credibility and careers. Students who indulge lose points and credibility as writers.

Bandwagon

Another emotional fallacy urges everyone "to jump on the bandwagon," to go along with the crowd. *Bandwagon* is the fallacy of common practice—the "everyone's doing it, so you should, too," argument. Peer pressure is exerted to exploit the desire to belong to a group or to do what other people are doing. The fallacy also capitalizes on the belief that the majority knows best.

Ads and commercials using the bandwagon appeal often show large groups of happy people using the same product and enjoying the results. For example, ads for soft-drink commercials feature explicit entreaties like "Join the Pepsi Generation." The bandwagon fallacy focuses on common ties of family, nationality, race, age, religion, gender, job, or special interest. Thus the propagandist may call upon us as United States citizens, Polish Americans, Catholics, Protestants, men, women, baby-boomers, truck drivers, or members of another group to do something.

Plain Folk Appeal/*ad Populum*

Awareness of the plain folk appeal, or *ad populum,* can be helpful in analyzing your reading audience. For example, this appeal is useful both in letter writing and argument. Establishing a common bond or "common ground" with the reader can have a positive and powerful influence.

The plain folk appeal stresses similarity to ordinary people or the so-called average citizen. A speaker wears ordinary clothing, adopts similar speech habits, and participates in everyday activities to show that someone of high status is just "a regular guy" at heart. For example, Fiorella La Guardia, who gained renown as mayor of New York City (1935–45), spoke three languages. When he visited various neighborhoods to campaign, he would vary his speech according to his audience. As a result, those who heard him felt he was one of them and truly their representative. The secret to effectiveness with the plain folk appeal is sincerity.

The plain folk appeal is seldom a problem in student essays, but you may encounter it being misused during your research. For now you should be prepared to recognize abuses and to apply the appeal appropriately.

Status Appeal

The old saying "Keeping up with the Joneses" illustrates status appeal, or snob appeal as it is sometimes called. *Status appeal* is a pitch to better oneself by wearing stylish clothes, driving expensive cars, taking exotic vacations, or buying whatever a company sells that requires lavish spending. For example, a commercial for a well-known car uses status appeal: "It's the difference between just getting there and truly arriving." Such commercials feature attractive people, dressed in stylish attire, who purchase top-of-the-line luxuries. The implication is that the viewer can be like them by buying and using the manufacturer's product.

Status appeal is the opposite of plain folk. Whereas plain folk can arouse friendly feelings when appropriately used, status appeal may antagonize, even when used appropriately. The applications for status appeal are limited. Unless you are a marketing major who creates advertising copy or writes sales brochures or a business communications student who writes sales letters, you will probably not use the status appeal in your college writing. Nonetheless, you need to be aware of it so that you can recognize it and deal with it appropriately.

Scare Tactics

Daily we encounter appeals that use *scare tactics*. These appeals attempt to manipulate us into accepting a product, message, or person. Often the danger is exaggerated, and other alternatives do exist. For example, some insurance ads use scare tactics to sell policies. One ad showed a mother holding a young child in her arms with the caption "What will they do when you are gone?"

But scare tactics can also warn the public of possible hazards. For example, warnings about the danger of small children drinking household cleaners or the danger of unhooked safety belts are a public service. In some cases, alarming statistics are given and frightening pictures shown (such as an accident caused by a drunk driver) to motivate people to protect themselves and their families.

In research papers, scare tactics are best avoided. A calm, objective tone and a logical approach that stresses benefits is the most effective way to persuade. In a process paper, a legitimate warning may be imperative.

Testimonial and Improper Appeal to Authority

Because Tiger Woods gives a testimonial for Nike apparel, a television viewer may be convinced to purchase some. Other athletes have plugged a variety of goods from shaving lotion to snuff. The *fallacy* inherent in a *testimonial* is the assumption that something is true or good just because a well-known person says so. Never forget that unless stated otherwise, the person giving the testimony has been paid by the sponsor.

Political testimonials for candidates are often given in election campaigns. Although a well-known public figure may endorse a relatively unknown candidate, we should keep in mind that endorsements are a form of patronage, an exchange of political favors. In student writing, testimonials seldom appear, but a related fallacy sometimes occurs—improper appeal to authority.

An *improper appeal to authority* is the giving of testimony by well-known persons about a particular field in which they are unqualified. The so-called authority, lacking relevant credentials, claims something is true. Some instances of this fallacy may be harmless; nonetheless, deception is inherent. For example, when physicians, researchers, or other professionals step outside their fields of expertise, their claims become meaningless. In writing papers, consider the qualifications of the researcher as well as the validity of the claim.

Glittering Generality

Glittering generalities proffer fuzzy phrases that sound good but lack substance. In other words, these vague generalizations "glitter," but have little meaning. A glittering generality contains an undefined term. If people were called upon to define the term, they might respond with different definitions. For instance, what is a "red-blooded American"? The "American way"? "Good government"? "Old-fashioned goodness"? All of these phrases can be stretched to mean whatever a writer wants.

Glittering generalities use positive words to persuade us to accept a product or proposal without thinking. Loaded with positive connotations, these statements stir emotions and cloud thinking. Propagandists often use glittering generalities to appeal to our sense of fair play, brotherhood, or love. They sprinkle their talk with virtuous words such as *freedom, liberty, loyalty, patriotism, progress, truth, honor, justice,* or *fairness*. These words suggest ideals that all "good" people believe in. Glittering generalities play on the emotions, urging us to do something without examining the facts.

CHECKLIST   USING APPEALS IN WRITING

To determine the difference between a legitimate appeal and propaganda, ask yourself these key questions:

1. Is the claim entirely truthful and accurate? Does the writing represent the claim fairly?

2. Does it have the interest of the audience at heart? Will it really protect or benefit them? Or is there a sly attempt to manipulate?

ETHICS: DEALING WITH FALLACIES

Fallacies are dishonest arguments that cheat on the facts or use an overdose of emotion to beguile an audience. Although there may be temptations to resort to fallacious persuasion, this path is unwise from both an ethical and a practical standpoint. Ethically, we have the obligation to give readers and listeners the facts. In the long run, deception is invariably impractical. Chances are the truth will eventually emerge, and the reputation of an unethical writer or speaker will be tarnished.

You may become fascinated by finding and categorizing fallacies, but if you find it difficult to label a particular case, don't worry. Recognizing deceit, manipulation, and misstatement is what is important, not the label. By learning about fallacies, you can develop healthy skepticism as well as thinking skills.

This chapter is much more than an intellectual exercise. The most important lesson is to *apply* your learning. Thinking skills can be applied almost anywhere. Critical thinking is valuable in writing and revising papers, in your personal life, and in the workplace. Critical thinking can improve your self-image and professional image. Critical thinking used wisely can give you *power*.

PRACTICE

SMALL GROUPS: Acceptable or Hasty Generalizations?

Directions: Mark A for acceptable generalization or H for hasty generalization. Discuss your answers.

1. Pit bulls are killers.
2. Women tend to score higher on vocabulary tests than men.
3. Most teenage drivers today are more reckless than those of other decades.
4. Left-handed folks are better at arithmetic than right-handed.
5. Beef is a versatile and nutritious food.

CASE PROBLEMS: Analyzing Logic

Directions: In small groups read the following cases aloud. Then discuss the main points and implications. Decide if the logic is valid or invalid. Give reasons for your decisions.

1. Is there a curse on presidents who are elected every twenty years, in years ending in zero? Since William Henry Harrison, elected 1840, all but one of the presidents elected in twenty-year cycles have either died in office or been shot: Abraham Lincoln, elected in 1860; James Garfield, elected in 1880; William McKinley, elected in 1900; Warren G. Harding, elected in 1920; Franklin D. Roosevelt, reelected in 1940; John F. Kennedy, elected in 1960; Ronald Reagan, elected in 1980 (seriously wounded but recovered). Just one other president died in office: Zachary Taylor, elected in 1850. Which fallacy is revealed in the idea of a curse?

2. After the November 2000 presidential election, Katherine Harris, Florida secretary of state, was disparaged by some journalists for her stand on ballot counting. Robin Givhan of the *Washington Post* described Harris at a press conference: "Her eyes, rimmed in liner and frosted with blue shadow, bore the telltale . . . spikes of false eyelashes. Caterpillars seemed to rise and fall with every bat of her eyelid, with every downward glance." What two fallacies are present in this comment?

3. In an essay entitled "Blue Jeans Are Here to Stay," a student made the following claims. Discuss their validity.

    The atmosphere at business meetings . . . is more casual when people dress in blue jeans. The fact that everyone feels comfortable eases the tension. Conversation is easily developed; ideas and thoughts flow more freely. The second factor that makes blue jeans popular is their quality. Everyone likes the thought of receiving the best value in clothing for the right price. Blue jeans have this feature. They are purchased for reasonable prices and provide excellent wear. . . .

The most influential factor that causes people to buy blue jeans is their comfort in wearing. Most people like to feel good in the clothing they wear. Blue jeans are made to give this feeling to all who wear them. There is an exact size to provide everyone with a unique fit. Then they are pleased with themselves and present a cheerful attitude toward life.

COLLABORATIVE LEARNING: Identify the Fallacies

Directions: Identify the fallacy or propaganda device in each example.

1. As a burglar entered a home, a black cat dashed across the room. The burglar opened a wall safe, emptied it, and continued to search. Suddenly, he was confronted by two policemen with drawn guns. At that moment he realized the cat was a bad omen. (The safe had an alarm.)

2. Mike wrote an argument paper using information from only two sources: a paid political advertisement and three pamphlets from the National Rifle Association. Discuss any problems you see in his sources and the quality of his evidence.

3. Excerpt from a student theme: "The mature person is *continuously* open, flexible, curious, and active." (*Hint:* See a dictionary.)

4. A ninety-year-old woman makes her own wine using whole grapes. Recently she had a minor stroke, but is now completely recovered. She attributes her recovery to drinking three small glasses of her homemade wine daily. Do you agree with this reasoning? Why or why not?

5. Four-year-old Jill Smythe has won twenty beauty contests. Her mother has enrolled Jill at a school of dance, for she believes that Jill will become a movie star. Discuss this path of reasoning and where it leads.

Reading Strategies and Responses to Literature

PART 5

"Reading without thinking is as nothing, for a book is less important for what it says than for what it makes you think."
Louis L'Amour,
The Walking Drum

Of all the books you have read, which one stands out the clearest in your mind? Why? How has it influenced you?

Reading Critically and Responding to Essays

> . . . the unexamined life is not worth living.
>
> —Socrates, in *Apology*, Plato

You may read essays in magazines, on editorial pages of newspapers, or as assignments. In college classes, essays are often referred to as readings. There you read critically, not just for enjoyment. The purpose of critical reading is to explore and examine ideas, to stimulate thinking. You share thoughts and opinions in discussions and write them in reaction papers or essay exams.

To assist you, this chapter presents an overview of essays and suggests strategies for critical reading.

It also provides help in writing a paper of reaction and long essay exam answers. (For further help with exams, see chapter 23.)

WHAT TO EXPECT IN ESSAYS

An *essay* is a short literary composition that focuses on one major idea. Essays range all the way from lighthearted spoof to political commentary to serious argument. Essayists reflect, reminisce, discuss incidents, or argue about daily life, trends, justice, values, and other subjects. Their words may echo nostalgia or disgust, cheeriness or sadness, cheekiness or humility. Often the ideas in essays are universal and timeless. An essayist may marvel at nature's beauty or decry its despoilment, explore humane acts or condemn inhumane acts, search for a purpose in life or wonder if there is one.

Essays are usually nonfiction. They often appear in op-ed columns, meditations, memoirs, diaries, journals, and letters. But some essays are fiction. They may appear in such forms as fables, parodies, or satire. For example, in 1729 after three years of drought and poor crops, Jonathan Swift wrote a satire entitled "A Modest Proposal." The essay raised quite a stir because many people took it seriously. The offending segment follows:

> I have been assured by a very knowing American of my acquaintance in London, that a young healthy child well nursed is at a year old a most delicious, nourishing, and wholesome food, whether stewed, roasted, baked, or boiled; and I make no doubt that it will equally serve in a fricassee or a ragout.

Although the general populace did not understand Swift's bitter irony, "A Modest Proposal" became famous. It is still widely read today as a classic example of satire.

Like fictional works, essays may contain figurative language and symbolism. Sometimes these devices are so cleverly used, the essay may seem like a short story. So how can you distinguish the two? First, check to see how the piece is categorized. In a magazine or book, turn to the table of contents or introduction. Consider that essays tend to be self-expressive and idea-centered. They often express an opinion about a significant topic. Stories, however, have a theme, which is invariably implicit. Rarely is there a direct attempt to share an opinion, as in an essay. (To analyze short stories, see chapter 21.)

PURPOSE OF ESSAYS

The chief purpose of an essay is to explore an idea and reflect upon it. Sometimes an essayist may simply seek a means of fresh expression, not necessarily agreement. Other essayists seek to inform or entertain. Others attempt to persuade the reader to agree with a position on an issue.

Personal (informal) essays often expose a human frailty or condition and attempt to elicit empathy or sympathy from the reader. Some essayists go against popular opinion in an attempt to surprise, shock, or arouse public indignation. Some writers use humor not only to entertain but also to make a point.

Formal essays invariably have an earnest, intent purpose. The writer seeks to stimulate thought and persuade the reader to agree or at least consider a point of view. Holman and Harmon's *A Handbook to Literature* describes the formal (impersonal) essay as having "seriousness of purpose, dignity, logical organization, length. . . . The technique of the formal essay is now practically identical with that of all factual or theoretical prose writing in which literary effect is secondary to serious purpose."

Characteristics of Personal Essays

Personal essays often appear to be spontaneous as they meander in and through a subject or circle it, coming closer and closer to the heart of the discussion. Others move along a time line, narrating an incident. You can identify personal essays by their conversational tone, self-disclosure, humor, freshness, and casual structure. They tend to be subjective and honest, inspiring trust in the reader.

The personal essay is essentially self-revelation. The writer, like a friend, shares personal details, opinions, and biases. In *The Art of the Personal Essay*, editor Phillip Lopate explains:

> The hallmark of the personal essay is its intimacy. The writer seems to be speaking directly into your ear, confiding everything from gossip to wisdom. . . . At the core . . . is the supposition that there is a certain unity to human experience.

Characteristics of Formal Essays

Despite the apparent spontaneity of many essays, the words are carefully chosen for a purpose. Typically, the language of a formal essay is restrained. Cynthia Ozick, in "Portrait of the Essay as a Warm Body" (*Atlantic Monthly* Sept. 1998), describes a "genuine" essay as a "fireside [chat], not a conflagration or a safari." Ozick says these essays have power, derived from an alluring use of language. She explains, "I may not be persuaded by Emersonianism as an ideology, but Emerson—his voice, his language, his music—persuades me."

Point of View and Voice

The perspective of the writer usually permeates an essay, although other viewpoints may be present. The way the topic is viewed affects the voice you hear from the printed page. This written voice may sound informal or formal, humble or arrogant, friendly or cantankerous, cheerful or cranky—just as the human voice reflects a range of emotion. Once in a great while, an essayist will assume a *persona*, a fictitious narrator, to tell a story. To determine how the words should be taken, seriously or in jest, you need to listen carefully to the written voice.

1. Whose perspective is presented?

2. How friendly does the speaker sound?

3. How is the subject treated? Seriously? Sympathetically? Ironically? With sly ridicule? How?

4. How does the speaker seem to feel about the subject?

5. Does the voice seem overly biased? Reasonably objective? How so?

QUESTIONS TO ANALYZE POINT OF VIEW AND VOICE

In "A Ride through Spain," a descriptive essay by Truman Capote, the reader hears a light, conversational voice like that of a friend. Capote writes from the point of view of a passenger on the train. His written voice reveals enjoyment of the experience. The opening and ending of this informal essay appear here:

A Ride through Spain

Certainly the train was old. The seats sagged like the jowls of a bulldog, windows were out and strips of adhesive held together those that were left; in the corridor a prowling cat appeared to be hunting mice, and it was not unreasonable to assume his search would be rewarded.

Slowly, as though the engine were harnessed to elderly coolies, we crept out of Granada. The southern sky was as white and burning as a desert; there was one cloud, and it drifted like a traveling oasis. . . .

It was like a party, and we all drifted back to the train as though each of us wished to be the last to leave. The old man, with my shirt like a grand turban on his head, was put into a first-class carriage. . . .

The train moved away so slowly butterflies blew in and out the windows.

Figurative Language

Comparison in the form of metaphor, simile, and analogy is often used in essays and other nonfiction writing. In the excerpt from "A Ride through Spain," Capote uses concrete images and figurative language, which enable the reader to share the train ride vicariously. Frequent similes ("sagged like the jowls of a bulldog") and other images enable the reader to visualize the trip and to sense the camaraderie of fellow travelers.

Assonance and other devices of sound contribute to the imagery and movement. An example of assonance appears in the last sentence. Here the sounds of the words reflect the movement of the train: the long *o* in *so* and *slowly* slows the rate of speech as do the three syllables of *butterflies* and the phrase *in and out the windows*. In fact, the language is rather like that of a lyric poem.

See chapter 22.

The Power of Plain Words

Many essays are more direct and plainspoken than Capote's "A Ride through Spain." In fact, the words of some may seem stark and unadorned. Nonetheless, the essays attain power as significant details accrue. The secret of that power resides in the telling—the skill of the essayist, not the method. Robert L. Rose, a staff writer for the *Wall Street Journal,* describes the predicament of a young mother in plain words:

Is Saving Legal?

A penny saved is a penny earned. Usually.

Take the case of Grace Capetillo, a 36-year-old single mother with a true talent for parsimony. To save on clothing, Ms. Capetillo dresses herself plainly in thrift-store finds. To cut her grocery bill, she stocks up on 67-cent boxes of saltines and 39-cent cans of chicken soup.

When Ms. Capetillo's five-year-old daughter, Michelle, asked for "Li'l Miss Makeup" for Christmas, her mother bypassed Toys 'R' Us, where the doll retails for $19.99. Instead, she found one at Goodwill—for $1.89. She cleaned it up and tied a pink ribbon in its hair before giving the doll to Michelle. Ms. Capetillo found the popular Mr. Potato Head at Goodwill, too, assembling the plastic toy one piece at a time from the used toy bin. It cost her 79 cents, and saved $3.18.

WHOSE MONEY?

Ms. Capetillo's stingy strategies helped her build a savings account of more than $3,000 in the last four years. Her goal was to put away enough to buy a new washing machine and maybe one day help send Michelle to college. To some, this might make her an example of virtue in her gritty North Side neighborhood, known more for boarded-up houses than high aspirations. But there was just one catch: Ms. Capetillo is on welfare—$440 a month, plus $60 in food stamps—and saving that much money on public aid is against the law. When welfare officials found out about it, they were quick to act. Ms. Capetillo, they charged, was saving at the expense of taxpayers.

Last month, the Milwaukee County Department of Social Services took her to court, charged her with fraud and demanded she return the savings—and thousands more for a total of $15,545. Ms. Capetillo says she didn't know it, but under the federal program Aid to Families with Dependent Children, she was ineligible for assistance after the day in 1985 when her savings eclipsed $1,000.

Uncle Sam wanted the money back.

"Tax dollars are going to support a person's basic needs on the AFDC program," says Robert Davis, associate director of the Milwaukee social services department. Federal rules, and the spirit of the program, don't intend for "people to take the money and put it in a savings account."

WELFARE'S ROLE

Ms. Capetillo's troubles began in 1988, when the social services department discovered the savings account she had opened in 1984. The tipoff: The department had matched its records with those supplied by her bank to the Internal Revenue Service.

Next, the sheriff department's welfare fraud squad went into action. Investigators contacted the M&I Bank two blocks from Ms. Capetillo's apartment and found she had "maintained $1,000 consistently" in her savings account from Aug. 1, 1985 through May 31, 1988.

In an interview that May with investigators, Ms. Capetillo admitted she hadn't reported the savings account to the department. After doing a little arithmetic, welfare officials figured she should repay $15,545—the amount of monthly aid she received after her bank balance passed $1,000. (The assistant district attorney later considered that harsh; he lowered the figure to $3,000.)

But the judge who got her case found it hard to believe Ms. Capetillo was motivated by fraud. Indeed, for Ms. Capetillo, thriftiness had been a way of life. Her father instilled the lessons of economizing, supporting his nine children on his modest income from a local tannery.

After Michelle was born, Ms. Capetillo began drawing aid—and saving in earnest. She says she rents the second floor of her father's duplex for $300 a month (though the welfare department says it suspects she was able to save so much by skipping at least some rent payments). In the summer, she looks for second-hand winter clothes and in the winter shops for warm-weather outfits to snare out-of-season bargains. When Michelle's T-shirts grew tight, her mother snipped them below the underarm so they'd last longer.

"She cared for her daughter well, but simply," says Donna Paul, the court-appointed attorney who defended Ms. Capetillo. "With inflation, all Grace could expect was for government aid to become more inadequate."

Now that Michelle is getting ready to enter the first grade, Ms. Capetillo says she will no longer have to stay home to care for the child. She says she plans to look for full-time work or go back to school to train to be a nurse's aide.

But her round face, framed by shoulder-length black hair, still brightens at the prospect of bargain-hunting. At her favorite supermarket, her eyes dart from item to item. She spots the display of generic saltine crackers. "See that? That's cheap," she pronounces, dropping a box in her grocery cart.

The total bill comes to $5.98, but Ms. Capetillo forgot the coupon that entitles her to free bacon for spending more than $5. She pockets the receipt, and vows to return for the bacon.

After the law caught up with her, Ms. Capetillo reduced her savings to avoid having her welfare checks cut off. She bought her new washing machine, a used stove to replace her hotplate, a $40 refrigerator and a new bedroom set for Michelle. But that didn't resolve the charge of fraud.

Finally, her day in court arrived. At first, Circuit Court Judge Charles B. Schudson had trouble figuring out Ms. Capetillo's crime. To him, welfare fraud meant double dipping: collecting full benefits and holding a job at the same time.

After the lawyers explained the rules about saving money, he made it clear he didn't think much of the rules. "I don't know how much more powerfully we could say it to the poor in our society: Don't try to save," he said. Judge Schudson said it was "ironic" that the case came as President Bush promotes his plan for Family Savings Accounts. "Apparently, that's an incentive that this country would only give to the rich."

THE LIMITS OF AID

Others differ. County welfare worker Sophia Partipilo says Ms. Capetillo's savings raise the question of whether she needed a welfare check at all. "We're not a savings and loan," says Ms. Partipilo, who handled the case. "We don't hand out toasters at the end of the month. We're here to get you over the rough times."

Ms. Capetillo could have fought the charge. Her lawyer and even the judge said later that there was a good chance a jury would have sided with the welfare mother. Even the prosecutor admits that had she simply spent the money, rather than saving it, she could have avoided a run-in with the law.

But for Ms. Capetillo, going to court once was enough. She was so frightened and her throat was so dry that the judge could barely hear her speak. She pleaded guilty to "failure to report change in circumstance." The judge sentenced her to one-year probation and ordered her to repay $1,000.

A few days later, Ms. Capetillo, who remains on welfare, returns from a shopping trip and is met by Michelle. Banana in hand, Michelle greets her mother with a smile and a gingerbread man she made at half-day kindergarten.

"Now you can see why I do what I do," says Ms. Capetillo.

QUESTIONS FOR DISCUSSION

1. Think about the opening anecdote. How does it affect your opinion when you hear the charge against Ms. Capetillo?

2. What is the effect of giving the price of every item down to the penny?

3. To what did Ms. Capetillo plead guilty? Why? Do you think she was guilty? Why or why not?

4. What is ironic about the case?

5. The author tells the story without interjecting opinion. Yet his opinion is apparent. Where and how?

CRITICAL READING

When you curl up with a novel or other leisure reading, you read primarily for pleasure. You may skim long descriptive passages and slow down to savor others. Rarely, if ever, do you take notes. But *critical reading* for college classes and the workplace is much more demanding. Critical reading requires you to think about ideas, ponder their meaning, and consider the writer's viewpoint.

Evaluating What You Read

Emotion can color the perceptions of a writer as well as a reader. When discussing an issue, a writer may not give the opposing belief a fair hearing. The critical reader's task is to spot any bias, illogic, or inaccuracy. This task requires knowledge, objectivity, and awareness of common fallacies and methods of propaganda.

Critical reading requires you not only to examine and weigh ideas but also to consider their implications. With a skeptical eye, you contemplate the writer's analysis, interpretation, or argument—while waiting to form your own opinion. To be fair to the author, you hold off making a judgment until all evidence has been carefully reviewed. With an open mind, you scrutinize inferences, data, results of studies, claims, reasons, examples, or whatever the author offers for support.

A Strategy for Critical Reading

Critical reading can be divided into three stages: prereading, rereading, and prewriting. Throughout this procedure, you will be trying to gauge the *reliability* of any quoted sources, to judge whether or not you can believe everything the author presents.

Stage 1: Prereading   A good place to start is with a brief background of the author. A synopsis of an author's background can give you a sense of the culture and era that influenced the essay, as well as personal information about the author.

- **Read a biographical sketch.** Background material may appear in a preface, introduction, or epilogue. Encyclopedias also contain biographical sketches of well-known authors. Or type the name into a good search engine, such as Google. Examine the writer's credentials. Is he or she an authority in the field? What else has the author written?

- **Look for the date of the essay.** A biographical sketch may yield the year an essay was written. Some essays may refer to events, which can help to determine the year. Then ask yourself whether or not the message is timely or dated. Some essays, regardless of age, remain timeless and *universal.* They continue to have relevance down through the centuries. Others soon become outdated.

- **Read the essay quickly.** To gain an overview and impression, preview the piece. A quick reading can improve your comprehension and retention during the second reading.

Stage 2: Rereading   Take your time so that you can read every word. The purpose of rereading is to examine the ideas and support the author presents.

- **Consider the title and other clues.** Essay titles often identify the topic and suggest an attitude or point of view. Sometimes a title is deliberately misleading. Watch for clues that point to double meanings or layers of meaning. As you read the body of an essay, think how it fits with the title.

- **Look for the thesis.** If the thesis is elusive, look at the first and last paragraphs. Once in a while, a thesis is unstated and implied—with just a hint in the title or elsewhere.

- **Note any headings, subheadings, or italicized phrases.** These spots contain ideas the author wishes to call attention to. Also watch for repetition. Are any names repeated or ideas echoed?

- **Watch for the unusual.** If you find an odd description or an apparent meandering, ask yourself how this relates to the main idea. An analogy or some other bit of symbolism may be hiding there.

- **Consider point of view and tone.** Try to view the subject through the author's eyes. Read the entire piece before making a judgment.

Consider how the writer's voice sounds. Does it seem serious, joking, or ironic? What values underlie the piece? For example, how does the author regard responsibility? Sanctity of human life? Other universal concerns?

www.mhhe.com/dietsch

For electronic resources on prewriting, check out: Writing>Prewriting

Stage 3: Prewriting   Prewriting will help you to question and clarify ideas. You can make prewriting notes in the margins or on a note pad or laptop computer as you read. Later you can use these notes to start your draft.

- **Underline.** Mark the thesis, key points, and any related clues. Then ask yourself, "What is this essay about?" Keep in mind that the first idea may merely introduce the topic. The main idea may come later.

- **Star any definitions or copy them.** Circle unfamiliar words and look them up. These notes will help you to understand and link details in the text.

- **Question.** Place a question mark beside any information that omits significant details or raises doubt. Write out brief questions. Then watch to see if the author answers your questions.

- **Watch for sources.** Does the author provide sources of information cited? If the essay cites research, ask questions: "Who did the study? When? Was the sample representative? Has anything been pulled out of context?"

- **Look for the premise of an argument.** Where is the starting point or basis of the discussion? On what vital point does the argument hinge? For example, the *premise* of an animal rights proposal might be the belief that animals have a right to enjoy their lives. From this premise, the proponents might argue that animals should not be eaten. But opponents might argue that this view conflicts with the traditional belief that humans should rule over animals and eat certain ones. If opposing factions cannot agree on a premise, they will be unable to convince the other side.

- **Write a synopsis or make an outline.** In your own words, summarize the content of the essay in a paragraph or two. Scan each topic sentence so that all key ideas are included. Or if you prefer, make a brief outline. Either technique will help to clarify your understanding.

- **Restate the thesis.** Ask yourself, "What is the author's thesis?" Try to reduce the main point of the essay to one or two sentences. This restatement should clarify the focus.

- **Check out new or doubtful ideas further.** If a reading topic is unfamiliar, find out what other authors have written about it. A quick search of periodicals in the library or on the Internet will usually yield information. If a claim differs from the general thinking of experts in the field, does the writer provide sufficient support to be convincing?

WRITING A PAPER OF REACTION OR ESSAY EXAM ANSWERS

www.mhhe.com/dietsch
For a wealth of electronic
writing resources, go to:
Writing

In your college courses, you may be asked to write short reaction papers and exam answers that *respond to ideas* in essays, short stories, histories, or other literature. Then you analyze the reading and contribute an *informed opinion*. That opinion should be based on facts and reasons, not emotion. A written reaction is expected to be logical, clear, and complete.

Two Types of Reactions

A reaction paper or an essay exam answer requires a thoughtful response to the writer's ideas. The purpose is to present a point of view and persuade the audience that the response is sound and reasonable. In one or two pages, you either comment or argue a point.

A Commentary   A reaction may be a *commentary* that considers *how* the reading presents the main idea. For example, you might discuss the originality of the piece, insights of the author, and the humor, if any; then give your response. On weightier matters, you consider the facts and possible consequences or implications of the main idea. Does the idea have relevance for you personally or for your field of study?

- **Summarize:** *To condense, giving only the chief points.* The purpose of a summary is to emphasize the main ideas and relationships between ideas (see chapter 29).

- **Paraphrase:** *To restate in your own words sentence by sentence.* The purpose of paraphrasing is to clarify, yet not lose the gist or the context (see chapter 29).

- **Quote:** *To copy someone's work and to give credit to the author.* That requires quotation marks and source identification (see chapter 28).

- **Analyze:** *To examine the parts of a whole.* Analysis goes beyond a summary. You may be asked to look closely at the structure and style, including figurative language (see chapters 21 and 22). The purpose is to understand and explain how the author achieves the effect/result (see chapter 16).

- **Evaluate:** *To rate, appraise, or judge.* The purpose is to attach an opinion of value or worth. For example, problem solving and argument require evaluation. (See chapters 17 and 18.)

**TASKS IN
RESPONDING
TO READINGS**

When appropriate, you might allude to historical figures or literary characters or cite quotations. You might compare or contrast, discuss cause and effect, give real-life examples, or organize in any way that is effective. There is no single way to organize a reaction.

An Argument   A reaction is often an argument. It examines, interprets, evaluates, and states an opinion. To be effective, an argument requires specific facts and reasons to defend and support a stand on an issue. Although a reaction paper or an exam answer may not be a full-fledged argument, an element of persuasion is inherent in many assignments. When an assignment is not explained, you may have to interpret it, as in the following example:

- React to the ethical questions Andrea Sachs raises in "When the Lullaby Ends" (p. 678). *Here you are to consider questions of responsibility and of right and wrong. Then comment and supply reasons for your opinion.*

Other assignments clearly call for an argument. They require you to take a position, defend it, and provide logical reasons:

- React to James T. Baker's "How Do We Find the Student in a World of Academic Gymnasts and Worker Ants?" (p. 621). *Do you agree or disagree with Baker's thesis? Why? How do you feel about his tone? Why?*

Those and similar questions are the sort to consider in your reaction paper. Then cite examples from the essay to support your opinions.

Prewriting and Outlining

To expand your prewriting notes, look at your questions in the margins. Did the author answer them? If not, you might raise them in your draft. Did any of the author's statements seem doubtful or inconsistent? Were you impressed by any descriptions or insights? Can you think of further comments to make? Asking yourself more questions will help you to expand your prewriting notes and start drafting.

QUESTIONS FOR PREWRITING

1. What is the main point of the essay?
2. Is the support convincing? Why or why not?
3. Has the writer omitted any significant facts? Are there implications or possible side effects that should be discussed?
4. What is especially interesting or challenging?
5. Is there any aspect I particularly like or dislike?
6. How does the author's voice sound?
7. How do I feel about the values underlying the essay? Why?
8. Might the ideas in the essay be applied to my field of study?

To make your draft go quickly, expand your working outline. If you haven't started an outline yet, just copy your thesis at the top of a clean sheet. Underneath, list your main points. Leave spaces between the points to add subpoints later. If a definition is required, write it on the outline. This framework will establish the direction of the paper. The outline on page 297 was drafted in reaction to a short story for a literature class paper.

Drafting

www.mhhe.com/dietsch

You can find advice online regarding drafting at: Writing>Drafting and Revising

There is no one way to start a draft, but it helps to know where you are going. Look over your working outline. Will you be writing a commentary, argument, or combination? What order is indicated? Revise your outline so that it clearly reflects a suitable order.

Writing a Commentary   To begin a commentary, you can identify the author and title of the work, then add a statement about the piece. (*Tip:* In your prewriting notes, find the one-sentence summary of the author's main point.) When you agree with an author, you might comment on a significant point or statement, the research, or an example. Or you might discuss the implications for you and your future career. The ending of a reaction paper can be brief, just a few well-stated sentences that give a sense of closure.

Question: Define *poetic justice* and explain how it functions in the "The Lady and the Tiger." What outcome would you predict?* Why? [In this short story by Frank Stockton, the main character has a chance to live and marry a lovely woman if he opens the right door. Behind one of the three doors lurks a tiger.]

WORKING OUTLINE:

Definition 1. Poetic justice—goodness is rewarded and evil is punished, often ironically.

Thesis 2. I think the tiger will come out the opened door.

Reasons 3. Why do I think so?
  a. Hints about "poetic justice." (Give examples)
  b. You can't believe the king—or his daughter? (Example)
  c. The princess is "semi-barbaric." (Explain)
  d. Nothing indicates she loves him so much she'll give him to another woman. She is jealous. (Give example)

Ending 4. Allude to "Nor hell a fury like a woman scorned." William Congreve, *The Mourning Bride* (1697) [Give the original source, regardless of where you find the line.]

  *The word *predict* implies a reaction. The question calls for an opinion that will provide a logical outcome to the story.

WORKING OUTLINE FOR A PAPER OF REACTION

Planning an Argument   If you disagree with an author, then you need to construct a reasonable argument and provide adequate support. Before plunging into the fray, list pros and cons on your outline. In the first paragraph, identify the author and title and summarize the issue or controversy. The tone of this description should be neutral. Next, briefly summarize the author's position, taking care to be fair. After that, give your rebuttal, answering the main points of the other side. Cite facts and other logical support. Use a summary ending, restating your thesis.

See chapter 28.

A paper of reaction rarely requires research. Usually, you are expected to study only one reading and draw from your own experience. If you do consult outside sources, however, proper documentation is always required.

Revision and Editing

www.mhhe.com/dietsch

For a wealth of revision and editing resources, check out:
Editing

Before you revise and edit a paper of reaction, it is often helpful to reread the directions for the assignment. Then as you revise, check to see if have fulfilled every one of them. Examine the organization, development, and logic of your paper. Would any sentence be more effective if moved elsewhere? Does more need to be said at any point? Is there needless repetition? Are the words clear?

Read your paper aloud to hear how your written voice sounds. Is the tone consistent with your purpose? Do you sound objective and knowledgeable? Can you find a better way to express an idea? Use a dictionary and a thesaurus to help you refine words so that you say what you intend in a suitable tone.

Edit each sentence with care. Even though you may have run a computer check for spelling, grammar, or punctuation, *proofread your paper carefully*. Software will not pick up all errors, and some packages may disagree with the rules your instructor advocates. Don't guess about spelling corrections—take a few seconds to open an up-to-date dictionary; also check the usage.

CHECKLIST   QUESTIONS FOR REVISING A REACTION PAPER

1. Is the thesis clear?

2. Is the order clear and logical?

3. Do I go beyond a summary and actually contribute to the discussion? Does my opinion sound informed?

4. If I am disagreeing, have I responded to all the writer's points?

5. Is my defense well supported?

6. Are facts correctly stated?

7. Are inferences logical and identifiable?

8. If there are allusions to other writers' works, have I given credit? If I consulted outside sources, are they properly documented?

9. Is my written voice appropriate?

10. Is there anything else that should be said?

STUDENT PAPER: REACTION

A college philosophy class was assigned a short paper of reaction with topics drawn from readings discussed in the classroom. One of the topics was to react to the philosophy of Martin Buber and to give practical applications. Scott Allen discusses the implication of Buber's beliefs for classroom teachers. He presents impressions, draws comparisons, and points out applications.

A Reaction to Martin Buber's Philosophy

Summary/Comparison

   Martin Buber's philosophy, as set forth in *Between Man and Man,* seems similar to Plato's in many respects. Although the philosophers disagree about the source of goodness, they both believe that goodness is an absolute, quite distinct from people. They believe we strive to attain goodness by making wise choices. Buber's philosophy has important applications for teachers.

   Buber feels that the formal teaching of values is worthless. Nonetheless, he believes that the teacher presents a selection from the real world and acts as a model to the pupil (indirect teaching). Buber develops the concept of "inclusiveness," which is the complete realization of the submissive person (i.e., the student).

   To develop the mental powers to make good choices, Plato suggests the [direct] study of mathematics, philosophy, and other disciplines. Plato attempts to outline an ideal society where everyone can live peacefully and develop to the fullest capacity.

Reaction and Implications

   In the educational situation, this inclusiveness means that educators must beware of the dangers of such a relationship. They must refrain from arbitrariness and must exercise responsibility in interpreting the real world to the pupil. I agree: Teachers should consider the needs and rights of their pupils and try to respond in a way that will benefit them. This goal requires not only responsibility in the selection of classroom material but also fairness in grading, settling disputes, and other situations which arise. I concur with Buber's theory about the teaching of values: values are caught, not taught. A teacher should be of good character and should act as a role model for students.

   How can educators accomplish this responsibility? Buber says they can do it by conscious and willed selection. In other words, educators should know what they want to achieve and select the proper means to achieve it. They should examine their basic principles and understand what is happening— not merely what they think they are doing. They must be objective as well as responsible.

   Finally, Buber believes that "Life lived in freedom is personal responsibility or it is a pathetic farce" ("Education," sec. 3). Rousseau, in a similar vein, says that pupils are obliged to develop their intellectual powers to learn a vocation and provide for themselves. Like Buber, Rousseau is greatly concerned about the educator's responsibility of keeping evil away from pupils. This idea of personal responsibility involves intellectual self-discipline as well as physical self-discipline, but it helps us to gain self-respect and stature in the eyes of others. It helps us to find a purpose beyond ourselves—and perhaps that is what life is really all about.

Conclusion

   In short, although Buber's traditional Judeo-Christian philosophy will not appeal to Ayn Rand fans or existentialists with leanings toward Nietzsche or Sartre, I believe it provides an excellent set of principles for undergirding education.

PRACTICE

ONE-MINUTE REACTIONS

Directions: Select one of the following topics or another and write until your instructor tells you to stop.

1. Are you satisfied or dissatisfied with your state's highways? Why?
2. What is the most annoying problem in your neighborhood or city?
3. What is your favorite make of automobile? Why?
4. How would you describe the president? Why?
5. Did you ever get into mischief in school? How did you react?

TWENTY IDEAS FOR REACTION PAPERS

All of the essays mentioned below are located in the Reader. Or you may prefer to react to another essay of your choice.

1 React to Deborah Tannen's "Gender Gap in Cyberspace." Do you agree or disagree? Why? Can you cite examples you have seen?

2 React to the analogy in Liane Norman's "Pedestrian Students and High-Flying Squirrels."

3 Respond to "Road Rage." Have you ever experienced a similar incident? What did you do?

4 React to "Mind over Munchies" and Brown's treatment of the topic.

5 React to James T. Baker's "How Do We Find the Student?" Comment on the perspective of the author. Do you agree or disagree? Why?

6 React to Phillip Lopate's "A Nonsmoker with a Smoker." How do you feel about banning smoking? Why?

7 Respond to Barbara Jordan's "Becoming Educated." What does an education mean to you?

8 Respond to Euell Gibbons's "How to Cook a Carp." What do you think of his method of fishing? Would you have been willing to taste all the dishes?

9 Respond to "Mother Tongue," by Amy Tan. Summarize her conclusions. Do you think her experience was unique, or does it have widespread implications? Why?

10 In "The Handicap of Definition," William Raspberry discusses the effects of stereotypes on black children. Do you agree or disagree with his thesis that we define our success by our beliefs and goals? Why?

11 React to "Why Marriages Fail," by Ann Roiphe. Can you cite any other reasons that marriages fail? Can you expand on Roiphe's points?

12 React to Daniel Henninger's "Street Fightin' Men Stomp the Quiet Virtues."

13 React to Andrea Lee's "Black and Well-to-Do." You might comment on the effect her sheltered lifestyle had upon her.

14 React to "We Have No 'Right to Happiness.'" What is C. S. Lewis's real point? Do you agree or disagree? Why?

15 React to Jean Huston's "The Art of Acknowledgment." Have you ever had a similar experience? How did you cope?

16 Select any other essay you wish and react to it.

17 Scan newspapers, magazines, or electronic bulletin boards for positions on political or educational issues, and react to one.

18 Has a poem, story, or other piece of literature caused you to ponder an aspect of your life? Might you find a topic there?

19 Describe your reaction to a hardship as a child. Has your perception changed over the years? If so, how?

20 React to a local zoning decision, traffic routing, or other concern.

Reading and Responding to Short Stories, Novels, and Plays

Genuine literature informs while it entertains. It manages to be both clear and profound.

—"Author's Note,"
*The Collected Stories
of Isaac Bashevis Singer*

Why do we read literature? The written word can be far more alluring than a video or movie screen. Literature challenges us to create a world on the screen of the mind. There we can meet intriguing characters, participate in an exciting plot, explore new ideas and sensations. We can watch and wonder about the unfamiliar and untried without undergoing the risks of reality. We can laugh at the foolishness and smile at the cleverness of human behavior and thought.

Literature often strips away pretenses that disguise intentions, motives, and values. It can help us to distinguish the insignificant from the significant. By sharing moments of human experience, we are prompted to reflect on the shape and direction of our own lives.

THE HUMAN CONDITION

Literature encourages us to think and consider concerns that arise from the *human condition*, which all people experience. Regardless of our culture, race, or creed, we share universal concerns: We wonder about the purpose of life and other vital questions:

- What is happiness?
- What is really worthwhile?
- What responsibilities do we have for each other? For animals? For planet earth?
- What causes conflict between people who love each other?
- Should I risk danger to protect someone else's life?
- What is ethical?
- What is moral—or do I really care?

THE ROLE OF THE READER

Many people assume a literary work has a single meaning or interpretation. The truth is that there is no one right answer about what a work means. Often a piece of literature is subtle, containing meanings of which even the author is unaware. Meaning is not limited to the text of a work; the reader plays an active role. As we read, we view ideas through our own window of experience—interpreting, inferring, evaluating—creating meaning. Our view is colored by our individual perception of the world, the topic, the treatment of the text, and the voice of the narrator.

Although readers create meaning to some extent, this is not an invitation to pull a passage out of context and distort it. To be valid, an interpretation must be supported by evidence and logical reasoning. This chapter explains an analytical approach that is applicable to short stories, novels, and plays.

How Do Short Stories Differ from Novels?

Since short stories have just a few pages for the action to unfold, every word must count. Descriptions and images must be pared to the essential. Time in a short story is constricted, often to a week or a day or less. There are few characters, and the reader is seldom told much about them. Most of the meaning is implicit, to be derived by the reader, who examines the juxtaposition of events, symbols, phrasing, or dialogue.

Sometimes the meaning is puzzling upon a first reading. The reader must be alert for clues cleverly concealed throughout the plot. Often plain, seemingly ordinary little stories are not ordinary at all; they contain clues that reveal surprising intensity and depth. Although similar clues exist in novels, the clues are seldom so important to the meaning as in the short story.

What Are the Major Characteristics of Novels?

A novel generally covers a much longer period than a short story or play. Novels of epic proportions may chronicle the life of the main character and the lives of descendants over several generations. Divided into chapters, novels usually have complex plots and subplots with several characters. The main characters tend to be well developed; the reader learns of their quirks and peers into their personal lives. The action may take place in various locales, often far-flung. Yet the skillful author weaves all the elements together into a compelling tale that has unity and coherence.

The opening of a novel may contain lengthy description and proceed at a slower pace than that of a short story or a play, where the action begins at once. The leisurely pace of some novels is due to the narrator's revelations about characters and a smaller percentage of dialogue. Once the conflict is introduced and the main character is beset with a problem, decision, or moral dilemma, the pace of the novel picks up. In the latter half, conflict builds to a climax, and the situation is usually resolved.

How Does Reading a Play Differ from Reading a Novel?

Plays are meant to be seen and heard. When you read a play, you are more or less on your own. Reading a play is rather like using a flashlight to view the action instead of watching it performed on a well-lit stage. You can't see the expressions on the faces of the characters or hear the intonations in their voices. In a novel there is a narrator who usually drops hints or explains from time to time. In a play there is usually no narrator.

Plays are often divided into one to three acts, which are divided into scenes. An introduction may precede the first act. Never skip this opportunity to preview the background, the plot, or other aspects. If the author is well known, you can consult an encyclopedia or look for a biography or a review of the play. Otherwise, you are handed only a list of characters before the action begins.

Scenes may shift abruptly with only a note such as "Venice. A street." Entrances, exits, and other sparse notes appear at intervals in parentheses. As you read, you are forced to rely chiefly on the words of the characters, which may be deceptive. A character may not tell the truth, or the words of the play may be from a different era. Shakespeare, for example, often uses common words, but they may have different meanings and connotations than do the same words today. Therefore, the reader is often obliged to interrupt the passage and consult a footnote to understand.

At times it is helpful to read puzzling bits of dialogue aloud and try to imagine the action in your mind's eye. What seems to be happening? Watch for subtleties and layers of meaning. Consider the craftsmanship of the play. Three important features to keep in mind are—

- **Sequencing of scenes.** How do scenes vary? For example, comedy may slow the pace in one scene, and a battle may rage in the next, as in *Henry IV.*
- **Character development.** What motivates the characters? Power? Greed? Love? What? Do they change? How?
- **Unveiling of the theme.** When does the theme become apparent? What is implied about the human condition? How would you state the theme?

Genre	Length	Plot	Span	Characters	Narrator
1. *Short story*	1–40 pp.	compact	1 day– a week	few	yes
2. *Novel*	150– 850 pp.	complex	may be years	many	yes
3. *Play*	2–3 hours (to view)	varies	1 day– a month	varies	rarely

FIGURE 21.1 General characteristics of three genres.

ELEMENTS OF LITERATURE

Despite obvious differences, short stories, novels, and plays have much in common. All three genres of literature usually consider some facet of the human condition. All have unity—a central idea and a pattern of development. And all can be analyzed according to seven basic elements: point of view, setting, plot, characters, symbolism, irony, and theme.

Point of View

See pages 288–89.

The outlook or *point of view* from which a work is told influences the effect of the story, novel, or play. Point of view is revealed through the narrator's voice or the voices of the characters. That means that the narrator's voice is *not* the voice of the author. The narrator may be one of the characters or someone outside the work. When the story is presented through the eyes of *a* character, you gain an *inside* view. You have access to one person's thoughts and observations. F. Scott Fitzgerald's *The Great Gatsby* opens with the narrator reminiscing in first person (italicized):

In *my* younger and more vulnerable years *my* father gave *me* some advice that *I've* been turning over in *my* mind ever since.

"Whenever you feel like criticizing any one," he told *me*, "just remember that all the people in this world haven't had the advantages that you've had."

He didn't say any more, but *we*'ve always been unusually communicative in a reserved way, and *I* understood that he meant a great deal more than that. In consequence, *I*'m inclined to reserve all judgments, a habit that has opened up many curious natures to *me* and also made *me* the victim of not a few veteran bores.

See page H-3.

Note that a first-person narrator observes or participates in the action. A third-person narrator, however, is outside the action. Usually, a third-person narrator enters the mind of just one character. But a third-person narrator with *limited omniscience* enters the minds of several characters. Sometimes a third-person narrator is *omniscient,* or all-knowing. You might think of an omniscient narrator as standing on a hill, looking down into the lives and minds of the characters, seeing everything that goes on.

Gauging the accuracy and truthfulness of a narrator, particularly one who is a character, is not always simple. Like human beings, characters may misjudge, understate, overstate, or deceive.

Setting

The time, place, atmosphere, weather, and culture make up the *setting.* Included in setting are the objects and articles the characters have and use. Symbolism is often intermingled with setting to create a mood. For example, Thomas Hardy's novels take place on wild and stormy moors, which set the scene for passion and outbursts of temper. Savvy readers know that the storms are omens of stormy relationships or tragic events.

As you read, note the setting of each action and the implications. Consider the area, time of year, and weather, all of which create a mood. What objects are present? What family, social, political, or religious obligations or conditions exist? How do they influence the plot and characters?

Plot

The series of actions and events that occur in a narrative make up the *plot.* Broadly defined, plot includes not only physical action but also words and thoughts. Conflicts arise not only from circumstance but also from human motivation. The main character may face an opponent or an impediment to a goal. The *conflict* may involve another individual, a natural force, an animal, or fate. Or the character may experience an *internal conflict* over ethical or moral issues.

Plots may move straight ahead, twist and turn, or pause for a *flashback* to a scene that happened before the story opened. Suspense increases as the turmoil caused by the conflict rises to a *climax,* the high point of the action. The ending may reveal a discovery or a reversal in the main character's fate, resulting in misfortune or success. Or the ending may resolve a problem between two enemies, imply a theme, or foreshadow a future event.

Sometimes plots are structured as letters, diaries, or other "found" writings. In Daniel Keyes's *Flowers for Algernon,* the main character, a mentally handicapped man named Charley, is asked by his doctor to prepare progress reports during the course of an experimental treatment. Early entries begin on a rudimentary level in Charley's diary:

progris riport 2—march 6

Dr. Strauss says I shud rite down what I think and evrey thing that happins to me from now on. I dont know why but he says its importint so they will see if they will use me. I hope they use me. Miss Kinnian says maybe they can make me smart. I want to be smart. My name is Charlie Gordon. I am 37 years old and 2 weeks ago was my birthday. I have nuthing more to rite now so I will close for today.

This early entry reveals not only Charley's low level of understanding and education but also his desire to learn. Although Charley is unable to explain what is happening, the phrase "use me" suggests to the alert reader that Dr. Strauss's purpose may not be in Charley's best interest. After surgery and intensive training, Charley's intelligence and learning escalate—revealed by later diary entries that are longer and more explicit. Toward the end, as Charley deteriorates, the concluding entries parallel his deterioration.

Foreshadowing   When authors use *foreshadowing* in a plot, they scatter clues that hint of events to come. In *Flowers for Algernon*, Algernon the mouse and Charley have the same operation. When Algernon's condition worsens, the alert reader suspects that Charley will suffer the same fate. The drastic changes in Algernon foreshadow the plot's irrevocable conclusion.

Characters

To seem realistic, characters are endowed with certain qualities and quirks. They may be portrayed as primarily good or evil, weak or strong, serious or fun-loving. Major characters are usually revealed indirectly through behavior whereas minor characters tend to be revealed directly through explanation. *Round characters* change and mature; they learn from events and circumstances. *Flat characters*, usually minor characters, do not change or grow. They may lack insight, remaining unaware and insensitive.

As you read, assess the characters. Do they seem true to life or stereotypic? Real people exhibit a blend of many traits. Do the characters act predictably or inconsistently? Are inconsistent acts explainable through motivation? Not every character needs to be well developed, but all need to have a reason for their existence.

Symbolism

A *symbol* may be a name, person, place, object, action, or situation that represents something else. In other words, a symbol has a significant meaning beyond the literal meaning. For example, if a character named Cain lives in the small town of Eden, there is probably an idyllic meaning attached to the locale, and other related clues may appear.

Public symbols are widely known and understood, such as our national flag, various commercial logos, and many religious symbols. Water is universally regarded as a symbol both of purification and of life. A bubbling fountain may represent youth and optimism. A stagnant pond may symbolize contamination or ebbing of life. The condition of water may also symbolize the status of a relationship: Lovers may meet by a placid lake, a river with rapids, or aboard ship on a storm-tossed sea. Or there may be *private symbols,* limited to the one work. When you think something might be a symbol, place a question mark beside it. Or if you understand the symbol, make a note.

Irony

Irony exists when something is inconsistent with what is apparent or believed and what is real. Irony consists of a discrepancy between expectations and reality. Sarcasm is a form of *verbal irony;* a character says one thing but means another. Using *dramatic irony,* a writer reveals to readers something that the characters do not know, which creates suspense. *Situational irony* refers to an event that is contrary to what is expected (often painfully so). The unexpected event may be a wry twist of the plot, as often found in the stories of Edgar Allan Poe or the films of Alfred Hitchcock. Sometimes the villain or central character is faced with an unanticipated and deserved dilemma of his or her own making.

Writers often use irony to suggest human fallibility—vanity, unwise judgment, and other limitations that keep us from recognizing the truth around us. Such susceptibility to error is at its most extreme in *cosmic irony,* or irony of fate. Cosmic irony is prevalent in Greek tragedies and other writings; the gods or destiny seem to control events so as to test and frustrate the protagonist.

Theme

The main idea or message embodied in a work of literature is called the *theme.* Some works have more than one theme. Theme reflects a universal belief about human life or the human condition. Theme may concern good or evil, love or hate, modesty or pride, beliefs or values.

More often than not, theme is implicit. Theme can be implied through a series of events, actions, or dialogue. Theme may be revealed as an observation, insight, doctrine, or general principle by a character or the narrator. For example, a devout character might murmur, "Evil has its own reward," meaning "Evil will be punished, sooner or later." In much modern literature, themes are complex and cannot be reduced to a simple moral or proverb. Theme is the common thread that unifies the other elements of literature; theme establishes order and coherence.

Figurative Language and Literary Devices

A figure of speech has a special meaning and construction that deviates from standard use of the language. *Similes* and *metaphors* are figures of speech that are unusual comparisons. Similes contain *like* or *as;* metaphors do not (for extensive examples, see the index). *Personification,* another common figure of speech, is the giving of human attributes to an object, abstraction, or animal. For example, the animals in George Orwell's *Animal Farm* represent people.

Special effects can be achieved with words by using *onomatopoeia, alliteration,* and *assonance.* These literary devices can emphasize and smooth phrases, as well as enhance the sound of words. All three devices are explained in chapter 22, since they are so often incorporated into poetry (see the analysis of a poem on pages 334–35).

READING AND TAKING NOTES ON A LITERARY WORK

To prepare for a paper in response to a literary work, you might mark the pages as you read, making notes in the margins. Or if you do not own the book, use a pack of file cards or large Post-its. Write a key phrase and page number across the top of the card or Post-it. Insert the note card so that it protrudes from the top of the book. Or stick your Post-it notes on pages as tabs. To start, consider these questions:

1. **Does anything seem *odd?*** If so, note with a question mark.

2. **Does the title contain a clue?** Is there a hint in the title?

3. **Is anything repeated or similar?** Watch for repetition and echoes of ideas. Note relationships and links to the central idea.

4. **Do you notice any symbolism?** Consider the setting and objects mentioned.

5. **What might the names mean?** Look up the origin and meaning of *names* of people, trains, ships, or other objects. Names often tie into the theme. If you can't find a book on names at the library, buy a paperback such as *10,000 Baby Names,* by Bruce Lansky.

6. **What motivates the main character?** What is the character seeking? Wealth? Power? Fame? Love? What? Jot down clues to motivation as you read.

7. **Do you notice any objects or anything else that might act as a symbol?** Look closely at the names of characters and places. Are there any other clues?

8. **Examine the dialogue.** What does it reveal about a character?

9. **Consider point of view.** Who is the narrator? How is the story told?

10. **Consider the ending.** Does it seem satisfactory and complete? How does the ending fit with the title and the opening?

PREPARING AN ANALYSIS OF LITERATURE

When your instructor assigns a paper of analysis, sometimes called a "paper of explication," select a topic that interests you, one that you understand. You can discuss point of view, setting, plot, characterization, symbolism, irony, theme, or a combination. You might compare and contrast two characters in one work, or compare the central characters of two works. Or you might discuss a combination of elements. An analytical paper comments on the form as well as the content of the work. You interpret meaning and estimate the significance of what happens.

To achieve a valid interpretation, look at events, actions, and clues—a chain of evidence upon which to base your thesis. Your discussion of the elements should fit the total context. The best interpretations consider the entire work and offer an explanation of passages that may seem contradictory or inconsistent. You might begin by examining the element(s) you selected as a topic. How does it influence the the work? As you write, observe three precautions:

1. **Avoid giving the impression that there is only one valid interpretation of a work.** Shun phrases such as "obviously" and "it is evident that." Use tentative words to leave the interpretation open to other possibilities.

2. **Analyze the work objectively.** Veto any inclination to give harsh criticism or sweet adoration. Be fair.

3. **Don't speculate about an author's intent.** A work may have a significance that the author was unaware of while writing, so don't attempt to mind-read. Instead, discuss the total effect. Describe the impression that is created. Supply reasons and examples.

suggests	suggesting	implies
indicates	indicating	signals
possibly	apparently	foreshadows
probably	may	represents
not entirely	seems	appears
hints	connotes	gesture
symbolizes	clue	sign

TENTATIVE WORDS FOR INTERPRETING LITERATURE

Writing about Point of View

A narrator may describe the story from inside or outside the action. The following example from a student paper focuses on the perspective of a lonely narrator who is outside the family circle and other groups, looking in. Gradually, the perspective of *The Grass Harp* changes, and the development of the central character, Collin, changes, too.

> *The Grass Harp*, by Truman Capote, is a beautifully written and sensitive account of a young boy, Collin, who becomes an orphan at age eleven. Collin goes to live with two aged cousins until he is eighteen. The novella chronicles the changes that occur in his life and the lives of people close to him. Written in first person with Collin as the narrator, the perspective of the book is cleverly done.
>
> Collin is a shy boy who does not make friends easily and who remains on the outer fringes of most groups. He literally stays outside the action, a spectator most of the time. In the Talbo household, he lives with his cousins, Dolly and Verena, and the black maid, Catherine. Collin spends much of his time up

in the attic, peering down through a knothole and cracks at the activities going on below. When the story opens, Collin is outside the action not only physically but also emotionally.

Collin is again a spectator when Riley Henderson, whom Collin greatly admires, confesses he is miserable. Riley would have killed himself if it were not for the responsibility of caring for his younger sisters. . . .

When Sister Ida invites the Judge and Dolly to go away with her, Collin feels left out, just as he has many times before; again he is on the outside of a circle, peering in. Again he is a spectator as he peers through a window at Riley, who is now his best friend and who is kissing a girl.

But later there are moments when Collin is accepted and moments when he is able to become an active participant. . . .

To start your prewriting notes on point of view, answer the questions in the checklist below after you complete your reading.

CHECKLIST   QUESTIONS FOR ANALYZING POINT OF VIEW

1.   Who is telling the story?

2.   Is the voice of the narrator consistent, or does it change? If it changes, how?

3.   How reliable is the narrator?

4.   Should the narrator be taken literally? Or is the piece a satire, tall tale, legend, myth, fable, or parable?

5.   Where is the narrator? Inside or outside the action? How does this perspective influence the plot, character, or theme?

Writing about Setting

To write about setting, specify the chief features of the place and time (era). Look for changes and contrasts in setting and wonder about their meaning. For example, if you were writing about *The Old Man and the Sea,* by Ernest Hemingway, you might examine how setting isolates the main character. You could explain how the old man copes with isolation and achieves a qualified success. Although you would also refer to plot, character, and symbolism, the focus would be on setting. Now let's take a look at how Hemingway sets the scene, introduces the main character, and prepares for the dramatic action of the novel all in one paragraph:

He was an old man who fished alone in a skiff in the Gulf Stream, and he had gone eighty-four days now without taking a fish. In the first forty days a boy had been with him. But after forty days without a fish the boy's parents had told him that the man was now definitely and finally *salao,* which is the worst form of unlucky, and the boy had gone at their orders in another boat which caught three good fish the first week. It made the boy sad to see the old man come in each day with his skiff empty and he always went down to help him carry either the coiled lines or the gaff and harpoon and the sail that was furled around the mast. The sail was patched with flour sacks and, furled, it looked like the flag of permanent defeat.

After you have taken notes on setting, you might reread them and write a quick draft, commenting on cause and effect and emphasizing your main idea. This exercise will spur thinking and should yield an overview of your forth-coming paper.

EXAMPLE OF A QUICK DRAFT

Hemingway's *The Old Man and the Sea* begins in a poor fishing village off the Gulf Stream. There superstition influences the thought and behavior of many residents, but not the old man. The belief in *salao,* or bad luck, has isolated him. Because he has had bad luck in fishing, going eighty-four days without a good fish, he is shunned. The old man has even been separated from his for-mer companion, the boy.

Alone on his skiff, the old man sits with his tattered flag and patched sail, which seem to be symbols—the sail "looked like a flag of permanent defeat." Two similarities between the boat and the old man stand out: both are old and both appear dysfunctional. Yet these appearances are deceiving. Despite the isolation and hardships imposed by weather, sea, and sharks, both en-dure. The old man continues his quest for a huge fish. Determined to succeed at any cost, he will not accept defeat.

Notes:

1. Need to discuss changes in setting at sea and effects on old man and the skiff.

2. Are sharks part of the setting? Not characters; must be setting.

3. Describe condition of the skiff, big fish, and old man when he returns to the harbor.

4. Is anything ironic?

5. What else should be mentioned?

CHECKLIST   **QUESTIONS FOR ANALYZING SETTING**

1. What in the setting is particularly significant? Features of the landscape? Time of year? Weather? What?

2. Do any parts of the setting seem to be symbolic?

3. How does setting contribute to the tone or mood?

4. Does the setting change? How does this influence the plot and the characters?

5. Do you notice any foreshadowing?

Writing about Plot

An analysis of plot is usually combined with one or more of the other elements of literature. The examples that follow are from an analysis of a novel. The stu-dent writer discusses plot, character, and theme. The title alludes to a nursery rhyme character, as explained in the opening sentence. The ending also hints at the analogy.

▶

Men, Chicks, and Eggshells

Introduction

Willie Stark, the main character of *All the King's Men,* by Robert Penn Warren, is the Humpty Dumpty who sits on top of the wall, the governorship of Louisiana. Here he reigns in his own anthropocentric world until he falls. The book has an epic quality in plot, character, and theme.

Willie is a farm boy with little education, but one who works hard and long to become a lawyer and achieve admittance to the bar. He believes in God, in honor, and in goodness. And at first he believes what people tell him. But Sadie Burke wises him up. He forsakes orange soda pop and a wholesome view of the world to embrace Scotch whiskey, a realistic view, and Sadie (as well as other mistresses). *[A major section of the paper, which appears later, empha-sizes character, although plot is mentioned throughout the paper. In the conclusion the student writer reacts to the novel, giving her response to plot and character.]*

Conclusion

All the King's Men, like a mighty river, snatches up the reader and thunders to the inexorable finish. When released, the reader is purged and saddened by the tragic mess which some characters have made of their lives, yet gladdened by the few who retain integrity and develop responsibility.

Rereading your notes and prewriting will help you trace the development of the plot. Look for cause and effect. Consider character flaws, impulses, values, goals, issues, or coincidences that influence the outcome. The checklist below will assist you.

CHECKLIST   **QUESTIONS FOR ANALYZING PLOT**

1. What is the major conflict, dilemma, or problem?

2. How does the main character cope?

3. What aspects of the plot create tension?

4. Where does the climax occur? What is the high point of the action?

5. Does the chief character lose or triumph? Why or why not?

Writing about Character

Analyzing character takes time and thought. Consider whether or not the character seems realistic. Start with the external events of existence and go to internal qualities. To discover personality traits, notice how the character treats other people. How does he or she speak and act? Modestly or arrogantly? Kindly or rudely? Thoughtfully or impulsively? What motivates the character? For example, Willie Stark seeks political power, but attaining that power has a hidden price, an undesirable consequence.

▶
Willie Stark is a complex character, a curious blend of good and evil, with Nietzsche-like overtones. As Stark gains power, he becomes a superman whose

reign is based on *argumentum ad hominem,* blackmail, and the premise that all men have erred. Yet Stark has a curious code of honor: he never frames anybody. He believes framing is unnecessary; all he does is dig deeply until he finds something.

Although Stark manipulates people and abuses power, he does work for the ultimate good of the people as he conceives it. He provides social services and allocates funds for a lavish hospital, which will be free to the poor.

Stark has an unusual philosophy: "Goodness. . . . You got to make it. . . . And you got to make it out of badness. . . . Because there isn't anything else to make it out of" (257). Although this idea is reminiscent of Romans 8:28 ("And we know that all things work together for good to them that love God, to them who are the called according to *His* purpose"), there is an essential difference that illustrates this character: Stark was a pragmatist who acted independently; he did not rely on his creator for direction.

To discuss character, make an assertion or claim about the character's role or personality. Then support this thesis with adequate examples and proof. You might examine how the character functions in the story. Is he the hero? Is she the heroine? Or does the character act as a *foil* or contrast for a major character? The questions in the checklist will help you to continue your analysis and start prewriting.

CHECKLIST   QUESTIONS FOR ANALYZING CHARACTER

1. What is significant about the character's history, home, or appearance?

2. How does the character achieve desires or goals? What values are revealed here?

3. What do you notice about the characters and their relationships with each other? Do they change?

4. What similarities and differences do you see in characters?

5. Do the characters seem convincing and realistic? Why or why not?

Writing about Symbols

Finding a symbol can lead the reader to look beneath a surface meaning for a deeper abstract meaning. The names of characters and places are often symbolic: they represent some aspect of plot, characterization, or theme. In *Jane Eyre*, the mansion of Edward Rochester, Thornfield, is the site of much trouble and pain. Besides the obvious meaning (field of thorns), Rochester's mad first wife, who is imprisoned on the top floor, is a thorn in his life.

You may recall another symbol Charlotte Brontë used in this novel—the giant horse chestnut tree, which stood in the orchard at Thornfield for many years. Near this tree Edward proposed marriage to Jane without telling her he already had a wife. After Jane accepted his proposal, a storm arose and the huge tree "writhed and groaned." That night the tree, which symbolized Edward, was struck by lightning and split, *foreshadowing* the impending tragedy.

A paper on symbolism alone could be difficult and inappropriate for some works. Unless you are adept at interpreting symbols, you may want to include other elements. To start thinking about possible symbols in a work, consider the questions below.

CHECKLIST   QUESTIONS FOR INTERPRETING SYMBOLS

1.   What features, objects, or persons might be symbols?

2.   Where and how do they appear?

3.   Do any of the symbols change? How?

4.   Are there any connections between symbols? If so, what are they?

5.   Are the symbols universal or individual? How are they related to the theme of the work?

Writing about Irony

If irony is a significant part of a story, you may want to analyze and categorize the types of irony embedded in the work. In Jane Austen's *Pride and Prejudice,* for example, verbal irony and situational irony appear throughout the novel. Verbal irony is habitual for the narrator as well as for Elizabeth Bennet and her father. The novel opens with the narrator speaking:

> It is a truth universally acknowledged that a single man in possession of a good fortune must be in want of a wife.
>
> However little known the feelings or views of such a man may be on his first entering a neighbourhood, this truth is so well fixed in the minds of the surrounding families, that he is considered as the rightful property of some one or other of their daughters.

Later Mr. Bennet, who assumes the role of an ironic spectator, says, "For what do we live, but to make sport for our neighbors, and laugh at them in our turn?" Elizabeth, like her father, categorizes people into the simple and the complex, finding amusement in the follies of the simple. Situational irony appears in minor incidents such as Lydia repeating much of her mother's behavior. The major example of irony evolves around Elizabeth, who begins by detesting Mr. Darcy but who finally loves and marries him.

Hemingway uses cosmic irony in *The Old Man and the Sea.* Even though the old man succeeds in catching the great fish and in taking it home, fate extracts an exorbitant price for success: not only do the sharks eat all the flesh off his prize, but the old man dies soon after.

If you should decide to write about irony, the prewriting checklist will help you begin.

CHECKLIST   **QUESTIONS FOR DETECTING IRONY**

1.   Does the reader or a character know something that another does not?

2.   Do any of the characters say the opposite of what they mean?

3.   Are there any inconsistencies between expectations and outcomes in the plot that create irony?

4.   Does fate or cosmic irony play a role in the plot?

5.   How does irony influence the work? What is the effect?

Writing about Theme

Theme is a continuing thread, the central meaning that winds through a work. A theme contains an observation about human life or the conditions that prevail. Usually, the theme is implicit and unstated, but you may find a theme directly stated, perhaps tucked into an obscure turn of the plot. In *All the King's Men*, an explicit statement of the theme reposes in a journal entry of a man long deceased:

> . . . the world is like an enormous spider web and if you touch it, however lightly, . . . the vibration ripples to the remotest perimeter and the drowsy spider feels the tingle . . . springs out to fling the gossamer coils about you . . . then injects the black, numbing poison under your hide. It does not matter whether you meant to brush the web of things. . . . what happens always happens. (188)

Briefly summarized, the theme is that even small unintentional acts and events can have consequences that reverberate, setting up a chain of cause and effect in our lives and the lives of others. (Willie Stark and others touch the web of circumstance.)

To write about theme, consider that it results from other elements. Look for a series of events and ideas that seem to be connected. Are there sets of circumstances that seem significant? What do they say about human life or values? Also keep in mind that there is not just one way to set forth a theme; readers' statements of theme from the same work will vary. Try writing several one-sentence versions of what seems to you to be the message of the work. Although theme is sometimes difficult to state, you can start your prewriting notes by answering the questions in the checklist.

CHECKLIST   **QUESTIONS FOR FINDING CLUES TO THEME**

1.   Does a set of related events, decisions, behavior, or symbols seem noteworthy? What might they mean?

2.   What do characters feel strongly about? What is important to them?

3.   What values are revealed by their responses?

4. What happens that strengthens or weakens human character? Could a universal statement be made about this?

5. What other aspects of plot and character challenge, entertain, or disgust readers? What do all these aspects seem to say about human life?

Revising

Accuracy, reasonableness, and fairness are key qualities to aim for in revising the draft of an analytical paper. Scrutinize your draft and add tentative words, qualifying phrases, and textual evidence to support claims and inferences. The following checklist will help you to avoid going out on the proverbial limb.

CHECKLIST   QUESTIONS FOR REVISING A LITERARY ANALYSIS

1. Is the thesis of my analysis clear? What elements will be discussed in the paper?

2. Is there enough evidence to support my thesis?

3. Are my main points clearly related to the thesis?

4. Is the discussion organized in a clear, logical order?

5. How familiar will the audience be with the work? How much do I need to explain?

6. How does the tone of the analysis sound? Is it serious? Is it overly critical or overly favorable?

7. Do I include at least one significant example (preferably more) to support each inference?

8. Are examples labeled correctly? (To check, see "Elements of Literature," near the beginning of this chapter.)

9. Has each inference been identified by a qualifier such as *indicates, suggests,* or another tentative term?

10. Do I explain how elements contribute to meaning?

11. Might I have overlooked any symbols or irony?

12. Have I identified the theme of the work?

STUDENT PAPER: LITERARY ANALYSIS

The writer of the next paper had difficulty in limiting her topic because Updike's story has such splendid unity. Each element is tightly linked to another. She wanted to focus on symbolism but found that impossible to discuss without mentioning plot and character. And since much of the symbolism is ambiguous, she selected only the clearest symbols.

Breaking Up Is Hard to Do

John Updike's short story "Still of Some Use" focuses on one day in the lives of a divorced couple and their children. The plot is simple, but the characterization and symbols are complex. Foster, his former wife, and their two grown sons are cleaning out the attic of the vacant house they once shared. The older son's girlfriend is also helping. Near the end, the former wife's friend Ted arrives. The story is revealed through Foster's eyes, although the omniscient narrator occasionally interjects a helpful comment.

To glimpse the conflicting emotions of the characters, the reader must peel back layers of symbolism, double meanings, and other clues. Implicit is an analogy between the contents of the attic and the former marriage: both are obsolete—the last tangible remnants of their lives together are being hauled to the dump. The characters' responses to this event vary. The older son seems unmoved, but the younger son, Tommy, is visibly upset. Although the older son and his girlfriend notice, neither seems empathetic. He remarks that Tommy has been "mooning over old stuff." She says Tommy is "very sensitive."

But the boys' mother is concerned and asks Foster to "talk to Tommy." She adds, "This is harder on him than he shows." Although Foster has kept a tight rein on his emotions, his inner conflict becomes evident when, "in a kind of agony," he shouts, "What shall we do with all these games?"

When his sons respond, "Trash 'em" and "Toss 'em," Foster is stunned. He stares at the "sad wealth of abandoned playthings" and remembers how "their lives had touched these tokens and counters once." He wishes they had played with them more often. Foster's former wife, too, seems reluctant to discard the games, asking, "Would Goodwill want them?"

Nor does she seem altogether happy about severing the marriage ties. Small clues hint at her emotional conflict. When Foster asks how she can bear to leave the house, she seems to reply a bit too quickly and flippantly to be convincing, saying, "Oh, it's fun once you get into it. Off with the old, on with the new." This response sounds defiant. She seems to still care for Foster. For instance, when he sits staring out the attic window, she asks, "What's the matter?" After listening a moment, she says, "You better stop now; it's making you too sad." Later she shares her drink with Foster—a gesture of intimacy.

There is little doubt about how Foster feels about the divorce. When he and his former wife are alone in the attic, regret overwhelms him. He looks at her, and the "attic tremble[s] slightly." Later he seems almost desperate as he begs, "Give me one sip." Only minutes before he had refused a drink. Does he want only to press his lips where hers have been?

Clearly, Foster is reluctant to part with the past. He wonders: What if they had "avoided divorce"? Then all the games would have stayed in the attic, their "sorrow [imperfections] unexposed." This passage suggests Foster would have preferred to remain in a marriage with his imperfections unexposed (to him).

So what does the reader actually learn about the breakup of the marriage? Not much, although the use of symbols is lavish. The most vivid is the image of games plummeting from the upstairs window to the truck bed: they "exploded," scattering "laughing children," "curious little faces," "hieroglyphs . . . whose code was lost." Like the games, the marriage undoubtedly started out with high expectations, but somehow the code to an enduring relationship was lost (or never found). Finally, the marriage "exploded" in divorce, scattering children and parents. Now the house is empty and the stove disconnected—just as the marriage has been abandoned and the family relationships disconnected.

The games, "aping the strategies of the stock market, of crime detection, of real estate speculation, of international diplomacy and war," seem to represent elements that marred the marriage. But the connection remains hazy and unclear. Had Foster speculated and lost family funds? What else happened? "War" seems to symbolize discord in the marriage.

The word *token* appears several times, suggesting Foster's minimal participation in the family. There are other hints he may have spent little time interacting with other family members: he says "he had not played enough with these games," and "now no one wanted to play." Yet he had spent many hours building a bookcase "so not a nailhead marred its smoothness." Did he devote more attention to objects than to family relationships? Was he an introvert who liked to go off alone? A stronger hint is that Foster never mentions his former wife's or his older son's names. This omission suggests that his relationships with them were not close.

In contrast, Ted is a "radiant brute," an extrovert, full of vitality and confidence, friendly even to Foster. Ted seems to prize time with his own children, visiting them instead of helping with the attic. He is charming and complimentary to Foster. Unlike Foster, Ted takes the initiative. Already he seems to have made himself a member of the family group: he gives fatherly advice, "Don't dawdle till the dump closes" and wipes away "a smudge of dirt along her [Mrs. Foster's] jaw." He even thanks Foster for helping clean the Foster attic, which seems unusual.

Foster realizes his former wife and Ted are now a "couple." Like the "cardboard spacemen" in the discarded games, Foster seems to feel he is a cardboard man, taking up space in a house no longer his. He feels he's "on the wrong square." He feels discarded—of no use as a husband or father. But as he is leaving, Tommy asks him to ride along to the dump. Foster declines, then asks, "This depresses you?"

Tommy admits, "Kind of," and adds, "It's changed since you left. They have all these new rules." Although Tommy is apparently talking about the dump, his face is clouded as if he's about to cry. His words seem to mirror a double meaning: Ted and his mother have new rules, and Tommy misses his father.

Foster senses these undercurrents, for suddenly he changes his mind and his mood. He jokes, "You win. I'll come along. I'll protect you." Foster seems pleased at the request—as if he is "still of some use."

The human desire to be needed and to be useful is a major theme in Updike's complex and disturbing story. Closely allied is the theme that divorce is not the perfect solution in such a situation. And even under amicable circumstances, divorce is never easy.

—Mae Mattix

TWENTY IDEAS FOR PAPERS OF LITERARY ANALYSIS

1. Analyze the main character of "Doves." How is Francine like the doves? How do they influence her?

2. Analyze the setting, symbolism, and theme of "Doves."

3. Discuss the characterization and plot of "Story of an Hour."

4. Discuss the plot and irony in "Story of an Hour."

5. Compare the main characters of "Doves" and "The Story of an Hour." How does fantasy influence the outcome of each story?

6. Discuss the influence of setting on plot and character in "Scheherazade."

7. Discuss the title and symbolism of "Scheherazade."

8. Compare the reality of "Scheherazade" with the fantasy.

9. Analyze the main character in "Scheherazade." Consider the line "It was like combat of a subtle kind."

10. Compare and contrast Foster and his former wife in "Still of Some Use."

11. Compare Foster with Francine ("Doves"). How are they similar in personality and behavior? How do they differ? (Hint: Consider initiative.)

12. Discuss the setting, plot, and characterization in "Still of Some Use."

13. Is there hope and a chance for reconciliation in "Still of Some Use"? Provide reasons and examples for your position.

14. Analyze the main character in "Still of Some Use."

15. Discuss the irony of a work and how it influences plot and character.

16 Compare two short stories with similar themes.

17 Analyze the symbolism and theme of a work.

18 Discuss the characterization of a novel.

19 Analyze a short story that contains suspense. How is it created?

20 Compare two characters from different works.

Reading and Responding to Poetry

> The poet is the stained glass window that transmits sunlight just as ordinary windows do, but colors it as it passes through.
>
> —Robert Hillyer, *In Pursuit of Poetry*

Poetry has taken a backseat in an age of electronic gadgets and cyberspace. We whiz from our homes to our jobs to other places in a whirlwind of activity. At night we tap away at a computer keyboard or collapse in front of the tube. If we read, it's often the headline news or the comics or self-help books, which poet Tess Gallagher calls "hamburger stands of the soul." Gone are the leisurely evenings and Sunday afternoons spent reading and staring into a wood-burning fire. Now there just doesn't seem to be time to read poetry and ponder tendrils of meaning.

Yet poetry can help us discover a hidden dimension of ourselves. Poetry can connect us more closely to nature and to the human race. In reading a poem, we can peer through a new window on our existence, savoring beauty taken for granted, sharing the warmth of unselfish love or the frigid chill left by death. Poetry acts as a link to the past by recapturing the pleasures and the pains of an earlier age. A poem can reach into the future, kindling desires, fueling dreams—providing the spark that transforms a wish into reality. A poem can fill the present with delight, appreciation, and anticipation. Poetry can yield contentment and acceptance of things we cannot change.

Here the purpose of reading poetry is *not* to classify dozens of literary devices or to analyze meter or to hunt for a message. *The purpose is to enter a poem, to experience it, to look at its parts, and to marvel at its artistry.* Despite careful analysis, any such knowledge is always incomplete. We can never comprehend all there is to know about a work of art—not that all poems are art. But if we approach each one as if it were, then we are more apt to give it a fair hearing.

HOW CAN A READER GET HOLD OF A POEM?

Great poetry has an essence that is elusive. Unlike expository writing, which is primarily concerned with fact and explanation, poetry is primarily feeling. With a few words poets often sketch scenes or wisps of ideas, leaving the reader to fill in the rest. These poets tend to show rather than tell. Great poems do not have excess words. Often the more passionate their feelings, the simpler their statements. Consider the first verse of one of Emily Dickinson's most famous poems:

> Success is counted sweetest
> By those who ne'er succeed.
> To comprehend a nectar
> Requires sorest need.

In the opening *couplet* (a set of two successive lines), the poet poses a *paradox* (a strange but true statement). The third and fourth lines restate the same idea in different words. Every word counts; every word is in perfect alignment and tension. The poet has said just enough in a unique and thoughtful way, balancing expectation with surprise.

When readers are required to analyze a poem, they often begin with the question "What does the poem mean?" In the title of his famous textbook, John Ciardi suggests a more effective starting point: "*How* does a poem mean?" For the meaning of a poem is derived not only from its words but also from its structure. Ciardi also suggests that to study a poem, the reader adopt a playful attitude—for much poetry, like dance, is "a performance" to be appreciated for the pleasure it brings. Ciardi believes the "best any analysis can do is to prepare the reader to enter the poem more perceptively."

To experience joy in comprehending a poem, we need a sense of curiosity, of wonder, and of play. For poets often frolic with words, pairing them in unexpected ways. A sense of play permeates the next poem. To appreciate the structure and sound, read it aloud.

On the Vanity of Earthly Greatness
by Arthur Guiterman

The tusks that clashed in mighty brawls
Of mastodons, are billiard balls.

The sword of Charlemagne the Just
Is ferric oxide, known as rust.

The grizzly bear whose potent hug
Was feared by all, is now a rug.

Great Caesar's bust is on the shelf,
And I don't feel so well myself.

Notice that the poem is composed of four rhyming couplets. Listen to the pace of the words, their slowness or quickness. The first line of each couplet tends to be slow and ponderous whereas the second is quick, especially the last phrase. Hear the sound and movement of certain words: "tusks that clashed," "billiard balls," and "grizzly bear whose potent hug." Note that other words suggest a lack of motion: "rust," "now a rug," and "bust is on the shelf." Each couplet contains surprises not only in sound but also in meaning.

QUESTIONS FOR DISCUSSION

1. Where does the biggest surprise occur?
2. What is the effect of the last line?
3. Does the poem seem to have a purpose other than to provoke amusement?
4. What do you notice about the title that is very different from the poem?
5. How would you state the main idea of Guiterman's poem?

The next poem, by Carl Sandburg, is more explicit and quite different in tone. Yet despite the macabre images, there is a spirit of sly playfulness, revealed in the grim irony and choice of narrator.

Grass

Pile the bodies high at Austerlitz and Waterloo.
Shovel them under and let me work—
   I am the grass; I cover all.

And pile them high at Gettysburg
And pile them high at Ypres and Verdun.
Shovel them under and let me work.
Two years, ten years, and passengers ask the conductor:
   What place is this?
   Where are we now?

   I am the grass.
   Let me work.

QUESTIONS FOR DISCUSSION

1. What has happened at all the places Sandburg names?

2. Who is the narrator? What is the "work"?

3. What is the significance of the passengers' questions to the conductor? What is the irony here?

4. How is "Grass" similar to "On the Vanity of Earthly Greatness"?

5. How do the treatments of the topic differ?

You may feel frustrated as you try to interpret the layers of meaning and glimpse the core of an apparently simple poem. But if you approach a poem as a work of art with form, sound, movement, and meaning and if you examine its parts with care, then you will begin to see its fusion and unity. Then you will be better prepared to appreciate its artistry.

READING NARRATIVE POEMS

Narrative poems are like miniature stories. They begin with a place and a situation. Often the scene is set very simply with a sparseness of detail. Characters are briefly introduced, and the action begins. The movement is usually from specific to general. At the end, concrete details or symbols often hint of a greater meaning, a *universal truth*.

See chapter 21.

The length of a narrative poem may vary from an anecdote such as Countée Cullen's "Incident" to a very long ballad such as "The Rime of the Ancient Mariner." Cullen was born in Louisville, Kentucky, in 1903. By 1925 he had become the most renowned black writer in the United States. Cullen completed theological study at Morgan State College in Baltimore. There he was a Methodist pastor for two years. Then he moved to New York City, where he formed a storefront mission and became politically active. His poem "Incident" deserves several readings.

Incident
by Countée Cullen

Once riding in old Baltimore,
    Heart-filled, head-filled with glee,
I saw a Baltimorean
    Keep looking straight at me.

Now I was eight and very small,
    And he was no whit bigger,
And so I smiled, but he poked out
    His tongue, and called me, "Nigger."

I saw the whole of Baltimore
    From May until December;
Of all the things that happened there
    That's all that I remember.

QUESTIONS TO ANALYZE "INCIDENT"

1. Vocabulary: *glee, incident.* (Also see *incidental.*)

2. How would you describe the tone of verse one?

3. What line in verse one conveys strong feeling?

4. Where does Cullen pair expectation with surprise? What is the effect?

5. Comment on the movement of the poem. (*Hint:* Examine the changes in tone from verse to verse.)

6. Ordinarily, a rollicking rhyme structure is not used in a serious poem. Why does it work well here?

7. Is this a child's poem? Why or why not?

As you examine this poem, keep in mind that understatement provides a wellspring of power for English poetry. *Understatement*, however, requires the reader to look beneath the surface of a poem to glimpse its essence. To assist in detecting understatement, keep a dictionary handy. Look up any unfamiliar words or any that might have more than one meaning. Consider all meanings of a word; poets often select ambiguous words that create layers of meanings. Also consider the historical period and the cultural norms that existed then.

READING LYRIC POEMS

Originally, lyric poems were sung by the Greeks to the accompaniment of a lyre, a stringed instrument. Lyric poetry, which includes most short poems, covers a broad array of subjects and forms. Rather than telling a story as narrative poetry does, lyric poetry expresses a state of mind, revealing thought and feeling. Since there is no plot, word choice and imagery must be powerful in a lyric poem.

Special Effects with Words

Poets select words not only for meaning but also for sound, movement, and color. All four aspects are inseparable. *Alliteration* (repeated consonant sounds), *assonance* (repeated vowel sounds), and rhyme are the most common devices of sound. Another device is *onomatopoeia*, whereby the sound of the word mimics its denotation. Listen to *hum, buzz,* and *crack* as you say them. These words sound like the actions they represent. Onomatopoeia supplies vitality to any poem.

Action verbs also give vitality to poetry, enhancing the image and varying the pace. Words may skip or skitter, slink or slither, sprint or stroll across a page. Let's pause for a moment and consider the verb pairs in the previous sentence. First, visualize the difference in movement between *skip* and *skitter*. A child might skip down a sidewalk, but an autumn leave skitters across a lawn, blown by the wind in quick irregular spurts.

Next listen to the sounds of the verb pairs. Notice the repetition of *sli* in *slink* and *slither*, which adds smoothness to their sound. Similarly, *ski* is repeated in *skip* and *skitter*. But the third pair sets up a little surprise. Instead of exact repetition at the beginning of the words, the *t* sound comes at a different place in each word: *sprint, stroll.* Finally, listen to the pace. The first word in each verb pair quickens the pace whereas the second slows it. For example, *sprint* with its short *i* is much quicker to say than *stroll* with the long *o* and *ll* sounds.

When you consider adjectives such as *red* and *ruby* or *green* and *emerald,* you note contrasts in color as well as sound and pace. The eye easily detects that red and green offer an array of shades whereas *ruby* and *emerald* are each a specific shade. As you listen to the sounds, you can hear the quickness of *red* and *green.* *Ruby* and *emerald* sound slower and richer.

Imagery in Lyric Poems

Our cave-dwelling ancestors drew primitive sketches to represent activities and events in their lives. Similarly, poets sketch images with words to represent significant occurrences, ideas, and emotions. In a poem with a single image, all words contribute. *Haiku,* an ancient Japanese form of lyric verse, always focus on a single image. The form generally consists of three lines of seventeen syllables, based on a metaphor. Implicit in the image is a comparison. Typical haiku describe nature or the seasons, much like the following examples:

<table>
<tr><td align="center">**The Barley Field**
by Joso</td><td align="center">**The Barley Field**
by Sora</td></tr>
<tr><td align="center">Bent down by the rain,
the ripe barley makes this
such a narrow lane!</td><td align="center">Up the barley rows,
stitching, stitching them together
a butterfly goes.</td></tr>
</table>

If you have seen wheat or oats growing in a field, then you can easily visualize a field of barley, which also grows in bearded, willowy stalks. To compare the two poems, jot down differences in the spaces below, beginning with concrete details. Then ask: How do the details influence the effect of each poem?

	(Joso)	(Sora)
Angle of stalks	_____	_____
Width of rows	_____	_____
Image (metaphor)	_____	_____
Punctuation	_____	_____
Connotations	_____	_____
	_____	_____
Repetition	_____	_____
Literary devices	_____	_____
	_____	_____
Tone	_____	_____

Poems with more than one image lack the splendid unity of poems with a single image. Yet multiple images can be skillfully unified by a central theme. All connotative meanings must, as Ciardi points out, "combine the overtone themes of the words and the images into a single unity."

Emily Dickinson (1830–1886) became famous for her lyric poems after her death. She was educated at Amherst Academy and Mount Holyoke Seminary. Her innovative style, characterized by whimsical daring and nimble skill, became a strong influence on twentieth-century poets. Yet Emily Dickinson was practically unknown during her lifetime; only a few of her poems were published in a local newspaper. The following poem is characteristic of her style:

[I never hear the word]
by Emily Dickinson

I never hear the word "escape"
Without a quicker blood,
A sudden expectation,
A flying attitude!

I never hear of prisons broad
By soldiers battered down,
But I tug childish at my bars
Only to fail again!
                    (c. 1859, 1891)

QUESTIONS TO ANALYZE "I NEVER HEAR THE WORD"

1. To what does "quicker blood" refer? (*Hint:* Today we would use a similar word and "pulse," rather than "blood.")
2. How would you describe the feeling in verse one?
3. Can you find the *slant rhyme* (imperfect rhyme) in verse one?
4. What other literary devices do you see?
5. Verse one introduces the idea of escape. Verse two contains the central idea of the poem. How would you state the theme of the poem?

More than a century later, an anonymous poet chose a similar theme but wrote a very different poem:

INCEPTION

Last night I dreamed
    my budding self
    flexed against
    its acorn walls
    and
    hurtled into light.

QUESTIONS TO ANALYZE "INCEPTION"

1. What does "budding self" convey to you?
2. Describe the imagery evoked by "flexed" and "hurtled."
3. Do you see a connection between "acorn walls" and "light"?
4. How is the title connected to the poem? (See a dictionary.)
5. How does this poem differ from Dickinson's?
6. What does the poem mean to you?

Although a spirit of play is less apparent in the poetry of Archibald MacLeish, still it is there. MacLeish won the Pulitzer Prize for poetry in both 1933 and 1953. He was not only a distinguished poet but also an author and statesman, working for UNESCO and other organizations. Born in Glencoe, Illinois, MacLeish graduated from Yale University and obtained a law degree from Harvard, where he became a professor. His most famous poem, "Ars Poetica" (Latin for *poetics,* the theory of writing poetry), written in 1926, contains a series of images. These involve sight, sound (or the lack of it), movement, and touch as well as meaning. Think about the texture of the images. What qualities do they have in common?

Ars Poetica
by Archibald MacLeish

A poem should be palpable and mute
As a globed fruit,

Dumb
As old medallions to the thumb,

Silent as the sleeve-worn stone
Of casement ledges where the moss has grown—

A poem should be wordless
As the flight of birds.
                    *

A poem should be motionless in time
As the moon climbs,

Leaving, as the moon releases
Twig by twig the night-entangled trees,

Leaving, as the moon behind the winter leaves,
Memory by memory the mind—

A poem should be motionless in time
As the moon climbs
                    *

A poem should be equal to:
Not true.

For all the history of grief
An empty doorway and a maple leaf.

For love
The leaning grasses and the two lights above the sea—

A poem should not mean
But be

QUESTIONS TO ANALYZE "ARS POETICA"

1. Vocabulary: *palpable, mute, medallion, casement, be* ("to have life or reality")

2. Why is *palpable* an excellent word for this poem? (Consider the medical meaning of the word as well as the old Latin.)

3. Consider the sound and imagery of "globed fruit," "sleeve-worn stone," "moon climbs," and "poem." What do you notice?

4. What do you notice about the pace of the pair of lines below?
   A poem should be wordless
   As the flight of birds.

5. What words convey the idea of silence?

6. The final line has no period. What is the effect? (*Clues:* What does a period do? What idea is conveyed through "motionless in time" and "history" that is similar to ending without a period?)

7. What else do you notice?

8. Each couplet specifies a quality that a poem should have. What are the qualities?

9. The final verse summarizes the meaning of the poem. How would you paraphrase it?

The Mysterious Fact of Poetic Energy

Josephine Jacobsen has not only won numerous awards but also published ten books of poetry and served two terms as Poetry Consultant to the Library of Congress. She writes: "Poetry is energy, and it is poetic energy that is the source of that instant of knowing that the poet tries to name" (*Writer* Jan. 1999). Jacobsen speaks of "the mysterious fact" that selected words, arrayed in an unusual rhythm, begin a "chain reaction explained by nothing in the words themselves or in their content." The cadence of the lines and the idea, perfectly expressed, can haunt us with their beauty and mystery.

For Jacobsen, an instant of knowing was followed by a strange chain reaction. She tells of stumbling upon an old cemetery in New Hampshire fifty years ago. Among the overgrown and broken tombstones, she saw a stone with a pair of clasped hands carved above a woman's name, a date, and two lines of poetry:

> It is a fearful thing to love
> What Death can touch.

These eleven words haunted Jacobsen; she tried to trace them but could not. Much later she wrote a lyric poem about a wartime cemetery and quoted the epitaph. Five years later she read a review of *Agamemnon,* a New York verse-play, which included the two lines from the tombstone. When asked, the author, William Alfred, said he had taken them from her poem. The energy in those eleven words had struck the poet-dramatist with such force that he placed them at the end of his play.

Jacobsen concludes: "A knowledge of what we already knew [before the poet said it] becomes for an instant so devastatingly fresh that it could be contained no more than a flash of lightning." Good poetry prompts that flash of knowing.

PREPARING AN ANALYSIS OF A POEM

As you browse through poems, choose one you like that offers possibilities for serious discussion. A fairly short poem is usually preferable if it has depth of thought. You may find different versions of the poem or possibly different titles. For example, one of William Wordsworth's poems has been widely printed under two titles: "Daffodils" or "I wandered lonely as a cloud." (Sometimes brackets are placed around the title of a poem to indicate it was originally untitled.)

TIPS FOR ANALYZING A POEM

1. *Copy the poem, enlarging it, but leaving 1½-inch margins.* Use the copy to make notes and gain an overview.

2. *Read biographical sketches.* Gaining insight into the author's background and the spirit of the times is often helpful in understanding the work. Encyclopedias, some poetry books, and the Internet offer brief biographies.

3. *Hold off on interpretation.* Going into a poem with preset ideas can close the mind. Withhold judgment; be open to newness.

4. *Look up unfamiliar words.* Read all definitions listed for a word. Poets often select words with double or triple meanings to enrich a poem. Jot definitions near the example if possible.

5. *Examine the words.* What is the level of language? Is dialect, jargon, or special terminology used? What does this usage imply?

6. *Listen to the feeling.* How does the voice of the narrator sound? From what point of view is the voice speaking? Listen to the nuances of the words. What emotion do you sense?

7. *Listen for devices of sound and movement.* Do you notice rhyme? Alliteration? Assonance? Any other device? How does the rhythm (pattern of sound) of the poem reinforce the meaning?

8. *Look for figurative language.* Do similes, metaphors, personification, symbolism, or other devices contribute to an image?

9. *Notice punctuation.* Poetry, like prose, is punctuated for a reason. Consider the effect of punctuation—or the lack of it.

10. *Keep the context of the poem in mind while looking at its parts.* Try to discover how each part is linked to the whole.

11. *Consider possible meanings.* Read the poem aloud. What does the imagery suggest? What do the words say? Might there be more than one interpretation? If so, which one fits best and why? Review your notes.

12. *What is the total effect of the poem?* What is your response to it?

Developing Your Analysis

Do a little research on the poet. After that, reread the poem silently. Then read it aloud and listen to the sound and movement. Who is speaking? Watch for clues to how the speaker feels about the subject. If the poem has rhyme, is there a pattern to the rhyme? Next, count the number of syllables in each line and write them at the side to determine how the lines compare. Do any have the same number of syllables? Is there a pattern to the arrangement of the lines?

After that, study the definitions and connotations of key words to see how they contribute to the meaning. Write the definitions and connotations near each word. Next, look for similes, metaphors, analogies, personification, symbols—or any other device that links one part of the poem with another. (For more about figurative language, see chapter 21.) Jot brief notes as you go. Write any questions you have at the bottom of the page or on the reverse side. You may find the answers later, or you might discuss the questions with someone else. By the time you have finished, you should have accumulated a page of notes to serve as raw material for a rough draft. (See "Critical Reading," chapter 20.)

Finally, reread the poem aloud to reassemble the parts in your mind and focus on the effect of the entire work. As you do, chances are that you will begin to see how the parts fuse into a central image or theme.

Organizing the Paper

Although there are many aspects to poetry, first-year college students are usually not expected to cover all them. Often an analytical paper on a poem is only one or two pages long. If your instructor allows a choice, select major elements that interest you. Then explain your impression of the way various elements contribute to the unity and meaning of the poem.

1. Identify the poem as narrative or lyric. If a special type, specify.
2. Follow the order of the poem as nearly as possible.
3. Explain how the word choice, symbolism, or other elements contribute to the overall effect of the poem.
4. Cite examples of elements.
5. State your perception of the central idea.
6. Describe your response to the poem.

**GUIDELINES:
ORGANIZING AND
DEVELOPING A
POETIC ANALYSIS**

If the poem is short, include the entire text in your paper. If over half a page, attach a copy to your paper unless the poem is in your textbook. To quote less than four lines, use quotation marks and indicate each line break between two or more lines by a slash mark: "I never hear the word 'escape' / Without a quicker blood" (Note: One space is placed before and after each slash.) If you quote four lines or more of poetry, indent and treat as a long direct quotation (with no quotation marks).

Revising an Analysis of a Poem

Even though your paper of analysis is only a page or two, check the organization and revise carefully. The following questions will help you revise your draft. Select the items that pertain to your subject.

CHECKLIST   REVISING AN ANALYSIS OF A POEM

1.   Do I have a clear thesis?

2.   Do I follow a logical order?

3.   Have I discussed the central image (or series of images)?

4.   Are any symbols present? Have I explained how they contribute?

5.   Have I discussed the devices of sound in the poem?

6.   Are there any similes, metaphors, or personification not yet discussed?

7.   Have I pointed out connections between related ideas?

8.   Have I considered how the poem appears on the page? How many stanzas there are? Their length and any other significant aspects?

9.   Have I interpreted the central idea of the poem?

STUDENT PAPER: ANALYSIS OF A POEM

The following example shows one way to organize an analytical paper. A poem of this length usually appears on a separate page, before the analysis. Wordsworth's poem was written about 1800 in the British Lake District. In the spring when the lake floods today, the blooming daffodils stand in water.

[I wandered lonely as a cloud]
by William Wordsworth

I wandered lonely as a cloud
That floats on high o'er vales and hills,
When all at once I saw a crowd,
A host of golden daffodils;
Beside the lake, beneath the trees
Fluttering and dancing in the breeze.

Continuous as the stars that shine
And twinkle on the milky way,
They stretched in never-ending line
Along the margin of a bay:
Ten thousand saw I at a glance,
Tossing their heads in sprightly dance.

The waves beside them danced; but they
Outdid the sparkling waves in glee;
A poet could not but be gay
In such a jocund company;
I gazed—and gazed—but little thought
What wealth the show to me had brought:

For oft, when on my couch I lie
In vacant or in pensive mood,
They flash upon that inward eye
Which is the bliss of solitude;
And then my heart with pleasure fills,
And dances with the daffodils.

Form and Meaning in "I wandered lonely as a cloud"

Every time I read William Wordsworth's poem "I wandered lonely as a cloud," it is a source of pleasure. The dazzling beauty of the daffodils is one that any reader can readily conceive and enjoy. But this lyric poem is much more than a vivid description with contrasts of sight and sound. The poem is alive with motion.

In the first line the narrator compares himself to the cloud that "floats on high." The tone of this line and the next differs greatly from that of other lines. The narrator's loneliness is juxtaposed to the happy sight of a "host of golden daffodils. . . . Tossing their heads in sprightly dance."

Light radiates throughout the poem in the words *golden, stars, shine, twinkle, milky way, sparkling waves,* and *flash.* Alliteration in *stars, shine, stretched, saw, sprightly* and in *Ten thousand . . . Tossing* focuses on this glorious sight.

Assonance contributes not only to the unity of the poem but also to the sound, varying the pace. The repetition of the long *o* in *lonely, floats, o'er,* and other examples slows the lines and suggests aloneness. The long *a* in *gazed* and its repetition reflect the narrator's reluctance to leave. In contrast is the short, quick *e,* in "Beside the lake, beneath the trees."

Personification and movement are major features of the poem. The daffodils toss their heads, dance, and laugh with *glee.* Movements of dance are conveyed by the words. *Fluttering* suggests short spurts of movement; *dancing,* a smooth glide. The rhyme scheme and the length of lines mimic the dance of the daffodils. Although the end rhyme is exact, the pattern of rhyming varies in the third stanza. No stanza has the same pattern, although some have the same number of syllables per line. These lines suggest the movement of dancers to music.

If there is a theme to the poem, it might be stated as "Beauty can nourish the spirit" or "Drink in every drop of beauty and store it to cheer the soul."

—Elizabeth D.

PRACTICE

IDEAS FOR WRITING

1. React to the two haiku entitled "The Barley Field." Which do you prefer? Why? Write a short essay giving your response.

2. Analyze Emily Dickinson's poem "I never hear the word."

3. Analyze another poem in this chapter and explain how some elements contribute to meaning.

4. Read and analyze another poem of your choice.

5. Research the life of your favorite poet and select one poem that reveals his or her philosophy. Write a short paper that summarizes his or her life and philosophy. Relate the poem to the philosophy.

PART 6

Survival Guide:
Preparing for Exams, Oral Presentations, and Employment

© Jeff Vanuga / CORBIS

The wolf has long had a bad reputation. Feared as "sheep killers," wolves have been hunted and killed for centuries. Farmers, ranchers, and others dislike the presence of wolves because they sometimes kill livestock, deer, and dogs. In 1973, when their extinction loomed in the United States, wolves were placed on the endangered species list. In the past decade, wolf packs have been introduced into Yellowstone National Park and other wildlife preserves. But the problem is that wolves do not stay in parks; they often roam over an area of fifty square miles or more. Lately, reports of wild wolf sightings in Wyoming, Wisconsin, Minnesota, Michigan, and other states indicate the wolf population is increasing.

WRITING EXERCISE

1. What connotations do you have for the word *wolf?* Are there "wolves" in your life? What (or who) are they?
2. Do you believe that the United States government should continue to reintroduce wolves into our national parks and wildlife refuges? Why or why not?

FENDING OFF THE WOLVES

The wolf of failure trails students who procrastinate and shirk the task of preparing well for exams. The wolf of fear stalks those who evade speech courses and avoid giving oral presentations. The wolf of poverty pursues those who seek jobs in the present economy.

The "Survival Guide" will help you elude these wolves. Chapter 23 shows you how to prepare effectively for both objective and essay exams. The time management section also shows *how to achieve more in less time*. Chapter 24 is a mini-manual, complete with instructions for preparing, practicing, and delivering professional oral presentations. Included, too, are tips for preparing audiovisuals, improving vocal variety, and building confidence. These skills can enhance your performance not only in college classes but also in job interviews.

Chapter 25, a guide to effective employment writing, shows the latest résumé styles, eye-catching cover letters, and letters of appreciation. It will help you focus on the needs of employers as you update your résumé. This chapter shows, step-by-step, how to research your career field, avoid common pitfalls, write a service-oriented job objective, and prepare effective employment documents. Included, too, are guidelines for writing e-mail, electronic and scannable résumés, a sheet of employment references, and a directory of career sites.

"The Survival Guide" is an essential part of this text. The chapter on preparing for exams and time management can help you immediately. Even if you are not looking for a job just now, you can save the book for future reference. By studying these chapters thoroughly, applying the principles, and exerting the necessary effort, you will be well on the road to success. Oh yes—you will need a bit of luck, but often we create our own luck through hard work.

Strategies to Prepare for Exams

> Procrastination is like a credit card; it's a lot of fun until you get the bill.
>
> —Christopher Parker

Many students procrastinate instead of preparing for exams. They wait until the night before and drink soda or coffee by the quart to stay awake while they study. The next day they are so exhausted they can barely keep their eyes open, much less focus their scattered thoughts to write complete essay answers. Pulling an all-nighter is not a good way to study for an exam—paced learning is more effective than cramming.

To do well on any exam, you need to prepare well throughout the term and get a good night's sleep beforehand. The journal *Nature* (9 Oct. 2003) reports that researchers at the University of Chicago and Harvard Medical School, in separate studies, found that a full night's sleep improves recall. Researchers believe that "sleep can rescue memories in a biological process of storing and consolidating them deep in the brain's complex circuitry."

TIME MANAGEMENT

The practical solution to the problem of procrastination is effective time management. By scheduling your time and studying regularly, you can increase your retention and decrease your stress. The rule of thumb for college study is "two hours out of class for every hour in class." This means that if you are taking sixteen hours of classes per week, you study thirty-two hours per week. Allotting this much time for study requires skillful planning.

If finding thirty-two hours or so a week to study seems impossible, don't despair. There are 168 hours in a week and many practical ways to become more efficient. The first step is simple—just *resolve early* in the term to manage your time wisely and to improve your study habits. The second step is to take control of your time by setting priorities and making a schedule.

Setting Priorities, Scheduling, and Implementing

Three keys to efficient scheduling are identifying your priorities early in the term, making a workable schedule, and disciplining yourself to follow it. Even though you might prefer to hang out with friends, go to a concert, or build a new sundeck, put study time first. To start managing your time effectively, you might follow this procedure:

- **Make a list of the activities you must do.** Include adequate daily study time. Postpone less urgent items, such as painting, shopping, and extra cleaning.

- **Rate essential activities in order of priority.** Mark high-priority items, such as deadlines for projects, papers, and exams, as **HP.** Include essential personal activities, such as doctor or dental appointments. Mark medium priorities as MP.

- **Mark a *monthly* calendar.** One big monthly calendar allows you to quickly check each day and spot possible conflicts early. If two high-priority items conflict, reschedule one or complete a paper or project early. Shuffle MP items around high priorities.

- **Make a *weekly* calendar.** This way you can develop an efficient routine. Mark your class hours, study times, work hours, and other high-priority items. Leave a little flextime in case of an emergency.

- **Make a daily to-do list the night before a high-pressure day.** Carry the day's list with you. As you complete an item, cross it off. If something is left undone, place it on the next day's list.

Setting priorities and following a schedule will help you develop a "can-do" attitude and self-confidence. Then you can enjoy the satisfaction that flows from being in control of your time.

1. **Study during your *prime time*.** Are you a night owl or a lark? When are you most alert and able to retain what you read? Is one hour of study in the early morning more effective for you than two hours late at night? Or is night your best time?

2. **Make *double use* of time.** Study at odd moments—on breaks at work, during lunch, and while waiting for appointments. You might listen to taped class notes as you drive. Or while a car-pool buddy drives, hit the books. What else might you do?

3. **Obtain help, especially during exam week.** A study buddy can ask questions and help review major concepts. If you are responsible for a family, is there someone who might assist while you study? Might you trade child care with a friend?

4. **Forgo leisure *temporarily*.** Say no to television, films, and computer games. Placing a high priority on learning and disciplining yourself will help you not only to achieve your college and career goals but also to develop constructive habits that can last a lifetime.

FOUR TIME-SAVERS

READING, NOTE-TAKING, AND REVIEW

To better understand the lesson, always read assignments *before* going to class. This prior study will allow you to participate and increase your efficiency in taking good class notes. (Some instructors include participation as part of your grade.) As you think and write, try to *associate* new learning with what you already know. Jot down your associations in parentheses. Creating a connection will help you retain the information over time.

Ten Ways to Improve Retention

Keep in mind that not everyone learns the same way. To discover which memory aids work well for you, try all ten of them:

1. **Keep a small notebook just for assignments, deadlines, and "to-do's."** After completing each assignment, cross it off. Jot down words you need to look up and questions you want to ask in the next class.

2. **Condense and reword for class notes.** Summarizing in your own words will enable you to recall material more easily than memorizing word for word.

3. **Develop your own code.** Since it is impossible to write down every word in a lecture, abbreviate some words and leave blanks. After class, fill them in. For example, b/c = because, i/t = into, w/o = without, b/t = between, c/ptr = computer.

4. **Keep a page of key terms.** For every course, start a page of key terms. Write out a definition for each one. Add to the list regularly and review.

5. **Make flash cards.** For difficult terms, make flash cards, using file cards and colored markers. Print the term on one side in large letters and the definition on the other. Then ask someone to flash the cards and quiz you.

6. **Create acronyms.** To memorize a short list, arrange the items to create an acronym. For example, if you have four skills to learn—*r*estatement/paraphrasing, *s*ummarizing, *r*esponding to nonverbal cues, *r*esponding to feelings—memorize the first letter of each word: *RSRR*.

7. **Break large chunks into parts.** To memorize quantities of material, look for a way to break it into manageable parts or categories. Adding capitalized headings to your class notes and numbering points will clarify. (Look at this chapter.)

8. **Color-code lists.** Break lists of several items into two columns. Then color the section numbers, such as 1–3 blue, 4–6 green, 7–9 yellow, and 10 orange. (Not all people are sensitive to color, but color-coding helps many.)

9. **Review and practice.** Think "see and say." Look at an item, then look away. Repeat the item aloud. *Hearing it will help to anchor the meaning in your memory.*

10. **Quiz and test yourself.** Type a list of questions you might be asked. The next day, print it out and answer the questions. Check your answers with the textbook.

Reviewing for Final Exams

If you study regularly throughout the term, attend classes, and take good notes (perhaps typing them each evening), then a week of review for final exams should be enough. A strategy to study effectively can help you organize your review.

A STRATEGY FOR EFFECTIVE STUDY

- **Plan the review.** First, scan the table of contents in your textbook. That gives an *overview* of the material. Note the headings and subheadings of chapters. Second, *mark HP (for high priority) by sections that need extensive review.* That way you can study the most difficult sections first and spend more time on them.

- **Think and question.** Think about major ideas and how they are related. *Turn your textbook headings and subheadings into questions* and try to answer orally. Then scan the section for the answer. This tactic will force you to examine and summarize ideas in your own words.

- **Highlight your notes.** Highlight main points. In some courses you will need to consider major events, changes, causes, influences, and trends. How have they affected the culture? What results or consequences have occurred?

- **Make a time line, a diagram, or another visual.** This will help you retain certain information. Some students type an outline of very difficult material. That device condenses and saves time in reviewing.

- **Review quizzes and handouts.** Look up answers to quiz questions missed and write them on the quiz. Review any handouts.

- **Encourage yourself.** Visualize completing the exam successfully. Refuse to succumb to negative thoughts and the "what if" syndrome ("What if I can't remember? What if I fail?") Negative thinking is a dead end. It sabotages your time and disrupts your focus. Reward yourself with brief breaks.

Predicting Exam Questions

Attending class regularly, particularly before exams, is essential. Many instructors share study hints and sample questions. Have pen poised, ready to record even casual remarks an instructor makes. Listen for hints disguised as joking, for example, a laughing comment such as "Memorize all the headings!" Translated, this usually means to study the major ideas of the textbook.

Or an instructor may smile and say, "Just remember *everything* I've covered in the lectures!" This means you can depend heavily on your class notes—if they are complete. If not, try to secure a good copy from someone else. Beware, however, of letting your own notes out of your sight unless you have them on a computer disk in a safe place. There is the danger of notes not being returned or of being lost or stolen.

Some instructors prepare a short study guide. Others volunteer only the time of the exam and vague suggestions for study. In either case, feel free to ask reasonable questions: Will the exam be on paper or computer? Will dictionaries, spelling checkers, or thesauruses be allowed? Will the exam contain only essay questions or a combination with multiple choice or short answers?

Before the Exam

To perform at your best, eat lightly but avoid meal skipping on exam day. Not eating can lower blood sugar, causing fatigue and inability to concentrate. Daily exercise, even walking a few blocks, contributes to a sense of well-being and helps to control test anxiety. Deep breathing and drinking cold water can also help you feel more alert and less anxious. Rested and energized, you will be able to think more clearly.

Avoid bringing coffee, soft drinks, or food to the exam. If you are nervous or someone bumps you, drinks may spill. Crumbs and smears stick to exams. Food wrappings can distract other students who are trying to concentrate.

Arrive about five minutes early with all your supplies on exam day. If you arrive too early, you may find yourself listening to someone wail about the upcoming exam. Take two pens (one may run dry), plenty of paper (the instructor may not supply it), a dictionary, and anything else you may need. If the exam is on a computer with a spelling checker, some supplies may seem unnecessary but still may be useful.

Check the chalkboard for messages. Sometimes an exam is moved to another room or even another building. Yet some students may sit and chat, not thinking to glance at the board. As a result, they lose time for completing the exam.

THREE KINDS OF EXAMS

College exams may include essay, fill in the blank, true or false, matching, short answer, or others. Three kinds are discussed here: open book, multiple-choice, and essay exams. All require adequate preparation.

Open Book Exams

Be forewarned that a question about open book exams may evoke laughter. To the uninitiated, an open book exam sounds as if it would not require much study. But the truth is that you have to prepare just as much or more! Although textbooks are permitted during an open book exam, the odds are stacked against your having time to use them.

Open book exams are so long that if you spend time searching for answers, finishing the exam is doubtful. Once, while taking one, I saw three students come in with textbooks loaded with colored slips of paper. During the exam they rapidly flipped pages, hunting for answers. None of the three completed the exam. There is no substitute for well-planned study and review.

Multiple-Choice Exams

To prepare for a multiple-choice exam, you need to memorize much specific data. Scan your class notes and quizzes. Highlight statistics, dates, events, names of important people, inventions, processes, procedures, or other vital facts, depending on the course and what the instructor has emphasized. In literature courses, pay strict attention to titles, names of authors, and dates, as well as names of characters, setting, plot, and theme.

Then type a list of these items or make a summary sheet to review. As you study the sheet, read each item, then look away and repeat it out loud to reinforce retention.

BEFORE THE TEST

1. **Take notes every class and date each entry.** Jot down all hints and tips teachers give. Type your notes after class, adding explanations as needed. Review.

2. **Study diagrams and figures in the textbook.** Don't overlook anything.

3. **Review old quizzes and exams.** Look up the correct answers for items missed.

DURING THE TEST

4. **Read directions twice.** Highlight the key terms, if permitted. Follow directions *exactly.* Answer only the number of parts required. Carelessness costs points.

5. **Determine whether or not to guess at answers.** On most tests there is no penalty for guessing. For some standardized tests, you may be ahead to leave an item blank if you do not know the answer.

6. **Cover possible answers with your hand. Read the question and think the answer.** Select the item that is closest to your answer.

7. **Read all the questions about an excerpt from literature before you read the excerpt.** Then reread and answer each question.

8. **Don't waste time looking for a pattern to answers.** Invariably, answers are lettered (a, b, c, d, or e) randomly.

9. **On timed tests, work fast.** If you have extra time, go back and look over just the items you are unsure of.

10. **Do not change an answer unless you are absolutely sure it is wrong.** Research has shown that a first answer is more likely to be correct than a second answer when the test taker is unsure.

TIPS FOR TAKING MULTIPLE-CHOICE EXAMS

Essay Exams

Most essay exams have several questions that require a paragraph or more to answer completely. Other exams have just one question that calls for a long essay. Regardless, you will need to memorize certain facts, details, and definitions, as well as understand key concepts. Essay exams often require that you understand cause and effect, organize, analyze, and comment. You may also be asked to make a claim and supply evidence to support it. The next section presents an overview of essay questions, definitions of certain verbs, key phrases, and a strategy for drafting complete essay answers, as well as other help.

A STRATEGY FOR MANAGING TIME DURING ESSAY EXAMS

1. **Preview the test.** Scan the entire test. If you have a choice of questions, mark the ones you will answer. *Do not spend time on extra questions that earn no credit.*

2. **Plan your time according to the worth of questions.** If all questions are weighted equally, allot equal time. If a question is worth more than others, spend more time there.

3. **Start with the easiest question.** Answering one completely will boost your confidence.

4. **When stalled, move on, or take a quick break.** Breathe deeply. Sip water. You may think of an answer.

5. **Keep your exam until the last possible moment.** Do not leave early. Instead, go back and check your answers. If you see any omissions or think of significant details, add them.

6. **If time is running out, outline your answers.** It is better to earn partial points than leave a question blank and earn none.

WRITING COMPLETE ESSAY EXAM ANSWERS

Before writing an exam answer, read the entire question. Thirty seconds spent considering the question can make the difference between an incomplete answer and a complete one. Two major causes of low grades on essay exams are that students misread or omit parts of questions. Hurrying through instructions is a path to disaster. To understand what is required, read *every* word carefully. Then follow directions.

Understanding the Question

To answer essay questions completely, you need to know the precise meanings of certain verbs. These words contain clues to the writing strategy that will best organize an essay answer. Listed in the box below are definitions of verbs frequently found on essay exams.

DEFINITIONS OF COMMON VERBS IN ESSAY QUESTIONS

Account for: to explain, as a cause and its effect; to justify

Analyze: to examine the parts of and determine their connections

Clarify: to explain; to present details, reasons, or examples

Defend, justify, support: to give reasons for; to offer evidence

Define: to give the meaning; to describe basic characteristics

Discuss: to examine and consider; to present details and reasons

Evaluate: to examine advantages and disadvantages; to rate or judge

Explain: to make clear; to define or offer reasons

Identify: to define; to give the characteristics of

Trace: to track or explain in chronological order

Exam questions may be broad or narrowly focused. Broad questions allow leeway in answering. They may ask you to *trace* or *state* influences, developments, or history. Such questions require listing a series of significant events or changes in *chronological* order, then explaining their evolution and effects. Or you may be asked to *analyze, discuss, explain, comment on,* or *account for* influences, changes, or trends:

- Trace the development of computers from the first practical model up to the present.
- Analyze the influence of World War II on women's lives from 1941 to 1950.

Narrowly focused questions are more specific. They may ask you to *identify, cite, compare, contrast, list, argue, defend, justify, support, evaluate,* and so on. These questions may be stated in one sentence or in more than one:

- Discuss the roller-coaster performance of the Dow Jones Index in 2003 and cite the chief causes of its wide fluctuations.
- Contrast Walter Mitty's real life with his secret life. Give two major reasons why he feels the need to escape from reality.

Instructors expect you to cite significant points, supply adequate support, and explain connections clearly. Omit trivial details. Clear, concise answers are better than long rambling padded ones. Strive for quality, not quantity.

Key Phrases	Writing Strategies
• Trace, give the history of	*Narration*
• Provide details, describe	*Description*
• Explain, list, provide examples of	*Illustration*
• Discuss or analyze the parts of	*Classification*
• Analyze, explain how, show how	*Process analysis*
• Discuss advantages/disadvantages	*Comparison-contrast*
• Show similarities/differences	*Comparison-contrast*
• Account for, analyze the results of	*Cause-effect*
• Discuss or explain reasons for	*Cause-effect*
• Identify, clarify, explain the term	*Definition*
• Defend, evaluate, justify, support	*Argument-persuasion*

WRITING STRATEGIES SUGGESTED BY KEY PHRASES

Writing Paragraph Essays

To begin an essay paragraph, write a clear topic sentence. Then draft support sentences, keeping in mind the *basic pattern of claim and evidence.* In other words, every detail and example in the paragraph should support the claim of the topic sentence. Use complete sentences. Fragments can lead to confusion and a loss of points. At the end of your answer, leave a few lines in case you think of more to add later.

When you are faced with writing several exam answers, focus on one question at a time. If you should think of information for another question before you finish the first, jot down the idea and put it aside. The precautions that follow will also help you write complete essay answers.

PRECAUTIONS FOR WRITING COMPLETE ESSAY ANSWERS

1. **Heed directions.** Listen to oral instructions. During the exam, check the board for any corrections or changes to the exam. Read each exam question *twice.*
2. **Highlight or underline key terms.** If you are permitted to write on an exam, mark special terms.
3. **Number the parts of multifaceted questions.** Be sure that no part is omitted.
4. **Check off numbers of parts after you answer each one.**
5. **When finished, check the answers you are least sure of.** If you think of more information, add it. Then proofread.

SAMPLE PARAGRAPH ESSAY

The three-part essay question below calls for definition, contrast, and division. The one-paragraph answer opens with a definition before the topic sentence. The support sentences follow.

Definition
Contrast
Topic Sentence

Support

Example

Summary

Question: Define *information interview.* How does it differ from an employment interview? State three specific advantages of this interview.

Answer: An information interview is a meeting with an employer for the direct purpose of gaining information about a career field, not to get a job. The information interview has three distinct advantages. It provides firsthand information about a position you hope to be working in some day. It allows you an inside look at a company to see whether or not you would enjoy working there. It allows access to employers whom you might not be able to contact otherwise. You may even be asked to bring your résumé or to come in for an employment interview. In fact, that is what happened to me last week. Tomorrow I start my new job as a medical transcriptionist. The information interview is truly an excellent technique for uncovering the "hidden jobs" that are never advertised.

Writing Long Exam Essays

Instead of several paragraph essays, you may be asked to write an in-class paper, either in longhand or on a computer. As soon as you are clear about what the essay question requires, start a tiny scratch outline, possibly in the margin or on the back of a paper exam. Then identify your main points and number them. This start will help you focus your thoughts. If writing by hand, place your first draft in the exam booklet, if given one; rarely is there time to recopy.

Always state your thesis early and cite examples to support main points. Questions about literature usually ask you to analyze elements of fiction such as theme, plot, or character. They may also ask about symbolism, irony, or other literary devices (see chapters 21 and 22). Some essay questions call for a *reaction*. A well-written reaction goes a step further than analysis. You include your opinion—based on examples from the text you are given or have read previously. If asked to react to a reading, respond to the main *idea* and add a well-reasoned comment (see chapter 20).

• "A Strategy for Critical Reading," page 293 • "Writing a Paper of Reaction or Essay Exam Answers," page 295 • "Reading and Taking Notes on a Literary Work," page 310	**FOR YOUR REFERENCE** **Study Aids** **for Literature**

PRACTICE

MAKE YOUR OWN STUDY QUESTIONS

To master the suggested study techniques for essay exams, make up your own study questions. Base them on the headings in this chapter. Leave spaces for your answers. After you have finished, check your answers with the text to see that you have included all significant points.

DRAFT AN ESSAY EXAM ANSWER

Sample Exam Question: Identify the chief obstacles you face when preparing for an essay exam. Which suggestions in this chapter might you adopt to alleviate these concerns and improve your study habits? Write a well-developed paragraph, citing specific details and reasons for your answer. You might also construct a plan for effective study.

Making Oral Presentations

In a survey of 480 companies, the National Association of Colleges and Employers asked what qualities were considered most important when hiring. The most frequent response was

> You gain strength, courage, and confidence by every experience in which you really stop to look fear in the face. . . . You must do the thing you think you cannot do.
>
> —Eleanor Roosevelt

"communication skills." Employers want applicants who can write well and speak effectively. To help meet this need, more and more colleges and universities are incorporating speaking skills, including oral presentations, into courses across the curriculum.

But many students quake at the thought of standing before a group and making a presentation.

WHETHER SPEAKING TO SIX OR TO SIXTY . . .

If your heart does a rapid tango and your face pales at the thought of giving an oral presentation, you will be glad to know that these responses are common and surmountable. And the fundamentals of speaking are easy to learn. In fact, many students discover they are better speakers than writers.

Whether facing six coworkers or sixty participants at a training seminar, you can learn to speak with confidence. The first key is to get your fear under control. By giving yourself a pep talk and applying the many guidelines in this chapter, you can ease the task of giving an oral presentation. The second key is to practice enough but not too much. We'll talk more about this point later.

The third key is to think of the audience as friends with whom you will share some interesting information. If you are enthusiastic, they will sit up and listen. Finally, the chances are good that your college classmates will be an empathic audience because they will be presenting, too. They are apt to encourage you by listening attentively, providing the kind of support they will want when they are speaking. Now are you ready to start?

HOW DO WRITING AND SPEAKING DIFFER?

If you are asked to present a paper orally to the class, rest assured that you have already accomplished a big chunk of the work. With a little tweaking, you can adapt the paper for presentation to a live audience. To start, you need to consider how your role as writer changes to that of speaker. For both rhetorical situations, the purpose and the topic remain the same, but three other factors—occasion, audience, and voice—change dramatically.

Writing and Speaking: Comparing Two Types of Rhetorical Situations

See chapter 1.   Three basic elements differ in the rhetorical situations of writing and speaking: the occasion, audience, and voice. These differences influence how an effective presenter prepares and how an audience receives the message.

OCCASION	PURPOSE	TOPIC	AUDIENCE	VOICE
• Writing	Same	Same	• Readers *see* words	*Writer's* voice
• Speaking	Same	Same	• Listeners *see* actions, *hear* words	*Speaker's* voice

In a paper the content, punctuation, and spelling are important. *In an oral presentation, however, the content and delivery are important.* Thus this chapter contains an overview of revising a paper for presentation as well as guidance for delivering the presentation. You will see examples of purpose statements, thesis statements, introductions, conclusions, and a student speech. Specific tips for preparing notes and audiovisuals; practicing; and improving eye contact, articulation, and vocal variety are also provided.

Presenting versus Reading

Any effective presentation requires that the speaker exude the energy, enthusiasm, and vocal variety found in animated conversation. Eye contact, facial expression, gestures, and tone of voice can make words come alive. A compelling speaker can make a message vibrant and persuasive in a way that differs radically from the mechanical reading of the same message.

Yet students who lack training in oral communication are often unsure of what is expected. Some assume they can just stand up and read their paper aloud, *little realizing that eye contact is an essential part of an effective presentation.* A scientist made that same mistake at a Society of Technical Communication conference in Chicago. After five minutes of his droning, people began to leave. As he continued in a monotone, head bowed with no eye contact, more and more left. By the end of the hour, two-thirds of the audience had gone.

By applying the guidelines in this chapter, you will be spared the embarrassment this man must have endured. As you gain experience in presenting, you will appear more confident and knowledgeable during job interviews. If asked to introduce yourself, report on a team project, give a sales presentation, or summarize a research paper or project, you will be able to smile, control the butterflies, and do a creditable job.

FOUR TYPES OF ORAL PRESENTATIONS

A speaker can choose from four types of oral presentations: *manuscript, memorized, extemporaneous,* and *impromptu.* Successful reading of a manuscript takes skill, training, and charisma. Memorized presentations are hazardous because they often lack spontaneity. Then too, nervousness can cause forgetfulness.

The most effective type of prepared presentation is extemporaneous. The secret of success for this type of presentation is sufficient preparation and speaking in a *conversational* manner. Although the presenter may glance at notes, the tone is informal and friendly. An impromptu speech is a spur-of-the-moment talk, given without more than a few moments of preparation. For example, you speak impromptu when introducing yourself to the class, when escorting visitors around your workplace, or when filling in for a master of ceremonies who is late or unexpectedly unable to attend an event. As you develop skill in speaking extemporaneously, your ease in impromptu speaking will increase.

**PREPARING A
PAPER FOR ORAL
PRESENTATION**

If you are asked to present a paper orally, don't panic! No radical changes are required. Here is an overview of the necessary steps. Tips and examples appear later in the chapter.

1. **Mark up your paper as you simplify and condense.** Most papers, especially research-based papers, will need to be simplified and condensed. Working on a printed copy of your paper, highlight the thesis, and sharpen it further (see "Define the Purpose" on page 358). Highlight statistics and brief anecdotes that lend support for your main point. Delete minor details and less relevant examples. Put brackets around extended discussions or complicated points, and jot summaries in the margins. Watch for an unusual fact or arresting quotation. Divide long sentences into shorter ones.

2. **Perk up your introduction.** To gain listeners' attention, you might start with an engaging quotation or example related to your topic. Then link the topic to the listeners. Emphasize the ways they can use the information.

3. **Include transition to your main points.** Prepare a link from your thesis to each main point, using numerical or embedded transition according to your purpose (see pages 156 and 80).

4. **Plan an effective and memorable conclusion.** Summarize the main idea, and then give your audience something extra to think about. You might add a bit of wisdom, a provocative thought, or a look to the future.

5. **Prepare an outline.** Using note cards, sheets of paper, or the notes pages tool of presentation software, work from your marked-up paper and written plans to prepare notes. Outline your main points and significant subpoints.

6. **Prepare audiovisuals.** People like to see as well as hear. If you are talking about coaching Little League baseball, wear your official shirt and bring a ball and bat. If you have access to PowerPoint or another presentation software program, you may want to use it to support your thesis (see "Creating Effective Audiovisuals").

7. **Time the presentation.** Pause slightly between sentences. If allowed four to six minutes, aim for five. The extra minute will give you time to pause for emphasis (or laughs). If needed, cut or condense points.

8. **Practice but do not overpractice.** Practice enough times so that you're comfortable but not so many that you memorize every word. Your presentation should seem fresh and spontaneous.

9. **Revise troublesome phrases.** Mark any words that cause stumbling. Use a thesaurus to find synonyms, so you can recast and shorten awkward or confusing sentences. Find words you can use comfortably and pronounce easily.

10. **Check arrangements and arrive early.** Have your notes and audiovisuals in order. Test all equipment to make sure it's hooked up and working properly. Good preparation will ease your mind.

PLANNING AN EXTEMPORANEOUS PRESENTATION

The first step toward an effective extemporaneous presentation is to analyze the rhetorical situation. The setting may impose limitations that can be circumvented, but if the topic is inappropriate for the occasion and the audience, the presentation has little chance for success.

Preview the Setting

To begin planning any presentation, find out where it will be held and the nature of the space. How large is the room? How will the seating be arranged? Is there a lectern for notes? Will you be using a microphone? Can projectors or any other necessary equipment be reserved? Is an Internet connection available? Are electrical outlets near the lectern, or are extension cords available? Is the lighting satisfactory?

The closer you can be to the audience, the more intimate and informal the setting. A semicircle is ideal because it allows you to establish eye contact with everyone. For very large audiences, a center aisle is desirable so that you can actually walk into the audience and involve individuals, particularly if there is a question-and-answer session.

If you will be using a microphone, try to practice at least a few minutes beforehand. Familiarizing yourself with the room and the equipment will not only diminish the fear of the unknown but also allow you to plan around any deficiencies and tailor the presentation to the setting.

Assess the Audience

Before definitely settling on a topic, consider the attitudes, beliefs, and values of the people to whom you will speak. Find out as much as you can about their demographics—age range, gender, ethnicity, occupation, education, or other relevant cultural factors. Then estimate how the audience will be likely to react to your topic. To analyze the audience, you might start with the familiar pattern of *who, what, why, where, when,* and *how:*

- Who will be attending? How many? (All men? All women? Mixed group?)
- What special interests or concerns do they have? (Consider age, education, and culture.)
- Why will I be making the presentation? (What do they expect and want?)
- How much will most listeners *likely know* about the topic?
- How do they *feel* about the topic? (Is the topic charged with emotion?)
- When will the presentation occur? How will the time of day, current events, or an upcoming holiday affect the rhetorical situation?

The answers to these questions will guide you in planning your approach—your thinking about how to stimulate listeners' interest. If you lack a topic or decide to switch to another, see "Twenty Ideas for Oral Presentations" at the end of the chapter.

**MURPHY'S LAW
IN ACTION**

Skipping audience analysis can invoke Murphy's law: "If anything can go wrong, it will." One student, who skipped this step, asked in a strong confident voice, "How many of you smoke? How many have tried to quit?" Only two of twenty-five classmates raised their hands. When the presenter realized that almost all of her audience were non-smokers, her face paled and her voice wavered. Her enthusiasm fled. The response of the audience was polite but lukewarm. With an audience of smokers, the how-to-quit-smoking presentation had the potential to earn an A, but it earned a C.

Consider the Occasion

When and why a presentation is given influences the length, approach to the topic, and organization. In the classroom, oral presentations will be much shorter than those generally given at work, for clients or prospective customers, or in the community. For a class you might give a one- to three-minute practice speech or a lab report. A graded presentation might run from four to eight minutes, depending on the time available and the size of the class. The purpose and audience will influence how you shape and organize the material for the presentation.

Define the Purpose

The *general* purpose of an oral presentation may be to inform, to persuade, to inspire, to dedicate, to celebrate, to entertain, to express appreciation, or a combination of these. The general purpose indicates the type of presentation. The *specific purpose statement* has three parts: purpose, topic, and desired result. Once you define your specific purpose, you can write a clear thesis statement reflecting that purpose. The thesis statement is the central idea you want to convey.

SPECIFIC PURPOSE STATEMENTS

- The purpose is to *inform* the audience about *common spiders* and
[purpose]　　　　　　　　　　　[topic]
[desired result]
show how to determine friend from foe.

- The purpose is to *persuade* the audience that since *most spiders are*
[purpose]　　　　　　　　　　　[topic]
[desired result]
harmless and beneficial, they should not be killed.

THESIS STATEMENTS

- Common spiders are harmless and easily distinguished from several poisonous varieties. (informative)
- Let's spare the beneficial and harmless spiders around our homes. (persuasive)

Notice that the examples above illustrate how the same subject can be approached in different ways, according to your general purpose. Before starting your outline or notes, write a specific purpose statement. It will clarify your intent and help you stay on track. Your thesis can be written later.

Select an Appropriate Topic

For a successful classroom presentation, the topic should be suitable for both you and the audience. Never speak on a subject that causes you to feel uneasy; discomfort blunts enthusiasm and dulls a presentation. Select a topic you can discuss rationally without excessive emotion—one that offers an opportunity for listeners to learn as well as to enjoy. Opinions about issues such as gun control, abortion, religion, and politics tend to be deeply ingrained and highly charged. There is little chance of changing anyone's mind; in fact, a shouting match may erupt and distract from your presentation.

Chances are that if you have already prepared a paper for another class, and it has been graded, then the topic is suitable for an oral presentation. If in doubt, ask your instructor. The following tips will help you to adapt the paper or select an entirely new topic.

Get Off the Beaten Path   Topics that have been highly publicized tend to make boring presentations. For example, most people already know quite a bit about illegal drugs, guns, and AIDS. Unless you can provide additional information that is fresh and interesting, the audience will be unlikely to listen closely. You may need to research your topic further (see chapter 27).

Sometimes you can freshen an old topic by researching the latest discoveries, such as advances in medicine. Or if you decide to look for another topic, you might share an area of personal expertise that would interest the audience, such as Web site design, genealogical research, or building a musical instrument.

Link the Topic to the Audience   During the introduction, effective presenters establish a link between the audience and the topic. To include listeners, use personal pronouns (*you, your, we, us*). State an advantage, benefit, or reason for them to listen. To search for a connection, you might ask yourself:

- Why should the audience listen to me?
- What benefit can they derive? (Learn, improve, enjoy, or what?)

- How can I make them eager to listen? (Start with the unusual or amusing.)

Role-Play   You might ask the class to assume a role. A bank manager wanted to practice a presentation she would be giving at work. Before the presentation, she asked the class to pretend they were managers of local branch banks who were attending a training seminar. This role-playing heightened their interest, and their attentive feedback enabled her to give an excellent presentation.

FINDING A LINK TO THE AUDIENCE

A student who collected antique glass wanted to share his hobby but doubted that the men in the audience would be interested. When he sought help in finding a link, his instructor asked, "What are men generally interested in?"

The student thought a moment, smiled, and replied, "Money?"

"Right! You could present antique glass not only as fun but also as an investment. Have you ever made a profit this way?"

"Yes, just last week," he replied. "I was driving through a village and spotted a general store. On a dusty bargain table I found a lovely old glass bowl that was hand signed. It cost just $5, but a catalog lists it for $100!" That anecdote became the opening for his presentation.

Audience Analysis: Make a Brief Written Plan

Writing down a plan or an overview of the rhetorical situation for your presentation will help to clarify the steps of preparation. In fact, your instructor may require that a plan be handed in. Below is a sample format for such a plan or overview.

PRESENTATION PLAN/RHETORICAL SITUATION OVERVIEW

1. General purpose: to _____
   Specific purpose: to _____

2. Demographics of audience:
   Estimated age range: _____ to _____ Gender: _____
   Relevant cultural factors: _____

3. What will most listeners be apt to know about the topic? _____

4. What else can you tell them? _____

5. How do they *feel* about the topic? _____
   Any touchy aspects? If so, what? _____

6. What are the implications of your audience analysis for this presentation?
   _____

7. *If* you use an argument format, how will you establish common
   ground? (See chapter 18.)

   _____

8. What audiovisual will you use? _____ When and how will
   you use it? _____

9. What factors influence your credibility? _____

10. What will be your biggest challenge? Why? _____

   _____

CREDIBILITY, ORGANIZATION, AND DEVELOPMENT

The aim of an extemporaneous presentation is to talk *with* an audience in a
forthright manner, not *at* them. This requires showing respect for their integrity,
intelligence, and values. To gain the trust of the audience and establish credibility, you need to show regard for accuracy, for ethics, and for the listeners. A
knowledgeable presenter who is poised, prepared, and considerate will earn respect. Preparation includes not only collecting reliable information, planning,
organizing, and practicing but also giving attention to other factors that influence credibility.

Considering Credibility

Your *credibility* (estimate of trustworthiness by the audience) is based upon the
quality of the information you present and the way you present it. To gain trust
and respect, you need to sound as if you know and believe what you say. That
means you collect reliable information, identify sources, and radiate sincerity.   See chapter 28.

Your credibility emanates not only from thorough preparation and reliable
information but also from professional demeanor and energy level. A clear
confident voice, proper pronunciation, and correct grammar promote respect.
Appropriate attire and a neat appearance also contribute to credibility. Look
professional, not flashy. To feel tip-top and maintain your energy level, get a full
night's rest and eat breakfast. To decrease anxiety, do some form of exercise.

Organizing an Informative Presentation

Clarity, logical reasoning, and flexibility are the chief factors to keep in mind as
you organize an oral presentation. Depending upon the rhetorical situation, an
informative presentation can be organized in various ways. For example, to explain a training procedure, use chronological order just as you would in a process paper.   See chapter 11.

If you are explaining something by giving three reasons, characteristics, or
other categories, you could arrange them according to importance. To describe   See "The Seven
the layout and features of a historical park, you could use spatial order or a com-   Basic Orders,"
bination of orders. As you practice a presentation, revise the order as needed.   chapter 4.

Organizing a Persuasive Presentation

A low-key argument is generally more effective than direct confrontation. The wise presenter downplays disagreement by starting with a neutral overview of an issue. A wise strategy is to follow with a point that both sides agree on. This *common ground* sets the stage for discussion. Next, state the points of the opposition *fairly* before presenting your proposition (see pages 249–50).

Treating an issue as a problem to be resolved will establish an air of objectivity and fairness. Try to find a common goal. Use the pronoun *we* whenever possible: "*We* all want Children's Services to keep on serving needy children in Hardin County. The question is, How do *we* continue services after the present operating levy expires?" This attitude will foster respect for the other side and keep tempers banked. To elicit cooperation, *ask* questions such as "What are the alternatives?" "What are the advantages and disadvantages of each alternative?" "What is the best overall solution?"

To shape an effective argument, determine the *area of resistance* and find a way around it. Why does the other side reject a proposal? Often the area of resistance is cost. You might point out "The operating levy on the ballot is a renewal. It will not increase your taxes." List the benefits and conclude with a summation such as "Anything worthwhile is going to cost money. Let's not be penny-wise and pound foolish. Let's plan for the future."

Considering Ethics, Logic, and Emotion

See chapter 18.   An important factor in any presentation is the blending of logic, ethics, and emotion. Yet there is no quick formula. First of all, appeals should be ethical. Second, most classroom presentations will require that logic predominate and emotion remain subordinate. Emotion should be subtle and suitable, used to reinforce the central point. The emphasis should be on facts, data, details, reasons, and examples.

Choosing the Right Words

When considering words, select a level of formality that is appropriate for the topic and the audience. This guideline rules out nonstandard English for classroom presentations. Informal Standard English is generally suitable for these presentations. Contractions will lend a conversational tone. If you need a technical term that the audience may not know, define it and perhaps give a brief **See chapter 2.**   example.

Sometimes you can make a presentation come alive with a vivid comparison—a simile, metaphor, or analogy. John F. Kennedy, in his inaugural address on January 20, 1961, used striking imagery. The excerpt that follows contains two metaphors:

> To our *sister republics* south of the border, we offer a special pledge: to convert our good words into good deeds—in a new alliance for progress—to assist free men and free governments in casting off the *chains of poverty*.

Shy away from buzzwords, slang, and clichés that may not be understood by some generations or ethnic groups. Avoid stereotypes and any language that might offend.

See chapter 8.

Improving Transition

To track the main idea, listeners need guide words even more than readers do. When there is a shift in meaning, place a transitional word or phrase at the head of the sentence. For example, "*But* the proponents believe that . . ." If you use chronological order or an order of importance, begin with numerical transition (*first, second, third*). For other situations involving time, you can insert transitions of time: *fifty years ago, today,* or *in the future.* If you speak of different places, begin with phrases such as *in Europe* or *at Madiera Beach.* (For lists of transitions, see the index.)

OPTIONS FOR INTRODUCTIONS AND CONCLUSIONS

Unless you plan carefully, the closing of your presentation may be the only part that an audience remembers. Unless you hook their attention early, some may daydream for the entire presentation. The attention of others may fade in and out like a weak radio signal. A successful introduction has three key ingredients:

1. **Attention-getter.** It must relate to the topic.
2. **Topic.** State the topic and the thesis unless there is a logical reason for delaying the thesis (see page 251).
3. **Relevance.** Link the topic to the audience. Whet their curiosity and interest.

Introductions

An attention-getter hooks listeners and stimulates interest, perhaps through a reference to the occasion, an anecdote or example, unfamiliar facts or fragments of history, a startling statistic or opinion, an intriguing question, an apt quotation, or original humor—something that happened to you.

Refer to the Occasion   Does the day of the presentation have historical significance? Is the occasion special for the audience or just for you? A reference to the occasion can provide an effective entry into the main idea. On September 7, 1953, George Meany, president of the American Federation of Labor, broadcast a message to our nation. He began by defining the day:

> Labor Day is the one national holiday which does not commemorate famous heroes or historic events. It is dedicated to the millions of men and women who work for wages, the people who have built America's towns and cities, the skilled and unskilled laborers who are responsible, in large measure, for the miracle of American industrial progress. As the representative of

nine million of these working men and women, it is my purpose to report to you on the issues which are of supreme importance on this Labor Day.

Offer an Anecdote or Example

A personal story that illustrates the main point allows you to ease into the topic. For example, if your purpose was to inspire and pay tribute, you might begin, "My uncle would have scoffed if someone had said he had great courage. He would have replied, 'I just did what needed to be done.'" Then the story or example would follow.

Provide an Unfamiliar Fact or Bit of History

Little-known information about a famous person, event, or place can provide an interesting opening. For example, an article from the *Wall Street Journal* (16 Oct. 1998) could serve as an opening for a persuasive presentation:

> Our Congressional Cemetery, 191 years old and located near Capitol Hill, has sunk into obscurity and decay. In fact, this cemetery—where John Philip Sousa, Mathew Brady, and other noted persons lie—was cited in 1997 as "one of the nation's 11 most endangered historic places." That fall volunteers worked for two days cutting shrubbery and sprucing up the grounds. Retired FBI agents placed a bench and fence on J. Edgar Hoover's plot, but major improvements are needed.

Give a Surprising Statistic or Opinion

To capture attention, begin with an unexpected fact or statement. This opening is handy if the topic is familiar to the audience. To interest them, you need something different, a fresh angle or an unusual comment to make them sit up and listen. Consider the following example:

> When my great-grandmother traveled from Pennsylvania to Ohio in a covered wagon in the 1800s, the family had to buy safe drinking water along the way. A typhoid epidemic was raging and people were dying. Today many of us are faced with polluted drinking water on a lesser scale, and we may not even know it. Arsenic is a naturally occurring element in our soil that flows into well water and reservoirs.

Ask a Question

Asking a *rhetorical question*, one you will answer in the presentation, can stimulate curiosity about the topic. For instance, if you were going to talk on beekeeping, you might ask, "Did you know that worker bees have to put the queen on a diet before she can fly and start a new hive? Normally, she is too heavy. They have to keep her from eating until she is light enough to fly."

Or you might ask a question and take an answer from the audience. If you take individual responses, limit them to three. Call on people who are unlikely to toss in a joke or hog the stage. The safest way is to ask a direct question of the entire audience, one that requires a brief yes or no, such as "How many of you have bought a lovely house plant only to have it die within a short time?" Then raise your own hand to indicate a show of hands.

Find an Apt Quotation

The right quotation at the beginning can lend a professional touch. In the first line of the introduction, repeat a key word or phrase from the quotation. This repetition will provide a direct lead to the main idea. If you cannot create a link, find a quotation that is relevant.

Use Humor   Using humor is like lighting a fire—you need to know what you are doing, or you may be burned. Original humor is best, especially brisk one-liners that bring you quickly to the main idea. Do not tell irrelevant jokes just because they are funny. Keep anecdotes and jokes short. A long-winded tale can create a top-heavy presentation. If you direct good-natured humor toward someone, choose a close friend or the head of the company—a self-confident person who will not take offense. Or better yet, tell jokes on yourself. The audience will love it, and it will keep you humble. Avoid ethnic, sexist, and off-color jokes. Be professional.

Inappropriate humor can blast a speaker's credibility. If you intend to use humor in a presentation, appraise it carefully, and follow these guidelines:

1. **Be original and relevant.** Relate humor closely to the main idea.
2. **Use humor like salt—sparingly.** Keep jokes and stories brief.
3. **Be kind.** Avoid remarks that might offend individuals or groups.
4. **Practice your timing.** If people do not laugh, go right on.
5. **Practice your punch line.** Pause before the punch line. Then say it clearly. Do not rush. Emphasize the important words.

GUIDELINES FOR USING HUMOR

Conclusions

In a serious presentation, the conclusion has two prime functions: to summarize and to provide closure. For most informative and persuasive presentations, the ending should *restate the main idea*. As you restate the thesis, allude to the importance of the topic to the audience. Be concise. Three guidelines can help you avoid common problems:

- Do not end abruptly.
- Do not introduce new points.
- Do not ramble.

To devise an effective closing, think about the impression you want to leave. What do you want listeners to remember? Six common endings are listed here. They can be combined in various ways, depending upon the presentation.

Summarize   For emphasis in a serious presentation, remind listeners of the thesis, either directly or by allusion. When you repeat the main idea, listeners are more apt to remember it. Or summarize your main points if appropriate. To spice up a summary ending, combine it with another type of closing.

End with a Quotation   A relevant quotation can provide a thoughtful conclusion. Do not quote an entire poem—use only a few lines that apply to the central idea of the presentation. If you began with a quotation, do not end with another. Chances are the two will conflict and detract from the presentation.

Loop to the Introduction   Allude to the opening in some way for closure. If you began with a rhetorical question, you might answer it briefly in the conclusion. If you began with a quotation, you might repeat a key phrase. Or if you began with a story, you might quickly finish it as Paul Harvey does in "the rest of the story."

Pose a Challenge or Question   A challenge or provocative question can motivate an audience. This ending is often used to persuade. For example, a presentation that reports the progress on a volunteer playground project might end with appreciation, a summary, and a question (note the emotional appeal):

> We appreciate your generosity. You have opened your pocketbooks and lent your hands. The job is almost complete. Will you come once more to help rake the site and spread mulch this Saturday or Sunday? Seeing the delight on the children's faces when they can use this playground will make you glad you did.

Call for Action   A persuasive presentation requires a restatement of the proposition. Often a call for action is also included to motivate the audience. For example, "Tonight set your alarm ten minutes early. Then stop by the voting booth on your way to class or to work. You owe it to yourself and your country."

Refer to the Future   Mentioning the future can lend an optimistic note. In "I Have a Dream," Martin Luther King combined three techniques in his ending: he summarized the main idea, alluded to the future, and quoted from an old song. Note, too, the use of *we* to unite listeners:

> When we let freedom ring, when we let it ring from every village and every hamlet, from every state and every city, we will be able to speed up that day when all of God's children, black men and white men, Jews and Gentiles, Protestants and Catholics, will be able to join hands and sing in the words of the old Negro spiritual, "Free at last! Free at last! Thank God almighty, we are free at last!"

PREPARING NOTES AND AUDIOVISUALS

Preparing careful notes and effective audiovisuals can enhance your presentation. Although some experienced speakers manage without notes, most carry them as insurance. Even professional presenters are not immune to sudden memory loss. Confidently, one presenter strode up to the lectern without his notes because he had practiced well. But when he looked out over a sea of five hundred faces, his mind went blank. While the audience waited, he walked back to his chair for the notes. That was a humbling experience.

Notes on Paper or Cards?

By now you should be convinced that notes are essential, even if your instructor does not require them. The one remaining question is whether to put the notes on paper or file cards. If you ever present a seminar, you might decide to type your outline on paper, double spaced in large type. If you're using presentation software, the program will include options for preparing notes.

A few sheets of paper are simpler to handle than a dozen note cards unless there will be air blowing near you. (Overhead projectors, for instance, can scatter pages.) Number the sheets in the upper right corner. Place them in a neat pile on one side of the lectern before you begin. As you finish covering the points on each page, *slide the page to the other side of the lectern while looking at your audience.* Continue in this way, and the audience will be unlikely to notice your notes. This method takes more skill and practice than using a few note cards.

For classroom presentations, carefully prepared note cards are easy to use. You just lay out the cards and leave them alone during the presentation. Six large cards will usually fit neatly on a lectern. Although six may seem like quite a few, beware of crowding words. *You need to be able to scan the cards quickly without picking them up or bending over.* Note cards should be legible from three feet away (unless you are very short).

1. **Use large 5- by 8-inch cards.** For easy reading, avoid crowding.
2. **Number the cards in the upper right corner.** Avoid mixups.
3. **Use an outline format.** Leave blank space to add key phrases later.
4. **Print neatly with black ink in large letters.** Use broad strokes.
5. **Use numbers or bullets to list points.** Enhance visibility.
6. **Use only one side of each card.** Turning cards over diverts attention.

TIPS FOR MAKING NOTE CARDS

Creating Effective Audiovisuals

Chances are that you will have a software program such as PowerPoint at your disposal for use in a presentation. Or you might use an overhead projector, a flip chart, a VCR, a tape player, or other audiovisual. (A chalkboard is not recommended because it lacks novelty and requires turning your back while the audience waits.) On the job you might use virtual meeting software, which allows remote participants on broadband networks to hear and see the speaker and the presentation materials.

The purpose of any audiovisual is to enhance a presentation, not overpower it. Include graphics not only to provide interest but also to support your points.

www.mhhe.com/dietsch

For help using PowerPoint to create audiovisuals, check out:
Writing>PowerPoint Tutorial

If you use tapes or videos, keep the clips short—a minute or less for a five- to seven-minute speech. Condense ideas and list only the major points. A common problem occurs when too many lines of print are included in a graphic. Use fragments that can be explained orally. Check the layout of posters, transparencies, and PowerPoint presentations with an eye to attractiveness:

- Use bullets to emphasize important points.
- As you plan graphics, check to see that each frame or sheet conveys a single idea.
- Avoid clutter. Limit the number of points per frame.
- If you have several statistics or other complex items, prepare a handout to pass out before you begin. *Do not interrupt your presentation to pass materials.* Less relevant information can be left near the door to be picked up later.

GUIDELINES FOR PLANNING VISUALS

1. **Predict the effect of the visual and test it.** *Run unusual ideas past your instructor.* Bring no snakes, guns, volatile liquids, or anything that might pose a threat to the audience or that violates campus policies.
2. **Limit the number of visuals and keep them fairly simple.** Otherwise, you may feel like a juggler with too many balls in the air.
3. **Limit tapes and videos to one minute in a five- to seven-minute presentation.**
4. **Make graphics neat and attractive.** Plan layouts so that they are clear, uncluttered, and pleasing to the eye. Limit each to one idea.
5. **Use color for a purpose.** Human eyes, like those of bees, are attracted to red and black. Use red for emphasis and dark colors for lettering.
6. **Check to see that visuals are clear to persons seated in the back row.** If you are discussing a small object, show an enlargement.
7. **Retain the element of surprise!** Keep visuals hidden until you use them. For example, reverse posters until you are ready to show them.

PRACTICING A PRESENTATION

Planning and practice are essential for an effective presentation. Attending to equipment at the last minute and dropping or misplacing items can give the impression of carelessness and incompetence. Careful preparation will boost your confidence and help fend off mishaps.

Practice your presentation several times, using your note cards and audiovisuals, but do not overpractice, or it may sound memorized. To lend a natural conversational tone, you might imagine you are talking to friends. *Act as if you feel calm, even if you don't.* If you have the opportunity to videotape a practice session, do so. Then you can critique your eye contact, posture, gestures, vocal variety, and use of notes and audiovisuals.

Using Audiovisuals

Plan how and when to use audiovisuals so that the audience does not have to wait. Can you set up and adjust PowerPoint, the VCR, or tape players before class? How will you prop up the antique doll? Can you get an easel so that the poster will not flop over? Other questions to consider are when to bring out objects and how long to leave them out.

As you speak, *look at the audience, not the visuals.* When using an overhead projector, use a pencil to point on the transparency. When slides or other visuals are projected on a screen behind you, use a longer object to point to areas of the screen. That way you can glance at it and look at the audience, not the screen. If you are describing an unfamiliar object or craft, such as punched tin, bring it out early. If the object will not distract, leave it out the entire time. Or some objects are more effective shown only at the end.

One student, who had won several trophies showing her horse, did not want to appear to be bragging, so she decided to display just one trophy. First she described the fun of displaying the horse in the ring; then she explained the unglamorous work behind the scenes. At the end she held up a large trophy and said, "But all the hard work was worthwhile, for I won first prize!" By then she had charmed the audience, and they were glad her efforts had been rewarded.

Revising Note Cards

As you practice your presentation, highlight key points on your notes with a colored marker. If you quote someone, highlight it. If certain terms are difficult to recall, print them in red. Reword any phrases or sentences that cause stumbling. Write the revision on your note card. Star the spots where audiovisuals will come. On the final card or page, write out the last sentence as a safety blanket. If your notes become messy from revision, recopy them as necessary for easy reading.

Improving Eye Contact, Posture, and Gestures

Before you ever open your lips, you send silent messages that enhance or diminish your credibility. Your eye contact, posture, and gestures greatly affect your presentation. Do you look at the audience—or do you stare at a point on the back wall? Do you stand erect or slumped? Do you have notes in hand ready to lay out, or do you fumble through a briefcase, backpack, or handbag?

Eye Contact   Smile and establish eye contact immediately before you say a word. During the presentation, look at one person for several seconds before moving on. Look at various people in different parts of the room, not just the front row. Avoid eye dart. You may *glance* at your note cards from time to time, but do not linger. Their purpose is merely to remind you of the next idea.

Gestures   Like your words, your gestures should appear spontaneous and natural. You might rest one hand on the lectern, but do not clutch it with both hands. The purpose of a lectern is to hold notes, not to lean on or hide behind. Once in a while you may want to walk out from behind the lectern, but beware of purposeless movement and repetitive gestures. Consider, too, that some gestures may have negative or humorous connotations. Three common stances have been identified as detrimental for speakers:

- **Fig leaf.** Avoid standing with hands clasped in front.
- **Parade rest.** Avoid standing with hands clasped behind the back like a general reviewing the troops.
- **Closed mind.** Avoid crossed arms on the chest. This posture may suggest coldness and a reluctance to admit new information.

While you speak, let you arms hang loosely at your sides so that you can use them naturally. Avoid nervous habits that dispel the illusion of spontaneity and distract. Common habits include scratching the nose, twisting long hair or beard, fidgeting with earrings, jingling coins, taking glasses on and off, or waving a note card around.

Improving Vocal Variety

The human voice is an instrument that conveys distinctive speech sounds that vary in volume, rate, and pitch. When we are relaxed and happy, the sounds are more pleasing than when we are tired or upset. Fear, anxiety, and anger tighten the vocal cords, producing a higher, thinner pitch than normal. With practice you can gain greater control of your voice. Volume and rate are easier to control than pitch, but all can be improved to some extent. Taping an entire presentation allows you not only to time it but also to hear how you sound.

Volume   A presenter's voice should be loud enough to be heard by everyone in the room, unless a microphone is available. To project your voice to the back row, you need plenty of air in the lungs. Shallow breathing interferes with vocal variety and quality. Try varying your volume according to the effect you wish to create. Emphasize important words. Be careful that your voice does not trail off at the ends of sentences, making them inaudible.

Rate   "Mallspeak" or immature speech patterns may be a concern for some readers. In "Taking Aim at Student Incoherence" (*Chronicle of Higher Education* 26 Mar. 1999), Alison Schneider cites this sample, delivered breathlessly: "Okay. Today I'm going to be talking to you guys about malaria." During the presentation the student fidgeted and giggled, ending with "So, in conclusion, I'd just like to say, malaria, you know, is the most prevalent of all tropical diseases."
Speaking too fast, fidgeting, and giggling may be due to nervousness or feelings of inadequacy, intensified by habit. If you have any of these concerns, give yourself a little pep talk. Reassure yourself that these minutes are yours and

you have an interesting topic to share. The audience is alert and waiting. You don't have to race to the finish line. Don't be afraid to pause at the right places, including a slight pause after periods. Pausing after an important point gives emphasis and allows the audience time to absorb the idea. Knowing that it is all right to pause naturally may help you delete unintentional fillers such as *uh, um, okay,* or *you know.*

Articulation   Practice and pausing can alleviate slurring (running words to-gether) or other problems in articulation. The lips, the tongue, and the teeth form speech sounds—they articulate the words. At the same time, the mouth has to open wide enough to let the words out or mumbling occurs. And *it must be empty*—chewing gum, candy, or cough drops interfere with clear delivery.

Common concerns are slurring and addition of or omission of syllables. Tape yourself and then check a dictionary for problem words. Listed here are common mispronunciations and the correct pronunciations:

INCORRECT	CORRECT
acrost	a-cross′
fishin′	fish′ing
gonna	go′ing to
pitchur	pic′ture
wanna	want to

Pitch   *Pitch* refers to the lowness or highness of the voice. We all have a natu-ral pitch that varies according to our emotions and health. Other factors also influence pitch. For example, if we ask a question, our voice goes up at the end of the sentence. At the end of a declarative sentence, the voice goes down. Most speakers, when relaxed, vary their pitch naturally. Those who speak in a mono-tone can add expression to their words through vocal exercise and practice (see the exercises at the end of the chapter).

GIVING A PRESENTATION

Enthusiasm and *sincerity* are two keys to an effective presentation. Enthusiastic speakers know and care about their topics. They vary their volume, rate, and pitch just as they would in casual conversation. Chances are that if you like your topic and prepare well, your enthusiasm will radiate from your face and your voice. And if you truly believe what you are saying, your sincerity will be apparent.

Arrive Early

Go early to the room where you will speak. Erase the board if necessary. Check to see that the equipment you need is in working order. (One mortified student forgot to plug in the VCR.) If you are supposed to sign equipment out somewhere else, go get it.

Take a Deep Breath . . .

When introduced, take a deep breath and approach the lectern. Put down your notes or, if you're using note cards, lay them out in sequence. Then look out over the audience and smile. Chances are that some people will smile back. If you come across as a friendly person, listeners will be more apt to give you their undivided attention. For some topics, smiling may be inappropriate.

On the job or in a community setting, extend an appropriate greeting, such as "Good Morning" or "Welcome." You may want to thank someone who has assisted or the group for inviting you. In the classroom these little courtesies are not expected.

Don't Apologize Unnecessarily

Even if you feel unprepared, rushed, or nervous, don't apologize or toss in unnecessary comments. Just ignore your feelings and begin with your planned opening. Once you get past that and the audience responds, speaking will become easier. If you should mispronounce a word, just correct yourself and go on. Avoid weak, *ineffective* remarks such as these:

- Uh, I guess I'm a little nervous.
- I didn't have as much time to prepare as I would have liked.
- I regret I am not an expert on this topic (false modesty).

Adapt to the Audience and Unexpected Events

Watching the audience will take your mind off yourself. Are they listening attentively? Or do they slump in their seats, gaze at the ceiling, or fidget? To regain lost attention, you can move out from behind the lectern, use more gestures, increase volume, or lower your voice to a whisper.

Handle unexpected incidents with poise. If a transparency falls, let it lie unless you need it. If the bulb in an overhead projector burns out, flip the switch for the spare bulb. If there is none, continue anyway. If computer equipment malfunctions, take a moment to resolve the problem. If the problem can't be fixed within a few moments, go on without the audiovisual. Seldom is there cause to interrupt a presentation. In the unlikely event of a power outage, sonic boom, or storm alert, stop and wait. Then when you resume the presentation, you might toss in a quick joke. The audience will admire your calm, professional demeanor and ability to function under duress.

End Purposefully and Gracefully

The last few words of a presentation tend to linger in the minds of the audience. Once in a while, an inexperienced presenter will skid to an abrupt stop with "That's it" or "that's all." Some go to the other extreme—tacking on afterthoughts, irrelevant jokes, or stories. Such tactics throw a presentation off balance and weaken its impact. Know when to stop.

Be Prepared for Questions

After a class presentation, there may not be time for questions. For presentations at work or in the community, however, question-and-answer sessions are often expected. In these cases, you should be prepared to say, "Are there any questions?"

Listen carefully to the entire question before answering. Maintain eye contact. If the question is unclear, ask for a restatement. Or you might paraphrase: "In other words, you are asking if . . . ?" Wait for a response. This tactic will allow you a little time to think. If you don't know the answer, you might reply, "That's an excellent question. I'd like to do a little research before responding. Can I get back to you?" Then ask for a phone number or an e-mail address.

STUDENT SAMPLE: A PERSUASIVE PRESENTATION
Carol Witzel gave the following presentation extemporaneously. She had outlined it on note cards but wrote out the draft later, when requested.

Give It More Respect!

Do you know what the hottest part of your body is? Do you know what part is the most dangerous if it becomes infected? The answer to both questions is your mouth, specifically your gums and teeth. Are you surprised? Like Rodney Dangerfield, your mouth and its contents get little respect. After you hear of my unfortunate experience, you should accord this part of your body much, much more respect.

During a regular checkup two years ago, my physician said that he did not like the looks of my gums and that I should have a dentist take a look at them. Immediately, I made an appointment with my regular dentist. I told him my mouth had a metallic taste, and my teeth seemed to hurt often. During the exam the dentist told me not to worry, everything was fine. He did not bother to take x-rays.

One year passed and the symptoms worsened. By then my gums were bleeding every time that I brushed my teeth. When I opened my mouth in cold air, my face and teeth hurt. Finally, I decided it was time to consult a different dentist. The second dentist did a quick exam—the results were dismal. Several teeth had advanced decay. Worst of all, my gums were in an advanced stage of periodontal disease or gingivitis. Gingivitis is inflammation and infection of the gingiva or gums. There are five stages of the disease, and I was in stage four.

What I needed was minor surgery on the gums to clear away the infection. Then he put in seven crowns to correct the problems with decayed teeth. After that came bridgework, which involved three additional crowns and two pontics (false teeth). The bridge was made to cover the loss of two teeth due to poor care. Correcting all these problems cost nearly $7,000.

Today you cannot tell my natural teeth from the crowns or bridgework. My teeth no longer hurt when I drink hot or cold liquids. I can actually breathe through my mouth without severe pain emitting from teeth to all points on my face.

Now you are probably wondering how you can prevent some of the problems I've experienced. The first step is to have regular dental checkups with a responsible dentist. Second, take good daily care of your teeth and mouth by brushing and flossing. Third, watch for any of these five symptoms:

1. **Bleeding in the mouth.** Have it checked just as you would if some other part of your body was bleeding regularly.
2. **A metallic taste.** If you already have fillings, this could mean you have decay under the filling, and the old filling is leaking.
3. **Extreme sensitivity** to hot and cold temperatures.
4. **Chronic bad breath.**
5. **Chronic tiredness, headaches, or white spots on the gums** could indicate infection. Those who use tobacco should watch these signs closely because of the risk of cancer in the mouth.

If your dentist does not stress good gum care, maybe you should consider finding another dentist. Just remember that your mouth is the gateway to your body. To have good health, respect and maintain your mouth, gums, and teeth. You will be glad you did!

QUESTIONS FOR DISCUSSION

1. How does Carol involve the audience in her opening?
2. What common order does she use to present information?
3. What signpost transitions indicate this order?
4. Can you find the transitional sentence that she uses to go from talking about herself to explaining about good dental care?
5. What do you notice about her ending?
6. React to the title of her speech.
7. How would you rate Carol's credibility? Why?

PRACTICE

EXERCISE: Articulation

To improve your articulation, say the alphabet aloud. Exaggerate each letter and say it distinctly. Listen and think about the position of your tongue and lips. They must be in the right position for a letter to be clear. To form an *l*, the tip of the tongue touches the roof of the mouth, and the mouth opens slightly. The *r* sound rumbles deep in the throat as the tongue is held up slightly and the mouth curls down, slightly open.

If dropping of *g*'s is a problem for you, practice words ending with *-ing* and think about the position of your tongue and mouth as you say them correctly, emphasizing *-ing*. As you attain greater self-awareness, your vocal variety will improve.

EXERCISE: Volume, Rate, Pitch

To improve vocal variety, you might read aloud to a child. To relax the vocal cords, exaggerate the sounds and have fun. *Goldilocks and the Three Bears* provides excellent practice, allowing the reader to assume different voices. Baby Bear's words tumble out in a high squeaky pitch. Mother Bear articulates clearly at a moderate rate in a medium-pitched voice. Papa Bear speaks in a slow, deep-pitched voice that rumbles with authority. (If the child can read, she can take Goldilocks's part. A boy might prefer a role in *The Three Little Pigs*.)

UNGRADED PRESENTATIONS

The chief purpose of an ungraded presentation is to alleviate speech fright. A one- or two-minute practice speech can use the basic claim-and-evidence order (opinion and support). For example, you might disagree with a news item, magazine article, political decision, or movie review. Give reasons. Close with a complete sentence, such as "See *Clint Rides Again* only if you want to be bored stiff." Or you might use one of the ideas below or one of your own.

1. Funny, exciting, or embarrassing moment
2. An unusual ancestor, neighbor, or boss
3. An incident: how your spouse proposed, prank at summer camp, et cetera
4. How a teacher (or someone else) influenced you
5. Anecdote: a lost pet, special birthday, or disastrous first date
6. Your first job or first car
7. Your first day at school
8. A scary experience
9. What you learned from . . .
10. Why you are attending college

TWENTY IDEAS FOR ORAL PRESENTATIONS

INFORMATIVE TOPICS

1 Present a research-based paper or project to the class (condense and simplify).

2 Present a lab report. Describe the process that you observed.

3 Practice a presentation you will be giving at work or elsewhere.

4 Present tips for improving something.

5 Describe your job and three things you have learned.

6 Explain what to look for in a diamond.

7 Suggest three interesting one-day trips to lesser-known spots.

8 Explain how to discourage burglars.

9 Describe your hobby. (Bring objects in stages of completion.)

10 Suggest three excellent restaurants in _____ .

PERSUASIVE TOPICS

11 Build a new firehouse.

12 Get a physical exam regularly.

13 Voting is a responsibility.

14 Neuter your pet.

15 Cut your sugar intake.

16 Preserve a historical landmark.

17 Take steps to prevent fires in your home.

18 Instant replay should (should not) be used by football referees.

19 Prevent skin cancer.

20 Be an organ donor.

Effective Employment Writing

> I hope I shall possess firmness and virtue enough to maintain what I consider the most enviable of all titles, the character of an "Honest Man."
>
> —George Washington (1732–1799)

With the Information Age, our culture catapulted into cyberspace. By accessing the Internet, you can research companies, read job listings, and secure help in writing employment documents. You can even post your own résumé on the Web, if you wish; but if you do, security precautions are advisable. This chapter provides practically everything you need to know about preparing an up-to-date résumé, an eye-catching cover letter, a letter of appreciation, and posthiring letters. Included, too, are suggestions for e-mail and maintaining privacy, as well as two Internet directories (see pages 382 and 400).

I. WRITING AN EFFECTIVE RÉSUMÉ

www.mhhe.com/dietsch

For online advice on writing in work settings, go to: Writing>Résumés/Writing at Work

Don't be misled into thinking that filling out a résumé form for an Internet posting is a one-hour shortcut to a job. Richard N. Bolles, whose *Net Guide* includes "The Fairy Godmother Report on Résumé Sites," says the chances are that an Internet résumé will go unread. Bolles' report emphasizes the fact that most job seekers need a printed résumé for mailing and faxing. If they apply to large companies that screen résumés with software, they will also need a scannable résumé. And since many companies request a résumé be sent by e-mail, a third version may be required.

Compiling different versions of a résumé is not as complicated as you might think, for all three have the same basic content. Only the format varies. This chapter presents suggestions for printed, scannable, and e-mailed résumés; various employment letters; and a list of references. Two career directories are also included. One will help you gain an overview of your career field. The other directory lists reliable Web sites, with a minimum of sales promotion, to help in writing employment documents.

Two fundamental guidelines for compiling an effective résumé are

1. To be honest and accurate in presenting your qualifications.
2. To focus the résumé toward the needs of the employer.

ETHICS, ACCURACY, AND RÉSUMÉS

Integrity has become a hidden agenda for employers. Flagrant abuses of truth on résumés have become common as more applicants fudge dates, magnify accomplishments, pad job duties, and invent college degrees. As employers scan résumés, they watch for anything that might indicate falsification, exaggeration, or carelessness. As they check references, they query former employers about the applicant's actual length of employment, kind of position, awards, promotions, and other items.

There is a demand for employees who are not only skilled but also reliable, trustworthy, and accurate. Therefore, allot plenty of time to prepare the best résumé possible. Then proofread it carefully several times before sending it. During an interview expect to be questioned closely about items on the résumé. You may also be tested and fingerprinted, depending upon the position. After hiring, some companies require a lie detector test.

Before you start your career research and writing, it will be valuable to know why many résumés are never read.

TEN REASONS RÉSUMÉS ARE DISCARDED

As you assemble personal data for your résumé, double-check all dates and consider the relevance of each item. Include only information that is accurate and pertinent to your job objective. Ten common reasons for discarding résumés are:

1. **Few or no dates.** When dates are missing, particularly dates of employment, the employer wonders what the applicant is trying to hide.

2. **Not following employers' directions.** Include requested information such as certification, licensure, bonding, or immigration status. Some employers request a cover letter be e-mailed before a résumé. Ads also list certain stipulations.

3. **Lack of focus.** Omission of a job objective, a haphazard résumé, and irrelevant information can leave an employer wondering if the applicant knows what he or she wants to do.

4. **Problems in format.** A résumé should be clear and easily scanned in twenty seconds or less. A summary of qualifications or "profile" should appear after the job objective. Avoid fancy fonts, crowding, lengthy paragraphs, and several pages.

5. **Skimpy listing of skills and experience.** Be succinct but specific. Start each listing with an active verb and include your accomplishments.

6. **Omission of keywords.** For the initial screening, many large companies use software that scans for keywords related to the position. Include them.

7. **Job hopping.** A series of short-term jobs may cause employers to wonder why you left and if you will do the same again. A functional résumé can de-emphasize this concern.

8. **Listing health problems.** One woman with an MBA and an impressive work history listed "2004–2005 Recovery from cancer. Cured." on her résumé. She received no calls until she removed the item, which she was not obligated to mention. (Instead, she stated "Personal obligations.") Legally, you must disclose *only disabilities that hinder your productivity,* not your medical history. Although such disabilities must be revealed before hiring, do not refer to them on your résumé.

9. **Discrepancies.** One woman accidentally misstated her college graduation date by one year. Her résumé, targeted for an accounting position, was weeded out.

10. **Spelling and grammatical errors.** Employers consider such errors inexcusable. Most positions for college graduates require accuracy and writing competency.

TWO POPULAR STYLES OF RÉSUMÉS

An excellent résumé is more than a work history; *it states what you can do to benefit the employer.* The résumé should reveal how you performed in the workplace or in the community if you did volunteer work. If you have a dual major or work experience in two areas and wish to apply for two different jobs, then you will need two different résumés, each focused on just one position.

Two current résumé styles are the chronological and the functional. Actually, both are hybrids of their forerunners of a few years ago. Acute differences between the two styles have blurred: Now both invariably contain a job objective, a summary of qualifications, and a listing of accomplishments and skills, as well as work experience and education.

The chief differences are that the chronological style emphasizes employment and skills gained on each job whereas the functional style emphasizes a mix of skills gained from work, education, and leisure. Both styles are quite flexible, and examples of each style vary widely. Still the basic principles for writing résumés apply, regardless of whether they are faxed, scanned, or e-mailed.

The Chronological Résumé

If you have worked in just one career field, progressed upward, and acquired the skills for your targeted position, then the chronological style is the best choice for you. The *chronological* style emphasizes solid qualifications and achievement on the job over several years. This style usually highlights work experience, setting forth what the applicant has accomplished (in reverse chronological order).

If you have a gap in employment, that does not necessarily raise a red flag, for layoffs have become routine at all ranks. If you have taken a job with less pay after such a gap, be prepared to supply a valid reason during an interview (illness of a family member, expense, time spent commuting, or a similar one). If you are switching career fields or have been fired (never mention on a résumé), then the functional résumé is definitely the better choice.

The Functional Résumé

The *functional* résumé style emphasizes skills and abilities—not when, where, or how you obtained them. When new college graduates have minimal work experience, they can fill out their résumé with groups of skills learned in classes, during internships, or from volunteer projects. Older students who are switching career fields can de-emphasize the disparity between their work experience and job objective by listing relevant achievements before their work history. Dates of work experience and education are listed in reverse chronological order.

A series of short-term jobs and gaps in employment receive less emphasis on a functional résumé (more help on this point a little later). The flexibility of the functional style makes it the best choice for most young students or others with little or no work experience in their chosen field.

RESEARCH AND PREWRITING FOR A RÉSUMÉ

The purpose of any résumé is to obtain an interview. To succeed, you need to package your qualifications in the most appealing way possible without deviating from the truth. Writing an effective résumé requires knowledge, skill, effort, and accuracy. You need to have a general knowledge of your career field, know what employers want, have certain skills, and present yourself well. From your résumé and during interviews, prospective employers will be trying to predict how you will fit in with the company and how well you will perform.

The first step to a successful résumé is preliminary research of your career field. You need background knowledge of possible positions, job duties, working conditions, and the correct terminology to use. New jobs are being created constantly, and new words are born every day.

Gaining an Overview of a Career Field

Although the Internet has a wealth of resources, you can fritter away hours online if your search is unfocused. The career resources directory on page 382 lists print, online, and database resources. In an hour or two, you can gain an overview of your career field and the range of positions within it. Special databases at the library can provide profiles of careers on state and national levels. A computerized index can assist you in locating career articles in journals and magazines.

After a preliminary search, you should have a general idea of your field, employment opportunities, correct job titles, and possible keywords to include on a résumé.

Identifying Employers' Needs

The more you know about the qualifications that employers seek, the better you can tailor your résumé to fit a company's specific needs. In addition to reading newspaper help-wanted ads, visit Web sites of employers in the field. Many post job descriptions of personnel they need. Jot down keywords relating to the job you would like. Print out copies of the ads that interest you so that you will know how to focus your résumé. This research will acquaint you with the expectations of employers.

It also helps to have an understanding of problems that employers commonly face but rarely discuss with applicants: theft, security of data, low productivity, and lawsuits, to name a few. Such items compose an invisible agenda that directs the appraisal of résumés and applicants. (The *Wall Street Journal* and other business publications often feature such concerns.)

PRINT SOURCES (To locate, ask the reference librarian.)

- *Encyclopedia of Careers and Vocational Guidance.* 12th ed. Ferguson Publishing Company, 2002. This four-volume set reviews 93 career fields and approximately 675 careers. The first volume includes finding a job, choosing a career, and networking. Well presented and up to date.

- *Occupational Outlook Handbook.* 2004–2005 ed. US Department of Labor, Bulletin 2570. Includes job educational requirements, duties, salaries, and outlook for the future.

- *O'Net Dictionary of Occupational Titles.* 3rd ed. JIST Works, 2004. A print version of the O'Net database. Source: US Department of Labor.

- **Specialized Encyclopedias.** Ask if there are any in your field of interest. For example, *Exploring Health Care Careers,* 2nd. ed., Ferguson Publishing Company, 2002, provides information on over 100 health care careers. Includes job descriptions, licensing requirements, salary and employment outlook.

- *VGM Opportunities Series.* VGM Career Books, 2001–2004. Covers a broad range of individual careers, including pharmacy, culinary, medical imaging, travel, eye care, veterinary medicine, and alternative medicine.

DIRECTORY 1: RELIABLE CAREER RESOURCES

INTERNET RESOURCES

The Web sites listed below are reliable and safe. They provide free, up-to-date help with minimal sales promotion. (Current browsers will fill in http://. Sometimes www. is not part of the URL.)

- **Career Onestop.** Free job and résumé postings. Information on wages, occupational trends, skills, abilities, et cetera. <www.careeronestop.org>

- *Occupational Outlook Handbook.* 2004–2005 ed. Printer-friendly version in HTML. <www.bls.gov/oco/home.htm>

- **O Net.** The replacement for the *U.S. Dictionary of Occupational Titles,* the *Directory of Occupational Titles,* and the *Occupational Job Outlook.* Online version of the print version (above). Updated periodically.

Note: Directory 2, "Online Employment Writing Resources," also lists sites that provide other career information (see page 400).

ONLINE DATABASES

Some libraries allow you to access these databases from your home computer, using your library card number. Ask the reference librarian.

- *EBSCOhost.* Offers articles and abstracts of periodicals from a range of disciplines. The *Vocational & Career Collection* provides the text of 400 trade- and industry-related periodicals.

- *Encyclopedia of Careers and Vocational Guidance.* Online version of the printed four-volume set (see above).

If you can adroitly show on your résumé how a company can benefit from hiring you, the targeted job may well be yours. As you research, watch for answers to the following questions:

1. What are the main duties of the positions?
2. What skills, qualities, and habits do potential employers seek?
3. What is likely to be the employer's chief concern? (Read your local newspapers carefully for news of businesses and other employers.)
4. What keywords recur in help-wanted ads?
5. Which kind of position is likely to be most appropriate for you?

Identifying Qualifications

A giant first step toward compiling an effective résumé is the identification of *transferable skills*, skills that can be applied on another job. A *skill* is an art, trade, or craft developed through extensive practice. Thinking tasks require mental abilities such as problem solving, decision making, designing, and the like. After identifying your skills and abilities, you can devise ways to attest to positive personal qualities and desirable work habits. Keep in mind that you need *concrete evidence* to back up these claims.

Transferable skills will become the heart of your résumé. To identify your skills, examine your experience in the workplace, in college, and during leisure hours. You can start by brainstorming. Take three sheets of paper and write three headings: "Work Skills," "Academic Skills," and "Leisure Skills." On the Work Skills page, jot down duties and the skills required to do them. Consider both paid and unpaid jobs, including military service and volunteer work. Leave an inch or so of space between items to add more details later. On the second sheet, list training and skills obtained during your education. On the third sheet, list hobbies and any skills you may have developed during leisure hours. To prod a sluggish memory, you might ask yourself questions.

Workplace Skills   As the questions below indicate, workplace skills include many abilities and responsibilities. Some may have been listed in your job description when you were hired, but others may have been additional tasks you took on.

- **What problems have I helped to solve or alleviate?** Include cost control, procedural changes, security, troubleshooting, or others.
- **What tasks can I perform effectively?** Include purchasing, data entry, network installations, software applications.
- **What equipment can I operate, maintain, or repair?** Include everything from oscilloscopes to cash registers to tractors.
- **What systems, layouts, or operations have I designed or executed?**
- **Have I ever inventoried, audited, or researched?** Include online research, lab or legal research, conducting surveys, and interviewing.

- **What writing did I do on the job?** Minutes or memos? Letters or newsletters? Procedures or manuals? Reports or proposals? Patient charts?

- **What oral communication skills have I developed?** Have I conducted meetings? Given presentations? Taught or trained? Screened applicants? Greeted clients? Do I speak a second language well?

- **What tasks have required interpersonal skill?** Handling difficult clients or patients? Negotiating? Making collections? Resolving problems?

- **What have I done that demonstrated responsibility?** Supervised or managed? Reorganized a department? Expanded? Resolved disputes? Budgeted? (State amount if large.) Hired? Scheduled? Coordinated projects?

- **How have I contributed to the success of projects and operations?** Decreased costs? Increased profits? Improved client or community relations?

- **Did I receive training in the military or in special courses on the job?**

- **Do I have any special licenses or certifications? Bonding? Security clearance?**

Academic Skills   Think of your college courses as training, but do *not* list courses. Look for *skills* you have gained—that's what employers want to know. Consider, too, any skills developed from internships, clinics, or other educational outside work. You might start by asking yourself questions such as these:

- **What equipment have I learned to operate? Repair? Maintain?**

- **What procedures have I performed?** Medical, legal, accounting, insurance billing, or others?

- **How have I used management skills?** What projects have I completed? Include work with campus organizations, fund-raising, event planning, tutoring, counseling, case work, and other projects.

- **What oral communication skills and interpersonal skills have I honed?** Giving presentations? Listening or questioning? Applying business etiquette training? Telephoning? Instructing clients? Handling complaints?

- **What research and writing skills have I demonstrated?** Include research papers, business report writing, independent study projects, published work in campus newspapers or magazines, and the like.

- **What other specialized training do I have?** Include skills such as "build prototypes," "diagnose electrical failures," or other special knowledge in your field.

Personal Skills   During leisure hours you may have acquired planning, leadership, financial, teaching, human relations, or other skills that are relevant to the position you seek. Consider activities and memberships in high school, college, or community organizations as well as hobbies. Then ask yourself other questions such as these:

- **What projects have I completed for my family and home?** You might list compiling a family genealogy, remodeling a kitchen, or building a patio. Then try to link the skill to the job objective. (All these tasks require planning and organizational skills.)

- **What community projects have I participated in?** Planning? Managing a scout troop? Coaching a team? Assisting in a day care center? Counseling on a hotline? Judging contests? Writing a newsletter? Organizing?

- **Have I developed special skills?** Photography, music, drawing, designing, writing, quilting, cooking, woodworking, or others?

- **What special training have I received?** Have I worked as a volunteer firefighter, librarian, pianist, or in another position? Do I have CPR or EMT training?

- **Do I have other knowledge derived from adult education courses, seminars, workshops, or conferences?**

Compiling a comprehensive skills list will require more than one session. Time is needed to mull over your experience. After you finish, you may have thirty or more specific, transferable skills. After that, pinpoint items that indicate positive qualities and work habits.

Personal Qualities and Work Habits   Employers look for positive personal qualities such as reliability, confidentiality, congeniality, and flexibility. However, you won't claim these directly on your résumé. Instead, give specific examples that imply or indicate these intangible qualities and sound work habits. For example, you might list items similar to the following:

- Never missed a day's work in five years
- Met all deadlines for reports and projects
- Collected cash receipts and made bank deposits
- Entrusted with keys to open and close business
- Maintained and monitored confidential client files
- Received two promotions within one year
- Acted as supervisor during boss's two-month leave

Or perhaps you had responsibility for security. You may have had access to certain keys, computer codes, valuable merchandise, formulas, procedures, or other private information. Avoid trite, unsubstantiated claims such as "work well with people," "honest," and "hard-working."

DRAFTING A RÉSUMÉ

The major parts of a résumé are *job objective, summary, accomplishments, skills, work experience,* and *education.* The job objective always comes first and the summary second, but other major parts follow in most- to least-important order, according to the applicant's qualifications. In other words, you organize these sections to your best advantage, using either the chronological or functional résumé style. Major sections containing dates are arranged in *reverse chronological order*. Thus the most recent date is listed first. Minor information, if any, follows.

A few experts suggest omitting the objective. But job objectives are generally regarded as essential in order to focus the résumé and save the employer's time. Few are going to spend time trying to figure out which position the applicant wants.

The Service-Oriented Job Objective

As you look at résumé samples, notice that good job objectives focus on just one career field, contain carefully worded fragments, and steer away from personal needs. They avoid trite, vague, and misdirected phrases such as "desire to work for a company that is a leader in the field," or "a position where I can hone my skills as a . . ." An employer watches for reasons to hire that will benefit the company, not fulfill your private agenda. A service-oriented job objective acts as a thesis statement with three parts:

- Job title with reference number, if there is one
- Type of business, industry, or institution (optional, especially when applying for a position with a reference number)
- Major skill areas of the applicant that can interest the employer

Shy away from underselling yourself. Avoid the phrase *entry-level*. Career consultants warn against it, lest you end up in a dead-end job. To prewrite your objective, ask yourself questions and jot down your answers:

1. How can I show that I am well qualified for the position?
2. What two or three qualities are especially needed for this job?
3. What major skills do employers seek for this position?
4. Do my qualifications fit the objective? (If not, look for another job.)
5. Is the terminology correct for the field? Have I included keywords?

SERVICE-ORIENTED OBJECTIVES

A service-oriented objective identifies the position and states how you can benefit the employer:

- Pediatric nursing position #2023. Skilled in postsurgical and terminal care; experienced in working with children.
- Accounting position requiring proficiency in medical terminology, insurance billing, legal applications, and customer relations.
- Office manager. Skilled in major software applications, written communication, problem solving, and conflict resolution.
- Medical laboratory technician in a clinic or hospital seeking reliability, interpersonal skills, and superior accuracy.

A Summary of Qualifications

A profile or *summary of qualifications* is a concise statement of the applicant's most important accomplishments and abilities that relate to the job objective. The summary and job objective may be the only sections that catch an employer's eye and rescue a résumé from oblivion. To fill just one position, employers may screen hundreds of résumés. Since they often spend twenty seconds or less on each one, a résumé must be well prepared to arouse interest.

The summary may be written as a short paragraph that sets forth the applicant's impressive achievements, awards, promotions, expertise, and professional qualities. More popular and easier to read is the summary with a list of three to five accomplishments, preceded by a brief statement of qualifications, usually including education. Volunteer projects as well as actual work experience may be listed.

If evidence is provided, claims about attitude and personality may be made, as in the example below, which is directed toward a high school teaching position. Although the new graduate has held various part-time jobs, she has no paid teaching experience. She explains this by adding "recently" to the statement about graduation (the date appears later under "Education"). Since her publications are not mentioned elsewhere, she puts the dates here in the summary. Note that she lists experience first.

Summary of Qualifications

BA in English education. Certified to teach English and speech. Recently graduated summa cum laude. Enthusiastic and dedicated to stimulating children to learn.

- Tutored dyslexic high school student who had been failing.
- Two years' experience teaching high school religious classes weekly.
- Won first prize in National Arts and Letters short story contest, 2004.
- Published five poems in little magazines in the past year.
- Active member of Toastmasters International. Made three presentations locally, using PowerPoint.

The next example summarizes the qualifications of an older student who has paid work experience in his chosen field and is still working at the same place while continuing his education. His job objective focuses on a supervisory position in the accounting department of a magazine subscription service. For emphasis, his most noteworthy achievements are placed first and last in the list:

Profile

Five years' accounting experience in retail store. Associate Degree, 3.6 GPA. Accounting major, business management minor. Auditor internship with Deloitte & Touche. Continuing course work toward a BS degree.

- Promoted to supervisor in one year. Oversee two assistants.
- Proficient in Windows XP, Quicken, TurboTax, and other related software.
- Prepare payroll and tax forms, maintain records, compile sales reports.

- Practice computer security precautions. No data loss due to viruses in five years.
- Made cost analysis and recommended cost-cutting procedure that saved the company $10,500 in just three months.

<table>
<tr><td>

WRITING A SUMMARY OF QUALIFICATIONS

</td><td>

To write a summary for your résumé, scan your lists of skills and achievements. Select the most impressive that relate to the specific position for which you apply. The following questions should help you prewrite and revise:

- What is the employers' greatest need for this position?
- Why am I well qualified to fill that need? What evidence can I present? (Don't be modest. If your draft is too strong, you can always tone it down.)
- Does the summary correlate closely with my job objective?
- Might I find an instructor or trusted co-worker to critique my job objective and summary?
- Have I revised sufficiently so that the summary presents my chief credentials in the best possible way?

</td></tr>
</table>

Grouping and Sharpening Skills

If you are fortunate enough to have work experience in your career field and are compiling a chronological résumé, list those work skills underneath the name of the employer. If the functional format is better for you, then revise and regroup your prewritten skills:

1. Sort skills according to the needs of potential employers. Sort and mix work, academic, and personal skills into groups.
2. Arrange the skills in neat columns under the group headings. Place the most important details at the beginning of each column.
3. Begin each skill entry with an appropriate action verb.

Citing Accomplishments   Employers seek people who can cut costs, solve problems, and perform quality work. If you have three to five distinctive achievements, you may list them in your summary of qualifications. To identify potential accomplishments, search your skills lists for superior work, especially in regard to finances or saving of resources, personnel, or time. Then *add a second part that provides specific data.* This addition can sometimes expand a skill to an accomplishment:

- *Skill:*   Decreased costs
  Add: 20% through selective bulk buying.
- *Skill:*   Generated sales
  Add: of $950,000 during the past year.

- *Skill:*   Upgraded outdated inventory system,

  Add: cutting storage time by one-half.

To fill out a list of accomplishments, you may also include honors, awards, and other distinctions you've received. Yana Parker suggests writing PAR (Problem-Action-Results) statements in *24 Hot Tips on Résumé Writing*. (Her Web site is listed in Directory 2, page 400.) PAR statements can be included under accomplishments.

For example, the manager of mail services revised her résumé and applied for a similar position elsewhere when her department was outsourced. She labeled her accomplishments a "Record of Productivity," which she placed after her job objective:

Record of Productivity

- Streamlined entire mail services operation for corporate headquarters of _____, Inc. This changeover included reorganizing job duties of all mail room personnel, developing new procedures, and reorganizing the physical layout for greater efficiency.

- Despite a 25% increase in mail flow, maintained quality service with no additional personnel. Increased number of in-house mail services for employees.

- Wrote and justified proposal for $80,000 for new equipment through equivalent savings in one year's time.

- As benefits approver at _____, maintained 97% accuracy and production criteria.

- At _____ Corporation, changed all accounts receivable functions from manual to computerized system.

Adding Action Verbs   Accurate, positive verbs can make skills attractive, parallel, and convincing. "Managed fifteen employees" indicates a skill; "excellent manager" is a claim without evidence. Skills are written in the past tense if you no longer have that job.

calculate	establish	maintain	record
compute	expand	operate	refine
conduct	implement	organize	reorganize
coordinate	increase	originate	repair
create	initiate	plan	research
decrease (costs)	innovate	prepare	schedule
develop	install	produce	support

ACTION VERBS FOR RÉSUMÉS

Education

When listing higher education on your résumé, provide names of institutions (and addresses of lesser known ones). Include dates, degrees, and major(s). Also state your minor concentration if relevant. Specify grade point average (GPA) if

B+ or more. GPA is usually stated in decimals such as "3.35/4.0," the second figure indicating the scale. If the GPA of your major is higher, you can cite it: "Major GPA 3.6/4.0."

List teaching certificates, nursing licensure, and other professional certification with education. For young applicants with little experience, a high school degree can be included if space allows. You might also list items such as "Took college preparatory courses," "Wrote for school newspaper," "Trained in debate." You can list high school honors here, too. (Do not note a GED.)

Work Experience

Experience in your targeted field should be emphasized on your résumé by allotting it more space than for other jobs. If you have had steady employment, include the employers' names and dates with months (Jan. 2003–present). State job title(s) and promotions, if any. For example: "Hired as crew member. In six months, promoted to assistant manager." After that you can list work skills. Include minor job experience because it indicates a desire to work and familiarity with the work world. If you have served in the military, place that under work experience. State term of service, branch, and rank upon leaving. Include training or travel relevant to your job objective.

Gaps in Work Experience   If you have gaps in your employment due to layoffs or downsizing, time off for parenting or other family obligations, or another valid reason, list the item with dates. State what you were doing. For seasonal items, preface the date with the season, as in the following individual examples:

- 2004–2005. Maternity leave and full-time parenting.
- 2003–2004. Layoff. Temporary work: Compiled tax forms for H & R Block, taught computer classes at Franklin Vocational High School, and started home business.
- Spring 2002–Summer 2003. Travel and full-time study.

A Series of Short-Term Jobs   If have held a succession of minor jobs, unrelated to your job objective, perhaps with gaps in employment, provide a short summary with a *range of dates*. Preface with one or two sentences *stating qualities you have developed and skills you have learned* from these jobs:

▶
Summary of Work Experience

During college years have held part-time employment that has developed initiative, accuracy, and flexibility. Have learned to budget, schedule, catalog books, find answers to research questions, service cars, make minor repairs, and provide courteous customer service.

2002–2005 **Library Assistant/Service Station Attendant:** BGSU main campus, Herbie's Marathon Station

2000–2001 **Server:** McMann's Restaurant, Burger Boy, Dolly's Coffee Shop

- **How far back should I go on work experience?** To avoid age discrimination, list only your last three jobs or the last ten years. That is usually enough unless you have earlier work in your targeted field. Label that section as "Relevant Work Experience."
- **Should any work experience ever be omitted?** Employment of one month or less can be omitted.
- **How can I make a job title sound better?** Retitle jobs such as dishwasher, cleaning lady, yard man, and bartender. For example: kitchen assistant, housekeeper, greenskeeper, and server. Avoid overstating the position, however.
- **What if I have no work experience?** Your best bet may be to head for the campus placement service or an employment agency to ask about temporary or part-time work in your targeted field, if possible.

Other Information on a Résumé

If you have extra space on your résumé, use it for minor, but relevant, information. Do not mention firings, demotions, ethnicity, handicaps, age, or medical disabilities on a résumé. Possible items to include are as follows:

- **Honors or awards.** If not listed elsewhere, group honors such as "Employee of the Month," "Top Salesperson of the Year," civic awards, dean's list, and other distinctions under "Honors."
- **Memberships.** Memberships in professional organizations related to your job objective imply commitment to a career. Do *not* list lodges, religious affiliations, or any membership that might arouse prejudice.
- **Activities and interests.** Optional. Include only those that are related to your job objective.
- **Salary.** Do not mention unless requested; then simply state "Negotiable" or "Open." Otherwise, you may price yourself out of a job or be hired at a low rate. (Research the salaries in your field and locale.)
- **References.** Place "References upon request" last. Optional.

ORGANIZING RÉSUMÉS

The job objective is the first item on any résumé after your name, home address, telephone number, and personal e-mail address. (Do not give your work number or e-mail address.) Next is the summary of qualifications. Arrange work experience, education, and skills in most- to least-important order, according to the format you choose.

ANTHONY R. ROGERS   (303) 222-3333   arogers@service.net
3945 East Front Street
Denver, CO 80200

Objective: Assistant systems manager position requiring experience in managing information systems, network communication, and problem solving

SUMMARY OF QUALIFICATIONS

Five years' experience using computers in various capacities, plus management experience. Soon to graduate with Bachelor of Science degree, *cum laude*. Majors: Database Management and Network Administration.

- Microsoft Certified Systems Engineer
- Program in Oracle, SQL, C++, and Visual Basic
- Use Microsoft Office XP and Open Systems Traverse accounting software with e-commerce
- Customized software for company and client needs
- Won the *Wall Street Journal* award for student achievement
- Designed systems and created documentation

Experience

April 2002
to
present

PROTECH ELECTRONICS, INC., Denver, Colorado
Promoted to Administrative Assistant to the President
- Perform financial analyses
- Assist in interviewing and hiring
- Assist in pricing and purchasing
- Track and report inventory
- Provide support for sales representatives
- Train employees
- Write brochures and design training literature
- Write proposals, business letters, and reports
- Make informative and persuasive presentations
- Provided support for end users
- Handled complaints and worked out compromises
- Performed user setup and maintenance on NT Server
- Detected and solved problems in software
- Improved systems of computer security

FIGURE 25.1 Chronological résumé.

Organizing a Chronological Résumé

After the job objective and summary, the next major part of a chronological résumé is usually a *reverse chronological listing* of work experience. Skills and achievements, including promotions, are listed under each employer. But for a teaching, a nursing, or another position that requires a certain degree and certification or licensure, *education* can come next. The general rule for both chronological and functional résumés is to place the most important major sec-

Anthony R. Rogers   3945 East Front Street   2

July 2000 to March 2002	**XYZ ELECTRONICS COMPANY,** Denver, Colorado Hired as a sales representative. Promoted to sales manager after one year.

- Supervised five employees
- Hired, dismissed, and trained personnel
- Sold, installed, and provided support for systems/software
- Made minor repairs on PC desktop computers
- Revised performance evaluation procedure
- Assisted potential users in defining system needs
- Answered application and support questions for customers
- Designed local area networks
- Designed customer survey, compiled results, and wrote report
- Created motivational plan that led to increased sales of 20%

May 1998 to June 2000	**WENDY'S,** Denver, Colorado Hired as customer service representative. Promoted to assistant manager after six months.

- Supervised six employees
- Kept sales records
- Ordered supplies
- Worked late shifts
- Balanced cash register
- Made bank deposits
- Opened and closed store

Education	**OLYMPIA UNIVERSITY,** Denver, Colorado
June 2005	Bachelor of Science, GPA 3.67/4.0 Majors: Database Management and Network Administration
Member	Small Business Association

References upon request

FIGURE 25.1 Chronological résumé. (continued)

tion first and the least important last. (For an example of a chronological résumé, see fig. 25.1.)

Organizing a Functional Résumé

The functional résumé style is quite flexible, suitable for anyone who lacks the qualifications needed for the chronological style. If you are close to graduation and have little work experience, you can emphasize your academic achievement

MELANIE A. ROBERTS
612 Greenlawn Drive
Marion, Ohio 43302
(614) 555-0755
maroberts@service.net

OBJECTIVE: Paralegal position with employer who seeks superior dedication, accuracy, and skill in paralegal duties, computer applications, and communications.

PROFILE

Recent graduate with Associate of Applied Business Degree, major in Paralegal Studies, GPA 3.7/4.0. Paralegal internship with Smith and Jones, Attorneys at Law. Apply basic accounting principles. Have notary public commission. Experienced in quality control.

- **Paralegal Experience:** Researched legal problems. Prepared and filed probate documents. Updated office filing system. Performed title searches. Proofread property descriptions and witnessed real estate closings. Wrote letters and contacted clients. Prepared corporation sales reports of securities.

- **Paralegal Training:** Investigated legal problems. Drafted contracts, complaints, and responses. Wrote and executed wills according to Ohio law. Prepared partnership agreements. Implemented debt collection practices. Applied problems in tort law and criminal law.

- **Computer Skills:** Use LEXIS, Access, Excel, Windows XP, TurboTax

- **Communication Skills:** Give quality oral presentations. Research and write arguments, essays, and reports. Trained in questioning and active listening. Surveyed opportunities for paralegals. Wrote for campus newspaper.

EDUCATION: Marion Technical College, Marion, Ohio, Associate Degree, June 2005. Dean's List. Served on student advisory board.

EARLY EXPERIENCE

1998–2003   Quality Control Inspector (promotion). A.O. Smith, Upper Sandusky, Ohio. Supervised 10 workers. Trained employees. Supplied parts.

1993–1997   Maintenance Supervisor/Receptionist. American Legion, Club 162; Howard Swink Advertising Agency, Marion, Ohio.

References upon request

FIGURE 25.2 Functional résumé, no paid experience in desired field.

by using the following order: *job objective, summary, education,* and *work experience* (with skills listed), as shown in fig. 25.2. Degreed applicants who are switching career fields might also use this order, particularly if their educational record matches well with the new career field. Or education might be included in the summary.

If you will be competing with applicants who have higher degrees than you and if you have some work in your targeted field, you can use a different arrangement: *job objective, summary, work experience* (listing skills), and *education.* College students who are *not* close to graduation but who have some work experience in their chosen field can use this same order.

MARK FOCUSES HIS FUNCTIONAL RÉSUMÉ

Mark, a young graduate with a bachelor's degree but little work experience, saw an ad for an administrative assistant that sounded interesting. The employer was seeking someone with three strengths: initiative, computer skills, and writing skills. Since Mark was strong in all three areas, he emphasized these categories in his summary of qualifications for his functional résumé:

PROFILE
Recent BA degree in Communications. Maintained a GPA of 3.6/4.0 while working twenty hours weekly.

- **Initiative:** Awarded full tuition scholarship for high school GPA of 4.0/4.0. Arose at 3 a.m. for disk jockey job for one year in college. Worked till midnight weekends at Burger King for two years.
- **Computer Skills:** Proficient in Word, Excel, PowerPoint, QuickBooks, and other software. At Champion Tile installed and maintained operating system, antivirus, and application software; entered data; compiled sales reports; and generated checks.
- **Writing Skills:** Wrote business letters, reports, research papers, and critiques of essays. Published two op-ed columns in a local paper.

Mark's effort won an interview and a job offer. He had tailored his summary of qualifications to the employer's specific needs.

Scannable Résumés

Sometimes human eyes never see a résumé. If your résumé will be scanned, prepare a scannable version that will keep it from being tossed out. Streamline your printed-style résumé. Keep margins rather narrow and do not center anything. (Length is seldom a concern as long as items are relevant.) Use a clear size 12 font such as Arial, Courier, or Verdana. *The general rule is "the plainer, the better."* That means no fancy fonts, bullets, italics, underlining, parentheses, brackets, graphics—anything that might end up as gibberish. Then place a keyword summary of your qualifications at the top of page 1.

Keyword Summary   Read ads and job boards to find the skills and abilities employers seek for different jobs. Then match these words with your qualifications and copy them into your keyword summary. The more matches you can provide, the more the scanner will select and the better your chances of having your résumé read. (Use hyphens in place of bullets to set off items.)

A KEYWORD SUMMARY

- 3 years' purchasing experience: vendors and wholesalers
- 2 years' client/customer service: corporate accounts
- Gave on-site training seminars, made installations and setups
- Wrote brochures, bulletins, reports, technical manuals to clients' specifications
- Proficient in Windows XP, Excel, Powerpoint, Microsoft Great Plains

Editing and Printing   After you finish a scannable version of your résumé, run a spelling check and proofread it again. Then save it as an ASCII file. Name the file *resume.txt.* Use any text editor (such as Appletext, MS Word, or Notepad) to edit the resume.txt file to resemble your original résumé. Print your scannable résumé, using a high-resolution laser printer. Do not bend or fold the résumé. Place it in a large manila envelope to protect it.

E-Mail Résumés

If you have a choice between submitting an e-mail résumé and sending a scannable résumé by regular mail, take e-mail. Scanning managers of GTE and other companies prefer e-mail résumés because there is less chance for error when storing them in a database. In fact, many ads specify "a plain text document sent in the body of your [e-mail] message." This means the résumé is not sent as an attachment. Attached files can be cumbersome to download and print out.

Preparation   An e-mail résumé does not need a keyword summary. Streamline the résumé as you would for a scannable version—taking out underlining, parentheses, brackets, graphics, bullets, centering, or anything that might become illegible. Run a spelling check and proofread thoroughly. Save the résumé as a text file (see "Scannable Résumés," on page 395). In this plain form, the résumé can be copied, pasted into e-mail, and read by unknown software. *Precaution:* Before e-mailing the résumé, insert a cover letter into the message first. Employers prefer to see the cover letter beforehand.

RESPONDING TO ONLINE ADS AND POSTING RÉSUMÉS ONLINE

The best way to find a job online is to visit the sites of the employers you wish to contact. Many post descriptions of jobs currently available and remove the ads as soon as the jobs are filled. Responding to listings on job boards can be a waste of time, however. Before you do, check the date of posting. If there is no date, consider that the listing may be two or three years old.

Although it is possible to post your e-mail résumé online at several sites, you need to consider the risks and take adequate precautions. Many sites share and sell personal information of applicants. Identity theft and scams do occur. (Never send money.) The online security guidelines below will help you to avert these problems.

The World Privacy Forum, a nonprofit organization based in California, provides the following guidelines for online security:

- **Read the privacy policy of the site carefully.** Know who can share your information.
- **Ensure that your résumé can be deleted.** If not, don't post it.
- **Get an e-mail address just for the online résumé.** Cancel later.
- **Reveal no private information** such as numbers on debit or credit cards, bank accounts, or Social Security. You may want to use your initials for this résumé. You can also omit your address and telephone number, leaving just an e-mail address.
- **Limit your résumé to a few sites.** Posting widely may limit your chances. If the résumé is widely circulated, employers may wonder what is the matter with the applicant.

ONLINE SECURITY GUIDELINES

FORMATTING A PRINTED RÉSUMÉ

Since your printed résumé is your ambassador, an immaculate appearance is imperative. Purchase high-quality 20-pound bond paper. Buy enough so that you have matching paper for cover and follow-up letters. White is best for résumés that will be duplicated or scanned. Otherwise, ivory is suitable. Employers tend to dislike unusual colors and extravagant layouts. You can vary the format by using capital letters, boldface, or underlining for headings. You can lead into each skill entry with a bullet (oversized dot), followed by one space.

To give a picture-frame look, use the same-size margins all around. Triple-space between sections, if possible, and double-space between subsections. You can center major headings or locate them at the side or mix the two arrangements. Work with your résumé until you have an effective layout that enhances your qualifications.

Never send pale or smudged copies of your résumé to an interviewer. Avoid script and difficult-to-read fonts. Select a popular font that is neat and clear; use a laser printer if possible. For students, a résumé of one or two pages is adequate. Yet expectations for acceptable résumés vary among employers, particularly government agencies. If your résumé is to work efficiently for you, determine what each employer expects and do your best to meet those expectations.

REVISING, EDITING, AND PROOFREADING A RÉSUMÉ

Chances are that a superficial résumé, hastily compiled, will not yield interviews. Employers assume a résumé reflects the intellect, competency, and attitude of the applicant. Take time to revise as much as necessary so that your résumé will outclass the competition and earn you the opportunities you deserve.

Checking Layout and Order

Layout does make a difference. Consider the order of items in columns. The first and last positions carry the most emphasis; the middle spot has the least emphasis. The *white* space throughout the résumé, not just the margins, influences appearance, readability, and credibility. Neat, aligned columns provide a balanced look. A crowded résumé is more difficult to read than a well-spaced one. For ease in reading, place dates on the left except when you want to de-emphasize them.

If your résumé runs more than one page, place your name and a page number at the top of the second page (reduce the font two sizes for that line). This precaution will prevent loss or confusion when the interviewer compares applicants' qualifications. (Never staple a résumé.) Revise your layout until you attain an appropriate order and look. The following checklist can help in editing your résumé.

CHECKLIST   **REVISING LAYOUT, ORDER, AND EMPHASIS**

1. Is the layout well-balanced, attractive, and easy to read?
    Is every column aligned? Is there enough white space?

2. Are dates accurate? Arranged in reverse chronological order?

3. Does each skill start with an action verb?

4. Are all major sections well-developed, positive, and accurate?

5. Are minor sections relevant? If not, discard.

Adjusting Length of Printed Résumés

"How long should a résumé be?" is a common question with no definite answer. Although many employers prefer one-page résumés for *entry-level* employees, this preference does not rule out longer résumés for applicants with extensive qualifications. Two-page résumés are increasingly common for newly graduated applicants. If you plan a second page, it should have sufficient information. A fraction of a page may appear to be the result of poor planning.

When expanding your résumé to fill a second page, be careful not to indulge in puffery. Wordiness and irrelevant details will detract from your purpose. A concise one-page résumé is far better than a puffed two-page one. The following options should help you to find more material and adapt the format, if you need a second page:

WAYS TO EXPAND A RÉSUMÉ

1. **Review the suggestions for identifying skills to find more.** Also consider adding more minor categories if relevant.

2. **Add white space.** Have you triple-spaced between sections? Have you centered your heading? A centered heading takes more space than one aligned on the left with items beside it. (See figs. 25.1 and 25.2)

3. **Expand the margins a bit,** keeping the same size all around.

4. **If you are not working, you can supply the addresses and telephone numbers of previous employers.** If working, reserve this information for a sheet of references.

5. **Expand a summary of minor work experience.** The names of employers could be added.

6. **If you are not working and have an extra half page or so,** you might add your list of references to the second page of the résumé, if the list will fit. (Or if possible, cut the résumé to one page.)

Or on the other hand, if you must cut the length of your résumé, start with the first suggestion below. Then go down the list just as far as needed; don't toss out good material unnecessarily. To adjust the length, you have several options:

WAYS TO CUT THE LENGTH OF A RÉSUMÉ

1. **Omit minor items.** Personal activities and interests are optional.

2. **Group similar skills on one line.** This technique is simple and quick.

3. **Place company name in bold with address in plain type on the same line.**

4. **Summarize unrelated work experience.** Beware of cutting too much; work experience of any kind can be an asset.

5. **Reduce the font one size.** You might use size 11 instead of size 12 font.

6. **Last resort.** Narrow the margins a bit or double-space between sections.

Eagle-Eyed Proofreading

You know and I know that errors can creep into a draft for a multitude of reasons, but that does not excuse them in an employer's eyes. When you are fresh and alert, proofread your finished résumé several times. Otherwise, you are unlikely to nab every error. Although a spell checker can catch misspellings, it cannot monitor usage. An eagle eye is needed to detect inappropriate words.

Scrutinizing Word Choice

Extra words dilute meaning. To interviewers, vague wordy phrases may imply that the applicant lacks confidence and competence. When reviewing the skill lists on your résumé, weigh every word. Delete unnecessary words and qualifiers, such as *very,* and unneeded prepositional phrases.

WEAK AND WORDY PHRASES

have a knowledge of	know about	familiar with
provided assistance	exposed to	very good with
acquainted with	had exposure to	worked on

Instead of the first phrase above, say *know*. Instead of "provided assistance," say *assisted*. Instead of "had exposure to," say *used* or *operated*. *Tip:* Watch for *of, to, on, with,* and other prepositions that often indicate unnecessary words. If you have the slightest doubt about spelling or usage, consult a dictionary. And run a spelling check after every revision.

CHECKLIST   **EDITING AND PROOFREADING A RÉSUMÉ**

1. Are all dates accurate?

2. Are months as well as years specified for work experience?

3. Is there any duplication of skills? (If so, cut.)

4. Is every word positive or neutral?

5. Is every word spelled and hyphenated correctly?

6. Are punctuation and capitalization consistent and correct?

DIRECTORY 2: ONLINE EMPLOYMENT WRITING RESOURCES

The Web sites listed below are reliable and safe from spyware. They provide free, up-to-date help with minimal sales promotion. View sample job objectives, résumés, letters, reference lists, and more. (Most browsers will fill in http://.)

*   **Career Journal.** Excellent advice for job seekers with experience. <www.careerjournal.com>
*   **The Damn Good Résumé.** Yana Parker's "Hot Tips for Résumés" and other excellent advice. <www.damngood.com/jobseekers/links.html>
*   **Distinctive Documents.** Sample résumés. <www.distinctiveweb.com>
*   **JobStar Central.** Excellent resource. <www.jobstar.org>
*   **The Net Guide.** Richard N. Bolles's "The Fairy Godmother Report on Résumé Sites" included. <www.JobHuntersBible.com>
*   **Rebecca Smith's eRésumés.** Electronic résumés. <www.eresumes.com>
*   **The Résumé Place.** Practical help with résumés, as well as federal job searches. <www.resume-place.com/>
*   **The Riley Guide.** Résumés, cover letters, and more. <www.rileyguide.com>
*   **The Résumé Guide.** Over sixty résumé samples. <www.susanireland.com>
*   **How to Write a Great Letter.** "Twenty-Eight Common Mistakes," "Friendship Letter," and others. <www.careerlab.com/letters/link002.htm>

II. WRITING LETTERS AND OTHER CORRESPONDENCE FOR EMPLOYMENT

An effective cover letter and a sincere letter of appreciation can help you win the job you want. The subtle aspects of your written voice reveal your attitude—influencing whether or not you will be considered for the position. Well-organized content; a neat format; and correct grammar, punctuation, and spelling convey an air of professionalism. When corresponding with potential employers whether through regular mail or e-mail, always take the time to produce your best work.

TEN COMMON MISTAKES IN LETTERS

Employers often draw inferences from incidentals, even careless, illegible signatures. Neat handwriting is essential for some tasks, such as writing numbers, invoices, notes, and checks. Regardless of the position you apply for, take extra pains to sign application forms and letters neatly. Employers may also cite a dozen or more other pet peeves, including these ten common mistakes in cover letters:

1. **Inappropriate salutations.** "Dear Sir," "Dear Madam," "To Whom It May Concern," and similar phrases are outdated. If possible, include a name. (Call and ask the receptionist who the human resource director is. If the name is unusual, ask how it is spelled.)

2. **Form letters.** Fill-in-the-blank letters or those copied from books or the Internet create a poor impression. Be original and tailor the message to the recipient.

3. **Grammatical errors.** Spelling errors, incorrect usage, unnecessary capitals, and unwieldy sentence structure also create a poor impression.

4. **Handwritten letters.** Short thank-you notes may be handwritten if they are neat and legible, but cover letters should be neatly typed and spaced.

5. **Hard-to-read format.** Omit clutter, graphics, and fancy fonts. Use a size 12 easy-to-read font. Use a balanced format with plenty of white space.

6. **Omissions.** Omitted signature, phone number, date, salutation, or résumé gives the impression of carelessness. Omissions may cause the letter to be discarded.

7. **Overuse of *I*.** Too many *I*'s can create a negative image. Instead, focus on the recipient and what you can do for the company. (See page 48.)

8. **Trite phrases.** Avoid wording such as "please find the attached résumé," "enclosed please find my résumé," "I'm excited about talking to you further," "yours truly," "yours sincerely," and similar outworn phrases.

9. **Abbreviations.** Avoid unnecessary abbreviations such as "St.," "Ave.," "Jan.," "Wed.," and others. Write out words.

10. **Long sentences and paragraphs.** Limit most sentences to fifteen words or less. Limit paragraphs to five lines or so.

WRITING E-MAIL MESSAGES

E-mail provides such convenience, economy, and speed that we tend to use it automatically—without the care we would give to a business letter. To save time, some writers clip their e-mail so much that it is difficult to decipher. Such carelessness and spur-of-the-moment responses can lead to embarrassment and other problems that are beyond the scope of this book. Still, five basic reminders are in order:

- All e-mail in your computer at work is the legal property of your employer.
- E-mail can be intercepted by your employer or by third parties on the Internet. In fact, the *New York Times* once fired twenty-two people for e-mailing offensive jokes. Such firings are not unusual at companies with harassment policies.
- E-mail can be misdirected to the wrong person through various errors.
- E-mail is often copied and sent on to dozens of people.
- E-mail messages linger. You may think you erase them through deletion, but this is not always true. And a copy is always stored on your provider's server.

Therefore, it is essential to keep this lack of privacy in mind. Although writing e-mail may seem intimate and personal, it is like conversing in public. E-mail is similar to memos that can be sent around, passed out at meetings, or tacked to a bulletin board. Unless you revise carefully, e-mail may come back to haunt you.

Without the standard openings, closings, and courtesy words used in business letters, e-mail may sound curt and abrupt. Some folks try to soften the tone with smiley faces and the like. But recipients may not care for the cutesiness, which is unsuitable for business messages. It is far better to take a few minutes to be cautious and complete.

WRITING AN EFFECTIVE COVER LETTER FOR A RÉSUMÉ

When hundreds of people vie for a single position, a résumé cover letter may be the only document in a job packet that an interviewer reads. If a cover letter contains even a whiff of incompetence or dishonesty, the résumé may well be tossed aside unread. Regardless of whether a résumé is mailed, faxed, e-mailed, or delivered in person, a cover letter is usually expected.

As you write your cover letter, keep in mind that the primary purpose is to motivate the interviewer to read your résumé. Express interest in the position, present an overview of your credentials, and make a courteous request for an interview. The tone of a well-written cover letter is professional and confident, never desperate, half-hearted, or arrogant. A confident letter may spark confidence in its reader—exactly the effect you wish to achieve. Like other business letters, cover letters have three basic parts: introduction, body, and closing.

1. **Keep e-mail short and focused.** Include a subject line. If you have two detailed topics to discuss, consider sending two messages.

2. **Start with a pleasant greeting:** "Hello," "Hi," "[name]," "Good morning!" "Dear Director," or whatever fits the occasion.

3. **Be friendly and courteous.** When appropriate, start with "Thank you for. . . ." If you make a request, ask a question with a question mark and include "May I" or "Will you please."

4. **Place the important part first unless it is negative.** In that case, build up to the bad news.

5. **After you make your point, close.** Don't ramble on. End on a positive note, even if you say no more than "So long," "Goodbye," or "Take care." For a more professional tone, use "Best regards," "Best wishes," "Sincerely," or other suitable closing.

6. **Don't send e-mail when very tired.** Avoid writing messages when exhausted, particularly those that are work-related.

7. **Reread each e-mail carefully before sending.** A hasty message may not say what you intend or carry the desired tone. If you tend to misspell or mistype, copy the message into a document and run a spelling check before sending.

8. **Wait twenty-four hours before replying to an irritating message.** Choose your words carefully. Reread several times. Consider how the reader may take them and whether the message merits a reply. Silence may be the best, and safest, response.

9. **If you use the "Reply" feature, check the message string.** Since strings often do not appear on-screen, they can accumulate and cause embarrassment, particularly when a third party is involved. *Send a string of messages only for a purpose.*

10. **Send e-mail by *blind carbon copy* (Bcc) when appropriate.** Some Internet messages accumulate long lists of names and addresses. Before forwarding, remove the list and direct the e-mail by using "Bcc," not "To." This small courtesy will be appreciated. It will also increase readability.

Effective Introductions

A pet peeve of interviewers is triteness in cover letters. Imagine having to read dozens of letters that begin: "I saw your ad in . . ." or some other predictable phrase. To make a cover letter stand out, hook the reader's interest with your very first words. Select them judiciously: the wrong words may steer you into a low-paying position. If you have experience in your desired field, shy away from "entry-level" or "trainee." These words peg you as having minimal skills and lacking experience. For inexperienced applicants, however, an entry-level position in your chosen field affords an opportunity to gain practical knowledge and skill.

A simple way to get up-to-date information about employers' needs is to clip job descriptions and ads. Underline the skills and abilities required for positions you would like. After that, draft an introduction that suggests how your training and experience meet those needs. Be sure that your description truly reflects your qualifications.

When you are applying for a particular position, specify the exact job title and number (if there is one) in the introduction of your cover letter. Otherwise, you can be less specific. To create a distinctive opening that will work for you, adapt one of the four basic openings for cover letters.

The Name Opening   You are fortunate, indeed, if you can begin with the name of a person the employer knows, one who has referred you or who will recommend you. Often a referral will open doors that might otherwise remain closed. If you learn of an available position from an executive or from someone else the employer respects, seize the opportunity! First, state the name of the person making the referral. Then mention the position and give the main areas of your qualifications:

- Jason Blank, systems manager of Incatech, spoke of an opening in your company for a junior accountant. He recommended I apply, for he is familiar with my accounting background and computer experience.
- Cynthia Jones, vice president of Blink's Advertising, has suggested I apply for the position of copywriter at your company. The requirements she mentioned match my training and experience in advertising.

The Creative Opening   To find just the right detail for an unusual opening, search your résumé and memory. Watch local papers for news items about potential employers, possibly the arrival of a new business or the expansion of a local company. Then match your experience, activities, and talent so as to spark the interest of an interviewer:

- Perserverance does pay off. After five years of attending night classes, working as a restaurant manager, and providing for a family, I am graduating *magna cum laude* with a BS degree in restaurant management. Would these qualifications plus confirmed workaholic tendencies equip me for the position of manager of your hotel's dining room?
- After Hastings, Holby, and Haberman move to the new downtown location, they may need more personnel. If so, please consider my legal training and work experience, which should qualify me for a paralegal position.

The Summary Opening   Although traditional, the summary opening can be quite workable when your strongest qualifications are linked to the desired position. You might give two or three main points taken from the headings of your résumé. But be sure the points are clearly connected to the current needs of potential employers. In the following summary openings, notice that the focus is upon *how the applicant can serve the employer:*

- Training in social work, an internship in student admissions, and a bachelor's degree in psychology should help me fulfill the responsibilities of Human Services Coordinator for Blinhard University.
- My management skills in nursing have been honed by supervision of nursing personnel, development of nursing policies and procedures, and preparation of six-figure budgets. This background, along with a recently acquired MSN degree, should qualify me for Director of Nursing at Memorial Hospital.

Employment consultants often advise clients to distinguish between "requirements" and "preferences" when applying for a job. If you don't have all the "preferences," apply anyway. Then shape your cover letter and interview responses to show that you fit the job:

1. **Secure the name of the interviewer.** If unknown, call the company. If unable to secure a name, send to "Human Resources Director." "Dear Director" can serve as your salutation.
2. **Write in a confident, courteous tone.** Select your words with care (see chapter 8).
3. **Individualize the letter.** Avoid trite phrases and examples from books. Be original.
4. **Type an individualized letter for each company.** Form letters without an inside name and address are inappropriate and ineffective.
5. **Point out transferable skills.** Don't expect an employer to infer how your skills will fit the job. Your cover letter should mention how these skills can be applied.
6. **Show prized qualities.** To *imply* flexibility, intellectual curiosity, and high energy level, share examples from your experience. For many positions, these three qualities have distinct advantages.
7. **Write with enthusiasm.** Your cover letter should try to convince the company that you are a good fit for the job, even if you are not an exact fit. *Note:* Never say "Although my skills don't exactly match" or "Although I am unqualified" (or inexperienced).
8. **Sign each letter neatly in *black* ink to match the type.** Never leave a letter unsigned. Employers tend to view the omission as carelessness and a disregard for detail.

DEVELOPING AN EFFECTIVE COVER LETTER

The Question Opening   Opening with a question is a popular method, but a word of caution is advisable. Some personnel directors say that question openings are "overused" and frequently "filled with clichés." One interviewer even went so far as to say he tossed letters that opened with stereotypic questions into the wastebasket unread. Still, an original question opening can serve as an attention-getter if it is fresh, appealing, and relevant.

Whatever opening you use, avoid any hint of overconfidence or presumption. Note, for example, that the sample introductions here use phrases such as "*should* quality me for the position" rather than "*will* qualify me." At the same time, an opening that seems doubtful or anxious is not likely to open many doors. Striking the proper balance can be tricky, so thoughtful applicants evaluate and revise their openings carefully, using their own words and avoiding threadbare phrases.

The Body of the Letter

The body of a cover letter explains the qualifications mentioned in the introduction. When you develop these points, retain the order set forth in your opening. After summarizing the highlights from the résumé, conclude the body with an *indirect* reference to the résumé.

Reference to the Résumé   A direct reference, such as "Please see the enclosed résumé," is awkward. An indirect reference, is worked smoothly into a sentence in a dependent clause or phrase. The indirect references below are italicized:

- For five years I have provided customer service and gained significant insights. For me, the customer is really number one. Supervision of eight employees has also offered opportunities to polish my interpersonal skills, *as indicated on the enclosed résumé.*
- On June 12, 2005, I will graduate *summa cum laude* from Buckeye University with a bachelor of arts degree in education. There I concentrated in English, specifically the teaching of high school literature and composition. In my senior year, I won first prize in the National Arts and Letters contest involving five area colleges. Seven poems have been published in little magazines, *as explained in the enclosed résumé.*

How to Handle the Salary Question

Although an ad may request "desired salary" or "salary history," you are not obligated to give a specific answer. In a cover letter, you might give an expected salary range, such as "$26,000 to $29,000" or "upper 20s." But before you do, consider that your answer may jeopardize your chances of being hired. The risk is twofold: If your figure is too high, employers may conclude you are overqualified or overpriced; if too low, they may think you underqualified. Even if you are aware of current salary ranges, a small business may not be able to comply.

In a telephone conversation, you might say that salary is "open" or sidestep questions about salary history (another can of worms) until the interview. In the conclusion of a cover letter, you can postpone your answer tactfully:

- At your convenience, may I set up an interview to discuss my qualifications, including expected salary [or salary history, if requested]? My telephone number is (000) 555-6721, and I'm available after 6:30 p.m. Or if you prefer, send an e-mail to the address above.

Sooner or later, you will confront the question of salary. Rather than be unprepared, begin to research salaries in your field. Then you'll know what you can expect locally, statewide, or nationally. Information about salary ranges can be gained from libraries, friends, employment agencies, information interviews, and temporary employment.

Effective Conclusions

The end of a cover letter is rather like a goodbye. As such, it should be brief, cordial, and courteous. Courtesy is integral to good business relations, yet many applicants fail to include courtesy words in cover letters. Instead, they border on arrogance without realizing it, sounding presumptuous or overly forceful. One applicant concluded with "I will be in town Tuesday and will stop by . . . ," presuming that he would be welcomed. Others thank in advance, assuming they will gain an interview, unaware that busy interviewers may take offense.

CHECKLIST   **EFFECTIVE CONCLUSIONS**

1. Is there a courteous request for an interview?

2. Are a home telephone number and e-mail address included? Protect your privacy and your job. Giving a work number poses hazards.

3. Did you specify the hours you can be reached at home?

You can transform a demand into a polite request with just a few courtesy words and a question mark:

- Demand: "E-mail me at . . ."
- Polite request: "Will you please e-mail me at . . .?"

A question with a question mark is more polite than a statement. A question is a request whereas a statement often sounds like a demand. You can set an appropriate tone in your letters by using questions with courtesy words such as *may, please, appreciate, appreciation,* and *your convenience.* Let consideration shine through your words as in the following examples:

- May I make an appointment at your convenience to further explain how I can benefit your company? Please e-mail <amy301@service.net> or call (611) 555-2121 Monday through Thursday from 4:30 to 8:30 p.m.

- If you think there might be a place for me in your firm, will you please e-mail <Brad42@service.net> or leave a message at (402) 555-2626?

Other Considerations

A job search may require dozens of mailings and many interviews before the right position is found. The wisest course may be to write two basic cover letters and see which elicits more responses. Each time you contact a potential employer, customize the basic letter with the current date and correct inside address and salutation as well as any other suitable changes. A cover letter should be limited to one uncrowded page with "picture frame" margins and plenty of white space. Before mailing, proofread your letter carefully, and check to see that it is signed. When contacting several employers, be sure each letter is correctly addressed, signed, and placed inside the right envelope.

E-Mail Cover Letters   If an employer requests an e-mail résumé, then prepare a cover letter for e-mail, too. You can take your printed cover letter and save another version as a plain text document (explained in "Scannable Résumés" and "E-mail Résumés"). Then e-mail the cover letter before the résumé, preferably in the same message.

Revising a Cover Letter

Rarely is an excellent cover letter dashed off in a few minutes. Chances are that you will need several drafts before the letter reflects your best work. Revising requires examining, editing, and proofreading the drafts several times. Whether or not you are granted an interview may hinge upon how effective your cover letter is—for if it is ineffective, your résumé may go unread.

> **CHECKLIST**   **REVISING A COVER LETTER**
>
> 1. Does the introduction focus on the employer's needs?
> 2. Does the introduction set up the main points of the body?
> 3. Does each paragraph center on one main idea?
> 4. Is the material well organized?
> 5. Are qualifications linked to job requirements?
> 6. Is the résumé referred to indirectly at the end of the *body?*
> 7. Is the tone confident without sounding overly confident?
> 8. Is an interview *requested* in the closing?
> 9. Are a phone number and e-mail address included? A time to call?
> 10. Are the words polite and appreciative? Do they conform to standard usage?

FORMAT FOR A BUSINESS LETTER

All business letters contain similar elements, but the positioning of the elements differs slightly. Letters typed with letterheads often follow the *block format* (fig. 25.3) with the date and all other typed elements aligned at the left margin. The *modified block format* (shown in fig. 25.4) is most common for letters that are *not* typed on letterhead stationery. Then the typed signature may be followed by a line of type indicating the writer's business title. A business title accords respect.

325 Cedar Lane
Anywhere, USA 00000
May 1, 2005

Tara Chase, Manager
Tara's Tall and Short Shop
332 State Street
Smalltown, USA 00000

Dear Manager Chase:

As an amateur artist, I have developed a keen eye for detail, line, and color, as well as an interest in people. These qualities along with my academic training and work experience should qualify me for the position of assistant manager of Tara's Tall and Short Shop.

Recently graduated from Washington State College, I have an Associate of Applied Business degree with a major in business management. I received training not only in small business management but also in business law, business ethics, accounting, and data processing. My training in interpersonal communication included active listening, questioning, and nonverbal communication.

For four years at Derrick's Designer Shop, I served customers, designed window displays, assisted in shop security, balanced the cash drawer, opened and closed the store, and made bank deposits. Whenever the owner was away, I managed the shop, supervising eight employees. Other experience is explained on the enclosed résumé.

May I have an appointment to discuss my qualifications? Please send an e-mail to <smbaker505@service.net> or phone (000) 555-1212 on Monday, Tuesday, or Thursdays from 4:30 to 8 p.m.

Sincerely,

Sabrina M. Baker

Sabrina M. Baker

FIGURE 25.3 Cover letter with creative opening. (Block format)

331 Patterson Avenue
Wintoska, Oregon 47000
March 27, 2005

Craig Withers, Office Manager
Baywood and Goldberg
1221 North Main Street
Wintoska, Oregon 47000

Dear Manager Withers:

When an old and respected law firm like Baywood and Goldberg advertises for
a junior accountant, I am interested. My three years' work experience and my training in accounting and information systems should enable me to perform successfully
for you.

As the only accountant for a local hardware store, I assume many responsibilities,
including writing a proposal that won a federally funded low-interest loan. During
my first year, I streamlined bookkeeping operations, converting from QuickBooks
to Microsoft Management System Headquarters. Currently, I am responsible for accounts receivable and accounts payable, insurance payments, and payroll. Quarterly,
I write reports and file tax returns.

On June 10, 2005, I will graduate from Franklin University with a bachelor's
degree in accounting. There I have received training not only in cost and corporate
accounting but also in finance and business law. Since my minor is in data processing,
I have experience with a wide range of microcomputers and accounting software, as
explained on the enclosed résumé.

At your convenience, I would like to set up an appointment to discuss how I can
serve your firm. Salary is open. Will you please call (000) 555-4689 between 5:30
and 9:00 p.m. Monday through Wednesday or weekends? Or if you prefer, e-mail
<jasmith@service.net>.

Sincerely,

Jon Alan Smith

Jon Alan Smith

**FIGURE 25.4 Cover letter with summary opening.
(Modified block format with indented paragraphs)**

MODIFIED BLOCK FORM

- **Heading.** Place your own address and the date on three lines in the top
  right corner.
- **Inside address.** Type the recipient's name and address—just as they
  appear on the envelope—several spaces below the heading at the left-
  hand margin.
- **Salutation:** Use a business title. The salutation falls two spaces below
  the heading, also at the left margin. In a business letter, the salutation is
  always followed by a colon.

- **Body.** Single-space the paragraphs. Double-space between paragraphs. Indentation is optional.

- **Complimentary close.** Double-space after the body and type "Sincerely," "Regards," "Best regards," or other suitable closing. Align the closing, followed by a comma, with the heading.

- **Signature.** Leave four lines after the complimentary close for the handwritten signature. Below this four-line space, type the signature.

PACKAGING JOB-SEARCH DOCUMENTS

A positive first impression is important not only for applicants but also for their job-search packet. Chances are the applicant will never meet the interviewer unless the documents in the packet are immaculate. Erasures, strikeovers, and smudges are unacceptable. The résumé, cover letter, and other items should be perfectly printed by a laser printer (if possible), a high-quality inkjet printer, or an up-to-date electric typewriter, preferably on *white* 20-pound bond paper. White paper transfers more clearly than colored when duplicated or scanned or faxed. Use a clear, conventional type style. Italics or unusual fonts are difficult for a scanner to read.

When finally satisfied with the quality of your résumé and cover letter, place them inside an 8½- by 11-inch manila envelope, unfolded. This precaution will protect against weather, wrinkling, fingerprints, or dropping. If you are employed, do *not* enclose a sheet of references, lest your employer be contacted prematurely. One applicant made this unfortunate mistake, only to find he had no job with either firm. The interviewer had telephoned the employer immediately, and the man was fired upon his return an hour later.

If unemployed, you can enclose references along with the résumé and cover letter; yet this is unnecessary, since most employers wait until after an interview to run a reference check. If you enclose letters of recommendation, do *not* send the originals, which could disappear into an employer's file. When an employer wants a grade transcript, order one and arrange to have it mailed directly to the company. Because oversized envelopes require extra postage, you can conserve by using standard envelopes for mailings to companies that seem less desirable.

PROVIDING A LIST OF REFERENCES

When you walk into an interview with an up-to-date, well-organized sheet of references, you have a definite advantage. This preparation not only boosts your confidence but also indicates to the interviewer your ability to plan ahead and organize. Yet relatively few job seekers are aware of the full significance of this important job-search tool, nor do they think to add *financial* references to the usual list of former employers, teachers, and the like. However, financial references are significant. From the employer's point of view, someone who is financially stable seems more likely to be trustworthy and reliable.

1. **Request permission before using names.** With teachers and others you have not seen for many years, try to meet in person to make sure you are remembered. Otherwise, telephone. If you must write, enclose a stamped, self-addressed envelope and politely request an early reply. (Employers expect to be contacted; it is unnecessary to ask for their permission.)

2. **Be sure the person is willing to give you a reference.** If you sense reluctance or a lack of enthusiasm, ask someone else. A lukewarm response can do harm.

3. **Provide employment references.** From your last two positions, list supervisors. If you know employees at the company to which you are applying who would give favorable references, include their names, too.

4. **Provide other references.** Include coworkers, teachers, coaches, scout leaders, or anyone else who can attest to your good qualities—except relatives and the clergy. For financial references, list banks, charge accounts, or paid-up loans.

5. **Indicate in parenthesis your relationship to the reference.**

6. **Organize the list of references in most- to least-important order.** Put employers first, character references second, and financial references third.

7. **Include your full name, address, telephone number, and e-mail address.** Place this information at the top of the sheet in a centered heading like the one on a résumé.

8. **If working, take precautions.** Across the top, before the heading with your name, type in capital letters: "PLEASE DO NOT CONTACT MY CURRENT EMPLOYER UNTIL THE FINAL STAGES OF INTERVIEWING." If using a résumé service, ask that neither your résumé nor your reference list be sent to your present employer.

WRITING A LETTER OF APPRECIATION

Several applicants had interviewed for the position of Financial Aid Director at Marion Technical College, but the search committee could not agree. Then a letter of appreciation for the interview arrived from Andrew Harper, who was the only applicant to send a thank-you. The committee reevaluated his credentials and called him for a second interview. Andy got the job. That one brief letter tipped the scales in his favor. Why? What is significant about a letter of appreciation?

First, a letter of appreciation reveals a sincere interest in a position. Since most applicants interview for several positions and seldom send follow-up notes, an employer does not know whether or not they are genuinely interested. Second, a thank-you conveys a message, implying the sender is considerate and appreciative. It also suggests motivation, perseverance, and a positive attitude. Third, the letter indicates good human relations skills. (See fig. 25.5 for an example.)

1122 Valley Road
Clearview, Washington 98222
February 6, 2005

Dr. Margaret Berman
Mad River Medical Association
1555 Main Street
Wenatchee, Washington 98555

Dear Dr. Berman:

Thank you for the opportunity to discuss the possibility of working at Mad River Medical Association. I enjoyed meeting with you and your staff; the friendly atmosphere and organization impressed me. After interviewing with you, I am even more eager to become a part of your medical team.

Once my program at Marion Technical College is complete on March 19, 2005, I will be available for employment. If accepted for the position of medical secretary, I am prepared to put all my efforts into achieving the goals set by your practice and to serving your patients accordingly.

If you should need any further information concerning my credentials, please contact me at (000) 555-1111 any time convenient for you or e-mail <tmcraig632@ service.net>.

Sincerely,

Trena M. Craig

Trena M. Craig

FIGURE 25.5 Letter of appreciation.

There is no standard format for a letter of appreciation, but *timing* and *tone* are important. Mail your letter the day of the interview or the next day. But keep your priorities straight: accuracy and appropriateness are more important than same-day mailing. Read the letter aloud to gauge the tone. Edit and proofread several times. Be sure the tone mirrors enthusiasm, not the image of a forlorn applicant sitting by a silent telephone. Avoid phrases such as "I eagerly look forward to hearing from you," or "If you are interested please call me," or "I'll be waiting to hear from you."

To write a successful letter of appreciation quickly, follow the outline below, including any of the six parts that are relevant to your situation.

OUTLINE: LETTER OF APPRECIATION

1. Thank you
2. I'm interested
3. I enjoyed . . . (or was impressed by . . .)
4. I'm available (give date)
5. Another item you might like to know (optional)
6. If you need more information (give telephone number, time to call, and e-mail address).

WORKPLACE CASE STUDY

CONNECT THE DOTS

During an interview, Valerie L. was asked if she had any grant-writing experience. She replied, "No, but I have had considerable experience writing letters, reports, and other documents. I would be glad to learn."

After the interview, Valerie went to the library, where she looked at sample grants. She realized that they were similar to the proposals that she had written at her previous job. In her letter of appreciation, she mentioned going to the library, the similarity between grants and proposals, as well as her proposal-writing experience.

As a result, she was hired.

Moral: Connect the dots of your experience to the job you apply for. Do not assume the interviewer will make the connections.

WRITING A LETTER OF ACCEPTANCE

Often employers notify successful applicants by telephone. If you should be called, be sure the terms of the job offer are clear before accepting. Acceptance over the telephone is an oral contract. During the call jot down the terms of the offer and ask for confirmation to ensure there is no misunderstanding. If you are unsure or if you have other offers pending, you can ask for one to three days to decide. Competitive offers will enhance your desirability.

After making a decision, call in your acceptance and send a letter accepting the job offer and the terms (see fig. 25.6). Specify the primary provisions of the offer and keep a copy. This letter not only protects the employer but also protects you by forestalling misunderstanding or friction later.

Dear Ms. Hendricks:

Thank you for the job offer. The staff nurse position, evening shift, on the surgical floor will be challenging and interesting since it offers numerous opportunities to learn. The salary of $_____ per hour with $_____ on weekends is more than acceptable.

On June 12, I will arrive early to fill out the insurance forms, receive instructions, and begin.

I am looking forward to working with you and the other members of the staff at Belvedere General Hospital.

Cordially,

Jonathan Jones

Jonathan Jones

FIGURE 25.6 Abbreviated letter of acceptance.

The following outline will help you organize a letter accepting a job offer.

OUTLINE: LETTER OF ACCEPTANCE

1. Thank-you or an expression of appreciation
2. Acceptance of the offer (sound pleased)
3. Main points of the job offer
4. Date and time to begin work
5. Courtesy closing

WRITING A LETTER OF REFUSAL

Never let the door slam on a job offer. Courtesy is important even in a refusal, for some day you may wish to reapply at the company. A refusal should be made promptly so that the company can continue the search. The refusal can be made over the telephone, but unless you are adept at speaking off the cuff, it is wiser to mail a decision, if possible.

Begin by tactfully expressing appreciation for the offer. But avoid an overly enthusiastic tone that might mislead the reader into thinking the letter is an acceptance. Provide a general reason for the refusal, without mentioning anything that might seem negative about the company or the offer. Close with a positive comment (see fig. 25.7).

OUTLINE: REFUSAL OF A JOB OFFER

1. Expression of appreciation for the job offer
2. Brief refusal
3. General reason for the refusal (optional)
4. Courtesy closing

Dear Ms. Plymale:

     Thank you for the informative tour of Tucker & Taylor's downtown facility and for the attractive offer of the junior accounting position.

     I have, however, accepted another offer that is more consistent with my career goals.

     Your time, consideration, and courtesy are appreciated.

Sincerely,

Raphael Perez

Raphael Perez

FIGURE 25.7 Abbreviated letter of refusal.

WRITING A LETTER OF RESIGNATION

Business etiquette requires that when an employee accepts another position, the present employer be notified in writing. When writing a letter of resignation, express appreciation and specify the date of leaving. Send the letter to the head of the department. If you are asked to go within the hour, don't be surprised or take offense. Many companies require that personnel working with computer records or other data requiring security depart immediately. Sometimes, however, when there is no immediate replacement, the employee is asked to stay longer.

    Try to leave on a friendly footing. Even if your employer does not take your resignation well, retain your dignity. If you are treated unprofessionally, be very careful that bitterness does not seep into your letter of resignation. Later you will be glad you retained your professional demeanor. The suggested outline below will be helpful.

OUTLINE: LETTER OF RESIGNATION

1. Express appreciation (possibly regret).
2. State the exact date of leaving.
3. If another job has been accepted, give a reason for leaving. State in general terms such as "opportunity" or "generous offer."
4. If you want to take accrued vacation time or holidays off, specify.
5. Keep the letter positive and end on an upbeat note.

Sometimes an employee is fired and given the opportunity to write a letter of resignation. Although this event is disheartening, the employee should take advantage of the offer unless prepared to contest the termination in court. A letter of resignation is a protection not only for the employer but also for the discharged employee. It gives the appearance that the employee is leaving of his or her own accord, which will work to the employee's advantage in future employment interviews.

The letter shown in fig. 25.8 was written by a company's star sales representative who had been asked to tender his resignation. A powerful client had complained over a refusal to be given a large discount and had arranged a deal with the sales manager. Then the client demanded the sales representative be fired, and the manager complied. Although filled with indignation, the discharged employee knew his future career depended upon subordinating feelings and conducting himself in a professional manner. To gain control, he waited a day to write the letter.

Mr. James Jones
Sales Manager
Mazdex, Incorporated
111 East Main Street
Anywhere, USA

Dear Jim:

My five years with Mazdex have been challenging and rewarding. This association has provided an opportunity for applying and developing my skills as well as gaining practical knowledge of the business world. It is with reluctance that I tender my resignation, effective immediately.

I have decided it is time to turn my career in a slightly different direction as an accounting software trainer/sales consultant. My experience with Mazdex has provided me with valuable skills and contacts.

Finally, Jim, I appreciate your assistance and training. You have helped to make our association pleasant and productive. I look forward to dealing with Mazdex in a different capacity.

Sincerely,

John R. Smith

FIGURE 25.8 Abbreviated letter of resignation.

PRACTICE

COLLABORATIVE EXERCISE: Revising Skills Lists

Directions: Working with a partner, check each other's drafts of skills. Questioning your partner will help each of you to find more transferable skills and an action verb for each skill.

1. Is the item a claim or a skill?

   Note: A skill tells what one can *do:* "type 60 wpm" and "monitored cash drawer" are skills. But "work well with others" and "honest" are vague claims. Instead, cite specific duties that point to a skill or an ability.

   Example of an interpersonal skill: "Resolved customer complaints."

2. Does each item begin with an action verb?

3. What else did you do that required accuracy, responsibility, communication skill, tact, problem solving, or trustworthiness?

4. How can that task be reworded for your skills list?

5. Is there anything else that you did at work, in class, or during leisure hours that might be transferable?

COLLABORATIVE EXERCISE: Revising a Job Objective

Directions: Using the criteria below, critique the job objectives of your group members. Place a question mark after any word or phrase that does not sound appropriate. Make suggestions.

1. Is the objective limited to *one* position or area?

2. Does the objective focus on service to an employer?

3. Is the objective written in third person?

4. Is the objective written as a fragment, not a sentence?

5. Are the skills in the objective the same as those in the skill headings?

6. Is the wording correct and appropriate?

A Research Guide for Writers

Whether you intend to use the library or a computer at home for secondary research, select a suitable topic and evaluate your sources for credibility, timeliness, and relevance. Look for a range of sources so that your paper can provide comprehensive coverage. If you plan to do field research, consider how you will gather information, whether through observation, a survey, or interviews.

PREWRITING EXERCISE

Brainstorm possible topics to explore for your research. Then stop and consider each possibility, asking questions such as these: Which one would be the most interesting? Does the topic need to be narrowed? Will I be able to find adequate information on the topic?

Planning Research

> Learning without thought is labour lost; thought without learning is perilous.
>
> —Confucius (6th century BC), *Analects*, 2.15, trans. James Legge

In the Information Age, learning often involves research. Professionals in business, law, engineering, medicine, and other fields gather, digest, and condense large quantities of information during the course of their workdays. In your professional life, you may observe sites and situations, interview prospective employees, or survey a group to gather opinions. You may analyze annual reports, budgets, government documents, court cases, medical journals, or other records.

In your college classes, you gather information for research papers and reports. A research project can help you acquire a wide range of career skills. It can afford opportunities to develop the ability to

- Plan and schedule your time
- Observe, interview, and survey
- Locate information in the library
- Find information on the Internet
- Summarize, paraphrase, and quote
- Analyze and evaluate
- Provide proper documentation for sources
- Meet deadlines

PRIMARY AND SECONDARY RESEARCH

www.mhhe.com/dietsch
For a wealth of online research resources, visit: Research

You can collect information in either of two general ways—primary research or secondary research. Or you can combine the two. Collecting data firsthand is called *primary research* or *field research.* You become the researcher and go to a *primary source,* one that has not been filtered through the eyes of another researcher. Whether you observe a class, interview someone, or survey a population sample, you go out in the "field" and conduct primary research. You may make careful notes, describing what happens and your perceptions. Or you may construct a questionnaire, administer it, and tabulate the responses. The data you collect becomes the basis of your report or paper.

See "Caterpillar Afternoon," p. 564.

Secondary research is the collecting of information that has passed through someone else's hands. You may find it in a library or on the Internet. When you use *secondary sources,* someone else has conducted the research and recorded the original data. Usually, this information has been published and printed.

See chapter 27.

BASIC GUIDELINES FOR RESEARCH

1. For research to be reliable, the researcher must be accurate and objective in presenting findings and interpreting results.
2. Sources must be clearly identified.
3. Primary sources are preferable to secondary sources.
4. Both primary and secondary research require *documentation,* a listing of the source, the date, the author, and other related data. Omission of documentation can result in plagiarism.

See chapter 28.

A basic concept to remember throughout your project is that for research to be reliable, the researcher must be accurate and objective in presenting findings and in interpreting results.

The Path to Objectivity

There are three sides to every story—yours, mine, and all that lie between.

—Jody Kern

Recently a National Public Radio panel discussed whether or not a reporter has the right to include opinion in a news report of an overseas conflict. The question was this: Should he give only the facts or should he put himself into the story as well? Traditionally, reporting and other research have constituted a quest for truth, a search for facts, not an opportunity to express a personal view.

Researchers are still expected to step back from their own beliefs and emotions—to be as objective and unbiased as possible. To maintain professional integrity and reliability, they must be observant and open to new information. They must be competent and honest, able to identify and describe data accurately, and able to understand what is occurring. They must be willing to question their own perceptions, for optical illusions and misperception can occur.

To check for bias, researchers need to be keenly aware that observation, description, interpretation, and writing are *separate* stages of primary research (see fig 26.1). Distortion can occur at any stage. To ensure accuracy, researchers check their perceptions, word choice, interpretation, and final draft carefully.

Objectivity Requires Checking Each Stage of Research

Observe   Describe   Interpret   Write

FIGURE 26.1 Path to objective research.

Fact or Idea?

Questioning the mental images, words, and inferences you derive through perception leads to objective writing. This doubting will help you differentiate fact from idea, which is not always easy. *Fact* is information generally accepted as real or true. But not all so-called facts are true. An *established fact* has been verified by substantial support/evidence. Some facts can be quickly verified through the five senses. Other facts are established through laboratory tests, control groups, and other measures.

See chapter 3.

In *The Modern Researcher*, fourth edition, Jacques Barzun defines an *idea* as "an image, inference, or suggestion that goes beyond the data [facts] nameable in conventional terms." This definition can guide you when the boundary between fact and idea blurs. Ask yourself if the information is entirely fact or if opinion has been injected. Is the information accepted by experts in the field as true or is it still in the realm of theory and unproven? Barzun explains, "An idea leads us on. . . . [It] suggests doubts and possibilities."

To test your alertness, consider the two sentences below. Which one is strictly fact? Which one mixes an idea with fact?

John F. Kennedy, a great president, was assassinated in 1963.

President John F. Kennedy was assassinated on November 22, 1963.

The first sentence contains the idea of greatness, which is a matter of opinion. Every word in the second sentence is factual. As you record data, do not mix ideas in with your concrete facts. Ideas belong to a later stage, when you make inferences and derive a conclusion. Descriptions of observations should be precise and factual. Keep in mind, too, that the *image* you perceive may be incomplete or distorted, depending upon your vantage point and your knowledge of the subject. Try to ensure that you will see all that happens.

Second, *choose words carefully*. Use neutral, concrete words, not emotionally charged language. Some words carry extra baggage—hidden meanings, associations, or opinions. For example, there is a big difference between "dozens of black-and-orange ladybugs have crept under my back door" (fact) and "dozens of spotted beetles have invaded my home" (idea). As you record data, avoid using words that reveal your opinion.

Third, *check interpretations and inferences*. Do they seem logical and reasonable, considering the observable facts? Do the inferences account for all the loose ends? Or are there conflicting data? If so, the conflict should be noted and discussed.

Fourth, *be tentative* in presenting interpretations and inferences. Use qualifiers such as *indicate, suggest, may, appear*, and *tend*. Remembering these precautions will help you attain objectivity.

SCHEDULING RESEARCH TASKS

Regardless of whether you do primary or secondary research, your project will require considerable time. If you interview, you will need to set up appointments, construct a list of questions, tabulate responses, and write a report of your findings. For secondary research, you will need to locate materials in the library or on the Internet. Reading, analyzing, and writing will require much time.

Is a Schedule Really Necessary?

Procrastination may be tempting when the deadline for a research report or paper seems distant—perhaps a month or more away. Yet don't be lulled into complacency by believing you can draft a questionnaire or find all the books you need in an hour. Such misconceptions can lead to anxiety and even panic as your deadline looms.

A flexible schedule, tailored to your needs, can alleviate anxiety and increase efficiency. The first step is to list the tasks involved. The second step is to make a realistic estimate of the time required for each one. Keep in mind that if you are doing secondary research, you will need to locate specific information, compile source cards, read, and take notes. Writing a paper based on either primary or secondary research will require drafting, revising, editing, and proofreading. If possible, allow a little leeway here and there in your schedule.

As a safeguard, plan research tasks so that your final draft can be completed a day or two early. That way you can revise, edit, and proofread thoroughly. And if a minor emergency should occur, you will not have to worry about finishing on time. Start soon so that you will have the time to write a quality paper.

TENTATIVE FIVE-WEEK SCHEDULE FOR SECONDARY RESEARCH

	Days Needed	Date to Complete
1. Select a topic. Locate materials. Do preliminary reading. Start note cards and source cards.	2–3	_____
2. Limit topic, read, and write a controlling question.	2	_____
3. Read. Start a scratch outline.	3	_____
4. As you read, continue making note and source cards.	3	_____
5. Revise outline. Write thesis and start draft.	3	_____
6. Reread notes. Refine outline. Finish first draft.	6	_____
7. Return unneeded materials. Get more if needed.	1	_____
8. Read. Revise draft. Print out.	4	_____
9. Revise draft. Check order and format. Print.	3	_____
10. Alphabetize source cards. Type list of works cited.	1	_____
11. Revise, edit, and proofread several times.	3	_____
12. *Tentative deadline:* Proof again. Print final copy.	1	_____
Final deadline: Submit research paper.		_____

Will the Internet Cut Research Time?

If you are adept at searching the Web and if you can find reliable and substantial information on your topic quickly, then you may save time in locating materials. But if you are a novice in cyberspace or if archives are huge, it may take longer to locate and load sources on the Net than to find them in the library. Research opportunities on the Internet are limited for several reasons:

1. Some sources on the Web are not reliable. The individual who posts the information may not be an authority and may misinterpret the results. Source listings may be incomplete.

2. Free information on the Internet may be scant and superficial, lacking significant details.

3. Many databases require *paid subscriptions.* They are available only at libraries or to patrons who have contracted for them.

4. Instructors often limit the number of online sources for a paper.

5. Some sources provide downloads that you may be unable to open without downloading additional software.

COLLECTING SOURCE INFORMATION

Whether you go to the library, go online, or do field research, you need to know what source information to collect. You also need to understand exactly what plagiarism is and the necessity of printing out any page you intend to summarize, paraphrase, or cite. (Chapters 27, 28, and 29 provide detailed instructions.) Gathering this data as you research provides the following advantages:

- **Saves time.** You don't have to retrace the original source. Instead, you can quickly scan printouts, select quotations, and double-check for accuracy.
- **Prevents unintentional plagiarism and worry.** *Avoids risky shortcuts.*
- **Enhances credibility.** Readers feel they can trust someone who supports a claim with adequate documentation.
- **Provides evidence.** If there should be any questions from an instructor, you have proof that you researched the sources for your paper.

Plagiarism is taking someone else's work and presenting it as your own. Whether intentional or unintentional, plagiarism is risky and impractical for the following reasons:

1. **Experienced instructors usually detect plagiarism.** When plagiarized material from professional writers is added to most undergraduate writing, the patchwork additions are readily apparent to the practiced eye.

2. **Papers that have been purchased from Web sites can be easily tracked.** And coincidences do occur. One professor, who was not suspicious, tells of awarding a history paper an A until another student submitted its duplicate. Both papers had been purchased at the same site.

3. **Search engines can quickly take instructors to plagiarized portions of online material.** If you can find it, so can your instructor.

HOW EASILY IS PLAGIARISM DETECTED?

A Note of Encouragement

Beginning a research project can be daunting. You can make your project satisfying and challenging by choosing a topic that interests you and pushes you to learn beyond what you already know. You can ease the pressure of the assignment by drafting a schedule early and by adjusting the schedule to your needs. A realistic plan for completing your project can enable you to become more efficient.

Hang in there! You should do just fine.

PRACTICE

DRAFTING A SCHEDULE

Directions: If your assignment calls for field research, read chapter 30, "Field Research: Observation, Interviews, and Surveys," before drafting your schedule. For other research, read chapter 27, "Locating Print and Electronic Sources."

1. Prewrite: List all the tasks you will need to complete your research project.

2. Draft: Copy your tasks in the order they will be done. At the bottom of the sheet, write *deadline*, followed by the date due.

3. If your instructor has included checkpoints, include those dates.

4. Determine the number of days until your deadline. Now allot a few days to each task, making sure you do not run over the total number of days. Include a *tentative deadline* to allow for an emergency.

5. Check to see that your estimates are realistic. Revise as needed. (See page 426.)

Locating Print and Electronic Sources

An open mind is an asset for research. To be open does not mean you accept everything you read. It just means you give new information and opposing beliefs a fair hearing. You consider unfamiliar data and dissenting views, rather than hastily rejecting them because they seem strange or different. You are willing to review a claim before you evaluate it. As you examine the evidence, you try to appraise the information impartially, yet question

> To be conscious that you are ignorant of the facts is a great step to knowledge.
>
> —Benjamin Disraeli (1845)

any point that seems doubtful. *The principal goal of research is to obtain an objective assessment of the facts—to discover the unvarnished truth.*

DETERMINING THE AIM OR PURPOSE

The first step to any research project is to determine the general aim or purpose. Your instructor may already have made this decision by assigning a particular kind of research paper. If not, consider whether you want to inform, investigate a problem, or persuade. All three kinds of papers require substantial reading, summary, paraphrase, quotation, and documentation of sources. As a result, the tone of research papers tends to be formal and less personal than undocumented papers.

Informative Research Papers

An *informative research paper* explores what is actually known about a topic and presents it in an objective manner. The paper ends with a logical conclusion, drawn from the research. The researcher boils down a wide range of information into a balanced summary, incorporating results of reputable studies and quoting opinion of authorities in the field, then points out the relevance to the reader.

For an informative research paper, you not only summarize and quote but also define, compare results, and paraphrase. You define terms not generally known and compare professional opinions. You report on areas of consensus or disagreement among experts. *You think about what the research means, how it can be applied, and what questions remain for future research.*

Research papers often require more than one kind of order. For example, you might use chronological order to summarize the onset of a disease and its symptoms, then use classification to list methods of treatment.

Problem-Solving Research Papers

Many topics for research papers center on problems. For example, you might investigate a business, medical, ethical, legal, social, or environmental problem. The problem might involve your campus, your community, your workplace, or a group to which you belong. You may do primary (field) or secondary research or a combination of both.

See chapters 17 and 30.

Like an informative paper, a *problem-solving paper* reports existing data and expert opinion. But it goes a step further: you evaluate the alternatives for solving or alleviating the problem. A *recommendation* may also be included. If your paper is based on secondary research, the recommendation is based on the majority opinion of experts in the field. If you conduct primary research yourself and if you are the expert, then you make the recommendation. A problem-solving paper often combines chronological order with description and classification.

Research Papers of Argument

An *argument paper* is quite different from either the informative or the problem-solving paper. In a paper of argument, you briefly summarize a controversy and argue for a point of view, belief, or course of action. In other words, you take a stand and support it with facts, reasons, and examples. An argument may open with a chronological summary, then use illustration and classification to organize the supporting details.

The tone of the argument depends upon the purpose, the topic, and the audience. How will you approach the topic so that your argument is effective? A fair and reasonable tone, adequate and reliable evidence, and logical organization will help to ensure that the argument is sound.

See chapter 18.

SELECTING AN APPROPRIATE TOPIC

Your research topic should be provocative, worthwhile, and challenging. This project should offer you the opportunity to learn and to draw a conclusion. Avoid a rehash of a topic you covered in high school or one well covered in a single source. As you mull over choices, consider three important questions:

> www.mhhe.com/dietsch
>
> For more information on choosing a topic, go to: Writing>Thesis/Central Idea

- **Can you find a topic that stirs your curiosity?** For example, if several of your family members have the same health problem, you might investigate the cause, effects, and current methods of treatment.

- **Can you find information that is unfamiliar to most readers?** Avoid familiar topics such as drinking and driving, abortion, or the death penalty, which have been widely publicized.

- **Can you locate conclusive support: data, studies, and expert opinion from several reliable sources?** A single source is not enough. (Ask your instructor how many sources are required.)

To determine whether or not a topic is feasible, do a *preliminary search* of possible sources. Can you secure enough suitable information within a few days? If a topic is quite new or old, you may find few sources.

> Look for a topic that you would like to know more about. What items have been in the news lately? You can also find ideas for topics in weekly news magazines such as *Time, Newsweek,* and *U.S. News and World Report.* Try online directories. The suggestions at the end of this chapter may also stimulate ideas.

WHERE TO FIND POSSIBLE TOPICS

LIMITING THE TOPIC

Limiting the topic for a research paper can be intimidating—rather like picking up an octopus. The crux of the problem is this: Where and how do you grasp it? Where do you start?

Starting Points

For some topics, you may need to acquire more general knowledge of a subject before you can limit your topic. Reading an overview in an encyclopedia, an abstract, or a digest is a quick and easy way to obtain leads. This broad view will list the main aspects of the topic. You can select one and search for more information on the narrowed topic. You may find that it, too, has several aspects that require narrowing the topic again. At the ends of articles, you may find lists of related sources and topics to investigate.

A good way to limit a subject is to consult the *Library of Congress Subject Headings,* a multivolume listing of headings used to catalog books. The *Library of Congress Subject Headings* (LCSH) is a very large book, usually located adjacent to the reference section. In the LCSH, under the subject headings for books, you can find subheadings to use in your search. You can also consult an online directory such as Yahoo. There you can find general topics, which can be narrowed according to your purpose and audience.

Writing a Controlling Question

After finishing your preliminary reading and deciding on a topic, you may find that it is too broad. Writing a *controlling question* will help you narrow the topic. A controlling question establishes limits. For example, the subject of breast cancer is much too broad. But you could restrict it by asking, "What are the advantages and disadvantages of various methods of treating breast cancer?" Here are more examples of controlling questions:

- How effective is solar energy for heating new homes?
- What should parents look for when selecting day care?
- What ethical issues are at stake in fetal stem cell research?

A controlling question will help you focus your research by specifying the direction your paper will take. Formulating the question early can cut both search and writing time. Then as you examine materials, list possible main points and start a scratch outline.

BALANCING PRINT AND ELECTRONIC SOURCES

Although you may be able to do much of your research from home via the Internet, your instructor may require that you also visit a library to obtain print sources. Both the library and the Internet have strengths and limitations. One important asset of the library is the staff. These professionals can help you find what you need quickly. On the Internet you are on your own. Then too, back issues of periodicals in Internet archives generally require a fee and a credit card number. Yet you can obtain the same information from a library database or print issues without charge. If you need to study an entire work, the library is probably better to obtain a novel or play.

But if you need to find a small item, say a line in one of Shakespeare's plays, the Internet is generally faster. The Internet may also be quicker for finding a famous quotation, but the campus library may have a broader selection. If you need to search for a current event, you might start with the Internet, then continue at the library. Many times the Internet offers a quick overview of a subject. It is not a substitute for the comprehensive sources available in the library.

FLORA NARROWS A VERY BROAD TOPIC

After preliminary reading on rain forests, Flora Kyle found that a number of rain forests exist around the world. She limited her topic to Amazon rain forests, but still she found too much information for the assignment of a 1,500–1,700-word paper. Feeling overwhelmed, she consulted her instructor, who suggested asking: How does deforestation of the Amazon rain forests affect residents of the United States? Then Flora was able to restate the question, limit her focus to three main reasons, and begin an outline:

SCRATCH OUTLINE

Controlling Question: Why should U.S. citizens be concerned about deforestation of the Amazon rain forest?

1. Habitat of many plants and animals destroyed
2. Spread of disease from fleas and mites that leave the deforested area
3. Effect on the ozone layer by greenhouse gases produced by burning in the rain forest
4. Worldwide climate changes

WORKPLACE CASE STUDY

THREE IMPORTANT PRECAUTIONS

During your research, you will come abreast of various pitfalls, but this chapter will help you skirt them safely. Three important preliminary precautions are provided here:

- **Use reliable Web sites that are secure.** To check the reliability of a Web site, see page 444. If you decide to purchase information online, be sure the site is safe. (See the directory of Web sites on page 445.)
- **Know how to obtain complete source information.** Prior to taking notes on any source, look over chapter 28 so that you know which source data are required.

- **Know how to quote, summarize, and paraphrase.** See chapter 29, which shows how to quote, summarize, and paraphrase. Then as you make notes, *insert quotation marks around copied material immediately.* This way you can avoid borrowing the author's words unintentionally.

AVOID PLAGIARIZING ONLINE MATERIALS

> **Warning:** If you stumble onto Web sites where you can view student papers or purchase professional research papers, beware. Some sites post a warning about *plagiarism;* others do not. Still, some errant students download and submit these papers to instructors, which is foolish and dangerous. Those who cheat not only rob themselves of an opportunity to learn but also run a high risk of detection and punishment for plagiarism. If you are tempted, consider these salient points:
>
> - **Free student papers on the Internet tend to be mediocre**— replete with errors in content, sentence structure, spelling, and grammar.
> - **Papers for sale tend to be poorly documented, listing few sources.** For example, one paper, "Evolution vs. Creationism," merely compares the content of two Web sites. Such methods constitute shoddy research.
> - **Few students have the writing proficiency of professionals.** If you buy a paper written by a professional, the differences in writing style are likely to be detected by experienced instructors.
> - **Instructors can easily check your paper with those on Web sites.** All they have to do is type an unusual sentence or phrase into a search engine. It can quickly find the original paper if copied.

www.mhhe.com/dietsch

For online resources related to using the library, go to:
Research>Using the Library

FINDING AND EVALUATING PRINT AND ELECTRONIC SOURCES AT THE LIBRARY

Libraries have resources on the premises, as well as access to resources at other libraries and on the Internet. Unless you are doing very advanced research, your college library should provide everything you need. As you search, do not assume a source is unavailable just because you cannot locate it. There may be a second copy elsewhere, or it may have been returned but not yet checked in. Or it may be available online. Old books and newspapers may be stored on microfilm or microfiche.

Be aware, too, that your library's central catalog may consist of one complete system or of segments, both printed and electronic. Ask at the information desk.

Finding Your Way around the Library

Many libraries provide a map of the facility and a brochure describing available services. Look for these materials near the main entrance or at the information desk. If you don't find what you need, inquire. In the periodical room, you'll find recent copies of magazines, journals, and newspapers. There may be several computer areas, each with a different function. Usually, there are computerized indexes, regional online networks, and Internet connections.

Libraries have four excellent sources for beginning a search: general references, indexes, catalogs, and bibliographies. If any of these resources is new to you, do not be dismayed. Library personnel tend to be quite helpful.

Preliminary Reading: General References

Brief reading in some general references will provide a quick overview of your topic and help you limit it. If the subject is not new, begin with short selections from dictionaries, encyclopedias, or abstracts. Many encyclopedias give not only an overview but also a bibliography for locating additional sources. They range from the *Encyclopedia of Chemistry* to the *Encyclopedia of Advertising* to the *Encyclopedia of Rock, Pop, and Soul.* Of course, some are available on the Internet. And many libraries subscribe to both general and specialized encyclopedias online and provide access to patrons in addition to having print copies on the premises.

> **TIP:** Some libraries offer home access to database subscriptions for patrons. This means patrons can log on from home computers, using their library card number or student ID as password. Ask library staff if any databases are available for home use and how to access them.

Electronic Central Catalog

After you have gained an overview, it is time to seek detailed material to flesh out your topic. Most libraries have transferred their old card catalogs to an *electronic central catalog.* This allows you to use a computer terminal to locate most of the holdings housed on the premises. You can search by subject, author, title, or keyword by pressing the appropriate keys. Most systems indicate the location of a book, availability, and date of return—if it has been borrowed.

Periodical Indexes and Abstracts

You can find recent information in newly published articles in periodicals (newspapers, magazines, journals, newsletters, and bulletins). To find these materials, consult indexes and abstracts. Indexes (printed and online) list articles alphabetically according to subject. Indexes give specific titles, authors, and publications—including magazines, newspapers, pamphlets, government publications, maps, pictures, records, tapes, films, and videos as well as books. Many specialized indexes list sources of information for science and technology, art, business, nursing, medicine, drama, education, and other areas.

Abstracts not only list subject headings but also summarize key information in a highly condensed form. For example, you might consult *Psychology Abstracts* (1927 to present) or *Historical Abstracts* (1955 to present).

General Indexes   General indexes list articles intended for a particular audience. For example, *The Readers' Guide to Periodical Literature* (1905 on) lists hundreds of early popular periodicals. Electronic directories list periodicals from the last decade or so, but if you want earlier articles, you will need to consult a print index or an electronic database with archives. Most libraries subscribe to an online periodical database such as EBSCOhost or InfoTrac. These are searchable by subject and keyword. They cover both general and scholarly resources. Articles in many cases are full-text and printable, eliminating the need to find the actual periodical and copy the article from it. Many of these online periodical indexes also offer the option of e-mailing to a home computer, where articles can be printed.

The *New York Times Index* and the *Wall Street Journal Index* can also guide you to articles of general interest. Both are in print and available online. Both offer free access to current articles, but for older, archived information, users must register and pay. Both include scientific, technical, and literary articles, but they are not as extensive as those found in more specialized indexes. If you use popular sources, you will need to supplement them with more scholarly sources.

Specialized Indexes   To find technical or scholarly research and government publications, consult specialized indexes and abstracts, either in print or online. For example, *The Humanities Index* (1974 to present) lists articles on archaeology, history, literature, the performing arts, philosophy, and religion. The *Social Sciences Index* (1974 to present) lists articles on economics, geography, government, law, political science, psychology, and sociology.

Prospective teachers might consult the *Education Index*. Medical technology students might search the *Cumulative Index to Nursing and Allied Health Literature*. The *Public Affairs Information Service* (PAIS) (1915 to present) carries subject listings of material by public and private agencies on economic and social concerns, international relations, and public administration.

Government Publications   These materials are cataloged according to a different system. Although there are indexes to these publications, such as the *Monthly Catalog of United States Publications* and *American Statistics Index,* the help of a librarian may be necessary.

Your library will not carry every periodical listed in every index. If you can't locate a periodical you need, ask if it can be borrowed from another library. Or you can go online and access various government agencies. The United States Census Bureau, in particular, has a wealth of statistical information <www.census.gov>. The Centers for Disease Control and Prevention <www.cdc.gov> provides reliable health information. For other reliable Web sites, see the Internet directory on page 445.

Bibliographies

These publications are similar to catalogs and indexes, but they may be more comprehensive. *Books in Print* lists every book in print in the United States, giving authors, titles, and subject area. *Paperbound Books in Print* is valuable in locating sources on recent topics. *The Bibliographic Index* is helpful for locating subjects you cannot find in other indexes.

Other sources may also use the *Library of Congress Subject Headings* as a guide, but often they have their own subject headings. Sometimes a thesaurus is handy for finding synonyms under which a subject may be listed.

Finding Print Sources

To use materials that are stored on site, print out your selections from the electronic central catalog or take your source cards to the stacks. The *stacks* are the rows of shelves where less recent periodicals and books are stored. To find the correct row, look up at the outside ends of the stacks. There the subject listing or the range of call letters for each row is found.

Books are shelved in numerical order by call numbers as well as alphabetical order by the author's last name. If books or other materials cannot be found on a shelf or in a file, consult the electronic central catalog for availability. If materials have been loaned, you can reserve them or perhaps borrow another copy through an interlibrary loan network (ask a librarian). For new books on recent topics, check with a bookstore.

The most recent periodicals are usually displayed on shelves in a reading area. They are arranged alphabetically according to title, left to right. The shelves, on which the latest copies rest, generally lift up. Underneath are recent copies. Older periodicals in the stacks are shelved by title and date or by subject, title, and date (alphabetically by title and numerically by year). They may be stored in open containers or in binders. Still older issues may be stored on microfilm or microfiche in drawers. Some libraries have you place an order, and the librarian gets them.

Scanning Sources and Evaluating Content

A brief preview in the library will avoid lugging home irrelevant materials. Check the copyright date, and skim introductory pages to discover the author's credentials and what the periodical or book covers. Then read a page here and there to sample the depth and tone. To obtain a variety of viewpoints, look for materials by several authors. Although they may all cite classic research, their interpretations may differ somewhat.

SELECTING SUITABLE SOURCES

Not all sources are equally suitable for academic research. While most of us are inclined to smile or shrug at supermarket headlines that proclaim "Man frozen in block of ice for 500 years recovers," we are less skeptical of most other print and Internet sources.

www.mhhe.com/dietsch
For a source evaluation
tutor, check out:
Research>Source
Evaluation Tutor CARS

Previewing Sources: Criteria

To research effectively, we need to preview all sources carefully. That is not so simple. Three preliminary questions will help you weed out unsuitable sources:

- **Is the source reliable?** Beware of any materials that do not include documentation. The date of the research, size of study, and names of researchers should be stated. If, however, authoritative groups such as the American Cancer Society, Mayo Clinic, or United States Census Bureau publish documents without an author, then you can depend on finding accurate information.

- **Does the source seem to provide comprehensive and fair coverage?** Some sources may give a brief overview of a topic. Coverage may be superficial with few details or significant points. Even though an article may purport to give both sides of an issue, the treatment may slant toward one view. Look for sources that give balanced coverage.

- **Is the source written on an appropriate level?** Reject material that is overly simplified; directed toward adolescents; or too technical, intended for specialists in the field. For a research paper, you need solid, reliable evidence—statistics, findings, examples, and expert opinion that you can summarize and paraphrase.

CHECKLIST   PREVIEWING SOURCES

1. **Is the material current or outdated?** Some fields need frequent updating. Material should be current and appropriate for the field.

2. **Is the material relevant?** Scan the table of contents, preface, and index. Read the chapter titles, a few paragraphs here and there, as well as subheadings. Consider your purpose and audience.

3. **Is the treatment of the topic evenhanded?** Differing viewpoints should be recognized and treated with respect. Consider the tone of each source.

See chapter 19.

4. **Is there solid support for the conclusions reached?** Watch for inconsistencies. Are any fallacies apparent?

See chapter 26.

5. **Is the source primary or secondary?** Try to obtain information from primary sources whenever possible.

Once you begin gathering potential sources for your research paper, whether from a library or a Web site, you will need a working bibliography to organize them.

Making a Working Bibliography

A *working bibliography* is a list of possible sources to consult. When you go to the library, take a pack of 3- by 5-inch index cards, rather than sheets of paper, so that you can start a bibliography. Cards work well because you can easily sort and alphabetize them. These source cards or your electronic file will help you find materials and develop an outline.

At this point, you may want to turn to chapter 28, which shows how to document sources required for research. You may follow the MLA or APA guidelines, depending on the course and the instructor. You might mark this chapter with a paper clip so that you can quickly refer to it while making your working bibliography.

How to Begin   To keep track of your sources, copy all information for each source onto one card, using only one side. Copy the call numbers from the catalog card or index entry onto the upper right corner of the source card. Underneath that, copy other pertinent data such as author, title, editor (if one), year of publication, publisher, city, and state. Making a working bibliography will give you a head start on your works-cited or reference list.

When you find a promising article, document, or book, make a source card or note and check the publication out right away before someone else borrows it. If the material is on the Internet, print it out immediately. If you delay, the materials may be gone. What you find on the Internet today may not be there tomorrow. *Be sure to obtain all essential documentation and keep it until your graded paper is returned.*

NEVER POSTPONE NOTING A SOURCE

After you select your reference materials, check your source cards to be sure all items are accurate and complete. For computerized listings, printouts will suffice temporarily, but make sure you get all needed information. *Write down not only the usual items but also the site address (URL) and access date.* Take pains to copy the URL exactly if it is not included on your printout.

MAKING SOURCE NOTES

1. For *books*, you need:
   a. Full name(s) of author(s)
   b. Full title (including subtitle, if any)
   c. Editor(s) or translator(s)
   d. Total volumes and specific volume number(s) you will use
   e. City of publication (if unfamiliar, also include state), name of publisher, date of publication
2. For *periodicals*, you need:
   a. Full name(s) of author(s)
   b. Full title of article (including subtitle, if any)
   c. Name of periodical
   d. Full date of periodical (for academic journals also include the volume and issue number, if listed)
   e. Inclusive page numbers (including section letters for newspapers)

3. For *special sources, such as nonprint material and online sources,* you need to jot down various items as explained in chapter 28. Note that most nonprint sources have *no page numbers.*

Accessing Networks to Borrow Materials

To locate materials at other campuses and libraries, you can use a computer connected to a regional network. Before searching, however, narrow your topic by writing a controlling question. For a search to be fruitful, the keywords should be fairly specific. You may be able to access a statewide hookup of colleges and universities. You may find that you can access more than one network from the same computer terminal. These networks allow patrons to borrow materials through an interlibrary loan system.

If you plan to order items from another site and face a deadline soon, be sure to ask about delivery dates and availability. You also need to inquire about notification. Does the library notify you of arrivals, or must you check a posted list? If you are to check a list, where will it be? You may also be able to order materials via OCLC, an international online network, which makes difficult-to-obtain materials available. You can request that a librarian access the OCLC network, or you can go to the Web site OCLC FirstSearch <www.oclc.org/support/documentation/firstsearch/using/refcard/default.htm>.

GUIDELINES FOR EVALUATING SOURCES

- When was the data collected? Is it relevant? Scientific and technological data tend to change rapidly. Not all early sources are outdated; some are classics.

- What is the author's professional status? Look for a brief biography in the introduction of a book or article. What else has the author written? What are his or her professional credentials?

- How credible is the publication? To assess the credibility of a nontechnical book, consult *Book Review Digest.* For reviews of technical works, see *Technical Book Review Digest.* Match the copyright date of the book with the volume of the digest. You can also check the next volume after that date.

- How much information is given about the research? What were the characteristics of the sample or study group? Size? Was the sample representative of the general population? Have other researchers obtained similar results? If an experiment was controlled in a laboratory, have other qualified personnel been able to replicate the experiment?

- If a topic is controversial, do sources examine various points of view? A balance of viewpoints is necessary to give comprehensive coverage. Does the tone seem impartial or biased?

- Are enough sources available to give comprehensive coverage? A few articles, even well-detailed ones, are inadequate for a research paper. To understand the thinking in a field and find adequate coverage, you need numerous sources with a variety of viewpoints.

FINDING AND EVALUATING INTERNET SOURCES

Since almost anything can be found on the Internet, reliability and quality are the primary concerns for researchers. This chapter discusses Internet services that are directly related to research. You'll find tips for searching, evaluating Web sites, and judging reliability. An Internet directory at the end of this chapter lists reliable Web sites for research. This is no guarantee you won't become sidetracked to an unreliable site. Just stay alert and apply the guidelines for evaluation that are provided on pages 443–444.

> **www.mhhe.com/dietsch**
>
> For advice on researching via the Internet, go to:
> Research>Using the Internet

Internet Directories

To find authoritative sources on the Internet, you can consult an online directory, which is a type of bibliography created to assist users. Usually organized by topic, online directories can be general or specialized. One example published annually by Omnigraphics is the *Web Site Source Book: A Guide to Major United States Businesses, Organizations, Agencies, Institutions and Other Information Resources on the World Wide Web*. A second title is *World War II on the Web: A Guide to the Very Best Sites* by J. Douglas Smith and Richard Jensen, published by Scholarly Resources, 2002. Both of those are examples of specialized sources.

Evaluating Web Sites

Although the need for controls on the Internet has been in the national spotlight, to date there are relatively few. Any individual who can construct a Web page can stake out a site and post almost anything—accurate or inaccurate, legitimate or fraudulent. Thus visitors must maintain vigilance, keeping an eye out for disclaimers, errors, doubtful information, and scams.

Clues to Sponsors of Web Sites   When visiting a Web site, look for the sponsor first. Sponsorship can give clues to the reliability of the posted information. Usually, the sponsor is listed on the home page. If you arrive on some other page, look for a link to go back. The suffix at the end of the URL is a clue to the type of site. You can recognize private sites by scanning the URL. If you see a tilde (~), this indicates a personal page. If a tilde is part of an *.edu* URL, it usually indicates the page of a faculty member or a graduate student.

PEANUTS reprinted by permission of United Feature Syndicate, Inc.

Domain Names   As you search, look for traditional sources. The last segment of the domain name of the URL can give you a clue. For example, in <http://www.mhhe.com>, the domain name <www.mhhe> tells you it is the address of a World Wide Web page, originated by a private company, McGraw-Hill. In the United States *.com* is used by companies; *.edu* is used by colleges and universities; *.gov* by government agencies; *.mil* by the military; *.net* by some Internet service providers; and *.org* by nonprofit groups.

Seven new domain name suffixes (TLDs), selected by the Internet Corporation for Assigned Names and Numbers (ICANN), recently went into effect: *.aero* (air-transport industry), *.biz* (businesses), *.coop* (cooperatives), *.info* (unrestricted use), *.museum* (museums), *.name* (individuals), and *.pro* (accountants, lawyers, physicians, and other professionals). For more information, see <http://www.icann.org/tlds>.

Additional hints for determining the source of a Web site include looking for a link that says "About This Page," "About Us," or "Home." Such links should take you to information about the sponsor. If there is no such link, try cutting the URL down to the domain name (using just the information before the first single slash).

TEN TIPS FOR SEARCHING THE INTERNET

1. **Before you start, check the spelling of your topic.** Typing errors and misspellings interfere with a search.

2. **Omit typing of *http://*.** Most browsers will usually take you to a Web address when you omit http://. *Note:* Not all sites have www and may require http://.

3. **Use long, specific phrases enclosed in quotation marks.** Use up to eight words to limit your search.

4. **Try several search engines.** Different ones will yield different topics. Google, Teoma, AltaVista, and Dogpile are among the most useful. To locate a search engine, just preface the name and add *.com, as* "teoma.com."

5. **Examine Web site listings carefully to avoid hazardous sites.** Beware of oddities, especially in domain names. Ignore any free offers that seem too good to be true. Spyware may be lurking there, ready to leap onto your hard drive.

6. **If you cannot reach a URL, try at a different time or even days later.** Heavy traffic flow and other factors can interfere with loading.

7. **When you find a relevant Web site, check for links to similar sites.** These leads may be significant.

8. **Keep searching until you find quality material from reliable sources.** If you cannot, then you will need to find another topic.

9. **Windows Tips.** Just type those two words into a search engine for help. Or you might start with <www.Annoyances.org>, which provides clear advice for beginners.

10. **Macintosh Tips.** Just type those two words into a search engine for a list of tips. Or start with the Apple site <www.Desktoppublishing.com/mactips.html>.

Evaluating the Reliability of Internet Sources

Unlike library books, periodicals, and other materials that have gone through a screening process to ensure reliability and accuracy, the Internet has no screen or controls. On the Net anyone with a computer and a modem can publish anything. Researchers need to scrutinize Web sites to see if they are accurate, expert, objective, timely, comprehensive, and responsible.

Check for a Monitor   Traditional sites of reputable companies, institutions, organizations, and government agencies are generally monitored for accuracy. For example, the Encyclopedia Britannica site has been vetted (verified) by editors. Some medical Web sites are screened by physicians. Some sites are maintained by librarians. Some news articles such as those in the *New England Journal of Medicine,* the *New York Times,* and the *Wall Street Journal* cite sources. But these sites are in a minority. Thus the researcher must be alert to discrepancies and wary of unreliable sites.

Watch for Credentials   Look for the name and qualifications of the author of the information. Reputable medical advice is available from physicians who publish the full text of articles related to their specialty. Notice that these professionals provide their names, cities, states, and credentials at the top of the articles they publish. You can check out the credentials of physicians by consulting the American Medical Association <www.ama-assn.org>. This site lists the education, residencies, and specialties of physicians.

Examine the Source Data   Are footnotes provided for quotations? Is the copyright listed for reprinted information? Examine claims and evidence closely. Have medicines been approved by the FDA? What side effects have occurred? If a study was done, who conducted it? Who paid for it? Companies that hire researchers may slant results to confirm their products.

Notice the Tone   Listen to the writer's voice. Are various theories, policies, methods, or other ideas discussed in an objective way? Or does the author seem bent on pushing an ideological or political agenda? Be suspicious if the document is filled with negativity or sensationalism. Watch out for special interests, such as info-ads and testimonials advocating a product.

Notice Dates   Look for dates on Web pages. Most reliable Web pages specify a date at the start or end. Lack of dates on a Web site and in the text of an article casts doubt on reliability and timeliness.

Evaluate the Coverage   To check comprehensiveness, look for a statement of purpose. What is the intent of the Web site? How specific is the material, and is it up to date? Does the material seem factual? If a treatment or topic is controversial, is the article well balanced, citing risks as well as advantages? Has the purpose been fulfilled? Finally, you can evaluate Internet information by comparing it to that gained from scholarly sources in a library.

GUIDELINES FOR EVALUATING THE RELIABILITY OF WEB SITES

ACCURACY

- Are sources of information properly cited?
- Are there bibliographic links to check against library holdings?
- Are spelling and grammar standard usage?

EXPERTISE

- Has the author been trained in this field?
- Is the author a member of an academic or professional organization?
- Has the document or site been reviewed by a peer or noted by a respected publication in print?
- Has the author published in print or electronic format?
- If the material is from a secondary source, are citations included for the original source?

OBJECTIVITY

- Does the language sound professional and fair?
- Does the site contain informational advertisements, testimonials, or other commercial interests?
- If research was conducted, who paid for it? (Be wary of studies paid for by the author or sponsor.)

TIMELINESS

- When was the site established?
- When was the material posted? Updated?
- Are there dead links on the page?

COVERAGE

- Is the material comprehensive, covering the main aspects of the topic?
- Does it give enough specific details to serve your purpose?
- Are references, bibliographies, or links included to access other current information on the topic? (Before deciding, check out the links to other pages.)

RESPONSIBILITY

- Is there a way to contact the author?
- Does the Web site list a Webmaster or a way to supply feedback?

Preserving Online Source Information

When you find a relevant and reliable article on the Internet, print it out immediately to ensure that you have all the information you need. If you wait, it may be gone when you return. Keep in mind these two points:

- **Obtain as much data about each source as possible.** You will need it later to construct a works-cited entry for each source.

- **Save Internet source documents until your paper is returned.** Your instructor may ask to see your sources before a grade is placed on a paper. If you cannot provide evidence, this lack may lead to embarrassing questions.

General Reference Web Sites

- **AcademicInfo.** Educational subject directory. <www.AcademicInfo.net/>
- **Advanced Search.** <www.search.msm.com>
- **Argus Clearinghouse.** Run by librarians. Links to academic and general-interest sites. <www.clearinghouse.net>
- **Encyclopedias.** <www.libraryspot.com/encyclopedias.htm>
- **Librarian's Index to the Internet.** This directory lists 7,000 sites relating to the arts, education, geography, literature, law, medicine, sports, and other subjects. <www.lii.org/>
- **Merlot: Multimedia Educational Resource for Learning and Online Teaching.** <www.merlot.org/home/SubjectCatIndex.po>
- **National Archives.** <www.archives.gov/index.html>
- **The World Wide Web Virtual Library.** <www.vlib.org/Overview.html>
- **US government agencies.** Access these agencies by either going directly to their individual sites or by going through <www.gpoaccess.gov>.

Literature and Media Web Sites

- **Bibliomania.** Browse the complete texts of literary classics, reference books, novels, short stories, drama, poetry, biographies, science texts, and other works. Keyword search available <www.bibliomania.com/>
- **Famous quotations.** Three excellent sites are <www.quotationspage.com>, <www.quoteland.com>, and <www.bartleby.com/100/>.
- **GreatBooks Online.** Verse, fiction, nonfiction, reference, and modern usage. <www.bartleby.com>
- **A Literary Index: Internet Resources in Literature.** <www.vanderbilt.edu/AnS/english/flackcj/Litmain.html>
- **MagPortal.com.** A categorized index of links to the latest magazine articles available on the Web <www.magportal.com>
- **Online Media Directory.** The Media Links database allows access to newspapers from various continents. <www.top100media.com/>
- **Your Dictionary.com.** Thesaurus, grammars, multilingual dictionaries, research, and more. <www.your dictionary.com>

continued

DIRECTORY OF SAFE, RELIABLE WEB SITES

**DIRECTORY OF
SAFE, RELIABLE
WEB SITES
(continued)**

Medical Web Sites

- **CancerNet.** Run by the National Cancer Institute. Sections for patients, health professionals, and basic researchers. <http://cancernet.nci.nih.gov>

- **Mayo Clinic.** Doctors respond to short queries through "Ask Mayo." <www.mayohealth.org>

- *New England Journal of Medicine.* Offers a partial text or an entire text of some articles. <www.nejm.org>

- **US National Library of Medicine.** World's largest medical library.

Career Web Sites: See pages 382 and 400.

PRACTICE

PRELIMINARY LIBRARY SEARCH

Directions: To become familiar with your campus library and start a working bibliography for your research paper, search the following sources.

1. *Determine which system of cataloging the library uses.* Write it here.

2. *Find your subject in the Library of Congress Subject Headings.* What headings could you use in your search?

3. *Electronic Periodical Index.* Type in a subject. Select sources that might be useful. Print out a list.

4. *Electronic Central Catalog or Network.* Select three books that might be useful. Print out (or copy) the bibliographic data.

5. *Encyclopedia.* Check an encyclopedia to find basic information. In three sentences, summarize the most important points. If a topic is not listed, try an almanac, atlas, or yearbook.

6. Consult a current government source or another in archives. Find and copy an entry that might be relevant to your research.

7–10. List four sources not listed on this quiz that you might consult. Specify the general area of the library where the material is located.

TWENTY IDEAS FOR RESEARCH

1 What career opportunities will you be qualified for after graduation? Discuss the advantages and disadvantages of two or three.

2 Investigate potential employers you might apply to after graduation. Discuss three or fewer. Cite advantages and disadvantages of each one. Or compare two.

3 How well do hybrid autos perform?

4 Investigate home security systems. Cite advantages and disadvantages.

5 How can obesity in children be prevented?

6 What side effects do artificial sweeteners have?

7 How risky is cosmetic surgery?

8   How does diet during pregnancy affect children later?

9   Does in-vitro fertilization lead to birth defects?

10   What can you do to prevent identity theft?

11   What are the chief factors that influence children's academic success?

12   Guidelines for selecting a quality nursing home for an aged parent

13   What are the benefits and risks of common herbal supplements?

14   How practical is solar energy in home construction?

15   What has happened in countries that have legalized drugs?

16   What possibilities exist for gene therapy? What risks does it pose?

17   Causes and prevention of burnout in nurses (or anyone else)

18   Pollution of the oceans (or another element of our environment)

19   Effects of sleep deprivation

20   What risks do maternal alcohol and drug use pose to unborn children?

Identifying Sources
Supplying Documentation

Careful documentation is a hallmark of professionalism. In the workplace, you need accurate and complete information not only to write checks and invoices but also to record daily business and legal transactions. Problems in safety, personnel, and other areas must be investigated and noted. Medical treatments, lab tests, and drug dosages must be logged. All these records constitute proof in case of complaints, disputes, or audits.

> Every [person] has a right to [an] opinion, but no [one] has a right to be wrong in . . . facts.
>
> —Bernard Baruch

In college classes you are required to supply documentation for all citations in speeches, reports, and papers, including those from dictionaries and encyclopedias.

WHAT PRECISELY IS DOCUMENTATION?

When a speaker or writer uses someone else's work and provides source information, this process is known as *documentation*. You give credit to the author and provide other data that allows listeners or readers to check facts and search further. For reports and papers, always state the author, title, place and date of publication. Volume numbers and other information may be needed for certain source entries. Entries for the Internet also vary. To scan the different MLA entries, turn to the directory on page 452. For APA entries, see the directory on page 473.

Most instructors prefer that you limit the number of quotations and use them only for a valid purpose. Legally, you may use small parts of copyrighted works (less than 10 percent of the entire work) for research if the author does not prohibit such use and if you document clearly what you summarize, paraphrase, or quote. *Enclose all copied material with quotation marks.* If you omit credit to an author or quotation marks around copied material, the offense is *plagiarism*. Why take unnecessary risks? Penalties for plagiarism in colleges and universities range from a failing grade to suspension.

THREE STEPS TO AVOID PLAGIARISM

Start early to collect source information. When making source cards or notes and when drafting your paper, include three forms of documentation:

1. **Cite sources within your paper.** Identify the author's name and other source information either in the text or in parentheses. (See pages 452–56 for MLA style or pages 473–75 for APA style.)

2. **Use quotation marks.** Enclose copied material with quotation marks.

3. **Make a list of sources (entries).** Place a works-cited list or a reference list (bibliographic data) at the end of your research report or paper. Identify all sources mentioned, summarized, paraphrased, or quoted. For an example, see pages 516–17.

WHICH DOCUMENTATION STYLE IS APPROPRIATE?

Documentation styles vary according to disciplines. For courses in the humanities, including freshman composition, the Modern Language Association (MLA) style is widely recommended. For the social and behavioral sciences, the American Psychological Association (APA) style is generally used. Models for citations and entries for both styles appear in this chapter. For more detailed information, see the *MLA Handbook for Writers of Research Papers*, sixth edition, 2003, by Joseph Gibaldi or the *Publication Manual of the American Psychological Association*, fifth edition, 2001. For online APA examples, visit <www.apastyle.org>. Some colleges and universities post MLA and APA documentation models online.

FREQUENTLY ASKED QUESTIONS: SOURCE INFORMATION

1. Where are the date and place of publication found?

   Answer: Near the beginning of the book, usually on the back of the title page.

2. What if there is more than one publication date?

   Answer: Take the latest one.

3. What if more than one city of publication is given?

   Answer: Cite the first one.

4. What if the book has been published by two companies?

   Answer: List both publishers in the order given.

5. What if no date, place, page, or publisher is given?

   Answer: Use *n.d.* to mean "no date," *n.pag.* for "no page." Use *n.p.* for "no publisher" or "no place."

6. What if a model for an entry is not shown?

   Answer: Construct a model similar to the one most like it.

7. What title is used for the source page?

   Answer: If MLA style is used, the page is called "Works Cited." The APA style has a page called "References."

8. Are Internet entries the same as those for printed sources?

   Answer: No. Construct an example according to the Internet models.

9. What extra information do Internet entries require?

   Answer: Web publication date (if available), date of access, URL (Web address), and other data may be required.

10. Which style of documentation should be used on the job?

    Answer: Follow the firm's guidelines. If none, use either the MLA or APA style.

For classes in other disciplines, your instructor may ask you to use some other citation style, such as that of the *Chicago Manual of Style* (CMS), often used in business, history, and other sciences. The Council of Biology Editors (CBE) style is used in the life sciences and explained in *Scientific Style and Format: The CBE Manual for Authors, Editors, and Publishers*. The Institute of Electrical and Electronic Engineers (IEEE) style is used in computer science and other fields.

MLA STYLE OF DOCUMENTATION

www.mhhe.com/dietsch
To read a student essay
written in MLA style, visit:
Research>Sample
Research Papers>Sample
Paper in MLA Style

The MLA has endorsed a style of documentation that has been widely adopted for research in the humanities. The MLA style requires brief source references within the text of a research paper. The paper concludes with a list of sources, entitled "Works Cited."

CHAPTER 28 MLA STYLE DIRECTORY

Parenthetical Citations: MLA Style

Source information placed within parentheses is called *parenthetical citation*. You will be using these citations throughout your research paper. For easy reading, keep citations brief. When feasible, insert the author's name into the text of your paper so that you can limit citations to just a page number (in parentheses). Key or match each of your citations to a source entry at the end of your paper. Several citations may refer to the same entry.

You may have used an earlier method of documentation that varied somewhat from the updated MLA style. As you construct MLA parenthetical citations to use in the text of your paper, keep these three guidelines in mind:

- If the source is from more than one page, cite the full range of pages (19–23).
- Use a parenthetical citation *each time* a source is cited. Some paragraphs may need several citations. Rarely will you have a paragraph without a citation.
- Optional: Cite one or more works within a paragraph in one parenthetical reference, using semicolons between citations: (Bernstein 17; Zinsser 59). If the citations are long and distracting, use a content note (see page 457).

One Author   When you identify the author in your text, put only the page number in parentheses. When you do not mention the author's name, include the author's last name inside the parentheses, before the page number. Do *not* separate the two with a comma (see example 2).

- Theodore Bernstein, assistant managing editor of the New York Times

  for seven years, points out that the word bandit "has a flavor of heroism."

  Bernstein advises: "Avoid any suggestion of glorifying outlaws" (17).

- One editor has advised against the use of the word bandit because its

  "flavor of heroism" has the effect "of glorifying outlaws" (Bernstein 17).

Work Cited

Bernstein, Theodore M. Watch Your Language. Great Neck, NY: Channel

   Press, 1958.

Two or More Works by the Same Author
To make citations for two or more works by the same author, place a comma after the author's name, followed by a condensed title and the page reference: (Barrett, "Claw" 123) (Barrett, "Sickness" 103).

Works Cited

Barrett, Deirdre. "The Claw of the Panther: Dreams and the Body." The

   Committee of Sleep. New York: Crown, 2001.

---. "Mourning Sickness." The Pregnant Man. New York: Random House,

   1998.

Two or More Authors
For works with two or more authors, include all last names; spell out *and:*

Four "aims of argument" are identified: "inquiry, convincing, persuasion, and

negotiation" (Crusius and Channell 8).

Some researchers recommend "rapid-fire questioning" during survey inter-

views (Kinsey, Pomeroy, and Martin 54).

For four or more authors, include only the first author's last name and the Latin abbreviation *et al.* ("and others"): (Klein et al. 53).

Works by Two Authors with the Same Last Name
When two authors have the same last name, give their full names in the text (preferred usage) with just

the page number in each citation. If names are not given in the text, then include the first initial in the parenthetical citation: (G. Mueller 24), (A. Mueller 36).

Entire Work   When citing an *entire* work, not a specific page, state only the author's name in the text and, if helpful, the title. Be sure the source is on your works-cited list.

> H. W. Fowler's Modern English Usage reflects his spartan life. Fowler believed
>
> in simplicity not only in living but also in writing a sentence. Clarity had top
>
> priority.

One-Page Articles   It is not necessary to include the page number when referring to an article that is a page or less long:

> According to its secretary, Michael Heyman, "the story of the Smithsonian
>
> is also the story of its volunteers."

Note that in the example below, only the volume number is cited:

> Work Cited
>
> Heyman, Michael. "Smithsonian Perspectives." Smithsonian Apr. 1996: 16.

Source with No Author Given   For unsigned works, shorten long titles. Begin with the word by which the work is alphabetized in works cited: ("China").

> Work Cited
>
> "China Banks Look to Diversify Ahead of Listing." Wall Street Journal 20 Jan.
>
> 2004, Midwest ed.: A13.

Corporate Author   Although a work by a group or an agency can be cited in parentheses, the preferred usage is to include the name in the text:

> Nuveen Investments' 2003 fall semiannual report stated: "The gross domestic
>
> product (GDP) expanded by 8.2% during the third quarter of 2003, the fastest
>
> quarterly advance in almost 20 years."

> Work Cited
>
> Nuveen Investments Municipal Bond Funds. Semiannual report dated October
>
> 31, 2003. Chicago: Nuveen Investments, 2003.

Indirect Source   When possible, use an original source rather than a secondhand one that quotes the original. If you are unable to obtain the original source and must use a secondary source, place *qtd. in* ("quoted in") before the citation for the secondary source.

> Ralph Waldo Emerson said: "Our best thoughts come from others" (qtd. in
>
> Cohen 9).

Work Cited

Cohen, Herb. You Can Negotiate Anything. New York: Bantam, 1980.

Quotations by Two or More Authors in One Sentence   Follow each quotation with a separate parenthetical citation:

> Zinsser says, "The most important sentence in any article is the first one" (59),
>
> and Bernstein suggests the writer "ask . . . what it is he is writing about" to
>
> find the focus for that sentence (75).

Two or More Sources in One Citation   If you cite information from two or more sources, include identifying information for each source in your parenthetical citation, separated by semicolons.

> All seem to agree that good writing is hard work (Bernstein 44; Trimble 54;
>
> Zinsser 33).

Work of More than One Volume   If your works-cited list includes more than one volume of a multivolume work, include the volume number, separated from the page number by a colon and a space: (Nicolson and Trautman 3: 25).

Literary Works   Because classic prose works may appear in different editions, include chapter (ch.), book (bk.), and part (pt.) in addition to page numbers. Place extra information after the page with a semicolon and a space between:

> In The Republic, Plato has Socrates ask: "What do you consider to be the
>
> greatest blessing which you have reaped from your wealth?" (221; bk. 1)

Work Cited

Plato. "The Republic." Five Great Dialogues. Trans. B. Jowett. Ed. Louise

> Ropes Loomis. Roslyn, NY: Classics Club-Black, 1942.

To cite classic verse plays, poems, and other works, leave out page numbers. Instead, give the division—canto, act, scene, book, part—and the line(s). Separate numbers by periods. For example, (*Waste Land* 1.35) refers to canto 1, line 35;

(*Electra* 1.60) refers to scene 1, line 60. Note that the word *line* is spelled out in citations:

> Dickinson ends her poem "Success Is Counted Sweetest" with a paradox: "The
>
> distant strains of triumph / Break, agonized and clear." (lines 11-12).

> Romeo and Juliet provides one of Shakespeare's most quoted lines: "But soft!
>
> What light through yonder window breaks?" (2.2.2).

Nonprint Sources   Works taken from a Web site are cited just like printed works. If Internet sources are not marked with page numbers, paragraph or section numbers may be included. If so, include those numbers, preceded by the proper abbreviation (*par.* or *sec.*).

If a nonprint source (interview, television program, compact disc, CD-ROM, or other) lacks page numbers, you can omit a parenthetical citation if you state the author's name in the text. A works-cited entry is still needed. If the author's or performer's name is not stated in the text, place it in a parenthetical citation: (Enya). For sound recordings, italicize the medium before the manufacturer's name: *Audiocassette*. If the medium is a compact disc, omit it in the works-cited entry:

> Work Cited
>
> Enya. Paint the Sky with Stars. Warner, 1996.

Long Quotations   Quotations of five lines or more are set off, indented ten spaces. After the final punctuation, type one space, then the parenthetical citation.

> Charles C. Moskos summarizes the argument well:
>
>> The principal argument raised against linking national service and
>>
>> federal educational aid is that it would have a regressive effect. . . .
>>
>> Students from wealthy families who do not need aid would be un-
>>
>> affected, while poor students would have to enter national service
>>
>> in order to get aid. (380)

Punctuation   For short quotations within the text, place a period or other punctuation *after* the parenthetical citation. For long block quotations, set off from the text, place the period and a space *before* the parenthetical citation.

Using Notes with MLA Parenthetical Citations

Content notes and bibliographic notes can be used along with parenthetical citations to provide more information. To insert a note, place a superscript arabic number at a suitable place in the text. Then at the bottom of the same page, place a matching number before the note. Keep the notes short and informative. Content notes and bibliographic notes can be mingled and numbered in sequence.

Content Notes   When a secondary source is cited, a content note can provide complete publication data on the original source. Or a necessary explanation may be included as in the example below:

> Several months ago when obesity specialist Dr. Frank Greenway from UCLA revealed that a thigh reduction cream really worked, several news accounts incorrectly reported reductions of as much as 1½ inches. The fact was that the most a woman's thighs shrunk was 1½ *centimeters* or approximately ½ inch. Furthermore, the safety of the cream has been questioned.[1]

Note

> [1] Several news sources have pointed out this misstatement.

Bibliographic Notes   To provide evaluative comments on sources or for references having several citations, use notes.

> The Wall Street Journal and many other newspapers carried articles about the resignation of David Howard, head of the District Office of Public Advocate, Washington, DC, over his use of a standard word that sounded like a taboo term.[1]

Note

> [1] For a sample of articles taken from editorial pages, see Dooling and Parker.

Works Cited

Dooling, Richard. "What a Niggling Offense! Oops, We Mean . . ." Wall Street
    Journal 29 Jan. 1999, Midwest ed.: A14.

Parker, Kathleen. "Must We Be So Niggling about Words?" Marion Star
    [Marion, OH] 7 Feb. 1999: A6.

PREPARING A LIST OF WORKS CITED: MLA STYLE

Use these general guidelines for the format of your works-cited page:

1. Type *Works Cited,* centered, at the top of the page.

2. Alphabetize entries according to the last name of the author. When an author's name is not known, alphabetize by the first word in the title except for *a, an,* or *the.*

3. Double-space the entire listing of works cited.

4. Do not indent the first line of an entry. Indent *five* spaces (or one-half inch on a word processor) for succeeding lines of the entry. This style of indention is called a "hanging indention."

5. Place a period after each subdivision of an entry and at the end of each entry.

6. *A, An,* or *The:* Retain as the first word in a book title. Omit in periodical titles (*Washington Post* not *The Washington Post*).

7. Underline the title of works such as books, magazines, newspapers, plays, paintings, and others.

8. Place quotation marks around titles of short works that appear in longer works, such as articles, chapters, stories, poems, and songs.

9. Cite inclusive page numbers (121–28) for specific essays, articles, short stories, and so forth that appear in a book or periodical.

10. Number the works-cited pages using arabic numerals, just as the other pages of the paper.

1. SAMPLE MLA ENTRIES: BOOKS AND OTHER NONPERIODICAL PUBLICATIONS

www.mhhe.com/dietsch

Bibliomaker can create MLA entries. Find it at:
Research>Bibliomaker

Include the author's name as it is printed on the title page. In the works-cited entry, reverse the name and place a comma between the last and first part: Bickford, Scott, Jr. Except for Jr. and roman numerals that are part of a name, leave out titles, affiliations, and degrees.

Underline the titles and subtitles of books. Separate the title and subtitle with a *colon* unless the main title ends with a question mark, an exclamation point, or a dash. An underline can be typed as a solid line under all the words in a title or name even when it contains a colon. Do *not* underline the period at the end of a title.

Specify the city of publication, publisher, and year of publication (or copyright date if publication date isn't listed). If the city is well-known, you can omit the state, country, or province if there is no chance of confusion.

1.1. A Book by One Author

The last name of a single author comes first.

▶ Reppetto, Thomas. American Mafia. New York: Henry Holt, 2004.

1.2. Two or More Books by One Author

List the name once in the first entry (alphabetically by title). For the second entry, type three hyphens and a period instead of the name.

Goldberg, Natalie. Wild Mind: Living the Writer's Life. New York: Bantam,

1990.

---. Writing Down the Bones: Freeing the Writer Within. Boston: Shambhala,

1986.

1.3. A Book by Two or Three Authors

When there are two or three authors, reverse only the first name. Spell out *and.* When citing the title for a research paper, capitalize the first and last words and all significant words. Do not reproduce special capitalization or lowercasing of all letters.

Curtis, Richard, and William Thomas Quick. How to Get Your E-book

Published. Cincinnati, OH: Writer's Digest, 2002.

1.4. A Book by Four or More Authors

For a book with four or more authors, you may include only the first author and add *et al.* ("and others"), or you may state all the authors in the order given on the title page.

Burrows, Thomas D., et al. Video Production: Disciplines and Techniques.

New York: McGraw-Hill, 2000.

1.5. Corporate Author: A Book by a Group

Boston Women's Health Book Collective. Ourselves and Our Children.

New York: Random, 1978.

1.6. Second or Later Edition of a Book

Specify any edition other than the first by number (2nd ed., 3rd ed.), by name (Rev. ed.), or by year (2005 ed.) after the book title. Or if the name of an editor, compiler, or translator follows, place the edition after the name.

Musciano, Chuck, and Bill Kennedy. HTML & XHTML: The Definitive Guide.

5th ed. Sebastopol, CA: O'Reilly, 2002.

1.7. A Work in a Compilation, an Anthology, or a Collection

Enclose in quotation marks the title of an essay, a short story, a poem, or another work collected in a book. The book title and editor(s) follow. State the inclusive page numbers for the specific piece at the end of the entry. If you are citing a previously published scholarly article, insert *Rpt. in* ("Reprinted in"), the title of the collection, and the new publication data.

▶ Glaspell, Susan. "A Jury of Her Peers." The Best Short Stories of the Century.

Eds. John Updike and Katrina Kenison. New York: Houghton Mifflin,

2000. 18-37.

PUBLISHERS' NAMES

Shorten the names of publishers, omitting *Inc., Company,* and so forth, and using only the first name when there is more than one name. *University Press* is shortened to *UP* (or *U of . . . P*). In some cases, initials are used. Some examples follow:

Appleton-Century-Crofts	Appleton
Beacon Press, Inc.	Beacon
Cambridge University Press	Cambridge UP
Henry Holt and Company	Henry Holt
Holt, Rinehart and Winston	Holt
New American Library	NAL
University of Chicago Press	U of Chicago P

STATES

Use state abbreviations without periods: NY, OH, CA.

GOVERNMENT PUBLICATIONS

Use the following abbreviations:

Congressional Record	Cong. Rec.
Government Printing Office	GPO
House of Representatives Report	H. Rept.
House of Representatives Document	H. Doc.
Library of Congress	LC
Senate Resolution	S. Res.
Senate Document	S. Doc.

1.8. A Book by an Anonymous Author

Go Ask Alice. New York: Prentice, 1971.

1.9. A Book with an Editor or Editors, No Author Listed

Parkyn, Neil, ed. The Seventy Wonders of the Modern World. New York:

Thames-Hudson, 2002.

1.10. A Book with an Author and an Editor

Tolkien, J. R. Unfinished Tales. Ed. Christopher Tolkien. Boston: Houghton,

1980.

1.11. A Book in Volumes

When using just one volume of a multivolume work, give that volume number before the place of publication (*Vol.* is capitalized).

Shakespeare, William. "Cymbeline." The Tragedies of Shakespeare.

Ed. Warren Chappell. Vol. 2. New York: Random, 1944.

When using two or more volumes of a work, include the total number of volumes after the title (vol. is not capitalized).

Nicolson, Nigel, and Joanne Trautmann, eds. The Letters of Virginia Woolf.

5 vols. New York: Harcourt, 1977.

1.12. An Article from a Reference Book

The place and publisher can be omitted for encyclopedias, dictionaries, and other well-known reference books. Page numbers can also be omitted if the entries are alphabetical. If the entry is signed, lead with the author's name.

"The Civil War." Encyclopedia Americana. 100th Anniversary Library Edition.

1995.

1.13. An Introduction, Preface, Foreword, or Afterword

Start with the author and title (if any) of the introduction, preface, foreword, or afterword, enclosing the title in quotation marks. Then state the part, using a capital letter but no underlining or quotation marks (Preface). If the book is by a different writer, place *By* before his or her full name. Place inclusive page numbers at the end. In the example here, the preface has no title and only one page.

▷   Hervé, de La Martinière. Preface. <u>Earth from Above</u>. By Yann Arthus-Bertrand.

  Trans. David Baker. New York: Abrams, 2003. i.

1.14. A Translation or Edited Edition

▷   Dostoevsky, Fyodor. <u>The Brothers Karamazov</u>. Trans. Constance Garnett. Ed.

  Manuel Komroff. New York: NAL, 1957.

1.15. A Pamphlet

Treat a pamphlet as a book, even if very short.

▷   Chao, Elaine L. US Dept. of Labor. <u>Employer's Pocket Guide on Youth</u>

   <u>Employment</u>. Washington: GPO, 2002.

1.16. Government Publications

When the writer is known, see 1.15. When the writer is unknown, list the government agency as author. If two or more works are issued by the same agency, place three hyphens in place of the author's name (---). Repeat if the works are by the same agency (---. ---.). Most congressional documents require the number and session of Congress, the house (S or HR), and the kind and number of publication (S. Res. 19, H. Res. 49). The *Congressional Record,* however, requires just the date and page.

▷   United States. Health Care Financing Administration. <u>Medicare & You 2005</u>.

   Washington: GPO, 2005.

   ---. Dept. of Justice. <u>FBI National Academy Directory of Graduates 2004</u>

   <u>Edition</u>. Quantico,VA.: FBI Academy, 2004.

1.17. Sacred Writings

The article, chapter, or "book" (as in books of the Bible) is placed before the verses (if applicable). The title of the entire work follows. (Titles of sacred writing are not underlined or enclosed with quotations marks.) If the work has more than one version, the abbreviation for the version is placed last.

▷   Proverbs 22 : 1. Bible. KJV.

   Genesis 1 : 3. Torah.

2. SAMPLE MLA ENTRIES: ARTICLES

Periodicals comprise journals, magazines, newspapers, newsletters, and similar publications. Scholarly journals, which are often published quarterly, are not aimed at a general audience. Since these articles often describe original research and give professional opinion, they are valuable sources for research papers. As you consult periodicals in your research, collect the following information on your note cards. Then you will be well prepared to construct works cited entries later.

1. Name of author, editor, compiler, or translator (if given)
2. Full title of article (enclose with quotation marks)
3. Name of source (underline or italicize title of periodical)
4. Series (if given)
5. Volume number (journals only)
6. Issue number (Number 2) or month or season before year (Spring 2005)
7. Journals with continuous paging: Omit issue numbers, months, or seasons.
8. Publication date
9. Edition (if given)
10. Inclusive page numbers of the article

As you construct entries for periodicals, the following guidelines will be helpful:

- Omit the introductory word *a, an,* or *the* from names of periodicals: *American Scholar* not *The American Scholar.*
- For a daily periodical, put the day before the month and year with no intervening punctuation (17 June 2005).
- If the article is from a source that is not a periodical, identify the type of article, such as *Letter* or *Editorial.* Reviews have a special format (see 2.7).

2.1. Journal Article with Continuous Paging

Many scholarly journals use continuous paging, starting in January and continuing throughout the year. The volume number and year are sufficient; do not include the issue or month. Give the range of pages.

Vastag, Brian. "Poised to Challenge Need for Sleep, 'Wakefulness Enhancer'

Rouses Concerns." Journal of the American Medical Association 291

(2004): 167-170.

2.2. Journal Article with Each Issue Paged Separately

Include issue numbers for journals that do *not* number pages continuously. After the volume number, place a period and the issue number together with no space: 10.3 (indicating volume 10, issue 3).

▶ Sea, Geoffrey. "A Pigeon in Piketon." American Scholar 73.1 (2004): 57-84.

2.3. Article from a Daily Newspaper

When a newspaper has different editions, specify the edition between the date and the page. If the article runs beyond one page, use a plus sign to indicate that it continues.

▶ Hwang, Suein. "As 'Doulas' Enter Delivery Rooms, Conflicts Arise." Wall

Street Journal 19 Jan. 2004, Midwest ed.: A1+.

2.4. Article from a Monthly Magazine

Include the cover date. Abbreviate all months except May, June, and July. If the paging of an article is interrupted, write only the first page and a plus sign. Otherwise, hyphenate the range of page numbers.

▶ Baker, John F. "Publishers Seek New Voices: Imprints Provide Opportunities

for Black, Hispanic Writers." Writer Feb. 2004: 46-48.

2.5. Article from a Weekly Newspaper or Weekly Magazine

▶ Omestad, Thomas. "Man on a Mission: Colin Powell Sets the Table for the

New Year." U.S. News and World Report 19 Jan. 2004: 31-33.

2.6. An Anonymous Article

When the author of an article is unstated, begin with the title and alphabetize by the first significant word in the title.

▶ "Pancreatic Cancer Update." Saturday Evening Post Apr. 2003: 32.

2.7. Review

▶ Holmes, Martha Stoddard. Rev. of The Fasting Girl: A True Victorian Medical

Mystery, by Michelle Stacy. New England Journal of Medicine 348

(2003): 870-71.

2.8. Abstract and a Review

The citation for the book appears before the citation for the abstract and the review. The periodical carrying the abstract and review is placed last. If the abstract has no review, omit *Rev. by.*

Monti, Daniel, J. The American City: A Social and Cultural History. Oxford,

UK: Blackwell, 1999. Rev. by J. C. Schneider, Journal of American

History 87 (2001): 1537-38. Book Review Digest 97.6 (2001): 157.

2.9. An Editorial

When citing a signed editorial, start with the author's name, then the title. Next, write *Editorial* (not underlined or italicized). When the editorial is unsigned, start with the title.

Bonnie Erbe. "Challenging the Idea of Gender." Editorial. Marion Star

[Marion OH] 19 Feb. 2003: A6.

2.10. A Letter to the Editor

Slott, Irving. "After Confession, What Next?" Letter. Washington Post

17 Jan. 2004: A 24.

2.11. Newsletter Article

Frazier, Ann. "If Walls Could Talk." Ohio Historical Society Newsletter 42

(Feb.-Mar. 2003): 1-2.

3. SAMPLE MLA ENTRIES: MISCELLANEOUS PRINT AND NONPRINT SOURCES

For broadcast, film, and recorded sources involving various personnel, you begin the entry with the name or title that is the primary subject of emphasis in your paper, as shown below:

Stouffer, Marty. "Cutthroat Trout." 2 episodes. Wild America. PBS.

WOSU-TV, Columbus, OH. 11 Sept.-12 Sept. 1995.

"Cutthroat Trout." 2 episodes. Marty Stouffer. Wild America PBS. WOSU-TV,

Columbus, OH. 11 Sept.-12 Sept. 1995.

3.1. Television or Radio Programs

The items in a works-cited entry for a television or radio program generally follow the order below. (Omit any items that are not relevant, but include relevant items such as performers, director, conductor, or number of episodes.)

1. Episode or segment title (Enclose in quotation marks. If there are two or more episodes, state the total.)
2. Author's name (in reverse order if it begins the entry)
3. Program title (underline)
4. Series title
5. Network (for example, CNN)
6. Local call letters and city (for example, WMAQ, Chicago)
7. Date of broadcast

> Kiss Me Kate. By Sam and Bella Spewak. Music and lyrics by Cole Porter. Perf.
>
> Nancy Anderson and Michael Berresse. Broadway performance. Great
>
> Performances. PBS. WOSU-TV, Columbus, OH. 26 Feb. 2003.

> Schama, Simon. "The Body of the Queen." 5 episodes. A History of Britain.
>
> Narr. Simon Schama. The History Channel. CNBC, Columbus, OH.
>
> 29 Oct. 2001.

> "Art of the Groove." Saturday at the Pops. Host and prod. Boyce Lancaster.
>
> WOSU-FM, Columbus, OH. 1 Mar. 2003.

If a transcript is available online, provide the information:

> Shaw, Bernard. "Clinton's Boom Era Not as Turbulent as LBJ's." Program
>
> segment. Inside Politics. CNN. 29 June 1999. Transcript. 1 July 1999
>
> <http://www.cnn.com/TRANSCRIPTS/9906/29/ip.06.html>.

For sound recordings of television or radio programs, see 3.2. For a videotape of a performance, see 3.3. For interviews conducted on television or radio, see 3.4.

3.2. Sound Recordings

If the recording is on compact disc, omit the medium. Specify audiocassette tape or LP. Include manufacturer and date. The name you place first depends on whom you want to emphasize—composer, conductor, or performer. Insert a comma between the manufacturer and the date.

> Beach Boys. The Greatest Hits: The Beach Boys. Capitol, 1999.

Strauss, Edvard. "The Merry Widow Waltz." <u>Viennese Favorites</u>. L.P. Cond.

Arthur Fiedler. Boston Pops Orchestra. Audiocassette. RCA Victrola,

1983.

3.3. Film or Video Recording

Include all pertinent information in an order that reflects your emphasis. For video recordings, include the original date of release as well as the date the recording was released.

a.   A Film, Video Recording, or Performance

<u>Enchanted April</u>. Dir. Mike Newell. Perf. Miranda Richardson, Josie Lawrence,

Polly Walker, and Joan Plowright. Screenwriter Peter Barnes. Warner

Brothers, 1992.

If material is not a film, specify the medium. Some materials may include an original release date, perhaps in another form. For example, some laser discs contain films in IMAX. If material has an original release date, include that date before the medium.

b.   Videocassette, DVD, Laser Disc, Slide Program, or Filmstrip

<u>My Fellow Americans</u>. Dir. Peter Segal. Perf. Jack Lemmon, James Garner, Dan

Aykroyd, John Heard, Wilford Brimley, and Lauren Bacall. 1996. Video-

cassette. Warner Home Video, 2000.

MacArthur Foundation, J. D. and C. T., National Science Foundation, and

Jostens Foundation. <u>Tropical Rainforest</u>. 1992. Laser disc. Denver:

Lumivision, 1994.

3.4. Interviews

Published interviews are treated as excerpts from anthologies and periodicals. Broadcast interviews are treated as television or radio programs. Personal and telephone interviews are listed as such. In all cases list the name of the person interviewed first.

MacLeish, Archibald. "Archibald MacLeish." Interview with Benjamin

De Mott. <u>Writers at Work: The Paris Review Interviews 5</u>. Ed. George

Plimpton. New York: Penguin, 1988. 23-48.

Senitko, Melanie. Personal interview. 1 June 2005.

Witzel, Carol. Telephone interview. 3 Apr. 2005.

3.5. Comic Strip or Cartoon

▶ Schulz, Charles. "Peanuts." Comic strip. <u>Marion Star</u> [Marion OH] 19 Jan.

 2004: B9.

3.6. Legal References

For papers requiring several legal citations, see the most recent edition of *The Blue Book: A Uniform System of Citation* (Cambridge: Harvard Law Rev. Assn.). A usual rule is to neither underline nor enclose in quotation marks any titles of laws, acts, or similar documents in the text or in the list of works cited. Works of this sort are generally cited by sections. The year is included when it is significant.

- 14 US Code. Sec. 77a. 1964
- US Const. Art. 2, sec. 1.

4. SAMPLE MLA ENTRIES: ELECTRONIC SOURCES

Entries for electronic sources begin with the author's name and title of the document, followed by print publication information (if any), electronic publication information, and access information. There is no punctuation between the access date and the URL. Place a period after the URL. For details about the components of an electronic source entry in MLA documentation style, see the guidelines on page 469.

4.1. An Entire Internet Site, Scholarly Project, Professional or Personal Site

a. *Entire Internet Site or Scholarly Project*

Cite what is given of the following information:

- Title of the site or project (underlined)
- Editor's name (preceded by "Ed.")
- Electronic publication information: version number (if not part of the title), publication date or latest update, and sponsor's name
- Date of access and URL

▶ CNN.com. 2005. Cable News Network. 10 Feb. 2005 <http://www.cnn.com/>.

Encyclopaedia Britannica Online. 2002. Encyclopaedia Britannica. 19 Nov.

 2004 <http://www.britannica.com>.

<u>Victorian Women Writers Project</u>. Ed. Perry Willett. 10 Dec. 2002. Indiana U.

 3 Feb. 2004 <http://www.indiana.edu/~letrs/vwwp/>.

When online material carries a printed source and date, cite that first, according to the MLA guidelines for books and periodicals (see 1.1 to 2.11 in the preceding discussion) before electronic information. All the information below may not be available in every situation.

1. **Author(s).** Reverse the name of the first (or only) author so that it can be alphabetized. If an editor is listed instead of an author, place *ed.* after the name (see 1.9).

2. **Title of an article, poem, short story, or similar item in a scholarly project, database, or periodical.** Enclose the title with quotation marks.

3. **Book title.** Underline both main title and subtitle.

4. **Editor, compiler, or translator.** If there is one, place *Ed., Comp., or Trans.* before the name (see 1.10, 1.14, and 4.3).

5. **Edition, version, volume, or issue.** If a version number is included in the title, do not repeat. For a journal include volume, issue, or any other number needed (see 2.1, 2.2, and 4.4).

6. **Title of a scholarly project, database, periodical, or professional or personal Web site.** Underline. If there is no title, write a description such as *Search page* or *Home page* (see 4.1.b).

7. **Other publication information.** Give publisher's name, place of publication, copyright date, and any other identification.

8. **Medium of publication.** If the source is on a CD-ROM, diskette, tape, DVD, or similar source, state the medium (see 4.11–4.13).

9. **Dates of information.** Include the dates of posting, electronic publication, and most recent update, if there is one.

10. **Article or work from a subscription service.** Identify the service, subscriber (often a library), and place of subscriber (see 4.14).

11. **Online posting or forum.** Supply name of list or forum (see 4.9).

12. **Range or number of pages, paragraphs, or sections.** Include if the material is numbered.

13. **Sponsor of the Web site.** Identify the individual, institution, organization, or agency sponsoring or associated with the Web site.

14. **Date of access.** Place the date you obtained the material right before the URL.

15. **URL of the source.** Place in angle brackets (< >), followed by a period. If the URL is long and complex, cite the search page URL. For a subscription service, use the home page URL. Or give the keyword of the service, preceded by *Keyword,* or give the sequence of links after the URL: *Path* and a semicolon (see 4.7).

MLA STYLE: DOCUMENTING ELECTRONIC SOURCES

b. Professional Site or Personal Site

First give the name of the person who created the site (if given) and the title of the site (underline). If there is no title, use a description such as *Home page* (no underlining). Next give the date of the last update, or, in the case of a course home page, give the dates of the course. Follow with the sponsor of the site (if applicable), date of access, and URL.

> Gates, Bill. Home page. 23 Jan. 2004. 26 Jan. 2004 <http://www.microsoft
>
> .com/billgates/default.asp>.
>
> Information Technology. Johns Hopkins Institutions. 3 Feb. 2004. 4 Feb. 2004
>
> <http://webapps.jhu.edu/hitswebsite/>.
>
> Barbour, Dennis. Useful Links. 11 Apr. 2002. 20 Jan. 2004 <http://www.bme
>
> .jhu.edu/~dbarbour/links.html>.

4.2. An Entire Online Book

The book below was originally published in 1878. In 1892 Harper published an edition. This information is placed in parentheses because it was not given on-line. Print information is optional if not provided online.

> James, Henry. Daisy Miller. [1878]. [New York: Harper, 1892]. 20 Jan. 2004
>
> <http://www.PageByPageBooks.com/Henry_James/Daisy_Miller/>.

4.3. A Poem, Short Story, or Other Short Work within a Book

The first example, a poem, lists the publication data of the original print version, which was on the Web site. The second example, a short story, is available online with no information about the author; the first date there is the date of posting.

> Frost, Robert. "Mending Wall." Boston: North, 1915. 20 Jan. 2004 <http://
>
> www.bartleby.com/104/64.html>.
>
> Poe, Edgar Allan. "The Cask of Amontillado." East of the Web. May 1999.
>
> 22 Jan. 2004 <http://www.short-stories.co.uk/>.

4.4. Online Article in a Scholarly Journal

The online article below was printed in *American Psychologist*, volume 58, January 2004. The Web site was accessed January 21, 2004.

> Oakley, Ray. "How the Mind Hurts and Heals the Body." American Psycholo-
>
> gist 58 (Jan. 2004). 21 Jan. 2004 <http://www.apa.org/journals/
>
> amp.html>.

4.5. Online Article in a Newspaper

Associated Press. "Massachusetts Court Clarifies Gay Marriage Ruling." New
York Times on the Web 24 Feb. 2003. 25 Feb. 2003 <http://www
.nytimes.com/>.

4.6. Online Article in a Magazine

Reeves, Jessica. "How to Beat the Gas Pump Blues." Time Online Edition
26 Feb. 2003. 27 Feb. 2003 <http://www.time.com/time/nation/
article/0,8599,426934,00 html>.

4.7. Online Abstract (showing a sequence of links)

The first example below shows a sequence of links after the URL.

Greene, Virginie. "How the Damoiselle d'Escalot Became a Picture."
Arthuriana 12.3 (Fall 2002): 31-48. Abstract. 5 Mar. 2003 <http://
www.smu.edu/arthuriana/>. Path: Abstracts; G-J.

Tavassolli, Nader T. "Spatial Memory for Chinese and English." Journal of
Cross-Cultural Psychology 33.4 (2002): 15-31. Abstract. 4 Mar 2003
<http://web26.epnet.com/citation.asp>.

4.8. Online Article from a Newsletter

Justice, Rod. "Hospital Workers Forget to Wash Hands between Patients."
In Touch Newsletter 3.4 (2000). In Touch. 21 Jan. 2004 <http://
www.intouchnews.com/sample.htm>.

4.9. Posting to a Discussion Group

Osheroff, J. A. "Computers in Medicine." Editorial and invitation to respond
by e-mail. 1996-2004. American College of Physicians–American
Society of Internal Medicine. 21 Jan. 2004. <http://www.acponline.org/
computer/sgim_edit.htm>.

4.10 E-Mail Communication

Dietsch, Betty M. "Reviewers." E-mail to Josh Feldman. 18 Jan. 2005.

4.11. Publication on CD-ROM, Diskette, or Magnetic Tape

Cite the print information first. Then add other available publication data: the medium; edition, release, or version; place of publication; name of publisher or vendor; and date of publication.

a. Periodical Published on CD-ROM

Some newspapers, magazines, journals, and other periodicals can be accessed from databases. Usually source information is provided at the beginning of the file.

▶ Hansen, Robert W. "Stigma, Conflict, and the Approval of AIDS Drugs."

> Journal of Drugs (Winter 1995): 129-39. CD-ROM. UMI-ProQuest,

> 1995.

b. Nonperiodical Publication on CD-ROM or Diskette

Many nonperiodical databases are published only once with no revisions or updates. Cite nonperiodical CD-ROMs the way you would cite a book but include the publication medium as well as the place, publisher, and date of publication.

▶ 1880 United States Census and National Index. CD-ROM. Salt Lake City:

> Intellectual Reserve, 2001.

> "Making a Will." Family Lawyer. CD-ROM. Hiawatha, IA: Parsons Technol-

> ogy, 1995.

> Bird, Alan. "TimeOut." Quickspell. Diskette. San Diego: Beagle Bros., 1987.

c. Updated Nonperiodical Publication on CD-ROM or Diskette

▶ Dr. Solomon's Virex 7 for Macintosh. CD-ROM. Network Associates. Santa

> Clara, CA: McAfee.com Corp, 2003.

4.12. A Work from a Library Subscription Service

To cite material found through an online service such as EBSCO, InfoTrac, and Lexis Nexis, follow the guidelines for citing online works and add the name of the database underlined (if known), the name of the service, the name of the library, and the date of access. Include the URL of the service's home page (if known).

▶ "About the U.S. Congress." 2000. Masterfile Premier. EBSCOhost. Marion

> Public Lib. 6 Mar. 2003 <http:www.web5.epnet.com>.

4.13. A Work in More than One Publication Medium

Some stores offer bundles of software in one package. Follow the directions for a nonperiodical CD-ROM (see 4.11a) and list the media in the package, the place, the publisher, and the copyright date.

> Newman, John J. "Ohio." Uncle, We Are Ready! Registering America's Men
>
> 1917-1918. CD-ROM and book. North Salt Lake, UT: Heritage Quest,
>
> 2001.

4.14 Other Electronic Sources

To document online sources that are not mentioned here, find a similar model and follow the general guidelines for citing print and electronic sources. Construct your entry appropriately, making changes as needed. For example, you may need to add a label such as *map or interview* (no quotation marks or underlining).

APA STYLE OF DOCUMENTATION

For research papers about the social sciences, many instructors prefer the American Psychological Association style of documentation. The explanations and examples shown here follow the guidelines in the *Publication Manual of the American Psychological Association,* fifth edition, 2001. You can also obtain up-to-date information and examples at <http://www.apastyle.org/elecref.html>.

SECTION TITLE	PAGE
• Parenthetical Citations: APA Style	473
• Preparing a Reference List: APA Style	475
A. APA Entries: Periodicals	475
B. APA Entries: Books, Brochures, and	
Government Publications	477
C. APA Entries: Audiovisual Media	480
D. APA Entries: Electronic Media	481

CHAPTER 28 APA STYLE DIRECTORY

Parenthetical Citations: APA Style

The APA style keys reference citations in a text to a list of sources. In parentheses, include the author's last name, the year of publication, the abbreviation for page (*p.* or *pp.* for pages), and the page number. Use ampersands (&) instead of *and.* Abbreviate *chapter* as *chap.* and *section* as *sec.* For quotations, always cite page numbers (Raines, p. 132).

Single Author   The author's name is usually mentioned in the text, followed by parentheses containing the year of publication and page. (Omit suffixes, such as *Jr.*) If the entire work is cited, no page numbers are needed. If the author is not listed in the text, include the author's last name in the parenthetical citation.

> Theodore Bernstein (1958) points out that the word *bandit* "has a flavor of
>
> heroism."

Research shows that experienced writers seem to have much stronger revision

habits than do student writers (Sommers, 2004).

Two or More Works by the Same Author   Distinguish different works by one author by their dates. For multiple references in the same year by one author, add *a, b,* or *c* in lowercase letters: 2004a, 2004b, and so forth.

Works by Two Authors with the Same Last Name   Distinguish by using initials: "C. A. Neff (2004) and J. Neff (2003) also found. . . ."

Source with No Author Name Given   For unsigned sources, use an abbreviated version of the title. Place article titles in quotation marks, and underline or italicize book and pamphlet titles: ("Timber Wolves," 2005), (*Recycling,* 1999).

Groups as Authors   In general, give the name of the group in full each time you cite it. If the name is long, abbreviate it in subsequent citations.

> First reference: (American Association of Retired People [AARP], 2005)
>
> Later references: (AARP, 2005)

Secondary Source   If you are citing an author quoted by another author, precede the secondary source with the phrase *as cited in.* Always give page numbers for quotations.

> Jameson's findings (as cited in Baure & Dinks, 2005, p. 124)

Two or More Sources in One Citation   List alphabetically by authors' last names, separated by semicolons: (Adams, 2000; Coates & Tan, 2001; Martiniu, 2004). If citations include two works by the same author, list the dates chronologically, separated by commas: (Wiggins 2001, 2003).

Personal Communications   E-mail, personal interviews, letters, and the like are cited only in the text, not on the reference list.

> According to the hospital's chief administrator, the procedure is no longer
>
> performed there (J. A. Wells, personal communication, May 28, 2005).

Long Quotations   Quotations of forty words or more are double-spaced and set off, indented five spaces. The parenthetical citation is placed one space after the final punctuation.

Moskos (2000) summarizes the argument well:

> The principal argument raised against linking national service and
> federal educational aid is that it would have a regressive effect. . . .
> Students from wealthy families who do not need aid would be un-
> affected, while poor students would have to enter national service
> in order to get aid. (p. 380)

Preparing a reference list is tricky, so keep the models and general guidelines below handy. Double check the order of entries, punctuation, capitalization, parentheses, and brackets in each entry. All references cited in the text, except personal communication, belong in the reference list. Here are general guidelines for the format:

- Type *Reference List,* centered, at the top of the page.
- Double-space entries.
- Alphabetize entries according to authors' last names or, when no author is listed, the first major word of the title. Use initials and the surname. Include Jr. or II after an author's name when applicable.
- After the author's name, enclose the date of publication (year, month, day) in parentheses, followed by a period.
- Do not indent the first line of each entry. Indent subsequent lines five spaces.
- Italicize the titles of periodicals, volume numbers, and book titles. If your keyboard does not italicize, underline.
- Place nonroutine information that is necessary to identify and recover a source in brackets after the article title.
- Use arabic numerals for volume (e.g., 4, not IV). Retain roman numerals that are part of a title.

PREPARING A REFERENCE LIST: APA STYLE

A. APA ENTRIES: PERIODICALS

www.mhhe.com/dietsch

Bibliomaker can create APA entries. Find it at: Research>Bibliomaker

Since entries for periodicals vary, check each item carefully after you type it. Compare it with the model in the textbook. Then proofread again when you are fresh. The guidelines below will help you type your entries correctly:

- Include *The* in the name of a periodical: *The New York Times.*
- Italicize the full name of the journal or magazine and the volume number (omit *Vol.*). Do not italicize issue numbers: *Book Review Digest, 97*(6).
- Capitalize just the first word of an article title and of a subtitle. Capitalize all proper nouns.
- Do not enclose article titles in quotation marks.
- Omit *p.* or *pp.* for references to journal and magazine articles.

- To list pages of newspapers, abbreviate as *p.* or *pp.* (p. B23).
- Place the range of pages at the end of the entry (352–357).
- Use an ampersand (&) instead of *and* when listing two or more authors.
- Spell out months.

1. Journal Article with One Author, Each Issue Paged Separately

Place issue numbers in parentheses after the volume number with no space between: *37*(3).

▶ Sea, G. (2004). A pigeon in piketon. *The American Scholar, 73*(1), 57–84.

2. Journal Article with Two to Six Authors, Continuous Paging

Omit issue numbers for journals with continuous paging. When citing the range of pages, include each full number. State all the authors up to and including six.

▶ Studdert, D. M., Mello, M. M., & Brennan, T. A. (2003). Medical monitoring

for pharmaceutical injuries. *Journal of the American Medical Association,*

289, 889–894.

More than six authors: Cite six authors, then *et al.* (not italicized), set off by a comma.

3. Magazine Article

▶ Baker, J. F. (2004, February). Publishers seek new voices: Imprints provide

opportunities for black, Hispanic writers. *The Writer,* 46–48.

4. An Unsigned Article in a Magazine

▶ Pancreatic cancer update. (2003, April). *Saturday Evening Post, 32.*

5. Newsletter Article

▶ Frazier, A. (2003, February/March). If walls could talk. *Ohio Historical Society*

Newsletter, 42: 1–2.

6. Daily Newspaper Article Continued to Other Pages

▶ Hwang, S. (2004, January 19). As 'doulas' enter delivery rooms, conflicts arise.

The Wall Street Journal, pp. A1, A10.

7. Editorial

After the article title, place nonroutine information necessary for identification in brackets.

> Erbe, B. (2003, February 19). Challenging the idea of gender [Editorial]. *The*
>
> *Marion Star* [Marion OH], p. A6.

8. Letter to the Editor

> Slott, I. (2004, January 17). After confession, what next? [Letter to the editor].
>
> *The Washington Post,* p. A24.

9. Abstract and Review from a Secondary Source (print periodical)

In scholarly research cite primary sources when possible. If an abstract has no review, omit *Review by.*

> Monti, Daniel, J. (1999). *The American city: A social and cultural history.*
>
> Review by J. C. Schneider (2001) in *Journal of American History, 87,*
>
> 1537–1538. Abstract and review obtained from *Book Review Digest,*
>
> *97*(6), 157.

B. APA ENTRIES: BOOKS, BROCHURES, AND GOVERNMENT PUBLICATIONS

Entries for books include author, date, title, place of publication (city and state), and publisher. Use all the surnames in a publishing company (Simon & Schuster, not just Simon), but don't include *Publishing Company, Inc.,* or other nonessential words. Retain *Books* and *Press.*

- Capitalize just the first word of the title and of the subtitle, as well as proper nouns.
- Use initials and the surname.
- Spell out names of associations and university presses: National Audubon Society, Oxford University Press.
- Do not invert the names of editors not in the author position. Identify the editor by (*Ed.*) after the surname.
- Italicize book titles (or underline if you lack that function).
- Do not enclose article or chapter titles in quotation marks.

10. A Book by One Author

▶ Reppetto, T. (2004). *American mafia.* New York: Henry Holt.

11. Two or More Books by One Author

Books by the same author are listed according to date, from least to most recent. The author's name is repeated in each subsequent entry.

▶ Goldberg, N. (1986). *Writing down the bones: Freeing the writer within.* Boston:

Shambhala.

Goldberg, N. (1990). *Wild mind: Living the writer's life.* New York: Random

House.

12. A Book by Two or More Authors

▶ Curtis, R., & Quick, W. T. (2002). *How to get your e-book published.* Cincinnati,

OH: Writer's Digest Books.

13. A Book by an Unknown Author

▶ *Go ask Alice.* (1971). New York: Prentice-Hall.

14. Book, Revised or Later Edition

▶ Musciano, C., & Kennedy, B. (2002). *HTML & XHTML: The definitive guide* (5th

ed.). Sebastopol, CA: O'Reilly.

15. Article or Chapter in a Book

Cite the inclusive pages of the article or chapter in parentheses after the book title.

▶ Ryan, T. (2001). Such a thing as destiny. In *The prize winner of Defiance, Ohio*

(pp. 283–289). New York: Simon & Schuster.

16. A Work in an Anthology

If you consult one book of a multivolume set, capitalize the volume number (Vol. 5) and place it after the volume title without parentheses. The example below is for a single-volume anthology:

▶ Glaspell, S. (2000). A jury of her peers. In J. Updike & K. Kenison (Eds.), *The*

best short stories of the century (pp. 18–37). New York: Houghton Mifflin.

17. Published Interview

Begin with the name of the person interviewed and the date of the interview, then the title (if any), and the identifying information in brackets. Place source information according to the guidelines for books (or periodicals if the interview was published in a periodical).

> MacLeish, A. (1974, Summer). Archibald MacLeish. [Interview with Benjamin
>
> De Mott]. In G. Plimpton (Ed.) (1988), *Writers at work: The Paris review*
>
> *interviews 5* (pp. 23–48). New York: Penguin.

18. Review

> Dickison, S. (2004, February). An entertaining primer for beginning writers
>
> [Rev. of the book *The pen commandments: A guide for the beginning writer*].
>
> *The Writer, 45.*

19. Dictionary or Encyclopedia

If a major reference work has a large editorial board, you may cite only the name of the executive editor and follow it with "et al." as in the first example.

A Single Volume with Several Editors

> Mish, F.C., et al. (Eds.). (2003). *Merriam-Webster's collegiate dictionary* (11th
>
> ed.). Springfield, MA: Merriam-Webster.

Entry in an Encyclopedia, No Author Given

> The Civil War. (1995). In *Encyclopedia Americana* (Vol. 6, pp. 782–819). Dan-
>
> bury, CT: Grolier.

20. Chapter in a Volume in a Series

> Moore, W. E. (1969). Social structure and behavior. In G. Lindzey & E. Aron-
>
> son (Eds.), *The handbook of social psychology: Vol. 4. Group psychology and*
>
> *phenomena of interaction* (2nd ed.). Reading, MA: Addison-Wesley.

21. Brochure, Corporate Author

Start with the name of the corporation or organization; then give the date and title. Identify the publication in brackets. List the place and publisher. If the publisher is the same as the author, write "Author" after the place.

> Personal Training Systems. (1992). *The official audio guide to Quicken for Macin-*
>
> tosh [Brochure]. San Jose, CA: Author.

22. Government Publications with a Group Author

▷ Health Care Financing Administration. (2004). *Medicare & you 2004.*

Washington, DC: U.S. Government Printing Office.

U.S. Department of Justice. (2004). *FBI National Academy directory of graduates*

2004 edition. Quantico, VA: FBI Academy.

C. APA ENTRIES: AUDIOVISUAL MEDIA

For broadcast, film, and recorded sources, enclose in *parentheses* the role of the contributing personnel and the date. Place the medium [Motion picture], [Television broadcast] or other in *brackets*.

23. Motion Pictures

Indicate the specific medium in brackets. Include the city and producing organization, if available.

▷ Newel, M. (Director), & Barnes, P. (Screenwriter). (1992). *Enchanted April*

[Motion picture]. Burbank, CA: Warner Brothers.

24. Television and Radio Broadcasts

Using brackets, identify the broadcast: [Television broadcast]. If you cite one episode of a series, use [Television series episode].

▷ Schama, S. (Writer, Narrator, & Producer). (2001, October 29). The body of

the queen [Television series episode]. In *A history of Britain.* Columbus,

OH: The History Channel.

Lancaster, B. (Host & Producer). (2003, March 1). Art of the groove [Radio

series episode]. On *Saturday at the pops.* Columbus, OH: WOSU-FM.

25. Music and Audio Recordings

When referring to specific lyrics or compositions, begin with the lyricist/composer, followed by the original copyright date. Then provide recording information, including the date if different from the copyright date. Or if appropriate, begin with the performer, conductor, or title. For nonmusical recordings, start with the original writer's name (if provided) or with the title. Include the medium and the number in brackets.

Blitzstein, M. (1941). In the clear [Recorded by D. Upshaw]. On *I wish it so*

[CD]. New York: Elektra Entertainment. (1994).

Official audio guide to Quicken. (1992). [Cassette Recording No. IQU4.00M-1-A].

San Jose, CA: Personal Training Systems.

D. APA ENTRIES: ELECTRONIC MEDIA

Whether you access a Web site or a database loaded onto a CD-ROM, stored on a college or library server, or supplied on the Internet, the general guideline is to attach a *retrieval statement* to the reference entry. A retrieval statement gives the date the material was obtained and the name and/or address of the source. *Exception:* The fifth edition of the *APA Publication Manual* says that if the print version of a work has been unchanged on the Internet (volume and page numbers are given) and "if you have viewed the article only in its electronic form," no retrieval statement is necessary. Just insert [Electronic version] in brackets after the title of the article (see example 26).

Since you may not know if the format differs, your instructor may prefer that a retrieval statement always be added. To make a retrieval statement, follow these guidelines:

- List print source (if any) before online data. (See examples 1–22.)
- When page numbers are not given or if the online format differs from the print version, add a retrieval statement with the date and URL (see examples 27, 28, and 29).
- Place *Retrieved,* the date, and *from* before the URL. Do not use angle brackets or add a period.
- Split URLs only at slash [/] or before a period.
- **Databases:** If you access the database online, provide a URL that links to the main search page. If there is an item or access number, place it at the end of the entry in parenthesis. For all databases, including CD-ROMS and software, provide the name of the database and date of access.

Note: You can obtain further information on APA-style electronic entries at <http://www.apastyle.org/elecref.html> or at <http://www.apastyle.org/elecsource.html>.

Periodicals on the Internet

26. Article in a Journal with a Print Version, Volume and Page Number Given

Oakley, R. (2004, January). How the mind hurts and heals the body

[Electronic version]. *American Psychologist, 58,* 29.

27. Article in a Magazine, No Page Numbers

Reeves, J. (2003, February 26). How to beat the gas pump blues. *Time.* Retrieved February 27, 2003, from http://www.time.com/time/nation/article/0,8599,426934,00 html

28. Daily Newspaper Article, No Page Number

Mars Spirit rover stops sending data. January 22, 2004. *CNN.com.* Retrieved January, 22, 2004, from http://www.cnn.com

29. Article in an Internet-Only Newsletter, No Page Numbers

Justice, R. (2000). Hospital workers forget to wash hands between patients. *In Touch Newsletter 3*(4). Retrieved January 22, 2004, from http://www.in-touchnews.com/sample.htm

30. Abstract, No Page Numbers

Greene, V. (2002, Fall). How the damoiselle d'Escalot became a picture. *Arthuriana, 12.* Abstract retrieved March 5, 2003, from http://www.smu.edu/arthuriana/

Nonperiodical Documents on the Internet

31. Chapter or Section in an Internet Document

The book below was originally published in 1878. The online source is based on Harper's 1892 edition.

James, H. (1878). Part I. *Daisy Miller.* Retrieved January 20, 2004, from http://www.PageByPageBooks.com/Henry_James/Daisy_Miller/

32. Online Anthology

Frost, R. (n.d.). Mending wall. Boston: North (1915). Retrieved January 20, 2004, from http://www.english.uluc.edu/maps/poets/a_f/frost/wall.htm

33. Collection of Short Stories

Poe, E. A. (n.d.). The cask of Amontillado. *East of the Web*. Retrieved January 22, 2004, from http://www.short-stories.co.uk/

34. Document Available on University Program or Department Web Site

Nesbit, E. (1922). Many voices. In P. Willett (Ed.), *Victorian women writers project*. Retrieved February 5, 2004, from the Indiana University Web site: http://www.indiana.edu/~letrs/vwwp/html

35. Entry in an Encyclopedia, No Volume or Page Number

Wild rice. (2003). *The Columbia encyclopedia* (6th ed.). New York: Columbia University Press. Retrieved January 27, 2004, from http://www.bartleby.com/65/

36. Professional or Personal Site

Hopkins Information Technology Services. Retrieved January 20, 2004, from the Johns Hopkins University Web site: http://webapps.jhu.edu/hitswebsite/

Barbour, D. (2004, January 7). *Dennis Barbour useful links* [Online directory]. Retrieved January 20, 2004, from http://www.bme.jhu.edu/~dbarbour/links.html

37. Message Posted to an Online Forum or Discussion Group

Kasworm, Evelyn. (2000, October 15). A totally implantable artificial heart. Message posted to http://www.med.utah.edu/ethics/

38. E-Mail

Online correspondence between individuals is cited as *personal communication* in the text of your paper only, as shown below. List the initials of the sender and the exact date.

(C. M. Smith, personal communication, May 1, 2005)

39. Material from a Library or Other Subscription Service

To cite a work found through an online library or other subscription service, include the author's name, the title of the work, and publication information about the printed version (if given). In the retrieval statement, include the name of the database, the name of the service, the date of access, and the URL of the service's home page.

▶ About the U.S. Congress. (2000). Retrieved February 5, 2004, from *Masterfile*

   Premier, EBSCOhost at http://www.web5.epnet.com/

Nonperiodical Publications on CD-ROMs

Cite nonperiodical CD-ROMs the way you would cite a book title and author. Include the publisher and disc or item number (if there is one).

40. CD-ROMs

The example below refers to one disc of a set of CD-ROMs that are available at many public libraries. Since the sets are stored on the premises, there is no URL. Still, there is a retrieval statement, naming the database.

▶ *1880 United States census and national index*. (2001). Retrieved February 5,

   2004, from Family Search Family History Resource File [CD-ROM]. Salt

   Lake City, UT: Intellectual Reserve.

41. Computer Software and Computer Programs

▶ Schulman, R., Schrader, J., & Jacobs, J. (1999). *Quicken Deluxe 99* [Computer

   software]. Menlo Park, CA: Intuit.

RECOGNIZING ITEMS THAT NEED TO BE DOCUMENTED

Directions: Go to a library or use some of your own materials to create examples of entries for an MLA-style list of works cited or an APA-style reference list. Follow the textbook models carefully, checking format and punctuation.

1. Book by two or three authors
2. Book with an editor or editors
3. A work in an anthology by several authors
4. Book with several volumes
5. Article from a daily newspaper
6. Article from a monthly magazine
7. Article from a journal with continuous paging
8. Videotape
9. One author quoting another author
10. Internet source: published newspaper, magazine, or journal article
11. Internet source: article from a professional Web site

Using Sources and Writing a Research Paper

> I have lived in this world just long enough to look carefully the second time into things that I am the most certain of the first time.
>
> —Josh Billings (1818–1885)
> (Henry Wheeler Shaw)

Research can be scientific investigation, as in primary research, or scholarly inquiry, as in secondary research. Both kinds require a fair and thorough consideration of existing facts before reaching a conclusion. When doing any research, be open to new evidence even if it conflicts with what you believe. Withhold judgment until you have examined the facts, noted inferences, and labeled theories. Otherwise, expensive mistakes may be made.

See chapter 26.

See "The Logical Appeal," chapter 25.

TRACKING THE TRUTH

As an employee was leaving a plant, security guards stopped him to search his brief-case. They found a $35 telephone. Assuming he had stolen the phone, the company fired him. Notices were placed on eleven bulletin boards and the electronic mail system, saying the phone was company property and the employee had violated work rule number 12 about theft. The employee filed suit against the company for libel.

At the trial a coworker testified to going with the defendant to a mall where he had purchased the phone. The defendant explained that his company phone had been damaged by a flood. But he had lost the sales slip for the new phone. His boss had said to just keep the phone. After the firing, the man had applied for a hundred jobs, but was rejected each time it was learned why he had been fired. The jury awarded the defendant $1.3 million in damages. The moral of this story is that an open mind is a prerequisite to tracking the truth.

WHEN IS A LIST OF SOURCES REQUIRED?

A paper based on secondary research always requires a list of the sources you consult, both printed and electronic. If you are doing field research, you may or may not need a list of sources, depending upon how you obtain your information. A paper based on personal observation or a survey alone does not require a list of sources (see chapter 30).

But if you conduct interviews, you need to list each interviewee's name, the place of the interview, and the date. (For telephone interviews, the place is omitted.) When primary (field) research and secondary research are combined, the different source entries can be integrated into one list. Then you make a works-cited list, following the MLA style guidelines on page 458 (or a reference list, following the APA style). Chapter 28 explains and shows model entries for both the MLA and APA documentation styles.

- **Start making source cards early.** Note the author, publication, volume, date, page numbers, URL, or other source information required.
- **To make entries, find the correct model in chapter 28.** Check the order and punctuation of each entry you construct.
- **Make a source entry for each quotation and parenthetical citation in your paper.**
- *Alphabetize* **source cards before typing your list of sources**. This saves time.
- **Double-space entries when typing your list of sources.** Do not indent the first line. Indent all succeeding lines.

TIPS FOR COMPILING A LIST OF SOURCES

RESEARCH READING

Reading for research, if you are absorbed in your topic, can be just as engrossing as the latest best-seller. By reading widely, you can gain not only a comprehensive view of your topic but also knowledge of the latest discoveries in a field. Research reading, however, requires an organized, analytical approach that reflects your purpose. At some points you need to be critical.

Examining Dates and Credentials

As new knowledge is discovered, previous knowledge may become dated. As you read, examine the dates of surveys, studies, and other research as well as the credentials of the writers and researchers. To find this background information, check the home page of a Web site and the preface, introduction, or any footnotes of printed materials.

CHECKLIST   EXAMINING SOURCES AND CREDENTIALS

1. **Is the author/researcher credible?** Does he or she have advanced degrees, licenses or certification, and a fine reputation in the field? Who sponsored the research?

2. **Is the information up-to-date and adequate?** When was the study, poll, or other research conducted? Are enough details provided to be convincing?

3. **Was the study or poll representative of the general population?** What was the size of the sample? Where was it taken?

4. **Does the interpretation of results seem logical?** Does the language seem objective? Or does the writer seem to have a hidden agenda?

5. **Have other researchers reported similar or conflicting results?** What do authorities in the field generally accept?

Using Tentative Words to Discuss Findings and Theories

The rhetorical situation of a research paper requires more precision in word choice than that of a less formal paper. As you read reputable accounts of polls, experiments, and studies, notice the tentative, or provisional, words that qualify discussions of results. These *uncertain* words indicate that evidence is *not* conclusive even though a growing body of research may indicate a conclusion or theory is probably true. Let's look at how the journal *Science* uses tentative words (italicized here) to discuss results of several studies about the cause of perfect pitch:

> A research team from Düsseldorf, Germany, *may* have located the physical basis of one exceptional form of mental performance: perfect pitch—the ability to identify any musical note without comparison to a reference note. . . .

A team led by neurologists Gottfried Schlaug and Helmuth Steinmetz of Düsseldorf's Heinrich Heine University *reports* that the planum temporale, a region of the brain cortex that processes sound signals, is far larger on the left side than on the right in professional musicians—and especially in those who have perfect pitch.

Overstatement undermines the credibility of research. Yet beginning writers sometimes assume that because a study or experiment *suggests* that something is true, it is, indeed, true. By the time they summarize their research notes, they have catapulted theory into the realm of fact. Often one word, *prove,* is what launches this assault upon truth. To discuss uncertain research findings competently, qualify your statements with tentative words. Use accurate terminology, as shown below.

TENTATIVE WORDS COMMONLY USED IN RESEARCH

Verbs	Nouns	Phrases
indicates	indication	probable cause
found	findings	possible influence
may	possibility	apparently is
reported	report	is often a sign of
suggest	suggestion	could indicate
influence	tendency	suggests that
theorize	theory	may affect
imply	implication	can produce
seems	symptoms	
appears	trend	

Recognizing Information That Must Be Acknowledged

The rhetorical situation of a secondary research paper requires that the majority of what you write will be based on outside sources. Careless noting of sources can result in unintentional plagiarism. Perhaps knowing that the Latin *plagiarius* means "kidnapper" will remind you not to kidnap absentmindedly any original words. The penalties for this offense can be severe, and the chances for detection are great. Take care in gathering all of the source information needed for parenthetical citations and works-cited entries.

See page 450.

Restating Common Knowledge   Factual information that is familiar to the general public is considered common knowledge. For example, it is common knowledge that orange juice is high in vitamin C, that Thomas A. Edison perfected the incandescent lightbulb, and that Alfred Hitchcock directed suspense films. So if you come across such facts in your research, you will not be expected to acknowledge the source for them—*unless you decide to quote the source directly.* If you copy an author's words, you need to enclose them in quotation marks and cite the source. In your early efforts at research, it is best to cite the source of any piece of information that you were unaware of before your reading.

Acknowledging Everything Else   Practically all other information gathered in research requires documentation. Here is a list of items to watch for so that you can make a source card for each item:

- Historical information that is not commonly known
- Current information based on a writer's direct observation or reporting
- Statistics
- Surveys and opinion poll results. Give the researcher, date, place, size of sample, and any other pertinent information in the text of the paper, if possible.
- Research results and interpretations. Give names of researchers, date.
- Expert opinion, estimates, predictions
- Theories. Identify the person who originated the theory, if possible.
- Artistic interpretations or criticisms
- Tables, charts, graphs, and other visual material
- Any statement that is subject to debate
- Footnote from printed material

Citing Professional Opinions and Conclusions   When doing secondary research and writing an *informative* research paper, you summarize the findings, or results, of the research and cite the opinions of authorities in the field. You do not interject your own personal opinion. Instead, you offer a logical interpretation of the evidence, as you understand it, using direct quotations to cite the words of experts as support. If you will be writing a *persuasive* paper or a paper of *argument*, however, check with your instructor, who may have other guidelines in regard to personal opinion. (Also see chapter 18.)

As you start your research reading, the following questions should be helpful in selecting information for your paper and in interpreting it:

- What are the main points (chief results) of my research?
- What points do most authorities in the field agree on?
- Why do some authorities disagree?
- Why are the findings significant?
- What are the implications?
- What does it all mean?

www.mhhe.com/dietsch

For more help taking notes while researching, visit:
Research>Researching
Techniques>Taking Notes

NOTE-TAKING, SUMMARIZING, PARAPHRASING, AND QUOTING

Take care to preserve the meaning of the original passage as you take notes, summarize, paraphrase, and quote. Distinguish fact from opinion. Transcribe numbers and other figures correctly. With thought and care, you can avoid five common problems in student research papers:

- Pulling ideas out of context
- Omitting significant information
- Using too many quotations
- Using too few quotations
- Inadequately documenting source

An informative freshman research paper is usually expected to consist mainly of summary. Paraphrase appears at times, and short direct quotations are sprinkled at appropriate intervals. One or more long direct quotations may be used, depending on the assignment and the material. An example of an informative research paper appears at the end of this chapter. To see researched arguments, turn to chapter 18.

Note-Taking and Critical Reading

The most important requirement as you take notes, either in the margins of photocopies or on note cards, is to *insert quotation marks around any material that you intend to copy into your research paper or report*. This chapter explains how to integrate quotations into a paper as well as use ellipsis, brackets, and explanatory notes. For extensive help with note-taking, commenting, and reacting to ideas, see "Critical Reading" in chapter 20. The Handbook provides grammar rules and examples of quotations, ellipsis, and brackets. (See the Handbook Directory, page 726.)

Summarizing

A well-written *summary* is clear, concise, and informative. It restates the main ideas of the original piece, omitting insignificant details. Brief quotations are sometimes included. To summarize your research findings, condense them and present them in your own words. Try to simplify the passage so that it is not too technical or too complex for the reader. Take care not to change the meaning.

As you make notes, retain the original order. Keep track of page numbers and quotations so that you don't have to hunt later for documentation. You might begin your draft by listing the chief ideas. Or you might copy the relevant topic sentences in order, then reword them. If you need some of the original words for a good reason, recopy those that are necessary. Place quotation marks around copied words immediately to avoid confusion later. As you summarize, *vary your sentence structure from the original*. (For help, see chapter 7.)

Using Major Words, Generic Nouns, and Minor Words   To summarize and paraphrase, you replace the original *major words* (specific nouns, verbs, adjectives, adverbs, and gerunds) with synonyms that mean the same. A thesaurus or two will help you find synonyms to replace an author's major words. If you have the slightest doubt about the accuracy of synonyms, check in a dictionary

to ensure they have the same meaning as the original words. Otherwise, the meaning or emphasis could be misconstrued.

You can, however, use generic nouns from the original without quotation marks. *Generic nouns* have no accurate synonym (dog, refrigerator, computer). Be careful though. Don't assume that a word is generic; use a thesaurus and a dictionary. For example, Kleenex is not generic; *facial tissue* is generic. *Car* may seem generic, but it has accurate synonyms: *auto* and *automobile*. According to the kind of vehicle, you might substitute *jalopy, SUV, sedan, Toyota Camry,* or another suitable word.

You can also include minor words from the original, as needed, without adding quotation marks. But try to vary your wording whenever possible. Still, do not create awkwardness or confusion just to avoid reusing a minor word. *Minor words* include the three articles (*a, an, the*), prepositions, conjunctions, relative pronouns, and some other pronouns. (To review the parts of speech, see the Handbook Directory, page 726.)

AVOIDING PLAGIARISM: USING MAJOR WORDS AND MINOR WORDS

To summarize and paraphrase, you need to be able to distinguish major words from minor words. Listed below are examples of each to help you avert unintentional plagiarism:

REPLACE MAJOR WORDS:

- **Specific nouns**
  boulder, mansion, edge, way, logic, photo

- **Adjectives**
  huge, fragile, dewy, quick, tiny, sad, happy

- **Verbs**
  hit, strolled, jogged, is, was lapped, ate, smile, slept, saw

- **Adverbs**
  very, quite, also, too, surely, where, fast, lately, certainly

- **Gerunds** (verbal nouns)
  steering, soaring, sunbathing
  (See page H-18)

MINOR WORDS (can be reused):

- *Prepositions*
  on, over, under, for, off, in, into, of, beneath, after

- *Conjunctions*
  but, and, either, for, or because, yet, when, until

- *Relative Pronouns*
  who, whom, which, whose, that, whomever, whoever

- *Other Pronouns*
  she, he, it, her, his, its, they, them, their, theirs

- *Articles*
  a, an, the

A Summary and the Original   A summary is often condensed 50 percent to 75 percent. The following example is slightly less than half as long as the original, yet it makes essentially the same points. Note that the author is identified in the first sentence of the summary. Synonyms replace major words. Generic nouns such as *horse, musical pitch,* and *alphabet* are reused because they have no close synonyms. At the end, the page number of the original source is placed in parentheses *before* the period. This source note, which specifies the page, is a link back to the related works-cited entry.

Summary

Mark L. Knapp tells an amazing story of a horse owned by Herr von Osten of Germany in the early 1900s. His owner taught Hans to do arithmetic, drummed out with a front hoof. Then von Osten began showing the horse in public, where Hans computed the total of persons with spectacles and did other tricks. He seemed to have learned the alphabet, for he could tap out a response to most queries. Many people were convinced Hans knew German well. In fact, he appeared brighter than many people (1).

Original

Herr von Osten purchased a horse in Berlin, Germany, in 1900. When von Osten began training his horse, Hans, to count by tapping his front hoof, he had no idea that Hans was soon to become one of the most celebrated horses in history. Hans was a rapid learner and soon progressed from counting to addition, multiplication, division, subtraction, and eventually the solution of problems involving factors and fractions. As if this were not enough, von Osten exhibited Hans to public audiences where he counted the number in the audience or simply the number of people wearing eyeglasses. Still responding only with taps, Hans could tell time, use a calendar, display an ability to recall musical pitch, and perform numerous other seemingly fantastic feats. After von Osten taught Hans an alphabet which could be coded into hoof beats, the horse could answer virtually any question—oral or written. It seemed that Hans, a common horse, had complete comprehension of the German language, the ability to produce the equivalent of words and numerals, and an intelligence beyond that of many human beings.

—Mark L. Knapp, *Nonverbal Communication in Human Interaction*

Example of Plagiarism   In the following example, major words were copied needlessly. Quotation marks around the copied words were omitted. Instead of synonyms, *variations* of major words were used. For instance, Knapp writes "began training," and the example uses "trained," which uses the same root word. And there is no source note at the end. The plagiarized portions are italicized.

Plagiarized Summary

According to Mark L. Knapp, in 1900 in Berlin, Germany, Herr von Osten *purchased* a horse. *When von Osten trained* the horse to *count* by rapping his hoof, he did not know that Hans would *become one* of the most famous horses *in history*. Hans was a *rapid learner* and *soon* could do arithmetic and other tricks. *After von Osten taught Hans a coded* alphabet, *it seemed that* Hans, a horse, understood German well and knew more than many people *[source note needed here]*.

Paraphrasing

Paraphrase is the restatement of an original passage, sentence by sentence. Thus a paraphrase is considerably longer than a summary, although you might condense somewhat. Paraphrasing requires the same precautions as those for summarizing. To paraphrase, you restate in your own words and revise using different sentence patterns if at all possible. As you paraphrase, take care to select synonyms, not variations of the original words. For example, if an author uses *defend*, do not write *defending*. Find another word such as *protect*. Retain the meaning of the original and avoid awkward rephrasing. Look up unfamiliar words.

Paraphrasing is time-consuming and can lead to wordiness. Therefore, limit paraphrasing and use it only when needed for the following reasons:

- **To emphasize important ideas.** Paraphrase significant points that will support your rhetorical purpose. For example, paraphrase topic sentences.
- **To clarify a difficult passage.** Reword and simplify; clarify ideas.
- **To combine details.** You may want to combine lesser ideas that are similar.

**GUIDELINES:
WRITING
SUMMARIES AND
PARAPHRASES**

1. **Read and reread the entire original carefully.** Take notes or mark the original, underlining topic sentences and key points. (For help, see "A Strategy for Critical Reading," chapter 20.)

2. **Rewrite and restate.** In your own words, restate the chief ideas from topic sentences and key points, using accurate synonyms.

3. **Retain the order of the original.** Changes in order may distort the meaning.

4. **Check your draft with the original.** Have you included all significant points? Have you retained the original order? Have you restated appropriately, or have you unwittingly copied material that should be paraphrased or quoted?

5. **Enclose all copied material in quotation marks.** Then use a thesaurus and a dictionary to help you paraphrase and summarize. If a few sentences are too technical, quote them directly.

6. **For a summary reduce material by 50 percent or more.** Restate major points. Combine and condense related ideas. Omit examples and minor details.

7. **Cite sources, pages, and dates.** Check to see that you have adequate documentation. (See chapter 28 for documenting print and Internet sources.)

8. **Read the summary or paraphrase aloud.** Is it clear? Has all important information been included? You might also ask someone else to read it for clarity.

9. **Run a spelling check after all revisions are made.** Spelling errors and typos are inexcusable flaws in this technological age.

10. **Proofread your final draft to be sure that every word is correct.** Have you omitted any words? Is the form of each word correct? Carelessness with spelling checkers can result in strange insertions.

Example of a Paraphrase If a passage seems impossible to paraphrase, you can include a few brief quotations. The following example paraphrases Knapp's original story about Hans:

Paraphrase with Brief Quotations

To explain how animals "read" nonverbal signals, Mark L. Knapp, tells a strange story. In 1900 Herr von Osten of Berlin, Germany, bought a horse. While teaching the horse, Hans, to rap out numbers with a fore hoof, von Osten did not suspect that the animal would ever become famous. But Hans learned so fast that he could soon do arithmetic. When von Osten showed Hans in public, the horse "counted the number of people wearing eyeglasses." He could even "tell time," read a calendar, remember musical pitch, and do other tricks. When von Osten drilled the horse in the alphabet, tapped out with a hoof, Hans responded to almost any query. He appeared not only to understand German well but also to know more than many people (1).

Using Quotations

Quotation is a respected practice that is used by educators, researchers, and other writers. Appropriate quotation in a research paper indicates responsible writing. Below are five reasons that you might include quotations. (The examples are from *The Writer,* January 2001.)

1. **To present technical words for which there is no accurate paraphrase.** Quoting the exact words prevents misunderstanding. In "Selling Your Work Online," Emily Vander Veer points out a new term:

   Stephen King single-handedly catapulted the term "e-publishing" into the mainstream last March when over half a million readers logged onto their computer and downloaded electronic copies of his novella *Riding the Bullet.*

2. **To allay any doubt about the accuracy of a surprising statement or evidence.** By giving the exact words, you avert the reader's suspicion. In "Take the Reader Along," Martha Sutro quotes a paradoxical truism to illustrate the risks that authors take in pitching their work to editors:

   Throughout the process, I remembered a helpful adage: "You have to increase your rate of failure in order to increase your rate of success." You have to be willing to put yourself out there.

3. **To capture the flavor of the original.** Paraphrase will often not do justice to a passage that is vivid and unusual. Aly Colón opens "Avoid the Pitfalls of Plagiarism" by quoting a distinctive phrase:

   Plagiarism is the "unoriginal sin," writes writing coach Roy Peter Clark, a senior scholar at the Poynter Institute, in an article first published in the March 1983 issue of *Washington Journalism Review.* And it seems to be a very common sin.

4. **To avoid an awkward or wordy paraphrase.** Do not abuse this privilege, however. Keep such quotations brief. Here Colón quotes a list of

criteria rather than attempting to paraphrase it. Because the material is identified and indented, no quotation marks are required. It is treated as a long quotation:

- Was there intent? Did the writer intend to pass the work off as his or her own?
- If there was no intent, then did the writer's work habits and methods lead to unintended replication?

5. **To enhance your credibility as a writer.** By including quotations appropriately, you demonstrate professionalism.

Use quotations for a purpose. Keep most quotations brief, according to your assignment and the difficulty of the material. Technical material may require more quotations than usual.

Making Changes in Quotations

Your readers expect that what you enclose in quotation marks will be the exact words of the original source. Yet some quotations may be too lengthy or detailed for your purpose. In that case you may be able to shorten the quotation by omitting unnecessary words and replacing them with an ellipsis. If you do, take care that the meaning does not change.

Ellipsis   An *ellipsis* is a set of three spaced dots used to replace insignificant or irrelevant material. You can use an ellipsis at the beginning, middle, or end of a sentence. The result should still be a complete sentence. If the ellipsis comes at the end of a sentence or if you omit more than an entire sentence, *then the period makes a fourth dot.* The example below shows the latest MLA style for ellipsis (see page H-36.) Written by Amal Kumar Naj, this excerpt from the *Wall Street Journal* is entitled "Chemicals Bad for Ozone Are Declining":

> "Dr. Montzka said the measurements . . . make it possible to predict when the ozone layer will recover. He said the rate of recovery will depend on stratospheric temperature and chemical emissions from volcanoes" (B4).

Brackets   If you need to add something to a quotation for clarity or logic, you can insert the explanatory words within brackets [ ]. Originally, the paragraph below used *he,* which has been replaced with the name of the researcher:

> "Barring unusual changes in temperature and emissions, [Dr. Montzka] estimated that it will take 50 to 60 years before the Earth's ozone layer is restored to the levels before 1970."

When the verb tense of a quotation differs from the text of your paper, you can resolve this inconsistency by substituting another tense in brackets. In the example below, the original was written in the present tense. For the sake of logic, two changes to the past tense (in brackets) replace the original wording.

> Farley Mowat describes the clothes of the Ihalmiut, a tribe that became extinct in the 1950s, as "two suits of fur, worn one over the other. . . . The inner suit [was] worn with the hair of the hides facing inward and touching the skin while the outer suit [had] its hair turned out to the weather" (422).

Once in a while, you may find an error in grammar or spelling in one of your sources. To indicate that you are reproducing the original error rather than creating one of your own, you may insert the Latin word *sic* ("thus") in brackets after the error, as shown after this grammatical mishap:

> An example of the radical nature of the organization is this advice from a pamphlet it published: "Thieves should be punished by having there [*sic*] hands cut off."

Keep in mind, however, that some words have two or more correct spellings. It is always a good idea to check two dictionaries to be sure a word is actually misspelled or misused.

Quotation within a Quotation   When your source contains a quotation, change the double quotation marks in the original to single marks (' '). Then enclose the full quotation in double quotation marks, as shown below:

> In *Strictly Speaking* Edwin Newman writes: "Most conversation these days is as pleasing to the ear as a Flash-Frozen Dinner is to the palate, consisting largely of 'You've got to be kidding,' 'It's a bad scene,' 'How does that grab you?' 'Just for openers . . .'" (16).

MAKING A WORKING OUTLINE

Once you have completed the bulk of your research and note-taking, you can use your note cards to start a working outline. A simple way to start is to classify your note cards. Sort through the cards according to subject and place related items in piles. Then examine each pile and label it with a category under which all items will fit. After that, organize the categories into a possible order. If you become puzzled, ask yourself questions as you draft your outline.

www.mhhe.com/dietsch
For online outlining help, check out:
Writing>Outlines

1. **What is the purpose of the paper?** How can I make the purpose clear?

2. **What are the main points of my research?** List them.

3. **What thesis can serve as an umbrella for all the main points?** Do I have irrelevant material? Do I need to narrow the topic?

4. **Is chronological order visible anywhere?** Are there historical items to place in chronological order? Might they make an interesting introduction, or should they come later? Will the overall order be chronological or just the introduction?

5. **How should the body of the paper be organized?** Should main points be arranged according to importance? Or should they go from concrete to abstract? Or would some other order, possibly problem solving, work best?

6. **Does the material seem comprehensive?** Are there significant gaps? Do I need more information to be complete?

QUESTIONS FOR DEVELOPING A THESIS AND AN OUTLINE

When you are comfortable with a tentative order, number your note cards and copy the categories and subcategories into outline form. Leave spaces for adding items. By the end of the writing process, your working outline will have become a formal outline, ready for submission along with your paper, if required. (An example of an outline submitted with a student paper appears near the end of this chapter.)

DRAFTING A RESEARCH PAPER

As you begin to draft, keep in mind that your working outline is subject to change. In the course of getting your thoughts on paper, you may make slight changes or even find a different organization emerging. If so, take the time to rethink your working outline before continuing to draft.

Drafting a Thesis and Introduction

www.mhhe.com/dietsch

Want online help with your introductions? Go to: Writing>Introductions

The sooner you can state a clear thesis, the sooner you can begin to organize and draft your research paper. If you are uncertain, reexamine your controlling question and rewrite it as a thesis statement. Or you might prefer to draft the introduction as a whole unit rather than in pieces. You may even find that your thesis has mushroomed out over several sentences as in Wilma Dunnington's introduction. Although her purpose is clearly informative, there is no one thesis sentence:

The Genome Project

Possible effects

Probably few readers can imagine a time when genetic profiles would be used as a basis for marriage or divorce, a time when genetic testing would be required by employers to screen applicants. It is easier to envision a world where children "diagnosed with cystic fibrosis would be spared their fate by a gene transplant," a world where cancers would be revealed and treated before a single cancer cell could grow (Bishop and Waldholz 22). These are the "threats and promises" of what could be the "most ambitious scientific research project ever undertaken" (22). The Human Genome Project is an effort to identify all of the genes in the human body.

Definition

In *Principles of Anatomy and Physiology*, Tortora and Anagnostakos report that the Human Genome Project will take an estimated fifteen years and cost three billion dollars. The overriding goal of the project is to "conquer genetic disease" (953). Marwick points out that in the human body are more than 100 thousand genes. Occasionally, a gene is injured, resulting in "abnormal features or disorders." Sometimes an embryo will not grow; other times children are born with defects. Some conditions caused by a damaged gene may not be apparent until a person becomes aged (3247).

Main goal

Explanation

Another way to begin an introduction is with a definition of a special term, followed by a brief history and explanation. Note, too, that Kathy Rummer includes a statement of purpose:

Dr. Nightingale: Nurse Practitioners in Primary Medical Care

The role of the nurse practitioner has evolved over several decades in response to a shortage of physicians and physician's assistants, escalating costs,

and a shortage of affordable health care. A nurse practitioner (NP) is a regis-   **Definition**
tered nurse who has completed an "accredited two-year program of study and
clinical practice," earned a master's degree in nursing, and passed a national
exam ("Nurse Practitioners" 4). In California, for example, NPs are certified to   **Example**
provide basic medical care, prenatal care, and family planning assistance. They
must pass a course in pharmacology and work for six months in an internship,
receiving intense supervised training, before they can write prescriptions
("Need a" 4).

The nurse practitioner program has evolved as a result of the short supply   **History**
of physician's assistants (PAs). In 1965 the physician's assistant program was
created to relieve the shortage of physicians. Using a physician's assistant for
routine medical care freed physicians to concentrate on more complex medical
problems (Sidel and Sidel 203, 204). But for some reason the program attracted relatively few medical students. In 1970 the American Medical Association asked the American Nurses Association (ANA) to supply nurses to be
trained as physician's assistants. Instead of complying with the request, the
ANA created its own alternative to the physician's assistant—the nurse practitioner (Sidel and Sidel 204).

The intent of the American Nurses Association was that this new health   **Purpose**
care professional's "training and philosophy [would reflect] nursing and not
medicine" (Sidel and Sidel 204). Dock and Stewart point out that this philosophy is based on the "Nightingale concept" of nursing in which there is "neither
independence nor subordination but interdependence and cooperation." According to the Nightingale philosophy, nursing is not a "subcaste of medicine." A nurse is not a "handmaid," but a "helpmate and partner" (367).

For other kinds of openings, see chapter 4.

Using Signal Phrases to Integrate Quotations into the Text

Every quotation you use requires transition to weave it into your text. Usually,
a *signal* phrase precedes the quotation. This introductory phrase signals the
reader that a direct quotation will be presented. To keep your signal phrases
strong and responsible, give the full name of the researcher, team, organization,
study, or poll whenever possible. To identify a person, give degrees, position, or
other credentials. The examples below illustrate signal phrases for introducing
quotations:

- According to Dr. Sheila S. Smith, a psychologist at Blake University,
- A study by an Ohio State University medical team found "...."
- In March 2005, the American Medical Association reported:
- James A. Bell, a scientist at Jones Laboratories of New York City, stated:
- Others, like Dr. H. R. Smythe, believe that "...."

More examples of signal phrases can be viewed in student examples
throughout the chapter as well as in the research paper at the end of the chapter.

Weak Phrases   Some popular magazines and newspapers omit vital source
information. Instead, they substitute vague transitional phrases and the word *it*.

All of the following examples are evasive and *inappropriate* for research papers and reports:

A study revealed . . .   (What study? Who conducted it?)

Experts/researchers/
authorities say . . .   (Who? All?)

It is believed . . .   (Who believes?)

It is estimated . . .   (Who estimated?)

It is predicted . . .   (Who predicted?)

"In my opinion" or "I feel"   (So what?)

VERBS IN SIGNAL PHRASES

The verb in a signal phrase should indicate the intent of the writer or speaker. Usually the verb is in the present tense unless the context requires the past tense *(found, reported, stated)*. The reference list of verbs below are all in the present tense:

admits	concedes	discloses	holds	observes
agrees	concludes	disputes	highlights	refuses
argues	concurs	emphasizes	insists	refutes
believes	denies	finds	maintains	reveals
claims	disagrees	grants	notes	stresses

Short Quotations   Quotations of four lines or fewer (three for poetry) are considered short. You can use short quotations to identify special terms or include vivid words and difficult-to-paraphrase segments. Short quotations, too, require transition to link them to the text.

Sometimes you may lack the name of a researcher to use as a transition to a quotation. Often popular magazines summarize research, giving only a minimum of details about several studies. When April Rausch was confronted with this problem, she presented the vital information that was available, using two short quotations:

> During 1991, thirty-seven babies in the United States died at home "while sleeping in bean-bag infant cushions." Although some of the babies were thought to have died of Sudden Infant Death Syndrome, others apparently smothered. After a research team headed by James S. Kemp and Bradley T. Thach tested bean-bag cushions for babies from two makers, using rabbits, the Consumer Product Safety Commission cited the cushions as a potential "asphyxiation hazard." In late 1991 infant bean-bag cushions were removed from the market (*USA Today* 5).

Block Quotations   A *block quotation* is a long quotation of five lines or more (four for poetry). For a research paper (MLA style), double-space and indent block quotations *ten* spaces on the left margin; none on the right. Do *not* use quotation marks for a block quotation because the indention and parenthetical citation alert the reader that the material has been borrowed. Careful writers use long quotations for a valid reason; overuse signals a hastily written paper. In the example below notice that (1) the source and author are identified in the text of the paper *before* the long quotation, (2) a *colon* is placed after the verb, (3) the period appears one space *before* the citation.

> In *The Managerial Woman,* management consultants Margaret Hennig and
>
> Anne Jardim state:
>
>> Studies of women who enroll in continuing college education
>>
>> programs show that many of the women who fail in these pro-
>>
>> grams . . . have never discussed their goals with their husbands.
>>
>> The husbands never really understood why their wives had gone
>>
>> back to school, and the wives on their own had attempted to
>>
>> maintain the same level of housework they had been accustomed
>>
>> to. (212)

Inserting Explanatory Notes

Once in a great while you may have material that is useful in discussing your subject but that seems to interrupt the text. In such cases you have the option of including the information in an explanatory note. To do so, insert a superscript numeral at an appropriate point in your text. Then you can place the note either at the bottom of the same page or on a separate page, headed "Note" or "Notes." Begin the note with a matching superscript number (see "Content Notes" on page 457).

Writing a Conclusion

The conclusion of a research paper may be longer than those of the other papers you have been writing. A graceful ending of three to five (or more) sentences is usually expected. Although new information is not introduced in the conclusion, a writer may leave the reader with a new thought. A brief summary or reference to the future may be appropriate. Peggy Bean combines these three techniques in her closing:

www.mhhe.com/dietsch
For more coverage of conclusions, check out:
Writing>Conclusions

> Although the fetal alcohol syndrome is a tragic disorder, it is also a preventable one. Therefore, it is important that the general public become aware of the risks ethanol poses to the developing fetus, especially to the fetus of a chronic alcoholic. Once families know the cause of this disorder, they can assist the alcoholic mother-to-be in securing professional help.

Bonnie L. Rice ends her research paper with a reference to the future and to what a reader might do to help in a similar situation:

▶ Efforts toward education, intervention, and prevention of adolescent suicide are being made. They must continue and expand. But can the individual do something to help? Yes, the greatest problem for the unhappy adolescent is isolation from close relationships; one person can be that caring friend who is missing from someone's lonely life.

Sometimes beginning writers tack on a quotation at the end without transition. Although the quotation may be appropriate, the gap between the body and the quotation halts the smooth flow of thought. To link a quotation to a conclusion, use a transitional segment, as italicized in the following example:

▶ *Child abuse is an ancient problem, but it is an occurrence that concerns us all, a problem that needs to be solved. For as James Agee wrote,* "In every child who is born, under no matter what circumstances, and of no matter what parents, the potentiality of the human race is born again; and in him, too once more, and of each of us, our terrific responsibility towards human life. . . ."

REVISING, EDITING, AND FORMATTING

When you finish the rough draft of your research paper, heave a sigh of relief, and take a break if possible. If not, perhaps you might alphabetize the entry cards for your works-cited list and start typing that or do some other related chore. Before you start to revise your paper, however, you need to gain distance so that you can come back and examine it objectively.

Revising

See chapter 5.

Persistence, time, and care are the keys to successful revision and proofreading. Yet you may be so preoccupied with content that order, documentation, and mechanics receive low priority. Several revisions spaced over several days will catch more errors than one intensive session the night before a deadline. The checklist below will prove helpful in assisting a tired brain to focus during this all-important stage.

CHECKLIST   REVISING SOURCE-BASED PAPERS

1.   Compare your outline and paper. Is the order the same? Is it sound?

2.   Now read the paper aloud. Is the introduction interesting and complete?

3.   Are the main ideas clear?

4.   Is there sufficient transition? Is each quotation linked to the text?

5.   Are there too many direct quotations? Should some be paraphrased or summarized instead?

6. Could the order of details within paragraphs be improved?

7. Is the conclusion logical and complete?

Checking Documentation

Every source you use in your research paper must be acknowledged according to a standard documentation style. Two of the most common—Modern Language Association (MLA) style and American Psychological Association (APA) style—are described in detail in chapter 28. Both use parenthetical citations within the text that are keyed to a complete bibliographical list.

In the course of drafting and revising, even the most conscientious writer may omit, misplace, or lose a text citation while rearranging sentences or paragraphs. If a problem occurs, don't panic! Remember you have your earlier drafts and note cards. Also check to see that every paragraph in your research paper has at least one text citation unless there is a reason for not including one. Remember, too, that if you split a paragraph you will probably have to make another citation.

CHECKLIST   USING PARENTHETICAL CITATIONS

1. Is there a citation for every source used?

2. Does every parenthetical citation for a printed source include a page number (except for single-page sources and entire works)?

3. Is the name of the author/researcher/group included either in the parenthetical citation or in an introductory phrase?

4. If there is more than one source by the same author, does a short form of the title appear in parenthetical citations?

Editing and Proofreading

To catch errors in a research paper, proofread when you are alert. Go over your paper several times—one sitting is seldom enough. For example, watch to see that you have the correct spelling of prefixes, as in words beginning with *per-* and *pre-*. To attain the high grades that most students desire, revise and proofread several times. If you follow the editing guidelines outlined in chapter 5 and provide the necessary effort, your paper should be a success.

www.mhhe.com/dietsch

You can find a wealth of editing resources at: Editing

Using an Appropriate Format

Some instructors may give few or no instructions for formatting a research paper; others may give precise instructions. Most expect good-quality white, 8½-by 11-inch paper. A title (cover) page may or may not be required. Some instructors like the title page format commonly used in the workplace (see the research paper at the end of this chapter). The APA style requires a title page, but the MLA does not. Both styles require that you double-space the entire manuscript, including quotations and list of sources. Some instructors also prefer that you staple or use a paper clip rather than a binder to keep pages together.

Margins and Indentation   Standard specifications for research papers call for one-inch margins (top, bottom, and sides). Pages numbers are placed one-half inch from the top right and flush with the right margin. Indent the first line of paragraphs one-half inch (5 spaces on a typewriter). For long quotations, the MLA style indents one inch (10 spaces) from the left margin. The APA style, however, indents long quotations one-half inch (5 spaces).

MLA-Style Heading, Title, and Page Numbering   If you decide not to have a title page, the MLA style advises starting the first page of the manuscript with your name, your instructor's name, the course number, and the date on consecutive lines one inch from the top left margin. Next, center the title. Capitalize the first and last words and major words of the title. Do not italicize any words unless you mention a book title or use a foreign phrase or other wording that requires italicizing. (Never italicize your own title.) Page numbers, in the upper right corner, are preceded by the writer's last name, as shown here.

> Bellows 1
>
> Susan N. Bellows
>
> Professor Raintree
>
> English Composition 112
>
> May 15, 2005
>
> New Sources of Antibiotics from Land and Sea
>
> Many of the wonder drugs of former decades are losing their
>
> effectiveness as bacteria acquire immunity to certain antibiotics.
>
> Thus there is a never-ending search for new medicines to replace
>
> older ones that have become obsolete.

FIGURE 29.1 Format for page 1 of a research paper, MLA style.

APA-Style Heading, Title, and Page Numbering   The APA style requires a title page with a "running head" (abbreviated title) of the first two or three words of the title, the full title, and the byline. The full title should summarize the main idea of the manuscript briefly and simply. The byline contains the writer's name and the institutional affiliation (college, university, or other site). In the byline use no extra words such as *by* or *from*. The preferred form of an author's name is first name, middle initial, and last name.

First, type the running head (the first two or three words of the title) and the page number one-half inch from the top right margin in upper and lowercase. Skip down about one-third of the page and type the full title, centered, in lowercase with capitals (if needed, on two lines. double-spaced). Double-space, then center the writer's name. Double-space again and center the name of the institution, as shown here.

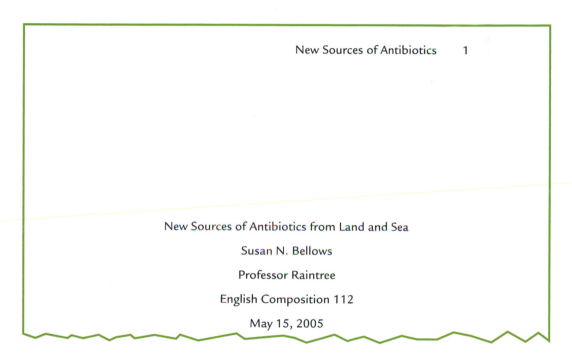

FIGURE 29.2 **Format for a title page, APA style.**

Page numbers in APA style are preceded by the running head from the title page on succeeding pages. This means that the first two or three words are taken from the title. Note that the page number appears five spaces after the head.

SAMPLE STUDENT RESEARCH PAPER: MLA STYLE

A complete student research paper using the Modern Language Association style follows; the title page is optional. The outline appears before the paper by Lois J. Gordon. For specific guidelines regarding the parenthetical citations in this paper, see chapter 28.

www.mhhe.com/dietsch

To read another student essay in MLA format, check out:
Research>Sample Research Papers>Sample Paper in MLA Style

Workers' Compensation: The Employee's Insurance Policy

by

Lois J. Gordon

CM 110 Research Writing

Professor Leslie Weichenthal

April 10, 2005

Gordon 1

Workers' Compensation: The Employee's Insurance Policy

<u>Thesis:</u> Over the years so many workers' compensation laws have been passed that volumes of information have accumulated, much of it written in legalese. Discerning what is directly relevant to an injured employee is an overwhelming task. And since laws differ so much from state to state, this paper is limited to an overview of workers' compensation in the United States, common problems in resolving claims, and basic suggestions for filing a claim.

I. Brief history of workers' compensation in the United States

II. Overview of workers' compensation

III. Common problems in resolving claims

    A. Prevalence of conditions causing musculoskeletal disorders and implementation of ergonomics rules. Explanation of ergonomics.

    B. Determining whether or not an injury is work-related

    C. Employers, even when negligent, may contest claims.

    D. Genetic testing

IV. Procedure for filing a claim, time limits, and liability

V. Suggestions for filing a claim

Gordon 2

Workers' Compensation: The Employee's Insurance Policy

Before workers' compensation programs came into effect, injured employees had no recourse except to sue for coverage of their medical bills and lost wages. This chore was not only extremely difficult but also unpleasant because of possible retaliation from the employer. Then too, coworkers were often hesitant to testify on behalf of the employee. Awards hinged upon the expertise of the lawyers involved, not actual losses. Cases could take years to settle while legal costs accumulated for the injured employee (Williams 4).

In 1908 President Theodore Roosevelt proposed that workmen's compensation be applied to all workers (Williams 43). In 1912 an amendment to the Constitution of the United States established Workmen's Compensation, which was changed to Workers' Compensation on January 17, 1977. The 1912 amendment required employers to provide insurance for work-related diseases, injuries, or death caused by mental, physical, and emotional factors. No longer would employees be required to prove that their employers intentionally harmed them (Swisher 283). But this amendment does not cover all categories of workers. For example, migrant or seasonal farm workers may or may not be covered according to the state and the employer ("Texas" 1). Some states make other exceptions.

Now, nearly a century after Roosevelt's recommendation, the United States has fifty-three workers' compensation systems in various stages of development with assorted rules and provisions. Two

Gordon 3

federal programs cover federal employees and longshore workers.
There are fifty state programs and another system that covers Washington, DC, because workers' compensation is a form of insurance   Summary
regulated by the state in which the company is located (Williams 43).
Congress regulates only the transactions that are considered interstate ("Insurance" 1).

    Over the years so many laws relating to workers' compensation
have been passed that volumes of information have accumulated,
much of it written in legalese. Discerning what is directly relevant to
an injured employee is an overwhelming task. And since these laws
differ so much from state to state, this paper is limited to an overview
of workers' compensation, common problems in resolving claims,   **Topic narrowed: Thesis sentence**
and basic suggestions for filing a claim.

    A short, convenient description of workers' compensation is
that it is an employee's insurance policy. An explicit definition of this
term is provided by William R. Tracey: **Authors' name pre- cedes the quotation**

        Workers' compensation—Statutes passed by all   **Extended quota- tion indented 10 spaces—no quo- tation marks**
    states designed to protect workers from the hazards and
    consequences of accidents, injuries, illnesses, and death
    to themselves and their families as a result of their em-   **Extended definition of workers' compensation**
    ployment. Benefits are paid to workers suffering job-
    related physical, mental, or emotional accidents, injuries,
    disabilities, or disfigurement or who aggravate preexisting
    physical or mental conditions at work. In addition to   **Quotation is double-spaced**

Gordon 4

death payments, they typically include weekly payments,

based on earnings and size of family, medical and hospi-

tal bills, scheduled loss (amputation, loss of use, or loss

of a bodily function), payments for scarring, rehabilita-

tion, retraining, settlements, travel expenses, and attor-

ney fees paid to the employee or his or her surviving

spouse or children. Businesses must either have adequate

funds to pay claims or carry appropriate workers' com-

pensation insurance coverage. The laws also provide some

Period precedes page of extended quotation

protection to employers against excessive liability. (375)

Employees who are injured on the job or disabled from work-

Summary: Eligibility and benefits explained

related mental or emotional illnesses or diseases are eligible for work-

ers' compensation benefits, according to state regulations, the em-

ployee's wages, and the severity of the disability. Financial benefits

may be awarded in a lump sum or a weekly check. For example, the

DIA Circular Letter No. 303 (2 Oct. 2000) cited Massachusetts's

weekly benefits as ranging from a minimum of $166.18 to a maxi-

mum of $830.89. A statute mandates that the minimum benefit be

Quotation

"at least 20% [of] the state average weekly wage" and the maximum

benefit "be set at 100%" of the SAWW ("Maximum" 1). Other com-

mon benefits include medical treatment, prosthetics, rehabilitation,

living expenses, job retraining, and funeral expenses. Some states pro-

vide allotments for attorneys' fees except for frivolous claims. Such

payments must be approved by the court before the case is heard.

Gordon 5

United States federal regulations override state laws whenever there is a contradiction in rules. The Occupational and Safety Health Act (OSHA) was passed to protect workers' safety and health while in the workplace, regardless of the state. OSHA laws regulate private employers that conduct business in interstate traffic. The federal government has also established health and safety laws for its own agencies. To guarantee that regulations are being followed, the secretary of labor has the authority to inspect workplaces, investigate complaints, and make decisions about needed laws. A citation may be given to employers who violate regulations. Fines may be imposed; the amount varies according to duration and type of violations ("OSHA Facts").

Problems have long existed in workers' compensations systems in the United States. In 1970 a national commission was set up to evaluate all fifty-three systems (Williams 43). The commission discovered many deficiencies and recommended that every state be required to meet nineteen essential standards by July 1, 1975. Most states still have some standards to be met (Williams 44).

One of the major health problems of employees is a group of conditions classified as musculoskeletal disorders. According to the United States Bureau of Standards, musculoskeletal disorders traceable to the workplace are responsible for "a third of the occupational illnesses reported." These conditions range from carpal tunnel syndrome to back and neck injuries (Pramik 1). In response to this find-

Summary: Role of federal government explained

Summary: Deficiencies in state systems and recommendations cited

Summary: Explanation of a major health problem

Gordon 6

ing, President Clinton's administration enacted regulations on ergo-

nomics that would require "companies to implement comprehensive

programs to protect their workers from repetitive-motion injuries" by

May 2001("Bush"). Almost two dozen states had begun making rules

Summary: Progress to date

to meet the deadline when Congress repealed the legislation in March

200l. The reasoning was that implementing the programs would be

so expensive that it would work an undue hardship on employers.

Three states—North Carolina, California, and Washington—had al-

ready enacted the ergonomics regulations ("Ergonomics").

Definition of ergonomics includes direct quotation

Ergonomics includes everything from office furniture to the

"walk through the parking lot to the relationships among coworkers."

Adjustable chair seats and backs, improved keyboards, a track ball in-

stead of a mouse, antiglare screens, glasses to reduce eyestrain, and

other features can alleviate strain and stress. Some companies furnish

recreation rooms, weight rooms, and jogging tracks (Pramik H4).

Cites examples

Problems in resolving workers' compensation claims often arise

when a determination is needed to prove an injury or disease is work-

related. This decision is particularly difficult in cases where the em-

ployee uses a home computer or other appliance that may lead to

musculoskeletal disorders. In such cases, a physician often considers

Explanation of how decisions are made on claims

the number of hours spent on each appliance and arrives at a split

estimate. The decision becomes more complicated when employers

urge the employee to see a company doctor. Although the law may

state that an injured employee can see his or her own physician, em-

Gordon 7

ployees may believe that this is their only choice. Even if they know better, they may feel pressured to see the company physician. Sometimes an injured employee sees several doctors who may disagree. Some states, like New York, require that an "impartial specialist" be appointed ("Rules" 1). Some states, such as California, identify specific criteria to classify the degree of incapacitation ("Levels 1").

Even when negligence seems clear-cut, an employer may dispute the claim for fear the employee will seek a large settlement. For example, an employee stepped into a puddle on a sunken sidewalk on company property. Ice lay beneath the water, causing her feet to fly out from under her. She suffered a mild concussion. The company contested, claiming the accident was "an act of God." The agency settled in her favor, finding that the walk constituted a hazard and should have been repaired. She asked only for payment of medical costs, which was awarded ("Anonymous"). In other cases, of course, employees often do receive large awards.

Interview to supplement research

Quotation

Yet another complication in the resolution of workers' compensation claims is DNA testing. In February 2001, the United States Equal Employment Opportunity Commission called for a stop to genetic testing of employees by the Burlington Northern Santa Fe Railroad. The commission's lawsuit, filed in the US District Court in Sioux City, Iowa, said a "nationwide policy of requiring employees who have submitted claims of work-related carpal-tunnel syndrome . . . to provide blood samples for DNA tests" infringes on

Court decision on DNA testing cited

Ellipsis to indicate omission in quotation

Gordon 8

rights to privacy and freedom from discrimination (Chen). The next day the company halted the tests (Machalaba).

The general procedure for filing a claim for workers' compensation is similar throughout the United States, although time limits and requirements vary. In Massachusetts, if an employee is unable to work for "five or more calendar days, or dies, as the result of a work-related injury or disease," the employer must submit a "First Report of Injury" to the Office of Claims Administration at the DIA, the insurer, and the employee within one week of the injury notification. Within 14 days of the report, the insurer must either settle the claim or contact the Department of Industrial Accidents (DIA), the employer, and the employee of the decision to deny the claim. A "pay without prejudice period" exists for 180 days, allowing the insurer to pay without accepting liability. This period encourages the early settlement of claims ("Maximum" 1).

A fact not generally known is that in the case of an employee's death, the law protects the employer. Ron Hayes, founder of Families in Grief Hold Together, said, "When I tell distraught families who just lost someone in a workplace fatality that they cannot sue the employer, they are shocked. . . . I've had families go to three or four attorneys until they would accept it" (Cullen).

To obtain specific information about workers' compensation laws in a state of residence or employment, visit WorkersCompensation.com or another Web site written in plain English. (Government

Gordon 9

sites contain legalese.) Some employers furnish such information.
Some basic suggestions for filing a claim, based on this research and
my experience, are presented here:

1. When an accident or illness occurs, record the exact time,
   conditions, cause, and names of any eyewitnesses. Photograph the accident scene if possible.

2. Secure medical treatment. If an on-site specialist sees you,
   secure a second opinion from your own physician.

3. Report the accident or illness to the employer as soon as
   possible.

4. Do not sign a waiver or take a quick settlement until the
   extent of injury is known. Some injuries may not become
   apparent until weeks later.

5. Fill out all necessary forms neatly and completely. Be polite
   and cooperative in follow-up meetings.

6. If necessary, secure the services of a competent attorney. If
   the state pays the fees, this step will have to be preapproved
   by the court.

Finally, an injured employee who is well-informed and proactive
will have a better chance of resolving a claim fairly with a minimum
of stress than the one who leaves everything to the employer and to
chance.

Writer makes suggestions for filing a claim, based on her experience and research

Cites a benefit of being well informed

Gordon 10

Works Cited

Anonymous. Personal interview. 16 Mar. 2004.

"Bush Could Move to Wipe Out Clinton's Final Actions." Wall Street
  Journal 19 Jan. 2001, Midwest ed.: A16.

Chen, Kathy. "U.S. Seeks to Halt Employee DNA Tests." Wall Street
  Journal 12 Feb. 2001, Midwest ed.: B2.

Cullen, Lisa. "The Myth of Workers' Compensation Fraud." Frontline,
  n.d. 2 Mar. 2004 <http://www.pbs.org/wgbh/pages/frontline/
  shows/workplace/etc./fraud.html>.

"Ergonomics Rules Still Alive in Many States." Wall Street Journal
  14 Mar. 2001: B15.

"Insurance Law: An Overview." LII: Law about . . . Insurance, 2003.
  12 Mar. 2004 <http://www.law.cornell.edu/topics.html>.

"Levels of Subjective Disability." WorkersCompensation.com, n.d.
  1 Mar. 2004 <http://www.workerscompensation.com/
  california/>.

Machalaba, Daniel. "Burlington Northern Ceases Its Genetic Testing." Wall Street Journal 13 Feb. 2001, Midwest ed.: B10.

"Maximum and Minimum Benefits" [Massachusetts].
  WorkersCompensation.com, n.d. 2 Mar. 2004 <http://
  www.workerscompensation.com/massachusetts/>.

"OSHA Facts." US Dept. of Labor, Occupational Safety and Health
  Administration. 2003. 10 Mar. 2004 <http://www.osha.gov/
  as/opa/oshafacts.html>.

Gordon 11

Pramik, Mike. "Health Risks Also Found in Modern Workplaces."

Columbus Dispatch 3 Sept. 2000: H1, H4.

"The Rules of New York: Workers' Compensation Subchapter A,

part 303." WorkersCompensation.com, n.d. 3 Mar. 2004

<http://www.workerscompensation.com/new_york/>.

Swisher, Thomas R. Ohio Constitution Handbook. Cleveland:

Baldwin, 1990.

"Texas Workers' Compensation Commission Rules."

WorkersCompensation.com, n.d. 4 Mar. 2004 <http://

www.workerscompensation.com/texas/>.

Tracey, William R. The Human Resources Glossary: A Complete Desk

Reference for HR [Human Resource] Professionals. New York:

American Management, 1991.

Williams, C. Arthur, Jr. An International Comparison of Workers'

Compensation. Boston: Kluwer, 1991.

"Workers' Compensation Overview" [Massachusetts].

WorkersCompensation.com, n.d. 2 Mar. 2004 <http://

www.workerscompensation.com/massachusetts/>.

Entry for state government online article

Entry for a book

Entry for book with one author

PRACTICE

TRANSITIONAL PHRASES TO INTRODUCE QUOTATIONS

Directions: For the following items, write a transitional phrase to introduce the quotation. For help, see "Using Signal Phrases to Integrate Quotations into the Text," in this chapter. (*Source for this exercise:* Siebert, Al. *The Survivor Personality.* New York: Berkley, 1996, page 64.)

1. Quotation: "The most direct access to the subconscious mind is through dreams. When we fall asleep, our rational, logical thinking relaxes."

2. Quotation: "Our dreams contain information about what is happening in our lives, our bodies, and the world around us."

WRITING A SUMMARY

Directions: Write a summary following "Guidelines: Writing Summaries and Paraphrases" in this chapter. Your tasks are as listed:

1. Find a one- or two-page article (three pages if much space is taken by pictures) in a popular magazine. Or if you prefer, select a short article from a journal to be used for your research paper.

2. Duplicate the article on a copier. This copy will be turned in to the instructor along with the summary.

3. Reread the article. Underline each topic sentence and essential supporting data. Number each topic sentence for convenience in writing your summary.

4. To begin your summary, write an introductory sentence that gives the author's name and the source. (Turn back to "Using Signal Phrases to Integrate Quotations into the Text.")

5. Make one entry for a works-cited list. Place at the bottom of your paper.

6. Staple the copy of the article to your completed summary.

Field Research
Observation, Interviews, and Surveys

CHAPTER 30

> A prudent question
> is one-half of wisdom.
>
> —Francis Bacon (1561–1626)

Recently a market research firm conducted focus groups of urban and suburban teens to determine what fads are in and what are out. The researchers asked questions, listened, and videotaped every word and gesture. From these observations and interviews, they will predict new teen trends in products from fast food to jeans. Corporate clients will use the report to shape commercials and products to teen tastes. Observation, interviews, and surveys are three methods of field research.

OBSERVATION

Observation can be done in other ways. In "Caterpillar Afternoon," Sue Hubbell, a naturalist, tells how she chanced upon a queer object, which appeared to be a snakeskin, lying on a dirt road. But when she knelt down, she found it was a mass of small white, hairless caterpillars that exhibited unusual behavior, especially when disturbed. Quite curious, she examined them and later searched through her library until she found a book that mentioned experiments with pine processionaries by a nineteenth-century entomologist. Later in an interview with another naturalist, Hubbell learned that such a sight was quite rare. Thus she combined primary and secondary research. (Hubbell's story is located on page 564.)

Observational research involves methodically watching a specimen, activity, interaction, or phenomenon and recording data. Observation can be done up close through the five senses or through cameras, tape recorders, X-ray machines, microscopes, radar, and other devices. The main advantage of observation is that the observer sees the subject firsthand. And if strict standards are maintained, findings can be quite reliable. The main disadvantage is that observation is limited to subjects verifiable through the senses. Observation is not a reliable method for testing attitudes or motives.

Selecting a Site

To accurately assess specimens, situations, or behavior, you need a certain amount of expertise. For instance, if enrolled in certain education courses, you might observe a class of schoolchildren. You could categorize their interactions with the teacher and each other, comment on patterns observed, and relate them to a course. Or as a student who has taken several college courses, you might observe the instructional styles of several professors who teach the same course and rate their effectiveness. This would require more than your opinion; you would need to survey other students, too. Then you could compare responses.

Or you might observe the instructional styles of one instructor who teaches in two areas, perhaps composition and speech. The findings for the two areas might vary considerably. The disparity might be due to greater competency in one area; attitude of the instructor and of the students toward the subject; potential to use audiovisuals, small groups, and humor; or other factors. Obtaining other students' opinions would make the research more valid.

Other projects for observation might be much simpler. You might watch various TV networks, perhaps ABC, CBS, and CNN, to see how each covers the same stories. Or you might watch several TV programs to classify and count actions that indicate courtesy as opposed to rudeness. Or you might play arcade games and categorize acts of violence and how they are treated. Is there fighting, blood, or killing? How much? Are gory scenes shown close up? How do characters respond to gore? How do the children/youth who play the games respond? Do the games seem to have redeeming value? If so, how would you rate them on a scale of one to ten?

Preparing to Observe

Some research requires obtaining permission and making appointments. If you would like to tape your observation, this privilege will require permission, which should be secured well in advance. Inquire as to when you should arrive and where you should sit so as to be unobtrusive.

Be prepared. Remember to take an extra pen and a note pad of convenient size. Devise a system to take notes, perhaps abbreviating, so that you can watch as much as possible. If you will be taping, check your supply of blank tapes and fresh batteries. Have the recorder working and ready to go with the flick of a switch. (Observing more than once will yield information to compare and to verify impressions.)

Keeping a Log

A detailed log of research data and results is essential. After you leave the site, rewrite and expand your notes as soon as possible. (The ability to recall falls off after one hour.) Flesh out the notes with precise details and examples of what happened. Your objective at this point is to record the facts, describing exactly what you saw and heard. Tell what occurred, under what conditions, the exact time of day, who was present, and other vital information. If an interaction occurred, describe it and the precise words said. Do not inject opinion.

Use quotation marks to enclose a comment or remark you include. Note nonverbal communication: gestures, frowns, smiles, touching, vocal intonations, and other nonverbal cues. Hold off on analysis and interpretation until you have the facts down on paper and have time to consider their meaning. To be as comprehensive and objective as possible, you need to look at the entire episode, not isolated fragments. The checklist below can help you expand your notes.

CHECKLIST   **MAINTAINING OBJECTIVITY**

1.   Observation

☐   What do I see?

☐   What do I hear?

☐   What do I smell?

☐   What do I taste?

☐   What do I perceive by touch?

☐   Is anything else significant?

2. Description

☐ What are the physical features?

☐ What behavior is observable?

☐ What interactions are occurring?

☐ Would someone else agree?

☐ Are the words neutral?

3. Interpretation

☐ What might it mean?

☐ What else might it mean?

☐ Are the inferences logical?

☐ Are the inferences unbiased?

☐ Do inferences account for all events/behavior?

4. Writing

☐ Is the description neutral?

☐ Is the interpretation logical?

☐ Does the conclusion flow logically from observable data?

☐ Is the conclusion fair?

Later you can analyze and look for links—common threads and patterns of behavior. If you observed more than once, did similar or dissimilar interactions occur on different days? Describe your overall impression each time. Date each observation as to the hour. In some cases, morning or afternoon can make a difference in activities and behavior.

INTERVIEWS

An interview is sometimes defined as a conversation with a purpose. Employers conduct interviews to hire, appraise, debrief, and fire employees. Computer sales reps interview clients to ascertain system needs. Journalists interview, seeking news and feature stories. Police officers interview witnesses and interrogate suspects. Lawyers interview clients to establish a defense. As a part of your field research, you might interview to learn more about a community problem, the history of your city, the underground railroad, or another topic.

Types of Interviews

Telephone interviews allow you to contact more people than face-to-face interviews do. But usually you gain less information since most people are less inclined to volunteer details to a faceless, unknown caller. Successful telephone interviews require lessening interviewees' suspicion and gaining their trust. Telephoning, however, may be a quick alternative when face-to-face interviews are canceled and you lack time to schedule more.

Talking face-to-face takes longer than telephoning but yields more information. Face-to-face interviews require planning and persistence. You have to call ahead, request appointments, and then travel. If an appointment is suddenly canceled, you may need to reschedule or find an alternative. Yet face-to-face interviews are worth the extra effort because you gain more details and make contacts that may prove beneficial.

Informational Interviewing   Informational interviews allow you to research family history, a product, or other topics. For a college research project, you might obtain preemployment information about your career field. If you do, keep in mind that informational interviews are not a job search although they may lead to a position later. An employer is apt to be kindly disposed to someone who is motivated to conduct preemployment research and to prepare a list of well-crafted questions. For example, you could ask about skills needed for a position, training offered, responsibilities, starting salary range, travel, chances for advancement, and related questions.

Before going to any interview, consider your choice of apparel carefully. If you are interviewing an elderly relative in her home, casual dress is appropriate. But if you are doing a preemployment interview, dress just as if you were applying for a job. Before you leave, convey your appreciation to the interviewee.

Unstructured versus Structured Interviews   *Unstructured* interviews are casual with no set format. They may elicit information that would not surface in a structured interview, but they are time-consuming and difficult to compare if you are doing a series. In an unstructured interview, interviewer and interviewee often contribute equally to the conversation. Yet authorities on interviewing recommend a 30 to 70 percent ratio with the interviewer doing the least talking, according to Charles J. Stewart and William B. Cash, Jr., in *Interviewing: Principles and Practices*. The interviewer's prime task is to listen.

The *structured* interview is based upon a list of prepared questions that is used for every interview. This approach not only saves time but also ensures coverage of all planned questions. A set of questions also provides a clear base for comparison.

Types of Questions

Well before your interviews start, read all you can on the subject to be discussed. You need to know enough to prepare a list of quality questions that will yield the information you seek. Using a format similar to that of a questionnaire will ease tabulation. Provide checklists for answers to allow comparison of responses.

Leave an extra space after each question for comments. Include some open questions to elicit unanticipated information.

Open questions are broad and unlimited. Their flexibility allows the interviewee to answer in several ways—for example, "Can you tell me about the duties of a bank teller?" Open questions may begin with phrases such as *what happened, how do you see this,* or *what experience have you. . . .* Often they are used at the beginning of interviews to decrease tension.

Closed questions limit an interviewee's response; they are more specific. For example, "What does a bank teller do when the day's accounts do not balance?" or "After one year what are the promotional opportunities for a teller?" These questions are so limited they have only one answer. Degrees of openness vary, as shown in the following examples:

OPEN: What types of crime have occurred in this neighborhood?

LESS OPEN: What types of vandalism have occurred in this neighborhood this year?

CLOSED: Have you had any vandalism on your property this year?

Avoid a series of closed questions that might cause defensiveness and cut off the flow of information. If questions about sensitive topics are necessary, ask them near the end of the interview. Be discreet. For example, if you ask about income or age, have the respondent indicate a range rather than a specific figure.

GUIDELINES FOR INTERVIEWING

1. **Call for an appointment.** Give full name and college or university. State the purpose of the call. Use courtesy words. (Reduces suspicion of unknown callers.)

2. **Arrive a few minutes early** to catch your breath and relax a bit.

3. **Shake hands.** A woman should extend her hand first so that the other person knows she is comfortable shaking hands.

4. **Do not sit until invited.**

5. **Politely decline an offer of a beverage.** Don't chance a spill.

6. **Have a typed list of questions handy.** Leave spaces to jot brief notes. Bring a clipboard or tablet for support. (Never use a corner of the person's desk.)

7. **Do not stay over the appointed time.** Ask important questions first.

8. **Thank the interviewee before you leave.**

9. **Write up your notes soon after the interview.** Expand. Include the date, place, and name of the interviewee. Use quotation marks to enclose exact words.

10. **Write a thank-you note to the interviewee.** Although this last tip is optional, it may be wise to cultivate some contacts for future reference. (See chapter 25.)

Leading questions indicate an expected answer. They yield little information and lead to dead ends. In the examples below, the tip-off word is italicized:

- Do you *dislike* filling out all those government forms?
- Do you *enjoy* flying to consulting sites?
- This seems like a progressive company. *Would you agree?*

Make several copies of your set of questions so that you have a clean sheet for each interview. During the interview, briefly note replies. Expand your notes soon afterward. With permission, you may tape-record. Be wary of promising copies of the results unless you have the time and resources to duplicate, mail, or deliver.

SURVEYS

Professional opinion polls and surveys are taken often. News organizations may survey a president's popularity every week; a magazine may survey readers' preferences; manufacturers may offer free coupons to entice you to reveal personal information. A survey requires a questionnaire, skillfully designed to yield the desired information. For your research project, you might conduct a student survey on campus. You would need good questions to elicit responses that reveal views and attitudes about a concern, a problem, an issue, or another topic. After you obtain the sample responses, you tabulate and interpret the results of the research.

Planning a Survey

In 1995, shortly after the Internet was opened to commercial activity, Jeanne Dietsch designed and conducted the first e-commerce market research study. The purpose of that study was "to determine whether any companies were actually making money online." Ms. Dietsch, founder of ActivMedia Research and CEO of ActivMedia Robotics, Inc., offers valuable advice for students: "Have a *specific* and *significant purpose* in mind as you draft questions. A major problem with many questionnaires is haphazard questions that yield trivial information."

Another major problem with some surveys is that the samples are neither random or representative. For example, over the years Alfred Kinsey has been widely criticized for his statistical sampling. The *Wall Street Journal* (31 Mar. 1993) reported that "about 25% of Kinsey's 5300 male subjects were former or present prisoners . . ." Yet Kinsey claimed that the results of the survey were representative of the general population. Ten years later, criticism of Kinsey's methods was still newsworthy. Robert Stacy McCain of the *Washington Times* (8 Sept. 2003) wrote: "The Kinsey Reports have been criticized for methodological flaws . . . [one] sample included hundreds of prison inmates. Those criticisms intensified after the admission by Kinsey Institute officials that the reports' information about children's sexual behavior was based on 'research' by sex offenders."

Representative and Random Samples

A *representative* sample is a group that is typical of the general population in age, gender, education, socioeconomic status, and other significant characteristics. The size of a sample should be statistically significant. This means that a reasonable number of instances should be examined before any inference is made—the larger the sample, the better. Ten percent of the population is considered ideal, but few professional surveys have that much. *Still, the typicality of the sample is more important than size.* For example, to be typical, a campus survey would include students of both genders, various age ranges and ethnic groups, all programs, and day and evening classes. In other words, the sample should represent the mix of the larger campus population.

A sample is *random* if all members of the population have equal chances of being chosen. If not, the results do not reflect the opinion of the larger population, only the group sampled. Random sampling is not simple. Even if you were to select every thousandth name in a telephone directory, you would omit the poor, those too ill to answer, and others who do not have telephones. To obtain a random sample, consider the place, the day, the time, and any other factors that influence randomness. The checklist below will help you plan.

CHECKLIST   PLANNING A SURVEY

1. **Have a significant purpose.** Find an interesting project that will supply meaningful information.

2. **Determine how the survey can be representative and random.** How large will the survey be? (Check with your instructor.) Where and how will you conduct it?

3. **How much time will the survey take?** Consider that you will need to design a questionnaire, duplicate, administer, tabulate, and interpret in addition to writing. If you have to do research to pose questions, that takes time, too.

4. **How much will paper and copying cost?** If you research a topic for a business, supplies might be furnished. One student even received $100 for conducting a customer survey for a barber shop.

5. **Will there be an additional cost for distribution?** Some students have been dismayed to find they spend over $50 for copies, envelopes, stamps, and gas for distributing and picking up questionnaires.

Constructing a Questionnaire

After you determine the topic, a group to sample, and a method of distribution, draft a set of questions. They should be appropriate for the topic, the situation, and the audience. Try to limit your questions to one page for easy answering.

1. Phrase questions clearly in *neutral* words. Be specific.
2. Ask for information that is easily recalled.
3. Keep questions *short*.
4. Ask only *one* question to a sentence.
5. Provide spaces, checklists, and multiple choices for *ease in answering*.
6. Plan *equal* ranges: 1–10; 11–20; 21–30. *Error: 1–10; 10–20; 20–30*
7. Use scale items (with a key) to circle for opinion:

   SA   A   N   D   SD

   SA = strongly agree, A = agree, N = neutral, D = disagree, SD = strongly disagree
8. Arrange questions in a *logical order*.
9. Place *sensitive* questions (age, salary, and so forth) near the end. Word them carefully.
10. Place any open-ended questions at the end for additional comments.
11. Limit questionnaire to one page if possible. (People dislike filling out long forms.)
12. If space allows, add a one-line thank-you.

GUIDELINES FOR CONSTRUCTING QUESTIONNAIRES

Next, write a brief set of *directions* for the questionnaire. Test the directions and questions to see whether or not they are clear and suitable. For some topics, you might seek feedback from half a dozen classmates, or you may need the expertise of an instructor or someone in the field. (See Figure 30.1.)

Dear Student,

   Help!!! Will you please take five minutes of your valuable time to assist a fellow student? I have to conduct a survey and write a report. Will you please complete this short questionnaire and drop it in the box labeled "Survey" in the student lounge by [date]?

Thanks loads,
[Your name]

FIGURE 30.1 Sample cover note for a student questionnaire.

Distributing Questionnaires

Mailing questionnaires is time-consuming and expensive. You need not only a cover letter but also a stamped, self-addressed envelope unless you plan to pick up the questionnaires. Another disadvantage is that mailed questionnaires usually have a low rate of return. Although dropping off and picking up takes time, the rate of return rises considerably. Handing out a questionnaire in a store, for return later, is apt to be unsuccessful. Instead, you might have customers write on a clipboard while you wait. One student set up a card table and chairs near the front of her parents' clothing store.

For a campus survey, you might select students at random in the student lounge, but you would need to spend equal time in the library and other places where students go. Otherwise, you would be unable to obtain a cross section. Or you might ask some instructors to distribute the questionnaire at the end of certain classes. If all students at your college are required to take freshman English, you might get a representative sample there. If you use that method, you will need a brief note to enlist cooperation and to direct respondents to an easily found box in the same building.

WORKPLACE CASE STUDY

NATHAN SURVEYS DRESS CODES FOR BANK EMPLOYEES

Nathan is majoring in business management. For his research project, he surveyed local bank managers to determine policies on attire.

Survey of Clothing Worn by Local Bank Employees

Directions: Please check *all* answers that apply to your bank.

1. Does the bank have a dress code?
   ☐ Dress code written in handbook or elsewhere.
   ☐ Unwritten dress code/guidelines given orally to employees.
   ☐ No dress code. Employees wear what they like.
2. Indicate all suitable attire for employees Monday through Thursday:
   ☐ suit   ☐ shirt/sweater, pants   ☐ jeans
   ☐ jacket & slacks   ☐ women wear skirts   ☐ no expectations
3. If you have casual Fridays, please indicate all suitable attire for Friday:
   ☐ jacket & slacks   ☐ shorts, miniskirts
   ☐ shirt/sweater, jeans   ☐ T-shirt/sweatshirt
4. What is the bank's policy on jewelry and tattoos?
   ☐ small earrings permitted ☐ no nose, tongue, or eyebrow piercing
   ☐ two-per-ear limit   ☐ no visible tattoos

continued

5. Does the bank provide financial assistance to encourage professional attire?
  ☐ gift certificate   ☐ other _____
                                                  (please explain)

  ☐ clothing bonus   ☐ no assistance

6. If an employee wears unsuitable attire, does the bank take action?
  ☐ sends home without pay   ☐ gives warning
  ☐ sends home to change   ☐ other _____
                                                  (please explain)

7. If an employee persists in wearing unsuitable attire, does the bank take action?
  ☐ may fire   ☐ warns of possible firing
  ☐ places on probation   ☐ other _____
                                                  (please explain)

8. Please indicate the approximate number of employees at this facility. (Do not count branch banks.)
  ☐ 101 or more   ☐ 61–80   ☐ 21–40
  ☐ 81–100   ☐ 41–60   ☐ 20 or fewer

9. Estimate the number of employees who have been notified of unsuitable attire in the past year:
  ☐ 21 or more   ☐ 11–15   ☐ 1–5
  ☐ 16–20   ☐ 6–10   ☐ none

10. Is your bank contemplating a change in the current policy on employee attire?
  ☐ yes   Comment: _____
  ☐ no   _____

Thank you for your courtesy and cooperation.

Drawing Conclusions from a Survey and Interviews

After you tabulate the results of your survey, you draw a logical conclusion based on the findings. This step requires interpreting the results: What do they mean and what are the implications? Then you make a reasonable generalization and possibly a prediction or recommendation, depending upon the rhetorical situation.

Let's assume Nathan's survey revealed that each of the ten banks had 21 to 40 employees. Six banks had written policies governing attire. Each bank's manager estimated five or fewer instances of improper attire in the past year. Warnings had been effective; no one was discharged.

But four banks had no policy. In follow-up interviews with the managers of these banks, Nathan learned that some employees repeatedly wore beach sandals, sheer blouses, visible tattoos, ponytails, or unusual haircuts. They were warned; this policy worked for a while. Three managers estimated a dozen instances of improper dress had occurred; one manager estimated two dozen instances. Nathan concludes that written policies are more effective than unwritten policies.

MAKING AN OUTLINE

Next, Nathan makes a working outline for his report. He follows a basic report format and lists the tabulation of each question in the original order:

I. **Introduction:** Purpose and scope of the project (list of 12 banks)

II. **Method of research:** Survey of six banks and interviews with six other bank managers

III. **Body of report**

    A. Summary of results of survey (results converted to percentages)

    B. Additional findings obtained through six interviews

IV. **Conclusion:** Enforced policies with warnings and penalties do work.

V. **Recommendation:** Banks lacking a policy on proper work attire should appoint a committee composed of bank officials and employees to write one. The policy should consider not only clothing and shoes but also jewelry, visible tattoos, body piercings, hairstyles, and hair colors.

To see student examples of a primary research paper and a report, turn to the end of this chapter. The section that follows will help you organize and interpret findings for your paper or report.

WRITING A PRIMARY RESEARCH PAPER OR REPORT

Whether you write a research paper or report, be sure you understand the assignment. Then examine your materials carefully. Do you have everything you need? If you made notes, have they been rewritten and amplified in your log so that you have all the data in front of you? If you used a set of questions, have they been tabulated? (For quick counting, use a blank copy of the questionnaire.)

If you did background reading, have you made a source card for each work (see chapter 27)? Is a list of works cited required (chapter 28), or can you state sources and dates in the text (see "Using Signal Phrases to Integrate Quotations into the Text," chapter 29).

Organizing and Interpreting Findings

Before starting to draft, consider what the findings of your research mean. Jot down your interpretation in a sentence or two. This prewriting exercise will help you focus on your thesis, the main idea of the research. Raw data is not sufficient to present in a paper or report. You not only summarize and explain the findings but also draw a conclusion. Then the reader who is unfamiliar with the subject will understand the purpose of the project and the meaning of the results.

Observation   If you observe a site or subjects, you might classify the examples from your log. Classification can help you organize by importance, such as *minor to major* or *mild to severe,* or in another way. For example, if you observe traffic at an intersection several times (for the purpose of proving that a stoplight is needed), you might begin by classifying your observations by the type of safety infraction. Then you could organize the categories according to severity of the consequences. Which infractions led to near misses? Which ones led to accidents? What was the extent of damages and injuries? Was a citation issued? Anything else?

If you observed animals or people, you might classify by physical characteristics, behavior, personality, or other traits that are relevant. For example, in a study of twins, physical characteristics and DNA results would be significant whereas for some other studies, these would be insignificant. What similarities and differences might you see? What categories of behavior would you note? Isolation? Positive interactions with others? Antisocial behavior? What else?

Next, look for patterns, trends, or tendencies. What links and connections can you spot? What do these seem to indicate? What logical inferences can you make? What is your overall impression?

Interviews and Surveys   After you add the responses to each question, convert the total into a percentage. Divide each total by the number of returned questionnaires. For example, if an item received 60 *yeses* out of 80 returns, divide 60 by 80, which equals 75 percent. (Divide the smaller number by the larger one.) Next consider whether a majority is large or small. Or is opinion almost evenly split? Look for attitudes, patterns, trends. Think about implications. What reasonable inferences can you derive from this data? What can you reasonably conclude? How will you state your findings in *tentative* terms, without overstating?

For example, two of the nation's top family scholars, Cynthia Harper at the University of California and Sara McLanahan at Princeton, conducted a longitudinal study, which was reported in the *Wall Street Journal* in December 1998. Using a large national database, Harper and McLanahan analyzed family breakdown and compared theories about "root causes" of crime. They found that "boys raised outside of intact marriages are, *on average,* more than twice as *likely* as other boys to end up jailed, even after controlling for other demographic factors. Each year spent without a dad in the home increases the *odds* of future incarceration by *about* 5%." (The tentative words are italicized here. For a list of tentative terms, see chapter 29.)

To simplify drafting of your report, make a working outline, based on classification or whatever organizational strategy you select. If you used a questionnaire, you may want to follow the order set up there. (An example of an outline appears with the student report later in this chapter.)

How Research Papers and Research Reports Differ

Research papers and reports differ considerably in format. The chief difference is that a research paper does not have internal headings. A research report is usually divided into three sections or more, each preceded by a heading.

The introduction of a research paper states the purpose and often gives an overview of the research. The methodology may be placed there, in a preface, in a content note at the bottom of a page, or at the end of the paper. The methodology tells what was observed, who was interviewed, or who was surveyed. For a survey the date, demographics, and size of the sample should also be provided. (For several interviews, your instructor may require a list of sources at the end of the report. See chapter 28 for MLA or APA style.)

The first section of a report, often called the "Purpose and Scope," states the purpose and tells why the research was conducted. This section also sets forth the range (coverage of the topic) of the research and may include the methodology. Or it may be placed in a separate section. Regardless of where this essential information is placed, it should be specific. State how the observation was made and under what conditions. For an interview or survey, tell how it was conducted, the number of questionnaires given out, and the rate of return.

The body of the research paper contains the findings and the discussion. There data and examples are presented; data is interpreted; patterns and trends are described. For a report, this material is also placed in the body, but in one section or more. The section may be entitled "Results of the Survey" or another suitable heading.

The conclusion of an informative research paper is a short summary of the results, the chief idea. The conclusion of a problem-solving paper recommends an alternative. In an argument, the conclusion restates the proposition. The final section of a report is often entitled "Conclusion" or "Recommendations." *Conclusion* implies a summary. *Recommendations* are suggestions for action. In student research reports, recommendations are usually those of professionals, such as physicians, engineers, or environmentalists.

A research paper may not be quite as concise as a report. A paper may spend more time explaining data, including definitions and examples, and may include several direct quotations—significant responses to open-ended questions. The following paper and report show two of many ways to organize and format. The structure you use will vary, depending on the assignment, the topic, and the method(s) of research.

STUDENT PAPER BASED ON OBSERVATION

Janet Burks, a volunteer playground supervisor at her children's school, observed the situation described here. She used a problem-solving strategy to organize her paper.

Playground Supervision

There was an old woman who lived in a shoe;
She had so many children she didn't know what to do.
                                        —MOTHER GOOSE

The old lady living in a shoe and a volunteer playground supervisor have a similar problem. Both have so many children they do not know what to do. Although Mother Goose does not tell readers how many children the old woman had, the number was certainly fewer than the 120 or so children for whom the playground supervisor is responsible.

What, specifically, can be done to solve this problem? Apparently, there are three possible solutions: soliciting additional volunteers, decreasing the number of children released for recess at any one time, or presenting a tax levy to pay the salaries for full-time supervisors. But any possible solution would be governed by two major constraints: cost and feasibility.

Presently, volunteers come to the playground to supervise during the hour-long midday recess (which includes lunch time). The supervisor's responsibility is to circulate among the children and either to help them or to maintain discipline. The job is physically, emotionally, and mentally draining because the supervisor's tasks vary all the way from tying a kindergartner's shoe to helping a child who has fallen off the slide to resolving disputes. During this vigil, children may approach the volunteer frequently with problems, complaints, or accident reports. The supervisor cannot be everywhere at once. Children can be hurt before he or she even knows about a fight.

A complication arises when the supervisor must handle an extreme disciplinary situation. He or she is not allowed to administer discipline, but instead escorts unruly (and often unwilling) children to the principal's office. While the supervisor is attending to one child, 119 or so are outside without supervision.

As the volunteer program has continued, more people have been quitting because of difficulties they confront. This factor has made the playground problem even worse. One proposal is to solicit the help of more volunteers. Having more would provide two supervisors each day. Then the child-to-supervisor ratio of 120 to 1 would decrease to 60 to 1. Although this proposal has the advantage of being inexpensive, it also has the disadvantage of being unlikely. Most parents are not volunteering to help (many work) and probably will not volunteer in the future.

A second proposal is to decrease the number of children released for recess at any one time. This proposal would involve shortening the midday recess to thirty minutes and staggering recess times. Only two classes (of the usual five) would be on the playground at once, cutting the number of children to supervise to approximately 40 per session. The others would return to their rooms for quiet play with teacher supervision. But the children would probably object, and teachers would not want to assume additional duties.

The third proposal would be to present a tax levy to pay the salaries of full-time supervisors. The rate per hour would be much less than the rate required to pay teachers to supervise the playground during their lunch break. At the same time, the rate would be high enough to attract people to the job. Full-time

www.mhhe.com/dietsch
You can find other examples of student writing at:
Writing>Writing Samples

volunteers sometimes do not come. Then, too, full-time supervisors would have standard rules, which the volunteers do not have. The main disadvantage is voter reluctance to approve higher taxes.

The writer's recommendation is a combination of the first and third proposals. First, information concerning the problem could be distributed to parents. They would know that if enough volunteers were not found, then a tax levy would be necessary. The levy would provide the necessary funds for employing full-time supervisors.

Although the old lady in the shoe did not know what to do, let it not be said that the same is true of Sycamore's parents and teachers. Let us solve this problem together.

In the student report that follows, notice that there are two sections in the body, entitled "Background Reading and Reactions" and "Self-Evaluation: Progress toward Objectives." These headings reflect the nature of the assignment and of the research.

STUDENT REPORT BASED ON READING AND OBSERVATION

The following report by Lisa White, a nursing student, was written for an oral communications class. The project required reading one book or more, applying principles learned in class and through reading to the student's personal or work life, and keeping a log. In their reports, students were to react to their reading, citing the most helpful ideas. Then they were to present and explain their findings as well as to evaluate progress toward their objectives. Before the project, they received an outline with suggested headings for formatting the report. (See Figure 30.3.)

No list of references was required although sources were to be provided. Lisa supplied her source information in the text of the report.

NONVERBAL COMMUNICATION WITH GERIATRIC PATIENTS

Prepared for Betty M. Dietsch, Prof.
CM 116 Oral Communications
Individual Goals Project

Prepared by Lisa White
February 28, 2002

FIGURE 30.2 Sample cover page of a student report.

Outline of the Report

I. Purpose and Scope
II. Methods of Research
III. Background Reading and Reactions
    A. *How to Win Friends and Influence People,* by Dale Carnegie
    B. *Nonverbal Communication with Patients,* by Marion Nesbitt Blondis
    C. *How to Stop Worrying and Start Living,* by Dale Carnegie
    D. *How to Manage Conflict,* by William Hendricks
IV. Self-Evaluation: Progress toward Objectives
    A. Appraisal of Progress
    B. Examples of Progress
V. Conclusion

FIGURE 30.3 Sample outline of a student report.

NONVERBAL COMMUNICATION WITH GERIATRIC PATIENTS

I. Purpose and Scope

Lake View Center (a pseudonym) is a geriatric care facility. The patients range from those needing postsurgical care to those needing care for Alzheimer's disease. As a nurse's aide, I daily encounter numerous situations that are taxing mentally, physically, and emotionally. Yet I lack the training to cope with them as I would like. I want to learn more about the importance of nonverbal communication and how to apply it to geriatric nursing. To become more skilled in interacting with patients and staff, I set the following objectives for this project:

1. To learn how to use nonverbal communication to enhance interactions with patients

2. To learn how to accept criticism

3. To develop ways to control anger

II. Methods of Research

Four library books supplied information on nonverbal communication. Most helpful were the specific suggestions that I could apply on the job. For three weeks (January 31 to February 19), I tried out the suggestions and kept a log. Every day after work, I recorded at least one incident, telling what happened, how I felt, how the other person reacted and seemed to feel. Then I stated what I had learned. As the days passed, I began to rate my progress. The log has twenty entries.

III. Background Reading and Reactions

A. *How to Win Friends and Influence People,* Dale Carnegie, 1981 (1964).

In this early book, Carnegie offers some fundamental techniques for dealing with people. The first is to remember that the deepest urge in human nature is the desire to be important. Sometimes we forget that other people besides us need to feel important. The second technique is to remember that everyone wants to be appreciated in one way or another. We can remember to thank people in small ways by words or by a quick note.

A third way to develop the best in another person is through encouragement. We all need to be encouraged, to know that we are heading in the right direction. Most helpful was Carnegie's reminder that other people need to feel important, too. I tend to get so wrapped up in trying to get everything done that I forget to try to help people feel valued, especially my patients.

B. *Nonverbal Communication with Patients,* Marion Nesbitt Blondis, 1977.

Blondis makes many excellent points about geriatric nursing. Her first suggestion is that when pausing to talk, one should speak patients' names, stand very close, look directly at them, and touch them lightly on the hand or arm. This sends a nonverbal message of "I am not too busy for you. You are important. I do care."

A second excellent point is that some elderly patients may not understand verbal communication due to hearing loss or mental impairment. But they are apt to note and understand nonverbal cues. Yet even when they understand, there is often a cultural gap of fifty or sixty years separating them from their young nurses. A word I say in one way may not be understood in the same context.

Third, patients will be more likely to judge us kindly when our nonverbal behavior is cheerful and effective. And it often seems that when one person is cheerful, the other person responds likewise. Fourth, Blondis warns that we should not confuse a patient's having a problem with the patient's being a problem. For example, some of the patients I take care of have been diagnosed as "hostile," "confused," or "senile." In reality, they may simply be unable to communicate verbally. Nevertheless, they still have thoughts and feelings.

C. *How to Stop Worrying and Start Living,* Dale Carnegie, 1984 (1970).

In his book, Carnegie explains several ways to accept and deal with criticism. The first is to remember that when we are "kicked" and criticized, it is often done because it gives the kicker a feeling of importance. Some people seem to derive satisfaction out of denouncing others who are better educated or more successful than they are. They are envious or jealous.

A second way to alleviate the sting of criticism is to remember that unjust criticism may be a compliment in disguise. We may just need to search for the motive behind it. If we keep that idea in mind, we will be less apt to worry so much about what some people say. A third suggestion is to just do the best we know how and can do when criticized unjustly—to retain dignity.

A fourth way is to keep a log of the foolish things we do and criticize ourselves for. After that, we can ask someone we respect and trust for unbiased, helpful, constructive criticism. I think this is a great idea because it helps us to improve.

D. *How to Manage Conflict,* William Hendricks, 1989.

Hendricks shares some practical tips on how to reduce and control anger through conflict management. His first suggestion is to have tolerance for diversity among people. We need to understand that other people's thoughts and ideas about issues may not reflect the same views we have. The second suggestion is to learn how to properly focus our anger on issues, not people.

This concept is difficult to apply, at least for me. I find that venting my anger on people is much easier than focusing on the issue.

Third, Hendricks points out that repressing anger will eventually lead to an explosion. Basically what he is saying is that we need to find a healthy way to handle anger. A good way, I think, is through exercise, cleaning, making crafts, or talking to a friend. This book has been very helpful because I have a quick temper.

IV. Self-Evaluation: Progress toward Objectives
A. Appraisal of Progress

Objective 1. I wanted to learn how to use nonverbal communication effectively on the job. Now when I talk to my patients, I look them in the face and smile. I speak in a cheerful tone. I also touch them on the hand to show I am not too busy for them and that I truly care. I have learned how powerful nonverbal cues can be.

Objective 2. I am learning to handle criticism in a calm, logical way. First, I assess the remark or comment to determine whether it is unjust or constructive criticism. If unjust, I take it as someone just being jealous or envious. If it is constructive criticism, I use it to improve myself and what I am doing. This procedure helps me to avoid taking offense.

Objective 3. I have been trying to focus my anger on the issue and not the person. I have also started activities to vent my emotion in a healthy manner. As soon as I get home after work, I exercise. Or if I am so angry, I cannot wait until I get home, I clean out the patients' closets. Talking to coworkers who have been in the same or a similar situation also helps.

B. Examples of Progress

Before I started this project, I used to become upset, worry, and sometimes cry. Now I do not let anybody's unjust criticism bother me. For example, a nurse at work was criticizing what I wear. I took it as her opinion and did not become upset. In fact, I used the "sponge" method, taught in class. I told her that she was probably right and that I probably could dress differently.

Another day a nurse criticized me because I was having trouble taking patients off the bedpan and keeping their beds dry. As a result, they were angry and complaining. I asked her if she would show me how she did it. She explained and then showed me. As a result of her constructive criticism and instruction, I learned to do the chore better and patients stopped complaining.

My log contains many other examples of progress, but two are especially significant. One evening a patient began yelling at me for not putting her to bed when she wanted. I tried using nonverbal communication in order to make her feel more important. It worked! I looked her in the eye while smiling and touching her hand. I explained it would be some time before I could put her to bed, but I would come back as soon as I could. Suddenly, she smiled and said that would be fine. Ever since then she has not given me any more problems.

The most trying incident occurred when I was trying to put a patient to bed. She slapped my face, scratched my arms, and bit me. I felt like screaming and hitting her back, but did not. Instead, I walked up and down the halls until I cooled down a bit. Then I went back and cleaned out her closet. (I cleaned out a lot of closets before the project was finished.)

V. Conclusion

This project has given me the opportunity to learn more about an important part of communication and to improve my work habits. My supervisor noticed the improvement and commended me. I told her about the communication project, and she seemed quite interested. Although I am well pleased with my success, I plan to continue the project. I want to learn more about nonverbal communication and continue to gain skill in accepting criticism.

TWENTY IDEAS FOR OBSERVATION, INTERVIEWING, AND SURVEYS

OBSERVATION

1. Observe a neighborhood problem such as litter control. Discuss possible alternatives and recommend action to alleviate the problem.

2. Observe a crossing that needs a stoplight. Count the cars that pass through at peak times. Describe reckless driving. What else? You might send the report to the editor of a local newspaper.

3. Observe a family communication problem. What is happening? What alternatives might alleviate the problem?

4. Local pollution problem: Combine observation with interviewing?

5. Observe a budget problem. Recommend cost-cutting actions. Pros and cons?

6. Preschool television: Time? Purpose? Themes? Hosts? Graphics? Value? Observe children viewing and record their responses, verbal and nonverbal.

7. Compare daily newscasts by different reporters. Divide topics: local, national, or international. Rate reporters and react (see "Critical Reading" in chapter 20).

INTERVIEWING

8. Jobs and salaries available locally in your career field. Will you need more training to qualify?

9. Qualities and training employers look for in _____ (your field).

10. Tour day-care centers: Interview personnel and observe. Which would be the best emotionally and educationally for your child?

11. What do you see as your state's biggest concern? Interview state officials.

12. Interview an elderly relative. Ask about his or her youth, parents, and grandparents. Record and analyze the anecdotes for your family history.

SURVEYS

13   Conduct a campus survey on the need for more litter control, parking lot surveillance at night, or another concern.

14   Campus opinion poll: Survey reactions to a no-smoking or other policy.

15   Survey student satisfaction with the bookstore. Convenience of layout, hours, service, competitive pricing, friendliness? What else?

16   Community poll: If your local library does not restrict Internet access for children, poll parents and determine what they would like to have done.

17   Community poll: How do parents feel about sex education in schools? When should it begin? Should the sexes be separated? What else?

18   Survey to determine major concerns of a community: More police/ deputies? Repair of schools? New schools? Street repair? Vandalism? What?

19   Customer survey: Ask your store manager for permission and input.

20   Investment survey: Contact a dozen banks for data on CDs, money market accounts, savings accounts, and checking accounts. Compare benefits.

THE READER

THE READINGS BY THEME

5. ANGER AND EMOTION

6. USING AND ABUSING LANGUAGE

7. TAKING RESPONSIBILITY FOR LEARNING

**THE READINGS
BY THEME**

**THE READINGS
BY THEME**

Introduction to the Reader

These forty-four essays and short stories open windows on different eras, cultures, problems, and points of view. All the readings have been carefully selected not only for interest but also for quality and significance. They cover unusual topics, ranging from flying squirrels to philosophical issues such as "Do we have a right to happiness?" But they also discuss contemporary problems such as road rage, gambling addiction, the decline of ethics, and other concerns. As you read, you will be challenged to think and question.

STRATEGIES FOR INSIGHTFUL READING

In your leisure reading, you have time to savor the passages you enjoy and the option to skip over those you don't. College reading is less flexible, but it can also be more rewarding. You will learn much about the craft of writing as you peruse these pages and later discuss the readings in class. You'll begin to notice how writers plant clues in openings, how they develop a thread of continuity that runs throughout a work, and how they shape endings appropriately. You'll also start to notice various sentence patterns and the expert use of transition to enhance the flow of an essay or narrative. You'll gain skill in spotting the clever use of literary devices (chapters 21 and 22) and in scrutinizing logic (chapters 3, 18, and 19).

The rhetoric section of this book explains two effective reading strategies, one for nonfiction and one for fiction. Chapter 20 provides a detailed strategy for *critical reading* of essays and other nonfiction. There you will find extensive help for improving reading comprehension, analysis, and note-taking. The three stages of critical reading are explained: prereading, rereading, and prewriting. An example of a short reaction paper shows how to respond critically to an essay.

Chapter 21 explains a strategy for reading, analyzing, and evaluating fiction. There you can learn about the seven elements of literature and consider how the content and structure of a narrative influence its meaning. As a result you will become more alert to symbols and subtle clues (objects, dialogue, and actions) that contribute to the central meaning, or theme, of a narrative.

HOW DO ESSAYS AND SHORT STORIES DIFFER?

An *essay* is a short literary commentary that focuses on a single idea. Usually, the author's opinion is present, perhaps as an evaluation or as an interpretation of an event or action and its consequences. An essay of argument may question one viewpoint and offer another. Essays tend to be direct with the thesis clearly stated, although irony may be present. Essays are organized in various ways, depending on the purpose and the topic.

A *short story*, however, is a fictitious narrative constricted by time. For example, Kate Chopin's story occurs in just one hour. Other short stories may span a day, a few days, or a few weeks. A good short story is compressed: every detail has a reason for being. To fully appreciate a work, the reader must interpret clues and ferret out the theme, the meaning that underlies the plot.

HOW DO THE WRITER'S PURPOSE
AND INTENT DIFFER?

The writer's purpose is usually *stated* in essays. You can find the purpose in the thesis statement, if there is one. A good thesis statement makes it clear whether the piece is to inform, entertain, define, or persuade. Often there are dual purposes, although just one may be stated. When the purpose is stated, then it is possible to evaluate whether or not the writer has achieved that purpose. In fiction the writer's purpose is rarely stated in the work itself, although some writers comment about the work elsewhere.

Even though a writer may state a purpose, we can seldom know what the writer really intended, for he or she may be reluctant to share the actual intent. Or *the result may be different from what the writer intended.* In *The Writer* (Nov. 1937), Wallace Stegner explains:

> I have found writing to be the most amazingly unpredictable exercise man can engage in. Characters are forever developing sinister neurotic tendencies under one's hands. Originally planned minor incidents expand and lengthen until they swallow up what was designed as the main action. Finished stories have a habit of meaning something different from, and frequently better than, the meaning one intended.

SECOND GUESSING

Sound critical reading does not second-guess an author's intent. As Stegner explains, writing may be richer and deeper than the writer had planned. Nor is it unusual for authors to admit they were unaware of certain symbols or themes in their works until someone else pointed them out. Therefore, all we can logically evaluate is the result—what a writer has achieved, *not what we think might have been intended.*

The more experience you gain, the more details you will notice as you read. Perhaps the best advice is to read quickly for enjoyment the first time. Then go back, reread, and ponder the piece. The better you understand the effect of a work, the more you will enjoy and appreciate its artistry.

Narrating Memorable Events

SOUND AND FURY

DAN GREENBURG

A sense of humor percolates through most of Dan Greenburg's novels, plays, magazine articles, and children's books. He has written for the *New Yorker, Esquire, Ms., Time, Newsweek, Life, New York, Cosmopolitan, Playboy, New York Times Book Review,* and *Vanity Fair.* His books for adults include *How to Be a Jewish Mother* (1993), *How to Avoid Love and Marriage* (1985), *How to Make Yourself Miserable* (1976), and others. Inspired by his young son, Greenburg has written over three dozen children's books with such intriguing titles as *Never Trust a Cat Who Wears Earrings* (1997) and *It's Itchcraft* (2003). In this essay he describes an incendiary incident that was deflected with adroit words.

1   We carry around a lot of free-floating anger. What we do with it is what fascinates me.

My friend Lee Frank is a stand-up comedian who works regularly in New York comedy clubs. Not long ago I accompanied him to one of these places, where he was to be the late-night emcee and where I myself had once done a stand-up act in a gentler era.

The crowd that night was a typical weekend bunch—enthusiastic, hostile and drunk. A large contingent of inebriated young men from Long Island had decided that a comedian named Rusty who was currently on stage was the greatest thing since pop-top cans and began chanting his name after almost everything he said: "Rus-TEE! Rus-TEE!"

My friend Lee knew he had a tough act to follow.

5   Indeed, the moment Lee walked on stage, the inebriated young men from Long Island began chanting "Rus-TEE! Rus-TEE!" and didn't give him a chance. Poor Lee, the flop sweat running into his eyes, tried every trick he knew to win them over, and finally gave up.

When he left the stage I joined him at the bar in the back of the club to commiserate.

"You did the best you could," I told him.

"I don't know," he said, "I could have handled it better."

"How?"

"I don't know," he said.   10

As we spoke, the young men who'd given him such a tough time trickled into the bar area. One of them spotted Lee and observed to a companion that Lee might want to do something about their heckling.

Lee thought he heard the companion reply, "I'm down," a casual acknowledgment that he was willing to have a fistfight. Lee repeated their remarks to me and indicated that he, too, was "down."

Though slight of frame, Lee is a black belt in Tae Kwon Do, has had skirmishes with three-card monte con men in Times Square, and once even captured a robber-rapist. I am also slight of frame but have had no training in martial arts. I did have one fistfight in my adult life (with a movie producer), but as Lee's best friend, I assumed that I was "down" as well.

Considering that there were more than a dozen of them and only two of us, the period of time that might elapse between our being "down" and our being down seemed exceedingly brief.

The young man who'd made the remark drifted toward Lee.   15

The eyes of everyone in the bar shifted slightly and locked onto the two men like heat-seeking missiles. Fight-or-flight adrenaline and testosterone spurted into dozens of male cardiovascular systems. Safeties snapped off figurative weapons. Red warning lights lit up dozens of DEFCON systems; warheads were armed and aimed. In a moment this bar area might very well resemble a saloon in a B grade western.

"How ya doing?" said Lee, his voice flat as unleavened bread, trying to make up his mind whether to be friendly or hostile.

"Okay," said the guy, a pleasant-looking, clean-cut kid in his mid-20s.

I was fascinated by what was going on between the two of them, each feeling the other out in a neutral, unemotional, slightly bemused manner. I saw no hostility here, no xenophobic loathing, just two young males jockeying for position, going through the motions, doing the dance, willing to engage at the slightest provocation. I had seen my cat do this many times when a stranger strayed onto his turf.

And then I had a sudden flash of clarity: These guys could either rip   20
each other's heads off now or they could share a beer, and both options would be equally acceptable to them.

I'd felt close to critical mass on many occasions myself. But here, feeling outside the action, I could see clearly that it had to do with the enormous reservoir of rage that we men carry around with us, rage that seethes just under the surface and is ready to be tapped in an instant, with or without just provocation.

"What're you in town for?" asked Lee casually.

The guy was watching Lee carefully, making minuscule adjustments on his sensing and triggering equipment.

"It's my birthday," said the guy.

25   Lee mulled over this information for a moment, still considering all his options. Then he made his decision.

"Happy birthday," said Lee finally, sticking out his hand.

The guy studied Lee's hand a moment. Then, deciding the gesture was sincere, he took the hand and shook it.

"Thanks," he said, and walked back to his buddies.

REFLECTING AND INTERPRETING

1. What do you notice about Greenburg's opening?

2. In narratives, we speak of "rising action" and "falling action." When does the action start to rise?

3. Note the change in structure and tone in paragraph 13. How does it differ from paragraphs 3 to 12?

4. How does the narrator think the fistfight will turn out? How long does he think it will last? Why?

5. What do you notice about paragraphs 18 and 19? Why are they significant?

6. Describe the emotions that hover beneath the surface of the conversation. How does the narrator explain them?

7. At what point does the action start to fall? Why?

8. How important are nonverbal signals in this episode? Why?

9. Which sentence serves as a transition to leap from this one episode to a universal statement about humankind?

10. Examine Greenburg's title. Do you think it appropriately reflects the point of the story? Why or why not?

A WRITER'S RESPONSE

1. Have you or any of your friends been the unwitting victim of such a hostile confrontation? If so, describe it.

2. Have you ever been able to turn a difficult situation to your advantage by using calming words and friendly signals? If so, how did you do it?

MOMMA'S ENCOUNTER   MAYA ANGELOU

This African-American poet, editor, essayist, songwriter, actress, and television producer speaks five languages. Born Marguerite Johnson in 1928, she lived most of her childhood with her grandmother, who ran a store in Stamps, Arkansas. Although she dropped out of school at age sixteen and got a job, she graduated from Mission High School in 1945. Later, while performing at a San Francisco night club, she chose the name of Maya Angelou. From 1961 to 1965 she lived in Africa, where she worked at the University of Ghana for a time. Later she wrote for the *African Review*, the *Ghanaian Times*, and the Ghanaian Broadcasting Company. Her five autobiographies describe her varied experiences. Her volumes of poetry include *Just Give Me a Cool Drink of Water 'Fore I Die'* (1971) and *And Still I Rise* (1978). In 1993 she delivered her poem "On the Pulse of Morning" at the inauguration of President William Clinton. The essay below is taken from *I Know Why the Caged Bird Sings* (1970).

"Thou shall not be dirty" and "Thou shall not be impudent" were the two commandments of Grandmother Henderson upon which hung our total salvation.

Each night in the bitterest winter we were forced to wash faces, arms, necks, legs and feet before going to bed. She used to add, with a smirk that unprofane people can't control when venturing into profanity, "and wash as far as possible, then wash possible."

We would go to the well and wash in the ice-cold, clear water, grease our legs with the equally cold stiff Vaseline, then tiptoe into the house. We wiped the dust from our toes and settled down for schoolwork, cornbread, clabbered milk, prayers and bed, always in that order. Momma was famous for pulling the quilts off after we had fallen asleep to examine our feet. If they weren't clean enough for her, she took the switch (she kept one behind the bedroom door for emergencies) and woke up the offender with a few aptly placed burning reminders.

The area around the well at night was dark and slick, and boys told about how snakes love water, so that anyone who had to draw water at night and then stand there alone and wash knew that moccasins and rattlers, puff adders and boa constrictors were winding their way to the well and would arrive just as the person washing got soap in her eyes. But Momma convinced us that not only was cleanliness next to Godliness, dirtiness was the inventor of misery.

The impudent child was detested by God and a shame to its parents and could bring destruction to its house and line. All adults had to be addressed as Mister, Missus, Miss, Auntie, Cousin, Unk, Uncle, Buhbah, Sister, Brother and a thousand other appellations indicating familial relationship and the lowliness of the addressor.

Everyone I knew respected these customary laws, except for the powhitetrash children.

Some families of powhitetrash lived on Momma's farm land behind the school. Sometimes a gaggle of them came to the Store, filling the whole room, chasing out the air and even changing the well-known scents. The children crawled over the shelves and into the potato and onion bins, twanging all the time in their sharp voices like cigarbox guitars. They took liberties in my Store that I would never dare. Since Momma told us that the less you say to whitefolks (or even powhitetrash) the better, Bailey and I would stand, solemn, quiet, in the displaced air. But if one of the playful apparitions got close to us, I pinched it. Partly out of angry frustration and partly because I didn't believe in its flesh reality.

They called my uncle by his first name and ordered him around the Store. He, to my crying shame, obeyed them in his limping dip-straight-dip fashion.

My grandmother, too followed their orders, except that she didn't seem to be servile because she anticipated their needs.

10 "Here's sugar, Miz Potter, and here's baking powder. You didn't buy soda last month, you'll probably be needing some."

Momma always directed her statements to the adults, but sometimes, Oh painful sometimes, the grimy, snotty-nosed girls would answer her.

"Naw, Annie . . ."—to Momma? Who owned the land they lived on? Who forgot more than they would ever learn? If there was any justice in the world, God should strike them dumb at once!—"Just give us some extry sody crackers, and some more mackerel."

At least they never looked in her face, or I never caught them doing so. Nobody with a smidgen of training, not even the worst roustabout, would look right in a grown person's face. It meant the person was trying to take the words out before they were formed. The dirty little children didn't do that, but they threw their orders around the Store like lashes from a cat-o'-nine tails.

When I was around ten years old, those scruffy children caused me the most painful and confusing experience I had ever had with my grandmother.

15 One summer morning, after I had swept the dirt yard of leaves, spearmintgum wrappers and Vienna-sausage labels, I raked the yellow-red dirt, and made half-moons carefully, so that the design stood out clearly and mask-like. I put the rake behind the Store and came through the back of the house to find Grandmother on the front porch in her big, wide white apron. The apron was so stiff by virtue of the starch that it could have stood alone. Momma was admiring the yard, so I joined her. It truly looked like a flat red-head that had been raked with a big-toothed comb. Momma didn't say anything but I knew she liked it. She looked over toward the school principal's house and to the right at Mr. McElroy's. She was hoping one of those community pillars would see the design before the day's business wiped it out. Then she looked upward to the school. My head had swung with hers, so at just about the same time we saw a troop of the powhitetrash kids marching over the hill and down by the side of the school.

I looked to Momma for direction. She did an excellent job of sagging from her waist down, but from the waist up she seemed to be pulling for the top of the oak tree across the road. Then she began to moan a hymn. Maybe not to moan, but the tune was so slow and the meter so strange that she could have been moaning. She didn't look at me again. When the children reached halfway down the hill, halfway to the Store, she said without turning, "Sister, go on inside."

I wanted to beg her, "Momma, don't wait for them. Come on inside with me. If they come in the Store, you go to the bedroom and let me wait on them. They only frighten me if you're around. Alone I know how to handle them." But of course I couldn't say anything, so I went in and stood behind the screen door.

Before the girls got to the porch I heard their laughter crackling and popping like pine logs in a cooking stove. I suppose my lifelong paranoia was born in those cold, molasses-slow minutes. They came finally to stand on the ground in front of Momma. At first they pretended seriousness. Then one of them wrapped her right arm in the crook of her left, pushed out her mouth and started to hum. I realized that she was aping my grandmother. Another said, "Naw, Helen, you ain't standing like her. This here's it." Then she lifted her chest, folded her arms and mocked that strange carriage that was Annie Henderson. Another laughed, "Naw, you can't do it. You mouth ain't pooched out enough. It's like this."

I thought about the rifle behind the door, but I knew I'd never be able to hold it straight, and the .410, our sawed-off shotgun, which stayed loaded and was fired every New Year's night, was locked in the trunk and Uncle Willie had the key on his chain. Through the fly-specked screen-door, I could see that the arms of Momma's apron jiggled from the vibrations of her humming. But her knees seemed to have locked as if they would never bend again.

She sang on. No louder than before, but no softer either. No slower or 20 faster.

The dirt of the girls' cotton dresses continued on their legs, feet, arms and faces to make them all of a piece. Their greasy uncolored hair hung down, uncombed, with a grim finality. I knelt to see them better, to remember them for all time. The tears that had slipped down my dress left unsurprising dark spots, and made the front yard blurry and even more unreal. The world had taken a deep breath and was having doubts about continuing to revolve.

The girls had tired of mocking Momma and turned to other means of agitation. One crossed her eyes, stuck her thumbs in both sides of her mouth and said, "Look here, Annie." Grandmother hummed on and the apron strings trembled. I wanted to throw a handful of black pepper in their faces, to throw lye on them, to scream that they were dirty, scummy peckerwoods, but I knew I was as clearly imprisoned behind the scene as the actors outside were confined to their roles.

One of the smaller girls did a kind of puppet dance while her fellow clowns laughed at her. But the tall one, who was almost a woman, said something very quietly, which I couldn't hear. They all moved backward from the porch, still watching Momma. For an awful second I thought they were going to throw a rock at Momma, who seemed (except for the apron strings) to have turned into stone herself. But the big girl turned her back, bent down and put her hands flat on the ground—she didn't pick up anything. She simply shifted her weight and did a hand stand.

Her dirty bare feet and long legs went straight for the sky. Her dress fell down around her shoulders, and she had on no drawers. The slick pubic hair made a brown triangle where her legs came together. She hung in the vacuum of that lifeless morning for only a few seconds, then wavered and tumbled. The other girls clapped her on the back and slapped their hands.

25   Momma changed her song to "Bread of Heaven, bread of Heaven, feed me till I want no more."

I found that I was praying too. How long could Momma hold out? What new indignity would they think of to subject her to? Would I be able to stay out of it? What would Momma really like me to do?

Then they were moving out of the yard, on their way to town. They bobbed their heads and shook their slack behinds and turned, one at a time:

"Bye, Annie."

"Bye, Annie."

30   "Bye, Annie."

Momma never turned her head or unfolded her arms, but she stopped singing and said, " 'Bye, Miz Helen, 'bye, Miz Ruth, 'bye, Miz Eloise."

I burst. A firecracker July-the-Fourth burst. How could Momma call them Miz? The mean nasty things. Why couldn't she have come inside the sweet, cool store when we saw them breasting the hill? What did she prove? And then if they were dirty, mean and impudent, why did Momma have to call them Miz?

She stood another whole song through and then opened the screen door to look down on me crying in rage. She looked until I looked up. Her face was a brown moon that shone on me. She was beautiful. Something had happened out there, which I couldn't completely understand, but I could see that she was happy. Then she bent down and touched me as mothers of the church "lay hands on the sick and afflicted" and I quieted.

"Go wash your face, Sister." And she went behind the candy counter and hummed, "Glory, glory, hallelujah, when I lay my burden down."

35   I threw the well water on my face and used the weekday handkerchief to blow my nose. Whatever the contest had been out front, I knew Momma had won.

I took the rake back to the front yard. The smudged footprints were easy to erase. I worked for a long time on my new design and laid the rake behind the wash pot. When I came back in the Store, I took Momma's hand and we both walked outside to look at the pattern.

It was a large heart with lots of hearts growing smaller inside, and piercing from the outside rim to the smallest heart was an arrow. Momma said, "Sister, that's right pretty." Then she turned back to the Store and resumed, "Glory, glory, hallelujah, when I lay my burden down."

REFLECTING AND INTERPRETING

1. What impression of Grandmother Henderson do you gain from the first sentence?

2. How does Maya's rearing differ from that of the "powhitetrash" children?

3. What clue in paragraph 16 reveals that Momma senses what is to come?

4. What do you learn about Maya in paragraph 17? Why can't she say anything?

5. What is the significance of the dialogue in paragraphs 28–31?

6. When does the action start to rise? Where does the climax occur?

7. How does Momma feel after the encounter? What nonverbal signals reveal her emotions?

8. What effect does the first-person point of view, rather than third person, have upon the narrative?

9. How might the final design in the yard be interpreted?

10. How would you state the point of or lesson to be gained from this narrative?

A WRITER'S RESPONSE

Compare and contrast "Momma's Encounter" with "Sound and Fury." How do they differ in tone? In the resolution of the problem?

THE ART OF ACKNOWLEDGEMENT   JEAN HOUSTON

Life is like a roller coaster that can take us from the depths of despair to the apex of joy— if we can just hang on. Clinging precariously, some hardy souls survive alone; others derive strength from the support of a family member, friend, or teacher. In this excerpt from *The Possible Human* (1982), Jean Houston, social scientist, describes the visiting professor who enabled her to surmount a devastating experience during her college years. This tale reminds us that we all have the ability to give a priceless gift to help others. Houston is the author of *A Mythic Life* (1996), *The Search for the Beloved* (1997), *The Passion of ISIS and OSIRIS* (1998), *A Passion for the Possible* (1998), *Jump Time* (2000), and *Mystical Dogs: Animals as Guides to Our Inner Life* (2005). Houston is the coauthor of numerous books and other publications.

I was eighteen years old and I was the golden girl. A junior in college, 1 I was president of the college drama society, a member of the student senate, winner of two off-Broadway critics' awards for acting and directing, director of the class play, and had just turned down an offer to train for the next Olympics (fencing). In class my mind raced and dazzled, spinning off facile but "wowing" analogies to the kudos of teachers and classmates. Socially, I was on top of the heap. My advice was sought, my phone rang constantly, and it seemed that nothing could stop me.

I was the envy of all my friends and I was in a state of galloping chutzpah.

The old Greek tragedies warn us that when hubris rises, nemesis falls. I was no exception to this ancient rule. My universe crashed with great suddenness. It began when three members of my immediate family died. Then a friend whom I loved very much died suddenly of a burst appendix while camping alone in the woods. The scenery of the off-Broadway production fell on my head and I was left almost blind for the next four months. My friends and I parted from each other, they out of embarrassment and I because I didn't think I was worthy. My marks went from being rather good to a D-plus average.

I had so lost confidence in my abilities that I couldn't concentrate on anything or see the connections between things. My memory was a shambles, and within a few months I was placed on probation. All my offices were taken away; public elections were called to fill them. I was asked into the advisor's office and told that I would have to leave the college at the end of the spring term since, clearly, I didn't have the "necessary intelligence to do academic work." When I protested that I had had the "necessary intelligence" during my freshman and sophomore years, I was assured with a sympathetic smile that intellectual decline such as this often happened to young women when "they became interested in other things; it's a matter of hormones, my dear."

5   Where once I had been vocal and high-spirited in the classroom, I now huddled in my oversized camel's-hair coat in the back of classes, trying to be as nonexistent as possible. At lunch I would lock myself in the green room of the college theater, scene of my former triumphs, eating a sandwich in despondent isolation. Every day brought its defeat and disacknowledgments, and after my previous career I was too proud to ask for help. I felt like Job and called out to God, "Where are the boils?" since that was about all I was missing.

These Jobian fulminations led me to take one last course. It was taught by a young Swiss professor of religion, Dr. Jacob Taubes, and was supposed to be a study of selected books of the Old Testament. It turned out to be largely a discussion of the dialectic between St. Paul and Nietzsche.

Taubes was the most brilliant and exciting teacher I had ever experienced, displaying European academic wizardry such as I had never known. Hegel, gnosticism, structuralism, phenomenology, and the intellectual passions of the Sorbonne cracked the ice of my self-noughting and I began to raise a tentative hand from my huddle in the back of the room and ask an occasional hesitant question.

Dr. Taubes would answer with great intensity, and soon I found myself asking more questions. One day I was making my way across campus to the bus, when I heard Dr. Taubes addressing me:

"Miss Houston, let me walk with you. You know, you have a most interesting mind."

10   "Me? I have a *mind?*"

"Yes, your questions are luminous. Now what do you think is the nature of the transvaluation of values in Paul and Nietzsche?"

I felt my mind fall into its usual painful dullness and stammered, "I d-don't know."

"Of course you do!" he insisted. "You couldn't ask the kinds of questions you do without having an unusual grasp of these issues. Now please, once again, what do you think of the transvaluation of values in Paul and Nietzsche? It is important for my reflections that I have your reactions."

"Well," I said, waking up, "if you put it that way, I think . . ."

I was off and running and haven't shut up since.   15

Dr. Taubes continued to walk me to the bus throughout that term, always challenging me with intellectually vigorous questions. He attended to me. I existed for him in the "realest" of senses, and because I existed for him I began to exist for myself. Within several weeks my eyesight came back, my spirit bloomed, and I became a fairly serious student, whereas before I had been, at best, a bright show-off.

What I acquired from this whole experience was a tragic sense of life, which balanced my previous enthusiasms. I remain deeply grateful for the attention shown me by Dr. Taubes. He acknowledged me when I most needed it. I was empowered in the midst of personal erosion, and my life has been very different for it. I swore to myself then that whenever I came across someone "going under" or in the throes of disacknowledgment, I would try to reach and acknowledge that person as I had been acknowledged.

I would go so far as to say that the greatest of human potentials is the potential of each one of us to empower and acknowledge the other. We all do this throughout our lives, but rarely do we appreciate the power of the empowering that we give to others. To be acknowledged by another, especially during times of confusion, loss, disorientation, disheartenment, is to be given time and place in the sunshine and is, in the metaphor of psychological reality, the solar stimulus for transformation.

The process of healing and growth is immensely quickened when the sun of another's belief is freely given. This gift can be as simple as "Hot Dog Thou Art!" Or it can be as total as "I know you. You are God in hiding." Or it can be a look that goes straight to the soul and charges it with meaning.

I have been fortunate to have known several of those the world deems   20 "saints": Teilhard de Chardin, Mother Teresa of Calcutta, Clemie, an old black woman in Mississippi. To be looked at by these people is to be gifted with the look that engenders. You feel yourself primed at the depths by such seeing. Something so tremendous and yet so subtle wakes up inside that you are able to release the defeats and denigrations of years. If I were to describe it further, I would have to speak of unconditional love joined to a whimsical regarding of you as the cluttered house that hides the holy one.

Saints, you say, but the miracle is that anybody can do it for anybody! Our greatest genius may be the ability to prime the healing and evolutionary circuits of one another.

It is an art form that has yet to be learned, for it is based on something never before fully recognized—deep psychological reciprocity, the art and science of mutual transformation. And all the gurus and masters, all the prophets, profs, and professionals, can do little for us compared to what we could do for each other if we would but be present to the fullness of each other. For there is no answer to anyone's anguished cry of "Why am I here, why am I at all?" except the reply, "Because I am here, because I am."

REFLECTING AND INTERPRETING

1. Notice the title. *Acknowledgement* is not commonly used in this way. What word would you use instead?

2. In the second paragraph, Houston says she was in a state of "galloping chutzpah." What does she mean?

3. Houston says, "I felt like Job and called out to God, 'Where are the boils?'" (See Job 2:1–10.) What do Houston's comparison and question reveal?

4. In the third paragraph, there is a sudden change in tone. What does Houston mean when she refers to hubris? Does this passage remind you of an old saying? (See Proverbs 16:18.) How does this proverb apply to Houston?

5. What do you think she means when she says, "I existed for him in the 'realest' of senses, and because I existed for him I began to exist for myself"? How does Dr. Taubes's attention affect Houston?

6. Houston says, "I acquired . . . a tragic sense of life, which balanced my previous enthusiasms" (paragraph 17). Can you explain this idea in your own words?

7. How would you describe Houston's attitude as she looks back on this troubling experience? Does she retain a sense of humor? Find examples to support your claim.

8. Notice Houston's alternating of colloquialisms with literary allusions. For example, what is the effect of "wowing" and "on top of the heap" in one paragraph and "hubris" and "nemesis" in another?

9. Note how she contrasts the "before and after" at several points. What is the effect of these contrasts as opposed to a simple chronological narrative?

10. Comment on Houston's last statement, which seems puzzling and somewhat contradictory to the ideas expressed in the essay.

A WRITER'S RESPONSE

Have you ever undergone a distressing experience and been helped by someone? Or perhaps you have been able to "prime the healing and evolutionary circuits" of someone. Describe what happened in an essay.

HOW TO GET OUT OF A LOCKED TRUNK | PHILIP WEISS

Metaphor plays a prominent role in this essay. By the end, the astute reader knows there is a deeper meaning to the experience than what is apparent. Weiss blends humor, suspense, and romance while explaining a process (in fact, several versions of it). In this clever piece, originally published in *Harper's* magazine and later in *The Best American Essays* (1993), Weiss begins with an investigation of one process of escape and uses it to reflect on another. He has written for *The New York Times Magazine*, *The New York Observer*, *Jewish World Review*, and other publications. Weiss is the author of *Religion & Art* (1964), *Modes of Being* (1968), *Art Deco Environment* (1976), *Cock-A-Doodle-Doo* (1995), and *American Taboo: A Murder in the Peace Corps* (2005).

On a hot Sunday last summer my friend Tony and I drove my rental car, 1 a '91 Buick, from St. Paul to the small town of Waconia, Minnesota, forty miles southwest. We each had a project. Waconia is Tony's boyhood home, and his sister had recently given him a panoramic postcard of Lake Waconia as seen from a high point in the town early in the century. He wanted to duplicate the photograph's vantage point, then hang the two pictures together in his house in Frogtown. I was hoping to see Tony's father, Emmett, a retired mechanic, in order to settle a question that had been nagging me: Is it possible to get out of a locked car trunk?

We tried to call ahead to Emmett twice, but he wasn't home. Tony thought he was probably golfing but that there was a good chance he'd be back by the time we got there. So we set out.

I parked the Buick, which was a silver sedan with a red interior, by the graveyard near where Tony thought the picture had been taken. He took his picture and I wandered among the headstones, reading the epitaphs. One of them was chillingly anti-individualist. It said, "Not to do my will, but thine."

Trunk lockings had been on my mind for a few weeks. It seemed to me that the fear of being locked in a car trunk had a particular hold on the American imagination. Trunk lockings occur in many movies and books— from *Goodfellas* to *Thelma and Louise* to *Humboldt's Gift*. And while the highbrow national newspapers generally shy away from trunk lockings, the attention they receive in local papers suggests a widespread anxiety surrounding the subject. In an afternoon at the New York Public Library I found numerous stories about trunk lockings. A Los Angeles man is discovered, bloodshot, banging the trunk of his white Eldorado following a night and a day trapped inside; he says his captors went on joyrides and picked up women. A forty-eight-year-old Houston doctor is forced into her trunk at a bank ATM and then the car is abandoned, parked near the Astrodome. A New Orleans woman tells police she gave birth in a trunk while being abducted to Texas. Tests undermine her story, the police drop the investigation. But so what if it's a fantasy? That only shows the idea's hold on us.

Every culture comes up with tests of a person's ability to get out of a 5 sticky situation. The English plant mazes. Tropical resorts market those straw finger-grabbers that tighten their grip the harder you pull on them, and Viennese intellectuals gave us the concept of childhood sexuality— figure it out, or remain neurotic for life.

At least you could puzzle your way out of those predicaments. When they slam the trunk, though, you're helpless unless someone finds you.

You would think that such a common worry should have a ready fix, and that the secret of getting out of a locked trunk is something we should all know about.

I phoned experts but they were very discouraging.

"You cannot get out. If you got a pair of pliers and bat's eyes, yes. But you have to have a lot of knowledge of the lock," said James Foote at Automotive Locksmiths in New York City.

Jim Frens, whom I reached at the technical section of *Car and Driver* in Detroit, told me the magazine had not dealt with this question. But he echoed the opinion of experts elsewhere when he said that the best hope for escape would be to try and kick out the panel between the trunk and the backseat. That angle didn't seem worth pursuing. What if your enemies were in the car, crumpling beer cans and laughing at your fate? It didn't make sense to join them.

10   The people who deal with rules on auto design were uncomfortable with my scenarios. Debra Barclay of the Center for Auto Safety, an organization founded by Ralph Nader, had certainly heard of cases, but she was not aware of any regulations on the matter. "Now, if there was a defect involved—" she said, her voice trailing off, implying that trunk locking was all phobia. This must be one of the few issues on which she and the auto industry agree. Ann Carlson of the Motor Vehicle Manufacturing Association became alarmed at the thought that I was going to play up a non-problem: "In reality this very rarely happens. As you say, in the movies it's a wonderful plot device," she said. "But in reality apparently this is not that frequent an occurrence. So they have not designed that feature into vehicles in a specific way."

When we got to Emmett's one-story house it was full of people. Tony's sister, Carol, was on the floor with her two small children. Her husband, Charlie, had one eye on the golf tournament on TV, and Emmett was at the kitchen counter, trimming fat from meat for lunch. I have known Emmett for fifteen years. He looked better than ever. In his retirement he had sharply changed his diet and lost a lot of weight. He had on shorts. His legs were tanned and muscular. As always, his manner was humorous, if opaque.

Tony told his family my news: I was getting married in three weeks. Charlie wanted to know where my fiancée was. Back East, getting everything ready. A big-time hatter was fitting her for a new hat.

Emmett sat on the couch, watching me. "Do you want my advice?"

"Sure."

15   He just grinned. A gold tooth glinted. Carol and Charlie pressed him to yield his wisdom.

Finally he said, "Once you get to be thirty, you make your own mistakes."

He got out several cans of beer, and then I brought up what was on my mind.

Emmett nodded and took off his glasses, then cleaned them and put them back on.

We went out to his car, a Mercury Grand Marquis, and Emmett opened the trunk. His golf clubs were sitting on top of the spare tire in a green golf bag. Next to them was a toolbox and what he called his "burglar tools," a set of elbowed rods with red plastic handles he used to open door locks when people locked their keys inside.

Tony and Charlie stood watching. Charlie is a banker in Minneapolis. He enjoys gizmos and is extremely practical. I would describe him as un-flappable. That's a word I always wanted to apply to myself, but my fian-cée had recently informed me that I am high-strung. Though that surprised me, I didn't quarrel with her.

For a while we studied the latch assembly. The lock closed in much the same way that a lobster might clamp on to a pencil. The claw portion, the jaws of the lock, was mounted inside the trunk lid. When you shut the lid, the jaws locked on to the bend of a U-shaped piece of metal mounted on the body of the car. Emmett said my best bet would be to unscrew the bolts. That way the U-shaped piece would come loose and the lock's jaws would swing up with it still in their grasp.

"But you'd need a wrench," he said.

It was already getting too technical. Emmett had an air of endless pa-tience, but I felt defeated. I could only imagine bloodied fingers, cracked teeth. I had hoped for a simple trick.

Charlie stepped forward. He reached out and squeezed the lock's jaw. They clicked shut in the air, bound together by heavy springs. Charlie now prodded the upper part of the left-hand jaw, the thicker part. With a rough flick of his thumb, he was able to force the jaws to snap open. Great.

Unfortunately, the jaws were mounted behind a steel plate the size of your palm in such a way that while they were accessible to us, standing outside the car, had we been inside the trunk the plate would be in our way, blocking the jaws.

This time Emmett saw the way out. He fingered a hole in the plate. It was no bigger than the tip of your little finger. But the hole was close enough to the latch itself that it might be possible to angle something through the hole from inside the trunk and nudge the jaws apart. We tried with one of my keys. The lock jumped open.

It was time for a full-dress test. Emmett swung the clubs out of the trunk, and I set my can of Schmidt's on the rear bumper and climbed in. Everyone gathered around, and Emmett lowered the trunk on me, then pressed it shut with his meaty hands. Total darkness. I couldn't hear the people outside. I thought I was going to panic. But the big trunk felt com-fortable. I was pressed against a sort of black carpet that softened the angles against my back.

I could almost stretch out in the trunk, and it seemed to me I could make them sweat if I took my time. Even Emmett, that sphinx, would give way to curiosity. Once I was out he'd ask how it had been and I'd just grin. There were some things you could only learn by doing.

It took a while to find the hole. I slipped the key in and angled it to one side. The trunk gasped open.

30   Emmett motioned the others away, then levered me out with his big right forearm. Though I'd only been inside for a minute, I was disoriented—as much as anything because someone had moved my beer while I was gone, setting it down on the cement floor of the garage. It was just a little thing, but I could not be entirely sure I had gotten my own beer back.

Charlie was now raring to try other cars. We examined the latch on his Toyota, which was entirely shielded to the trunk occupant (i.e., no hole in the plate), and on the neighbor's Honda (ditto). But a 1991 Dodge Dynasty was doable. The trunk was tight, but its lock had a feature one of the mechanics I'd phoned described as a "tailpiece": a finger-like extension of the lock mechanism itself that stuck out a half inch into the trunk cavity: simply by twisting the tailpiece I could free the lock. I was even faster on a 1984 Subaru that had a little lever device on the latch.

We went out to my rental on Oak Street. The Skylark was in direct sun and the trunk was hot to the touch, but when we got it open we could see that its latch plate had a perfect hole, a square in which the edge of the lock's jaw appeared like a face in a window.

The trunk was shallow and hot. Emmett had to push my knees down before he could close the lid. This one was a little suffocating. I imagined being trapped for hours, and even before he had got it closed I regretted the decision with a slightly nauseous feeling. I thought of Edgar Allan Poe's live burials, and then about something my fiancée had said more than a year and a half before. I had been on her case to get married. She was divorced, and at every opportunity I would reissue my proposal—even during a commercial. She'd interrupted one of these chirps to tell me, in a cold, throaty voice, that she had no intention of ever going through another divorce: "This time, it's death out." I'd carried those words around like a lump of wet clay.

As it happened, the Skylark trunk was the easiest of all. The hole was right where it was supposed to be. The trunk popped open, and I felt great satisfaction that we'd been able to figure out a rule that seemed to apply about 60 percent of the time. If we publicized our success, it might get the attention it deserved. All trunks would be fitted with such a hole. Kids would learn about it in school. The grip of the fear would relax. Before long a successful trunk-locking scene would date a movie like a fedora dates one today.

35   When I got back East I was caught up in wedding preparations. I live in New York, and the wedding was to take place in Philadelphia. We set up camp there with five days to go. A friend had lent my fiancée her BMW, and we drove it south with all our things. I unloaded the car in my parents' driveway. The last thing I pulled out of the trunk was my fiancée's hat in its

heavy cardboard shipping box. She'd warned me I was not allowed to look. The lid was free but I didn't open it. I was willing to be surprised.

When the trunk was empty it occurred to me I might hop in and give it a try. First I looked over the mechanism. The jaws of the BMW's lock were shielded, but there seemed to be some kind of cable coming off it that you might be able to manipulate so as to cause the lock to open. The same cable that allowed the driver to open the trunk remotely . . .

I fingered it for a moment or two but decided I didn't need to test out the theory.

REFLECTING AND INTERPRETING

1. Where is the thesis statement located?

2. Do you see any foreshadowing? (Hint: Notice where he parks the Buick.)

3. In paragraph 5 there is a hint that the essay may be about more than finding a way out of a locked trunk. Where is the hint?

4. Can you see a link between the epitaph on the tombstone and Emmett's bit of wisdom? If so, what is it?

5. What qualities does the narrator see in Charlie and Emmett that he would like to develop?

6. Climbing out of the trunk, he was "disoriented . . . someone had moved my beer. . . ." What does this incident suggest about his personality?

7. Examine paragraph 34. What is the implication?

8. What does Weiss mean by "You would think such a common worry would have a ready fix . . . something we should all know about." What might it symbolize?

9. In Philadelphia, he decided he "didn't need to test out the theory" on the BMW his fiancée had borrowed. What are the implications of this decision?

10. By the end of the story, do you see any change in Weiss? If so, what?

A WRITER'S RESPONSE

1. Freewrite about physical states that mimic social or emotional entrapment.

2. *Small Groups:* The steps of the process are intermingled with a narrative. What are the six steps?

Describing Significant Impressions

SUE HUBBELL

Sue Hubbell is a naturalist, a commercial beekeeper, who lives in the Ozark Mountains. She is the author of numerous books, including *A Book of Bees* (1988), *On This Hilltop* (1991), *Far-Flung Hubbell: Essays from the American Road* (1997), *Waiting for Aphrodite* (2000), *Shrinking the Cat* (2001), and *From Here to There and Back Again* (2005). One day as Hubbell was walking down a dusty country road, she spied what appeared to be a snakeskin lying in the road. Curious, she bent down and saw, instead, a strange procession of maggoty-like caterpillars. "Caterpillar Afternoon," from *A Country Year* (1999), illustrates one way primary and secondary research can be combined.

1   A year ago, on an afternoon late in springtime, I was walking on the dirt road that cuts across the field to the beehives. I noticed a light-colored, brownish dappled something-or-other stretched across the roadway ahead of me, and decided that it was a snakeskin. I often find them, crumpled husks shed by snakes as they grow. They are fragile and delicate, perfect but empty replicas of the snakes that once inhabited them. I started to turn it over with the toe of my boot, but stopped suddenly, toe in air, for the flecked, crumpled-looking empty snakeskin was moving.

It gave me quite a start and I was amused at my own reaction, remembering that Ronald Firbank wrote somewhere that the essence of evil was the ordinary become unnatural, the stone in the garden path that suddenly begins to move.

I squatted down to see what queer thing I had here, and found that my supposed snake skin was a mass of maggoty-like caterpillars, each one no more than half an inch long. They were hairless, with creamy white smooth skin, black heads and brown stripes along their backs. They were piled thickly in the center, with fewer caterpillars at the head and rear end of the line, which was perhaps eighteen inches long. They moved slowly, each caterpillar in smooth synchrony with its fellows, so that a wave of motion undulated down the entire length of the line.

They seemed so intensely social that I wondered what they would do on their own. I gently picked up half a dozen or so, and isolated them a few inches from the column. Their smooth, easy movements changed to frantic, rapid ones, and they wriggled along the ground quickly until they rejoined the group. They certainly were good followers. How did they ever decide where to go? The single caterpillar in the lead twisted the forepart of his body from side to side as though taking his bearings; he appeared to be the only one in the lot capable of going in a new direction, of making a decision to avoid a tuft of grass here, of turning there. Was he some special, super-caterpillar? I removed him from the lead position and put him off to the side, where he became as frantic as had the others, wriggling to rejoin the group somewhere in the middle, where he was soon lost to view, having turned into just another follower. At the head, the next caterpillar in line had simply assumed leadership duties and was bending his body from side to side, making the decision about the direction the column was to take. I removed three leaders in a row with the same result: each time, the next caterpillar in line made an instant switch from loyal and will-less follower to leader.

What were they doing? Were they looking for food? If so, what kind? 5 What manner of creature were they? The beework that I had set out to do could wait no longer, so I went back to the hives. When I returned along the road, the caterpillars, if that is what they were, had disappeared.

Back in my cabin, none of the books on my shelves were much help explaining what I had seen, except one by Henri Fabre, the nineteenth-century French entomologist who had conducted one of his famous experiments with pine processionaries, one of the Thaumatopoeidae. Fabre's caterpillars were *Thaumatopoea processionea,* "the wonder maker that parades"; eventually they become rather undistinguished-looking moths.

The pine processionaries are a European species, but their behavior was similar to that of my caterpillars, although not identical. Pine processionaries travel to feed in single file, not massed and bunched, but they do touch head to rear and have only one leader at a time. Fabre found them so sheeplike that he wondered what they would do if he could somehow manage to make them leaderless. In a brilliant experiment, he arranged them on the upper rim of a large vase a yard and a half in circumference, and waited until the head end of the procession joined the tail end, so that the entire group was without a leader. All were followers. For seven days, the caterpillars paraded around the rim of the vase in a circle. Their pace slowed after a while, for they were weary and had not been able to feed, but they continued to circle, each caterpillar unquestioningly taking his direction from the rear of the one in front, until they dropped from exhaustion.

However, even Fabre never discovered what it was that could turn one caterpillar into a leader as soon as he was at the head of the line.

It was not until several months later, when I was talking to Asher, that I was able to find out anything about the caterpillars I had found in the roadway. He said that I probably had seen one species or another of sawfly larvae. They are gregarious, he told me, and some are whitish with brown stripes. Sure identification could only be made by counting the pairs of their prolegs, and of course I had not known enough to look at them that closely. Asher said that they were a rare sight and that I would probably never see them again, but if I did I should gather up a few and put them in a solution of 70 percent alcohol; then he would help me identify them. He had read about Fabre's experiment too, but knew nothing more about their behavior.

He added, "If you ever find out what makes processionary caterpillars prosesh, please enlighten me. Maybe it's the same thing that makes people drive in Sunday traffic or watch TV or vote Republican."

10   It is springtime again. I would like to count the caterpillars' prolegs and am prepared to pickle a few to satisfy my curiosity, but mostly I should just like to watch them again. This time I should let the beework go. I should like to know where these caterpillars go, and what it is they are looking for. I wonder if I could divide them up into several small columns that would move along independently, side by side. I have more questions about them than when I first saw them.

This spring I often walk along, eyes to the ground, looking for them. There may have been nobler quests—white whales and Holy Grails—and although the Ahabs and Percivals of my acquaintance are some of my most entertaining friends, I am cut of other stuff and amuse myself in other ways. The search for what may or may not be sawfly larvae seems quite a good one this springtime.

REFLECTING AND INTERPRETING

1. What two strategies of exposition does Hubbell use to explain her research?

2. Note the distinctive way that Hubbell describes the caterpillars. What device does she use in the third sentence?

3. What was unusual about the physical appearance of the caterpillars?

4. What spur-of-the-moment experiments did Hubbell conduct? How did the individual caterpillars react?

5. What paragraph presents the questions that Hubbell wants to research?

6. What transition shifts the reader to the next scene, where Hubbell continues her research?

7. How and when did Hubbell gain more specific information about the kind of caterpillars she had seen? By what name are they tagged?

8. What had Henri Fabre discovered in the nineteenth century about a similar caterpillar?

9. What experiment does Hubbell plan to do if she ever finds more of these strange caterpillars?

10. Do you see any similarities between the behavior of the caterpillars and some people? What kinds of events can cause people to suddenly become leaders?

A WRITER'S RESPONSE

1. Have you ever been thrust into a circumstance where you suddenly had to assume a leadership role? If so, write an essay describing your experience.

2. *Small Groups:* Have you ever seen something that appeared to be something else at first? What does this reveal about the process of perception? Can you list a few precautions to promote objectivity? (After the group is finished, turn to "Checklist: Maintaining Objectivity" on pages 521–22.)

ONE WRITER'S BEGINNINGS   EUDORA WELTY

Eudora Welty (1909–2001) published her first short story in 1936. After writing short fiction for ten years, she published a novel, *Delta Wedding*, in 1946. She has written twenty-six books, receiving a Pulitzer Prize in 1971. In 1980 she received the National Medal for Literature and the Presidential Medal of Freedom. In this excerpt from *One Writer's Beginnings* (1984), she explores the connection between reality and the imagination in an attempt to trace her origin as a writer.

I had the window seat. Beside me, my father checked the progress of 1
our train by moving his finger down the timetable and springing open his pocket watch. He explained to me what the position of the arms of the semaphore meant; before we were to pass through a switch we would watch the signal lights change. Along our track, the mileposts could be read; he read them. Right on time by Daddy's watch, the next town sprang into view, and just as quickly was gone.

Side by side and separately, we each lost ourselves in the experience of not missing anything, of seeing everything, of knowing each time what the blows of the whistle meant. But of course it was not the same experience: what was new to me, not older than ten, was a landmark to him. My father knew our way mile by mile; by day or by night, he knew where we were. Everything that changed under our eyes, in the flying countryside, was the known world to him, the imagination to me. Each in our own way, we hungered for all of this: my father and I were in no other respect or situation so congenial.

In Daddy's leather grip was his traveler's drinking cup, collapsible; a lid to fit over it had a ring to carry it by; it traveled in a round leather box. This treasure would be brought out at my request, for me to bear to the water cooler at the end of the Pullman car, fill to the brim, and bear back to my seat, to drink water over its smooth lip. The taste of silver could almost be relied on to shock your teeth.

After dinner in the sparkling dining car, my father and I walked back to the open-air observation platform at the end of the train and sat on the folding chairs placed at the railing. We watched the sparks we made fly behind us into the night. Fast as our speed was, it gave us time enough to see the rose-red cinders turn to ash, each one, and disappear from sight. Sometimes a house far back in the empty hills showed a light no bigger than a star. The sleeping countryside seemed itself to open a way through for our passage, then close again behind us.

5   The swaying porter would be making ready our berths for the night, pulling the shade down just so, drawing the green fishnet hammock across the window so the clothes you took off could ride along beside you, turning down the tight-made bed, standing up the two snowy pillows as high as they were wide, switching on the eye of the reading lamp, starting the tiny electric fan—you suddenly saw its blades turn into gauze and heard its insect murmur; and drawing across it all the pair of thick green theaterlike curtains—billowing, smelling of cigar smoke—between which you would crawl or dive headfirst to button them together with yourself inside, to be seen no more that night.

When you lay enclosed and enwrapped, your head on a pillow parallel to the track, the rhythm of the rail clicks pressed closer to your body as if it might be your heart beating, but the sound of the engine seemed to come from farther away than when it carried you in daylight. The whistle was almost too far away to be heard, its sound wavering back from the engine over the roofs of the cars. What you listened for was the different sound that ran under you when your own car crossed on a trestle, then another sound on an iron bridge; a low or a high bridge—each had its pitch, or drumbeat, for your car.

Riding in the sleeper rhythmically lulled me and waked me. From time to time, waked suddenly, I raised my window shade and looked out at my own strip of the night. Sometimes there was unexpected moonlight out there. Sometimes the perfect shadow of our train, with our car, with me invisibly included, ran deep below, crossing a river with us by the light of the moon. Sometimes the encroaching walls of mountains woke me by clapping at my ears. The tunnels made the train's passage resound like the "loud" pedal of a piano, a roar that seemed to last as long as a giant's temper tantrum.

But my father put it all into the frame of regularity, predictability, that was his fatherly gift in the course of our journey. I saw it going by, the outside world, in a flash. I dreamed over what I could see as it passed, as well as over what I couldn't. Part of the dream was what lay beyond, where the path wandered off through the pasture, the red clay road climbed and went over the hill or made a turn and was hidden in trees, or toward a river whose bridge I could see but whose name I'd never know. A house back at its distance at night showing a light from an open doorway, the morning faces of the children who stopped still in what they were doing, perhaps picking blackberries or wild plums, and watched us go by—I never saw with the thought of their continuing to be there just the same after we were out of sight. For now, and for a long while to come, I was proceeding in fantasy.

REFLECTING AND INTERPRETING

1. What do we learn about Welty and her father in the first and second paragraphs? Do they seem similar or different? How?

2. As Welty attempts to trace her origins as a writer, why does this train trip seem significant?

3. How do Welty's childhood dreams differ from the reality of the train?

4. The description of the porter making up the berths is filled with similes and metaphors. Which ones do you especially like?

5. Welty spends a paragraph describing the sounds of the engine, rails, whistle, and structures that vary the "pitch, or drumbeat, for your car." What device is used here? What do these details reveal about her, even as a child?

6. Note the alternating of images when she describes riding in the sleeper. How do these images and sounds reflect the rhythm of the train?

7. Is the essay written, for the most part, from the point of view of a ten-year-old or from an adult in retrospect? Where does a shift occur? What was "his fatherly gift"? Why does Welty seem to need that?

8. Images that connote safety and seclusion while experiencing the world from a distance appear throughout this essay. Which ones do you notice?

9. Welty was interested in photography. How is this excerpt of her writing like a series of photos?

10. What might the author mean at the end when she says, "For now, and for a long while to come, I was proceeding in fantasy"?

A WRITER'S RESPONSE

1. Describe a trip you took as a child that was memorable. Use vivid images and sensory language to recapture the experience and your feelings at the time.

2. Welty opens with "I had the window seat." Later she says, "I saw it going by, the outside world, in a flash." You might say we all have a window seat from which we view life as it flashes by. Select one vivid "flash" from your window on life to describe in an essay.

DAWN WATCH   JOHN CIARDI

A renowned poet, essayist, and translator, John Ciardi (1916–86) wrote over fifty books. He received the Prix de Rome of the American Academy of Arts and Letters, the Harriet Monroe Memorial Award, and the NCTE Award for Children's Poetry. He first published a book of poems entitled *Homeward to America* (1940). Two years later he enlisted in the Army Air Force and served with distinction as an aerial tail gunner during World War II. He taught at Harvard and Rutgers; spent twenty years as poetry editor for the *Saturday Review* magazine; wrote children's books, poetry textbooks, and others; and translated *The Divine Comedy* and other classic works. Some of his well-known works are *Mid-Century American Poets* (1950), *How Does a Poem Mean* (1959), *Selected Poems* (1984), *Saipan: The War Diary of John Ciardi* (1988), *The Birds of Pompeii* (1988), and *The Selected Letters of John Ciardi* (1991), some of which were published posthumously. In this essay from *Manner of Speaking* (1972), Ciardi praises a magical time of day.

1   Unless a man is up for the dawn and for the half hour or so of first light, he has missed the best of the day.

The traffic has just started, not yet a roar and a stink. One car at a time goes by, the tires humming almost like the sound of a brook a half mile down in the crease of a mountain I know—a sound that carries not because it is loud but because everything else is still.

It isn't exactly a mist that hangs in the thickets but more nearly the ghost of a mist—a phenomenon like side vision. Look hard and it isn't there, but glance without focusing and something registers, an exhalation that will be gone three minutes after the sun comes over the treetops.

The lawns shine with a dew not exactly dew. There is a rabbit bobbing about on the lawn and then freezing. If it were truly a dew, his tracks would shine black on the grass, and he leaves no visible track. Yet, there is something on the grass that makes it glow a depth of green it will not show again all day. Or is that something in the dawn air?

5   Our cardinals know what time it is. They drop pure tones from the hemlock tops. The gang of grackles that makes a slum of the pin oak also knows the time but can only grate at it. They sound like a convention of broken universal joints grating uphill. The grackles creak and squeak, and the cardinals form tones that only occasionally sound through the noise. I scatter sunflower seeds by the birdbaths for the cardinals and hope the grackles won't find them.

My neighbor's tomcat comes across the lawn, probably on his way home from passion, or only acting as if he had had a big night. I suspect him of being one of those poolroom braggarts who can't get next to a girl but who likes to let on that he is a hot stud. This one is too can-fed and too lazy to hunt for anything. Here he comes now, ignoring the rabbit. And there he goes.

As soon as he has hopped the fence, I let my dog out. The dog charges the rabbit, watches it jump the fence, shakes himself in a self-satisfied way, then trots dutifully into the thicket for his morning service, stopping to sniff everything on the way back.

There is an old mountain laurel on the island of the driveway turnaround. From somewhere on the wind a white morning-glory rooted next to it and has climbed it. Now the laurel is woven full of white bells tinged pink by the first rays through the not quite mist. Only in earliest morning can they be seen. Come out two hours from now and there will be no morning-glories.

Dawn, too, is the hour of a weed I know only as day flower—a bright blue button that closes in full sunlight. I have weeded bales of it out of my flower beds, its one daytime virtue being the shallowness of its root system that allows it to be pulled out effortlessly in great handfuls. Yet, now it shines. Had it a few more hours of such shining in its cycle, I would cultivate it as a ground cover, but dawn is its one hour, and a garden is for whole days.

There is another blue morning weed whose name I do not know. This one grows from a bulb to pulpy stems and a bedraggled daytime sprawl. Only a shovel will dig it out. Try weeding it by hand and the stems will break off to be replaced by new ones and to sprawl over the chosen plants in the flower bed. Yet, now and for another hour it outshines its betters, its flowers about the size of a quarter and paler than those of the day flower but somehow more brilliant, perhaps because of the contrast of its paler foliage.

And now the sun is slanting in full. It is bright enough to make the leaves of the Japanese red maple seem a transparent red bronze when the tree is between me and the light. There must be others, but this is the only tree I know whose leaves let the sun through in this way—except, that is, when the fall colors start. Aspen leaves, when they first yellow and before they dry, are transparent in this way. I tell myself it must have something to do with the red-yellow range of the spectrum. Green takes sunlight and holds it, but red and yellow let it through.

The damned crabgrass is wrestling with the zinnias, and I stop to weed it out. The stuff weaves too close to the zinnias to make the iron claw usable. And it won't do to pull at the stalks. Crabgrass (at least in a mulched bed) can be weeded only with dirty fingers. Thumb and forefinger have to pincer into the dirt and grab the root-center. Weeding, of course, is an illusion of hope. Pulling out the root only stirs the soil and brings new crabgrass seeds into germinating position. Take a walk around the block and a new clump will have sprouted by the time you get back. But I am not ready to walk around the block. I fill a small basket with the plucked clumps, and for the instant I look at them, the zinnias are weedless.

Don't look back. I dump the weeds in the thicket where they will be smothered by the grass clippings I will pile on at the next cutting. On the way back I see the cardinals come down for the sunflower seeds, and the jays join them, and then the grackles start ganging in, gatecrashing the buffet and clattering all over it. The dog stops chewing his rawhide and makes a dash into the puddle of birds, which splashes away from him.

I hear a brake-squeak I have been waiting for and know the paper has arrived. As usual, the news turns out to be another disaster count. The function of the wire services is to bring us tragedies faster than we can pity. In the end we shall all be inured, numb, and ready for emotionless programming. I sit on the patio and read until the sun grows too bright on the page. The cardinals have stopped singing, and the grackles have flown off. It's the end of birdsong again.

15   Then suddenly—better than song for its instant—a hummingbird the color of green crushed velvet hovers in the throat of my favorite lily, a lovely high-bloomer I got the bulbs for but not the name. The lily is a crest of white horns with red dots and red velvet tongues along the insides of the petals and with an odor that drowns the patio. The hummingbird darts in and out of each horn in turn, then hovers an instant, and disappears.

Even without the sun, I have had enough of the paper. I'll take that hummingbird as my news for this dawn. It is over now. I smoke one more cigarette too many and decide that, if I go to bed now, no one in the family need know I have stayed up for it again. Why do they insist on shaking their heads when they find me still up for breakfast, after having scribbled through the dark hours? They always do. They seem compelled to express pity for an old loony who can't find his own way to bed. Why won't they understand that this is the one hour of any day that must not be missed, as it is the one hour I couldn't imagine getting up for, though I can still get to it by staying up? It makes sense to me. There comes a time when the windows lighten and the twittering starts. I look up and know it's time to leave the papers in their mess. I could slip quietly into bed and avoid the family's headshakes, but this stroll-around first hour is too good to miss. Even my dog, still sniffing and circling, knows what hour this is.

Come on, boy. It's time to go in. The rabbit won't come back till tomorrow, and the birds have work to do. The dawn's over. It's time to call it a day.

REFLECTING AND INTERPRETING

1. Ciardi's essay has an argumentative edge that is apparent in his thesis statement. Where is it?

2. What is the dominant impression of "Dawn Watch"?

3. Can you find similes?

4. Can you find an example of personification?

5. Throughout the essay, Ciardi's carefully chosen words create sensory descriptions that convey an essence of the scene. How many types of appeals to the senses can you find?

6. What is the primary order used to organize details?

7. Ciardi alternates subjectivity with objectivity at times in his description. Can you find examples of each?

8. Instead of presenting only beautiful images of the morning, Ciardi pairs negative images with positive ones and presents other unusual contrasts. What are the effects?

9. Does Ciardi make his reversed schedule seem logical? Has he supplied enough support for his claim to be convincing? Give reasons for your answer.

10. Describe the voice of the writer. Where does he seem to be poking fun at himself?

A WRITER'S RESPONSE

1. Whether you agree or disagree with Ciardi's belief that early morning is the best time of all may depend upon whether you are a "lark" or "night owl." What time of day do you like best? Why?

2. List favorite spots where you can be alone. Focus on one and freewrite about the atmosphere there, incorporating as many sights, sounds, and other sensory images as possible. Next add a chronological structure, similar to Ciardi's, describing the "events" of a typical visit from beginning to end. How does the passing of time affect what happens there? What time of day is best? Rewrite your draft into a revised essay.

PEDESTRIAN STUDENTS AND HIGH-FLYING SQUIRRELS

LIANE ELLISON NORMAN

So what do high-flying squirrels and many college students have in common? What is a significant difference? Liane Ellison Norman creates this unique analogy to illustrate a common view of first-year college students, intent on obtaining the necessary skills to land a good job. Thought-provoking, the essay examines certain traditional beliefs and questions their practicality. Norman is also the author of *Hammer of Justice: Molly Rush and the Plowshares Eight* (1989), *Mathland: The Expert Version* (1994), *Mathland: The Novice Version* (1994), and *Stitches in Air: A Novel about Mozart's Mother* (2001).

The squirrel is curious. He darts and edges, profile first, one bright 1 black eye on me, the other alert for his enemies on the other side. Like a fencer, he faces both ways, for every impulse toward me an impulse away. His tail is airy. He flicks and flourishes it, taking readings of some subtle kind.

I am enjoying a reprieve of warm sun in a season of rain and impending frost. Around me today is the wine of the garden's final ripening. On the zucchini, planted late, the flagrant blossoms flare and decline in a day's time.

I am sitting on the front porch thinking about my students. Many of them earnestly and ardently want me to teach them to be hacks. Give us ten tricks, they plead, ten nifty fail-safe ways to write a news story. Don't make us think our way through these problems, they storm (and when I am insistent that thinking *is* the trick, "You never listen to us," they complain). Who cares about the First Amendment? they sneer. What are John Peter Zenger and Hugo Black to us? Teach us how to earn a living. They will be content, they explain, with know-how and jobs, satisfied to do no more than cover the tedium of school board and weather.

Under the rebellion, there is a plaintive panic. What if, on the job—assuming there is a job to be on—they fearlessly defend the free press against government, grand jury, and media monopoly, but don't know how to write an obituary? Shouldn't obituaries come first?

I hope not, but even obituaries need good information and firm prose, 5 and both, I say, require clear thought.

The squirrel does not share my meditation. He grows tired of inquiring into me. His dismissive tail floats out behind as he takes a running leap into the tree. Up the bark he goes and onto a branch, where he crashes through the leaves. He soars from slender perch to slender perch, shaking up the trees as if he were the west wind. What a madcap he is, to go racing from one twig that dips under him to another at those heights!

His acrobatic clamor loosens buckeyes in their prickly armor. They drop, break open, and he is down the tree in a twinkling, picking, choosing. He finds what he wants and carries it, an outsize nut which is burnished like a fine cello, across the lawn, up a pole, and across the tightrope telephone line to the other side, where he disappears in maple foliage.

Some inner clock or calendar tells him to stock his larder against the deep snows and hard times that are coming. I have heard that squirrels are fuzzy-minded, that they collect their winter groceries and store them, and then forget where they are cached. But this squirrel is purposeful; he appears to know he'd better look ahead. Faced with necessity, he is prudent, but not fearful. He prances and flies as he goes about his task of preparation, and he never fails to look into whatever startles his attention.

Though he is not an ordinary pedestrian, crossing the street far above, I sometimes see the mangled fur of a squirrel on the street, with no flirtation left. Even a high-flying squirrel may zap himself on an aerial live wire. His days are dangerous and his winters are lean, but still he lays in provisions the way a trapeze artist goes about his work, with daring and dash.

10   For the squirrel, there is no work but living. He gathers food, reproduces, tends the children for a while, and stays out of danger. Doing these things with style is what distinguishes him. But for my students, unemployment looms as large as the horizon itself. Their anxiety has cause. And yet, what good is it? Ten tricks or no ten tricks, there are not enough jobs. The well-trained, well-educated stand in line for unemployment checks with the unfortunates and the drifters. Neither skill nor virtue holds certain promise. This being so, I wonder, why should these students not demand, for the well-being of their souls, the liberation of their minds?

It grieves me that they want to be pedestrians, earthbound and always careful. You ask too much, they say. What you want is painful and unfair. There are a multitude of pressures that instruct them to train, not free, themselves.

Many of them are the first generation to go to college; family aspirations are in their trust. Advisers and models tell them to be doctors, lawyers, engineers, cops, and public-relations people; no one ever tells them they can be poets, philosophers, farmers, inventors, or wizards. Their elders are anxious too; they reject the eccentric and the novel. And, realism notwithstanding, they cling to talismanic determination; play it safe and do things right and I, each one thinks, will get a job even though others won't.

I tell them fondly of my college days, which were a dizzy time (as I think the squirrel's time must be), as I let loose and pitched from fairly firm stands into the space of intellect and imagination, never quite sure what solid branch I would light on. That was the most useful thing I learned, the practical advantage (not to mention the exhilaration) of launching out to find where my propellant mind could take me.

A luxury? one student ponders, a little wistfully.

Yes, luxury, and yet necessity, and it aroused that flight, a fierce unap- 15 peasable appetite to know and to essay. The luxury I speak of is not like other privileges of wealth and power that must be hoarded to be had. If jobs are scarce, the heady regions of treetop adventure are not. Flight and gaiety cost nothing, though of course they may cost everything.

The squirrel, my frisky analogue, is not perfectly free. He must go on all fours, however nimbly he does it. Dogs are always after him, and when he barely escapes, they rant up the tree as he dodges among the branches that give under his small weight. He feeds on summer's plenty and pays the price of strontium in his bones. He is no freer of industrial ordure than I am. He lives, mates, and dies (no obituary, first or last, for him), but still he plunges and balances, risking his neck because it is his nature.

I like the little squirrel for his simplicity and bravery. He will never get ahead in life, never find a good job, never settle down, never be safe. There are no surefire tricks to make it as a squirrel.

REFLECTING AND INTERPRETING

1. Examine the first sentence of the essay. Is this sentence significant, or is it merely specifying a characteristic of a squirrel? Give a reason for your answer.

2. Why is the second paragraph relevant? Would some other season have done just as well to set the scene? Why or why not?

3. What is the fear that Norman senses in many of her students? What do they assume they should be learning about writing? (What does *obituary* symbolize?)

4. How are the squirrel's activities that Norman observes similar to those of college students?

5. Is Norman advising students not to listen to advisers' and parents' advice about an occupation? What is she recommending?

6. Why is Norman sad? What does she mean when she says students "want to be pedestrians"? (Check the adjective meaning of this word.) What does she say was the most practical advantage she gained in college?

7. Norman says she had "a fierce unappeasable appetite to know and to essay." What does she mean? (Check the verb meaning of *essay*.) How are these qualities related to finding and keeping a job? Or are they?

8. What qualities does Norman admire in the squirrel? She ends with "There are no sure-fire tricks to make it as a squirrel." Is she just being flippant, or is there a deeper meaning here? Why or why not?

9. How does the tone change in the paragraphs where Norman considers the squirrel and then her students? See paragraphs 1, 4, and 8 for examples.

10. What rhetorical strategies are used in this essay along with description?

SMALL GROUP DISCUSSION

1. With your group, discuss whether or not most jobs are entirely "safe." Once you get the necessary skills in your field, will you be immune to job turnover? Before answering, list major factors that affect the job market. What are they?

2. What personal qualities are necessary to survive fluctuations in the job market? How will the qualities that Norman mentions help us to regain our equilibrium after a downsizing?

Analyzing a Process

FAST TRACK TO PERFECTION IAN DUNBAR

Veterinarian, animal behaviorist, and dog trainer, Ian Dunbar has attained international renown. A graduate of the Royal Veterinary College (London University), he completed his doctorate at the University of California in Berkeley. He is a columnist, the host of the British television show *Dogs with Dunbar,* and the founder of several dog-training organizations. Dr. Dunbar has given more than 750 seminars and workshops around the globe. He has made over a dozen videos and written numerous books, including *Doctor Dunbar's Good Little Dog Book* and a set of behavior booklets on dog-owner concerns. His *How to Teach a New Dog Old Tricks* and *Sirius Puppy Training* won Best Book and Best Video awards. His dog-friendly training method is based upon "six crucial developmental deadlines." He advocates "off-leash socialization" classes, "lure/reward," and games training for puppies and dogs. In this essay Dr. Dunbar explains how to encourage good habits while training puppies.

Puppies mature at an astounding rate. Don't let yours fall behind on the developmental curve. Nearly everything a puppy needs to learn must be taught in 12 weeks—between the ages of 2 and 5 months. You can buy yourself time by knowing what and how to teach the puppy before you bring it home. Go to puppy classes, read behavior and training books, watch instructional videos and consult your veterinarian. Then raise your puppy perfectly by meeting these six training deadlines. 1

Deadline 1: Before You Bring Home a Puppy
Your puppy should be accustomed to a domestic environment before you bring it home—at around 8 weeks of age. Make sure it has been raised indoors and in close contact with people. It should be prepared for the

clamor of everyday life—the noise of the vacuum cleaner, the hoopla surrounding sports programs on the television, children crying, adults arguing. Early exposure—before the pup's eyes and ears have fully opened—allows the puppy to gradually assimilate sights and sounds that otherwise might frighten.

The window for socializing begins to close by the time the pup turns 3 months of age, and its most impressionable learning period starts to fade by its fifth month.

Deadline 2: Puppy's First Day at Home

Misbehavior is the most common reason dogs end up in shelters. This is especially sad because owners can prevent most behavior problems. For instance, if you avoid leaving the pup unsupervised, it won't chew furniture and belongings or soil your house; while teeny accidents do little damage in themselves, they may set a precedent for habits in months to come.

5   When you cannot watch your pup, confine it to a crate or a puppy-proofed room, which should contain:

- a comfortable bed.

- a bowl of fresh water.

- a doggie toilet placed away from the bed and which simulates the outdoors. Lay down a sheet of linoleum and cover it with a disposable plastic sheet. Next lay newspaper or something absorbent. Top the three layers with dirt or sod to teach the pup to relieve itself on grass (or concrete slabs for city pups that relieve themselves curbside).

- Hollow chew toys with kibble inside to reward your puppy for chewing toys rather than furniture. During its first few weeks at home, a marvelous training ploy is to serve your puppy's food only in chew toys. After it's a chew toy-aholic—and has not had a chewing mishap for at least three months—begin to serve its dinner in a bowl.

At least every hour, release your puppy from its crate, quickly leash it and hurry it to its outdoor toilet area. Stand still and give the pup three minutes to produce. When it does, lavishly praise and offer *three* extra special treats. Freeze-dried liver treats work well because dogs love their strong smell.

If your puppy eliminates, it may be allowed supervised exploration of the house. If it does not eliminate, lead it back to its crate or puppy-proof room and try again in half an hour.

Keep up the once an hour schedule until your pup is at least 3 months old to make certain it never eliminates indoors. After 3 months of age pups start to develop the bladder control necessary for longer waits between potty breaks, but you must still be vigilant. One mistake can set a bad precedent.

Always reward your puppy for using its outdoors toilet area, but wait until it has completed its shots before taking it to public property; otherwise it can pick up other dogs' diseases. A pup must not walk or sniff where other dogs have been until it has developed sufficient immunity (between 3 and 4 months old).

Deadline 3: Puppy at 3 Months

By 3 months your pup must master socialization and basic manners. [10] Pups that do not will have a hard time picking up these skills later in life. Unfortunately, the risk of disease means dog-to-dog socialization must wait. Meanwhile, teach your pup to be people-friendly.

As a general rule, your pup should socialize with at least 100 people before it is 3 months old. This is easier than it sounds. Invite eight friends over each Sunday to watch sports on the television. Each Monday invite eight different friends to watch *Ally McBeal* and *Dateline.* Catch up on outstanding social obligations by inviting family, friends and neighbors to weekly puppy parties. On another night, invite some neighborhood children. Socializing a puppy is great because it does wonders for *your* social life.

Show your guests how to hand feed the puppy's kibble to encourage and reward it for coming, sitting and lying down. Ask your puppy to come. Praise profusely as it approaches and offer a piece of kibble when it arrives. Back up, then do it again—and again and again. Then say "Puppy, Sit" and slowly move a piece of kibble from in front of the puppy's nose to between its eyes. As the puppy raises its nose to sniff, it will lower its rear and sit. If the puppy jumps up, you're holding the food too high. When your puppy sits, say "Good dog" and offer the kibble. Now say "Puppy, Down" and lower a piece of kibble from in front of the puppy's nose to between its forepaws. As the puppy lowers its head to follow the food, it will usually lie down. If your puppy stands, hide the kibble in your palm until it lies down. Then say "Good dog" and offer the food. Coach your guests until each can get the puppy to come, sit and lie down three times for a piece of kibble.

When a puppy approaches promptly and happily, it is a sign the dog is people-friendly. Sitting and lying down on request indicates respect for the person issuing instructions. If your puppy is regularly hand-fed by guests, it will learn to enjoy people's company.

Deadline 4: Puppy at 4½ Months

Seemingly overnight, puppies become adolescents. Enroll in a training class before yours is 14 weeks old—that is, before it starts to test your limits. A professional will teach it to stop nipping and other behavior no-no's, as well as temper its hyper-turbo energy.

Most puppies can start classes at 3 months. Classrooms are generally [15] safe places; the puppies are vaccinated, the floors regularly sterilized. I advise delaying walks in public places until your puppy is 4 months old because of the risk of disease.

Puppy classes develop canine social savvy through play with other puppies in a controlled setting. Most classes are family-oriented, offering pups opportunities to socialize with all sorts of people—men, women and children. The number of behaviors your pup learns in its first training lesson will amaze you. Shy and fearful pups gain confidence. Bullies tone it down and become gentle. All dogs learn to come, sit and lie down when requested and listen to their owners and ignore distractions.

Deadline 5: Puppy at 5 Months

Take your dog everywhere—errands around town, car trips to visit friends, picnics in the park and especially to explore the neighborhood. And bring a little bag of kibble. Give a couple of pieces to each stranger who wants to meet your dog. Ask each person to offer the kibble only after your pup sits to say hello.

At this point, you may come to believe the canine weight-pulling record exceeds 10,000 pounds. Your dog also may begin to ignore you. A few tips:

- **Make your dog walk for its dinner.** With kibble in hand, stand still and wait for the dog to sit. Ignore everything else your dog does; it will sit eventually. When it does, say "Good dog," offer the kibble, take one giant step forward, stand still and wait for your dog to sit again. Repeat this until your dog sits each time you stop. Now take two giant steps before your stop. Then three steps, five, eight, 10, 20, and so on. *Voilá,* your dog walks calmly and attentively by your side and sits each time you stop.

- **Take a few time-outs on each walk.** Sit down, relax and allow the dog to settle down and watch the world go by. If your pup is not the sit-still type, take along a treat-stuffed chew toy as an incentive.

- **Never take your dog's sound temperament for granted.** Outdoors can be scary and offer the occasional surprise. Give your dog a piece of kibble every time a big truck, noisy motorcycle or child on a skateboard whizzes by and your dog doesn't overreact.

- **Don't make a habit of letting your dog off-leash to run and play with other dogs;** your dog may eventually refuse to come when called. Instead, take your dog's dinner to the park and, throughout its play session, call your dog every minute or so and have it sit for a couple of pieces of kibble. It will soon get the idea and its enthusiastic response will be the talk of the park.

Deadline 6: Now and Forever

Continue walking your dog at least once a day and take it to a dog park several times a week. Find different walks and dog parks to meet a variety of dogs and people. If your dog always sees the same people and dogs, it may regress socially and become intolerant of strangers.

20   Now enjoy life with your good-natured, well-mannered companion. Give your dog a special bone—Good dog!—and yourself a pat on the back—Good owner!

REFLECTING AND INTERPRETING

1. Consider the second sentence. What is its purpose?
2. What is the first step that Dr. Dunbar advocates?
3. What does he mean by the "window of socializing"? When is this?
4. What does he believe about puppy misbehavior?
5. What procedure should you follow to train the puppy in elimination?
6. Why does Dunbar recommend that your dog meet many other people and dogs?
7. What two incentives does Dunbar stress to promote good puppy behavior?
8. At one point he compares puppies to adolescents. Why? What do they need?
9. Consider his ending. How would you rate it? Why?
10. After reading this article, would you adopt a puppy? Why or why not?

A WRITER'S RESPONSE

Write an essay giving directions, perhaps for training a horse, a farm dog to herd, or a helping dog for the handicapped. Or if you have had success in training a cat or another animal, you might write about that.

HOW TO COOK A CARP   EUELL GIBBONS

This essay has the air of an old-time western movie with cowhands sitting around a campfire in the evening, spinning yarns. Only this time, they vie with each other to describe the best way to cook a carp—a fish that has been commonly regarded in the United States as a "trash fish," unfit for eating. Born in Clarksville, Texas, Euell Gibbons (1911–75) worked as a cowboy, carpenter, harvest hand, and trapper. He served a two-year hitch in the U.S. Army from 1934 to 1936. During World War II, he helped build ships for the U.S. Navy. When he was thirty-six years old, he enrolled at the University of Hawaii as a freshman. He later taught, wrote, and lectured about wild foods and living off the land. His amusing narratives include *Stalking the Wild Asparagus* (1962), from which "How to Cook a Carp" has been taken; *Stalking the Blue-Eyed Scallop* (1964); *Stalking the Healthful Herbs* (1966); and *Euell Gibbons' Beachcomber's Handbook* (1967). More than thirty years later, these books were reprinted.

When I was a lad of about eighteen, my brother and I were working 1 on a cattle ranch in New Mexico that bordered on the Rio Grande. Most Americans think of the Rio Grande as a warm southern stream, but it rises among the high mountains of Colorado, and in the spring it is fed by melting snows. At this time of the year, the water that rushed by the ranch was turbulent, icy-cold and so silt-laden as to be semisolid. "A little too thick to drink, and a little too thin to plow" was a common description of the waters of the Rio Grande.

A few species of fish inhabited this muddy water. Unfortunately, the most common was great eight- to ten-pound carp, a fish that is considered very poor eating in this country, although the Germans and Asiatics have domesticated this fish, and have developed some varieties that are highly esteemed for the table.

On the ranch where we worked, there was a drainage ditch that ran through the lower pasture and emptied its clear waters into the muddy Rio Grande. The carp swimming up the river would strike this clear warmer water and decide they preferred it to the cold mud they had been inhabiting. One spring day, a cowhand who had been riding that way reported that Clear Ditch was becoming crowded with huge carp.

On Sunday we decided to go fishing. Four of us armed ourselves with pitchforks, saddled our horses and set out. Near the mouth of the ditch, the water was running about two feet deep and twelve to sixteen feet wide. There is a saying in that part of the country that you can't get a cowboy to do anything unless it can be done from the back of a horse, so we forced our mounts into the ditch and started wading them upstream, four abreast, herding the carp before us.

5   By the time we had ridden a mile upstream, the water was less than a foot deep and so crystal clear that we could see our herd of several hundred carp still fleeing from the splashing, wading horses. As the water continued to shallow, our fish began to get panicky. A few of the boldest ones attempted to dart back past us and were impaled on pitchforks. We could see that the whole herd was getting restless and was about to stampede back downstream, so we piled off our horses into the shallow water to meet the charge. The water boiled about us as the huge fish swirled past us and we speared madly in every direction with our pitchforks, throwing each fish we managed to hit over the ditch bank. This was real fishing—cowhand style. The last of the fish herd was by us in a few minutes and it was all over, but we had caught a tremendous quantity of fish.

Back at the ranch house, after we had displayed our trophies, we began wondering what we were going to do with so many fish. This started a series of typical cowboy tall tales on "how to cook a carp." The best of these yarns was told by a grizzled old *vaquero,* who claimed he had made his great discovery when he ran out of food while camping on a tributary of the Rio Grande. He said that he had found the finest way to cook a carp was to plaster the whole fish with a thick coating of fresh cow manure and bury it in the hot ashes of a campfire. In an hour or two, he said, the casing of cow manure had become black and very hard. He then related how he had removed the fish from the fire, broken the hard shell with the butt of his Winchester and peeled it off. He said that as the manure came off the scales and skin adhered to it, leaving the baked fish, white and clean. He then ended by saying, "Of course, the carp still wasn't fit to eat, but manure in which it was cooked tasted pretty good."

There were also some serious suggestions and experiments. The chief objection to the carp is that its flesh is full of many forked bones. One man said that he had enjoyed carp sliced very thin and fried so crisp that one could eat it, bones and all. He demonstrated, and you really could eat it without the bones bothering you, but it was still far from being an epicurean dish. One cowboy described the flavor as "a perfect blend of Rio Grande mud and rancid hog lard."

Another man said that he had eaten carp that had been cooked in a pressure cooker until the bones softened and became indistinguishable from the flesh. A pressure cooker is almost a necessity at that altitude, so we had one at the ranch house. We tried this method, and the result was barely edible. It tasted like the poorest possible grade of canned salmon flavored with a bit of mud. It was, however, highly appreciated by the dogs and cats on the ranch, and solved the problem of what to do with the bulk of the fish we had caught.

It was my brother who finally devised a method of cooking carp that not only made it fit for human consumption, but actually delicious. First, instead of merely scaling the fish, he skinned them. Then, taking a large pinch, where the meat was thickest, he worked his fingers and thumb into the flesh until he struck the median bones, then he worked his thumb and fingers together and tore off a handful of meat. Using this tearing method, he could get two or three goodsized chunks of flesh from each side of the fish. He then heated a pot of bland vegetable shortening, rubbed the pieces of fish with salt and dropped them into the hot fat. He used no flour, meal, crumbs or seasoning other than salt. They cooked to a golden brown in a few minutes, and everyone pronounced them "mighty fine eating." The muddy flavor seemed to have been eliminated by removing the skin and the large bones. The forked bones were still there, but they had not been multiplied by cutting across them, and one only had to remove several bones still intact with the fork from each piece of fish.

For the remainder of that spring, every few days one or another of the 10 cowboys would take a pitchfork and ride over to Clear Ditch and spear a mess of carp. On these evenings, my brother replaced the regular *cocinero* and we enjoyed some delicious fried carp.

The flavor of carp varies with the water from which it is caught. Many years after the above incidents I attended a fish fry at my brother's house. The main course was all of his own catching, and consisted of bass, catfish and carp, all from Elephant Butte Lake farther down the Rio Grande. All the fish were prepared exactly alike, except that the carp was pulled apart as described above, while the bass and catfish, being all twelve inches or less in length, were merely cleaned and fried whole. None of his guests knew one fish from another, yet all of them preferred the carp to the other kinds. These experiences have convinced me that the carp is really a fine food fish when properly prepared.

Carp can, of course, be caught in many ways besides spearing them with pitchforks from the back of a horse. In my adopted home state, Pennsylvania, they are classed as "trash fish" and one is allowed to take them almost any way. They will sometimes bite on worms, but they are vegetarians by preference and are more easily taken on dough balls. Some states allow the use of gill nets, and other states, because they would like to reduce the population of this unpopular fish, will issue special permits for the use of nets to catch carp.

A good forager will take advantage of the lax regulations on carp fishing while they last. When all fishermen realize that the carp is really a good food fish when prepared in the right way, maybe this outsized denizen of our rivers and lakes will no longer be considered a pest and will take his rightful place among our valued food and game fishes.

REFLECTING AND INTERPRETING

1. In what general locale does the story take place? Where on the ranch do the cowboys start their fishing trip?

2. What is the effect of including the common description of the waters of the Rio Grande in the spring? How does it influence the tone?

3. How does Gibbons's use of first person influence the narrative? How would it have differed if it he had used third person?

4. In paragraph 4, a common saying is included. What is the effect?

5. What is the chief objection to eating a carp? What two methods are tried to overcome these objections but are unsuccessful?

6. An old *vaquero* claims that he has discovered the best way to cook a carp. How does he claim to have done it? Is there anything that makes you doubt the story?

7. What method does Gibbons's brother devise that makes the carp delicious and easy to eat? The removal of what two parts improves the flavor? Later Gibbons finds another significant factor that influences the flavor. What is it?

8. What proof does Gibbons offer to support his claim that carp is a "fine food fish"?

9. The actual procedure of cooking a carp successfully is not explained until paragraph 9. How do paragraphs 1 through 8 function?

10. Gibbons's books were first published in the 1960s and reprinted over thirty years later. How do you explain the popularity of his writing?

A WRITER'S RESPONSE

1. Alone or with your group members, write a step-by-step analysis of something you do. For example, you might consider a morning or evening ritual such as caring for a pet or a Sunday afternoon activity. Create a list of the steps in chronological order. Then discuss ways in which you can use point of view and humor to make the essay more engaging.

2. Try rewriting some of Gibbons's paragraphs using third person only. For instance, rewrite paragraph 1, deleting all first-person pronouns (*we, I,* etc.). How difficult is this rewriting? How does the third-person point of view change those paragraphs?

WRITE YOUR OWN SUCCESS STORY   CAROL CARTER

Coasting through high school, seldom studying, seventeen-year-old Carol Carter was yanked from a career disaster by a conversation with her brother. This vivid essay from *Majoring in the Rest of Your Life: Career Secrets for College Students* (1999) relates how she suddenly changed direction, "determined to learn all she could." Since graduating from the University of Arizona, Carter has also written *Student Planner* (1998) and *Keys to Success* (2000). She has coauthored and collaborated on more than a dozen other books designed to help students increase their effectiveness.

Who am I to talk to high school graduates and college freshmen about planning? As a high school student in Tucson, Arizona, I never planned. I just coasted along letting things happen to me. Sure, I was spontaneous. I spent weeknights talking on the phone and studied only when I felt like it— i.e., seldom. On weekends my friends and I roamed shopping malls and partied in the mountains. The typical irresponsible high school student. 1

And then BOOM. The ax fell. The ax was not some accident, scandal, or divine intervention. It was simply a conversation with my older brother Craig during the first week of my senior year in high school. Our talk changed the course of my life.

At seventeen, I was intimidated by my four older brothers. I saw them as bright, motivated, and respected achievers—the opposite of me. Whenever one of them asked me about what I was doing or thinking, I'd answer with a one-liner and hope he'd soon leave me alone.

This conversation with Craig was different. He didn't give up after five minutes despite my curt, vague responses.

"Carol, what are you interested in?" 5

"I dunno."

"What do you think about all day?"

"I dunno."

"What do you want to do with your life?"

"I'll just let things happen." 10

Craig persisted. His voice grew indignant. He criticized me for talking on the phone, for spending too much time at pep rallies and rock concerts, for not studying, for not challenging myself. He pointed out that I hadn't read an unassigned book in three years. He asked if I intended to approach college the way I'd approached high school—as one continuous party. If so, he warned, I'd better start thinking of a career flipping burgers at the local hamburger stand because no respectable employer would ever take me seriously. He asked me if that was what I wanted to do with my life. He cautioned that out of laziness and lack of planning I would limit my options so narrowly that I would never be able to get a real job. I had wasted three years of high school, he said. College was a new start, since employers and graduate schools seldom check as far back as high school for records. So he advised me to quit making excuses, decide what I wanted and plan how to achieve it. My only limitations would be self-imposed.

Craig then left my room—sermon completed. I didn't speak to him before he flew back to New York that afternoon to finish his senior year at Columbia. I hated him for interfering in my life. He made me dissatisfied with myself. I was scared he was right. For the first time, I realized that "typical" was not necessarily what I wanted to be.

The next day, still outraged but determined to do something, I went to the library and checked out six classics: *Pride and Prejudice* by Jane Austen; *The Great Gatsby* by F. Scott Fitzgerald; *A Farewell to Arms* and *For Whom the Bell Tolls* by Ernest Hemingway; *A Portrait of the Artist as a Young Man* by James Joyce; and *Sister Carrie* by Theodore Dreiser. Then I wrote down in a notebook a few goals that I wanted to accomplish. They all seemed boldly unattainable: earn straight A's (previously I had made B's and C's), study every week including one weekend night, keep reading classics on my own. If I couldn't make it in my senior year of high school, why should I waste time and money in college? I'd beat fate to the door and begin my career at the hamburger stand directly.

Three weeks later I got a letter from Craig. He knew how angry I was with him. He told me our conversation wasn't easy for him either but if he hadn't cared, he wouldn't have bothered to say anything. He was right. I needed that sermon. If I didn't come to terms with my problems, I could never have moved from making excuses to making things happen.

15   I worked hard and got results. The second semester of my senior year I made all A's (except for a B in physics). I finished the six classics and others as well. I started reading newspapers and magazines. I had to move the *Vogue* on my nightstand to make room for *Time, Harper's,* and *Fortune.* I found that I could set goals and attain them, and I started to realize that I wasn't so different from my brothers after all.

To my utter astonishment, I discovered that for the first time I enjoyed learning. My world seemed to open up just because I knew more about different kinds of people, ways of thinking and ways of interpreting what I had previously assumed to be black-and-white. (If you are a shy person, joining a club and getting to know—and actually like—a few people whom you originally perceived as unfriendly or uninteresting may astonish you as much as my newfound appreciation for learning astonished me.)

The summer before college, I thought about what I wanted to do with my life, but couldn't decide on a direction. I had no notion of what I wanted to major in. What to do . . . what to do?

I turned to Craig, a phone call away in New York City. He told me not to worry in my first year of college about what I wanted to do. The main priority: learn as much as I could. College, he told me, was my golden opportunity to investigate all kinds of things—biology, psychology, accounting, philosophy. He told me I'd become good at writing and critical thinking techniques—skills that would help me learn any job after graduation. And though I could continue to expand my educational horizons throughout life, college was the best opportunity to expose myself to the greatest minds and movements of our civilization.

Craig also warned me that being a scholar, though important, wouldn't be enough. (He had just graduated from Columbia as a Phi Beta Kappa, but since he hadn't gained any real-world experience in college, it took him several months to find his first job.) To maximize options upon graduation, I would have to do three things:

1. Learn as much as possible from classes, books, professors, and other people
2. Participate in extracurricular activities
3. Get REAL-WORLD experience by working part-time and landing summer internships

If I did these three things reasonably well, Craig assured me, I could 20 choose from a number of career opportunities at the end of my senior year. And even if I only did two of the three full-force and one half-speed, I'd be in good shape. The effort in each area, and a modest outcome, was an attainable goal. That way I could balance my college experience and open options for the future.

Craig advised me that I should look ahead and develop a plan of action for each of my four years of college. He told me that foresight—the ability to consider the bigger picture beyond short-term challenges and intermittent goals—is invaluable in most jobs; it distinguishes outstanding people from the rest of the pack. . . . Most important, you'll learn that everyone— including YOU—has his or her own set of skills, abilities, passions and talents to tap. Finding the career and lifestyle that allows you to cultivate and nurture them is one of the most important success secrets.

So Take Action!

A good way to start is to assess your shortcomings and strengths. As I've already told you, one of my shortcomings in high school was not learning all I could from my classes and teachers. Your shortcoming may have been that you focused entirely on your studies without developing many outside interests. Someone else may feel that he concentrated so much on an outside activity—such as training for a particular sport—that he had no time for studies or friends. What was your major shortcoming in high school?

Now think about three things:

1. What pleased you in high school?
2. What could you have done better?
3. What do you want to improve upon in the future?

Identifying these areas will help you strike a good balance during col- 25 lege. Once you get in the habit of analyzing past experiences, you will have a clearer notion of what you do and don't want in the future. That's important.

As a high school senior, a college freshman, or a college senior, the next thing you must do is decide to take action. Don't worry if you don't know what you want to do. Just commit yourself to the process. If you do, you'll eventually find out which careers might be best for you and how you could best prepare for them.

RECAP: The priorities

1. Gain knowledge

2. Participate in activities

3. Get REAL-WORLD experience

Making It Happen

"Luck is the residue of design," said Branch Rickey, known as the baseball mahatma for his strategic methods for playing and organizing baseball. He developed the farm system on which the minor leagues were formed. His PLANS OF ACTION took a handful of disjointed teams in faraway cities and banded them into an organization which has left its mark on American culture.

Nothing happens magically. If you want to be a success, you are going to have to take personal responsibility for your life. Why do some graduates get twenty job offers and others receive none?

30   While successful people may appear lucky, they, in fact, illustrate the maxim that "luck favors the prepared mind."

Joe Cirulli agrees. He is the owner of the successful Gainesville Health and Fitness Center in Florida. Early on in his life, exercise was a priority, an essential part of his day. So he followed his interests and put his talents to work to start his own health club. While many other clubs have folded around him, he has experienced enormous success—his membership continues to grow, and he is able to keep his club filled with the best equipment and the most knowledgeable professionals.

When Joe was twenty, he worked as an assistant manager and a sales representative for a health club. One of his responsibilities was to train new sales representatives for the club. He worked hard to prepare them for their jobs only to have to compete with them once they were trained.

He remembers talking with the vice president of the company about his frustration. The vice president, a person Joe respected, advised him to keep on putting his best efforts into his work. "Right now you may not see the benefit of your hard work, but one day you will."

Joe followed his advice. Less than five years later his skill at training people in the health club industry paid off—he was able to put his expertise to work for his own health club. "Knowing how to motivate employees to do their best, to care about the quality of their work, and to care about our customers has had an enormous impact on the success of my own company."

35   Joe believes the secret to his success is giving 100 percent of himself in everything he does. "Success is the culmination of all your efforts. There are thousands of opportunities for people who give their all."

How do you arrange to have the most options when you leave college? Plan, develop foresight, and take charge of your life, and you will become one of the lucky ones. Most important, decide that you want to succed—and believe it.

Charles Garfield a clinical psychologist who has spent his career studying what motivates people to superior effort, says that the drive to excel comes primarily from within. Can "peak performances" be learned? Yes, says Garfield. High achievers are not extraordinarily gifted superhumans. What they have in common is the ability to cultivate what the German writer Johann Wolfgang von Goethe termed "the genius, power, and magic" that exists in all of us. These doers increase the odds in their favor through simple techniques which anyone can cultivate:

1. Envision a mission
2. Be result-oriented
3. Tap your internal resources
4. Enlist team spirit
5. Treat setbacks as stepping stones

First Things First

The first thing to keep in mind when planning: accept the world the way it is. Your plans should be based on a realistic assessment of how things are, not some starry-eyed vision of how they should be. You can dream, but there's a happy medium between cold reality and pie in the sky. That's why you must be open to opportunity. Indeed, you must create it. Although you can't change the hand you were dealt, you can play it as wisely as possible.

So start today. Start now.

The more questions you ask now, the better prepared you'll be in four 40 years. You don't want to be stuck in a boring job or wondering why you can't find work.

Are you going to make mistakes? I hope so, unless you're not of the human species. Making mistakes is the process by which we learn. And whenever we're disappointed by the outcome, we have to maintain a positive attitude, log the information, and keep going. The key is to learn from mistakes without letting them slow us down.

REFLECTING AND INTERPRETING

1. What rhetorical strategy does Carter use in the first sentence? What is the effect?
2. How did Carol's careless attitude in high school affect her self-image?
3. What three main points did Craig make in his criticism?
4. How did Carol react to her brother's advice? Why? What did she do the next day?
5. What three things did Carol discover about herself?

6. When Craig pointed out that high grades alone were not enough to land a job, what three actions did he recommend?

7. What four actions does Carol recommend readers take to "have the most options when you leave college"?

8. Does the author seem convincing? Why or why not?

9. What type of support does she provide other than personal experience?

10. What is appealing about her writing style?

A WRITER'S RESPONSE

What is the most significant point that you derived from this essay? Did you learn anything that can help you be more successful in college? On the job? What do you plan to do differently to improve your grades and chances for success? Write an essay that responds to these questions and any other points Carter raises.

HOW DO YOU KNOW IT'S GOOD?   MARYA MANNES

What makes writing, art, music, or theater good? One popular approach denies the existence of any valid criteria to measure the quality of a work. This approach claims that decisions about value are merely a matter of personal taste. But Marya Mannes disagreed, saying there are standards to determine value. She said that the prime function of art is "to create order out of chaos—again, not the order of neatness or rigidity or convention or artifice, but the order of clarity. . . ." There is room for "incredible diversity of forms" within a universal pattern and rhythm. Mannes (1904–90) was born into a family of prominent musicians and chemists. She was a columnist, editor, and television commentator for PBS. She wrote two novels, *Message from a Stranger* (1948) and *They* (1968), as well as an autobiography, *Out of My Time* (1971). Best known was her collection of essays, *But Will It Sell?* (1964), in which "How Do You Know It's Good?" was first published.

1   Suppose there were no critics to tell us how to react to a picture, a play, or a new composition of music. Suppose we wandered innocent as the dawn into an art exhibition of unsigned paintings. By what standards, by what values would we decide whether they were good or bad, talented or untalented, successes or failures? How can we ever know that what we think is right?

For the last fifteen or twenty years the fashion in criticism or appreciation of the arts has been to deny the existence of any valid criteria and to make the words "good" or "bad" irrelevant, immaterial, and inapplicable. There is no such thing, we are told, as a set of standards, first acquired through experience and knowledge and later imposed on the subject under discussion. This has been a popular approach, for it relieves the critic of the responsibility of judgment and the public of the necessity of knowledge. It pleases those resentful of disciplines, it flatters the empty-minded by calling them open-minded, it comforts the confused. Under the banner of democracy and the kind of equality which our forefathers did *not* mean, it says, in effect, "Who are you to tell us what is good or bad?" This is the same cry used so long and so effectively by the producers of mass media who insist that it is the public, not they, who decides what it wants to hear and see, and that for a critic to say that *this* program is bad and this program is good is purely a reflection of personal taste. Nobody recently has expressed this philosophy more succinctly than Dr. Frank Stanton, the highly intelligent president of CBS television. At a hearing before the Federal Communications Commission, this phrase escaped him under questioning: "One man's mediocrity is another man's good program."

There is no better way of saying "No values are absolute." There is another important aspect to this philosophy of *laissez faire:* It is the fear, in all observers of all forms of art, of guessing wrong. This fear is well come by, for who has not heard of the contemporary outcries against artists who later were called great? Every age has its arbiters who do not grow with their times, who cannot tell evolution from revolution or the difference between frivolous faddism, amateurish experimentation, and profound and necessary change. Who wants to be caught *flagrante delicto* with an error of judgment as serious as this? It is far safer, and certainly easier, to look at a picture or a play or a poem and to say "This is hard to understand, but it may be good," or simply to welcome it as a new form. The word "new"— in our country especially—has magical connotations. What is new must be good; what is old is probably bad, and if a critic can describe the new in language that nobody can understand, he's safer still. If he has mastered the art of saying nothing with exquisite complexity, nobody can quote him later as saying anything.

But all these, I maintain, are forms of abdication from the responsibility of judgment. In creating, the artist commits himself; in appreciating, you have a commitment of your own. For after all, it is the audience which makes the arts. A climate of appreciation is essential to its flowering, and the higher the expectations of the public, the better the performance of the artist. Conversely, only a public ill-served by its critics could have accepted as art and literature so much in these last years that has been neither. If anything goes, everything goes; and at the bottom of the junkpile lie the discarded standards, too.

But what are these standards? How do you get them? How do you 5 know they're the right ones? How can you make a clear pattern out of so many intangibles, including that greatest one, the very private I?

Well for one thing, it's fairly obvious that the more you read and see and hear, the more equipped you'll be to practice that art of association which is at the basis of all understanding and judgment. The more you live and the more you look, the more aware you are of a consistent pattern— as universal as the stars, as the tides, as breathing, as night and day— underlying everything. I would call this pattern and this rhythm an order. Not order—an order. Within it exists an incredible diversity of forms. Without it lies chaos. I would further call this order—this incredible diversity held within one pattern—health. And I would call chaos—the wild cells of destruction—sickness. It is in the end up to you to distinguish between the diversity that is health and the chaos that is sickness, and you can't do this without a process of association that can link a bar of Mozart with the corner of a Vermeer painting, or a Stravinsky score with a Picasso abstraction; or that can relate an aggressive act with a Franz Kline painting and a fit of coughing with a John Cage composition.

There is no accident in the fact that certain expressions of art live for all time and that others die with the moment, and although you may not always define the reasons, you can ask the questions. What does an artist say that is timeless; how does he say it? How much is fashion, how much is merely reflection? Why is Sir Walter Scott so hard to read now, and Jane Austen not? Why is baroque right for one age and too effulgent for another?

Can a standard of craftsmanship apply to art of all ages, or does each have its own, and different, definitions? You may have been aware, inadvertently, that craftsmanship has become a dirty word these years because, again, it implies standard—something done well or done badly. The result of this convenient avoidance is a plenitude of actors who can't project their voices, singers who can't phrase their songs, poets who can't communicate emotion, and writers who have no vocabulary—not to speak of painters who can't draw. The dogma now is that craftsmanship gets in the way of expression. You can do better if you don't know *how* you do it, let alone *what* you're doing.

I think it is time you helped reverse this trend by trying to rediscover craft: the command of the chosen instrument, whether it is a brush, a word, or a voice. When you begin to detect the difference between freedom and sloppiness, between serious experimentation and ego-therapy, between skill and slickness, between strength and violence, you are on your way to separating the sheep from the goats, a form of segregation denied us for quite a while. All you need to restore it is a small bundle of standards and a Geiger counter that detects fraud, and we might begin our tour of the arts in an area where both are urgently needed: contemporary painting.

10   I don't know what's worse: to have to look at acres of bad art to find the little good, or to read what the critics say about it all. In no other field of expression has so much double-talk flourished, so much confusion prevailed, and so much nonsense been circulated: further evidence of the close interdependence between the arts and the critical climate they inhabit. It will be my pleasure to share with you some of this double-talk so typical of our times.

Item one: preface for a catalogue of an abstract painter:

"Time-bound meditation experiencing a life; sincere with plastic piety at the threshold of hallowed arcana; a striving for pure ideation giving shape to inner drive; formalized patterns where neural balances reach a fiction." End of quote. Know what this artist paints like now?

Item two: a review in the *Art News:*

"... a weird and disparate assortment of material, but the monstrosity which bloomed into his most recent cancer of aggregations is present in some form everywhere. ..." Then, later, "A gluttony of things and processes terminated by a glorious constipation."

Item three, same magazine, review of an artist who welds automobile 15 fragments into abstract shapes:

"Each fragment . . . is made an extreme of human exasperation, torn at and fought all the way, and has its rightness of form as if by accident. *Any technique that requires order or discipline would just be the human ego.* No, these must be egoless, uncontrolled, undesigned and different enough to give you a bang—fifty miles an hour around a telephone pole. ..."

"Any technique that requires order or discipline would just be the human ego." What does he mean—"just be"? What are they really talking about? Is this journalism? Is it criticism? Or is it that other convenient abdication from standards of performance and judgment practiced by so many artists and critics that they, like certain writers who deal only in sickness and depravity, "reflect the chaos about them . . ."? Again, whose chaos? Whose depravity?

I had always thought that the prime function of art was to create order *out* of chaos—again, not the order of neatness or rigidity or convention or artifice, but the order of clarity by which one will and one vision could draw the essential truth out of apparent confusion. I still do. It is not enough to use parts of a car to convey the brutality of the machine. This is as slavishly representative, and just as easy, as arranging dried flowers under glass to convey nature.

Speaking of which, i.e., the use of real materials (burlap, old gloves, bottletops) in lieu of pigment, this is what one critic had to say about an exhibition of Assemblage at the Museum of Modern Art last year:

> Spotted throughout the show are indisputable works of art, account- 20
> ing for a quarter or even half of the total display. But the remainder are
> works of non-art, anti-art, and art substitutes that are the aesthetic coun-
> terparts of the social deficiencies that land people in the clink on charges
> of vagrancy. These aesthetic bankrupts . . . have no legitimate ideological
> roof over their heads and not the price of a square intellectual meal,
> much less a spiritual sandwich, in their pockets.

I quote these words of John Canaday of *The New York Times* as an example of the kind of criticism which puts responsibility to an intelligent public above popularity with an intellectual coterie. Canaday has the courage to say what he thinks and the capacity to say it clearly: two qualities notably absent from his profession.

Next to art, I would say that appreciation and evaluation in the field of music is the most difficult. For it is rarely possible to judge a new composition at one hearing only. What seems confusing or fragmented at first might well become clear and organic a third time. Or it might not. The only salvation here for the listener is, again, an instinct born of experience and association which allows him to separate intent from accident, design from experimentation, and pretense from conviction. Much of contemporary music is, like its sister art, merely a reflection of the composer's own fragmentation: an absorption in self and symbols at the expense of communication with others. The artist, in short, says to the public: If you don't understand this, it's because you're dumb. I maintain that you are not. You may have to go part way or even halfway to meet the artist, but if you must go the whole way, it's his fault, not yours. Hold fast to that. And remember it too when you read new poetry, that estranged sister of music.

> A multitude of causes, unknown to former times, are now acting with a combined force to blunt the discriminating powers of the mind, and, unfitting it for all voluntary exertion, to reduce it to a state of almost savage torpor. The most effective of these causes are the great national events which are daily taking place and the increasing accumulation of men in cities, where the uniformity of their occupations produces a craving for extraordinary incident, which the rapid communication of intelligence hourly gratifies. To this tendency of life and manners, the literature and theatrical exhibitions of the country have conformed themselves.

This startingly applicable comment was written in the year 1800 by William Wordsworth in the preface to his "Lyrical Ballads"; and it has been cited by Edwin Muir in his recently published book, *The Estate of Poetry*. Muir states that poetry's effective range and influence have diminished alarmingly in the modern world. He believes in the inherent and indestructible qualities of the human mind and the great and permanent objects that act upon it, and suggests that the audience will increase when "poetry loses what obscurity is left in it by attempting greater themes, for great themes have to be stated clearly." If you keep that firmly in mind and resist, in Muir's words, "the vast dissemination of secondary objects that isolate us from the natural world," you have gone a long way toward equipping yourself for the examination of any work of art.

25   When you come to theatre, in this extremely hasty tour of the arts, you can approach it on two different levels. You can bring to it anticipation and innocence, giving yourself up, as it were, to the life on the stage and reacting to it emotionally, if the play is good, or listlessly, if the play is boring; a part of the audience organism that expresses its favor by silence or laughter and its disfavor by coughing and rustling. Or you can bring to it certain critical faculties that may heighten, rather than diminish, your enjoyment.

You can ask yourselves whether the actors are truly in their parts or merely projecting themselves; whether the scenery helps or hurts the mood; whether the playwright is honest with himself, the characters, and you. Somewhere along the line you can learn to distinguish between the true creative act and the false arbitrary gesture; between fresh observation and stale cliché; between the avant-garde play that is pretentious drivel and the avant-garde play that finds new ways to say old truths.

Purpose and craftsmanship—end and means—these are the keys to your judgment in all the arts. What is this painter trying to say when he slashed a broad band of black across a white canvas and lets the edges dribble down? Is it a statement of violence? Is it a self-portrait? If it is *one* of these, has he made you believe it? Or is this a gesture of the ego or a form of therapy? If it shocks you, what does it shock you into?

And what of this tight little painting of bright flowers in a vase? Is the painter saying anything new about flowers? Is it different from a million other canvases of flowers? Has it any life, any meaning, beyond its statement? Is there any pleasure in its forms or texture? The question is not whether a thing is abstract or representational, whether it is "modern" or conventional. The question, inexorably, is whether it is good. And this is a decision which only you, on the basis of instinct, experience, and association, can make for yourself. It takes independence and courage. It involves, moreover, the risk of wrong decision and the humility, after the passage of time, of recognizing it as such. As we grow and change and learn, our attitudes can change too, and what we once thought obscure or "difficult" can later emerge as coherent and illuminating. Entrenched prejudices, obdurate opinions are as sterile as no opinions at all.

Yet standards there are, timeless as the universe itself. And when you have committed yourself to them, you have acquired a passport to that elusive but immutable realm of truth. Keep it with you in the forest of bewilderment. And never be afraid to speak up.

REFLECTING AND INTERPRETING

1. Where is the thesis statement located?

2. Mannes says a denial of the existence of criteria to evaluate the arts has been popular for several reasons. What are they?

3. What is the general fear of observers of all forms of art? Yet what danger lies in accepting a critic's verdict of "exquisite complexity" without evaluation?

4. Mannes says that appreciation is necessary for the arts to flower. How do the expectations of the public influence art? Are there any other factors that Mannes does not mention?

5. What two basic criteria can be used to judge any piece of art? (Hint: See paragraphs 6 and 7.)

6. What does Mannes mean when she says, "The dogma now is that craftsmanship gets in the way of expression."

7. How does Mannes define *craft*? She says that an audience needs to be able to distinguish what from what?

8. Mannes gives a final piece of advice. What is it?

9. Mannes suggests we ask, "What does an artist say that is timeless; how does he say it?" Using these guidelines, how would you explain Jane Austen's popularity?

10. What four steps does Mannes suggest the reader take to acquire the standards needed to distinguish good art from bad art?

SMALL GROUP DISCUSSION

With your group explore the criteria you use to rate a film as good or bad—one that you would or would not recommend to friends. Have a recorder jot down the proceedings and tabulate the votes for each criterion. After the discussion, the recorder should read the results.

Illustrating with Effective Examples

<table>
<tr><td>INTRODUCTION OF
MOTHERS OF INVENTION</td><td>ETHLIE ANN VARE
GREG PTACEK</td></tr>
</table>

Sometimes an author's best fuel is a powerful load of examples and dry wit—especially when those examples loudly decry the opposition's assertions. In this excerpt from *Mothers of Invention* (1988), Vare and Ptacek effectively shoot down an unjust stereotype, presenting impressive facts. They have also coauthored *Women Inventors and Their Discoveries* (1993), *Patently Female: More Women Inventors and Discoveries* (1998), and *Patently Female* (2001). Vare has written *Adventurous Spirit* (1992) and *Diva: Barbra Streisand and the Making of a Superstar* (1996), as well as television scripts and several biographies. Greg Ptacek is corporate communications director for the American Film Marketing Association. Formerly a marketing executive for Walt Disney Studios, he has also worked as a Hollywood reporter. He has written for a range of publications, as well as published several nonfiction books, including *Champions for Children's Health* (1993).

The first inventor introduced in every grammar-school primer is Eli Whitney, the genius who invented the cotton gin in 1793. Fact is, Mr. Whitney *didn't* invent the cotton "engine" in 1793—or any other year. Eli Whitney built a device conceived, perfected, and marketed by Mrs. Catherine Littlefield Greene, a Georgia belle who, unlike her Massachusetts-born houseguest, was quite familiar with the cotton boll.

Some accounts have it that Mrs. Greene handed Whitney a virtual set of plans for the cotton gin; others believe she "merely" suggested the idea and financed the work. Either way, Catherine Littlefield Greene somehow got lost on her way to those sixth-grade history texts.

Women have been inventing in America [since] before there was a United States, and in other parts of the world [since] before there was an

America. Catherine Littlefield Greene is not the only innovative lady whose accomplishments have slipped through the cracks. Western society has decreed that women do not invent despite facts to the contrary, and makes it a self-fulfilling prophecy by overlooking a few of those facts.

Even in our Smithsonian Museum, the painting honoring America's great inventors—"Men of Progress" by John Lawrence Mott, c. 1856— depicts exactly that: men, all white, and all over the age of forty. By 1856 a young widow named Martha Coston had already patented the Navy's signal flare; Ada Lovelace had designed the prototype computer; Mary Montagu had introduced smallpox inoculation; Nicole Clicquot had invented pink champagne and Elizabeth Flanagan the cocktail; and a Madame Lefebre synthesized the first nitrate fertilizer.

5   Nor can we look back and laugh at nineteenth-century male chauvinism. In his 1957 book *Inventors and Inventions,* C. D. Tuska, then director of RCA patent operations, said: "I shall write little about female inventors . . . most of our inventors are of the male sex. Why is the percentage [of women] so low? I am sure I don't know, unless the good Lord intended them to be mothers. I, being old-fashioned, hold that they are creative enough without also being 'inventive.' They produce the inventors and help rear them, and that should be sufficient."

By 1957 Eleanor Raymond and Maria Telkes had perfected solar heating; Grace Murray Hopper created the basis of computer software; Melitta Bentz invented the modern coffeepot; Mary Engle Pennington developed refrigeration; Margaret Knight invented the square-bottomed bag; Katherine Burr Blodgett patented invisible glass; Gladys Hobby produced the first usable penicillin; Kate Gleason designed the first tract housing; and Hattie Alexander had cured meningitis.

The National Inventors' Hall of Fame in Washington, D.C., boasted a total of fifty-two inductees in 1984; none was a woman. William Coolidge, the inventor of the vacuum tube, is mentioned . . . but not Marie Curie, who invented what we now call the "Geiger" counter and discovered radioactivity. Enrico Fermi makes the grade for building the first atomic reactor . . . but not Lise Meitner, who first created—and named—nuclear fission. Leo Bakeland is honored for inventing Bakelite . . . but not Madame Dutillet, who created cultured marble a century before. . . .

Since 1880, the U.S. Patent Office has officially recognized not only mechanical devices as inventions per se, but also substances, techniques, and processes. . . .

In this volume, we expand the definition of Inventor to include the Discoverers, those who advanced humankind by recognizing the value of things that were in front of everyone else all along.

10   The list of female inventors includes dancers, farmers, nuns, secretaries, actresses, shopkeepers, housewives, military officers, corporate executives, schoolteachers, writers, seamstresses, refugees, royalty, and little kids. All kinds of people can and do invent. The idea that one's gender somehow precludes the possibility of pursuing any technological en-

deavor is not only outdated but also dangerous. In the words of 1977 No-
bel Prize winner Rosalyn Yalow: "The world cannot afford the loss of the
talents of half of its people if we are to solve the many problems which
beset us."

REFLECTING AND INTERPRETING

1. What do you note about the pairing of facts in the first paragraph? Read the last two lines and the second paragraph aloud. How would you describe the tone?

2. Can you find a thesis statement in this essay? How does the delay affect the effectiveness of the opening?

3. What is a "self-fulfilling prophecy" (paragraph 3)?

4. What other groups of inventors were ignored by artist John Lawrence Mott, whose painting hangs in the Smithsonian Museum?

5. We tend to think of the latter half of the twentieth century as being enlight-ened. What evidence do the authors cite that indicates stereotypes about women inventors were widespread at that time?

6. Were the omissions that the authors speak of generally true for your school's history books? Were any women inventors mentioned? If so, which ones do you recall?

7. Look at each place where the authors list women inventors. Note how as-sertions about male inventors contrast with lists of women whose lives dis-prove the assertions. Do the contrasts always follow the same structure? Map the examples to show two ways they are presented.

8. Although twentieth-century history books recognize the work of Marie Curie, she has never received what honor that the authors think she deserves?

9. What is the stereotype that long governed the recognition of inventors and discoverers? By 1977 this assumption had run aground. How do you know?

10. Typically, fewer girls than boys take electives in mathematics and science. More men than women obtain degrees in medicine, biochemistry, and en-gineering. Might these facts influence the number of people who become in-ventors? Why or why not?

A WRITER'S RESPONSE

1. Discrimination appears in many shapes and forms. Have you ever been a victim? How did you cope? Write an essay, giving at least three examples.

2. Since the equal rights movement began, many changes have occurred. Has your life been affected by this movement? If so, how? Write an essay based on examples. (You might contrast your opportunities with those of a parent.)

ROAD RAGE

JASON VEST
WARREN COHEN
MIKE THARP

Have you ever been crowded onto a shoulder of the road, insulted, or assaulted by an angry driver? If so, you were a victim of "road rage," an ever-increasing phenomenon that sometimes results in fatalities. Vest, Cohen, and Tharp researched this problem for *U.S. News & World Report* and reported their findings in an article, first published June 2, 1997. Jason Vest is a Washington DC-based reporter for *The Nation*. He has also written for the *Washington Post, Miami New Times, Boston Phoenix, U.S. News & World Report, Village Voice, Atlantic Monthly*, and others. He also covered the Eritrea-Ethiopia border war. Warren Cohen is a journalist who has written for *U.S. News & World Report, Common Cause, Rolling Stone, Fortune, New Republic, Washington Monthly, Pittsburgh Post-Gazette, Washington City Paper*, and others. Mike Tharp is a communications professor at California State Fullerton. A former reporter for *U.S. News & World Report, Tharp* has worked in Japan and served as president of the Foreign Correspondents' Club there. He also covered Somalia and the Gulf War.

1   Some of the incidents are so ludicrous you can't help but laugh—albeit nervously. There was the case in Salt Lake City, where 75-year-old J. C. King—peeved that 41-year-old Larry Remm Jr. honked at him for blocking traffic—followed Remm when he pulled off the road, hurled his prescription bottle at him, and then, in a display of geriatric resolve, smashed Remm's knees with his '92 Mercury. In tony Potomac, Md., Robin Ficker—an attorney and ex-state legislator—knocked the glasses off a pregnant woman after she had the temerity to ask him why he bumped her Jeep with his.

Other incidents lack even the element of black humor. In Colorado Springs, 55-year-old Vern Smalley persuaded a 17-year-old boy who had been tailgating him to pull over; Smalley decided that, rather than merely scold the lad, he would shoot him. (And he did. Fatally—after the youth had threatened him.) And last year, on Virginia's George Washington Parkway, a dispute over a lane change was settled with a high-speed duel that ended when both drivers lost control and crossed the center line, killing two innocent motorists.

Anyone who spent the Memorial Day weekend on the road probably won't be too surprised to learn the results of a major study to be released this week by the American Automobile Association. The rate of "aggressive driving" incidents—defined as events in which an angry or impatient driver tries to kill or injure another driver after a traffic dispute—has risen by 51 percent since 1990. In those cases studied, 37 percent of offenders used "firearms" against other drivers, an additional 28 percent used other weapons, and 35 percent used their cars.

Fear of (and participation in) aggressive driving has grown so much that in a poll last year residents of Maryland, Washington, D.C. and Virginia listed it as a bigger concern than drunk driving. The Maryland highway department is running a campaign called "The End of the Road for Aggressive Drivers," which, among other things, flashes anti-road-rage messages on electronic billboards on the interstates. Delaware, Pennsylvania, and New Jersey have initiated special highway patrols targeting aggressive drivers. A small but busy community of therapists and scholars has arisen to study the phenomenon and counsel drivers on how to cope. And several members of Congress are now trying to figure out ways to legislate away road rage.

Lest one get unduly alarmed, it helps to put the AAA study's numbers 5 in context: Approximately 250,000 people have been killed in traffic since 1990. While the U.S. Department of Transportation estimates that two-thirds of fatalities are at least partially caused by aggressive driving, the AAA study found only 218 that could be directly attributable to enraged drivers. Of the more than 20 million motorists injured, the survey identified 12,610 injuries attributable to aggressive driving. While the study is the first American attempt to quantify aggressive driving, it is not rigorously scientific. The authors drew on reports from 30 newspapers—supplemented by insurance claims and police reports from 16 cities—involving 10,037 occurrences. Moreover, the overall trendlines for car accidents have continued downward for several decades, thanks in part to increases in the drinking age and improvements in car technology like high-mounted brake lights.

But researchers believe there is a growing trend of simple aggressive behavior—road rage—in which a driver reacts angrily to other drivers. Cutting them off, tailgating, giving the finger, waving a fist—experts believe these forms of nonviolent fury are increasing. "Aggressive driving is now the most common way of driving," says Sandra Ball-Rokeach, who codirects the Media and Injury Prevention Program at the University of Southern California. "It's not just a few crazies—it's a subculture of driving."

In focus groups set up by her organization, two-thirds of drivers said they reacted to frustrating situations aggressively. Almost half admitted to deliberately braking suddenly, pulling close to the other car, or taking some other potentially dangerous step. Another third said they retaliated with a hostile gesture. Drivers show great creativity in devising hostile responses. Doug Erber of Los Angeles keeps his windshield-wiper-fluid tank full. If someone tailgates, he turns on the wipers, sending fluid over his roof onto the car behind him. "It works better than hitting the brakes," he says, "and you can act totally innocent."

Mad Max

While the AAA authors note there is a profile of the lethally inclined aggressive driver—"relatively young, poorly educated males who have criminal records, histories of violence, and drug or alcohol problems"—road-rage scholars (and regular drivers) believe other groups are equally represented in the less violent forms of aggressive driving. To some, it's tempting to look at this as a psychologically mysterious Jekyll-and-Hyde phenomenon; for others, it's simply attributable to "jerk drivers." In reality, there's a confluence of emotional and demographic factors that changes the average citizen from mere motorist to Mad Max.

First, it isn't just your imagination that traffic is getting worse. Since 1987, the number of miles of roads has increased just 1 percent while the miles *driven* have shot up by 35 percent. According to a recent Federal Highway Administration study of 50 metropolitan areas, almost 70 percent of urban freeways today—as opposed to 55 percent in 1983—are clogged during rush hour. The study notes that congestion is likely to spread to currently unspoiled locations. Forty percent of the currently gridlock-free Milwaukee County highway system, for example, is predicted to be jammed up more than five hours a day by the year 2000. A study by the Texas Transportation Institute last year found that commuters in one-third of the largest cities spent well over 40 hours a year in traffic jams.

10   Part of the problem is that jobs have shifted from cities to suburbs. Communities designed as residential suburbs with narrow roads have grown into "edge cities," with bustling commercial traffic. Suburb-to-suburb commutes now account for 44 percent of all metropolitan traffic versus 20 percent for suburb-to-downtown travel. Demographer and *Edge City* author Joel Garreau says workers breaking for lunch are essentially causing a third rush hour. He notes that in Tysons Corner, Va., it takes an average of four traffic signal cycles to get through a typical intersection at lunchtime. And because most mass transit systems are of a spoke-and-hub design, centering on cities and branching out to suburbs, they're not really useful in getting from point A to point B in an edge city or from one edge city to another. Not surprisingly, fewer people are relying on mass transit and more on cars. In 1969, 82.7 percent drove to work; in 1990, 91.4 percent did. Despite the fact that the Washington, D.C., area has an exemplary commuter subway system, it accounts for only 2 percent of all trips made.

Demographic changes have helped put more drivers on the road. Until the 1970s, the percentage of women driving was relatively low, and many families had only one car. But women entered the work force and bought cars, something developers and highway planners hadn't foreseen. From 1969 to 1990 the number of women licensed to drive increased 84 percent. Between 1970 and 1987, the number of cars on the road more than doubled. In the past decade, the number of cars grew faster (17 percent) than the number of people (10 percent). Even carpooling is down despite HOV lanes and other preferential devices. The cumulative effect, says University of Hawaii traffic psychology professor Leon James, is a sort of sensory overload. "There are simply more cars—and more behaviors—to deal with," says James.

As if the United States couldn't produce enough home-grown lousy drivers, it seems to be importing them as well. Experts believe that many immigrants come from countries that have bad roads and aggressive styles. It's not just drivers from Third World countries, though. British drivers are considered among the safest in Europe, yet recent surveys show that nearly 90 percent of British motorists have experienced threats or abuse from other drivers. Of Brits who drive for a living, about 21 percent report having been run off the road. In Australia, one study estimates that about half of all traffic accidents there may be due to road rage. "There are different cultures of driving all over the world—quite clearly, if we mix new cultures in the melting pot, what we get is a culture clash on the roadway," says John Palmer, a professor in the Health Education and Safety Department at Minnesota's St. Cloud University.

The peak moment for aggressive driving comes not during impenetrable gridlocks but just before, when traffic density is high but cars are still moving briskly. That's when cutting someone off or forcing someone out of a lane can make the difference (or so it seems) between being on time and being late, according to Palmer.

Unfortunately, roads are getting more congested just as Americans feel even more pressed for time. "People get on a time line for their car trips," says Palmer. "When they perceive that someone is impeding their progress or invading their agenda, they respond with what they consider to be 'instructive' behavior, which might be as simple as flashing their lights to something more combative."

Suburban Assault Vehicles

This, uh, "instruction" has become more common, Palmer and others   15
speculate, in part because of modern automotive design. With hyperadjustable seats, soundproof interiors, CD players, and cellular phones, cars are virtually comfortable enough to live in. Students of traffic can't help but wonder if the popularity of pickup trucks and sport utility vehicles has contributed to the problem. Sales have approximately doubled since 1990. These big metal shells loom over everything else, fueling feelings of power and drawing out a driver's more primal instincts. "A lot of the anecdotal evidence about aggressive driving incidents tends to involve people driving sport utility vehicles," says Julie Rochman of the Insurance Institute for Highway Safety. "When people get these larger, heavier vehicles, they feel more invulnerable." While Chrysler spokesman Chris Preuss discounts the notion of suburban assault vehicles being behind the aggressive-driving phenomenon, he does say women feel more secure in the jumbo-size vehicles.

In much of life, people feel they don't have full control of their destiny. But a car—unlike, say, a career or a spouse—responds reliably to one's wish. In automobiles, we have an increased (but false) sense of invincibility. Other drivers become dehumanized, mere appendages to a competing machine. "You have the illusion you're alone and master, dislocated from other drivers," says Hawaii's James.

Los Angeles psychologist Arnold Nerenberg describes how one of his recent patients got into an angry road confrontation with another motorist. "They pulled off the road and started running toward each other to fight, but then they recognized each other as neighbors," he says. "When it's just somebody else in a car, it's more two-dimensional; the other person's identity boils down to, 'You're someone who did something bad to me.'"

How can aggressive driving be minimized? Some believe that better driver's education might help. Driver's ed was a high school staple by the 1950s, thanks to federal highway dollars given to states. But a 1978 government study in De Kalb County, Ga., found no reduction in crashes or traffic violations by students who took a driver's ed course compared with those who didn't. Rather than use these results to design better driver's ed programs, the feds essentially gave up on them and diverted money to seat belt and anti-drunk-driving programs. Today, only 40 percent of new drivers complete a formal training course, which may be one reason 20 percent to 35 percent of applicants fail their initial driving test.

The Inner Driver

But governments are looking anew at the value of driver's education. In April, Michigan passed sweeping rules that grant levels of privilege depending on one's age and driving record. States with similar systems, like California, Maryland, and Oregon, have seen teen accident rates drop.

20   Those who lose their licenses often have to return to traffic school. But some states have generous standards for these schools. To wit: California's theme schools. There, errant drivers can attend the "Humor's My Name, Traffic's My Game," school, in which a mock jury led by a stand-up comic decides who the worst drivers are; the "Traffic School for Chocoholics," which plies errant drivers with chocolate and ice cream; and the gay and lesbian "Pink Triangle Traffic School."

But the real key to reducing road rage probably lies deep within each of us. Professor James of the University of Hawaii suggests that instead of emphasizing defensive driving—which implies that the other driver is the enemy—we should focus on "supportive driving" or "driving with the aloha spirit." Of course that's hard to do if (a) someone has just cut you off at 60 mph or (b) you live in Los Angeles instead of Hawaii. Nerenberg, the Los Angeles psychologist, has published an 18-page booklet called "Overcoming Road Rage: The 10-Step Compassion Program." He recommends examining what sets off road rage and to "visualize overcoming it." Other tips: Imagine you might be seeing that person at a party soon. And remembering that other drivers "are people with feelings. Let us not humiliate them with our aggression." In the chapter titled, "Peace," he suggests, "Take a deep breath and just let it go." And if that doesn't work, the windshield-wiper trick is pretty clever.

REFLECTING AND INTERPRETING

1. Comment on the incidents described in the opening. Do you think such conflicts are common or isolated? Do they seem to occur more often in certain areas? If so, where?

2. How does the American Automobile Association define an "aggressive driving" incident?

3. When does the peak moment for aggressive driving occur?

4. What do the authors cite as major causes of the increase in aggressive driving?

5. Do the authors of the AAA research believe that aggressive drivers tend to have criminal records, histories of violence, or drug or alcohol problems?

6. What did the drivers in focus groups set up by the University of Southern California admit?

7. How does the type of vehicle seem to influence a driver's feelings and behavior?

8. Since 1987, the miles of roadway in the USA have increased by 1 percent, but the miles driven have increased 35 percent. What conclusions can you draw from these statistics?

9. What is the predominant rhetorical strategy used in this article?

10. How do the authors support their claims?

SMALL GROUP DISCUSSION

1. What tends to set off road rage? What can a driver do to forestall arousing his or her own impatience and irritating other drivers?

2. Discuss possible ways of self-preservation when risky on-the-road situations occur. How can you diffuse the wrath of a driver? What should you do if that person signals you to stop?

3. Have you ever witnessed an incident of road rage? If so, write an essay describing what happened. Is there a moral to the tale?

BLACK AND WELL-TO-DO   ANDREA LEE

Too often in the past, blacks have been dogged by stereotypes. In this essay Andrea Lee strikes a different note as she describes her life in the upper-middle-class integrated suburb of Yeadon, on the edge of Philadelphia. Sheltered from prejudice, she attended Quaker schools and spent summers on Martha's Vineyard. At Harvard she earned both bachelor's and master's degrees. A former staff writer for *The New Yorker*, Lee has also written for the *New York Times Magazine*, *New York Times Book Review*, *Oxford American*, *Vogue*, and *Time*. She and her husband spent nearly a year in Russia in 1978–79, where she started writing *Russian Journal* (1981). In 1984 she received the Jean Stein Award and American Academy and Institute of Arts and Letters Award. Her other books include *The Lady Cavaliers* (1979), *Sarah Phillips* (1984), and *Interesting Women* (2002).

I grew up in the kind of town few people believe exists: a black upper-   1
middle-class suburb full of colonial-style houses and Volkswagen Rabbits. Yes, Virginia, there is a black bourgeoisie, it has existed for years, and it summers on Martha's Vineyard.

The Philadelphia suburb of Yeadon, my home through childhood and adolescence, is one of many black enclaves that someday will make a very interesting study for a sociologist.

After World War II, housing speculators found it profitable to scare off white residents and sell whole streets of Yeadon to black professionals who were as eager as anyone else at that time to pursue the romantic suburban dream of fieldstone patios and eye-level ovens. In the 1950's, half the black doctors and lawyers in Philadelphia crowded into this rather small town, which was one of the few integrated suburbs, and we Yeadon kids grew up with tree houses and two-car garages and fathers who commuted into the city.

Our parents had a vision of pastoral normalcy for their children that was little different from the white ideal laid out in the Dick and Jane readers. Their attempts to provide this and to protect us from the slightest contact with race prejudice left us extraordinarily, perhaps unhealthily, sheltered: We were sent to Quaker schools and camps where race and class were discounted with eager innocence. When the Yeadon Civic Association (my father was president) discovered that a local swimming club was discriminating against blacks, the parents in my neighborhood simply built another club, which they christened "The Nile Swim Club." When we asked about the name, my father explained gravely: "This is a club only for Egyptians."

5   Childhood in Yeadon was a suburban idyll of shady streets and bicycles and ice cream from a drugstore called Doc's. This was the early 1960's, and as my friends and I grew older, we became dimly aware that the rest of the world was not necessarily Yeadon. Most of our parents were active in the civil rights movement, and at gatherings we listened avidly to their campaign references: Birmingham, Selma, Greensboro.

Occasionally, we kids would travel into the city and stare in horrified fascination at slums. When my generation of Yeadon preppies was graduated from high school in the late 1960's and early 1970's, however, we quickly realized that our vague concern was not enough, and many of us became radicalized. (Most of us were attending Ivy League colleges, and this increased our sense of guilt.)

During college holidays, Yeadon's driveways were colorful with dashikis and other, more complicated African garments, and a great deal of talk went on about the brothers and sisters of the urban community. Yeadon parents were edgy and alienated from their children at this time, and a common conversation between mothers began: "Yes, she used to look so sweet, and now she's gone and gotten one of those . . . Afros."

In the 1970's, our guilt evaporated, and Yeadon became a place where parents vied with one another to produce tidbits about surgeon daughters and M.B.A. sons. Now, early in the 1980's, I find that in some circles, Yeadon is a synonym for conservatism and complacency, a place famed as being the hunting-ground of the AAP (Afro-American Prince or Princess), but I don't care.

Yeadon was a great town to grow up in, was as solid a repository of American virtues and American flaws as any other close-knit suburban community; moreover, it had, and still has, its own peculiar flavor—a lively mixture of materialism, idealism, and ironic humor that prevents the minds of its children from stagnating. I feel a surge of well-being when I return there in the summer to hear the symphony of lawn mowers and to find that the Nile Swim Club remains "for Egyptians only."

REFLECTING AND INTERPRETING

1. Examine the first paragraph. What tone does "Yes, Virginia, there is . . ." set?
2. What is the "romantic suburban dream" that Lee speaks of?
3. What types of people lived in Yeadon? Describe their lifestyle.
4. How were Lee and other children in Yeadon sheltered from racial prejudice?
5. How did the youth of Yeadon become aware of racial prejudice?
6. What message was implicit in Lee's father's explanation of the name of the swim club?
7. What did the new swim club symbolize? Why was it unusual and significant?
8. Why did Lee and her friends feel guilty when they were attending Ivy League colleges?
9. How does Lee feel about Yeadon and her childhood there?
10. Andrea Lee has two degrees from Harvard and is a staff writer for *The New Yorker*. After reading this essay, what do you think were the prime factors that influenced her success?

A WRITER'S RESPONSE

1. Write an essay describing the place where you grew up. How did you feel about it? Have your feelings stayed the same or changed over the years?
2. *Small Groups:* What kinds of discrimination exist in your state? What changes in societal attitudes have occurred there during your lifetime? What other changes would you like to see?

GOING FOR BROKE

MATEA GOLD
DAVID FERRELL

Staff writers for the *Los Angeles Times*, Matea Gold and David Ferrell have a variety of publications to their credit. Gold specializes in political reporting but has also written about food safety, Yiddish literature, and language. She wrote a "First Person" column for the *Times* and won Sacramento Press awards in 1994 and 1995. Ferrell was a finalist in 1996 for the Investigative Reporting and Editors Award. He has been a member of two news teams that won Pulitzer prizes. In 1998 his work was included in *Best American Sports Writing*. His black comedy baseball novel, *Screwball*, was published in 2003. The essay that follows is based upon data from a seven-month investigation of legalized gambling nationwide.

1   Rex Coile's life is a narrow box, so dark and confining he wonders how he got trapped inside, whether he'll ever get out.

He never goes to the movies, never sees concerts, never lies on a sunny beach, never travels on vacation, never spends Christmas with his family. Instead, Rex shares floor space in cheap motels with other compulsive gamblers, comforting himself with delusional dreams of jackpots that will magically wipe away three decades of wreckage. He has lost his marriage, his home, his Cadillac, his clothes, his diamond ring. Not least of all, in the card clubs of Southern California, he has lost his pride.

Rex no longer feels sorry for himself, not after a 29-year losing streak that has left him scrounging for table scraps to feed his habit. Still, he agonizes over what he has become at 54 and what he might have been.

Articulate, intellectual, he talks about existential philosophy, the writings of Camus and Sartre. He was once an editor at Random House. His mind is so jampacked with tidbits about movies, television, baseball and history that card room regulars call him "Rex Trivia," a name he cherishes for the remnant of self-respect it gives him. "There's a lot of Rexes around these card rooms," he says in a whisper of resignation and sadness.

5   And their numbers are soaring as gambling explodes across America, from the mega-resorts of Las Vegas to the gaming parlors of Indian reservations, from the riverboats along the Mississippi to the corner mini-marts selling lottery tickets. With nearly every state in the union now sanctioning some form of legalized gambling to raise revenues, evidence is mounting that society is paying a steep price, one that some researchers say must be confronted, if not reversed.

Never before have bettors blown so much money—a whopping $50.9 billion last year—five times the amount lost in 1980. That's more than the public spent on movies, theme parks, recorded music and sporting events combined. A substantial share of those gambling losses—an estimated 30% to 40%—pours from the pockets and purses of chronic losers hooked on the adrenaline rush of risking their money, intoxicated by the fast action of gambling's incandescent world.

Studies place the total number of compulsive gamblers at about 4.4 million, about equal to the nation's ranks of hard-core drug addicts. Another 11 million, known as problem gamblers, teeter on the verge. Since 1990, the number of Gamblers Anonymous groups nationwide has doubled from about 600 to more than 1,200.

Compulsive gambling has been linked to child abuse, domestic violence, embezzlement, bogus insurance claims, bankruptcies, welfare fraud and a host of other social and criminal ills. The advent of Internet gambling could lure new legions into wagering beyond their means.

Every once in a while, a case is so egregious it makes headlines: A 10-day-old baby girl in South Carolina dies after being left for nearly seven hours in a hot car while her mother plays video poker. A suburban Chicago woman is so desperate for a bankroll to gamble that she allegedly suffocates her 7-week-old daughter 11 days after obtaining a $200,000 life-insurance policy on the baby.

But these tragedies that flash before the public eye are just lightning 10 strokes of a roiling night storm. Far more often, compulsive gambling bends lives more subtly, less sensationally, over the course of years.

Gwen, one of the unseen masses trying to keep her head above water, sits on an easy chair in the living room of her worn Jefferson Park bungalow, watching the movie "Titanic" on an old TV. Her hair is uncombed and there are bags under her eyes. She puffs on a cigarette and shakes her foot nervously. On the screen, the great ship begins to founder.

"That's me," she says, tears rolling down her checks. "I'm sinking."

Gwen has just come off a three-day bender at the Hollywood Park Casino in Inglewood. She blew a paycheck, emptied out her new checking account, gambled right through her work shift. Driving home from the casino, she contemplated veering off the road, ending it all. "I just don't want to be here," she mumbles, watching Titanic's Rose and Jack struggling to hold on to a piece of driftwood in the freezing sea. "I just feel like I'm living a hopeless life. So hopeless."

She's written bad checks and maxed out her credit cards. One bank closed her checking account after she put too many fake deposit slips in the ATM to withdraw cash. She lies. She tells her boss she needs a salary advance because her son is in the hospital. Late on the rent, she parks a block from the house to duck the landlord. For the last eight years, this has been her life, one so empty of joy and options that the card clubs have become her only hope of filling the hole.

She thinks back to that night a few years ago when, desperate to re- 15 coup her gambling losses, she pilfered several thousand dollars from the safe of a restaurant where she was working. She just needed something to get herself started, she told herself. She'd pay it back with the winnings. She blew it all in one weekend.

Overwhelmed by guilt, she came clean with her manager. She was booked, fingerprinted and briefly thrown behind bars. "It was the worst experience of my life," she says.

Gwen now makes monthly $75 restitution payments to the restaurant as part of her court-ordered probation.

"I have hurt so many people with my gambling," says Gwen. "I have lost best friends. After all the pain I've caused everybody, the pain I caused myself, I still have the urge to gamble. I never know what I'm going to do. I'm so afraid. I'm really afraid."

Science has begun to uncover clues to compulsive gambling—genetic predispositions that involve chemical receptors in the brain, the same pleasure pathways implicated in drug and alcohol addiction. But no amount of knowledge, no amount of enlightenment, makes the illness any less confounding, any less destructive. What the gamblers cannot understand about themselves is also well beyond the comprehension of family members, who struggle for normality in a world of deceit and madness.

Money starts vanishing: $500 here, $200 there, $800 a couple of weeks 20 later. Where is it? The answers come back vague, nonsensical. It's in the desk at work. A friend borrowed it. It got spent on family dinners, car repairs, loans to in-laws. Exasperated spouses play the sleuth, combing through pockets, wallets, purses, searching the car. Sometimes the incriminating evidence turns up—a racing form, lottery scratchers, a map to an Indian casino. Once the secret is uncovered, spouses usually fight the problem alone, bleeding inside, because the stories are too humiliating to share.

"Anybody who is living with a compulsive gambler is totally overwhelmed," says Tom Tucker, president of the California Council on Problem Gambling. "They're steeped in anger, resentment, depression, confusion. None of their personal efforts will ever stop a person from their [sic] addiction. And they don't really see any hope because compulsive gambling in general is such an under-recognized illness."

One Los Angeles woman, whose husband's gambling was tearing at her sanity, says she slept with her fists so tightly clenched that her nails sliced into her palms. She had fantasies of death—first her own, thinking he'd feel sorry for her and stop gambling. Later, she harbored thoughts of turning her rage on her husband. She imagined getting a gun, hiding in the closet and blasting him out of her life.

"The hurt was so bad I think I would have pulled the trigger," she says. "There were times the pain was so much I thought being in jail, or being in the electric chair, would be less than this."

Five years in Gam-Anon, the 12-step support group for family and friends of compulsive gamblers, has only begun to heal her. "I don't think I'm even halfway there," she says.

25　　Too often, families of gambling addicts endure more than warped finances and wrecked psyches. They have come to fear for their physical safety.

Trena, a 42-year-old Whittier homemaker, is among them. Several months ago, after years of agony, she filed for divorce. Her husband, a manager in an industrial plant, was making decent money and took pride in his job. He had two good children and a nice home, an airy bungalow with hardwood floors and a white-brick fireplace. Inside him, though, was a fearsome need to fulfill some glossy vision.

Lottery keno became the rhythmic pulse of his life. For five years, Trena says, she awoke in an empty bed every weekend. Her husband would be gone by 5:30 or 6, joining other keno regulars at the neighborhood doughnut shop, watching the numbers flash on an overhead monitor. He'd shuffle home hours later, refusing to divulge his losses.

Trena did what tens of thousands of spouses do: She struggled desperately to pay the bills. She hid money in Cheerios boxes, books, couch cushions, under the doormat. She drew up household budgets—hundreds of them. They became her obsession. She drafted a new one almost every day, never able to get one to work.

Absurd dramas were played out. On paydays, when her husband's check was directly deposited into their account, they would race each other to the bank. Trena would go to one branch, he'd head to another. She would sit at the drive-up window, jamming her withdrawal slip in the pneumatic tube the moment the bank opened. If she got the money, they could pay the utilities and keep the phone connected. If not, he'd be off to the races, the casinos or the doughnut shop.

Like a caged animal, she threw things—smashed a clock against the 30 wall, broke the portable TV in the bedroom. She yelled, clawed and sometimes just sank down and cried. Trena had no money for herself, for the important personal things. She got nothing for her mom on Mother's Day.

Increasingly reclusive, she stopped returning calls. Chit-chatting with friends seemed a frivolous distraction when dealing with foreclosure notices, filing for bankruptcy or, worse, fending off her husband's angry demands for cash.

He would burst into the house shouting, "Give me my money!" Pacing, following her, tipping over plants, rifling through drawers, dumping them out to try to find it. "Don't you touch my money!"

Joining Gam-Anon, where Trena receives emotional support from the spouses of other gamblers, has helped her deal with her decade-long ordeal. She says she is not bitter and understands that compulsive gambling is an illness.

While her husband now lives with his parents, she remains in their home of 19 years, a place filled with memories as wistful as they are painful.

With drug or alcohol abusers, there is the hope of sobering up, an ac- 35 complishment in itself, no matter what problems may have accompanied their addictions. Compulsive gamblers often see no way to purge their urges when suffocating debts suggest only one answer: a hot streak. "They have nowhere to turn—they feel cornered," says Dr. Richard J. Rosenthal, a Beverly Hills psychiatrist who founded the California Council on Problem Gambling. "Very often they are motivated by their shame into more and more desperate attempts to avoid being found out."

David Phillips, a UC San Diego sociology professor, studied death records from 1982 to 1988—before legalized gambling exploded across America—and found that people in Las Vegas, Atlantic City and other gambling meccas showed significantly higher suicide rates than people in non-gambling cities.

Rex Trivia is not about to kill himself, but like most compulsive gamblers, he occasionally thinks about it. Looking at him, it's hard to imagine he once had a promising future as a smart young New York book editor. His pale eyes are expressionless, his hair yellowish and brittle. In his fifties, his health is failing: emphysema, three lung collapses, a bad aorta, rotting teeth.

His plunge has been so dizzying that at one point he agreed to aid another desperate gambler in a run of bank robberies—nine in all, throughout Los Angeles and Orange counties. When the FBI busted him in 1980, he had $50,000 in cash in a dresser drawer and $100,000 in traveler's checks in his refrigerator's vegetable crisper. Rex, who ended up doing a short stint in prison, hasn't seen that kind of money since.

At 11 P.M. on a Tuesday night, with a bankroll of $55—all he has—he is at a poker table in Gardena. With quick, nervous hands he stacks and unstacks his $1 chips. The stack dwindles. Down $30, he talks about leaving, getting some sleep. Midnight comes and goes. Rex starts winning. Three aces. Four threes. Chips pile up—$60, $70. "A shame to go when the cards are falling my way." He checks the time: "I'll go at 2. Win, lose or draw."

40   Fate, kismet, luck—the cards keep falling. At 2 A.M., Rex is up $97. He stands, leaves his chips on the table and goes out for a smoke. In the darkness at the edge of the parking lot, he loiters with other regulars, debating with himself whether to grab a bus and quit.

"I should go back in there and cash in and get out of here," he says. "That's what I should do."

A long pause. Crushing out his cigarette, Rex turns and heads back inside. He has made his decision.

"A few more hands."

REFLECTING AND INTERPRETING

1. Where is the thesis statement located?

2. Identify the two sentences that provide transition from the opening example to the thesis statement.

3. In paragraph six Gold and Ferrell provide a comparison to the statistic of $50.9 billion spent last year on gambling. What is the effect of the comparison?

4. Is compulsive gambling generally regarded as a bad habit or as an illness? Why?

5. Why is compulsive gambling a social and criminal problem rather than just a problem of individuals?

6. How did compulsive gambling affect death records near gambling meccas?

7. Consider the analogy in paragraphs 11 to 13. Is it apt? Why or why not?

8. What is the effect of including direct quotations such as those in paragraph 31?

9. Examine the opening example and its continuation at the ending. How does it function? What is the effect of the last sentence?

10. Consider the title. Have you ever heard that expression? Why is it ironic here?

A WRITER'S RESPONSE

1. Do you regard gambling as a harmless pastime? If so, defend your point of view.

2. Do you consider gambling to be a problem in your state? Why or why not?

Classifying
Sorting into Groups

MIND OVER MUNCHIES	NORMAN BROWN

"Food cravings are like fingerprints," or so Norman Brown has decided. We all have individual food cravings that surface, perhaps at a particular time of day or under certain conditions. He presents research about "comfort foods," "mood foods," and "happy foods" but with no definitive results. Although researchers do not agree about what causes food cravings, they do agree that excessive cravings of certain foods and nonfoods are a good reason to consult a physician. "Mind Over Munchies" was first published in *Northwest Airlines* (June 1992) and later in *The Thoughtful Reader* (1994).

Got any favorite foods? They can reveal a lot about your personality, [1] say experts who have been digging into our "edible complex" ever since Cleopatra's milk baths and fig outs. Not surprisingly, those gastronomical urges are also the subject of considerable debate.

Some researchers believe there are strong physiological links to food cravings. But others feel that our urges are not that deep-rooted or overwhelming. How much is scientific fact—and should we be that concerned about "mood foods" which are supposed to make us happier, smarter or sexier?

Current research lends support to both sides. Scientists now believe that food cravings are a smorgasbord of biological and psychological events that help the body regulate its intake of nutrients. The notion, though controversial, has obvious appeal. Whether you crave a pizza or nachos, it's comforting to think the body is getting a desired carbohydrate fix—or quick salt injection.

Food cravings are like fingerprints. In those sluggish hours when there's nothing better to do than imagine the perfect entrée, our choices are as varied as they are precise: McDonald's fries, subgum chow mein, or chocolate chip cookies.

Necessary Comforts

5   "Comfort foods are really an individual thing," says Dr. Kelly Brownell, professor of nutrition at Yale University in New Haven. He compares cravings to a wave in the ocean—starting small, building to a peak, then rapidly subsiding. If you track where you are in the cycle, or if the urge strikes at the same time each day, you can ward it off by taking a brisk walk.

Brownell admits he's not sure whether cravings are in the head or stomach. "It's possible that there's nothing physiological about them," he says. "Even if you buy that argument, our protein intake is amazingly steady. What varies wildly is fat and sugar consumption—and which foods you choose depends on habit."

In a survey for the *Wall Street Journal,* half of all respondents said they did seek solace in food when depressed. First choice: ice cream or chocolate bars (with 34 percent of the vote). Pizza, beer, soft drinks, hot soup, peanut butter and burgers completed the list of comforting edibles.

Other scientists agree that what we eat (or don't eat) is often rooted in the nurturing, warmth and security we felt in childhood. "Some cravers want a little taste of what Mom gave them to feel better," explains Dr. Tom Castonguay, associate professor of nutrition at the University of Maryland. "Others use food to be bad."

The very word "craving" conjures up an addiction, but that's not the kind of thing a person with a sweet tooth is experiencing. "Cravings are not that deep-rooted or overwhelming," says Castonguay. "But people are making money talking about them in that way."

Eat for Success?

10   Every fad diet for "cravers" that hits the bookstores claims to rely on scientific proof and it all has to do with those elusive brain chemicals that can send you to the sack—or to the refrigerator. Among the strongest proponents of "mood foods" is Dr. Judith Wurtman, nutritional biochemist at the Massachusetts Institute of Technology.

Her research over the past several years seems to indicate that irrational desires for certain foods may indeed be biologically based. Carbohydrate cravers, she says, feel calmer—and less tired and depressed—after satisfying their need.

Wurtman notes that dietary needs vary from person to person, but suggests that carbohydrate craving may be linked to the activity of serotonin, a chemical produced in the brain when sugar or starch is ingested. When cravers were given a substance that increases serotonin, she says, "the cravings went down to nothing."

Her books and advice have become immensely popular, but she's quick to point out that food is not a panacea for all our ills. "There are myths to confront," says Wurtman. One is that sugar causes anxiety. Her research has shown that sugar or starch actually has a calming effect and may be an unconscious attempt at self-medication.

She advises stress-plagued executives to cut down on "dumb" foods and eat smart: low-fat carbohydrates like bananas and crackers to chase away tension, or high-protein snacks (peanut butter or cottage cheese) for the alertness chemicals dopamine and norepinephrine.

Happy Foods

Campbell Soup Co. is also investigating how food may affect people's moods, and is doing research projects with Tufts University School of Medicine. "We feel mood is going to be really big in the 90s and that positioning foods as making one smarter or happier could be a gold mine," says Tony Adams, marketing research chief.   15

The company is studying carbohydrates, caffeine and other components of food. "But the research puts some folks at Campbell in a nervous mood. "People here worry about making claims," says Adams. "We'll have to be careful to separate fact from witch doctoring."

Other researchers think carbohydrate cravers may be deluding themselves. What they really yearn for are those fat-sugar mixtures, says Dr. Adam Drewnowski, nutrition professor at the University of Michigan School of Public Health.

"Hardly anyone craves pure carbohydrates such as macaroni or cabbage," he says. "But almost everybody can identify with an uncontrollable desire for a Snickers bar or piece of cheesecake." He has demonstrated that such food cravings can be blocked by the drug naloxone, which is also given to addicts to ease opiate cravings.

Other scientists are studying a hormone (cholecystokinin) that may hold the key to why we pig out. They believe that the hormone, secreted during digestion, sends signals to the brain that cause the can't-eat-another-bite sensation. The trick in stopping binges is to make this reaction happen sooner—not later.

And behaviorists argue that we *learn* our food fixations. "Taste may be more addictive than calories or nutrients," says Dr. Stephen Chang, food science professor at Rutgers University. The brain is more interested in what's happening on the tongue than in the stomach. "If the tongue is happy, then the brain will be happy," he says.   20

Brain Chemicals

Drewnowski and others speculate that in some people, food cravings increase the output of endorphins, mood-altering brain chemicals with potent effects similar to narcotics. Not only do endorphins soothe headaches and calm frazzled nerves, they can sweep us into euphoria—or kindle destructive behavior such as excruciating workouts or compulsive gambling.

Childbirth would be unbearable without the easing effects of these natural opiates, which increase four or five times during labor. After the baby is born, endorphins return to their former levels. Not surprisingly, people with chronic pain have only half the endorphins of a healthy person.

It's not that cravings are significantly more common during pregnancy. Rather, women are more likely to satisfy them at that time, explains Dr. Judith Rodin, professor of psychology at Yale. Pregnant women do require the extra salt and calories that pickles and ice cream provide as fetal development begins.

Aversions, the flip side of cravings, are particularly strong during the first trimester. Since that's when the fetus is most vulnerable, aversions to coffee or alcohol are very protective, says Rodin.

25   When food cravings (or aversions) have an obsessional quality, or are persistent, it may indicate a more serious eating disorder such as bulimia or anorexia, she says. For most of us, cravings are either short-lived or the result of temporary stress.

Food intolerances also can cause anxiety, food cravings and obesity. Additives, irritants and toxins are common culprits. But there may be an acquired biochemical defect, such as the inability to digest milk sugar (lactase deficiency). Finding *healthy* ways to boost our moods through endorphins and other brain chemicals could even keep us from falling into dangerous addictions.

Mood Medicine

Food cravings can be the undoing of even the most conscientious eaters. So, how do we deal with them? "You can't control the fact that cravings occur," says Dr. Harvey Ross, psychiatrist and author of *The Mood Control Diet* (Prentice Hall, 1990). "But you can control how you react to them."

His research shows that certain foods, or substances concentrated from them, can be used in the same way as drugs to improve your sleep or the way you handle stress. Avoiding "trigger" foods can be effective in treating disorders as varied as depression and yeast infections.

The most controversial aspect of food cravings or intolerances is the claim that they are often the underlying causes of such disorders as hypoglycemia (low blood sugar), allergies, anemia, and chronic fatigue. Most allergists dispute such claims, but additional studies may eventually bear out many of them.

30   If you find yourself craving inordinate amounts of the following, consult your physician to rule out any serious medical condition:

> *Salt.* Excessive cravings can be a sign of adrenal insufficiency in which tissues and blood are depleted of saltwater, and blood pressure plummets.

Water. Constant thirst may signal juvenile or adult-onset diabetes. Weight loss may also occur despite constant hunger or voracious eating.

Sugar. Severe cravings may be a symptom of reactive hyperglycemia and the body's inability to maintain adequate levels of blood sugar (glucose).

Ice. Persistent need can be a sign of anemia (sore mouth or tongue) or chronic kidney disease due to disturbances in blood chemistry.

Nonfoods. Abnormal cravings for items such as laundry starch by pregnant   35
women and paint chips by children is known as pica. Fetal risk and lead poisoning are possible effects.

REFLECTING AND INTERPRETING

1. What rhetorical device does Brown use in the first and second paragraphs?
2. Dr. Judith Wurtman advises eating certain foods to alleviate stress and increase alertness. What are they? What four examples does she give?
3. Dr. Wurtman claims that sugar has a calming effect. Do you agree or disagree? Is it possible that different people react differently to sugar?
4. What hormone is thought to "hold the key to why we pig out"? Yet what do behaviorists argue as being more "addictive than calories and nutrients"?
5. Researchers speculate that in some people, food cravings increase the output of endorphins, mood-altering brain chemicals. How can endorphins affect us?
6. What is the most controversial aspect of food cravings or intolerances?
7. The author cites five kinds of cravings that deserve the attention of a physician. What are they?
8. You may have to hunt to find Brown's thesis. What is the main idea of this essay? How would you state it in your own words?
9. Although the author cites research, this is not a technical article. How does he achieve the light tone?
10. How would you rate Brown's objectivity in presenting this research?

A WRITER'S RESPONSE

1. Before your group begins, appoint someone to chart categories of individual food cravings and the times they occur. Then share experiences. What factors seem to affect your cravings? Do you attempt to control them? What seems to work best? After the discussion, tally the responses and read them to the group.
2. What are your favorite foods? Do you experience cravings at particular times? Do you think they reveal anything about your personality? Write a short essay analyzing and classifying your eating habits.

WHERE DO WE STAND?   LISA DAVIS

Have you noticed any slight differences in behavior or conversational style among students of varying cultures on your campus? In this essay, first published in *Health* magazine, Lisa Davis discusses how different spatial needs and eye contact can cause hasty judgments and misunderstanding. Davis graduated with a BA in psychology from the University of California and an MS in education and psychology from California State University. She served as editor of *Health* magazine and as advisor to the San Joaquin Family Preservation and Family Support Program. She received awards from the Sierra Health Foundation (1995), City of Manteca (1995), and University of California (1992), as well as an Excellence award (1998). Davis has published *Journeys Within: Source Book of Guided Meditations* (1997) and articles in the *Los Angeles Times*, *Science News*, *Discover*, *More*, *Reader's Digest*, and *O*, the Oprah magazine.

1   Call it the dance of the jet set, the diplomat's tango: A man from the Middle East, say, falls into conversation with an American, becomes animated, takes a step forward. The American makes a slight postural adjustment, shifts his feet, edges backward. A little more talk and the Arab advances; a little more talk and the American retreats.

"By the end of the cocktail party," says Middle East expert Peter Bechtold of the State Department's Foreign Service Institute, "you have an American in each corner of the room, because that's as far as they can back up."

What do you do when an amiable chat leaves one person feeling vaguely bullied, the other unaccountably chilled? Things would be simpler if these jetsetters were speaking different languages—they'd just get themselves a translator. But the problem's a little tougher, because they're using different languages of space.

Everyone who's ever felt cramped in a crowd knows that the skin is not the body's only boundary. We each wear a zone of privacy like a hoop skirt, inviting others in or keeping them out with body language—by how closely we approach, the angle at which we face them, the speed with which we break a gaze. It's a subtle code, but one we use and interpret easily, indeed automatically, having absorbed the vocabulary from infancy.

5   At least, we *assume* we're reading it right. But from culture to culture, from group to group within a single country, even between the sexes, the language of space has distinctive accents, confusing umlauts. That leaves a lot of room for misinterpretations, and the stakes have gotten higher as business has become increasingly international and populations multicultural. So a new breed of consultants has appeared in the last few years, interpreting for globe-trotters of all nationalities the meaning and use of personal space.

For instance, says international business consultant Sondra Snowdon, Saudi Arabians like to conduct business discussions from within spitting distance—literally. They bathe in each other's breath as part of building the relationship. "Americans back up," says Snowdon, "but they're harming their chances of winning the contracts." In seminars, Snowdon discusses the close quarters common in Middle Eastern conversations and has her students practice talking with each other at very chummy distances.

Still, her clients had better be careful where they take their shrunken "space bubble," because cultures are idiosyncratic in their spatial needs. Japanese subways bring people about as close together as humanly possible, for instance, yet even a handshake can be offensively physical in a Japanese office. And, says researcher and writer Mildred Reed Hall, Americans can even make their business counterparts in Japan uncomfortable with the kind of direct eye contact that's normal here.

"Not only do most Japanese businessmen not look at you, they keep their eyes down," Hall says. "We look at people for hours, and they feel like they're under a searchlight."

The study of personal space got under way in the early 1950s, when anthropologist Edward Hall described a sort of cultural continuum of personal space. (Hall has frequently collaborated with his wife, Mildred.) According to Hall, on the "high-contact" side of the continuum—in Mediterranean and South American societies, for example—social conversations include much eye contact, touching and smiling, typically while standing at a distance of about a foot. On the other end of the scale, say in Northern European cultures, a lingering gaze may feel invasive, manipulative or disrespectful; a social chat takes place at a remove of about 2½ feet.

In the middle-of-the-road United States, people usually stand about 10 18 inches apart for this sort of conversation—unless we want to win foreign friends and influence people, in which case, research shows, we'd better adjust our posture. In one study, when British graduate students were trained to adopt Arab patterns of behavior (facing their partners straight on, with lots of eye contact and smiling), Middle Eastern exchange students found them more likable and trustworthy than typical British students.

In contrast, the misuse of space can call whole personalities into suspicion: When researchers seated pairs of women for conversation, those forced to talk at an uncomfortably large distance were more likely to describe their partners as cold and rejecting.

Don't snuggle up too fast, though. Men in that study were more irritated by their partners when they were forced to talk at close range. Spatially speaking, it seems men and women are subtly foreign to each other. No matter whether a society operates at arm's length or cheek-to-jowl, the women look at each other more and stand a bit closer than do the men.

Anthropologist Hall suggests that a culture's use of space is evidence of a reliance on one sense over another: Middle Easterners get much of their information through their senses of smell and touch, he says, which require a close approach; Americans rely primarily on visual information, backing up in order to see an intelligible picture.

Conversational distances also tend to reflect the standard greeting distance in each culture, says State Department expert Bechtold. Americans shake hands, and then talk at arm's length. Arabs do a Hollywood-style, cheek-to-cheek social kiss, and their conversation is similarly up close and personal. And, at a distance great enough to keep heads from knocking together—about two feet—the Japanese bow and talk to each other. On the other hand, the need for more or less space may reflect something of a cultural temperament. "There's no word for privacy in Arab cultures," says Bechtold. "They think it means loneliness."

15   Whatever their origin, spatial styles are very real. In fact, even those who set out to transgress find it uncomfortable to intrude on the space of strangers, says psychologist John Aiello at Rutgers University. "I've had students say, 'Boy, that was the hardest thing I ever had to do—to stand six inches away when I was asking those questions.'"

Luckily, given coaching and time, it seems to get easier to acculturate to foreign habits of contact. Says Bechtold, "You often see men holding hands in the Middle East and walking down the street together. It's just that they're concerned and don't want you to cross the street unescorted, but I've had American pilots come in here and say, 'I don't want some SOB holding my hand.' Then I see them there, holding the hand of a Saudi."

"Personal space isn't so hard for people to learn," Bechtold adds. "What is really much harder is the business of dinner being served at midnight."

REFLECTING AND INTERPRETING

1. How does Davis classify people in this essay?

2. What divisions of conversational distances are discussed?

3. What is unusual about the way the first example is given? Describe the tone.

4. How does Davis establish credibility in the second paragraph and again later?

5. What function does paragraph 3 serve?

6. Davis makes unusual comparisons. Identify the literary devices in "a zone of privacy like a hoop skirt" and "bathe in each other's breath."

7. How do the personal space needs of Americans and those of Middle Eastern people generally differ? What American habits make Japanese uncomfortable?

8. Who studied the use of personal space in the 1950s? At what average distance do Americans converse? How does this distance vary with gender?

9. What danger exists in nonverbal communication?

10. How do greetings and other habits influence personal space? How does this vary from culture to culture? Is it difficult to learn about this topic? To adapt?

A WRITER'S RESPONSE

In your future career, will it be beneficial for you to be keenly aware of cultural diversity? Why or why not? Write an essay explaining your point of view.

HOW DO WE FIND THE STUDENT IN A WORLD OF ACADEMIC GYMNASTS AND WORKER ANTS?	JAMES T. BAKER

Categorizing individuals is risky business, especially if you are not a member of the group you are classifying. Study carefully how James Baker delineates types of college students he has known and think about the implications. This essay, in which Professor Baker reveals as much about himself as about his students, was first published in *The Chronicle of Higher Education*. Baker has also written *Brooks Hays* (1989), *Studs Terkel* (1992), and *Eleanor Roosevelt: First Lady* (1998). He has coauthored five books including *A Headstart: Study Tips for the Student of Western Civilization: A Brief History since 1300* (1998).

Anatole France once wrote that "the whole art of teaching is only the art of awakening the natural curiosity of young minds." I fully agree, except I have to wonder if, by using the word "only," he thought that the art of awakening such natural curiosity was an easy job. For me, it never has been—sometimes exciting, always challenging, but definitely not easy.

Robert M. Hutchins used to say that a good education prepares students to go on educating themselves throughout their lives. A fine definition, to be sure, but it has at times made me doubt that my own students, who seem only too eager to graduate so they can lay down their books forever, are receiving a good education.

But then maybe these are merely the pessimistic musings of someone suffering from battle fatigue. I have almost qualified for my second sabbatical leave, and I am scratching a severe case of the seven-year itch. About the only power my malaise has not impaired is my eye for spotting certain "types" of students. In fact, as the rest of me declines, my eye seems to grow more acute.

Has anyone else noticed that the very same students people college classrooms year after year? Has anyone else found the same bodies, faces, personalities returning semester after semester? Forgive me for violating my students' individual "personhoods," but reality makes it so tempting to see them as types. Doubtless you will recognize at least some of them. They have twins, or perhaps clones, on your campus, too.

There is the eternal Good Time Charlie (or Charlene), who makes every party on and off the campus, who by November of his freshman year has worked his face into a case of terminal acne, who misses every set of examinations because of "mono," who finally burns himself out physically and mentally by the age of 19 and drops out to go home and recuperate, and who returns at 20 after a long talk with Dad to major in accounting.

There is the Young General Patton, the one who comes to college on an R.O.T.C. scholarship and for a year twirls his rifle at basketball games while loudly sniffing out pinko professors, who at midpoint takes a sudden but predictable, radical swing from far right to far left, who grows a beard and moves in with a girl who refuses to shave her legs, who then makes the just as predictable, radical swing back to the right and ends up preaching fundamentalist sermons on the steps of the student union while the Good Time Charlies and Charlenes jeer.

There is the Egghead, the campus intellectual who shakes up his fellow students—and even a professor or two—with references to esoteric formulas and obscure Bulgarian poets, who is recognized by friend and foe alike as a promising young academic, someday to be a professional scholar, who disappears every summer for six weeks ostensibly to search for primeval human remains in Colorado caves, and who at 37 is shot dead by Arab terrorists while on a mission for the C.I.A.

There is the Performer—the music or theater major, the rock or folk singer—who spends all of his or her time working up an act, who gives barely a nod to mundane subjects like history, sociology, or physics, who dreams only of the day he or she will be on stage full time, praised by critics, cheered by audiences, who ends up either pregnant or responsible for a pregnancy and at 30 is either an insurance salesman or a housewife with a very lush garden.

There is the Jock, of course—the every-afternoon intramural champ, smelling of liniment and Brut, with bulging calves and a blue-eyed twinkle, the subject of untold numbers of female fantasies, the walking personification of he-man-ism—who upon graduation is granted managerial rank by a California bank because of his golden tan and low golf score, who is seen five years later buying the drinks at a San Francisco gay bar.

10   There is the Academic Gymnast—the guy or gal who sees college as an obstacle course, as so many stumbling blocks in the way of a great career or a perfect marriage—who strains every moment to finish and be done with "this place" forever, who toward the end of the junior year begins to slow down, to grow quieter and less eager to leave, who attends summer school, but never quite finishes those last six hours, who never leaves "this place," and who at 40 is still working at the campus laundry, still here, still a student.

There is the Medal Hound, the student who comes to college not to learn or expand any intellectual horizons but simply to win honors—medals, cups, plates, ribbons, scrolls—who is here because this is the best place to win the most the fastest, who plasticizes and mounts on his wall every certificate of excellence he wins, who at 39 will be a colonel in the U.S. Army and at 55 Secretary of something or other in a conservative Administration in Washington.

There is the Worker Ant, the student (loosely rendered) who takes 21 hours a semester and works 49 hours a week at the local car wash, who sleeps only on Sundays and during classes, who will somehow graduate on time and be the owner of his own vending-machine company at 30 and be dead of a heart attack at 40, and who will be remembered for the words chiseled on his tombstone:

All This Was Accomplished Without Ever Having So Much As Darkened The Door Of A Library

There is the Lost Soul, the sad kid who is in college only because teachers, parents, and society at large said so, who hasn't a career in mind or a dream to follow, who hasn't a clue, who heads home every Friday afternoon to spend the weekend cruising the local Dairee-Freeze, who at 50 will have done all his teachers, parents, and society said to do, still without a career in mind or a dream to follow or a clue.

There is also the Saved Soul—the young woman who has received, 15 through the ministry of one Gospel freak or another, a Holy Calling to save the world, or at least some special part of it—who majors in Russian studies so that she can be caught smuggling Bibles into the Soviet Union and be sent to Siberia where she can preach to souls imprisoned by the Agents of Satan in the Gulag Archipelago.

Then, finally, there is the Happy Child, who comes to college to find a husband or wife—and finds one—and there is the Determined Child, who comes to get a degree—and gets one.

Enough said.

All of which, I suppose, should make me throw up my hands in despair and say that education, like youth and love, is wasted on the young. Not quite.

For there does come along, on occasion, that one of a hundred or so who is maybe at first a bit lost, certainly puzzled; who may well start out a Good Timer, an Egghead, a Performer, a Jock, a Medal Hound, a Gymnast, a Worker Ant; who may indeed have trouble settling on a major, who will be distressed by what sometimes passes for education, who might even be a temporary dropout; but who has a vital capacity for growth and is able to fall in love with learning, who acquires a taste for intellectual pleasure, who becomes in the finest sense of the word a Student.

This is the one who keeps the most jaded of us going back to class after 20 class, and he or she must be oh-so-carefully cultivated. He or she must be artfully awakened, given the tools needed to continue learning for a lifetime, and let grow at whatever pace and in whatever direction nature dictates.

For I try always to remember that this student is me, my continuing self, my immortality. This person is my only hope that my own search for Truth will continue after me, on and on, forever.

REFLECTING AND INTERPRETING

1. Do you agree with Anatole France's definition of the art of teaching? Why or why not?

2. What is the question behind the opening paragraph? In paragraph 2?

3. The third paragraph is self-deprecating. How does he feel? Yet he makes a claim. What is it?

4. Paragraphs 5 to 16 set forth categories of students. Are all categories equally well done? Are any underdeveloped? Do any overlap or lack clarity?

5. What is the tone of the description about the "Lost Soul"?

6. What literary device is present in the description of the Jock?

7. Evaluate the objectivity of each category. Is Baker harder on some types of students than others? Which remarks border on insult?

8. In using humor there is always the risk of offending someone. How did you feel when you read his classifications? Would the humor be suitable for Baker's intended audience of college faculty?

9. Can you recognize yourself or your peers in any of these categories? What are the categories? What does this say about Baker's essay?

10. Did your response change when you came to the last four paragraphs? Why or why not? What does the author reveal about himself and his values?

A WRITER'S RESPONSE

1. Turn the tables on Baker! Sort professors into categories similar to his categories for students. Add a final, positive example, called "The Teacher." For help in writing the essay, see chapter 14.

2. Would you have liked a different ending for Baker's essay? Perhaps you could allude to the title in some way or write an ending that has universal appeal.

3. *Small Groups:* Discuss how you decide when someone is crossing the line on humor in writing or in conversation. Can you devise some guidelines?

THE MYTH OF THE LATIN WOMAN: I JUST MET A GIRL NAMED MARIA
JUDITH ORTIZ COFER

At age four Judith Ortiz Cofer came with her family to the United States from Puerto Rico. Now a professor of English at the University of Georgia, Cofer has written a dazzling array of books, short stories, essays, and poetry. Her writings have garnered numerous awards, including the Anisfield Wolf Book Award for *The Latin Deli: Prose and Poetry* (1993), the PEN/Martha Albrand Special Citation in nonfiction for *Silent Dancing* (1995), Best Book of the Year 1995–96 for *An Island Like You: Stories of the Barrio*, and the Paterson Book Prize for *The Year of Our Revolution: New and Selected Stories and Poems* (1998). Her work has been published in the *Kenyon Review, Southern Review, Georgia Review,* and *Glamour,* as well as numerous anthologies and textbooks. This essay, taken from *The Latin Deli,* explores the stereotypes often appended to Latinas.

1   On a bus trip to London from Oxford University where I was earning some graduate credits one summer, a young man, obviously fresh from a pub, spotted me and as if struck by inspiration went down on his knees in the aisle. With both hands over his heart he broke into an Irish tenor's rendition of "Maria" from *West Side Story.* My politely amused fellow passengers gave his lovely voice the round of gentle applause it deserved. Though I was not quite as amused, I managed my version of an English smile: no show of teeth, no extreme contortions of the facial muscles—I

was at this time of my life practicing reserve and cool. Oh, that British control, how I coveted it. But Maria had followed me to London, reminding me of a prime fact of my life: you can leave the Island, master the English language, and travel as far as you can, but if you are a Latina, especially one like me who so obviously belongs to Rita Moreno's gene pool, the Island travels with you.

This is sometimes a very good thing—it may win you that extra minute of someone's attention. But with some people, the same thing can make *you* an island—not so much a tropical paradise as an Alcatraz, a place nobody wants to visit. As a Puerto Rican girl growing up in the United States and wanting like most children to "belong," I resented the stereotype that my Hispanic appearance called forth from many people I met.

Our family lived in a large urban center in New Jersey during the sixties, where life was designed as a microcosm of my parents' casas on the island. We spoke in Spanish, we ate Puerto Rican food bought at the bodega, and we practiced strict Catholicism complete with Saturday confession and Sunday mass at a church where our parents were accommodated into a one-hour Spanish mass slot, performed by a Chinese priest trained as a missionary for Latin America.

As a girl I was kept under strict surveillance, since virtue and modesty were, by cultural equation, the same as family honor. As a teenager I was instructed on how to behave as a proper señorita. But it was a conflicting message girls got, since the Puerto Rican mothers also encouraged their daughters to look and act like women and to dress in clothes our Anglo friends and their mothers found too "mature" for our age. It was, and is, cultural, yet I often felt humiliated when I appeared at an American friend's party wearing a dress more suitable to a semiformal than to a playroom birthday celebration. At Puerto Rican festivities, neither the music nor the colors we wore could be too loud. I still experience a vague sense of letdown when I'm invited to a "party" and it turns out to be a marathon conversation in hushed tones rather than a fiesta with salsa, laughter, and dancing—the kind of celebration I remember from my childhood.

I remember Career Day in our high school, when teachers told us to 5 come dressed as if for a job interview. It quickly became obvious that to the barrio girls, "dressing up" sometimes meant wearing ornate jewelry and clothing that would be more appropriate (by mainstream standards) for the company Christmas party than as daily office attire. That morning I had agonized in front of my closet, trying to figure out what a "career girl" would wear. . . . I knew how to dress for school: at the Catholic school I attended we all wore uniforms; I knew how to dress for Sunday mass, and I knew what dresses to wear for parties at my relatives' homes. Though I do not recall the precise details of my Career Day outfit, it must have been a composite of the above choices. But I remember a comment my friend (an Italian-American) made in later years that coalesced my impressions of that day. She said that at the business school she was attending the Puerto Rican girls always stood out for wearing "everything at once." She meant, of course, too much jewelry, too many accessories. On that day at school, we were simply made the negative models by the nuns who were themselves not credible fashion experts to any of us. But it was painfully obvious to me that to the others, in their tailored skirts and silk blouses, we must have seemed "hopeless" and "vulgar." Though I now know that most adolescents feel out of step much of the time, I also know that for the Puerto Rican girls of my generation that sense was intensified. The way our teachers and classmates looked at us that day in school was just a taste of the culture clash that awaited us in the real world, where prospective employers and men on the street would often misinterpret our tight skirts and jingling bracelets as a come-on.

Mixed cultural signals have perpetuated certain stereotypes—for example, that of the Hispanic woman as the "Hot Tamale" or sexual firebrand. It is a one-dimensional view that the media have found easy to promote. In their special vocabulary, advertisers have designated "sizzling" and "smoldering" as the adjectives of choice for describing not only the foods but also the women of Latin America. From conversations in my house, I recall hearing about the harassment that Puerto Rican women endured in factories where the "boss men" talked to them as if sexual innuendo was all they understood and, worse, often gave them the choice of submitting to advances or being fired.

It is custom, however, not chromosomes, that leads us to choose scarlet over pale pink. As young girls, we were influenced in our decisions about clothes and colors by the women—older sisters and mothers who had grown up on a tropical island where the natural environment was a riot of primary colors, where showing your skin was one way to keep cool as well as to look sexy. Most important of all, on the island, women perhaps felt freer to dress and move more provocatively, since, in most cases, they were protected by the traditions, mores, and laws of a Spanish/Catholic system of morality and machismo whose main rule was: *You may look at my sister, but if you touch her I will kill you.* The extended family and church structure could provide a young woman with a circle of safety in her small pueblo on the island; if a man "wronged" a girl, everyone would close in to save her family honor.

This is what I have gleaned from my discussion as an adult with older Puerto Rican women. They have told me about dressing in their best party clothes on Saturday nights and going to the town's plaza to promenade with their girlfriends in front of the boys they liked. The males were thus given an opportunity to admire the women and to express their admiration in the form of *piropos:* erotically charged street poems they composed on the spot. I have been subjected to a few piropos while visiting the Island, and they can be outrageous, although custom dictates that they must never cross into obscenity. This ritual, as I understand it, also entails a show of studied indifference on the woman's part; if she is "decent," she must not acknowledge the man's impassioned words. So I do understand how things can be lost in translation. When a Puerto Rican girl dressed in her idea of what is attractive meets a man from the mainstream culture who has been trained to react to certain types of clothing as a sexual signal, a clash is likely to take place. The line I first heard based on this aspect of the myth happened when the boy who took me to my first formal dance leaned over to plant a sloppy overeager kiss painfully on my mouth, and when I didn't respond with sufficient passion said in a resentful tone: "I thought you Latin girls were supposed to mature early"—my first instance of being thought of as a fruit or vegetable—I was supposed to *ripen,* not just grow into womanhood like other girls.

It is surprising to some of my professional friends that some people, including those who should know better, still put others "in their place." Though rarer, these incidents are still commonplace in my life. It happened to me most recently during a stay at a very classy metropolitan hotel favored by young professional couples for their weddings. Late one evening after the theater, as I walked toward my room with my new colleague (a woman with whom I was coordinating an arts program), a middle-aged man in a tuxedo, a young girl in satin and lace on his arm, stepped directly into our path. With his champagne glass extended toward me, he exclaimed, "Evita!"

Our way blocked, my companion and I listened as the man half-recited, 10 half-bellowed "Don't Cry for Me, Argentina." When he finished, the young girl said: "How about a round of applause for my daddy?" We complied, hoping this would bring the silly spectacle to a close. I was becoming aware that our little group was attracting the attention of the other guests. "Daddy" must have perceived this too, and he once more barred the way as we tried to walk past him. He began to shout-sing a ditty to the tune of "La Bamba"—except the lyrics where about a girl named María whose exploits all rhymed with her name and gonorrhea. The girl kept saying "Oh Daddy" and looking at me with pleading eyes. She wanted me to laugh along with the others. My companion and I stood silently waiting for the man to end his offensive song. When he finished, I looked not at him but at his daughter. I advised her calmly never to ask her father what he had done in the army. Then I walked between them and to my room. My friend complimented me on my cool handling of the situation. I confessed to her that I really had wanted to push the jerk into the swimming pool. I knew that this same man—probably a corporate executive, well educated, even worldly by most standards—would not have been likely to regale a white woman with a dirty song in public. He would perhaps have checked his impulse by assuming that she could be somebody's wife or mother, or at least *somebody* who might take offense. But to him, I was just an Evita or a María: merely a character in his cartoon-populated universe.

Because of my education and my proficiency with the English language, I have acquired many mechanisms for dealing with the anger I experience. This was not true for my parents, nor is it true for the many Latin women working at menial jobs who must put up with stereotypes about our ethnic group such as: "They make good domestics." This is another facet of the myth of the Latin woman in the United States. Its origin is simple to deduce. Work as domestics, waitressing, and factory jobs are all that's available to women with little English and few skills. The myth of the Hispanic menial has been sustained by the same media phenomenon that made "Mammy" from *Gone with the Wind* America's idea of the black woman for generations; María, the housemaid or counter girl, is now indelibly etched into the national psyche. The big and the little screens have presented us with the picture of the funny Hispanic maid, mispronouncing words and cooking up a spicy storm in a shiny California kitchen.

This media-engendered image of the Latina in the United States has been documented by feminist Hispanic scholars, who claim that such portrayals are partially responsible for the denial of opportunities for upward mobility among Latinas in the professions. I have a Chicana friend working on a Ph.D. in philosophy at a major university. She says her doctor still shakes his head in puzzled amazement at all the "big words" she uses. Since I do not wear my diplomas around my neck for all to see, I too have on occasion been sent to that "kitchen," where some think I obviously belong.

One such incident that has stayed with me, though I recognize it as a minor offense, happened on the day of my first public poetry reading. It took place in Miami in a boat-restaurant where we were having lunch before the event. I was nervous and excited as I walked in with my notebook in my hand. An older woman motioned me to her table. Thinking (foolish me) that she wanted me to autograph a copy of my brand new slender volume of verse, I went over. She ordered a cup of coffee from me, assuming that I was the waitress. Easy enough to mistake my poems for menus, I suppose, I know that it wasn't an intentional act of cruelty, yet of all the good things that happened that day, I remember that scene most clearly, because it reminded me of what I had to overcome before anyone would take me seriously. In retrospect I understand that my anger gave my reading fire, that I have almost always taken doubts in my abilities as a challenge—and that the result is, most times, a feeling of satisfaction at having won a convert when I see the cold, appraising eyes warm to my words, the body language change, the smile that indicates that I have opened some avenue for communication. That day I read to that woman and her lowered eyes told me that she was embarrassed at her little faux pas, and when I willed her to look up at me, it was my victory, and she graciously allowed me to punish her with my full attention. We shook hands at the end of the reading, and I never saw her again. She has probably forgotten the whole thing but maybe not.

Yet I am one of the lucky ones. My parents made it possible for me to acquire a stronger footing in the mainstream culture by giving me the chance at an education. And books and art have saved me from the harsher forms of ethnic and racial prejudice that many of my Hispanic *compañeras* have had to endure. I travel a lot around the United States, reading from my books of poetry and my novel, and the reception I most often receive is one of positive interest by people who want to know more about my culture. There are, however, thousands of Latinas without the privilege of an education or the entrée into society that I have. For them life is a struggle against the misconceptions perpetuated by the myth of the Latina. . . . We cannot change this situation by legislating the way people look at us. The transformation, as I see it, has to occur at a much more individual level. My personal goal in my public life is to try to replace the old pervasive stereotypes and myths about Latinas with a much more interesting set of realities. Every time I give a reading, I hope the stories I tell, the dreams and fears I examine in my work, can achieve some universal truth which will get my audience past the particulars of my skin color, my accent, or my clothes.

I once wrote a poem in which I called us Latinas "God's brown daugh-   15 ters." This poem is really a prayer of sorts, offered upward, but also, through the human-to-human channel of art, outward. It is a prayer for communication, and for respect. In it, Latin women pray "in Spanish to an Anglo God / with a Jewish heritage," and they are "fervently hoping / that if not omnipotent, / at least He be bilingual."

REFLECTING AND INTERPRETING

1. Does the opening anecdote influence your feeling toward the narrator? If so, how?
2. Where is the thesis statement?
3. Did Cofer's parents help her to blend in with her American peers? Cite examples.
4. What assumption did the teachers make about Career Day that caused problems for the Puerto Rico girls? What should the teachers have done?
5. Explain the "circle of safety" that existed for women in Puerto Rico. What underlying premise protected women there?
6. What are the stereotypic classifications that Cofer has been subjected to?
7. How has Cofer channeled her anger? Cite an example.
8. Does the anecdote in paragraph 13 seem incomplete? What else would you like to know?
9. Why does Cofer say she is "one of the lucky ones"? What is her personal goal?
10. Examine the title. How do "myth" and "Maria" work together?

A WRITER'S RESPONSE

1. Have you ever been stereotyped? How did you react?
2. In the past decade, have expectations for appearance in job interviews changed? If so, how?

Comparing and Contrasting for a Purpose

| DEBORAH TANNEN

Internationally recognized, Deborah Tannen is a prolific author as well as a linguistics professor at Georgetown University in Washington, DC. Her nineteen works not only cover a range of communication styles but also offer fascinating insights and helpful suggestions. *You Just Don't Understand* (1990) held the top spot on the best-seller list for eight months and remained on the list for nearly four years. Some of her better-known books include *That's Not What I Meant!* (1987), *The Argument Culture* (1999), *I Only Say This Because I Love You* (2001), and *Talking from 9 to 5: Women and Men in the Workplace: Language, Sex, and Power* (2001). She has also written for many major newspapers and magazines. This essay, first printed in *Newsweek* (16 Apr. 1994), compares the attitudes of men and women toward computers.

1   I was a computer pioneer, but I'm still something of a novice. That paradox is telling.

I was the second person on my block to get a computer. The first was my colleague Ralph. It was 1980. Ralph got a Radio Shack TRS-80, I got a used Apple II+. He helped me get started and went on to become a maven, reading computer magazines, hungering for the new technology he read about, and buying and mastering it as quickly as he could afford. I hung on to old equipment far too long because I dislike giving up what I'm used to, fear making the wrong decision about what to buy, and resent the time it takes to install and learn a new system.

My first Apple came with videogames; I gave them away. Playing games on the computer didn't interest me. If I had free time I'd spend it talking on the telephone to friends.

Ralph got hooked. His wife was often annoyed by the hours he spent at his computer and the money he spent upgrading it. My marriage had no such strains—until I discovered E-mail. Then I got hooked. E-mail draws me the same way the phone does: it's a souped-up conversation.

E-mail deepened my friendship with Ralph. Though his office was next 5 to mine, we rarely had extended conversations because he is shy. Face to face he mumbled so, I could barely tell he was speaking. But when we both got on E-mail, I started receiving long, self-revealing messages: we poured our hearts out to each other. A friend discovered that E-mail opened up that kind of communication with her father. He would never talk much on the phone (as her mother would), but they have become close since they both got on line.

Why, I wondered, would some men find it easier to open up on E-mail? It's a combination of the technology (which they enjoy) and the oblique-ness of the written word, just as many men will reveal feelings in dribs and drabs while riding in the car or doing something, which they'd never talk about sitting face to face. It's too intense, too bearing-down on them, and once you start you have to keep going. With a computer in between, it's safer.

It was on E-mail, in fact, that I described to Ralph how boys in groups often struggle to get the upper hand whereas girls tend to maintain an appearance of cooperation. And he pointed out that this explained why boys are more likely to be captivated by computers than girls are. Boys are typically motivated by a social structure that says if you don't dominate you will be dominated. Computers, by their nature, balk; you type a perfectly appropriate command and it refuses to do what it should. Many boys and men are incited by this defiance: "I'm going to whip this into line and teach it who's boss! I'll get it to do what I say!" (and if they work hard enough, they always can). Girls and women are more likely to respond, "This thing won't cooperate. Get it away from me!"

Although no one wants to think of herself as "typical"—how much nicer to be *sui generis*—my relationship to my computer is—gulp—fairly typical for a woman. Most women (with plenty of exceptions) aren't excited by tinkering with the technology, grappling with the challenge of eliminating bugs or getting the biggest and best computer. These dynamics appeal to many men's interest in making sure they're on the top side of the inevitable who's-up-who's-down struggle that life is for them. E-mail appeals to my view of life as a contest for connections to others. When I see that I have fifteen messages, I feel loved.

I once posted a technical question on a computer network for linguists and was flooded with long dispositions, some pages long. I was staggered by the generosity and the expertise, but wondered where these guys found the time—and why all the answers I got were from men.

Like coed classrooms and meetings, discussions on E-mail networks 10 tend to be dominated by male voices, unless they're specifically women-only, like single-sex schools. On line, women don't have to worry about getting the floor (you just send a message when you feel like it), but, according to linguists Susan Herring and Laurel Sutton, who have studied this, they have the usual problems of having their messages ignored or attacked. The anonymity of public networks frees a small number of men to send long, vituperative, sarcastic messages that many other men either can tolerate or actually enjoy, but that turn most women off.

The anonymity of networks leads to another sad part of the E-mail story: there are men who deluge women with questions about their appearance and invitations to sex. On college campuses, as soon as women students log on, they are bombarded by references to sex, like going to work and finding pornographic posters adorning the walls.

Most women want one thing from a computer—to work. This is significant counterevidence to the claim that men want to focus on information while women are interested in rapport. That claim I found was most often true in casual conversation, in which there is no particular information to be conveyed. But with computers, it is often women who are more focused on information, because they don't respond to the challenge of getting equipment to submit.

Once I had learned the basics, my interest in computers waned. I use it to write books (though I never mastered having it do bibliographies or tables of contents) and write checks (but not balance my checkbook). Much as I'd like to use it to do more, I begrudge the time it would take to learn.

Ralph's computer expertise costs him a lot of time. Chivalry requires that he rescue novices in need, and he is called upon by damsel novices far more often than knaves. More men would rather study the instruction booklet than ask directions, as it were, from another person. "When I do help men," Ralph wrote (on E-mail, of course), "they want to be more involved. I once installed a hard drive for a guy, and he wanted to be there with me, wielding the screwdriver and giving his own advice where he could." Women, he finds, usually are not interested in what he's doing; they just want him to get the computer to the point where they can do what they want.

15   Which pretty much explains how I managed to be a pioneer without becoming an expert.

REFLECTING AND INTERPRETING

1. What type of opening does Tannen use? Yet one word in the first paragraph hints that the direction of the essay is more than that. What is the word?

2. Where does the contrast start?

3. What is ironic about paragraph 5? (Tip: Consider the lack of privacy in e-mail.)

4. & 5. Summarize the contrasting generalizations in paragraphs 7 and 8.

6. What type of support does Tannen supply to reinforce her generalizations?

7. What often happens to women's online postings on networks?

8. Examine Tannen's ending. What is the effect of using a fragment and the colloquial "pretty much"? Do you think a complete sentence using standard English would have been more effective? Why or why not?

9. Tannen describes some of the effects of anonymity in e-mail. Have you noticed any of these happening? Are there any other effects you have noticed?

10. This essay was written more than ten years ago. Do you think that the tendencies Tannen describes are still generally true, or have they changed somewhat? If so, how have they changed?

A WRITER'S RESPONSE

Describe your relationship with your computer. Is it like Tannen's or more like Ralph's? Or does it vary?

A NONSMOKER WITH A SMOKER | PHILLIP LOPATE

Essayist, novelist, poet, and film critic, Phillip Lopate has published several books, including *The Eyes Don't Always Want to Stay Open* (1972), *Being with Children* (1975), *Confessions of Summer* (1979), *The Rug Merchant* (1989), *The Ordering Mirror: Readers and Contexts* (1993), *Totally, Tenderly, Tragically: Essays and Criticism from a Lifelong Love Affair with the Movies* (1998), and *John Koch: Painting a New York Life* (2001). Lopate is also the editor of several anthologies of essays. His writing has appeared in *The Best American Short Stories*, *The Paris Review*, *Harvard Educational Review*, and numerous other publications. This essay is taken from *Against Joie De Vivre: Personal Essays* (1989). Lopate, a nonsmoker, ponders his thoughts on smoking, contrasting the feelings and views of smokers and nonsmokers. He creates a kaleidoscope of images which cause us to feel—not merely see—clearly first one side of smoking and then the other. The result? A remarkably balanced viewpoint.

Last Saturday night my girlfriend, Helen, and I went to a dinner party 1
in the Houston suburbs. We did not know our hosts, but were invited on account of Helen's chum Barry, whose birthday party it was. We had barely stepped into the house and met the other guests, seated on a U-shaped couch under an A-framed ceiling, when Helen lit a cigarette. The hostess froze. "Uh, could you please not smoke in here? If you have to, we'd appreciate your using the terrace. We're both sort of allergic."

Helen smiled understandingly and moved toward the glass doors leading to the backyard in a typically ladylike way, as though merely wanting to get a better look at the garden. But I knew from that gracious "Southern" smile of hers that she was miffed.

As soon as Helen had stepped outside, the hostess explained that they had just moved into this house, and that it had taken weeks to air out because of the previous owner's tenacious cigar smoke. A paradigmatically awkward conversation about tobacco ensued: like testifying sinners, two people came forward with confessions about kicking the nasty weed; our scientist-host cited a recent study of indoor air pollution levels; a woman lawyer brought up the latest California legislation protecting nonsmokers;

a roly-poly real estate agent admitted that, though he had given up smokes, he still sat in the smoking section of airplanes because "you meet a more interesting type of person there"—a remark his wife did not find amusing. Helen's friend Barry gallantly joined her outside. I did not, as I should have; I felt paralyzed.

For one thing, I wasn't sure which side I was on. I have never been a smoker. My parents both chain-smoked, so I grew up accustomed to cloudy interiors and ever since have been tolerant of other people's nicotine urges. To be perfectly honest, I'm not crazy about inhaling smoke, particularly when I've got a cold, but that irritating inconvenience pales beside the damage that would be done to my pluralistic worldview if I did not defend smokers' rights.

5   On the other hand, a part of me wished Helen *would* stop smoking. That part seemed to get a satisfaction out of the group's "banishing" her: they were doing the dirty work of expressing my disapproval.

As soon as I realized this, I joined her in the garden. Presently a second guest strolled out to share a forbidden toke, then a third. Our hostess ultimately had to collect the mutineers with an announcement that dinner was served.

At the table, Helen appeared to be having such a good time, joking with our hosts and everyone else, that I was unprepared for the change that came over her as soon as we were alone in the car afterward. "I will never go back to that house!" she declared. "Those people have no concept of manners or hospitality, humiliating me the moment I stepped in the door. And that phony line about 'sort of allergic'!"

Normally, Helen is forbearance personified. Say anything that touches her about smoking, however, and you touch the rawest of nerves. I remembered the last time I foolishly suggested that she "think seriously" about stopping. I had just read one of those newspaper articles about the increased possibility of heart attacks, lung cancer, and birth deformities among women smokers, and I was worried for her. My concern must have been maladroitly expressed, because she burst into tears.

"Can't we even talk about this without your getting so sensitive?" I had asked.

10   "You don't understand. Nonsmokers never understand that it's a real addiction. I've tried quitting, and it was hell. Do you want me to go around for months mean and cranky outside and angry inside? You're right, I'm sensitive, because I'm threatened with having taken away from me the thing that gives me the most pleasure in life, day in, day out," she said. I shot her a look: careful, now. "Well, practically the most pleasure. You know what I mean." I didn't. But I knew enough to drop it.

I love Helen, and if she wants to smoke, knowing the risks involved, that remains her choice. Besides, she wouldn't quit just because I wanted her to; she's not that docile, and that's part of what I love about her. Sometimes I wonder why I even keep thinking about her quitting. What's it to me personally? Certainly I feel protective of her health, but I also have selfish motives. I don't like the way her lips taste when she's smoked a lot. I associate her smoking with nervousness, and when she lights up several cigarettes in a row, I get jittery watching her. Crazy as this may sound, I also find myself becoming jealous of her cigarettes. Occasionally, when I go to her house and we're sitting on the couch together, if I see Helen eyeing the pack I make her kiss me first, so that my lips can engage hers (still fresh) before the competition's. It's almost as though there were another lover in the room—a lover who was around long before I entered the picture, and who pleases her in mysterious ways I cannot.

A lit cigarette puts a distance between us: it's like a weapon in her hand, awakening in me a primitive fear of being burnt. The memory is not so primitive, actually. My father used to smoke absentmindedly, letting the ash grow like a caterpillar eating every leaf in its path, until gravity finally toppled it. Once, when I was about nine, my father and I were standing in line at a bakery, and he accidentally dropped a lit ash down my back. Ever since, I've inwardly winced and been on guard around these little waving torches, which epitomize to me the dangers of intimacy.

I've worked hard to understand from the outside the satisfaction of smoking. I've even smoked "sympathetic" cigarettes, just to see what the other person was experiencing. But it's not the same as being hooked. How can I really empathize with the frightened but stubborn look Helen gets in her eyes when, despite the fact we're a little late going somewhere, she turns to me in the car and says, "I need to buy a pack of cigarettes first"? I feel a wave of pity for her. We are both embarrassed by this forced recognition of her frailty—the "indignity," as she herself puts it, of being controlled by something outside her will.

I try to imagine myself in that position, but a certain smugness keeps getting in the way (I don't have that problem and *am I glad*). We pay a price for our smugness. So often it flip-flops into envy: the outsiders wish to be included in the sufferings and highs of others, as if to say that only by relinquishing control and surrendering to some dangerous habit, some vice or dependency, would one be able to experience "real life."

Over the years I have become a sucker for cigarette romanticism. Few 15 Hollywood gestures move me as much as the one in *Now Voyager,* when Paul Henreid lights two cigarettes, one for himself, the other for Bette Davis: these form a beautiful fatalistic bridge between them, a complicitous understanding like the realization that their love is based on the inevitability of separation. I am all the more admiring of this worldly cigarette gallantry because its experiential basis escapes me.

The same sort of fascination occurs when I come across a literary description of nicotine addiction, like this passage in Mailer's *Tough Guys Don't Dance:* "Over and over again I gave them up, a hundred times over the years, but I always went back. For in my dreams, sooner or later, I struck a match, brought flame to the tip, then took in all my hunger for existence with the first puff. I felt impaled on desire itself—those fiends trapped in my chest and screaming for one drag."

"Impaled on desire itself"! Such writing evokes a longing in me for the centering of self that tobacco seems to bestow on its faithful. Clearly, there is something attractive about having this umbilical relation to the universe—this curling pillar, this spiral staircase, this prayer of smoke that mediates between the smoker's inner substance and the alien ether. Inwardness of the nicotine trance, sad wisdom ("every pleasure has its price"), beauty of ritual, squandered health—all those romantic meanings we read into the famous photographic icons of fifties saints, Albert Camus or James Agee or James Dean or Carson McCullers puffing away, in a sense they're true. Like all people who return from a brush with death, smokers have gained a certain power. They know their "coffin nails." With Helen, each cigarette is a measuring of the perishable, an enactment of her mortality, from filter to end-tip in fewer than five minutes. I could not stand to be reminded of my own death so often.

REFLECTING AND INTERPRETING

1. What is the effect of the anecdote as an opening to the essay?
2. How does Lopate feel about an issue on which most people have clear-cut opinions? Describe the tone.
3. What happens after Helen leaves the room?
4. Comment on the contrast between Helen's behavior and her feelings.
5. Lopate admits that he has selfish reasons for wanting Helen to quit smoking. What are they? Comment on the image near the end of paragraph 11.
6. Can you find two vivid similes that dramatize Lopate's deep feelings about *tobacco?*
7. What is the "cigarette romanticism" that he mentions? Do you think it is still prevalent? Why or why not?
8. Despite Lopate's attraction to a smoker and smoking, he does not smoke. Why?
9. After reading the essay, how do you feel about the author? How does he sound?
10. For Lopate, cigarettes have also acquired a deadly symbolism: "an enactment of . . . mortality." Where does he explain this?

A WRITER'S RESPONSE

1. Using some of Lopate's techniques, compare and contrast two views in an essay. For example, you might discuss a habit you disapprove of but, nonetheless, tolerate in someone you love.
2. *Small Groups:* Summarize the viewpoint of the host and hostess, listing their reasons. Then summarize the view of smokers. Now analyze. Which reasons are based on fact? On emotion? What about etiquette? Who was being rude?

MOTHER TONGUE   AMY TAN

Born and raised in California, Amy Tan (1952–) graduated from high school in Montreux, Switzerland. She earned a master's degree in linguistics from San Jose State University. For five years she served as a language development consultant and directed programs for young disabled children. Next she turned to freelance writing, including corporate communications for companies such as AT&T, IBM, and Pacific Bell. Her first novel *The Joy Luck Club* (1989), brought her international acclaim. Her other works include *The Kitchen God's Wife* (1991), *The Hundred Secret Senses* (1995), *The Bonesetter's Daughter* (2001), *The Opposite of Fate: A Book of Musings* (2003) and two children's books– *The Moon Lady* (1992) and *The Chinese Siamese Cat* (1994). "Mother Tongue" was selected for *Best American Essays 1991*.

1   I am not a scholar of English or literature. I cannot give you much more than personal opinions on the English language and its variations in this country or others.

I am a writer. And by that definition, I am someone who has always loved language. I am fascinated by language in daily life. I spend a great deal of my time thinking about the power of language—the way it can evoke an emotion, a visual image, a complex idea, or a simple truth. Language is the tool of my trade. And I use them all—all the Englishes I grew up with.

Recently, I was made keenly aware of the different Englishes I do use. I was giving a talk to a large group of people, the same talk I had already given to half a dozen other groups. The nature of the talk was about my writing, my life, and my book, *The Joy Luck Club*. The talk was going along well enough, until I remembered one major difference that made the whole talk sound wrong. My mother was in the room. And it was perhaps the first time she had heard me give a lengthy speech, using the kind of English I have never used with her. I was saying things like, "The intersection of memory upon imagination" and "There is an aspect of my fiction that relates to thus-and-thus"—a speech filled with carefully wrought grammatical phrases, burdened, it suddenly seemed to me, with nominalized forms, past perfect tenses, conditional phrases, all the forms of standard English that I had learned in school and through books, the forms of English I did not use at home with my mother.

Just last week, I was walking down the street with my mother, and I again found myself conscious of the English I was using, the English I do use with her. We were talking about the price of new and used furniture and I heard myself saying this: "Not waste money that way." My husband was with us as well, and he didn't notice any switch in my English. And then I realized why. It's because over the twenty years we've been together I've often used that same kind of English with him, and sometimes he even uses it with me. It has become our language of intimacy, a different sort of English that relates to family talk, the language I grew up with.

5   So you'll have some idea of what this family talk I heard sounds like, I'll quote what my mother said during a recent conversation which I video-

taped and then transcribed. During this conversation, my mother was talking about a political gangster in Shanghai who had the same last name as her family's, Du, and how the gangster in his early years wanted to be adopted by her family, which was rich by comparison. Later, the gangster became more powerful, far richer than my mother's family, and one day showed up at my mother's wedding to pay his respects. Here's what she said in part:

"Du Yusong having business like fruit stand. Like off the street kind. He is Du like Du Zong—but not Tsung-ming Island people. The local people call putong, the river east side, he belong to that side local people. That man want to ask Du Zong father take him in like become own family. Du Zong father wasn't look down on him, but didn't take seriously, until that man big like become a mafia. Now important person, very hard to inviting him. Chinese way, came only to show respect, don't stay for dinner. Respect for making big celebration, he shows up. Mean gives lots of respect. Chinese custom. Chinese social life that way. If too important won't have to stay too long. He come to my wedding. I didn't see, I heard it. I gone to boy's side, they have YMCA dinner. Chinese age I was nineteen."

You should know that my mother's expressive command of English belies how much she actually understands. She reads the *Forbes* report, listens to *Wall Street Week,* converses daily with her stockbroker, reads all of Shirley MacLaine's books with ease—all kinds of things I can't begin to understand. Yet some of my friends tell me they understand 50 percent of what my mother says. Some say they understand 80 to 90 percent. Some say they understand none of it, as if she were speaking pure Chinese. But to me, my mother's English is perfectly clear, perfectly natural. It's my mother tongue. Her language, as I hear it, is vivid, direct, full of observation and imagery. That was the language that helped shape the way I saw things, expressed things, made sense of the world.

Lately, I've been giving more thought to the kind of English my mother speaks. Like others, I have described it to people as "broken" or "fractured" English. But I wince when I say that. It has always bothered me that I can think of no way to describe it other than "broken," as if it were damaged and needed to be fixed, as if it lacked a certain wholeness and soundness. I've heard other terms used, "limited English," for example. But they seem just as bad, as if everything is limited, including people's perceptions of the limited English speaker.

I know this for a fact, because when I was growing up, my mother's "limited" English limited *my* perception of her. I was ashamed of her English. I believed that her English reflected the quality of what she had to say. That is, because she expressed them imperfectly her thoughts were imperfect. And I had plenty of empirical evidence to support me: the fact that people in department stores, at banks, and at restaurants did not take her seriously, did not give her good service, pretended not to understand her, or even acted as if they did not hear her.

My mother has long realized the limitations of her English as well. 10 When I was fifteen, she used to have me call people on the phone to pretend I was she. In this guise, I was forced to ask for information or even to complain and yell at people who had been rude to her. One time it was a call to her stockbroker in New York. She had cashed out her small portfolio and it just so happened we were going to go to New York the next week, our very first trip outside California. I had to get on the phone and say in an adolescent voice that was not very convincing, "This is Mrs. Tan."

And my mother was standing in the back whispering loudly, "Why he don't send me check, already two weeks late. So mad he lie to me, losing me money."

And then I said in perfect English, "Yes, I'm getting rather concerned. You had agreed to send the check two weeks ago, but it hasn't arrived."

Then she began to talk more loudly. "What he want, I come to New York tell him front of his boss, you cheating me?" And I was trying to calm her down, make her be quiet, while telling the stockbroker, "I can't tolerate any more excuses. If I don't receive the check immediately, I am going to have to speak to your manager when I'm in New York next week." And sure enough, the following week there we were in front of this astonished stockbroker, and I was sitting there redfaced and quiet, and my mother, the real Mrs. Tan, was shouting at his boss in her impeccable broken English.

We used a similar routine just five days ago, for a situation that was far less humorous. My mother had gone to the hospital for an appointment, to find out about a benign brain tumor a CAT scan had revealed a month ago. She said she had spoken very good English, her best English, no mistakes. Still, she said, the hospital did not apologize when they said they had lost the CAT scan and she had come for nothing. She said they did not seem to have any sympathy when she told them she was anxious to know the exact diagnosis, since her husband and son had both died of brain tumors. She said they would not give her any more information until the next time and she would have to make another appointment for that. So she said she would not leave until the doctor called her daughter. She wouldn't budge. And when the doctor finally called her daughter, me, who spoke in perfect English—lo and behold—we had assurances the CAT scan would be found, promise that a conference call on Monday would be held, and apologies for any suffering my mother had gone through for a most regrettable mistake.

I think my mother's English almost had an effect on limiting my possi- 15 bilities in life as well. Sociologists and linguists probably will tell you that a person's developing language skills are more influenced by peers. But I do think that the language spoken in the family, especially in immigrant families which are more insular, plays a large role in shaping the language of the child. And I believe that it affected my results on achievement tests, IQ tests, and the SAT. While my English skills were never judged as poor, compared to math, English could not be considered my strong suit. In grade school I did moderately well, getting perhaps B's, sometimes

B-pluses, in English and scoring perhaps in the sixtieth or seventieth percentile on achievement tests. But those scores were not good enough to override the opinion that my true abilities lay in math and science, because in those areas I achieved A's and scored in the ninetieth percentile or higher.

This was understandable. Math is precise; there is only one correct answer. Whereas, for me at least, the answers on English tests were always a judgment call, a matter of opinion and personal experience. Those tests were constructed around items like fill-in-the-blank sentence completion, such as, "Even though Tom was _____, Mary thought he was _____." And the correct answer always seemed to be the most bland combinations of thoughts, for example, "Even though Tom was shy, Mary thought he was charming," with the grammatical structure "even though" limiting the correct answer to some sort of semantic opposites, so you wouldn't get answers like, "Even though Tom was foolish, Mary thought he was ridiculous." Well, according to my mother, there were very few limitations as to what Tom could have been and what Mary might have thought of him. So I never did well on tests like that.

The same was true with word analogies, pairs of words in which you were supposed to find some sort of logical, semantic relationship—for example, "*Sunset* is to *nightfall* as _____ is to _____." And here you would be presented with a list of four possible pairs, one of which showed the same kind of relationship: *red* is to *stoplight, bus* is to *arrival, chills* is to *fever, yawn* is to *boring*. Well, I could never think that way. I knew what the tests were asking, but I could not block out of my mind the images already created by the first pair, "*sunset* is to *nightfall*"—and I would see a burst of color against a darkening sky, the moon rising, the lowering of a curtain of stars. And all the other pairs of words—red, bus, stoplight, boring—just threw up a mass of confusing images, making it impossible for me to sort out something as logical as saying: "A sunset precedes nightfall" is the same as "a chill precedes a fever." The only way I would have gotten that answer right would have been to imagine an associative situation, for example, by being disobedient and staying out past sunset, catching a chill at night which turns into feverish pneumonia as punishment, which indeed did happen to me.

I have been thinking about all this lately, about my mother's English, about achievement tests. Because lately I've been asked, as a writer, why there are not more Asian Americans represented in American literature. Why are there few Asian Americans enrolled in creative writing programs? Why do so many Chinese students go into engineering? Well, these are broad sociological questions I can't begin to answer. But I have noticed in surveys—in fact, just last week—that Asian students, as a whole, always do significantly better on math achievement tests than in English. And this makes me think that there are other Asian-American students whose English spoken in the home might also be described as "broken" or "limited." And perhaps they also have teachers who are steering them away from writing and into math and science, which is what happened to me.

Fortunately, I happen to be rebellious in nature and enjoy the challenge of disproving assumptions made about me. I became an English major my first year in college, after being enrolled as pre-med. I started writing nonfiction as a freelancer the week after I was told by my former boss that writing was my worst skill and I should hone my talents toward account management.

But it wasn't until 1985 that I finally began to write fiction. And at first 20 I wrote using what I thought to be wittily crafted sentences, sentences that would finally prove I had mastery over the English language. Here's an example from the first draft of a story that later made its way into *The Joy Luck Club,* but without this line: "That was my mental quandary in its nascent state." A terrible line, which I can hardly pronounce.

Fortunately, for reasons I won't get into today, I later decided I should envision a reader for the stories I would write. And the reader I decided upon was my mother, because these were stories about mothers. So with this reader in mind—and in fact she did read my early drafts—I began to write stories using all the Englishes I grew up with: the English I spoke to my mother, which for lack of a better term might be described as "simple"; the English she used with me, which for lack of a better term might be described as "broken"; my translation of her Chinese, which could certainly be described as "watered down"; and what I imagine to be her translation of her Chinese if she could speak in perfect English, her internal language, and for that I sought to preserve the essence, but neither an English nor a Chinese structure. I wanted to capture what language ability tests can never reveal: her intent, her passion, her imagery, the rhythms of her speech and the nature of her thoughts.

Apart from what any critic had to say about my writing, I knew I had succeeded where it counted when my mother finished reading my book and gave me her verdict: "So easy to read."

REFLECTING AND INTERPRETING

1. Note how the author opens the first two paragraphs. What parallel pattern does she use to precede the definition? ("I am not . . . I am.") What technique is this?

2. How does Amy Tan define *writer?*

3. How did her mother's English influence Amy?

4. Amy Tan and her husband sometimes use her "mother's tongue" to communicate when they are alone. Why?

5. Does Amy's mother's English reflect the depth of her understanding of the language? How do you know?

6. How did the public and hospital employees react to Mrs. Tan's broken English?

7. What does Amy Tan notice about math and English test scores of Asian students? How does this affect course scheduling in high schools?

8. How does Amy Tan react to disillusionment?

9. What advantages does Standard English have over broken English?

10. If this essay had been written in third person by a biographer, how would that change have affected the essay?

A WRITER'S RESPONSE

1. Have you ever turned disillusionment or failure into something positive? Write an essay describing how you achieved this feat.

2. *Small Groups:* How many tips for good writing can you glean from this essay?

CONVERSATIONAL BALLGAMES   NANCY MASTERSON SAKAMOTO

Living in Japan for twenty-four years with her husband, a Japanese artist and Buddhist priest, Nancy Masterson Sakamoto learned much about Japanese culture. At the University of Osaka, as a visiting professor, she provided in-service training to Japanese teachers of English and gave intercultural seminars to business and women's groups. She wrote articles for Japanese publications teaching English and coauthored research backed by the Japanese Ministry of Education. Her book *Polite Fictions: Why Japanese and Americans Seem Rude to Each Other* (1981) is still in print and used as a university textbook in Japan. She also coauthored *Mutual Understanding of Different Cultures* (1981). Now living in Hawaii with her family, she holds the position of professor of American Studies at Shitennorji Gkuen University. In the following essay, she explains the major differences in conversation styles between Japanese and Americans.

1   After I was married and had lived in Japan for a while, my Japanese gradually improved to the point where I could take part in simple conversations with my husband and his friends and family. And I began to notice that often, when I joined in, the others would look startled, and the conversational topic would come to a halt. After this happened several times, it became clear to me that I was doing something wrong. But for a long time, I didn't know what it was.

Finally, after listening carefully to many Japanese conversations, I discovered what my problem was. Even though I was speaking Japanese, I was handling the conversation in a western way.

Japanese-style conversations develop quite differently from western-style conversations. And the difference isn't only in the languages. I realized that just as I kept trying to hold western-style conversations even when I was speaking Japanese, so my English students kept trying to hold Japanese-style conversations even when they were speaking English. We were unconsciously playing entirely different conversational ballgames.

A western-style conversation between two people is like a game of tennis. If I introduce a topic, a conversational ball, I expect you to hit it back. If you agree with me, I don't expect you simply to agree and do nothing more. I expect you to add something—a reason for agreeing, another example, or an elaboration to carry the idea further. But I don't expect you always to agree. I am just as happy if your question me, or challenge me, or completely disagree with me. Whether you agree or disagree, your response will return the ball to me.

And then it is my turn again. I don't serve a new ball from my original starting line. I hit your ball back again from where it has bounced. I carry your idea further, or answer your questions or objections, or challenge or question you. And so the ball goes back and forth, with each of us doing our best to give it a new twist, an original spin, or a powerful smash. 5

And the more vigorous the action, the more interesting and exciting the game. Of course, if one of us gets angry, it spoils the conversation, just as it spoils a tennis game. But getting excited is not all the same as getting angry. After all, we are not trying to hit each other. We are trying to hit the ball. So long as we attack only each other's opinions, and do not attack each other personally, we don't expect anyone to get hurt. A good conversation is supposed to be interesting and exciting.

If there are more than two people in the conversation, then it is like doubles in tennis, or like volleyball. There's no waiting in line. Whoever is nearest and quickest hits the ball, and if you step back, someone else will hit it. No one stops the game to give you a turn. You're responsible for taking your own turn.

But whether it's two players or a group, everyone does his best to keep the ball going, and no one person has the ball for very long.

A Japanese-style conversation, however, is not at all like tennis or volleyball. It's like bowling. You wait for your turn. And you always know your place in line. It depends on such things as whether you are older or younger, a close friend or a relative stranger to the previous speaker, in a senior or junior position, and so on.

When your turn comes, you step up to the starting line with your bowling ball, and carefully bowl it. Everyone else stands back and watches politely, murmuring encouragement. Everyone waits until the ball has reached the end of the alley, and watches to see if it knocks down all the pins, or only some of them, or none of them. There is a pause, while everyone registers your score. 10

Then, after everyone is sure that you have completely finished your turn, the next person in line steps up to the same starting line, with a different ball. He doesn't return your ball, and he does not begin from where your ball stopped. There is no back and forth at all. All the balls run parallel. And there is always a suitable pause between turns. There is no rush, no excitement, no scramble for the ball.

No wonder everyone looked startled when I took part in Japanese conversations. I paid no attention to whose turn it was, and kept snatching the ball halfway down the alley and throwing it back to the bowler. Of course the conversation died. I was playing the wrong game.

This explains why it is almost impossible to get a western-style conversation or discussion going with English students in Japan. I used to think that the problem was their lack of English language ability. But I finally came to realize that the biggest problem is that they, too, are playing the wrong game.

Whenever I serve a volleyball, everyone just stands back and watches it fall, with occasional murmurs of encouragement. No one hits it back. Everyone waits until I call on someone to take a turn. And when that person speaks, he doesn't hit my ball back. He serves a new ball. Again, everyone just watches it fall.

15   So I call on someone else. This person does not refer to what the previous speaker has said. He also serves a new ball. Nobody seems to have paid any attention to what anyone else has said. Everyone begins again from the same starting line, and all the balls run parallel. There is never any back and forth. Everyone is trying to bowl with a volleyball.

And if I try a simpler conversation, with only two of us, then the other person tries to bowl with my tennis ball. No wonder foreign English teachers in Japan get discouraged.

Now that you know about the difference in the conversational ball-games, you may think that all your troubles are over. But if you have been trained all your life to play one game, it is no simple matter to switch to another, even if you know the rules. Knowing the rules is not at all the same thing as playing the game.

Even now, during a conversation in Japanese I will notice a startled reaction, and belatedly realize that once again I have rudely interrupted by instinctively trying to hit back the other person's bowling ball. It is no easier for me to "just listen" during a conversation, than it is for my Japanese students to "just relax" when speaking with foreigners. Now I can truly sympathize with how hard they must find it to try to carry on a Western-style conversation.

If I have not yet learned to do conversational bowling in Japanese, at least I have figured out one thing that puzzled me for a long time. After his first trip to America, my husband complained that Americans asked him so many questions and made him talk so much at the dinner table that he never had a chance to eat. When I asked him why he couldn't talk and eat at the same time, he said that Japanese do not customarily think that dinner, especially on fairly formal occasions, is a suitable time for extended conversation.

20   Since westerners think that conversation is an indispensable part of dining, and indeed would consider it impolite not to converse with one's dinner partner, I found this Japanese custom rather strange. Still, I could accept it as a cultural difference even though I didn't really understand it. But when my husband added, in explanation, that Japanese consider it extremely rude to talk with one's mouth full, I got confused. Talking with one's mouth full is certainly not an American custom. We think it very rude,

too. Yet we still manage to talk a lot and eat at the same time. How do we do it?

For a long time, I couldn't explain it, and it bothered me. But after I discovered the conversational ballgames, I finally found the answer. Of course! In a western-style conversation, you hit the ball, and while someone else is hitting it back, you take a bite, chew, and swallow. Then you hit the ball again, and then eat some more. The more people there are in the conversation, the more chances you have to eat. But even with only two of you talking, you still have plenty of chances to eat.

Maybe that's why polite conversation at the dinner table has never been a traditional part of Japanese etiquette. Your turn to talk would last so long without interruption that you'd never get a chance to eat.

REFLECTING AND INTERPRETING

1. What is the purpose of the first paragraph?
2. In paragraph 2, notice the wording of the first sentence: "I discovered what my problem was." (She could have said "the problem.") What does this phrasing reveal about Sakamoto?
3. To what games does she compare Western conversation? Why?
4. To what game is Japanese conversation similar? In what ways?
5. How does status affect Japanese conversation?
6. Paragraphs 10 and 11 explain why the nature, pace, and participation in Japanese conversation is so different. How does etiquette enter in? What is the result?
7. How many rules of Japanese conversation does the author cite? List them.
8. How many rules for Western conversation does she cite? Can you think of any others?
9. Do you agree with Sakamoto's statement "Knowing the rules is not at all the same thing as playing the game"? Why or why not?
10. Think about the title and the analogy that runs throughout the piece. How does it function? (What is the result?)

A WRITER'S RESPONSE

1. Have you ever experienced a culture clash with a relative, friend, or acquaintance? If so, explain.
2. Sometimes generations clash as a result of different rules. Can you give an example?

Definition
Identifying Basic Characteristics

DAVID RAYMOND

ON BEING 17, BRIGHT, AND UNABLE TO READ

Someone who has experienced a disability can give an insider's view, providing insights that increase an outsider's understanding in a way that a technical definition cannot. David Raymond was a junior in high school when his essay on dyslexia was published in the *New York Times*. Dyslexics think in pictures and experience problems in perceiving letters or numbers. Words may appear jumbled, upside down, backwards, or in other ways that hinder reading. Symptoms vary in range and intensity. Special programs are now available to help dyslexics.

1   One day a substitute teacher picked me to read aloud from the textbook. When I told her "No, thank you," she came unhinged. She thought I was acting smart, and told me so. I kept calm, and that got her madder and madder. We must have spent 10 minutes trying to solve the problem, and finally she got so red in the face I thought she'd blow up. She told me she'd see me after class.

Maybe someone like me was a new thing for that teacher. But she wasn't new to me. I've been through scenes like that all my life. You see, even though I'm 17 and a junior in high school, I can't read because I have dyslexia. I'm told I read "at a fourth-grade level," but from where I sit, that's not reading. You can't know what that means unless you've been there. It's not easy to tell how it feels when you can't read your homework assignments or the newspaper or a menu in a restaurant or even notes from your own friends.

My family began to suspect I was having problems almost from the first day I started school. My father says my early years in school were the worst years of his life. They weren't so good for me, either. As I look back on it now, I can't find the words to express how bad it really was. I wanted to die. I'd come home from school screaming, "I'm dumb. I'm dumb—I wish I were dead!"

I guess I couldn't read anything at all then—not even my own name— and they tell me I didn't talk as good as other kids. But what I remember about those days is that I couldn't throw a ball where it was supposed to go, I couldn't learn to swim, and I wouldn't learn to ride a bike, because no matter what anyone told me, I knew I'd fail.

Sometimes my teachers would try to be encouraging. When I couldn't 5 read the words on the board they'd say, "Come on, David, you know that word." Only I didn't. And it was embarrassing. I just felt dumb. And dumb was how the kids treated me. They'd make fun of me every chance they got, asking me to spell "cat" or something like that. Even if I knew how to spell it, I wouldn't; they'd only give me another word. Anyway, it was awful, because more than anything I wanted friends. On my birthday when I blew out the candles I didn't wish I could learn to read; what I wished for was that the kids would like me.

With the bad reports coming from school, and with me moaning about wanting to die and how everybody hated me, my parents began looking for help. That's when the testing started. The school tested me, the child-guidance center tested me, private psychiatrists tested me. Everybody knew something was wrong—especially me.

It didn't help much when they stuck a fancy name onto it. I couldn't pronounce it then—I was only in second grade—and I was ashamed to talk about it. Now it rolls off my tongue, because I've been living with it for a lot of years—dyslexia.

All through elementary school it wasn't easy. I was always having to do things that were "different," things the other kids didn't have to do. I had to go to a child psychiatrist, for instance.

One summer my family forced me to go to a camp for children with reading problems. I hated the idea, but the camp turned out pretty good, and I had a good time. I met a lot of kids who couldn't read and somehow that helped. The director of the camp said I had a higher I.Q. than 90 percent of the population. I didn't believe him.

About the worst thing I had to do in fifth and sixth grade was go to a 10 special education class in another school in our town. A bus picked me up, and I didn't like that at all. The bus also picked up emotionally disturbed kids and retarded kids. It was like going to a school for the retarded. I always worried that someone I knew would see me on that bus. It was a relief to go to the regular junior high school.

Life began to change a little for me then, because I began to feel better about myself. I found the teachers cared; they had meetings about me and

I worked harder for them for a while. I began to work on the potter's wheel, making vases and pots that the teachers said were pretty good. Also, I got a letter for being on the track team. I could always run pretty fast.

At high school the teachers are good and everyone is trying to help me. I've gotten honors some marking periods and I've won a letter on the cross-country team. Next quarter I think the school might hold a show of my pottery. I've got some friends. But there are still some embarrassing times. For instance, every time there is writing in the class, I get up and go to the special education room. Kids ask me where I go all the time. Sometimes I say, "to Mars."

Homework is a real problem. During free periods in school I go into the special ed room and staff members read assignments to me. When I get home my mother reads to me. Sometimes she reads an assignment into a tape recorder, and then I go into my room and listen to it. If we have a novel or something like that to read, she reads it out loud to me. Then I sit down with her and we do the assignment. She'll write, while I talk my answers to her. Lately I've taken to dictating into a tape recorder, and then someone— my father, a private tutor or my mother—types up what I've dictated. Whatever homework I do takes someone else's time, too. That makes me feel bad.

We had a big meeting in school the other day—eight of us, four from the guidance department, my private tutor, my parents and me. The subject was me. I said I wanted to go to college, and they told me about colleges that have facilities and staff to handle people like me. That's nice to hear.

15　　As for what happens after college, I don't know and I'm worried about that. How can I make a living if I can't read? Who will hire me? How will I fill out the application form? The only thing that gives me any courage is the fact that I've learned about well-known people who couldn't read or had other problems and still made it. Like Albert Einstein, who didn't talk until he was 4 and flunked math. Like Leonardo da Vinci, who everyone seems to think had dyslexia.

I've told this story because maybe some teacher will read it and go easy on a kid in the classroom who has what I've got. Or, maybe some parent will stop nagging his kid, and stop calling him lazy. Maybe he's not lazy or dumb. Maybe he just can't read and doesn't know what's wrong. Maybe he's scared, like I was.

REFLECTING AND INTERPRETING

1. Rather than calling on one person to read, what might the teacher have done?

2. At no point does the author give the technical definition of dyslexia. Should he? What is the effect of this omission?

3. What is dyslexia? Does it vary in how it affects people?

4. What experience was a turning point for David? How did it help?

5. What changes occurred in David's life during junior high school?

6. Why is he confident that he can graduate from college? What does he fear?

7. Why does he mention Albert Einstein and Leonardo da Vinci?

8. David includes many colloquialisms in the essay. How do "blow up" and "didn't talk as good as other kids" affect the tone?

9. What is the author's purpose in writing the essay?

10. What factor do you think is most influential in David's or anyone's success?

A WRITER'S RESPONSE

Have you had a long, difficult experience that makes you somewhat of an expert? Write an essay that gives an insider's view. If you haven't, perhaps a close family member has. How did the problem affect you and other family members?

THE HANDICAP OF DEFINITION — WILLIAM RASPBERRY

Born in a small town in Mississippi in 1935, William Raspberry knows firsthand about the various connotations that have been attached to his race. In this essay, taken from *Instilling Positive Images* (1982), he explores the ways *black* is used in regard to race and the meaning of *blackness*. At the end he issues a challenge to blacks and mainstream Americans to expect more from black youth, encourage them, and expand the definition of *black*. Raspberry worked his way through Indiana Central College as a reporter, photographer, and editor for the *Indianapolis Recorder*. After a two-year stint in the Army, he joined *The Washington Post*, where he writes a column, now syndicated in 225 newspapers. He has won Journalist of the Year (1965), a Citation of Merit in Journalism (1967), and the Pulitzer Prize for Distinguished Commentary (1994). Fifty of his favorite columns were published in *Looking Backward at Us* (1991). Raspberry has also served as a television commentator and taught journalism classes at Howard University.

I know all about bad schools, mean politicians, economic deprivation 1 and racism. Still, it occurs to me that one of the heaviest burdens black Americans—and black children in particular—have to bear is the handicap of definition: the question of what it means to be black.

Let me explain quickly what I mean. If a basketball fan says that the Boston Celtics' Larry Bird plays "black," the fan intends it—and Bird probably accepts it—as a compliment. Tell pop singer Tom Jones he moves "black" and he might grin in appreciation. Say to Teena Marie or The Average White Band that they sound "black" and they'll thank you.

But name one pursuit, aside from athletics, entertainment or sexual performance in which a white practitioner will feel complimented to be told he does it "black." Tell a white broadcaster he talks "black," and he'll sign up for diction lessons. Tell a white reporter he writes "black," and he'll take a writing course. Tell a white lawyer he reasons "black" and he might sue you for slander.

What we have here is a tragically limited definition of blackness, and it isn't only white people who buy it.

5   Think of all the ways black children can put one another down with charges of "whiteness." For many of these children, hard study and hard work are "white." Trying to please a teacher might be criticized as acting "white." Speaking correct English is "white." Scrimping today in the interest of tomorrow's goals is "white." Educational toys and games are "white."

An incredible array of habits and attitudes that are conducive to success in business, in academia, in the non-entertainment professions are likely to be thought of as somehow "white." Even economic success, unless it involves such "black" undertakings as numbers banking, is defined as "white."

And the results are devastating. I wouldn't deny that blacks often are better entertainers and athletes. My point is the harm that comes from too narrow a definition of what is black.

One reason black youngsters tend to do better at basketball, for instance, is that they assume they can learn to do it well, and so they practice constantly to prove themselves right.

Wouldn't it be wonderful if we would infect black children with the notion that excellence in math is "black" rather than white, or possibly Chinese? Wouldn't it be of enormous value if we could create the myth that morality, strong families, determination, courage and love of learning are traits brought by slaves from Mother Africa and therefore quintessentially black?

10   There is no doubt in my mind that most black youngsters could develop their mathematical reasoning, their elocution and their attitudes the way they develop their jump shots and their dance steps: by the combination of sustained, enthusiastic practice and the unquestioned belief that they can do it.

In one sense, what I am talking about is the importance of developing positive ethnic traditions. Maybe Jews have an innate talent for communication; maybe the Chinese are born with a gift for mathematical reasoning; maybe blacks are naturally blessed with athletic grace. I doubt it. What is at work, I suspect, is assumption, inculcated early in their lives, that this is a thing our people do well.

Unfortunately, many of the things about which blacks make this assumption are things that do not contribute to their career success—except for that handful of the truly gifted who can make it as entertainers and athletes. And many of the things we concede to whites are the things that are essential to economic security.

So it is with a number of assumptions black youngsters make about what it is to be a "man": physical aggressiveness, sexual prowess, the refusal to submit to authority. The prisons are full of people who, by this perverted definition, are unmistakably men.

But the real problem is not so much that the things defined as "black" are negative. The problem is that the definition is much too narrow.

Somehow, we have to make our children understand that they are in- 15
telligent, competent people, capable of doing whatever they put their
minds to and making it in the American mainstream, not just in a black
subculture.

What we seem to be doing, instead, is raising up yet another generation of young blacks who will be failures—by definition.

REFLECTING AND INTERPRETING

1. Where is the transitional sentence that spans the chasm between the positive examples and the negative ones?

2. How does the construing of saving money, pleasing the teacher, having educational toys, and speaking correct English as "white" prove detrimental
   to blacks?

3. What reasons does Raspberry cite for blacks' success in basketball? Do you
   agree or disagree? Why?

4. What rhetorical strategy does Raspberry use in paragraph 9?

5. What image, in particular, is harmful for young black males?

6. Notice the three-word sentence "I doubt it" in paragraph 11. What is the
   effect?

7. See paragraph 15. In 1987 Raspberry pinpointed a crucial aspect of the problem: For most black children, the subculture is their world, meaning they do
   not see themselves as an integral part of a larger society. Do you think this
   perspective has changed since 1987? Since September 11, 2001? How?

8. How would you classify Raspberry's ending? (Hint: See "Writing an Effective Conclusion," chapter 4.)

9. How would you describe the writer's voice? How does the tone differ from
   that of many other black writers?

10. Raspberry says that "an incredible array of habits and attitudes are conduc-
    tive to success in business, in academia, and in the nonentertainment pro-
    fessions." Can you specify some of these?

A WRITER'S RESPONSE

How does a person's attitude and behavior define his or her chances for success?
Write an essay explaining these vital influences. Cite positive and negative examples as Raspberry does.

BECOMING EDUCATED	BARBARA JORDAN

Barbara Charline Jordan (1936–96) was born in an all-black neighborhood in Houston,
Texas. In an era when relatively few women attended college, she earned a bachelor's degree from Texas Southern University and a law degree from Boston University Law School
(1959). Seven years later she became the first black woman to be elected to the Texas Senate. In 1972 she won a seat in the US House of Representatives, where she served on the

Judiciary Committee. Her powerful speech in favor of impeaching President Nixon during the Watergate affair gained national attention. Some constituents were so impressed with her dedication and ethics that they urged her to run for president, but she declined. In 1978 she left Congress to teach at the University of Texas at Austin. In 1992 at the Democratic National Convention, she spoke eloquently about making the American Dream come true for both whites and blacks. Her *Selected Speeches* (1999) was published posthumously. In this extract from her autobiography, *Barbara Jordan: A Self Portrait* (1979), she defined what an education meant to her.

1   So I was at Boston University in this new and strange and different world, and it occurred to me that if I was going to succeed at this strange new adventure, I would have to read longer and more thoroughly than my colleagues at law school had to read. I felt that in order to compensate for what I had missed in earlier years, I would have to work harder, and study longer, than anybody else. I still had this feeling that I did not want my colleagues to know what a tough time I was having understanding the concepts, the words, the ideas, the process. I didn't want them to know that. So I did my reading not in the law library, but in a library at the graduate dorm, upstairs where it was very quiet, because apparently nobody else there studied. So I would go there at night after dinner. I would load my books under my arm and go to the library, and I would read until the wee hours of the morning and then go to bed. I didn't get much sleep during those years. I was lucky if I got three or four hours a night, because I had to stay up. I had to. The professors would assign cases for the next day, and these cases had to be read and understood or I would be behind, further behind than I was.

I was always delighted when I would get called upon to recite in class. But the professors did not call on the "ladies" very much. There were certain favored people who always got called on, and then on some rare occasions a professor would come in and would announce: "We're going to have Ladies Day today." And he would call on the ladies. We were just tolerated. We weren't considered really top drawer when it came to the study of the law.

At some time in the spring, Bill Gibson, who was dating my new roommate, Norma Walker, organized a black study group, as we blacks had to form our own. This was because we were not invited into any of the other study groups. There were six or seven in our group—Bill, and Issie, and I think Maynard Jackson—and we would just gather and talk it out and hear ourselves do that. One thing I learned was that you had to talk out the issues, the facts, the cases, the decisions, the process. You couldn't just read the cases and study alone in your library as I had been doing; and you couldn't get it all in the classroom. But once you had talked it out in the study group, it flowed more easily and made a lot more sense.

And from time to time I would go up to the fourth floor at 2 Rawley Street to check on how Louise was doing. She was always reading *Redbook.* Every time I was in there and wanted to discuss one of the cases with her, she was reading a short story in *Redbook.* I don't know how she could do that. She was not prepared in class when the professors would call on her to discuss cases, but that did not bother her. Whereas it was a matter of life and death with me. I had to make law school. I just didn't have any alternatives. I could not afford to flunk out. That would have been an unmitigated disaster. So I read all the time I was not in class.

Finally I felt I was really learning things, really going to school. I felt that I was getting educated, whatever that was. I became familiar with the process of thinking. I learned to think things out and reach conclusions and defend what I had said.

In the past I had got along by spouting off. Whether you talked about debates or oratory, you dealt with speechifying. Even in debate it was pretty much canned because you had, in your little three-by-five box, a response for whatever issue might be raised by the opposition. The format was structured so that there was no opportunity for independent thinking. (I really had not had my ideas challenged ever.) But I could no longer orate and let that pass for reasoning. Because there was not any demand for an orator in Boston University Law School. You had to think and read and understand and reason. I had learned at twenty-one that you couldn't just say a thing is so because it might not be so, and somebody brighter, smarter, and more thoughtful would come out and tell you it wasn't so. Then, if you still thought it was, you had to prove it. Well, that was a new thing for me. I cannot, I really cannot describe what that did to my insides and to my head. I thought: I'm being educated finally.

REFLECTING AND INTERPRETING

1. In the first paragraph, what do we learn about Barbara Jordan's early education? What decision did she make? What does this reveal about her attitude?

2. Why didn't she study in the law library? What does this reveal about her?

3. How did the professor at Boston University treat women in his classes? What was "Ladies Day"?

4. Why did Jordan and her friends form a study group? Describe the results.

5. How did Louise differ from Barbara Jordan? What is the effect of including this paragraph in the essay?

6. How had Jordan gotten along in former debate classes? How did her performance change at Boston University Law School?

7. How did Jordan feel as a result of this experience?

8. In one brief paragraph, Jordan defined what becoming educated meant to her. Can you find it?

9. How would you describe Jordan's attitude toward learning?

10. How would you describe the writer's voice in this essay?

1. In a paragraph, define and explain what an education means to you.

2. *Small Groups:* What were your early expectations for your college courses? What was the reality? Are there any similarities between Jordan's experience at Boston University and your college experience? If so, what?

THE INSUFFICIENCY OF HONESTY   STEPHEN L. CARTER

The *New York Times* has termed Stephen L. Carter one of the foremost intellectuals in the USA. Born black in Washington, DC, in 1954, he first distinguished himself by earning a bachelor's degree from Stanford and a law degree from Yale (1979). After gaining experience as a law clerk for the United States Court of Appeals and later for Supreme Court Justice Thurgood Marshall, Carter joined the Yale faculty in 1982. He has taught constitutional law, contracts, law and religion, law and science, and legal ethics—framing debate on national issues ranging from the role of religion in politics to the influence of civility and integrity in everyday life. His nonfiction and fiction writings have been critically acclaimed. Best known are *Reflections of an Affirmative Action Baby* (1991), *The Culture of Disbelief: How American Law and Politics Trivialize Religious Devotion* (1993), *Civility: Manners, Morals, and the Etiquette of Democracy* (1998), *God's Name in Vain* (2000), and *The Emperor of Ocean Park* (2002). In this essay Carter defines integrity, differentiating it from honesty.

1   A couple of years ago I began a university commencement address by telling the audience that I was going to talk about integrity. The crowd broke into applause. Applause! Just because they had heard the word "integrity": that's how starved for it they were. They had no idea how I was using the word, or what I was going to say about integrity, or, indeed, whether I was for it or against it. But they knew they liked the idea of talking about it.

Very well, let us consider this word "integrity." Integrity is like the weather: everybody talks about it but nobody knows what to do about it. Integrity is that stuff that we always want more of. Some say that we need to return to the good old days when we had a lot more of it. Others say that we as a nation have never really had enough of it. Hardly anybody stops to explain exactly what we mean by it, or how we know it is a good thing, or why everybody needs to have the same amount of it. Indeed, the only trouble with integrity is that everybody who uses the word seems to mean something slightly different.

For instance, when I refer to integrity, do I mean simply "honesty"? The answer is no; although honesty is a virtue of importance, it is a different virtue from integrity. Let us, for simplicity, think of honesty as not lying; and let us further accept Sissela Bok's definition of a lie: "any intentionally deceptive message which is *stated.*" Plainly, one cannot have integrity without being honest (although, as we shall see, the matter gets complicated), but one can certainly be honest and yet have little integrity.

When I refer to integrity, I have something very specific in mind. Integrity, as I will use the term, requires three steps: discerning what is right and what is wrong; acting on what you have discerned, even at personal cost; and saying openly that you are acting on your understanding of right and wrong. The first criterion captures the idea that integrity requires a degree of moral reflectiveness. The second brings in the ideal of a person of integrity as steadfast, a quality that includes keeping one's commitments. The third reminds us that a person of integrity can be trusted.

The first point to understand about the difference between honesty   5
and integrity is that a person may be entirely honest without ever engaging in the hard work of discernment that integrity requires: she may tells us quite truthfully what she believes without ever taking the time to figure out whether what she believes is good and right and true. The problem may be as simple as someone's foolishly saying something that hurts a friend's feelings; a few moments of thought would have revealed the likelihood of the hurt and the lack of necessity for the comment. Or the problem may be more complex, as when a man who was raised from birth in a society that preaches racism states his belief in one race's inferiority as a fact, without ever really considering that perhaps this deeply held view is wrong. Certainly the racist is being honest—he is telling us what he actually thinks—but his honesty does not add up to integrity.

Telling Everything You Know

A wonderful epigram sometimes attributed to the filmmaker Sam Goldwyn goes like this: "The most important thing in acting is honesty; once you learn to fake that, you're in." The point is that honesty can be something one *seems* to have. Without integrity, what passes for honesty often is nothing of the kind; it is fake honesty—or it is honest but irrelevant and perhaps even immoral.

Consider an example. A man who has been married for fifty years confesses to his wife on his deathbed that he was unfaithful thirty-five years earlier. The dishonesty was killing his spirit, he says. Now he has cleared his conscience and is able to die in peace.

The husband has been honest—sort of. He has certainly unburdened himself. And he has probably made his wife (soon to be his widow) quite miserable in the process, because even if she forgives him, she will not be able to remember him with quite the vivid image of love and loyalty that she had hoped for. Arranging his own emotional affairs to ease his transition to death, he has shifted to his wife the burden of confusion and pain, perhaps for the rest of her life. Moreover, he has attempted his honesty at the one time in his life when it carries no risk; acting in accordance with what you think is right and risking no loss in the process is a rather thin and unadmirable form of honesty.

Besides, even though the husband has been honest in a sense, he has now twice been unfaithful to his wife: once thirty-five years ago, when he had his affair, and again when, nearing death, he decided that his own peace of mind was more important than hers. In trying to be honest he has violated his marriage vow by acting toward his wife not with love but with naked and perhaps even cruel self-interest.

10   As my mother used to say, you don't have to tell people everything you know. Lying and nondisclosure, as the law often recognizes, are not the same thing. Sometimes it is actually illegal to tell what you know, as, for example, in the disclosure of certain financial information by market insiders. Or it may be unethical, as when a lawyer reveals a confidence entrusted to her by a client. It may be simple bad manners, as in the case of a gratuitous comment to a colleague on his or her attire. And it may be subject to religious punishment, as when a Roman Catholic priest breaks the seal of the confessional—an offense that carries automatic excommunication.

In all the cases just mentioned, the problem with telling everything you know is that somebody else is harmed. Harm may not be the intention, but it is certainly the effect. Honesty is most laudable when we risk harm to ourselves; it becomes a good deal less so if we instead risk harm to others when there is no gain to anyone other than ourselves. Integrity may counsel keeping our secrets in order to spare the feelings of others. Sometimes, as in the example of the wayward husband, the reason we want to tell what we know is precisely to shift our pain onto somebody else—a course of action dictated less by integrity than by self-interest. Fortunately, integrity and self-interest often coincide, as when a politician of integrity is rewarded with our votes. But often they do not, and it is at those moments that our integrity is truly tested.

Error

Another reason that honesty alone is no substitute for integrity is that if forthrightness is not preceded by discernment, it may result in the expression of an incorrect moral judgment. In other words, I may be honest about what I believe, but if I have never tested my beliefs, I may be wrong. And here I mean "wrong" in a particular sense: the proposition in question is wrong if I would change my mind about it after hard moral reflection.

Consider this example. Having been taught all his life that women are not as smart as men, a manager gives the women on his staff less-challenging assignments than he gives the men. He does this, he believes, for their own benefit: he does not want them to fail, and he believes that they will if he gives them tougher assignments. Moreover, when one of the women on his staff does poor work, he does not berate her as harshly as he would a man, because he expects nothing more. And he claims to be acting with integrity because he is acting according to his own deepest beliefs.

The manager fails the most basic test of integrity. The question is not whether his actions are consistent with what he most deeply believes but whether he has done the hard work of discerning whether what he most deeply believes is right. The manager has not taken this harder step.

Moreover, even within the universe that the manager has constructed for himself, he is not acting with integrity. Although he is obviously wrong to think that the women on his staff are not as good as the men, even were he right, that would not justify applying different standards to their work. By so doing he betrays both his obligation to the institution that employs him and his duty as a manager to evaluate his employees.

The problem that the manager faces is an enormous one in our practical politics, where having the dialogue that makes democracy work can seem impossible because of our tendency to cling to our views even when we have not examined them. As Jean Bethke Elshtain has said, borrowing from John Courtney Murray, our politics are so fractured and contentious that we often cannot even reach *disagreement.* Our refusal to look closely at our own most cherished principles is surely a large part of the reason. Socrates thought the unexamined life not worth living. But the unhappy truth is that few of us actually have the time for constant reflection on our views—on public or private morality. Examine them we must, however, or we will never know whether we might be wrong.

None of this should be taken to mean that integrity as I have described it presupposes a single correct truth. If, for example, your integrity-guided search tells you that affirmative action is wrong, and my integrity-guided search tells me that affirmative action is right, we need not conclude that one of us lacks integrity. As it happens, I believe—both as a Christian and as a secular citizen who struggles toward moral understanding—that we *can* find true and sound answers to our moral questions. But I do not pretend to have found very many of them, nor is an exposition of them my purpose here.

It is the case not that there aren't any right answers but that, given human fallibility, we need to be careful in assuming that we have found them. However, today's political talk about how it is wrong for the government to impose one person's morality on somebody else is just mindless chatter. *Every* law imposes one person's morality on somebody else, because law has only two functions: to tell people to do what they would rather not or to forbid them to do what they would.

And if the surveys can be believed, there is far more moral agreement in America than we sometimes allow ourselves to think. One of the reasons that character education for young people makes so much sense to so many people is precisely that there seems to be a core set of moral understandings—we might call them the American Core—that most of us accept. Some of the virtues in this American Core are, one hopes, relatively noncontroversial. About 500 American communities have signed on to Michael Josephson's program to emphasize the "six pillars" of good character: trustworthiness, respect, responsibility, caring, fairness, and citizenship. These virtues might lead to a similarly noncontroversial set of political values: having an honest regard for ourselves and others, protecting freedom of thought and religious belief, and refusing to steal or murder.

Honesty and Competing Responsibilities

20   A further problem with too great an exaltation of honesty is that it may allow us to escape responsibilities that morality bids us bear. If honesty is substituted for integrity, one might think that if I say I am not planning to fulfill a duty, I need not fulfill it. But it would be a peculiar morality indeed that granted us the right to avoid our moral responsibilities simply by stating our intention to ignore them. Integrity does not permit such an easy escape.

Consider an example. Before engaging in sex with a woman, her lover tells her that if she gets pregnant, it is her problem, not his. She says that she understands. In due course she does wind up pregnant. If we believe, as I hope we do, that the man would ordinarily have a moral responsibility toward both the child he will have helped to bring into the world and the child's mother, then his honest statement of what he intends does not spare him that responsibility.

This vision of responsibility assumes that not all moral obligations stem from consent or from a stated intention. The linking of obligations to promises is a rather modern and perhaps uniquely Western way of looking at life, and perhaps a luxury that only the well-to-do can afford. As Fred and Shulamit Korn (a philosopher and an anthropologist) have pointed out, "If one looks at ethnographic accounts of other societies, one finds that, while obligations everywhere play a crucial role in social life, promising is not preeminent among the sources of obligation and is not even mentioned by most anthropologists." The Korns have made a study of Tonga, where promises are virtually unknown but the social order is remarkably stable. If life without any promises seems extreme, we Americans sometimes go too far the other way, parsing not only our contracts but even our marriage vows in order to discover the absolute minimum obligation that we have to others as a result of our promises.

That some societies in the world have worked out evidently functional structures of obligation without the need for promise or consent does not tell us what *we* should do. But it serves as a reminder of the basic proposition that our existence in civil society creates a set of mutual responsibilities that philosophers used to capture in the fiction of the social contract. Nowadays, here in America, people seem to spend their time thinking of even cleverer ways to avoid their obligations, instead of doing what integrity commands and fulfilling them. And all too often honesty is their excuse.

REFLECTING AND INTERPRETING

1. In one sentence, summarize the gist of the first two paragraphs.
2. What simple definition of honesty does Carter put forth?
3. What three steps are essential to achieve integrity?
4. If a person omits step one, what is the risk?

5. Can a person be honest yet lack integrity? Explain.

6. Examine and summarize paragraph 10 in one sentence.

7. Carter cites two obligations that a manger must fulfill in order to have integrity. What are they?

8. Carter speaks of an "American Core" that has six values necessary for good character. What are they?

9. What "further problem" does he point out when honesty is honored too highly? Do you believe that honesty can be misused? How?

10. Consider the title of this essay. What is the effect?

A WRITER'S RESPONSE

1. Have you ever worked at a place where you knew fraud was occurring? What did you do? Now through hindsight, would you have followed the same course of action? Why or why not?

2. Select a quality such as reliability, faithfulness, or loyalty as a topic for an essay. Use examples to clarify and support your purpose.

Investigating Cause and Effect

<table>
<tr><td>THE STUBBORN TWIG:
MY DOUBLE DOSE OF SCHOOLING</td><td>MONICA SONE</td></tr>
</table>

Born in Seattle in 1917, Monica Sone lived her first five years in "amoebic bliss" with her parents in an old hotel on the waterfront. At age six she was shocked to learn of her Japanese descent. In 1942, after World War II broke out, she and her family were forced to relocate to a prison camp in Idaho, along with other Japanese Americans. There they lived in drafty tar-paper barracks heated by coal-burning stoves. The 950-acre camp was guarded by barbed wire, watchtowers, armed guards, and dogs. In 1943 Monica Sone was allowed to leave to take a job in Chicago as a dental assistant. In 1953 she published *Nisei Daughter*, an autobiography. Later she became a clinical psychologist. This essay describes her reaction to attending both an American and a Japanese school when she was six years old.

1   The inevitable, dreaded first day at Nihon Gakko [Japanese school] arrived. Henry and I were dumped into a taxicab, screaming and kicking against the injustice of it all. When the cab stopped in front of a large, square gray-frame building, Mother pried us loose, though we clung to the cab door like barnacles. She half carried us up the hill. We kept up our horrendous shrieking and wailing, right to the school entrance. Then a man burst out of the door. His face seemed to have been carved out of granite and with turned-down mouth and nostrils flaring with disapproval, his black marble eyes crushed us into a quivering silence. This was Mr. Ohashi, the school principal, who had come out to investigate the abominable, un-Japanesey noise on the school premises.

Mother bowed deeply and murmured, "I place them in your hands."

He bowed stiffly to Mother, then fastened his eyes on Henry and me and again bowed slowly and deliberately. In our haste to return the bow, we nodded our heads. With icy disdain, he snapped, "That is not an *ojigi*." He bent forward with well-oiled precision. "Bow from the waist, like this."

I wondered, if Mr. Ohashi had the nerve to criticize us in front of Mother, what more he would do in her absence.

School was already in session and the hallway was empty and cold. Mr. Ohashi walked briskly ahead, opened a door, and Henry was whisked inside with Mother. I caught a glimpse of little boys and girls sitting erect, their books held upright on the desks.

As I waited alone out in the hall, I felt a tingling sensation. This was the moment for escape. I would run and run and run. I would be lost for days so that when Father and Mother finally found me, they would be too happy ever to force me back to Nihon Gakko. But Mr. Ohashi was too cunning for me. He must have read my thoughts, for the door suddenly opened, and he and Mother came out. He bowed formally again, "*Sah,* this way," and stalked off.

My will completely dissolved, I followed as in a terrible nightmare. Mother took my hand and smiled warmly, "Don't look so sad, Ka-chan. You'll find it a lot of fun when you get used to it."

I was ushered into a brightly lighted room which seemed ten times as brilliant with the dazzling battery of shining black eyes turned in my direction. I was introduced to Yasuda-sensei, a full-faced woman with a large, ballooning figure. She wore a long, shapeless cotton print smock with streaks of chalk powder down the front. She spoke kindly to me, but with a kindness that one usually reserves for a dull-witted child. She enunciated slowly and loudly, "What is your name?"

I whispered, "Kazuko," hoping she would lower her voice. I felt that our conversation should not be carried on in such a blatant manner.

"*Kazuko-san desuka?*" she repeated loudly. "You may sit over there." She pointed to an empty seat in the rear and I walked down an endless aisle between rows of piercing black eyes.

"Kazuko-san, why don't you remove your hat and coat and hang them up behind you?"

A wave of tittering broke out. With burning face, I rose from my seat and struggled out of my coat.

When Mother followed Mr. Ohashi out of the room, my throat began to tighten and tears flooded up again. I did not notice that Yasuda-sensei was standing beside me. Ignoring my snuffling, she handed me a book, opened to the first page. I saw a blurred drawing of one huge, staring eye. Right above it was a black squiggly mark, resembling the arabic figure one with a bar across the middle. Yasuda-sensei was up in front again, reading aloud, "*Meh!*" That was "eye." As we turned the pages, there were pictures of a long, austere nose, its print reading *"hana,"* an ear was called *"mi-mi,"* and a wide anemic-looking mouth, *"ku-chi."* Soon I was chanting at the top of my voice with the rest of the class, *"Meh! Hana! Mi-mi! Ku-chi!"*

Gradually I yielded to my double dose of schooling. Nihon Gakko was so different from grammar school I found myself switching my personality back and forth daily like a chameleon. At Bailey Gatzert School I was a jumping, screaming, roustabout Yankee, but at the stroke of three when the school bell rang and doors burst open everywhere, spewing out pupils like jelly beans from a broken bag, I suddenly became a modest, faltering, earnest little Japanese girl with a small, timid voice. I trudged down a steep hill and climbed up another steep hill to Nihon Gakko with other black-haired boys and girls. On the playground, we behaved cautiously. Whenever we spied a teacher within bowing distance, we hissed at each other to stop the game, put our feet neatly together, slid our hands down to our knees and bowed slowly and sanctimoniously. In just the proper, moderate tone, putting in every ounce of respect, we chanted, *"Konichi-wa, sensei.* Good day."

15 For an hour and a half each day, we were put through our paces. At the beginning of each class hour, Yasuda-sensei punched a little bell on her desk. We stood up by our seats, at strict attention. Another "ping!" We all bowed to her in unison while she returned the bow solemnly. With the third "ping!" we sat down together.

There was *yomi-kata* time when individual students were called upon to read the day's lesson, clear and loud. The first time I recited I stood and read with swelling pride the lesson which I had prepared the night before. I mouthed each word carefully and paused for the proper length of time at the end of each sentence. Suddenly Yasuda-sensei stopped me.

"Kazuko-san!"

I looked up at her confused, wondering what mistakes I had made.

"You are holding your book in one hand," she accused me. Indeed, I was. I did not see the need of using two hands to support a thin book which I could balance with two fingers.

20 "Use both hands!" she commanded me.

Then she peered at me. "And are you leaning against your desk?" Yes, I was slightly. "Stand up straight!"

"*Hai!* Yes, ma'am!"

I learned that I could stumble all around in my lessons without ruffling sensei's nerves, but it was a personal insult to her if I displayed sloppy posture. I must stand up like a soldier, hold the book high in the air with both hands, and keep my feet still.

We recited the Japanese alphabet aloud, fifty-one letters, over and over again. "Ah, ee, oo, eh, *OH!* Kah, kee, koo, key, *KOH!* Sah, shi, soo, seh, *SOH!*" We developed a catchy little rhythm, coming down hard on the last syllable of each line. We wound up the drill with an ear-shattering, triumphant, "Lah, lee, loo, leh, *Loh!* WAH, EE, OO, EH, OH! UN!"

Yasuda-sensei would look suspiciously at us. Our recital sounded a 25 shade too hearty, a shade rhythmic. It lacked something . . . possibly restraint and respect.

During *kaki-kata* hour, I doubled up over my desk and painfully drew out the *kata-kanas,* simplified Japanese ideographs, similar to English block printing. With clenched teeth and perspiring hands, I accentuated and emphasized, delicately nuanced and tapered off lines and curves.

At five-thirty, Yasuda-sensei rang the bell on her desk again. "Ping!" We stood up. "Ping!" We bowed. "Ping!" We vanished from the room like magic, except for one row of students whose turn it was to do *otohban,* washing blackboards, sweeping the floor, and dusting the desks. Under sensei's vigilant eyes, the chore felt like a convict's hard labor.

As time went on, I began to suspect that there was much more to Nihon Gakko than learning the Japanese language. There was a driving spirit of strict discipline behind it all which reached out and weighed heavily upon each pupil's consciousness. That force emanated from the principal's office.

Before Mr. Ohashi came to America, he had been a zealous student of the Ogasawara Shiko Saho, a form of social conduct dreamed up by a Mr. Ogasawara. Mr. Ohashi himself had written a book on etiquette in Japan. He was the Oriental male counterpart of Emily Post. Thus Mr. Ohashi arrived in America with the perfect bow tucked under his waist and a facial expression cemented into perfect samurai control. He came with a smoldering ambition to pass on this knowledge to the tender Japanese saplings born on foreign soil. The school-teachers caught fire, too, and dedicated themselves to us with a vengeance. It was not enough to learn the language. We must talk and walk and sit and bow in the best Japanese tradition.

As far as I was concerned, Mr. Ohashi's superior standard boiled down 30 to one thing. The model child is one with deep *rigor mortis* . . . no noise, no trouble, no back talk.

We understood too well what Mr. Ohashi wanted of us. He yearned and wished more than anything else that somehow he could mold all of us into Genji Yamadas. Genji was a classmate whom we detested thoroughly. He was born in Seattle, but his parents had sent him to Japan at an early age for a period of good, old-fashioned education. He returned home a stranger among us with stiff mannerisms and an arrogant attitude. Genji boasted that he could lick anyone, one husky fellow or ten little ones, and he did, time and time again. He was an expert at judo.

Genji was a handsome boy with huge, lustrous dark eyes, a noble patrician nose, jet crew-cut setting off a flawless, fair complexion, looking every bit the son of a samurai. He sat aloof at his desk and paid strict attention to sensei. He was the top student scholastically. He read fluently and perfectly. His handwriting was a beautiful picture of bold, masculine strokes and curves. What gnawed at us more than anything else was that he stood up as straight as a bamboo tree and never lost rigid control of his arms or legs. His bow was snappy and brisk and he always answered "*Hai!*" to everything that sensei said to him, ringing crisp and clear with respect. Every time Mr. Ohashi came into our room for a surprise visit to see if we were under control, he would stop at Genji's desk for a brief chat. Mr. Ohashi's eyes betrayed a glow of pride as he spoke to Genji, who sat up erect, eyes staring respectfully ahead. All we could make out of the conversation was Genji's sharp staccato barks, "*Hai! . . . Hai! . . . Hai!*"

This was the response sublime to Mr. Ohashi. It was real man to man talk. Whenever Mr. Ohashi approached us, we froze in our seats. Instead of snapping into attention like Genji, we wilted and sagged. Mr. Ohashi said we were more like "*konyaku,*" a colorless, gelatinous Japanese food. If a boy fidgeted too nervously under Mr. Ohashi's stare, a vivid red stain rose from the back of Mr. Ohashi's neck until it reached his temple and then there was a sharp explosion like the crack of a whip. "*Keo-tsuke!* Attention!*" It made us all leap in our seats, each one of us feeling terribly guilty for being such an inadequate Japanese.

I asked Mother, "Why is Mr. Ohashi so angry all the time? He always looks as if he had just bitten into a green persimmon. I've never seen him smile."

35   Mother said, "I guess Mr. Ohashi is the old-fashioned schoolmaster. I know he's strict, but he means well. Your father and I received harsher discipline than that in Japan . . . not only from schoolteachers, but from our own parents."

"Yes, I know, Mama." I leaned against her knees as she sat on the old leather davenport, mending our clothes. I thought Father and Mother were still wonderful, even if they had packed me off to Nihon Gakko. "Mrs. Matsui is so strict with her children, too: She thinks you spoil us." I giggled, and reassured her quickly, "But I don't think you spoil us at all."

Mrs. Matsui was ten years older than Mother, and had known Mother's father in Japan. Therefore she felt it was her duty to look after Mother's progress in this foreign country. Like a sharp-eyed hawk, she picked out Mother's weaknesses. . . . It was impossible for us to remember the endless little things we must not do in front of Mrs. Matsui. We must not laugh out loud and show our teeth, or chatter in front of guests, or interrupt adult conversation, or cross our knees while seated, or ask for a piece of candy, or squirm in our seats. . . .

Mr. Ohashi and Mrs. Matsui thought they could work on me and gradually mold me into an ideal Japanese *ojoh-san,* a refined young maiden who is quiet, pure in thought, polite, serene, and self-controlled. They made little headway, for I was too much the child of Skidrow. As far as I was concerned, Nihon Gakko was a total loss. I could not use my Japanese on the people at the hotel. Bowing was practical only at Nihon Gakko. If I were to bow to the hotel patrons, they would have laughed in my face. Therefore promptly at five-thirty every day, I shed Nihon Gakko and returned with relief to an environment which was the only real one to me. Life was too urgent, too exciting, too colorful for me to be sitting quietly in the parlor and contemplating a spray of chrysanthemums in a bowl as a cousin of mine might be doing in Osaka.

REFLECTING AND INTERPRETING

1. What impression do you gain of the two children from the opening paragraph?
2. How does Kazuko feel that first day of school? Why?
3. What method of teaching was used?
4. How did Kazuko's behavior differ at the two schools?
5. What seems to be the primary emphasis of the Japanese school? How did it affect Sone?
6. Why were some students required to stay after school?
7. What literary devices does the author use in paragraphs 14 and 23 to describe her behavior?
8. To avoid having their mother criticized by a neighbor, what seven things must the children not do?
9. What does Sone say about the effect of the Japanese school upon her?
10. How might the strict discipline of the Japanese school have helped Sone later in life? (Tip: Reread the introduction.)

A WRITER'S RESPONSE

1. Describe your first day of school. How did you feel at the beginning and end of the day?
2. Have you attended more than one school? If so, compare them and their influence on you.

WHY MARRIAGES FAIL   ANNE RICHARDSON ROIPHE

Born in New York City, Anne Roiphe graduated from Sarah Lawrence College with a BA degree. In the past four decades, she has published a dozen fiction and nonfiction books, as well as collaborated on several others. Her latest works include *If You Knew Me* (1995), *Lovingkindness* (1997), *Fruitful: Living the Contradictions: A Memoir of Modern Motherhood* (1997), *For Rabbit, with Love and Squalor: An American Read* (2000), and *1185 Park Avenue: A Memoir* (2000). Roiphe writes a column for the *New York Observer*. Her articles and

reviews have appeared in *Vogue, Redbook, Glamour, Family Circle,* and *Working Woman.*
In this essay, which first appeared in *Family Weekly* (27 Feb. 1983), she analyzes the factors
that lead to divorce.

1   These days so many marriages end in divorce that our most sacred
vows no longer ring with truth. "Happily ever after" and "Till death do us
part" are expressions that seem on the way to becoming obsolete. Why
has it becomes so hard for couples to stay together? What goes wrong?
What has happened to us that close to one-half of all marriages are des-
tined for the divorce courts? How could we have created a society in which
42 percent of our children will grow up in single parent homes? If statistics
could only measure loneliness, regret, pain, loss of self-confidence and
fear of the future, the numbers would be beyond quantifying.

Even though each broken marriage is unique, we can still find the
common perils, the common causes for marital despair. Each marriage has
crisis points and each marriage tests endurance, the capacity for both intimacy and change. Outside pressures such as job loss, illness, infertility,
trouble with a child, care of aging parents and all the other plagues of life
hit marriage the way hurricanes blast our shores. Some marriages survive
these storms and others don't. Marriages fail, however, not simply because of the outside weather but because the inner climate becomes too
hot or too cold, too turbulent or too stupefying.

When we look at how we choose our partners and what expectations
exist at the tender beginnings of romance, some of the reasons for disaster become quite clear. We all select with unconscious accuracy a mate who
will recreate with us the emotional patterns of our first homes. Dr. Carl A.
Whitaker, a marital therapist and emeritus professor of psychiatry at the
University of Wisconsin explains, "From early childhood on, each of us
carried models for marriage, femininity, masculinity, motherhood, fatherhood and all the other family roles." Each of us falls in love with a mate
who has qualities of our parents, who will help us rediscover both the psychological happiness and miseries of our past lives. We may think we have
found a man unlike Dad, but then he turns to drink or drugs, or loses his
job over and over again or sits silently in front of the T.V. just the way Dad
did. A man may choose a woman who doesn't like kids just like his mother
or who gambles away the family savings just like his mother. Or he may
choose a slender wife who seems unlike his obese mother but then turns
out to have other addictions that destroy their mutual happiness.

A man and a woman bring to their marriage bed a blended concoction
of conscious and unconscious memories of their parents' lives together.
The human way is to compulsively repeat and recreate the patterns of the
past. Sigmund Freud so well described the unhappy design that many of
us get trapped in: the unmet needs of childhood, the angry feelings left
over from frustrations of long ago, the limits of trust and the recurrence of
old fears. Once an individual senses this entrapment, there may follow a
yearning to escape, and the result could be a broken, splintered marriage.

Of course people can overcome the habits and attitudes that devel- 5 oped in childhood. We all have hidden strengths and amazing capacities for growth and creative change. Change, however, requires work— observing your part in a rotten pattern, bringing difficulties out into the open—and work runs counter to the basic myth of marriage: "When I wed this person all my problems will be over. I will have achieved success and I will become the center of life for this other person and this person will be my center, and we will mean everything to each other forever." This myth, which every marriage relies on, is soon exposed. The coming of children, the pulls and tugs of their demands on affection and time, place a considerable strain on that basic myth of meaning everything to each other, of merging together and solving all of life's problems.

Concern and tension about money take each partner away from the other. Obligations to demanding parents or still-depended-upon parents create further strain. Couples today must also deal with all the cultural changes brought on in recent years by the women's movement and the sexual revolution. The altering of roles and the shifting of responsibilities have been extremely trying for many marriages.

These and other realities of life erode the visions of marital bliss the way sandstorms eat at rock and the ocean nibbles away at the dunes. Those euphoric, grand feelings that accompany romantic love are really self-delusions, self-hypnotic dreams that enable us to forge a relationship. Real life, failure at work, disappointments, exhaustion, bad smells, bad colds and hard times all puncture the dream and leave us stranded with our mate, with our childhood patterns pushing us this way and that, with our unfulfilled expectations.

The struggle to survive in marriage requires adaptability, flexibility, genuine love and kindness and an imagination strong enough to feel what the other is feeling. Many marriages fall apart because either partner cannot imagine what the other wants or cannot communicate what he or she needs or feels. Anger builds until it erupts into a volcanic burst that buries the marriage in ash.

It is not hard to see, therefore, how essential communication is for a good marriage. A man and a woman must be able to tell each other how they feel and why they feel the way they do; otherwise they will impose on each other roles and actions that lead to further unhappiness. In some cases, the communication patterns of childhood—of not talking, of talking too much, of not listening, of distrust and anger, of withdrawal—spill into the marriage and prevent a healthy exchange of thoughts and feelings. The answer is to set up new patterns of communication and intimacy.

At the same time, however, we must see each other as individuals. "To 10 achieve a balance between separateness and closeness is one of the major psychological tasks of all human beings at every stage of life," says Dr. Stuart Bartle, a psychiatrist at the New York University Medical Center.

If we sense from our mate a need for too much intimacy, we tend to push him or her away, fearing that we may lose our identities in the merging of marriage. One partner may suffocate the other partner in a childlike dependency.

A good marriage means growing as a couple but also growing as individuals. This isn't easy. Richard gives up his interest in carpentry because his wife, Helen, is jealous of the time he spends away from her. Karen quits her choir group because her husband dislikes the friends she makes there. Each pair clings to each other and are angry with each other as life closes in on them. This kind of marital balance is easily thrown as one or the other pulls away and divorce follows.

Sometimes people pretend that a new partner will solve the old problems. Most often extramarital sex destroys a marriage because it allows an artificial split between the good and the bad—the good is projected on the new partner and the bad is dumped on the head of the old. Dishonesty, hiding and cheating create walls between men and women. Infidelity is just a symptom of trouble. It is a symbolic complaint, a weapon of revenge, as well as an unraveler of closeness. Infidelity is often that proverbial last straw that sinks that camel to the ground.

All right—marriage has always been difficult. Why then are we seeing so many divorces at this time? Yes, our modern social fabric is thin, and yes the permissiveness of society has created unrealistic expectations and thrown the family into chaos. But divorce is so common because people today are unwilling to exercise the self-discipline that marriage requires. They expect easy joy, like the entertainment on TV, the thrill of a good party.

15   Marriage takes some kind of sacrifice, not dreadful self-sacrifice of the soul, but some level of compromise. Some of one's fantasies, some of one's legitimate desires have to be given up for the value of the marriage itself. "While all marital partners feel shackled at times, it is they who really choose to make the marital ties into confining chains or supporting bonds," says Dr. Whitaker. Marriage requires sexual, financial and emotional discipline. A man and a woman cannot follow every impulse, cannot allow themselves to stop growing or changing.

Divorce is not an evil act. Sometimes it provides salvation for people who have grown hopelessly apart or were frozen in patterns of pain or mutual unhappiness. Divorce can be, despite its initial devastation, like the first cut of the surgeon's knife, a step toward new health and a good life. One the other hand, if the partners can stay past the breaking up of the romantic myths into the development of real love and intimacy, they have achieved a work as amazing as the greatest cathedrals of the world. Marriages that do not fail but improve, that persist despite imperfections, are not only rare these days but offer a wondrous shelter in which the face of our mutual humanity can safely show itself.

REFLECTING AND INTERPRETING

1. Reread the first paragraph. What rhetorical strategy is used here? How does it function?

2. In paragraph 3, Roiphe cites expert opinion. Why?

3. Do you agree or disagree with Dr. Whitaker's theory? Why?

4. What is the basic marriage myth that Roiphe wrote about two decades ago? Do you think the myth still exists? Why or why not?

5. What five qualities does Roiphe identify that are essential for a marriage to endure? Can you think of any others?

6. What pretense does a partner often use to "solve old problems"? How effective is it? What are the risks? (Think about the opening sentence.)

7. What are some of the factors that have created more tension in marriages than those of a century ago?

8. Roiphe says that divorce is so common for one chief reason. What is it? What can couples do to evade divorce? Can you think of some ways that she does not name?

9. What is the basic question that couples must resolve in order for a marriage to succeed?

10. What advantages does a successful marriage offer a family? Consider effects on children, education, health, and others.

A WRITER'S RESPONSE

1. If you are married, analyze the growth that you have attained since your wedding vows. Write an essay analyzing the cause and effects. If you are single, describe the kind of marriage you would like to have some day. Then analyze the responsibilities you will need to assume and the changes you will need to make.

2. *Small Groups:* Roiphe points out that growth must take place for a marriage to succeed. What kind of growth does she mean? How do changes in perception and perspective figure in? Can you give some examples?

THE TEACHER WHO CHANGED MY LIFE   NICHOLAS GAGE

Running barefoot through minefields with his three sisters, Nicholas Gage left his Greek village to escape communist guerrillas. The children stayed in a refugee camp until their father, who lived in the United States, located them. When nine-year-old Nicholas Gage arrived in the United States, he did not expect to be placed in a class for the mentally retarded. Non-English speaking, he and his sisters learned English. Four years later Gage met a teacher who changed his life. He won a scholarship to Boston University and later attended Columbia's Graduate School of Journalism. He worked for the Associated Press, *Boston Herald Traveler, Wall Street Journal,* and *New York Times,* which sent him to Greece as a foreign correspondent. His book *Eleni* (1987), which relates his early experiences, was a best-seller and later produced as a film. He has written several other books, including *Hellas: A Portrait of Greece* (1987), *Greece: Land of Light* (1998), and *Greek Fire* (2001). The following excerpt is from *A Place for Us* (1990).

1   The person who set the course of my life in the new land I entered as a young war refugee—who, in fact, nearly dragged me onto the path that would bring all the blessings I've received in America—was a salty-tongued, no-nonsense schoolteacher named Marjorie Hurd. When I entered her classroom in 1953, I had been to six schools in five years, starting in the Greek village where I was born in 1939.

When I stepped off a ship in New York Harbor on a gray March day in 1949, I was an undersized 9-year-old in short pants who had lost his mother and was coming to live with the father he didn't know. My mother, Eleni Gatzoyiannis, had been imprisoned, tortured and shot by Communist guerrillas for sending me and three of my four sisters to freedom. She died so that her children could go to their father in the United States.

The portly, bald, well-dressed man who met me and my sisters seemed a foreign, authoritarian figure. I secretly resented him for not getting the whole family out of Greece early enough to save my mother. Ultimately, I would grow to love him and appreciate how he dealt with becoming a single parent at the age of 56, but at first our relationship was prickly, full of hostility.

As Father drove us to our new home—a tenement in Worcester, Mass.—and pointed out the huge brick building that would be our first school in America, I clutched my Greek notebooks from the refugee camp, hoping that my few years of schooling would impress my teachers in this cold, crowded country. They didn't. When my father led me and my 11-year-old sister to Greendale Elementary School, the grim-faced Yankee principal put the two of us in a class for the mentally retarded. There was no facility in those days for non-English-speaking children.

5   By the time I met Marjorie Hurd four years later, I had learned English, been placed in a normal, graded class and had even been chosen for the college preparatory track in the Worcester public school system. I was 13 years old when our father moved us yet again, and I entered Chandler Junior High shortly after the beginning of seventh grade. I found myself surrounded by richer, smarter and better-dressed classmates who looked askance at my strange clothes and heavy accent. Shortly after I arrived, we were told to select a hobby to pursue during "club hour" on Fridays. The idea of hobbies and clubs made no sense to my immigrant ears, but I decided to follow the prettiest girl in my class—the blue-eyed daughter of the local Lutheran minister. She led me through the door marked "Newspaper Club" and into the presence of Miss Hurd, the newspaper adviser and English teacher who would become my mentor and my muse.

A formidable, solidly built woman with salt-and-pepper hair, a steely eye and a flat Boston accent, Miss Hurd had no patience with layabouts. "What are all you goof-offs doing here?" she bellowed at the would-be journalists. "This is the Newspaper Club! We're going to put out a *newspaper*. So if there's anybody in this room who doesn't like work, I suggest you go across to the Glee Club now, because you're going to work your tails off here!"

I was soon under Miss Hurd's spell. She did indeed teach us to put out a newspaper, skills I honed during my next 25 years as a journalist. Soon I asked the principal to transfer me to her English class as well. There, she drilled us on grammar until I finally began to understand the logic and structure of the English language. She assigned stories for us to read and discuss; not tales of heroes, like the Greek myths I knew, but stories of underdogs—poor people, even immigrants, who seemed ordinary until a crisis drove them to do something extraordinary. She also introduced us to the literary wealth of Greece—giving me a new perspective on my war-ravaged, impoverished homeland. I began to be proud of my origins.

One day, after discussing how writers should write about what they know, she assigned us to compose an essay from our own experience. Fixing me with a stern look, she added, "Nick, I want you to write about what happened to your family in Greece." I had been trying to put those painful memories behind me and left the assignment until the last moment. Then, on a warm spring afternoon, I sat in my room with a yellow pad and pencil and stared out the window at the buds on the trees. I wrote that the coming of spring always reminded me of the last time I said goodbye to my mother on a green and gold day in 1948.

I kept writing, one line after another, telling how the Communist guerrillas occupied our village, took our home and food, how my mother started planning our escape when she learned that the children were to be sent to re-education camps behind the Iron Curtain and how, at the last moment, she couldn't escape with us because the guerrillas sent her with a group of women to thresh wheat in a distant village. She promised she would try to get away on her own, she told me to be brave and hung a silver cross around my neck, and then she kissed me. I watched the line of women being led down into the ravine and up the other side, until they disappeared around the bend—my mother a tiny brown figure at the end who stopped for an instant to raise her hand in one last farewell.

I wrote about our nighttime escape down the mountain, across the 10 minefields and into the lines of the Nationalist soldiers, who sent us to a refugee camp. It was there that we learned of our mother's execution. I felt very lucky to have come to America, I concluded, but every year, the coming of spring made me feel sad because it reminded me of the last time I saw my mother.

I handed in the essay, hoping never to see it again, but Miss Hurd had it published in the school paper. This mortified me at first, until I saw that my classmates reacted with sympathy and tact to my family's story. Without telling me, Miss Hurd also submitted the essay to a contest sponsored by the Freedoms Foundation at Valley Forge, Pa., and it won a medal. The Worcester paper wrote about the award and quoted my essay at length. My father, by then a "five-and-dime-store chef," as the paper described him, was ecstatic with pride, and the Worcester Greek community celebrated the honor to one of its own.

For the first time I began to understand the power of the written word. A secret ambition took root in me. One day, I vowed, I would go back to Greece, find out the details of my mother's death and write about her life, so her grandchildren would know of her courage. Perhaps I would even track down the men who killed her and write of their crimes. Fulfilling that ambition would take me 30 years.

Meanwhile, I followed the literary path that Miss Hurd had so forcefully set me on. After junior high, I became the editor of my school paper at Classical High School and got a part-time job at the Worcester *Telegram and Gazette.* Although my father could only give me $50 and encouragement toward a college education, I managed to finance four years at Boston University with scholarships and part-time jobs in journalism. During my last year of college, an article I wrote about a friend who had died in the Philippines—the first person to lose his life working for the Peace Corps—led to my winning the Hearst Award for College Journalism. And the plaque was given to me in the White House by President John F. Kennedy.

For a refugee who had never seen a motorized vehicle or indoor plumbing until he was 9, this was an unimaginable honor. When the Worcester paper ran a picture of me standing next to President Kennedy, my father rushed out to buy a new suit in order to be properly dressed to receive the congratulations of the Worcester Greeks. He clipped out the photograph, had it laminated in plastic and carried it in his breast pocket for the rest of his life to show everyone he met. I found the much-worn photo in his pocket on the day he died 20 years later.

15   In our isolated Greek village, my mother had bribed a cousin to teach her to read, for girls were not supposed to attend school beyond a certain age. She had always dreamed of her children receiving an education. She couldn't be there when I graduated from Boston University, but the person who came with my father and shared our joy was my former teacher, Marjorie Hurd. We celebrated not only my bachelor's degree but also the scholarships that paid my way to Columbia's Graduate School of Journalism. There, I met the woman who would eventually become my wife. At our wedding and at the baptisms of our three children, Marjorie Hurd was always there, dancing alongside the Greeks.

By then, she was Mrs. Rabidou, for she had married a widower when she was in her early 40s. That didn't distract her from her vocation of introducing young minds to English literature, however. She taught for a total of 41 years and continually would make a "project" of some balky student in whom she spied a spark of potential. Often these were students from the most troubled homes, yet she would alternately bully and charm each one with her own special brand of tough love until the spark caught fire. She retired in 1981 at the age of 62 but still avidly follows the lives and careers of former students while overseeing her adult stepchildren and driving her husband on camping trips to New Hampshire.

Miss Hurd was one of the first to call me on Dec. 10, 1987, when President Reagan, in his television address after the summit meeting with Gorbachev, told the nation that Eleni Gatzoyiannis' dying cry, "My children!" had helped inspire him to seek an arms agreement "for all the children of the world."

"I can't imagine a better monument for your mother," Miss Hurd said with an uncharacteristic catch in her voice.

Although a bad hip makes it impossible for her to join in the Greek dancing, Marjorie Hurd Rabidou is still an honored and enthusiastic guest at all family celebrations, including my 50th birthday picnic last summer, where the shish kebab was cooked on spits, clarinets and *bouzoukis* wailed, and costumed dancers led the guests in a serpentine line around our Colonial farmhouse, only 20 minutes from my first home in Worcester.

My sisters and I felt an aching void because my father was not there to 20 lead the line, balancing a glass of wine on his head while he danced, the way he did at every celebration during his 92 years. But Miss Hurd was there, surveying the scene with quiet satisfaction. Although my parents are gone, her presence was a consolation, because I owe her so much.

This is truly the land of opportunity, and I would have enjoyed its bounty even if I hadn't walked into Miss Hurd's classroom in 1953. But she was the one who directed my grief and pain into writing, and if it weren't for her I wouldn't have become an investigative reporter and foreign correspondent, recorded the story of my mother's life and death in *Eleni* and now my father's story in *A Place for Us,* which is also a testament to the country that took us in. She was the catalyst that sent me into journalism and indirectly caused all the good things that came after. But Miss Hurd would probably deny this emphatically.

A few years ago, I answered the telephone and heard my former teacher's voice telling me, in that won't-take-no-for-an-answer tone of hers, that she had decided I was to write and deliver the eulogy at her funeral. I agreed (she didn't leave me any choice), but that's one assignment I never want to do. I hope, Miss Hurd, that you'll accept this remembrance instead.

REFLECTING AND INTERPRETING

1. Where is Gage's thesis statement?

2. Although this essay is primarily about a teacher that Gage had the year he was thirteen, he talks about virtually his entire life. Why?

3. What order does Gage use to present the events of so many years? At times he uses what device to weave in past events? How does he accomplish these shifts so that readers can easily follow?

4. How did Miss Hurd (later Mrs. Rabidou) occasionally make a "project" of one of her students?

5. What are stories of "underdogs"? Can you think of one of our presidents who was an underdog?

6. What skills did Gage develop as a result of Miss Hurd's instruction? How did one of her assignments change his life?

7. Trace Miss Hurd's influence on Gage after he left her junior high class.

8. When Gage uses "salty-tongued, no-nonsense" to describe Miss Hurd, what do you think he means? What other glimpses of her personality do you gain from her interaction not only with Gage but also with other students?

9. An excerpt from Gage's book *Eleni* was quoted on national television. Who referred to it? What was the occasion? How did one of her assignments change his life?

10. How would you describe Gage's attitude and the tone of the essay?

A WRITER'S RESPONSE

1. Have you ever changed schools and felt uncomfortable among students who seemed quite different? Describe the experience and how you adjusted. Was any particular person helpful in making you feel comfortable? Write an essay describing the experience and how it affected you.

2. Consider the people who have influenced your life. Write an essay identifying the incidents that were particularly significant to you. Explain why.

THE EMOTIONAL QUADRANT   ELISABETH KÜBLER-ROSS

"Big boys don't cry!" We've all heard it, and perhaps some of us have said it without an inkling of the possible effects on a child who has a vital need to cry. The following essay by Elisabeth Kübler-Ross (1926–2004), one of the world's foremost authorities on death and dying, traces the effect of a parent's death on a young child. Kübler-Ross, born in Zurich, Switzerland, received her MD from Zurich University in 1957. Four years later she became a naturalized American citizen. A physician, educator, and writer, she published her watershed work, *On Death and Dying*, in 1969. Since then she has published twelve other books, including *On Life after Death* (1991), *On Children and Death* (1993), *Working It Through* (1997), *Remember the Secret* (1998), *The Tunnel and the Light* (1999), and *Life Lessons* (2000).

1   Very young children have no fear of death, although they have the two innate fears of sudden loud noises and of falling from high places. Later on children are naturally afraid of separation, since the fear of abandonment and the absence of a loving caretaker is very basic and meaningful. Children are aware of their dependency, and those who have been exposed to early traumas in life are scarred. They will need to relive the trauma and learn to let go of the panic, pain, anxiety and rage of the abandonment.

These violent feelings arise often, not solely when a member of the family dies. Abandonments of all sorts happen thousands of times over in our society, and if the loss is not associated with the death of a loved one, few people will recognize this. The emergency support systems or shoulders to lean on will not be called into action, and there will be no sympathy visits by neighbors. So the child who feels abandoned in some manner is left vulnerable; his future mind-set could include a general mistrust, a fear of ever allowing a close relationship, an alienation from the person who is blamed for the separation, and a deep grief over the absence of love.

Rene was such a child, and he needed thirty years to heal. He was only five years old when his father told him to get into the car, because they were going somewhere together. Rene was very excited. His father had been drinking for many years; his mom had been in and out of mental hospitals, and there had been very little laughter and happiness in his life. And now his dad was going to take him somewhere. He did not dare to ask him where they were going. To the zoo? To the park? To a football game? He could not understand why Dad had come home in the middle of the week, but he knew that his mom was very sick again, because she had slept all day and never came down even to fix him a sandwich.

In the car, Rene and his father approached a huge building and parked. His father silently opened the car door and let Rene out. The father was very quiet; he did not even smile once. Rene wondered if his father was mad at him. He remembered he had fixed his own breakfast. He had even put the dishes in the sink. He was never noisy when his mom and dad had their fights, and he stayed in the den and out of the way. He had not heard them fighting today, and therefore Rene had hoped it would be a good day.

His dad took him by the hand and led him into a strange room with a funny smell. A Catholic sister came and talked to his father, but no one talked to him. Then his father left the room, and a short time later the sister left also. Rene sat very quietly and waited, but no one came. Maybe his dad had to go to the bathroom. Finally he got up, and out the window he saw his dad walking out of the house toward the car. He ran as fast as he could: "Dad, Dad, don't leave me!" But the car door shut, and he saw the old familiar car turn the corner—out of sight. 5

Rene never saw his mother again. She returned to the mental hospital, where two years later she killed herself. He didn't see his father again for many years. It was much later that a strange woman came to visit him one day; she told him that his dad had married her and that they had planned to take him out of the home of the sisters to see if it could "work out."

Rene tried to please his dad in every way he could. He painted the new house and worked every free moment he had to get a nod of approval from him. But his dad remained as silent as he had always been. This silence always brought back to Rene the memory of that nightmarish day when he had been taken away from home without so much as an explanation, much less a good-bye or last hug from his mom.

His father never said "thank you" or "I am pleased with you," just as he never brought up the reasons for Rene's placement in the home and the lack of warning. So Rene grew up trying to please, not knowing that the fear of rejection and abandonment was still with him in adulthood. But Rene was afraid of alcoholism, afraid of mental illness, afraid of getting close to anyone. His whole life consisted of work and more work to please his father. He never allowed himself to get angry, to speak up, to express displeasure. The only time his face lit up was at the sight of a parent playing with a child in the park or swinging on a swing in a schoolyard. He spent his free time in those places, vicariously enjoying the laughter of these children, unaware of why he could not experience love and laughter in his own life.

As a mature adult he took an opportunity to look at his pain, anguish, despair, and incomprehension of this totally unexpected abandonment in early childhood, and he emerged a free man. It took him only one week, touched by others who shared their agonies in a safe place where it was regarded as a blessing to get rid of old tears and anger. During that week, Rene felt loved unconditionally. This man has just resolved his conflicts and has begun to understand his inability to trust and relate.

10   If someone—preferably his parents—had talked with this little boy and made an effort to understand his play, his drawings, his sullen withdrawal and isolation, much pain and unresolved conflict, carried within for decades, could have easily been avoided. You think those things happened in the last century? No, they still happen every day in our society.

Many, many adults suffer from never having resolved the hurts of their childhood. So children need to be allowed to grieve without being labeled crybaby or sissy, or hearing the ridiculous statement "Big boys don't cry." If children of both sexes are not allowed to express their natural emotions in childhood, they will have problems later on in the form of self-pity and many psychosomatic symptoms. Grief and fear, when allowed to be expressed and shared in childhood, can prevent much future heartache.

REFLECTING AND INTERPRETING

1. In the anecdote about five-year-old Rene, from whose point of view is the story told? What is the effect?

2. Where is the thesis statement?

3. How does Rene try to win his father's approval?

4. Describe Rene's early home life and his relationship with his father. Did the relationship improve when his father remarried? How effective is this extended example in supporting the thesis?

5. As an adult, what three things did Rene fear?

6. Although the essay devotes only one paragraph to the startling change in Rene, what can we surmise?

7. What danger does Dr. Kübler-Ross point to in the conclusion of her essay?

8. The author says that after a week of treatment, "Rene felt loved unconditionally." What does this phrase mean to you?

9. When tragedy strikes in a family, why should it be discussed with even very young children?

10. The author does not define "emotional quadrant" in this essay. Consider the meaning of *quadrant*. To what does emotional quadrant seem to refer?

A WRITER'S RESPONSE

1. Has something ever happened to you that you felt you could not tell anyone? What was the effect on your peace of mind and behavior? What finally happened? Write an essay describing the event and your reaction to it.

2. Perhaps you have survived a traumatic event with the support of kind friends and family. Write an essay describing the experience and its effect on you.

Shaping an Effective Argument

<table>
<tr><td>WHEN THE LULLABY ENDS</td><td>ANDREA SACHS</td></tr>
</table>

Should someone be allowed to return a child to an adoption agency if the child turns out to be defective? That is the question Andrea Sachs raises in this essay. A member of the New York Bar, the Illinois Bar, and the United States Supreme Court Bar, Sachs has a degree not only in law but also in journalism. Sachs has written for the *Los Angeles Times*, the *Washington Post*, *New York Newsday*, the *Columbia Journalism Review*, and the *American Bar Association Journal*. Currently, she covers the Supreme Court and legal issues for *Time* magazine. In 2000 she received special recognition for her reporting for an article in *Time*.

1   Most eleven-year-olds don't have a lawyer, but Tony is a special case. His adoptive parents decided five years after his adoption that Tony had not properly "bonded" with them, and returned him to the state in March. They kept Sam, Tony's natural younger brother. Patrick Murphy, the Chicago public guardian who was appointed to serve as Tony's attorney, says the youngster is an "absolute joy to be around." But there have been scars. Says Murphy: "One of the tragic things is that Tony blames himself."

Tony is one of at least 1,000 children adopted in the U.S. each year who will be returned to agencies by their new parents. Some are sent back because of unmet expectations, others because they have severe emotional problems the parents cannot handle. In a risk-averse age when consumer standards have become more exacting and family commitments seem less binding, there is a danger that adopted children could be viewed as commodities that come with an implied warranty. The problem presents a major challenge for the legal system. "This is not a question of damaged goods; it's a matter of what's in the best interest of the child," says Neil Cogan of Southern Methodist law school.

Social workers used to believe that all an adopted child needed was a loving home. But now many admit that even the most committed parents may be overwhelmed by unexpected problems. In 1986 Dan and Rhonda Stanton adopted a blond baby girl they named Stacey René. "We thought we had a perfect baby because she didn't cry," says Dan, an insurance agent in suburban Dallas. Their contentment faded as the months passed and Stacey did not develop properly. She didn't babble and laugh like their friends' babies and couldn't pinch with her individual fingers. The tentative diagnosis: Rett's syndrome, a rare genetic disorder in which the brain stops growing. Devastated, the Stantons took Stacey back to the agency and have not seen her since. "We made a commitment to her, but we were not able to live up to that commitment," says Rhonda. "She turned out to be totally different from what we thought we had adopted."

If adoptive parents are saddled with an unforeseen defect, who should shoulder the load? Most experts put the onus on the adoptive parents. "Families, having decided to do an adoption, assume a certain risk," says Professor William Winslade of the University of Texas Medical School in Galveston. "If it is an incredibly difficult burden, it seems unfair not to give parents, who have provided the benefit to society by making the adoption, some special help. But I don't think the burden should be totally given back to the state either. Parents adopt because they want the joys—and the sorrows—of having children."

About 2% of all adoptions in the U.S. fail. But for older children and 5 children with special needs, the numbers are far higher. For children older than two, 10% of the adoptions are dissolved. For ages 12 to 17, the rate shoots up to around 24%. This poses a special problem, since healthy adoptable babies are increasingly scarce due to the fact that more single women now opt to have abortions or to keep their infants. More families are therefore adopting older or handicapped children. This seems to be a main cause of the growing return-to-sender phenomenon.

As the problem of disrupted adoptions spreads, specialists are looking more closely at agency methods. One cause for failure is a practice that Berkeley Professor Richard Barth describes as "stretching." In essence, it is a bait-and-switch game: would-be parents are encouraged to adopt a child different from the one they wanted by the withholding of some negative information. For example, a couple who want a baby are persuaded to take an older child and never told that several earlier placements have not worked out because of emotional problems. Though the motive is benevolent—finding a home for a hard-to-place child—Barth regards the tactic as unethical.

Some disappointed parents have begun to fight back in the courts. The notion of "wrongful adoption"—which claims that agencies are liable for damages if they place children without fully disclosing their health backgrounds—is gaining legal recognition. Frank and Jayne Gibbs of Philadelphia are suing two agencies for $6 million, following their adoption of a seven-year-old boy who turned out to be violently disturbed. After the adoption, say the couple, they discovered that he had been horribly abused, including an attempt by his natural mother to cut off his genitals.

Many states have passed medical disclosure laws, which make it easier to obtain accurate information about a child. Agencies themselves are attempting to gather more data. The Golden Cradle adoption agency, in Cherry Hill, N.J., requires natural mothers to fill out 10-page medical histories that ask about everything from hay fever and heavy drinking to Down's syndrome and blood transfusions. Genetic counselors are often called in as consultants. "We believe an ounce of prevention is worth a pound of cure," says agency supervisor Mary Anne Giello.

Still, there are no warranties on adoptions. Those who set out looking for perfect "designer" children are likely to be disappointed. Nor is it possible—or even necessary—to know everything about a child. "People shouldn't get the idea that they can't be parents unless they have a DNA portrait of a kid," says Professor Joan Hollinger of the University of Detroit law school. Instead, adoptive parents, armed with as much information as possible, should face the inevitable mysteries—just as all parents do.

REFLECTING AND INTERPRETING

1. Examine the first paragraph. Does it raise any questions in your mind? Is there anything more you would like to know about that particular case?

2. Approximately how many adopted children are returned each year? What are three reasons children are returned?

3. Which age range of children has the greatest rate of return? Which factors might lead to their return? Are these factors similar to the ones that natural parents face?

4. What, according to Neil Cogan of Southern Methodist law school, is the key question that should be asked when an adopted child is about to be returned?

5. Should an alternative or support be offered to adoptive parents in these circumstances? If so, what?

6. Who should assume the responsibility for unforeseen problems in children? What do most experts say in answer to this question?

7. What factors contribute to the growing problem of returns?

8. Define "stretching" as practiced by some adoption agencies. Is this an ethical tactic?

9. What is "wrongful adoption"?

10. If agencies allow the return of adopted children, should a time limit be set? If so, what is a reasonable limit? (Answers may vary.)

A WRITER'S RESPONSE

1. Should adoptive parents be allowed to return children? Write an essay taking a stand on this question and defend your position. To gain more information, you may want to do research.

2. *Small Groups:* What can a couple do to forestall unnecessary risks in adopting a child? Should they depend only on the agency to provide information? Should they be allowed access to the medical histories of the parents?

STREET FIGHTIN' MEN STOMP THE QUIET VIRTUES

DANIEL HENNINGER

Born in Cleveland, Ohio, Daniel Henninger earned a bachelor's degree from Georgetown University's School of Foreign Service. In 1971 he hired on as a staff writer for the *National Observer*. In 1978 he joined *the Wall Street Journal* as an editorial-page writer. After a series of promotions, he became deputy editor of the editorial page in 1989. Henninger has won wide recognition for his commentary and editorial writing, including the Gerald Loeb Award (1985), Scripps Howard Foundations's Walker Stone Award (1998), and American Society of Newspaper Editors' Distinguished Writing Award (1995). A finalist for a Pulitzer Prize in editorial writing in 1987 and 1996, Henninger shared in the *Journal*'s 2002 Pulitzer Prize for reporting on the September 11 attacks. The following essay, first printed on December 3, 2004, in the *Wall Street Journal*, analyzes the effects of the graphic and electronic media upon our culture.

By now, you've probably seen the tape of the fight between Ron Artest 1 and the Detroit Pistons fans. Just kidding. You've seen it.

You've seen it in real time, in slo-mo and—my favorite—super slo-mo. In super slo-mo, Ron Artest's $50-million arm flows into the head of the (apparently innocent) fan like a bird's feather landing lightly on a fireplug. As aesthetics, rather than street fighting, it's hard not to gape and admire. The art director at Sports Illustrated also noticed how TV's compulsion to bathe us in images, no matter the subject, had transformed the fight into something else.

For this week's cover story on "SPORTS-RAGE," SI's art director blew up the TV images of the fighting Pacers in a way that changed the brawling bodies into lurid, splattered pixels—something bizarre and not quite real. Like much else in the culture today.

The very next day, after the football players from Clemson and South Carolina staged their own swirling TV fight across the green turf, everyone jumped on Clemson coach Tommy Bowden for suggesting the players had been brainwashed into violence by watching replays of the Artest video. But I think Tommy Bowden had it right. He said almost everything one needs to know about how American culture swooned from the on-court dignity of an Oscar Robertson to the choreographed road-rage and stylish personal exhibitionism you see no matter where you look these days. The only thing Coach Bowden left out were the preceding 18 years and probably 30,000 hours of similar images his players had watched.

Like Tommy Bowden, Marshall McLuhan was laughed at in 1967 with 5 the publication of "The Medium Is the Massage," his aphoristic summary of what electronic media were going to do to us. "All media works us over completely," McLuhan said. The book's subtitle was "An inventory of effects." It's a good time for another inventory, because no one's laughing now.

Much of the "culture" we consume is graphic and electronic. Most of us have watched more screens of entertainment—on TV, in movies, videogames and computers—than any other activity not required to sustain life. A cable company like Time Warner now offers about 500 channels. This is relatively new. It must have an effect. But what is "it"?

It is mostly entertainment. As with movies, TV from the first days was primarily a performance medium. That means it is a medium of exaggeration. It exists to go over the top. Professionals will tell you that like any staged performance, TV requires exaggeration, or sharpened behavior, to succeed. On a TV screen or the silver screen, normal "performance" doesn't "come across." To compensate for the screen's odd, deadening effect, all actors ham it up. Actors from Jackie Gleason to Telly Savalas to John Belushi have all painted their characters in broad, "unreal" strokes—to put them across.

Violence is also one of the medium's most basic tools. Since the slapstick figures of Europe's old Commedia dell'Arte, violence has been a staple of exaggerated effects—the Three Stooges, the Marx Brothers and today "South Park." But of course no one in the 17th century watched such stuff every night.

Until recently, only actors trained in artful exaggeration did any of this. Everyone else just watched. Now, from the basketball courts in Detroit to reality TV, amateurs are "performing." Untrained in performance art, the audiences default to what they know—being loud, flamboyant or making fools of themselves. But that's OK with TV, too. On TV, a loud fool is more watchable than a quiet fool.

10   To hold channel-surfing audiences, much performance on television is more exaggerated than ever. Exhibitionism is encouraged. ESPN's afternoon sports-talk show, "Around the Horn," features sports writers for major newspapers yelling like drunks at the corner bar. Stephen A. Smith, who shouts basketball commentary for ESPN, is the new model, overwhelming a more normal colleague like Greg Anthony.

Not-normal people are becoming the norm. Exhibitionism is routine. Last Sunday, Giants' tight end Jeremy Shockey caught a 15-yard pass across midfield and danced and pranced like he'd won the Super Bowl. It was weird and pathetic. The Giants got killed. But the same commentators appalled at Ron Artest routinely write that sport "needs more characters," meaning more egomaniacs.

Sports figures are in the news now, but unreal, jacked-up, cartoonlike performance and behavior is everywhere in the culture now. Computer assisted graphics produce cyber-streams of hyper-real, speeded-up pictoids of humanlike figures—"The Matrix," videogames like "Grand Theft Auto," automobile commercials. The fashion industry transmits the stagey flamboyance of hip-hop culture and pop-diva culture straight to the street now. Hip-hop artists, having forgotten what's up, morph from pretend criminals into real criminals. This, too, is among the "inventory of effects."

Reality TV recruits its "stars" from the audience, and they scream and vamp on cue. The guy alleged to have thrown the [plastic cup] at Artest got his 8.5 minutes of fame with Greta Van Susteren. He was obviously thrilled to be there, notwithstanding his ban for life from the Palace of Auburn Hills.

McLuhan said media would change us. He was right. There are simple words to describe what we are seeing lots of now: vanity, anger, impatience, envy, egocentrism, arrogance. Oh yes, vices are not crimes. But standing under a constant electronic shower of them will wash away what might be called the smaller, quieter virtues, such as humility, restraint, modesty, respect, tact, patience, generosity, prudence, piety—that stuff.

Does it matter? Two years after "The Medium Is the Massage," Supreme Court Justice Hugo Black issued a famous dissent in the *Tinker* case, which elevated the speech rights of very young students and lowered the inclination of teachers to civilize their students. Justice Black warned this would make the schools vulnerable "to the whims and caprices of their loudest-mouthed, but maybe not their brightest, students." So what? They're all stars now. 15

REFLECTING AND INTERPRETING

1. The author opens with a reference to the Ron Artest incident with Pistons fans. What exactly occurred? Do you remember what other team members did?

2. Can you find the transitional sentence that begins to switch the topic from Artest to the effects of the electronic media? In the fourth paragraph, point out the sentence that continues this transition.

3. What analogy did Coach Bowden make? Who was Oscar Robertson? Why is this comparison significant?

4. In 1967 who predicted that television and other media would change our culture drastically? How was his prediction received?

5. The author points out that "TV from the first days was primarily a performance medium. That means it is a medium of exaggeration." What does he mean? What examples does he cite? Can you think of others?

6. What other element does the author cite as a "basic tool" of the medium. Can you think of other examples? What important distinction does he make between these early performances and those we are exposed to today?

7. What significant change is pointed out in paragraphs 9 and 10?

8. React to the opinions expressed in paragraph 11. Do you agree or disagree? Why?

9. Reread paragraph 14. Do you agree with Henninger's conclusion? Why or why not?

10. What do you notice about the words in the title of this essay? What is the effect of the disparity there?

A WRITER'S RESPONSE

Consider Justice Hugo Black's statement in paragraph 15. Do you believe that the graphic and electronic media have contributed to unruliness in school children? Why or why not? How much freedom should teachers have to discipline young students?

HISTORICAL PERSPECTIVE
OF THE WAL-MART CONTROVERSY

1   In 1945 Sam Walton purchased a Ben Franklin five-and-dime store in Newport, Arkansas. After this store flourished, he opened his first "Wal-Mart" store in 1962. The first public stock offering occurred in 1970. During the 1980s, Wal-Mart became a national chain. By 2002 Wal-Mart had mushroomed into the largest corporation in the world. During the twentieth century, Wal-Mart's expansion was regarded quite favorably by consumers, primarily because of low prices.

But in the past few years, widespread doubt has arisen about long-term effects of Wal-Mart's presence, particularly in small communities. After a decade, many areas have reported tax losses because of abatements afforded Wal-Mart, yet their fire and police protection costs have risen. Then too, some small businesses have closed or gone bankrupt because of an inability to compete with Wal-Mart, contributing to downtown decay.

According to Congressman George Miller, 7th District, California (16 Feb. 2004), the average hourly wage for Wal-Mart grocery store workers is $8.23, "compared to $10.35 for an average supermarket worker." Other sources cite wages as low as $7.80 per hour for some Wal-Mart employees. Since many are allowed to work only a twenty-eight hour week, they do not have health insurance. Many communities report that Wal-Mart's low wages have increased the demand for social services—free lunches, housing, children's health insurance, Medicaid, and other assistance. These costs are borne by taxpayers.

Wal-Mart, like many large corporations, has had its share of lawsuits. Hundreds of claims have been filed against Wal-Mart and are pending, including patent infringement, liability for accidents, unsafe parking lots, disability discrimination, sexism, hiring of illegal workers, child labor violations, and unpaid overtime. Wal-Mart has settled few of these lawsuits and disputed most. In 2002 in Portland, Oregon, however, a federal jury found that Wal-Mart had made employees work overtime without pay during 1994–1999. Over 400 workers at twenty-four of Oregon's twenty-seven Wal-Marts had filed the class action suit. Since this victory, similar lawsuits have been filed in several states, claiming forced unpaid overtime work during breaks, lunch hours, and after-shift hours. Wal-Mart has denied some of these charges, citing company policy and saying that managers are expected to enforce it.

5   Now as Wal-Mart seeks approval, coast to coast, to build "supercenters" that include grocery stores, many communities are lobbying to keep out the discount Goliath. The city council of Hartford, Connecticut, however, welcomed Wal-Mart. They even waived the city's living-wage ordinance, allowing Wal-Mart to establish its own wage scale. The two essays that follow give differing accounts of the Hartford controversy and opposing views of an unregulated Wal-Mart.

WAL-MART'S BIG CITY BLUES   DAN LEVINE

Based in Hartford, Connecticut, Dan Levine is a staff writer for the *New Haven Advocate*, an alternative weekly newspaper. Levine's stories have appeared in a variety of local and national outlets, including *In These Times*, *The Nation*, *Valley Advocate*, *Fairfield County Weekly*, and *Connecticut Law Tribune*. His journalism career began at the *Village Voice* in New York City. He writes on social and political issues—everything from deadbeat dads to Saddam Hussein's banning of labor unions. The following op-ed column was published in *The Nation* (8 Dec. 2003), soon after Hartford city officials suspended the city's living-wage ordinance to lure Wal-Mart there.

Having plundered America's countryside and suburbs for decades, 1 Wal-Mart is now setting its sights on unfamiliar urban territory: a grassy lot in Hartford, Connecticut. But as the mega-corporation expands out of America's conservative strongholds, it must contend with a phenomenon it hasn't previously encountered—an opposition armed with a living-wage ordinance.

Forging a countermovement to the retailer's one-step-from-welfare wage policy, activists have successfully pushed living-wage ordinances in 110 cities and counties across the country since the mid-1990s, most often in Northern, urban areas—like Hartford—and in California. Typically those laws require companies seeking city contracts, property tax abatements or other public subsidies to pay their employees a living wage, which can come to several dollars above hourly minimum-wage rates.

Other big-box developers have made a mockery of similar guidelines. When politicians in St. Paul, Minnesota, granted Target Corporation a $6.3 million subsidy in 2001 to redevelop a downtown department store, the city council simply waived its own living-wage policy. But in Hartford, a coalition of progressive advocacy groups is determined not to let Wal-Mart secure the same sort of pass.

Wal-Mart has not sought a property tax break in Hartford, but the city's housing authority owns the meadow where the store will sit. And the living-wage ordinance covers real estate deals, according to the coalition, which includes the United Food and Commercial Workers Local 371, ACORN and the state Working Families Party, among other organizations. It is a natural campaign to launch, because the unions and community groups advancing living-wage ordinances are usually part of the same crowd that opposes construction of new Wal-Mart stores. Their task is a difficult one: convincing unfriendly city officials to make the mega-retailer abide by the law.

And the corporation did its groundwork in Hartford, lining up a segment 5 of community leaders to support the development before the plans became public. So shifting focus from prohibition of a Wal-Mart store to regulation of its labor standards is a significant change in strategy for an anti-big-box campaign. It is a shift that acknowledges how hard it is to convince residents of a depressed city to oppose the lure of economic development.

"If it's a question of nothing versus Wal-Mart, that's sort of a losing battle for us. So the question is: Should Wal-Mart provide living-wage jobs and [affordable] health benefits, or not?" says Jon Green, director of the Working Families Party in Connecticut. "That's a different kind of question than, 'Should there be nothing, or should there be a massive retail development?' Politically, we think that's a better wedge for us."

Wal-Mart's vital statistics are remarkable. Annual sales ($244 billion) comparable to the gross domestic product of Austria. Plans to open a new Supercenter every two days. No unionized American workers.

The last bit is one of Wal-Mart's keys to profitability. By keeping wages close to subsistence level, the Arkansas-based retailer offers low prices that draw herds of gleeful shoppers away from the competition. Little wonder the company dispatches squads of unionbusters whenever its happy "associates" breathe the phrase "living wages."

But ubiquitous as it seems, Wal-Mart operated none of its Supercenters (giant structures that include grocery stores) in urban areas at the end of 2001. And more than half of those existing stores could be found in one region: the eleven states of the Old South, according to a study by Retail Forward, an industry analysis group. California had none. To maintain its fantastic growth rate, Wal-Mart is beginning to target territory that it had previously neglected.

10   In Hartford—an economically depressed city with a 73 percent Puerto Rican and African-American population—the retailer plans to break ground by the end of July on a 165,000 square-foot store; without a supermarket, at first, but with enough room to build one in the future. A massive effort to build forty Supercenters is under way in California. Key to the activists' success is explaining the hidden societal costs of allowing an unregulated Wal-Mart into town. Since workers don't make enough money to afford company health insurance, taxpayers end up footing the bill by subsidizing Medicaid coverage and other economic assistance.

Hartford's economic development chief says his office looked at the city's living-wage ordinance but decided it was moot. Why? Wal-Mart indicated their wages would be high enough to comply. As a backup, city lawyers argue that the ordinance doesn't apply to the corporation, because it only covers city land, not city housing authority land. Never mind that the city manager appoints the authority's entire board.

Living-wage campaigns are geared specifically toward companies like Wal-Mart. It would be devastating if activists who have already achieved victory in 110 localities let skittish politicians eviscerate their hard-won ordinances.

REFLECTING AND INTERPRETING

1. Examine the opening sentence. What do you learn about the writer?
2. What is a "living-wage ordinance"?
3. Levine does not use the classic argument opening. What does he do?

4. What is the pivotal question that the city leaders of Hartford had to decide?

5. Why was it so difficult to convince Hartford residents to oppose the development?

6. What is the key to Wal-Mart's profitability?

7. Does Levine acknowledge Wal-Mart's point of view? If so, where?

8. Is Hartford the only city with a living-wage ordinance that has caved in to Wal-Mart's demands? Have you heard of any areas that have refused to let Wal-Mart in?

9. What kind of ending does Levine use? How objective does the tone sound to you?

10. How would you rate the tone of his entire argument? Why?

A WRITER'S RESPONSE

Write a paragraph or an essay setting forth your position on the Wal-Mart controversy. Give specific reasons. Do you shop there? Why or why not?

THE WAR ON WAL-MART   STEVEN MALANGA

Presently a contributing editor of *City Journal* and a senior fellow at the Manhattan Institute, Steven Malanga writes articles and op-ed columns about intersection urban economies, business communities, and public policy. For seven years prior, he served as managing editor and executive editor of Crain's *New York Business*. In 1998 he cowrote "Tort-ured State," a series about trial lawyers in the state of New York that AABP cited as the "best investigative story of the year." Malanga has written articles for the *New York Post*, *New York Daily News*, *Newsday*, and other publications. This op-ed column was published in the *Wall Street Journal* (7 Apr. 2004) several months after Hartford City Council had decided to welcome Wal-Mart.

Here is a story you're unlikely to read in the spate of press attacks on 1
Wal-Mart these days:

When Hartford, Conn., tore down a blighted housing project, city officials hatched an innovative redevelopment plan: Lure Wal-Mart to the site, entice other retailers with the promise of being near the discount giant, and then use the development's revenues to build new housing. After Wal-Mart agreed, city officials and residents celebrated the idea of better shopping, more jobs and new housing in one of America's poorest cities.

But then outsiders claiming to represent the local community began protesting the project. Astonished city leaders and residents quickly discovered the forces fueling the campaign: a Connecticut chapter of the United Food and Commercial Workers Union; and ACORN, the radical community group. Outraged residents denounced outside interference. "These people looked for every possible reason to stop a project that the community wants," says Jackie Fongemie, a resident.

Though Wal-Mart has encountered opposition for years from anti-sprawl activists or small-town merchants, the Hartford drama exemplifies a new form of opposition, a coordinated effort of the Left in which unions, activist groups like ACORN and the National Organization of Women, and even plaintiffs' attorneys work together in alliances. They are fighting the giant retailer in statehouses, city halls and courts.

5   More than just a skirmish over sites, theirs is an assault on a company that embodies the productivity-driven, customer-oriented economy that emerged in the '90s, by opponents who argue that there is a hidden cost to business's increasing emphasis on low prices and high employee output. Opponents seek government or court edicts to force Wal-Mart and others like it to raise wages and offer workers more benefits, and they are rushing into battle just as the company expands to underserved urban communities, making the conflict a vital issue not just in Wal-Mart's traditional rural and suburban markets but, increasingly, in American cities.

Few would have imagined that when Sam Walton started Wal-Mart more than 40 years ago, he was hatching anything that would become so controversial. Though his first Wal-Marts, opened in the early '60s, were chaotic, with goods piled high on tables, the stores charged unparalleled low prices and crowds flocked to them. The company's success rested on "Mr. Sam's" formula of scouring the marketplace for the best prices and keeping a relentless rein on expenses. But the folksy country retailer, recognizing the importance of efficient systems, also led a technology revolution, installing computerized ordering and distribution that others quickly imitated. So efficient did the system become that Wal-Mart was soon selling goods in its stores even before it had to pay suppliers for them.

Pursuing this formula, Wal-Mart has led a productivity revolution in retailing which super-charged the American economy. Warren Buffett even declared that Wal-Mart—not Microsoft—has contributed more than any other business to the health of the economy.

Because non-union Wal-Mart represents the leading edge of this American business revolution, the left's crusade against it has emerged as a clash of worldviews, as unions and their allies try to convince the public that super-efficient operators like Wal-Mart lower workers' standard of living. The left has especially targeted Wal-Mart's push into grocery super centers, which have been pulverizing unionized grocery stores. In an age when supermarkets already operate on single-digit profit margins, Wal-Mart's entry into a market can still drive down grocery prices 15%.

A coalition of more than 30 unions and left-wing groups kicked off the campaign with a national day of protest in October 2002, urging shoppers to boycott the company as a "Merchant of Shame." The boycott got no results, but the coalition has more effectively waged legislative battles around the country. In California, the anti-Wal-Mart coalition has successfully lobbied more than a dozen cities and towns to pass ordinances to keep Wal-Mart out, while dozens of other such bills are in the legislative hopper.

10   The real issue in this battle is union wages. Unions argue that supermarkets in California pay store workers from $18 to $25 an hour (though

Wal-Mart says those wages represent the high end of the union scale), while Wal-Mart pays its California store associates about $10 on average. The effect of Wal-Mart entering the market, union advocates say, would be a vast reduction in the wage pool. "While charging low prices obviously has some consumer benefits . . . these benefits come at a steep price for American workers," alleged a recent diatribe by California Democratic Congressman George Miller. Instead, union think tanks argue, Wal-Mart should be made to pay "sustainable" or "self-sufficiency" wages, a popular idea with the left, which holds that wages should be based on an area's cost of living. In many parts of California, liberal economists estimate, that means up to $38,000 a year for a worker supporting a spouse.

But the left's case ignores the greater benefit that an efficient operator like Wal-Mart brings to an entire economy by driving down prices and forcing other stores to perform better. A Wal-Mart-sponsored study, undertaken by the Los Angeles Economic Development Council, estimates that Wal-Mart's entry into the local market would save southern California shoppers $3.76 billion annually, or nearly $600 per household, creating up to 36,000 new jobs.

Despite opponents' charges, Wal-Mart has had little trouble recruiting workers, in part because the gap between its pay and union wages isn't as large as opponents claim, and because Wal-Mart is growing so rapidly that it attracts ambitious workers looking for a career. In particular, workers in minority communities traditionally friendly to the left's agenda have shocked opponents by welcoming Wal-Mart. Unions tried to stop the opening of the company's store in Crenshaw Plaza, Los Angeles, even unsuccessfully urging the Urban League not to work with Wal-Mart on a job-training program; but more than 10,000 locals applied to work at the store. "It's those who don't live in this community who did the most objecting to this store," says councilman Bernard Parks. "The community has clearly spoken, and it supports this store."

Though union-sponsored campaigns have meant little to consumers, the constant attacks are scoring in the elite media, whose members rarely go to Wal-Mart and can't understand the importance of the stores to middle-American shoppers. Once celebrated in the press for Sam Walton's folksy wisdom, Wal-Mart today is just as likely to be the subject of stories with headlines such as: "Is Wal-Mart Too Powerful?"—which advance the left's line that Wal-Mart's business model is undermining the buying power of the American worker. So striking have the attacks been that a Kansas City newspaper columnist recently suggested that the national press is "angry that average Americans don't share their perceptions of Wal-Mart as the bad guys."

Not surprisingly, the press downplays Wal-Mart's virtues: that it has never been accused of funny accounting; that it doesn't reward its executives with exorbitant salaries or perks; that not only do other executives call it the most admired company in America, but shopping surveys show it is the consumer's favorite store. But acclaim from common folk may not protect a company when elite opinion turns against it, influencing legislators, regulators and the courts. That's why Wal-Mart has become the chief private-sector target of trial lawyers, sued more than any other company, as the plaintiff's bar and its allies seek to achieve through litigation what activists struggle to accomplish in organizing drives. And every battle they win will cost the American consumer.

REFLECTING AND INTERPRETING

1. What type of opening does Malanga use? Does it arouse your interest?
2. Malanga does not follow the classic argument format. What do you notice about the structure of the third paragraph?
3. How does the account set forth in Malanga's third paragraph differ from Levine's? What vital information has Malanga omitted?
4. Where does Malanga summarize the opposing view?
5. Malanga contends that opponents have ignored what long-term benefit that a Wal-Mart store brings. How might opponents answer this point? (Tip: Refer to "Historical Perspective.")
6. He believes that Wal-Mart is a leader in a "clash of world views." Explain.
7. Malanga claims that the "elite media, whose members rarely go to Wal-Mart," are behind the "constant attacks." Examine the word choice and claim. Are most reporters highly paid? What do you make of this charge?
8. Examine the last paragraph. Does the press tend to report more bad news than good, or is this tendency limited only to reporting about Wal-Mart?
9. Examine the word choice and selected examples throughout the piece. Rate Malanga's objectivity on a scale of 1–10, with 10 being most objective.
10. What type of location will Wal-Mart occupy in Hartford? (Refer to Levine's and Malanga's descriptions.) How does this location differ from the typical Wal-Mart location? Is the difference significant? Why or why not?

A WRITER'S RESPONSE

Reread "Historical Perspective," then Levine's and Malanga's arguments. Which argument do you find more convincing? Why?

WHAT IS THE "PURSUIT OF HAPPINESS"?

HISTORICAL BACKGROUND

In 1776 Thomas Jefferson drafted the Declaration of Independence, which contains the momentous phrase: *"We hold these truths to be self-evident, that all men are created equal, that they are endowed by their Creator with certain unalienable Rights, that among these are Life, Liberty and the pursuit of Happiness.—"*   1

In 1789 Congress adopted the American Bill of Rights, which specifies basic rights and freedoms of all citizens. These amendments to the United States Constitution act as safeguards for our freedoms, but they do not mention the "pursuit of happiness." Yet this right is generally accepted as inborn and covered by the Bill of Rights. In the following arguments, two authors ask "What is the 'pursuit of happiness'?" and "Does the right to pursue happiness have limits?"

SUMMARY OF TWO ARGUMENTS

C. S. Lewis, an author of world renown, claims "We Have No 'Right to Happiness.'" In this essay he and "Clare" discuss an affair—Mr. A's getting a divorce to marry Mrs. B. and her divorcing to marry him—followed by his first wife's suicide. Mr. A., though shocked, defended his action with "A man has a right to happiness."

Clare agrees. Lewis analyzes her belief, knowing that Clare thinks Mr. A. "had not only a legal but also a moral right to act as he did." Lewis disagrees about the moral right to "sexual happiness" and explains why he thinks Mr. A's actions were wrong. Implicit is Lewis's belief in marital fidelity and upholding of the marriage contract. He presents a strong argument, based upon the deleterious effects that uncontrolled erotic passion and sexual permissiveness wreak upon society, as well as individuals. He points out that certain impulses must be curbed if [civilized] society is to endure.

In the other essay on the *pursuit of happiness*, Andrew Sullivan, a well-   5
known political commentator, dissects this weighty phrase. He explores its meaning and implications—not from a moral/social perspective as Lewis does—but from a political perspective. Sullivan points out that in former centuries, tyrants and religious fanatics ruled with an iron hand. Personal freedom for ordinary citizens was greatly limited, and the idea of pursuing happiness was "revolutionary." Yet our early settlers uprooted the traditional authority of divine right and the church—replacing it with the United States Constitution.

Sullivan examines various meanings of the pursuit of happiness and whether or not it is connected to virtue. Then he looks at the effects of American culture and dominance around the globe, ending with an explanation of why the American pursuit of happiness is so repulsive to Muslim nations.

WHAT DOES "PURSUIT OF HAPPINESS" MEAN TO YOU?

Is happiness simply self-indulgence? Or a "sense of well-being"? What else might happiness be? Does true happiness require virtue and a recognition of responsibility? Regardless of whether you agree or disagree with the opinions of these authors, you will be challenged to think as you consider how the pursuit of happiness has affected our culture and that of other nations around the world.

WE HAVE NO "RIGHT TO HAPPINESS"   C. S. LEWIS

A writer of world renown, Clive Staples Lewis (1898–1963) taught literature courses at Oxford and Cambridge Universities. His work includes fiction, children's books, poetry, and numerous books and essays on Christianity. Some of his best-known works are *The Allegory of Love: A Study in Medieval Tradition* (1936), *The Screwtape Letters* (1942), *Mere Christianity* (1943), *Miracles: A Preliminary Study* (1947), and the seven *Chronicles of Narnia* (1950–56). In this essay Lewis raises questions of morality that are even more pertinent today than four decades ago: What exactly did the writers of the Declaration of Independence mean in the phrase "pursuit of happiness"? What are the limitations of this freedom in regard to individual behavior?

1   "After all," said Clare, "they had a right to happiness."

We were discussing something that once happened in our own neighborhood. Mr. A. had deserted Mrs. A. and got his divorce in order to marry Mrs. B., who had likewise got her divorce in order to marry Mr. A. And there was certainly no doubt that Mr. A. and Mrs. B. were very much in love with one another. If they continued to be in love, and if nothing went wrong with their health or their income, they might reasonably expect to be very happy.

It was equally clear that they were not happy with their old partners. Mrs. B. had adored her husband at the outset. But then he got smashed up in the war. It was thought he had lost his virility, and it was known that he had lost his job. Life with him was no longer what Mrs. B. had bargained for. Poor Mrs. A., too. She had lost her looks—and all her liveliness. It might be true, as some said, that she consumed herself by bearing his children and nursing him through the long illness that overshadowed their earlier married life.

You mustn't, by the way, imagine that A. was the sort of man who nonchalantly threw a wife away like the peel of an orange he'd sucked dry. Her suicide was a terrible shock to him. We all knew this, for he told us so himself. "But what could I do?" he said. "A man has a right to happiness. I had to take my one chance when it came."

5   I went away thinking about the concept of a "right to happiness."

At first this sounds to me as odd as a right to good luck. For I believe—whatever one school of moralists may say—that we depend for a very great deal of our happiness or misery on circumstances outside all human control. A right to happiness doesn't, for me, make much more sense than a right to be six feet tall, or to have a millionaire for your father, or to get good weather whenever you want to have a picnic.

I can understand a right as a freedom guaranteed me by the laws of the society I live in. Thus, I have a right to travel along the public roads because society gives me that freedom; that's what we mean by calling the roads "public." I can also understand a right as a claim guaranteed me by the laws, and correlative to an obligation on someone else's part. If I have a right to receive £100 from you, this is another way of saying that you have a duty to pay me £100. If the laws allow Mr. A. to desert his wife and seduce his neighbor's wife, then, by definition, Mr. A. has a legal right to do so, and we need bring in no talk about "happiness."

But of course that was not what Clare meant. She meant that he had not only a legal but a moral right to act as he did. In other words, Clare is—or would be if she thought it out—a classical moralist after the style of Thomas Aquinas, Grotius, Hooker and Locke. She believes that behind the laws of the state there is a Natural Law.

I agree with her. I hold this conception to be basic to all civilization. Without it, the actual laws of the state become an absolute, as in Hegel. They cannot be criticized because there is no norm against which they should be judged.

The ancestry of Clare's maxim, "They have a right to happiness," is august. In words that are cherished by all civilized men, but especially by Americans, it has been laid down that one of the rights of man is a right to "the pursuit of happiness." And now we get to the real point.

What did the writers of that august declaration mean?

It is quite certain what they did not mean. They did not mean that man was entitled to pursue happiness by any and every means—including, say, murder, rape, robbery, treason and fraud. No society could be built on such a basis.

They meant "to pursue happiness by all lawful means"; that is, by all means which the Law of Nature eternally sanctions and which the laws of the nation shall sanction.

Admittedly this seems at first to reduce their maxim to the tautology that men (in pursuit of happiness) have a right to do whatever they have a right to do. But tautologies, seen against their proper historical context, are not always barren tautologies. The declaration is primarily a denial of the political principles which long governed Europe: a challenge flung down to the Austrian and Russian empires, to England before the Reform Bills, to Bourbon France. It demands that whatever means of pursuing happiness are lawful for any should be lawful for all; that "man," not men of some particular caste, class, status or religion, should be free to use them. In a century when this is being unsaid by nation after nation and party after party, let us not call it a barren tautology.

But the question as to what means are "lawful"—what methods of pursuing happiness are either morally permissible by the Law of Nature or should be declared legally permissible by the legislature of a particular nation—remains exactly where it did. And on that question I disagree with Clare. I don't think it is obvious that people have the unlimited "right to happiness" which she suggests.

For one thing, I believe that Clare, when she says "happiness," means simply and solely "sexual happiness." Partly because women like Clare never use the word "happiness" in any other sense. But also because I never heard Clare talk about the "right" to any other kind. She was rather leftist in her politics, and would have been scandalized if anyone had defended the actions of a ruthless man-eating tycoon on the ground that his happiness consisted in making money and he was pursuing his happiness. She was also a rabid teetotaler; I never heard her excuse an alcoholic because he was happy when he was drunk.

A good many of Clare's friends, and especially her female friends, often felt—I've heard them say so—that their own happiness would be perceptibly increased by boxing her ears. I very much doubt if this would have brought her theory of a right to happiness into play.

Clare, in fact, is doing what the whole western world seems to me to have been doing for the last forty-odd years. When I was a youngster, all the progressive people were saying, "Why all this prudery? Let us treat sex just as we treat all our other impulses." I was simple-minded enough to believe they meant what they said. I have since discovered that they meant exactly the opposite. They meant that sex was to be treated as no other impulse in our nature has ever been treated by civilized people. All the others, we admit, have to be bridled. Absolute obedience to your instinct for self-preservation is what we call cowardice; to your acquisitive impulse, avarice. Even sleep must be resisted if you're a sentry. But every unkindness and breach of faith seems to be condoned provided that the object aimed at is "four bare legs in a bed."

It is like having a morality in which stealing fruit is considered wrong— unless you steal nectarines.

20   And if you protest against this view you are usually met with chatter about the legitimacy and beauty and sanctity of "sex" and accused of harboring some Puritan prejudice against it as something disreputable or shameful. I deny the charge. Foam-born Venus . . . golden Aphrodite . . . Our Lady of Cyprus . . . I never breathed a word against you. If I object to boys who steal my nectarines, must I be supposed to disapprove of nectarines in general? Or even of boys in general? It might, you know, be stealing that I disapproved of.

The real situation is skillfully concealed by saying that the question of Mr. A.'s "right" to desert his wife is one of "sexual morality." Robbing an orchard is not an offense against some special morality called "fruit morality." It is an offense against honesty. Mr. A.'s action is an offense against good faith (to solemn promises), against gratitude (toward one to whom he was deeply indebted) and against common humanity.

Our sexual impulses are thus being put in a position of preposterous privilege. The sexual motive is taken to condone all sorts of behavior which, if it had any other end in view, would be condemned as merciless, treacherous and unjust.

Now though I see no good reason for giving sex this privilege, I think I see a strong cause. It is this.

It is part of the nature of a strong erotic passion—as distinct from a transient fit of appetite—that it makes more towering promises than any other emotion. No doubt all our desires make promises, but not so impressively. To be in love involves the almost irresistible conviction that one will go on being in love until one dies, and that possession of the beloved will confer, not merely frequent ecstasies, but settled, fruitful, deep-rooted, lifelong happiness. Hence *all* seems to be at stake. If we miss this chance we shall have lived in vain. At the very thought of such a doom we sink into fathomless depths of self-pity.

Unfortunately these promises are found often to be quite untrue. Every 25 experienced adult knows this to be so as regards all erotic passions (except the one he himself is feeling at the moment). We discount the world-without-end pretensions of our friends' amours easily enough. We know that such things sometimes last—and sometimes don't. And when they do last, this is not because they promised at the outset to do so. When two people achieve lasting happiness, this is not solely because they are great lovers but because they are also—I must put it crudely—good people; controlled, loyal, fairminded, mutually adaptable people.

If we establish a "right to (sexual) happiness" which supersedes all the ordinary rules of behavior, we do so not because of what our passion shows itself to be in experience but because of what it professes to be while we are in the grip of it. Hence, while the bad behavior is real and works miseries and degradations, the happiness which was the object of the behavior turns out again and again to be illusory. Everyone (except Mr. A. and Mrs. B.) knows that Mr. A. in a year or so may have the same reason for deserting his new wife as for deserting his old. He will feel again that all is at stake. He will see himself again as the great lover, and his pity for himself will exclude all pity for the woman.

Two further points remain.

One is this. A society in which conjugal infidelity is tolerated must always be in the long run a society adverse to women. Women, whatever a few male songs and satires may say to the contrary, are more naturally monogamous than men; it is a biological necessity. Where promiscuity prevails, they will therefore always be more often the victims than the culprits. Also, domestic happiness is more necessary to them than to us. And the quality by which they most easily hold a man, their beauty, decreases every year after they have come to maturity, but this does not happen to those qualities of personality—women don't really care twopence about our *looks*—by which we hold women. Thus in the ruthless war of promiscuity women are at a double disadvantage. They play for higher stakes and are also more likely to lose. I have no sympathy with moralists who frown at the increasing crudity of female provocativeness. These signs of desperate competition fill me with pity.

Secondly, though the "right to happiness" is chiefly claimed for the sexual impulse, it seems to me impossible that the matter should stay there. The fatal principle, once allowed in that department, must sooner or later seep through our whole lives. We thus advance toward a state of society in which not only each man but every impulse in each man claims *carte blanche.* And then, though our technological skill may help us survive a little longer, our civilization will have died at heart, and will—one dare not even add "unfortunately"—be swept away.

REFLECTING AND INTERPRETING

1. Examine paragraph 3. What irony do you see?
2. What implicit question is the central idea of this essay? (Look at the first sentence and the title.)
3. Can you find an example of negation, a technique of definition?
4. Is there a difference between a right to happiness and the right to pursue happiness? If so, what is it?
5. Clare believes that "behind the laws of the state there is a Natural Law." Does Lewis agree or disagree? Why?
6. In paragraph 10 Lewis begins to trace the history of Clare's belief and where it leads. What is the pivotal question on which he disagrees?
7. How does Lewis view the marrige vow?
8. What kind of happiness does Lewis believe Clare means? Why does this kind raise moral questions?
9. What does Lewis say is necessary for two people to achieve lasting happiness?
10. What six rhetorical patterns does Lewis combine to organize his complex argument?

A WRITER'S RESPONSE

Lewis says, "In the ruthless war of promiscuity, women are at a double disadvantage." Write an essay agreeing or disagreeing with his position. Cite facts and examples to support your claim.

THE PURSUIT OF HAPPINESS: FOUR REVOLUTIONARY WORDS
ANDREW SULLIVAN

Born in Great Britain in 1963, Andrew Sullivan earned a bachelor's degree at Oxford. At Harvard he earned a doctorate in political science (1990). A well-known political commentator, he has written for the *New York Times, Washington Post, New York Post, Daily Telegraph, Wall Street Journal, New York Times Magazine, Sunday Times* of London, and others. Editor of the *New Republic* from 1991 to 1996, he was named *AdWeek*'s Editor of the Year in 1996. Sullivan is the editor of three anthologies and the author of several books, including *Sound and Fury: The Making of the Punditocracy* (2000, 1992), which won the 1992 Orwell Award. In this essay he discusses the broad political implications of four words in the Declaration of Independence.

It's a small phrase when you think about it: "the pursuit of happiness." It's somewhat overshadowed in the Declaration of Independence by the weightier notions of "life" and "liberty." In today's mass culture, it even comes close to being banal. Who, after all, doesn't want to pursue happiness? But in its own day, the statement was perhaps the most radical political statement ever delivered. And when we try and fathom why it is that the United States still elicits such extreme hatred in some parts of the world, this phrase is as good a place to start as any.

Take the first part: pursuit. What America is based on is not the achievement of some goal, the capture of some trophy, or the triumph of success. It's about the process of seeking something. It's about incompletion, dissatisfaction, striving, imperfection. In the late eighteenth century, this was a statement in itself. In the Europe of the preceding centuries, armies had gone to war, human beings had been burned at stakes, monarchs had been dethroned, and countries torn apart because imperfection wasn't enough. From the Reformation to the Inquisition, religious fanatics had demanded that the state enforce holiness, truth and virtue. Those who resisted were exterminated. Moreover, the power and status of rulers derived from their own perfection. Kings and queens had artists portray them as demi-gods. Dissenters were not merely troublemakers, they were direct threats to the perfect order of the modern state. This was a political order in which everything had to be perfectly arranged—even down to the internal thoughts of individual consciences.

Enter the Americans. Suddenly the eternal, stable order of divine right and church authority was replaced by something far more exclusive, difficult, even intangible. Out of stability came the idea of pursuit. To an older way of thinking, the very idea is heretical. The pursuit of what? Where? By whom? Who authorized this? By whose permission are you off on some crazy venture of your own? Think of how contemporary Islamic fundamentalists must think of this. For them, the spiritual and intellectual life is not about pursuit; it's about submission. It's not about inquiry into the unknown. It's about struggle for the will of Allah. Since the result of this struggle is literally the difference between heaven and hell, there can be no doubt about what its content is, or the duty of everyone to engage in it. And since doubt can lead to error, and error can lead to damnation, it is also important that everyone within the community adhere to the same struggle—and extend the struggle in a fight against unbelievers.

Today, we find this religious extremism alien. But it was not alien to the American founders. The European Christians of the sixteenth and seventeenth centuries were not so different in their obsessiveness and intolerance from many Islamic fundamentalists today. And against that fundamentalist requirement for uniformity, the Founders of a completely new society countered with the notion of a random, chaotic, cacophonous pursuit of any number of different goals. No political authority would be able to lay down for all citizens what was necessary for salvation, or even for a good life. Citizens would have to figure out the meaning of their own lives, and search for that meaning until the day they died. There would be no certainty; no surety even of a destination. Pursuit was everything. And pursuit was understood as something close to adventure.

5   And then comes the even more radical part. The point of this pursuit was happiness! Again, this seems almost banal to modern ears. But it was far from banal in the eighteenth century and it is far from banal when interpreted by the radical mullahs of political Islam. Here's the difference. Before the triumph of American democracy, governments and states and most philosophers viewed happiness as incidental to something else. For Christians, happiness was only achieved if you were truly virtuous. Happiness was the spiritual calm that followed an act of charity; the satisfied exhaustion after a day caring for others. For Aristotle, happiness was simply impossible without virtue. Happiness was an incidental experience while pursuing what was good and true. The idea of pursuing happiness for its own sake would have struck Aristotle as simple hedonism. The happiness someone feels drinking a cold beer on a hot day or bungee-jumping off a bridge was not a happiness he recognized. And for almost every pre-American society, other goals clearly had precedence over the subjective sense of well-being. Remember Cromwell's England? Or Robespierre's France? Or Stalin's Russia? They weren't exactly pleasure-fests. Again, in radical Islam today, American notions of happiness—choice, indulgence, whimsy, humor, leisure, art—always have to be subjected to moral inspection. Do these activities conform to religious law? Do they encourage or discourage virtuous behavior, without which happiness is impossible and meaningless? These are the questions human beings have always historically asked of the phenomenon we call happiness.

6   Not so in America. Here, happiness is an end in itself. Its content is up to each of us. Some may believe, as American Muslims or Christians do, that happiness is still indeed only possible when allied to virtue. But just as importantly, others may not. And the important thing is that the government of the United States take no profound interest in how any of these people define their own happiness. All that matters is that no-one is coerced into a form of happiness he hasn't chosen for himself—by others or by the state. Think of this for a moment. What America means is that no-one can forcibly impose a form of happiness on anyone else—even if it means that some people are going to hell in a hand basket. Yes, there have been many exceptions to this over the years—and America has often seen religious revivals, spasms of cultural puritanism, cultural censorship, and so on. But the government has been barred from the deepest form of censorship—the appropriation of any single religion under the auspices of the state. You can call this all sorts of things. In my book, it's as good a definition of freedom as any. But to others—countless others—it seems

a callous indifference to the fate of others' souls, even blasphemy and degeneracy. This view is held by some Christian fundamentalists at home. And it is surely held by Islamic fundamentalists abroad. We ignore this view at our peril.

There are, of course, many reasons why America evokes hostility 7 across the globe. There are foreign policies; there are historical failings. There is resentment of American wealth and power. There is fear of the social dislocation inherent in globalization. But there is also something far deeper. What we have forgotten is how anomalous America is in the history of the world. Most other countries have acquired identity and culture through ancient inheritance, tribal loyalty, or religious homogeneity. Even a country very like the United States, Britain, still has a monarchy and an established church. If you told the average Brit that his government was designed to help him pursue "happiness," he'd laugh. Other developed countries, like Germany, have succumbed to the notion of race as a purifying and unifying element. Many others, like Pakistan or India, cling to a common religious identity to generate a modicum of political unity. In none of these countries is "happiness" even a political concept. And in none of these places is the pursuit of something in and of itself an admirable goal, let alone at the center of the meaning of the state and Constitution.

And when the society which has pioneered this corrosively exhilarat- 8 ing idea of happiness becomes the most powerful and wealthy country on earth, then the risks of backlash increase exponentially. In the late eighteenth century Europeans could scoff at banal American encomiums to happiness as an amusing experiment doomed to failure. At the beginning of the twenty-first century, with the products of such happiness—from McDonald's to Starbucks to MTV—saturating the globe, foreigners can afford no such condescension. Happiness is coming to them—and moral, theological certainty is departing. In response to this, they can go forward and nervously integrate—as countries like China, South Korea, and Russia are attempting. Or they can go back, far, far back to a world where such notions of happiness were as alien as visitors from outer space.

Far, far back is where some in the Middle East now want to go. The 9 roots of Islamic fundamentalism go back centuries and bypass many more recent, and more open, strains of Islam. And we are foolish if we do not see the internal logic of this move. The fundamentalist Muslims are not crazy. They see that other cultures are slowly adapting to the meme of the pursuit of happiness—from Shanghai to Moscow, from Bombay to Buenos Aires. They see that they are next in line. But they also see that such a change would deeply alter their religion and its place in society. So they resist. They know that simply accommodating piece-meal to slow change will doom them. So they are pulling a radical move—a step far back into the past, allied with a militarist frenzy and rampant xenophobia to buttress it. This move is the belated response of an ancient religious impulse to the most-radical statement of the Enlightenment, which is why it is indeed of such world-historical importance. As I write I have no idea as to the conclusion of this new drama in world history—except that it will have ramifications as large and as lasting as the end of the Cold War.

10   What power four little words still have. And what carnage they must still endure to survive.

REFLECTING AND INTERPRETING

1. Sullivan makes a claim and then supplies support. Where does the claim first appear? Where is his thesis statement?

2. He points out that in the United States the elusive concept of "pursuit of happiness" replaced what historical concept of authority?

3. What basic requirement of many Islamic fundamentalists does Sullivan mention?

4. What responsibility does the "pursuit of happiness" impose on individuals?

5. For Aristotle, Christians, and "American Muslims," what is an essential requirement for happiness?

6. What is Sullivan's point in paragraph 6? Does he agree or disagree with C. S. Lewis on this point?

7. What is the "deepest form of censorship" that our government forbids?

8. How does this definition of freedom appear to some countries?

9. Does Sullivan's essay provide insight into Muslim resistance to the USA's attempt to establish a democracy in Iraq? If so, how?

10. Look up *carnage* in the dictionary. What is Sullivan saying in his final sentence?

A WRITER'S RESPONSE

What is happiness? Write an essay defining your idea of happiness. Give examples. What conditions are needed for you to be happy?

TAKING A CLOSE LOOK AT THE STARS AND STRIPES

The American flag has become a universal symbol that stirs passionate emotions and reactions. Our flag flies from military bases in far-flung lands, government buildings, and sports arenas. Our national banner flutters from windows of vehicles and flagstaffs, hangs on porches, and drapes politicians' platforms. Our flag leads parades, and we stand at attention as it passes by. Some citizens wear the flag on T-shirts, jeans, and tattooed arms. Since September 11, 2001, our flag has become ever more visible across the land, a symbol of patriotism and pride that tugs at our hearts.

But the American flag is not universally revered or respected. Our history and our flag have been torn with violence and spattered with blood many times. In our own country, the flag has been burned more than once to protest various causes. In 1984 Gregory Lee Johnson was "convicted of desecrating a flag in violation of Texas law."

In 1989, after a series of appeals, the case came before the United States Supreme Court. The question was this: Is flag burning as a political protest protected by the First Amendment? Justice Brennan and Chief Justice Rehnquist differed greatly in their opinions of this "symbolic speech." Their arguments provide compelling reading in the "Majority Opinion of the U.S. Supreme Court in Texas v. Johnson" and the "Dissenting Opinion. . . ."

Their arguments illuminate the illusive nature of the First Amendment and raise a related question: What are the criteria for limiting freedom of speech?

MAJORITY OPINION OF THE U.S. SUPREME COURT IN TEXAS V. JOHNSON (1989)

JUSTICE WILLIAM J. BRENNAN, JR.

After receiving a law degree from Harvard, William J. Brennan (1906–97) practiced law. During World War II, he served in the military. Afterward he resumed his law practice and later served on the New Jersey State Supreme Court. Then President Eisenhower appointed him to the United States Supreme Court, where he served for thirty-three years. Justice Brennan retired in 1990. He was a strong supporter of civil rights and an advocate of individual rights, as revealed in this Supreme Court decision.

After publicly burning an American flag as a means of political protest, Gregory Lee Johnson was convicted of desecrating a flag in violation of Texas law. This case presents the question of whether his conviction is consistent with the First Amendment. We hold that it is not.

While the Republican National Convention was taking place in Dallas in 1984, respondent Johnson participated in a political demonstration dubbed the "Republican War Chest Tour." . . .

The demonstration ended in front of Dallas City Hall, where Johnson unfurled the American flag, doused it with kerosene and set it on fire. While the flag burned, the protestors chanted, "America, the red, white,

U.S. Marines of the 28th
Regiment of the Fifth
Division raise the American
flag atop Mt. Suribachi,
Iwo Jima, on Feb. 23, 1945.

The U.S. flag is set on fire during a massive
demonstration in front of the former U.S.
embassy in Tehran, November 3, 1996.

and blue, we spit on you." After the demonstrators dispersed, a witness to the flag burning collected the flag's remains and buried them in his backyard. No one was physically injured or threatened with injury, though several witnesses testified that they had been seriously offended by the flag burning.

Of the approximately 100 demonstrators, Johnson alone was charged with a crime. The only criminal offense with which he was charged was the desecration of a venerated object in violation of Texas Penal Code Ann. Sec. 42.09 (a)(3) (1989) ["Desecration of a Venerated Object"]. After a trial, he was convicted, sentenced to one year in prison and fined $2,000. The Court of Appeals for the Fifth District of Texas at Dallas affirmed Johnson's conviction, but the Texas Court of Criminal Appeals reversed, holding that the State could not, consistent with the First Amendment, punish Johnson for burning the flag in these circumstances. . . .

State Asserted Two Interests

To justify Johnson's conviction for engaging in symbolic speech, the State asserted two interests: preserving the flag as a symbol of national unity and preventing breaches of the peace. The Court of Criminal Appeals held that neither interest supported his conviction.

Acknowledging that this Court had not yet decided whether the Government may criminally sanction flag desecration in order to preserve the flag's symbolic value, the Texas court nevertheless concluded that our decision in West Virginia Board of Education v. Barnette, 319 U.S. 624 (1943), suggested that furthering this interest by curtailing speech was impermissible.

The First Amendment literally forbids the abridgement only of "speech," but we have long recognized that its protection does not end at the spoken or written word. . . .

Especially pertinent to this case are our decisions recognizing the communicative nature of conduct relating to flags. Attaching a peace sign to the flag, Spence v. Washington, 1974; saluting the flag, Barnette, and displaying a red flag, Stromberg v. California (1931), we have held, all may find shelter under the First Amendment. . . . That we have had little difficulty identifying an expressive element in conduct relating to flags should not be surprising. The very purpose of a national flag is to serve as a symbol of our country; it is, one might say, "the one visible manifestation of two hundred years of nationhood." . . .

Pregnant with expressive content, the flag as readily signifies this nation as does the combination of letters found in "America."

The Government generally has a freer hand in restricting expressive conduct than it has in restricting the written or spoken word. . . . It may not, however, proscribe particular conduct because it has expressive elements. . . . It is, in short, not simply the verbal or nonverbal nature of the expression, but the governmental interest at stake, that helps to determine whether a restriction on that expression is valid.

The State offers two separate interests to justify this conviction: preventing breaches of the peace, and preserving the flag as a symbol of nationhood and national unity. We hold that the first interest is not implicated on this record and that the second is related to the suppression of expression. . . .

We thus conclude that the State's interest in maintaining order is not implicated on these facts. The State need not worry that our holding will disable it from preserving the peace. We do not suggest that the First Amendment forbids a state to prevent "imminent lawless action." And, in fact, Texas already has a statute specifically prohibiting breaches of the peace, Texas Penal Code Ann. Sec. 42.01 (1989), which tends to confirm that Texas need not punish this flag desecration in order to keep the peace.

If there is a bedrock principle underlying the First Amendment, it is that the Government may not prohibit the expression of an idea simply because society finds the idea itself offensive or disagreeable. . . .

We have not recognized an exception to this principle even where our flag has been involved. In Street v. New York, 394 U.S. 576 (1969), we held that a state may not criminally punish a person for uttering words critical of the flag. . . .

15   Nor may the Government, we have held, compel conduct that would evince respect for the flag. . . .

We never before have held that the Government may insure that a symbol be used to express only one view of that symbol or its referents. . . . To conclude that the Government may permit designated symbols to be used to communicate only a limited set of messages would be to enter territory having no discernible or defensible boundaries.

Which Symbols Warrant Unique Status?

Could the Government, on this theory, prohibit the burning of state flags? Of copies of the Presidential seal? Of the Constitution? In evaluating these choices under the First Amendment, how would we decide which symbols were sufficiently special to warrant this unique status? To do so, we would be forced to consult our own political preferences, and impose them on the citizenry, in the very way that the First Amendment forbids us to do.

There is, moreover, no indication—either in the text of the Constitution or in our cases interpreting—that a separate juridical category exists for the American flag alone. Indeed, we would not be surprised to learn that the persons who framed our Constitution and wrote the Amendment that we now construe were not known for their reverence for the Union Jack.

The First Amendment does not guarantee that other concepts virtually sacred to our nation as a whole—such as the principle that discrimination on the basis of race is odious and destructive—will go unquestioned in the marketplace of ideas. We decline, therefore, to create for the flag an exception to the joust of principles protected by the First Amendment.

We are fortified in today's conclusion by our conviction that forbidding 20 criminal punishment for conduct such as Johnson's will not endanger the special role played by our flag or the feelings it inspires. . . .

Reaffirmation of Principles

We are tempted to say, in fact, that the flag's deservedly cherished place in our community will be strengthened, not weakened, by our holding today. Our decision is a reaffirmation of the principles of freedom and inclusiveness that the flag best reflects, and of the conviction that our toleration of criticism such as Johnson's is a sign and source of our strength.

The way to preserve the flag's special role is not to punish those who feel differently about these matters. It is to persuade them that they are wrong. . . .

We can imagine no more appropriate response to burning a flag than waving one's own, no better way to counter a flag-burner's message than by saluting the flag that burns, no surer means of preserving the dignity even of the flag that burned than by—as one witness here did—according its remains a respectful burial. We do not consecrate the flag by punishing its desecration, for in doing so we dilute the freedom that this cherished emblem represents.

REFLECTING AND INTERPRETING

1. Where is Brennan's thesis statement?
2. What two criteria does he use to evaluate the seriousness of Johnson's act?
3. What crime was Johnson charged with? What was his sentence?
4. How did the State of Texas justify Johnson's conviction?
5. What broad interpretation of the First Amendment did the Court of Appeals issue?
6. How did the Court of Appeals justify its decision?
7. Consider the inference, a personal opinion, in paragraph 18. Does this remark seem strange in this document? Why or why not?
8. Why does Brennan think that his decision will strengthen regard for the flag?
9. What does he recommend that onlookers do as a sign of respect while a flag burns as a political protest?
10. Examine Brennan's argument. Which of the three classic appeals (*logos, ethos, pathos*) does he use? Which appeal is predominant?

A WRITER'S RESPONSE

Research the legality of cross burning. What distinctions have been made in court decisions? Is cross burning similar to or different from flag burning? How?

DISSENTING OPINION OF THE U.S. SUPREME COURT IN TEXAS V. JOHNSON (1989)

CHIEF JUSTICE WILLIAM H. REHNQUIST

From 1943 to 1946, William Benjamin Rehnquist (1924–) served in the United States Army Air Corps. After obtaining two masters' degrees, one from Stanford (1948) and the other from Harvard (1950), he returned to Stanford to earn a law degree (1952). He practiced law in Arizona, specializing in civil litigation. In 1969 President Nixon appointed him assistant attorney general, Office of Legal Counsel. In 1971 President Reagan nominated Rehnquist as associate justice of the US Supreme Court, and in 1986 nominated him as chief justice. Rehnquist believes that historical values and the will of the people should influence decisions on "symbolic speech."

1   In holding this Texas statute unconstitutional, the Court ignores Justice Holmes's familiar aphorism that "a page of history is worth a volume of logic." For more than 200 years, the American flag has occupied a unique position as the symbol of our nation, a uniqueness that justifies a governmental prohibition against flag burning in the way respondent Johnson did here.

At the time of the American Revolution, the flag served to unify the 13 colonies at home while obtaining recognition of national sovereignty abroad. Ralph Waldo Emerson's Concord Hymn describes the first skirmishes of the Revolutionary War in these lines:

> By the rude bridge that arched the flood,
> Their flag to April's breeze unfurled,
> Here once the embattled farmers stood,
> And fired the shot heard round the world.

In the First and Second World Wars, thousands of our countrymen died on foreign soil fighting for the American cause. At Iwo Jima in the Second World War, United States Marines fought hand to hand against thousands of Japanese. By the time the marines reached the top of Mount Suribachi, they raised a piece of pipe upright and from one end fluttered a flag. That ascent had cost nearly 6,000 American lives. . . .

The flag symbolizes the nation in peace as well as in war. It signifies our national presence on battleships, airplanes, military installations and public buildings from the United States Capitol to the thousands of county courthouses and city halls throughout the country. . . .

5   No other American symbol has been as universally honored as the flag. In 1931 Congress declared "The Star Spangled Banner" to be our national anthem. In 1949 Congress declared June 14th to be Flag Day. In 1987 John Philip Sousa's "The Stars and Stripes Forever" was designated as the national march. Congress has also established "The Pledge of Allegiance to the Flag" and the manner of its deliverance. . . . all of the states now have statutes prohibiting the burning of the flag. . . .

The result of the Texas statute is obviously to deny one in Johnson's frame of mind one of many means of "symbolic speech." Far from being a case of "one picture being worth a thousand words," flag burning is the equivalent of an inarticulate grunt or roar that, it seems fair to say, is most likely to be indulged in not to express any particular idea, but to antagonize others. . . .

The Texas statute deprived Johnson of only one rather inarticulate symbolic form of protest—a form of protest that was profoundly offensive to many—and left him with a full panoply of other symbols and every conceivable form of verbal expression to express his deep disapproval of national policy. . . .

But the Court today will have none of this. The uniquely deep awe and respect for our flag felt by virtually all of us are bundled off under the rubric of "designated symbols" that the First Amendment prohibits the Government from "establishing." But the Government has not "established" this feeling; 200 years of history have done that. The Government is simply recognizing as a fact the profound regard for the American flag created by that history when it enacts statutes prohibiting the disrespectful public burning of the flag.

The Court concludes its opinion with a regretably patronizing civics lecture, presumably addressed to the members of both houses of Congress, the members of the 48 state legislatures that enacted prohibitions against flag burning, and the troops fighting under that flag in Vietnam who objected to its being burned: "The way to preserve the flag's special role is not to punish those who feel differently about these matters. It is to persuade them that they are wrong."

The Court's role as the final expositor of the Constitution is well established, but its role as a platonic guardian admonishing those responsible to public opinion as if they were truant school children has no similar place in our system of government. . . . **10**

Even if flag burning could be considered just another species of symbolic speech under the logical application of the rules that the Court has developed in its interpretation of the First Amendment in other contexts, this case has an intangible dimension that makes those rules inapplicable.

A country's flag is a symbol of more than "nationhood and national unity." It also signifies the ideas that characterize the society that has chosen that emblem, as well as the special history that has animated the growth and power of those ideas. . . .

So it is with the American flag. It is more than a proud symbol of the courage, the determination and the gifts of nature that transformed 13 fledgling colonies into a world power. It is a symbol of freedom, of equal opportunity, of religious tolerance and of good will for other peoples who share our aspirations. . . .

The value of the flag as a symbol cannot be measured. Even so, I have no doubt that the interest in preserving that value for the future is both significant and legitimate. . . . The creation of a Federal right to post bulletin boards and graffiti on the Washington Monument might enlarge the market for free expression, but at a cost I would not pay.

Similarly, in my considered judgment, sanctioning the public desecration of the flag will tarnish its value—both for those who cherish the ideas for which it waves and for those who desire to don the robes of martyrdom by burning it. That tarnish is not justified by the trivial burden on free expression occasioned by requiring that an available, alternative mode of expression—including uttering words critical of the flag—be employed.

15   The ideas of liberty and equality have been an irresistible force in motivating leaders like Patrick Henry, Susan B. Anthony, and Abraham Lincoln, schoolteachers like Nathan Hale and Booker T. Washington, the Philippine Scouts who fought at Bataan, and the soldiers who scaled the bluff at Omaha Beach. If those ideas are worth fighting for—and our history demonstrates that they are—it cannot be true that the flag that uniquely symbolizes their power is not itself worthy of protection from unnecessary desecration.

REFLECTING AND INTERPRETING

1. Examine the first page of this argument. How does Rehnquist begin?

2. What item of support do you find most convincing in paragraphs 1–5? Why?

3. How does he justify denying Johnson this symbolic act of protest?

4. What is Rehnquist's thesis? Where does he restate his thesis later?

5. Why does he believe that our flag represents "more than 'nationhood and national unity'"?

6. Do you agree or disagree with his belief that the "value of the flag as a symbol cannot be measured"? Why or why not?

7. Consider paragraph 12. How is the comparison of graffiti on the Washington Monument similar to flag burning? How is it different?

8. Rehnquist believes that "sanctioning the public desecration of the flag" will lead to what?

9. What is Rehnquist's criterion for weighing the seriousness of Johnson's act? (Tip: See the final point.)

10. Examine Rehnquist's argument. Which of the three classic appeals does he use? Which appeal is predominant?

A WRITER'S RESPONSE

After reading the opinions of both Supreme Court justices, which opinion do you find to be the most convincing? Why?

Short Stories

DOVES URSULA HEGI

When *Tearing the Silence: Being German in America* (1997) was selected for Oprah Winfrey's book club, Ursula Hegi gained widespread fame. She was born in Germany after World War II but immigrated to the United States at age eighteen. Now a professor at Eastern Washington University, she teaches creative writing. Her other books include *Intrusions* (1981), *Floating in My Mother's Palm: A Novel* (1990), *Salt Dancers* (1995), *Stones from the River* (1997), *The Vision of Emma Blau* (2000), and *A Sacred Time: A Novel* (2003). In addition, she has published two collections of short stories, *Unearned Pleasures* (1997) and *Hotel of the Saints: Stories* (2001). "Doves," the story which appears here, was first published in *Prairie Schooner* 65, no. 4 (Winter 1992).

Francine is having a shy day, the kind of day that makes you feel sad 1 when the elevator man says good afternoon, the kind of day that makes you want to buy two doves.

Her raincoat pulled close around herself, Francine walks the twelve blocks to Portland Pet And Plant. She heads past the African violets, past the jade plants and fig trees, past the schnauzers and poodles, past the hamsters and turtles, past the gaudy parrot in the center cage who shrieks: "Oh amigo, oh amigo . . ."

What Francine wants are doves of such a smooth gray that they don't hurt your eyes. With doves like that you don't have to worry about being too quiet. They make soft clucking sounds deep inside their throats and wait for you to notice them instead of clamoring for your attention.

Six of them perch on the bars in the tall cage near the wall, two white with brownish speckles, the others a deep gray tinged with purple. Above the cage hangs a sign: Ring Neck Doves $7.99. Doves like that won't need much; they'll turn their heads toward the door when you push the key into the lock late in the afternoon and wait for you to notice them instead of clamoring for your attention.

5   "Oh amigo, oh amigo . . . ," screeches the parrot. Francine chooses the two smallest gray doves and carries them from the store in white cardboard boxes that look like Chinese takeout containers with air holes. The afternoon has the texture of damp newspaper, but Francine feels light as she walks back to her apartment.

In her kitchen she sets the boxes on top of her counter, opens the tops, and waits for the doves to fly out and roost on the plastic bar where she hangs her kitchen towels. But they crouch inside the white cardboard as if waiting for her to lift them out.

She switches on the radio to the station where she always keeps it, public radio, but instead of Tuesday night opera, a man is asking for donations. Francine has already sent in her contribution, and she doesn't like it when the man says, "None of you would think of going into a store and taking something off the shelves, but you listen to public radio without paying. . . ." The doves move their wing feathers forward and pull their heads into their necks as if trying to shield themselves from the fund-raising voice.

Francine turns the dial past rock stations and commercials. At the gaudy twang of a country-western song, the doves raise their heads and peer from the boxes. Their beaks turn to one side, then to the other, completing a nearly full circle. Low velvet sounds rise from their throats. Francine has never listened to country-westerns; she's considered them tacky, but when the husky voice of a woman sings of wanting back the lover who hurt her so, she tilts her head to the side and croons along with the doves.

Before she leaves for her job at K-Mart the next morning, Francine pulls the radio next to the kitchen sink and turns it on for the doves. They sit in the left side of her double sink which she has lined with yellow towels, their claws curved around folds of fabric, their eyes on the flickering light of the tuner that still glows on the country-western station. When she returns after working all day in the footwear department, they swivel their heads toward her and then back to the radio as if they'd been practicing that movement all day.

10   At K-Mart she finds that more people leave their shoes. It used to be just once or twice a week that she'd discover a worn pair of shoes half pushed under the racks by someone who's walked from the store with stolen footwear. But now she sees them almost every day—sneakers with torn insoles, pumps with imitation leather peeling from the high heels, work shoes with busted seams—as if a legion of shoe thieves had descended on Portland.

Francine keeps the discarded shoes in the store's lost and found crate out back, though no one has ever tried to claim them. But some are still good enough to donate to Goodwill. She murmurs to the doves about the shoes while she refills their water and sprinkles birdseed into the porcelain soap dish. Coming home to them has become familiar. So have the songs of lost love that welcome her every evening. A few times she tried to return to her old station, but as soon as the doves grew listless, she moved the tuner back. And lately she hasn't felt like changing it at all. She knows some of the lines now, knows how the songs end.

Francine has a subscription to the opera, and after feeding the doves, she takes a bubble bath and puts on her black dress. In the back of the cab, she holds her purse with both hands in her lap. Sitting in the darkened balcony, she feels invisible as she listens to *La Traviata,* one of her favorite operas. For the first time it comes to her that it, too, is about lost love and broken hearts.

In the swell of bodies that shifts from the opera house, Francine walks into the mild November night, leaving behind the string of waiting taxicabs, the expensive restaurants across from the opera house, the stores and the bus station, the fast-food places and bars.

A young couple saunters from the Blue Moon Tavern hand in hand, steeped in amber light and the sad lyrics of a slow-moving song for that instant before the door closes again. Francine curves her fingers around the doorhandle, pulls it open, and steps into the smoky light as if she were a woman with red boots who had someone waiting for her. Below the Michelob clock, on the platform, two men play guitars and sing of betrayed love.

On the bar stool, her black dress rides up to her knees. She draws her 15 shoulders around herself and orders a fuzzy navel, a drink she remembers from a late night movie. The summer taste of apricots and oranges soothes her limbs and makes her ease into the space her body fills.

A lean-hipped man with a cowboy hat asks Francine to dance, and as she sways in his arms on the floor that's spun of sawdust and boot prints, she becomes the woman in all the songs that the men on the platform sing about, the woman who leaves them, the woman who keeps breaking their hearts.

REFLECTING AND INTERPRETING

1. What do you learn in the first two sentences about the setting and the main character?

2. Why is Francine attracted to the doves rather than the parrot? What does the narrator say?

3. What does the parrot screech at her? Notice that he repeats the same words in paragraph 5. What do they mean (translated)? What is their significance?

4. What is the significance of paragraph 6? What do you learn about Francine and the doves?

5. What do you learn about Francine's values in paragraph 7?

6. A paragraph and a half is spent describing shoes, which seems odd in a story so short. Do you see any similarities between the shoes and something else? (See also paragraph 8.)

7. How does the footwear in Francine's fantasy differ from the shoes left at K-Mart? What connotations do the red boots carry?

8. How does Francine feel as she dances? How has she changed since she bought the doves?

9. What kind of night is described? Compare this night with the day the story opens. How does Francine feel?

10. What is the theme of this story?

A WRITER'S RESPONSE

Have you ever made a small purchase or made a slight variation in your daily routine that has had far-reaching effects? Or perhaps you made a small decision that led to a big change. What motivated or inclined you to take the action that initiated the change? Share your experience with your group.

SCHEHERAZADE   CHARLES BAXTER

A prolific writer, Charles Baxter is also the director of the MFA program in creative writing at the University of Michigan. Baxter is the author of four novels, *Shadow Play* (1994), *First Light* (1995), *The Feast of Love* (2001), and *Saul and Patsy* (2003). He has also written poems, essays, and five collections of short stories: *A Relative Stranger* (1991), *Harmony of the World* (1997), *Believers* (1998), *Through the Safety Net* (1998), and *Feast of Love* (2001). Five of his stories have been selected for *Best American Short Stories*. "Scheherazade," which appears here, was first published in *A Relative Stranger*.

1   She leaned down to adjust his respirator tube and the elastic tie around his neck that kept it in place. "Don't," he said, an all-purpose warning referring to nothing in particular, and she heard Muzak from down the hall, a version of "Stardust" that made her think of cold soup. A puddle outside his window reflected blue sky and gave the ceiling of his room a faint blue tint.

He was looking sallow and breathing poorly; she would have to lie again to perk him up.

"Do you remember," she said, sitting in the chair next to his chair, "my goodness, this would have been fifty years ago, that trip we made to Hawaii?"

"Don't remember it," he said. "Don't think I've been there."

5   "Yes, you have," she said, patting his hand where the wedding ring was. "We took the train, it had 'Zephyr' in its name somewhere, one of

those silver trains that served veal for dinner. We had a romantic night in the Pullman car; I expect you don't remember that."

"Not just now," he said.

"Well, we did. We took it to Oakland or San Francisco, I forget which, and from there we took the boat to Honolulu."

"What boat? I don't remember a boat. Did it have a name?"

She leaned back and stared at the ceiling. Why did he always insist on the names? She couldn't invent names; that always caused her trouble. And her bifocals were hurting her. She would have to see that nice Dr. Hauser about them. "The name of the ship, dear, was *Halcyon Days,* not very original, I must say; we were on the C deck, second-class. The first night out you were seasick. Then you were all right. The ship had an orchestra and we danced the fox-trot. You flirted with that woman whose room was down the hall. You were quite awful about it."

The outline of a smile appeared on his face. "Who?"

She saw the smile and was pleased. "I don't remember," she said. "Why should I remember her name? She was just a silly woman with vulgar dark-red hair. She let it fly all over her shoulders."

"What was her name?"

"I told you I don't remember."

"Please," he said. His mouth was open. His filmy eyes looked in her direction.

"All right," she said. "Her name was Peggy."

"Peggy" he said, briefly sighing.

"Yes, Peggy," she said, "and you made yourself quite ridiculous around her, but I think she liked you, and I remember I once caught you two at the railing, looking at the waters of the Pacific go by as the ship churned westward."

"Was I bad?"

"You were all right, dear. You were just like any man. I didn't mind. Men are like that. You bought her drinks."

"What did she drink?"

"Old-fashioned," she said, but she felt herself going too far and hauled herself back in. "What *I* minded was that she would not always close the door to her stateroom. You would look in, and there she was."

"Yes," he said. "There she was."

"There she was," she continued, "in her bathrobe, or worse, with that terrible red hair of hers billowing down to her shoulders. In her white bathrobe, and you, standing in the hallway like any man, staring at her."

"You caught me."

"Yes, I did, but I didn't blame you. You were attractive to women."

"I was?"

"Yes, you were. You were so handsome in those days, and so witty, and when you sat down at the piano and sang those Cole Porter tunes, it was hard for women to resist."

"Could I play the piano?" He was smiling, perhaps thinking of the Pacific, or Peggy.

"Very well, dear. You could play and sing. Though I've heard better, I have certainly heard worse. You sang to me. You'd sing to anybody."

30 "To Peggy?"

"To anyone," she said. When she saw his smile fade, she said, "And to her, too. In an effort to charm. You sang 'You're the Top.' I daresay she liked it. Who knows what trouble you two got into? I was not a spy. All I know now is, it's been over fifty years."

He closed his eyes and stretched his thin legs. She saw a smile cross his face again and was pleased with herself.

"In Hawaii," she said, "we stayed at the Royal Palm Hotel." Although she had once been on a ship, she had never been in Hawaii and was speaking more slowly now as she tried to see the scene. "It was on the beach, the famous one with the name, and the sands were white, as white as alabaster. We played shuffleboard."

"I remember that," he said.

35 "Good. We drove around the island and climbed the extinct volcano, Mount Johnson. There's a lake inside Mount Johnson, and you went swimming in it, and there were large birds, enormous blue birds, flying over our heads, and you called them the archangel birds and said that God had sent them to us as a sign."

"A sign of what?"

"A sign of our happiness."

"Were we happy?"

"Yes," she said. "We were."

"Always?"

40 "It seems so to me now. Anyway, Mount Johnson was one day, and on another day we went diving for pearls. You found an oyster with a pearl in it. I still wear it on a pin."

He looked over at her and searched her face and chest and arms.

"Just not today," she said. "I'm not wearing it today."

The sound of the oxygen hissing out of the respirator tube fatigued her. She would not be able to continue this much longer. It was like combat of a subtle kind. She hurried on. "On the island we picked enormous flowers, and every evening we sat down for dinner by the water, and you put a gardenia in my hair one night. We ate pineapples and broke open coconuts, and at moonrise the sea breezes came in through the window of our room where we were lying on the bed. We were so in love. We had room service bring us champagne and you read poetry to me."

45 "Yes," he said. "What did you look like?"

She clasped her hands in her lap. "I was beautiful." She paused. "You said so."

"The sound," he said.

"What sound?"

"There was a sound."

"I don't remember a sound," she said.   50

"There was one," he insisted.

"Where?"

"In the room."

"Yes?"

"It came in through the window," he whispered.   55

"From where?"

"From the sea. Do you hear it?"

"No."

"Listen."

She sat listening. The Muzak from the hallway had fallen silent. From 60 outside there was a faint, low humming.

"Hear it?"

"Yes," she said faintly.

"I heard it first there. In Hawaii."

"So did I."

"I feel a little better," he said. "I feel sleepy."   65

"Go to sleep, dear," she said. "Take a little nap."

"You'll be back?"

"Yes, tomorrow."

"Where else did we go?"

"We went," she said, "to Egypt, where we crawled through the pyra- 70 mids. We went through the fjords in Norway. We saw wonders. We saw many wonders."

"Tell me tomorrow."

"I will." She kissed him on the forehead, stood up, and walked to the doorway. She looked back at him; he seemed to be about to fall asleep, but he also seemed to be listening to the sound. She gazed at him for a moment, and then went down the hallway, past the nurses, bowing her head for a moment before she went out the front door to the bus stop, thinking of tomorrow's story.

REFLECTING AND INTERPRETING

To understand the allusion in the title of "Scheherazade," the reader needs to know that it alludes to the *Arabian Nights,* a collection of 200 folktales. The *Arabian Nights* begins with a story about King Shahriyar, who has vowed to marry a new wife every night and have her beheaded in the morning. When Scheherazade becomes his bride, however, she tells him a tale that is so entertaining he lets her live another day so that she can finish it. Her storytelling continues for one thousand and one nights. By that time the king is so in love with her that he lets her live.

1. Describe the setting of "Scheherazade." (Consider the weather outside as well as the atmosphere inside.)

2. What in the story indicates that the old man is terminally ill? (Hint: Think about the title.)

3. Why does the old woman tell her husband the tale about their going to Hawaii? Is this the first time that she has lied to him?

4. With a dictionary, look up the meaning of the names of the train and the ship. How do these names form a connection to the setting and the old man?

5. What direction did the ship head? What other connections do you see to this direction? What is the significance of this direction?

6. What are the archangel birds a sign of? Was the marriage always a happy one?

7. Examine the description of Hawaii. Do you notice any symbolism?

8. What does "It was like combat of a subtle kind" refer to? Who (or what) was the old woman's adversary?

9. What does the old woman's tale reveal about her?

10. What element of this story lends a note of universality?

A WRITER'S RESPONSE

The author is very careful to name objects but not the main characters. What is the effect of calling them *she* and *he* rather than giving their names? Does this detract or enhance the image of the hospital room for you? Why?

THE STORY OF AN HOUR   KATE CHOPIN

A prolific writer, Kate Chopin (1850–1904) did not start writing until age thirty-eight, when she wrote her first poem "If It Might Be" and began the story "Euphrasie." She married at age twenty and had six children before her husband died in 1882. In 1889 the poem and two stories, "Wiser than a God" and "A Point at Issue," were published and well received. In 1890 her novel, *At Fault*, appeared in print. She was unable to find a publisher for another novel, *Young Dr. Gosse*, and destroyed the manuscript. Other successful writing—"Désirée's Baby" (1893), *Bayou Folk* (1894), "Athénaise" (1895), and *A Night in Acadie* (1897)—made her acclaimed in St. Louis, where she lived. In 1899, however, the reviews of *The Awakening* were scathing. Critics deemed it "immoral," and her popularity faded. In the past few decades, her writing has again gained favor in the United States.

1   Knowing that Mrs. Mallard was afflicted with a heart trouble, great care was taken to break to her as gently as possible the news of her husband's death.

It was her sister Josephine who told her, in broken sentences: veiled hints that revealed in half concealing. Her husband's friend Richards was there, too, near her. It was he who had been in the newspaper office when intelligence of the railroad disaster was received, with Brently Mallard's name leading the list of "killed." He had only taken the time to assure himself of its truth by a second telegram, and had hastened to forestall any less careful, less tender friend in bearing the sad message.

She did not hear the story as many women have heard the same, with a paralyzed inability to accept its significance. She wept at once, with sudden, wild abandonment, in her sister's arms. When the storm of grief had spent itself she went away to her room alone. She would have no one follow her.

There stood, facing the open window, a comfortable, roomy armchair. Into this she sank, pressed down by a physical exhaustion that haunted her body and seemed to reach into her soul.

She could see in the open square before her house the tops of trees 5 that were all aquiver with the new spring life. The delicious breath of rain was in the air. In the street below a peddler was crying his wares. The notes of a distant song which some one was singing reached her faintly, and countless sparrows were twittering in the eaves.

There were patches of blue sky showing here and there through the clouds that had met and piled one above the other in the west facing her window.

She sat with her head thrown back upon the cushion of the chair, quite motionless, except when a sob came up into her throat and shook her, as a child who has cried itself to sleep continues to sob in its dreams.

She was young, with a fair, calm face, whose lines bespoke repression and even a certain strength. But now there was a dull stare in her eyes, whose gaze was fixed away off yonder on one of those patches of blue sky. It was not a glance of reflection, but rather indicated a suspension of intelligent thought.

There was something coming to her and she was waiting for it, fearfully. What was it? She did not know; it was too subtle and elusive to name. But she felt it, creeping out of the sky, reaching toward her through the sounds, the scents, the color that filled the air.

Now her bosom rose and fell tumultuously. She was beginning to rec- 10 ognize this thing that was approaching to possess her, and she was striving to beat it back with her will—as powerless as her two white slender hands would have been.

When she abandoned herself a little whispered word escaped her slightly parted lips. She said it over and over under her breath: "free, free, free!" The vacant stare and the look of terror that had followed it went from her eyes. They stayed keen and bright. Her pulses beat fast, and the coursing blood warmed and relaxed every inch of her body.

She did not stop to ask if it were or were not a monstrous joy that held her. A clear and exalted perception enabled her to dismiss the suggestion as trivial.

She knew that she would weep again when she saw the kind, tender hands folded in death; the face that had never looked save with love upon her, fixed and gray and dead. But she saw beyond that bitter moment a long procession of years to come that would belong to her absolutely. And she opened and spread her arms out to them in welcome.

There would be no one to live for during those coming years; she would live for herself. There would be no powerful will bending hers in that blind persistence with which men and women believe they have a right to impose a private will upon a fellow-creature. A kind intention or a cruel intention made the act seem no less a crime as she looked upon it in that brief moment of illumination.

15   And yet she had loved him—sometimes. Often she had not. What did it matter! What could love, the unsolved mystery, count for in face of this possession of self-assertion which she suddenly recognized as the strongest impulse of her being!

"Free! Body and soul free!" she kept whispering.

Josephine was kneeling before the closed door with her lips to the keyhole, imploring for admission. "Louise, open the door! I beg; open the door—you will make yourself ill. What are you doing, Louise? For heaven's sake open the door."

"Go away. I am not making myself ill." No; she was drinking in a very elixir of life through that open window.

Her fancy was running riot along those days ahead of her. Spring days, and summer days, and all sorts of days that would be her own. She breathed a quick prayer that life might be long. It was only yesterday she had thought with a shudder that life might be long.

20   She arose at length and opened the door to her sister's importunities. There was a feverish triumph in her eyes, and she carried herself unwittingly like a goddess of Victory. She clasped her sister's waist, and together they descended the stairs. Richards stood waiting for them at the bottom.

Some one was opening the front door with a latchkey. It was Brently Mallard who entered, a little travel-stained, composedly carrying his grip-sack and umbrella. He had been far from the scene of accident, and did not even know there had been one. He stood amazed at Josephine's piercing cry: at Richards' quick motion to screen him from the view of his wife.

But Richards was too late.

When the doctors came they said she had died of heart disease—of joy that kills.

REFLECTING AND INTERPRETING

1. Might there be more than one kind of "heart trouble" involved?

2. Often denial is the first stage of grief. How does Mrs. Mallard react to the news?

3. Describe the scene outside her open bedroom window. How does that scene symbolize what she is experiencing?

4. As she sits, facing the window, Mrs. Mallard feels ambivalent. Why? (Consider the lines in her face and "fearfully.")

5. How does her outlook on life change? How does this change affect her behavior?

6. Reread the story. Do you see any foreshadowing?

7. Do you notice any changes in the way the narrator refers to the main character? What is the significance of these various forms?

8. How does the staircase function in the story?

9. How is the story ironic?

10. What is curious about the use of "abandonment" and "abandoned"? How do these words relate to the ending—or do they?

A WRITER'S RESPONSE

Essay or Small Group: Consider that this story was written in 1894. How do you think it might have been received by the general public if it had been published then? What is your reaction to the story?

STILL OF SOME USE   JOHN UPDIKE

In an interview for *Salon* magazine, Dwight Garner wrote: "There is indeed something snow-capped and oddly angelic about [John] Updike; he seems to hover over the contemporary literary scene like an apparition from another era, the last great American man of letters." In 1981 John Updike (1932–) won the Pulitzer Prize for *Rabbit Is Rich*, the third of a series of Rabbit novels. Over four decades Updike has won numerous awards for his books (more than fifty), which include novels, collections of short stories, poems, and criticism. Some of his best-known works include *Rabbit Run* (1960), *Pigeon Feathers* (1962), *Couples* (1968), *Bech: A Book* (1970), *Bech Is Back* (1982), *In the Beauty of the Lilies* (1997), *Bech at Bay: A Quasi-Novel* (1998), *Gertrude and Claudius* (2000), and *Seek My Face* (2002). The following short story was first published in *Trust Me* (1987).

When Foster helped his ex-wife clean out the attic of the house where   1
they had once lived and which she was now selling, they came across dozens of forgotten, broken games. Parcheesi, Monopoly, Lotto; games aping the strategies of the stock market, of crime detection, of real-estate speculation, of international diplomacy and war; games with spinners, dice, lettered tiles, cardboard spacemen, and plastic battleships; games bought in five-and-tens and department stores feverish and musical with Christmas expectations; games enjoyed on the afternoon of a birthday and for a few afternoons thereafter and then allowed, shy of one or two pieces, to drift into closets and toward the attic. Yet, discovered in their bright flat boxes between trunks of outgrown clothes and defunct appliances, the games presented a forceful semblance of value: the springs of their miniature launchers still reacted, the logic of their instructions would still generate suspense, given a chance. "What shall we do with all these games?" Foster shouted, in a kind of agony, to his scattered family as they moved up and down the attic stairs.

"Trash 'em," his younger son, a strapping nineteen, urged.

"Would the Goodwill want them?" asked his ex-wife, still wife enough to think that all of his questions deserved answers. "You used to be able to give things like that to orphanages. But they don't call them orphanages anymore, do they?"

"They call them normal American homes," Foster said.

5 His older son, now twenty-two, with a cinnamon-colored beard, offered, "They wouldn't work anyhow; they all have something missing. That's how they got to the attic."

"Well, why didn't we throw them away at the time?" Foster asked, and had to answer himself. Cowardice, the answer was. Inertia. Clinging to the past.

His sons, with a shadow of old obedience, came and looked over his shoulder at the sad wealth of abandoned playthings, silently groping with him for the particular happy day connected to this and that pattern of colored squares and arrows. Their lives had touched these tokens and counters once; excitement had flowed along the paths of these stylized landscapes. But the day was gone, and scarcely a memory remained.

"Toss 'em," the younger decreed, in his manly voice. For these days of cleaning out, the boy had borrowed a pickup truck from a friend and parked it on the lawn beneath the attic window, so the smaller items of discard could be tossed directly into it. The bigger items were lugged down the stairs and through the front hall; already the truck was loaded with old mattresses, broken clock-radios, obsolete skis and boots. It was a game of sorts to hit the truck bed with objects dropped from the height of the house. Foster flipped game after game at the target two stories below. When the boxes hit, they exploded, throwing a spray of dice, tokens, counters, and cards into the air and across the lawn. A box called Mousetrap, its lid showing laughing children gathered around a Rube Goldberg device, drifted sideways, struck one side wall of the truck, and spilled its plastic components into a flower bed. A set of something called Drag Race! floated gently as a snowflake before coming to rest, much diminished, on a stained mattress. Foster saw in the depth of downward space the cause of his melancholy: he had not played enough with these games. Now no one wanted to play.

Had he and his wife avoided divorce, of course, these boxes would have continued to gather dust in an undisturbed attic, their sorrow unexposed. The toys of his own childhood still rested in his mother's attic. At his last visit, he had crept up there and wound the spring of a tin Donald Duck; it had responded with an angry clack of its bill and a few stiff strokes on its drum. A tilted board with concentric grooves for marbles still waited in a bushel basket with his alphabet blocks and lead airplanes—waited for his childhood to return.

10 His ex-wife paused where he squatted at the attic window and asked him, "What's the matter?"

"Nothing. These games weren't used much."

"I know. It happens fast. You better stop now; it's making you too sad."

Behind him, his family had cleaned out the attic; the slant-ceilinged rooms stood empty, with drooping insulation.

"How can you bear it?" he asked, of the emptiness.

15 "Oh, it's fun," she said, "once you get into it. Off with the old, on with the new. The new people seem nice. They have *little* children."

He looked at her and wondered whether she was being brave or truly hard-hearted. The attic trembled slightly. "That's Ted," she said.

She had acquired a boyfriend, a big athletic accountant fleeing from domestic embarrassments in a neighboring town. When Ted slammed the kitchen door two stories below, the glass shade of a kerosene lamp that, though long unused, Foster hadn't had the heart to throw out of the window vibrated in its copper clips, emitting a thin note like a trapped wasp's song. Time for Foster to go. His dusty knees creaked when he stood. His ex-wife's eager steps raced ahead of him down through the emptied house. He followed, carrying the lamp, and set it finally on the bare top of a bookcase he had once built, on the first-floor landing. He remembered screwing the top board, a prize piece of knot-free pine, into place from underneath, so not a nailhead marred its smoothness.

After all the vacant rooms and halls, the kitchen seemed indecently full of heat and life. "Dad, want a beer?" the bearded son asked. "Ted brought some." The back of the boy's hand, holding forth the dewy can, blazed with fine ginger hairs. His girl friend, wearing gypsy earrings and a NO NUKES sweatshirt, leaned against the disconnected stove, her hair in a bandanna and a black smirch becomingly placed on one temple. From the kind way she smiled at Foster, he felt this party was making room for him.

"No, I better go."

Ted shook Foster's hand, as he always did. He had a thin pink skin and   **20** silver hair whose fluffy waves seemed mechanically induced. Foster could look him in the eye no longer than he could gaze at the sun. He wondered how such a radiant brute had got into such a tame line of work. Ted had not helped with the attic today because he had been off in his old town, visiting his teen-aged twins. "I hear you did a splendid job today," he announced.

"They did," Foster said. "I wasn't much use. I just sat there stunned. All these things I had forgotten buying."

"Some were presents," his son reminded him. He passed the can his father had snubbed to his mother, who took it and tore up the tab with that defiant-sounding *pssff.* She had never liked beer, yet tipped the can to her mouth.

"Give me one sip," Foster begged, and took the can from her and drank a long swallow. When he opened his eyes, Ted's big hand was cupped under Mrs. Foster's chin while his thumb rubbed away a smudge of dirt along her jaw which Foster had not noticed. This protective gesture made her face look small, pouty, and frail. Ted, Foster noticed now, was dressed with a certain comical perfection in a banker's Saturday outfit—softened blue jeans, crisp tennis sneakers, lumberjack shirt with cuffs folded back. The youthful outfit accented his age, his hypertensive flush. Foster saw them suddenly as a touching, aging couple, and this perception seemed permission to go.

He handed back the can.

"Thanks for your help," his former wife said.   **25**

"Yes, we do thank you," Ted said.

"Talk to Tommy," she unexpectedly added, in a lowered voice. She was still sending out trip wires to slow Foster's departures. "This is harder on him than he shows."

Ted looked at his watch, a fat, black-faced thing he could swim under water with. "I said to him coming in, 'Don't dawdle till the dump closes.'"

"He loafed all day," his brother complained, "mooning over old stuff, and now he's going to screw up getting to the dump."

30 "He's very sensi-tive," the visiting gypsy said, with a strange chiming brightness, as if repeating something she had heard.

Outside, the boy was picking up litter that had fallen wide of the truck. Foster helped him. In the grass there were dozens of tokens and dice. Some were engraved with curious little faces—Olive Oyl, Snuffy Smith, Dagwood—and others with hieroglyphs—numbers, diamonds, spades, hexagons—whose code was lost. He held out a handful for Tommy to see. "Can you remember what these were for?"

"Comic-Strip Lotto," the boy said without hesitation. "And a game called Gambling Fools there was a kind of slot machine for." The light of old payoffs flickered in his eyes as he gazed down at the rubble in his father's hand. Though Foster was taller, the boy was broader in the shoulders, and growing. "Want to ride with me to the dump?" Tommy asked.

"I would, but I better go." He, too, had a new life to lead. By being on this forsaken property at all, Foster was in a sense on the wrong square, if not *en prise.* He remembered how once he had begun to teach this boy chess, but in the sadness of watching him lose—the little furry bowed head frowning above his trapped king—the lessons had stopped.

Foster tossed the tokens into the truck; they rattled to rest on the metal. "This depresses you?" he asked his son.

35 "Naa." The boy amended, "Kind of."

"You'll feel great," Foster promised him, "coming back with a clean truck. I used to love it at the dump, all that old happiness heaped up, and the seagulls."

"It's changed since you left. They have all these new rules. The lady there yelled at me last time, for putting stuff in the wrong place."

"She did?"

"Yeah, it was scary." Seeing his father waver, he added, "It'll only take twenty minutes." Though broad of build, Tommy had beardless cheeks and, between thickening eyebrows, a trace of that rounded, faintly baffled blankness babies have, that wrinkles before they cry.

40 "O.K.," Foster said. "You win. I'll come along. I'll protect you."

REFLECTING AND INTERPRETING

"Still of Some Use" is a rather puzzling story because so much that is important is left unsaid. The reader must watch for clues and listen to the nuances of dialogue to detect the turbulent emotions beneath the calm exterior of the main characters. As you make inferences, be sure to base each one on evidence from the story. Qualify your statements to make them tentative as you discuss the questions that follow.

1. Only one of Foster's family members is named. What does the lack of names imply?
2. What does Foster discover as he flips the games down to the truck?
3. Why are Foster's old toys and bookcase significant in the story? (Consider their condition.)
4. What does Foster's sarcastic response to his ex-wife indicate?
5. How does Foster feel about his ex-wife? What signs do you see?
6. Why might Foster's wife drink beer when she does not like it? What does her sharing her drink with him indicate?
7. What change does Foster show in his conversation with Tommy?
8. How are the title, the first paragraph, and the last sentence linked?
9. What is the analogy that underlies this story?
10. What themes do you see?

SMALL GROUP DISCUSSION

With your group, discuss the change in societal attitudes toward divorce. In the 1930s, divorce was relatively rare and viewed askance. Now at the start of the twenty-first century, divorce is commonplace, with nearly half of all marriages disintegrating. What causes have contributed to the change? What subtle changes often occur in the way children are regarded and treated after divorce? Should any changes be made in laws regarding marriage and divorce?

THE HANDBOOK

A Guide to Grammar, Punctuation, Mechanics, and Usage

HANDBOOK DIRECTORY

INTRODUCTION

This concise handbook is a handy guide to frequently asked questions about standard written English. You won't find complicated explanations of rarely used rules. Instead, basic information, examples, and common errors are explained. Whether you write essays, papers, letters, reports, or other documents, you can easily find answers to most of your usage questions either in this reference section or in related parts of the textbook.

What Is the Best Way to Use This Handbook?

To find quick answers to usage questions, first turn to the Handbook Directory, which appears on the opposite page. Next, scan the headings to locate the section you need and the page number, such as *H-2*. Then turn to that page and scan until you find the appropriate rule. Or you may wish to brush up on all of the rules in a particular section. If you desire more help, look for cross-references in the handbook that direct you to other explanations and examples in chapters of this text. You can also consult the *subject index* in the back of the book.

> www.mhhe.com/dietsch
> To assess the skills you need the most help with, go to:
> Editing>Diagnostic Tests

Should a Writer Ever Break a Rule?

If you deliberately break a stylistic rule, it should be done to promote effective writing. To estimate how effective a change might be, consider the rhetorical situation (chapter 1). Two key questions will help in predicting the result:

- What do readers expect?
- Is the writing appropriate for the occasion?

If readers expect traditional usage and you punctuate creatively, they may think you are uneducated. As a result, your ideas may not receive the attention they deserve. When in doubt about usage, consult this book, your instructor, the campus writing center, or an online site:

- *The American Heritage Book of English Usage* Covers grammar, diction, style, words, gender, and pronunciation <http://www.bartleby.com/64/>
- *Guide to Grammar and Writing* <http://ccc.commnet.edu/grammar>
- *Merriam-Webster's Collegiate Dictionary* <http://www.m-w.com/dictionary>

1.   Grammar and Usage

English grammar classifies words into eight major parts of speech: *nouns, pronouns, adjectives, verbs, adverbs, prepositions, conjunctions,* and *interjections.* Other constructions such as gerunds, phrases, and clauses also serve as minor parts of

www.mhhe.com/dietsch

For further coverage of the parts of speech, visit: Editing>Parts of Speech

speech. This section defines these terms and provides examples of structures that often cause problems and raise questions. The guidelines presented here are generally used for college composition in the United States, although some instructors may vary them slightly to fit various rhetorical situations. If you are in doubt, check with your instructor.

1a. Nouns

A noun is the name of a person, place, or thing. Nouns serve as the subject of a sentence, object of a verb (also called a direct object), and object of a preposition. For explanations of these three structures, see chapter 7.

▶ The *hammer* is in the tool chest. [subject]

▶ Hank hit the *ball* over the back fence. [object of verb]

▶ The ball rolled under a lilac *bush.* [object of a preposition]

Note: For *specific nouns,* see "Moving from General to Specific," chapter 8.

1b. Pronouns

www.mhhe.com/dietsch

For online coverage of pronouns, go to: Editing>Pronouns

A pronoun is a handy substitute for a noun. By using a pronoun, you can avoid unnecessary repetition of the noun. Notice that a pronoun needs an *antecedent*— a noun to directly precede to avoid confusion. If there is another intervening noun, do not use a pronoun to refer to the first noun.

Exception: Once in a while the pronoun *it* is clear and needs no antecedent: *It* is snowing!

1.   **Make sure that what each pronoun refers to is clear.**

A pronoun needs a clear antecedent (sometimes called referent). The meaning of a pronoun is clear only when the reader or listener knows to what or to whom the pronoun refers.

www.mhhe.com/dietsch

For more examples of pronouns and antecedents, visit: Editing>Pronoun- Antecedent Agreement

UNCLEAR

❯ The law firm of Creager and Colvin failed after *he* withdrew the operating capital and fled to Switzerland.

❯ Teresa proofread my paper, but she didn't find a single *one.*

❯ He believes in reincarnation, but he does not believe that *they* appear to the living.

❯ *It* said in the newspaper that the election would be close.

CLEAR

▶ The law firm of Creager and Colvin failed after *Colvin* withdrew the operating capital and fled to Switzerland.

▶ Teresa proofread my paper, but she didn't find a single *error.*

▶ He believes in reincarnation, but he does not believe that *the dead* appear to the living.

▶ The newspaper reported that the election would be close.

2. **Use the correct case of pronouns.**

Because pronouns have different uses, they have different forms. A pronoun that is the subject of a sentence is in the *subjective* case. A pronoun that shows ownership is in the *possessive* case. A pronoun that acts as an object is in the *objective* case.

Case of Pronouns

	Subjective	Possessive	Objective
Singular			
First person	I	my, mine	me
Second person	you	you, yours	you
Third person	he, she, it	his, her, hers, its	him, her, it
Plural			
First person	we	our, ours	us
Second person	you	your, yours	you
Third person	they	their, theirs	them

Use the subjective case for the following:

SUBJECTS OF MAIN OR SUBORDINATE CLAUSES

▶ *I* will act as chairman during Brad's absence. [subject of main clause]

▶ Hope's party was the best that *I* have ever attended. [subject of subordinate clause]

APPOSITIVES THAT IDENTIFY WORDS IN THE SUBJECTIVE CASE

▶ Only two people—*Ray and I*—decided to go.

SUBJECT COMPLEMENTS FOLLOWING LINKING VERBS (*BE* VERBS, *SEEM*, *APPEAR*, *FELT*, ETC.)

▶ The winners were *he* and Joan.

Use the possessive case to designate ownership and before a gerund (see section 1j):

▶ The hat is *hers.*

▶ The committee was late in finishing *its* report.

▶ *Your* not writing upset Mother. (*writing* is the gerund)

▶ *Her* drum playing angers the neighbors. (*playing* is the gerund)

Use the objective case for direct objects, indirect objects, and objects of prepositions (see sections 1a and 1f):

▶ Bradley reimbursed *him* for the roll of stamps. [direct object]

▶ Jack sent *her* flowers. [indirect object]

▶ The letter was addressed to *me.* [object of preposition]

Use the objective case in an appositive that identifies the object:

▶ The club elected two new members, Erin and *her.*

Note: An *appositive* is a noun or pronoun, often with modifiers, that follows another noun or pronoun to identify it. (*Appositive:* Erin and her.)

Use the pronoun case that correctly completes your meaning after *than* or *as:*

▶ My mother understands my sister better than *I.* ("than I do")

▶ My mother understands my sister better than *me.* ("than she understands me")

Note: *We* or *us* before a noun takes the same case it would if you dropped the noun.

▶ *We* students have complained to the administration about this problem before.

▶ It is difficult for *us* registered Independents to affect the primary process.

3.   Use the correct person of pronouns.

First person

First person *I* and *we* refer to the individual who is speaking (*I* sold my old car). *My, mine, our,* and *ours* show ownership. *Me* and *us* are used as objects.

▶ *I* will leave soon. *We* will meet at the inn. [subjective case]

▶ *My* suitcase is packed. *Our* children are going, too. [possessive case]

▶ Rick will pick *them* up at the airport. [objective case]

▶ I brought Tim and let *him* ride up front. [objective case]

Second person

Second person *you* refers to the individual spoken to (*You* will be in charge). *Your* and *yours* show ownership. Sometimes a subject in *second person* is omitted; this usage is called *understood you* (also see chapter 11).

▶ *You* are very thoughtful [subjective case]

▶ [*You*] Clean the bathroom before turning on the computer. [understood you]

▶ The supermarket is right on *your* way home. [possessive case]

▶ Where did the rubber band hit *you*? [objective case]

Third person

Third person refers to the people or things mentioned by the preceding noun that agrees with it in person, number, and gender.

▶ Neil planned to bring *his* running shoes but forgot. [possessive case]

▶ Kristin had intended to put *them* in the big suitcase. [objective case]

▶ *They* both thought to bring *their* tickets for the dinner. [subjective, possessive case]

4. Avoid inappropriate shifts of person.

A careless shift in person can confuse your reader and disrupt the flow of the sentence. Maintain a consistent point of view by writing in the same person. If you make a shift in person, do so skillfully for a purpose.

INAPPROPRIATE

I always spend the morning hours on work that requires mental effort, for *your* mind is freshest in the morning.

REVISED

I always spend the morning hours on work that requires mental effort, for *my* mind is freshest in the morning.

5. Make pronouns and their antecedents agree in gender, person, and number.

Pronouns must have the same gender, number, and person as the word they refer to. Because gender and person seldom pose problems with pronouns (but see section 1b.6 on sexist usage), the discussion here is limited to agreement in number. The rule is simple: Use plural pronouns to refer to plural antecedents. Use singular pronouns to refer to singular antecedents.

RECOGNIZING SINGULAR PRONOUNS

▶ *Anyone* who intends to go should be prepared to stay overnight.

▶ *Everybody* who is coming needs to make a reservation.

▶ *Neither* one brought matches to light the campfire.

USING INDEFINITE PRONOUNS CORRECTLY

Most indefinite pronouns indicate number. The plural forms seldom pose problems, but the singular forms are confusing, sometimes violating logic. For example, the word *everyone* means all, but *everyone* is singular and *all* is plural. Listed below are the most common *singular* pronouns:

anyone	everybody	somebody
anybody	everyone	one
either	someone	each
neither	no one	

An easy way to recall these eccentricities of usage is to remember that any pronoun containing *one* or *body* is singular. If you have trouble with *either, neither,* or *each,* then mentally add *one* and think *either one, neither one, each one.* Likewise, in a word that has the suffix *body,* substitute *one.* For *anybody,* think *anyone.* For *somebody,* think *someone.*

COMPOUND ANTECEDENTS AND PRONOUNS

Use a singular pronoun to refer to *singular* antecedents linked by *or* or *nor*:

▶ A cat or a dog needs *its* own bowl of fresh water, especially during the summer.

Use a plural pronoun to refer to *plural* antecedents linked by *neither* and *nor*:

▶ Neither friends nor family members gave *their* approval to the marriage.

Use a plural pronoun to refer to compound antecedents linked by *and*:

▶ Kerry and Daniel are taking *their* time.

Exception: Use a singular pronoun and a singular verb when a compound antecedent is preceded by *each* or *every*:

▶ Every cafe and restaurant in town *has seen its* business suffer.

▶ Each beauty salon and barber shop owner *has paid his* or *her* license fee.

6. **Avoid sexist use of pronouns.**

Since the early 1970s, we have become more aware that the English language discriminates against women in many ways. Some people object to word forms that contain the generic form *man* (meaning all people—the human race) and the use of the pronoun *he* when the referent could be female, as in "Everyone brought *his* cell phone." Below are two possible ways to handle the problem:

Use *he or she* and *his or her* sparingly.

One *he or she* or one *his or her* will not disrupt the flow of a sentence, but the repeated use of these terms can distract the reader. Instead, rewrite sentences, avoiding male and female pronouns. You can omit the third-person pronoun and repeat the noun. Consider the following correct examples:

▸ If a person is insincere, chances are that *his or her* insincerity will be detected.

▸ If a person is insincere, chances are that *the* insincerity will be detected. (preferable)

Write in the plural.

▸ If *people* are insincere, chances are that *their* insincerity will be detected. (preferable)

Some folks misuse *their* when referring to a singular subject. This colloquial usage is heard in sentences such as "*Everyone* should remember to take *their* ground cloth and hunting knife." For most writing, this sentence would be considered incorrect. Standard English is as follows:

- *Everyone* should remember to take *his* or *her* ground cloth and hunting knife.
- *All* should remember to pack *their* rain gear.
- Not *one* of the runners felt *she* had run *her* best.

USING *THEIR* CORRECTLY

---

7. **Use relative pronouns correctly.**

There are only six relative pronouns. You can easily memorize them as the "five *W*'s and a *T*." The six are *who, whom, whose, which, what,* and *that.*

Use *who* and *whom* correctly in questions.

▸ *Who* is calling? [subject]

▸ *Whose* gerbil is that? [possessive]

▸ *Whom* did Shelley call? [direct object]

▸ To *whom* am I speaking? [object of preposition]

▸ Will you give the message to *whomever* answers? [object of preposition]

Use *which* and *that* correctly.

That always introduces an essential clause and provides emphasis. *Which* carries less emphasis and can introduce either an essential or a nonessential clause. In the first sentence below, *that* introduces the *essential* adjective clause— no commas are needed. In the second example, *which* introduces the *nonessential* adjective clause and requires commas. Since a nonessential clause just gives extra information, the clause is enclosed by a pair of commas.

▶ The dog *that is wearing the collar* is mine. [essential clause]

▶ A dog, *which had no collar,* followed me home. [nonessential clause]

CASES OF RELATIVE PRONOUNS

Most relative pronouns have different case forms. When you write, choose the correct form of a pronoun, according to its use in the sentence—as a subject, object, or possessive.

Subjective	Objective	Possessive
who	whom	whose
which	which	whose
that	whom or which	whose
what	what	what

NOTE: *Who* and *whom* generally refer only to people. *That* can refer to anything. *Which* can refer to animals, places, or things. Sometimes *who* is used to refer to animals with names, but such usage is unusual.

1c. Adjectives

www.mhhe.com/dietsch

For online coverage of adjectives, check out: Editing>Adjectives and Adverbs

Adjectives modify nouns and pronouns. An adjective may modify in any of three ways: (1) by identifying the kind (*taupe* leather), (2) by indicating something (*this* cat, *that* dog, *those* men), (3) by stating how many (*nine* players, *few* customers). Usually, an adjective directly precedes the word it modifies.

▶ Jenny is wearing a *two-carat* diamond in *that* necklace.

▶ The *tall, elderly* man limped along.

Exceptions:

▶ Ian is *precocious.* [predicate adjective]

▶ The moon, *full* and *bright,* lighted our path. [stylistic reason]

www.mhhe.com/dietsch

You can find additional material on articles at: Editing>Articles

A, an, and *the*

These three little words are similar to adjectives because they modify nouns. *A* and *an* are actually classified as *indefinite articles*—they are not specific. *The* is classified as a *definite article* because it points to one certain item or person. *A* is used to precede words beginning with consonants. *An* precedes words that begin with vowels.

▶ *a* kitten   (general, nonspecific)

▶ *an* apricot   (general, nonspecific)

▶ *the* tiger-striped kitten   (one specific kitten)

1d. Verbs

www.mhhe.com/dietsch

If you want additional help using verbs and verb voice correctly, check out: Editing>Verb and Voice Shifts

Most verbs show action. These verbs can be written in the *active* or *passive voice,* although the active voice is generally used. *Be* verbs do not show action; they relate to our existence, to our being here on earth.

1. **Use the active voice of verbs unless there is a good reason for using the passive voice.**

When the subject performs the action, the verb is in the active voice. The passive voice occurs when the subject is not the doer of the action expressed by the verb.

▶ Sergei Grinkov *won* an Olympic gold medal twice. [active voice]

▶ Twice an Olympic gold medal *was won* by Sergei Grinkov. [passive voice]

Note: For a detailed explanation of active and passive voice, see chapter 7.

2. **Make subjects and verbs agree in number.**

www.mhhe.com/dietsch

You will find additional coverage of agreement at: Editing>Subject/Verb Agreement

Use singular verbs with singular subjects; use plural verbs with plural subjects. Verb agreement is sometimes a problem, particularly for international students. Although adding an *s* to a noun makes it plural, the opposite is true of verbs. Adding an *s* to a verb makes it *singular,* as shown here:

Singular	Plural
is	are
was	were
has	have
skates	skate
drives	drive

Words between the subject and verb

Words and phrases that appear between the subject and the verb sometimes mislead. In the following sentence, the verb is plural to agree with the plural subject:

▶ The letters, along with the package, *were* mailed today.

The word *package* is not the subject. But because *package* comes immediately before the verb, it may seem natural to use *was.* But this usage is incorrect. In the following sentences, *were* is correct:

▶ The letters and the package *were* mailed this morning.

▶ The package and the letters *were* mailed this morning. [preferable]

Compound subject linked with *or* or *nor*

Another troublemaker is the sentence that has a singular and a plural subject without *and*. Then the *subject nearest the verb* determines the agreement of the verb:

▶ Neither the cookies nor the fruitcake *was* fresh.

▶ Neither the fruitcake nor the cookies *were* fresh.

Inverted word order

In questions and in statements beginning with *there*, the subject usually follows the verb. Be careful that the verb agrees with the subject in such constructions.

▶ *Is* the box labeled and ready to go? (box *is*)

▶ There *are* three cashiers on duty right now. (cashiers *are*)

Relative pronoun subjects

In a clause beginning with a relative pronoun—*who, which,* or *that*—look for the antecedent of the pronoun to decide whether the verb is singular or plural.

▶ People who *litter* should be fined heavily. (people *litter*)

▶ This house, which *needs* some work, could be a bargain. (house *needs*)

3. **Use the correct tense of a verb.**

Most verbs pose no problem in regard to tense. But several require cautious use. Those verbs are the ones we focus on here. (If you have a question about the tense of a verb, consult your dictionary. Be aware that two or more forms are sometimes considered acceptable.)

Four verbs—*can, may, will,* and *shall*—are frequently misused because the tenses are mixed improperly. The lists below will help you keep the tenses straight.

Present Tense	Past Tense
can	could
may	might
will	would
shall	should

Six verbs—*lie, lay, sit, set, rise, raise*—commonly cause havoc for inexperienced writers. The following chart and explanation will help you use them correctly. Perhaps the best advice is to say the tenses for each verb aloud so that you become used to hearing each one correctly.

Six Troublesome Verbs

	Present Tense	Past Tense	Past Participle
	lie (to recline)	lay	(have) lain
	lay (to place an object)	laid	(had) laid
	sit (to take a seat)	sat	(has) sat
	set (to place an object)	set	(have) set
	rise (to get up)	rose	(had) risen
	raise (to list)	raised	(has) raised

To use the "troublesome six" correctly, just remember that *lay, sat,* and *raise*—when used in the active voice—all require direct objects. *Lie, sit,* and *rise* do not take objects. In the examples below, the direct objects are italicized.

Direct Objects	No Direct Objects
Please lay the *book* there.	Lie down, Rags.
Sharon laid her *coat* on the bed.	Jada has lain in the sun two hours.
Barry set his *briefcase* on my desk.	Harry sat there.
Connor raised the *blind*.	The sun rises at 6:30 a.m.

4. **Use the correct helping verb according to number and tense.**

Helping verbs assist other verbs in showing action or making a statement. Two or more verbs used together make up a *verb phrase.* The parts of a verb phrase may have intervening words.

▶ The bomb *had been concealed* underneath a cart of melons.

▶ The soldier *would* not *submit* to an anthrax vaccination. (*would submit* is the verb phrase)

Helping verbs must agree in number (be singular or plural) with the main verb and show the same tense.

The verbs below can work either alone or with other verbs as helpers. When these verbs are used alone, they are not helping verbs.

am	did	may	would
are	do	shall	will
is	has	has been	might
was	had	have	might have
were	can	could	

COMMON HELPING VERBS

5.   **Use verb forms correctly.**

It is not uncommon for individuals to grow up hearing incorrect verb forms. To them, standard verb forms sound strange. If you are in doubt about the correct verb form, check it out in a recent dictionary. A few usages have changed over time.

All verbs have four basic forms. These principal parts are the *infinitive, present participle, past,* and *past participle.* These basic forms can be varied by the addition of helping verbs or the preposition *to. To* indicates the infinitive, which is in the present tense (see page H-18).

Four Principal Parts

Infinitive	Present Participle	Past	Past Participle
(to) live	(is) living	lived	(has, have, or had) lived

Principal parts of irregular verbs

The following list of irregular verbs and their principal parts is based on the *American Heritage Dictionary,* 3rd edition. These verbs are used with helping verbs (such as *is, are, was, were, have, has, had, have been*) to form various tenses.

Present	Present Participle	Past	Past Participle
bear	(is, are) bearing	bore	(has, have, had) borne
beat	beating	beat	beaten
become	becoming	became	become
begin	beginning	began	begun
bite	biting	bit	bitten
blow	blowing	blew	blown
break	breaking	broke	broken
bring	bringing	brought	brought
burst	bursting	burst	burst
buy	buying	bought	bought
catch	catching	caught	caught
choose	choosing	chose	chosen
come	coming	came	come
cut	cutting	cut	cut
creep	creeping	crept	crept
dive	diving	dived	dived, dove

Present	Present Participle	Past	Past Participle
do	doing	did	done
draw	drawing	drew	drawn
drink	drinking	drank	drunk
drive	driving	drove	driven
eat	eating	ate	eaten
fall	falling	fell	fallen
find	finding	found	found
fling	flinging	flung	flung
fly	flying	flew	flown
forget	forgetting	forgot	forgot, forgotten
freeze	freezing	froze	frozen
get	getting	got	gotten, got
give	giving	gave	given
go	going	went	gone
grow	growing	grew	grown
hang (suspend)	hanging	hung	hung
hang (execute)	(is being) hanged	hanged	hanged
hit	hitting	hit	hit
hurt	hurting	hurt	hurt
keep	keeping	kept	kept
know	(is) known	knew	known
lead	leading	led	led
leave	leaving	left	left
lend	lending	lent	lent
let	letting	let	let
pay	paying	paid	paid
lose	losing	lost	lost
ride	riding	rode	ridden
ring	ringing	rang	rung
rise	rising	rose	risen

Present	Present Participle	Past	Past Participle
run	running	ran	run
say	saying	said	said
see	seeing	saw	seen
shake	shaking	shook	shaken
shine (the sun)	shining	shone	shone
shine (to polish)	shining	shined	shined
sing	singing	sang or sung	sung
sink	sinking	sank or sunk	sunk
speak	speaking	spoke	spoken
spring	springing	sprang, sprung	sprung
stand	standing	stood	stood
steal	stealing	stole	stolen
sting	stinging	stung	stung
strike	striking	struck	struck
swear	swearing	swore	sworn
swim	swimming	swam	swum
swing	swinging	swung	swung
take	taking	took	taken
teach	teaching	taught	taught
tear	tearing	tore	torn
tell	telling	told	told
throw	throwing	threw	thrown
wear	wearing	wore	worn
write	writing	wrote	written

6. **Use *be* correctly.**

The verb *be* should not be used as if it were a complete verb. Except in a few special instances (see the discussion of the subjunctive mood in the next section (1d.7), some other form of *be* or a helping verb such as *will* is required.

NONSTANDARD

I *be* a college student.

I *be* going there.

Mrs. Beck, you *be* leaving soon?

I *am* a college student.

I *am* going there.

Mrs. Beck, *will* you *be* leaving soon?

7.   Use the subjunctive mood correctly.

Verbs may show three moods: *indicative* (almost all verbs are in the indicative mood), *imperative* (expresses a request or command), or *subjunctive.* The subjunctive mood is commonly used in two ways: to express (1) a situation contrary to fact (unreal condition) or (2) a request, suggestion, wish, or order. Once in a while, the subjunctive mood is used to introduce a few idioms.

UNREAL CONDITIONS

▶ My husband acted as though he *were* an expert at ironing until he scorched a shirt.

▶ In Chicago's traffic jams, I felt as if I *were* having a bad dream.

▶ Terry could fix that leak if he *were* here.

REQUESTS, SUGGESTIONS, WISHES, OR ORDERS

▶ Her boss asked that she *remain* in the building during her coffee break.

▶ I wish I *were* going to Chicago with my friends.

▶ The company requires that I *be* on duty at 6:30 a.m.

▶ The committee agreed that Jane *be* given extra time to complete the project.

▶ Henry moved that the meeting *be* adjourned.

Note: *That* usually introduces the clauses above.

A FEW IDIOMS

▶ If this *be* true

▶ *Come* what may

▶ Far *be* it from me

▶ Long *wave* the stars and stripes!

8.   Avoid inappropriate shifts of tense, voice, or mood.

Inappropriate shifts in the tense, voice, or mood of verbs can be distracting and even confusing for the reader.

INAPPROPRIATE

▷ Before he *went* to class, he *drinks* three cups of coffee. [needless shift from past to present tense]

▷ A cocoon was sighted on a liatris plant, and in the spring a beautiful moth crept out. [needless shift from active to passive voice]

> *Go* to school, and *you should* take an umbrella. [needless shift from imperative to indicative mood]

APPROPRIATE

▶ Before he *goes* to class, he *drinks* three cups of coffee. [Both verbs are in the present tense.]

▶ On a liatris plant, I *found* a cocoon; and in the spring a beautiful moth *crept* out. [Both verbs are in the past tense and active voice.]

▶ *Go* to school and *take* an umbrella. [Both verbs are in the imperative mood.]

1e. Adverbs

www.mhhe.com/dietsch

For online coverage of adverbs, visit: Editing>Adjectives and Adverbs

An adverb is a word that modifies a verb, an adjective, or another adverb. An adverb may express how, where, when, to what degree, or under what conditions. *Not* is an adverb that makes an exception. Since adverbs are flexible, they may appear at various spots in a sentence. The usual place is after a verb or before an adjective or adverb.

▶ Tanya is *not* the one who threw the snowball. [adverb modifies verb; makes an exception]

▶ *Tomorrow* Riley will arrive. [adverb modifies verb; tells when]

▶ *Quickly,* Troy stepped out into the darkness. [adverb modifies verb; tells how]

▶ Kaia is a *very* good singer. [adverb modifies adjective; tells degree]

▶ Wade studied *quite* often and aced the exam. [adverb modifies adverb: tells how often]

Conjunctive adverbs

These adverbs link elements of equal rank. They can show addition, similarity, contrast, effect or result, time, emphasis, or example.

▶ We had intended a simple cookout; *however,* my sister brought all sorts of goodies.

▶ Shawn wrote an outstanding report; *in fact,* he edited it without staff help.

▶ Rags is well trained; *for example,* he will not accept food from strangers.

1f. Prepositions

A preposition usually precedes a noun or pronoun to make a prepositional phrase, as *for her.* In the phrase, the noun or pronoun is the object of the preposition. Sometimes a prepositional phrase also has other words:

See chapter 7.

▶ *under* the chair

▶ The cupboard *above the refrigerator* is hard to reach.

▶ *Near the barn* stood a large buck deer.

about	around	beside	from	on
above	at	between	in	over
across	before	beyond	like	past
after	behind	by	near	to
against	below	down	of	until
among	beneath	except	off	up

COMMON PREPOSITIONS

1g. Conjunctions

A conjunction is a word that connects words, phrases, or clauses. There are three types of conjunctions: *coordinating, correlative,* and *subordinating.* For detailed explanations, see chapter 7, "Restyling Sentences."

1. **Use coordinating conjunctions to join words, phrases, or main clauses.**

    ▶ Jan invited several neighbors, including you *and* me. [connects two pronouns]

    ▶ Over the bridge *and* through the tunnel, we go. [connects two prepositional phrases]

    ▶ Most of us sang carols on the ride home, *but* grandpa slept. [connects two main clauses]

2. **Use correlative conjunctions to join elements of equal grammatical importance.**

    Notice that correlative conjunctions always work in pairs.

    ▶ Ryan was *not only* the tallest player on the squad *but also* the best.

    ▶ *Either* we leave in plenty of time to reach the airport early *or* I'm not going.

3. **Use a subordinating conjunction to join a minor clause to a main clause.**

    ▶ Dustin bought municipal bonds *because* they are triple tax free.

    ▶ We stayed in the basement *until* the tornado had passed.

    Note: For *conjunctive adverbs,* see section 1e, "Adverbs."

1h. Interjections

An interjection is a word or phrase that conveys emotion yet has no grammatical connection to the sentence. Interjections are followed by an exclamation point or a comma, depending on the degree of emotion expressed.

▸ *Oh!* We just missed our train.

▸ *Ouch!* A splinter went into my finger.

▸ *Oh dear,* we are out of sugar.

1i.   Infinitives

An infinitive is a verb form that is preceded by *to*. An infinitive can be used as a noun or a modifier.

▸ *To travel* to Switzerland would be fascinating! [infinitive as the subject]

▸ However, my husband does not want *to go.* [infinitive as the object of a verb]

▸ Bret's motive for late-hours trading was *to gain* quick profits. [infinitive as a predicate nominative]

▸ She had the foresight *to reject* his offer. [infinitive acts as an adjective; modifies *foresight*]

▸ All her life Carrie has studied *to learn.* [infinitive modifies the verb *studied*]

Notes:

1. When complements or modifiers are added to an infinitive, an *infinitive phrase* results:

   ▸ *To save money,* she clips coupons.

2. Notice that an infinitive phrase differs from a prepositional phrase. A prepositional phrase never contains a verb.

Split infinitives

When a word intrudes between the parts of an infinitive, the result is a *split infinitive.* Authorities disagree about the use of a split infinitive. Since it sometimes impedes the flow of a sentence and offends readers, many instructors prefer that students avoid this construction. In rare cases, if the traditional use of the infinitive is unclear or awkward, then split the infinitive.

UNTRADITIONAL

▸ *To properly work,* a curling iron needs to heat for a few minutes. [split infinitive]

TRADITIONAL

▸ *To work* properly, a curling iron needs to heat for a few minutes.

1j.   Gerunds and Gerund Phrases

A gerund is a *verbal noun,* formed by adding *-ing* to certain verbs. For example, if you add *-ing* to *drive,* you have *driving,* which can be used as a noun, as in

"*Driving* can be dangerous." You can tell when the same word is used as a verb because it requires a helping verb, as in "He *is driving* a new car."

1. **Use a gerund as you would a noun.**

    Like a noun, a gerund can be used as a subject, object of a verb, object of a preposition, or predicate nominative.

    ▸ *Coasting* down a high hill on a sled is fun. [subject]

    ▸ Haley quietly watched his *juggling* of five balls. [object of a verb]

    ▸ The neighbors objected to his *practicing* on the drums outside. [object of a preposition]

    ▸ Happiness for Rachel was *winning!* [predicate nominative]

2. **Use a gerund phrase as you would a noun.**

    A gerund phrase consists of a gerund and its modifiers or complements. A gerund phrase can be used in four ways:

    ▸ *Finding a four-leaf clover* is thought by some folks to bring good luck. [subject]

    ▸ Caitlin and Michael went *mushroom hunting.* [object of verb]

    ▸ Nikki's goal in *fishing for bass* was to catch enough for supper. [object of preposition]

    ▸ Happiness for Jerry was *winning the race.* [predicate nominative]

1k. Dangling Participles and Other Misplaced Modifiers

Dangling participles interfere with clarity and logic. Other modifiers such as misplaced participial phrases, adverb clauses, and adverbs can also cause problems. These errors can be found not only in student writing but also in advertisements, newspaper articles, and other media.

1. **Avoid dangling modifiers.**

www.mhhe.com/dietsch
For additional coverage of modifiers, check out:
Editing>Dangling Modifiers

    Dangling modifiers are phrases that lack a referent. The noun or pronoun needed to make the phrase clear and logical has been omitted or placed somewhere else in the sentence. Usually, a dangling modifier clings precariously at the beginning of a sentence with an incorrect subject following it.

Dangling participles and participial phrases

A *participle* is a verb form that ends in -*ing* or -*ed*. When used with other words as a modifier, the result is a *participial phrase*. Whenever you begin a sentence with a participle or participial phrase, check to see that the correct subject follows.

INCORRECT

▸ *Lifting her over the fence,* her coat caught on the barbed wire. (Who is lifting her?)

> After standing up well under the two-year exposure test, the *manufacturers* were convinced that the paint was sufficiently durable. (The manufacturers stood up well?)

> Absorbed in a mystery novel, the oven timer went unheard. (Who is absorbed?)

REVISED

▸ As *he lifted* her over the fence, her coat caught on the barbed wire.

▸ After *the paint* stood up well under the two-year exposure test, the manufacturers were convinced that it was sufficiently durable.

▸ Absorbed in a mystery novel, *he did not hear* the oven timer.

Dangling adverb clause

INCORRECT

> When only a youngster in grade school, *my father* instructed me in the art of boxing. (Who was in grade school?)

REVISED

▸ When *I was* only a youngster in grade school, my father instructed me in the art of boxing.

2. Avoid other misplaced modifiers.

Misplaced modifiers are simply out-of-place words or phrases. They sneak into places they do not belong. For example, *only* is an impudent pest that cuts into line ahead of other words. Although *only* may seem small and harmless in the wrong place, don't overlook its misbehavior. Yank it back to where it belongs, close to the word it limits. Consider some examples:

MISPLACED

> "Who says kids *only* like junk food?" (ad for spaghetti)

> "If *only* your feet could talk." (ad for podiatrist)

> "If you *only* inspect your draft sentence by sentence, you can easily overlook how its parts work together." (a textbook)

REVISED

▸ Who says kids like *only* junk food?

▸ If your feet could *only* talk.

▸ If you inspect your draft *only* sentence by sentence, you can easily overlook how its parts work together.

The adverbs *almost* and *even* are other frequent offenders. Like *only*, they should precede the word they modify:

MISPLACED

▶ She *almost* used the entire bottle of bath oil for one bath.

▶ I *even* felt worse after I took the medicine.

REVISED

▶ She used *almost* the entire bottle of bath oil for one bath.

▶ I felt *even* worse after I took the medicine.

Clauses and phrases may also be misplaced in sentences, leading to humorous misreadings:

MISPLACED

▶ Faith wore a flower in her hair that was pink. (What was pink?)

▶ Jerry kept an odd-shaped piece of jade in his jacket pocket, *which he considered lucky.* (What was lucky?)

▶ I easily spotted the rare bird *using highly powered binoculars.* (Was the bird using binoculars?)

REVISED

▶ In her hair Faith wore a flower that was pink. (Or: pink flower)

▶ Jerry kept an odd-shaped piece of jade, which he considered lucky, in his jacket pocket.

▶ Using highly powered binoculars, I easily spotted the rare bird.

Note: Probably the best way to find such tangled syntax is to read your writing aloud and listen carefully. Does each sentence make sense? Beware of answering in the affirmative too quickly. Writers know what they mean. *The question is whether each sentence will be clear and logical to readers.*

1l. Use *Like* Correctly

1. **Use *like* as a preposition.**

   ▶ Jenny looks *like* her aunt.

   ▶ *Like* me, Bill enjoys jazz.

   ▶ It is not *like* him to be late.

   ▶ I feel *like* resting.

2. **Use *like* as an adjective, meaning "similar, equal, or alike."**

   ▶ I used one-half cup of butter and a *like* amount of flour.

   ▶ My grandmother used to say, "*Like* father, *like* son."

3. Use *as if*, not *like*, as a conjunction to connect two independent clauses.

INCORRECT

> None of the teenagers lit their cigarettes *like* they were used to smoking.

> Lola acted *like* she was angry with me.

CORRECT

▶ None of the teenagers lit their cigarettes *as if* they were used to smoking.

▶ Lola acted *as if* she were angry with me.

1m. Sentence Fragments

www.mhhe.com/dietsch

If you want more information on sentence fragments, go to:

Editing>Sentence Fragments

A fragment is a portion of a sentence that is punctuated as if it were an entire sentence. Lacking a subject, a verb, or both, a fragment is an incomplete thought. A fragment may be a word, a phrase, a dependent clause, or any combination of words that deviate from the basic requirement of a subject and verb (or verb-subject) needed for a complete sentence.

Traditionally, sentence fragments have been frowned on and complete sentences advocated except in dialogue, conversation, and other informal situations. In formal writing, fragments are avoided in all but a few special circumstances.

USING FRAGMENTS FOR A PURPOSE

To be effective, a fragment should have a purpose consistent with the rhetorical situation. The writer who uses fragments carelessly risks not only appearing unknowledgeable but also being misunderstood. The most important special uses of the fragment are exclamations, requests, commands, or answers to questions.

- *No! Not really!* **[exclamation]**
- *Please, no smoking.* **[request]**
- *Ready, get set, go!* **[command]**
- [When is the next meeting?] *Thursday at 2:30 p.m.* **[answer to a question]**

1. Avoid using *-ing* words or *infinitives* as main verbs, thus creating a fragment.

INCORRECT

> *Driving* 100 miles a day to and from classes, *doing* complex assignments, and *raising* a family. I found that my undergraduate days were exhausting. [The first group of words is a fragment.]

> Owen and Shane stayed home last night. The reason *being* that they were broke. [The second group of words is a fragment.]

> First, the proper equipment *to get* out on the lake or pond. A canoe with a paddle or chest waders will do the job. [The first group of words is a fragment.]

CORRECT

▸ *Driving* 100 miles a day to and from classes, *doing* complex assignments, and *raising* a family, I found that my undergraduate days were exhausting. [Join the fragment to the sentence with a comma.]

▸ Owen and Shane stayed home last night *because* they had no money. [The fragment and the sentence could be joined with a comma, but the result would be wordy.]

▸ First, *gather* the proper equipment to get out on the lake or pond. Either a canoe with a paddle or chest waders will do the job. [Add a verb to the first word group; the subject is understood to be *you,* meaning "you gather."]

2. **Avoid treating phrases that merely add additional details as complete sentences.**

INCORRECT

> Then there is the high-speed driver. *A real maniac.*

> Brayden called his father collect last night. *To ask for a loan.*

> The company refused to honor the warranty. *Even though I purchased the lawn mower only six months ago.*

CORRECT

▸ Then there is the high-speed driver, a real maniac.

▸ Brayden called his father collect last night to ask for a loan.

▸ The company refused to honor the warranty even though I purchased the lawn mower only six months ago. [The fragment is added to the complete sentence that precedes it.]

3. **Avoid treating dependent clauses as complete sentences.**

INCORRECT

> *After I learned the market price for comparable antique tables.* I decided to rescue mine from the attic and refinish it.

CORRECT

▸ After I learned the market price for comparable antique tables, I decided to rescue mine from the attic and refinish it. [The introductory adverb clause is made a part of the sentence with a comma.]

2. Punctuation

The purpose of punctuation is to clarify the meaning of a sentence. Even punctuation so small as a comma can be significant. The omission of a comma in a contract can change the interpretation—possibly leading to a loss or a lawsuit. In the following sentence, notice how the insertion of punctuation changes the meaning:

- ▶ Woman without her man is nothing.

- ▶ Woman: without her, man is nothing.

Unnecessary punctuation can obscure the meaning, distract, and annoy. To improve your writing, learn the basic rules and use punctuation for a purpose.

2a. Comma (,)

www.mhhe.com/dietsch

For online coverage of commas, go to: Editing>Commas

The primary task of the comma is to clarify by indicating sentence structure. Commas should be used for a reason. (The old general rule to insert a comma for a pause does not always work.) In fact, many comma errors are due to unnecessary commas. To guide you, here are three "Don'ts":

- ❭ Do not place a comma before a parenthesis.
- ❭ Do not place a comma between a verb and a direct object.
- ❭ Do not insert a comma if you lack a reason.

1. **Use a comma to separate a series of coordinate words, phrases, and clauses.**

   - ▶ The Delany children were named *Lemuel, Sarah, Elizabeth, Julia, Henry, Lucius, Manross, Hubert, Laura,* and *Samuel.* [a series of nouns]

   - ▶ A 1994 book by Sadie and Bessie Delany *made the best-selling nonfiction list, ran as a successful play,* and *won several awards.* [a series of verb phrases]

   - ▶ Sarah "Sadie" Delany, *by completing normal school, graduating from Columbia University's Teachers College,* and *circumventing prejudice,* gained a teaching position in an all-white New York City school during the Depression. [a series of participial phrases]

   - ▶ *If Sadie had accepted the stereotypes of the times, if she had succumbed to the racial barriers, if she had rejected the long hours of work and study,* she would have remained in the South, uneducated and unknown. [a series of adverb clauses]

   (For more information and examples of coordination, see "Parallel Items in a Series," chapter 7.)

2. **Use a comma to separate addresses, dates, and titles.**

   - ▶ In the late 1890s Henry and Nanny Delany lived with their ten children in a small house on the campus of *Saint Augustine's School, Raleigh, North Carolina.*

▸ Elizabeth "Bessie" Delany was born on *September 3, 1891.*

▸ In 1918 Henry Beard Delany, *Jr.,* encouraged his sister to become a dentist, too.

▸ Bessie Delany, *DDS,* became the second black woman licensed in New York City to practice dentistry.

3. **Place a comma before a coordinating conjunction that joins independent clauses (clauses that could be complete sentences).**

The coordinating conjunctions are *for, and, nor, but, or, yet, so.* (See chapter 7 for more on joining independent clauses.)

▸ In 1869 the territory of Wyoming granted women the right to vote, *but* Amendment 19 to the Constitution did not become law until August 1920.

4. **Use a comma to separate an introductory subordinate clause from the main part of the sentence.**

When the introductory clause is short and will not be misread, the comma may be omitted. (See chapter 7 for more on subordinate clauses.)

▸ *After Victoria Claflin Woodhull became one of the first two female stock-brokers in the United States,* she became, in 1872, the first woman to run for the presidency.

5. **Use a comma after an introductory participial phrase or infinitive phrase.**

▸ *Living in Tasmania and southern Australia,* wombats are marsupials that feed on roots, leaves, and vegetables.

▸ *To see a wombat,* you must look at night.

6. **Use a comma after two or more introductory prepositional phrases or a long introductory prepositional phrase (a good rule of thumb is four words or more).**

▸ *In the icy waters of the North Atlantic,* the savage wolf fish grows up to three feet long. *Along the sea bottom,* the sea robin walks on its breast fin rays, looking for food.

7. **Use commas to set off transitional expressions and conjunctive adverbs.**

Transitional expressions include phrases such as *in fact* and *for example.* Conjunctive adverbs include words such as *however, consequently,* and *therefore.*

▸ *Finally,* the floodwaters receded after ten days of rain.

▸ It was, *in fact,* the worst flooding on record in the region.

▸ Flooding is common in the area; *consequently,* people are being discouraged from rebuilding homes there.

8. Use commas to set off nonessential (nonrestrictive) elements.

Use a comma to set off tag words such as *well, yes,* and *isn't it* at the beginning or end of a sentence.

▶ *Yes,* you really did win a new Lexus.

▶ You are a very lucky fellow, *aren't you?*

Use a *pair* of commas to set off nonessential phrases and clauses that interrupt the flow of a sentence.

▶ One department head, *working late,* inadvertently erased the weekly sales report.

▶ Ricardo Alvarez, *a business owner,* joined our Toastmasters' Club last week.

▶ Our students, *who come from surrounding counties,* usually commute daily.

9. Use a comma to set off a contrasting expression.

▶ My billfold is lying on the dresser, *not the chair.*

10. Use a comma to prevent misreading.

Sometimes a comma is needed for clarity.

▶ Inside, the stereo was going full blast.

▶ Outside, the children were roaring around the house on their motorbikes.

11. Use commas to set off a speaker tag or source tag from a direct quotation.

A speaker tag or source tag identifies the speaker or writer and includes a verb of saying, such as *said, called, asked,* or *wrote.*

▶ *Derek yelled,* "Get out! The rear tire is on fire!"

▶ "The law must be stable," *wrote Roscoe Pound,* "but it must not stand still."

Note that when the speaker tag follows a quotation or part of a quotation, the comma preceding it is placed inside the quotation marks.

2b. Semicolon (;)

www.mhhe.com/dietsch

For more help using semicolons, visit:
Editing>Semicolons

Basically, the semicolon has only two uses. If you understand the rules governing it, you should be able to use the semicolon with confidence. Remember that the semicolon is a stronger mark of punctuation than the comma and that it is used for the *larger* divisions within a sentence.

1. **Use a semicolon to connect two closely related independent clauses not joined by a comma and a coordinating conjunction (*and, but, or, nor, for, so,* and *yet*). (See "Compound Sentences," chapter 7.)**

   ▸ Representatives from every state attended the Democratic Convention; the majority voted against "open rule."

2. **Use a semicolon between two independent clauses joined by a conjunctive adverb or other transitional expression.**

   ▸ Sue is an accounting major; *however,* she plans to switch to engineering.

   ▸ Kevin was not feeling well; *nonetheless,* he went to the dance.

   Note that using a comma instead of a semicolon before a conjunctive adverb such as *nevertheless, however,* or *therefore* at the junction of two independent clauses results in an error called a comma splice. (For more on comma splices, see the box in chapter 7, "Avoiding Comma Splices and Fused Sentences.")

3. **Replace commas with semicolons for clarity when items in a series already contain commas.**

   ▸ Here is our new slate of officers: *Jean Henson, president; Mike Henry, vice president; Scott Trainor, treasurer; and Mary Wiley, secretary.*

4. **If there are commas within the independent clauses of a sentence, use a semicolon rather than a comma before the coordinating conjunction.**

   ▸ The Harvest House, a new restaurant on Center Street, features ethnic foods; and the crowds, surprisingly large for a small town, flock in.

2c. Colon (:)

A colon is used after an independent clause to signal that something will follow.

1. **Use a colon to precede a list or series that does not fit smoothly into a sentence.**

   ▸ Sue ordered the following items: *one pair of scissors, two yards of denim, one thimble, and one tape measure.*

   ▸ Nanette will need these tools: *needle-nose pliers, a monkey wrench, a claw hammer, and a hacksaw.*

   Note: Do not use a colon after a verb or preposition.

   INCORRECT

   ▸ My grocery list included: zucchini, papaya, mangoes, and sunflower seeds. [The colon is not needed.]

www.mhhe.com/dietsch

To learn more about colon use, check out:
Editing>Colons

2. **Use a colon to formally introduce a quotation.**

▸ My point can be summarized in the words of Edward Haines: "With every civil right there has to be a corresponding civil obligation."

3. **Use a colon between independent clauses when the second explains the first.**

▸ Jim has a real problem: his hair started falling out last month.

▸ "Let the world slip: we shall ne'er be younger." (William Shakespeare, *The Taming of the Shrew*)

4. **Use a colon in biblical references, in expressions of time, and after salutations in business letters.**

▸ Psalm 27:3   ▸ 6:05 p.m.   ▸ Dear Ms. Brown:

2d. Apostrophe (')

www.mhhe.com/dietsch

For additional coverage of apostrophes, go to:
Editing>Apostrophes

The little apostrophe is one of the most abused marks of punctuation. Often apostrophes are inserted where they are unneeded. The apostrophe has *three* basic uses: to form possessives, to form a few plurals, and to indicate certain omissions.

1. **Use an apostrophe with *s* to form the possessive of singular nouns and irregular plural nouns not ending in *s*.**

▸ today's fashions   ▸ children's toys

▸ men's clothing   ▸ the city's attractions

▸ my mother's life   ▸ mice's life spans

Note: When adding *s* to form the possessive sounds awkward in speech, some writers add only an apostrophe in writing: *Mr. Rogers' neighborhood, Charles' sons.* But it is never incorrect to add both an apostrophe and *s* for such words. Whichever practice you adopt, be consistent.

2. **Add only an apostrophe to form the possessive of a plural noun ending in *s*.**

▸ boys' jeans   ▸ horses' manes   ▸ butterflies' wings

3. **Indefinite pronouns (*anyone, everyone, everybody, nobody, one*) in the possessive case are treated like singular nouns and require an apostrophe before *s*.**

▸ Everyone's invitation was mailed.

▸ Anybody's guess is as good as mine.

▸ Someone's coat was left outside.

▸ Each one's jacket was labeled.

▶ No one's car was ticketed.

▶ Nobody's name was omitted.

4. **To show joint possession and to show possession with hyphenated terms and names of organizations, make only the last word possessive.**

▶ Bill and Thad's boat   ▶ father-in-law's car

▶ Cutter and Holt's Welding Company

5. **To show individual possession, use an apostrophe with each name.**

▶ Sue's and Joan's themes are late.

6. **Use an apostrophe to form the possessive of words referring to time or to amounts of money.**

▶ a minute's rest   ▶ two years' time

▶ two hours' work   ▶ one cent's worth

▶ three days' pay   ▶ two dollars' worth

▶ a week's wages   ▶ a dime's worth

▶ one month's rent

7. **Use an apostrophe to form the plurals of numbers, letters, symbols, and words referred to as words. (Sometimes the apostrophe is omitted if there is no problem of clarity.)**

▶ My house number is simply three 7's, or 777.

▶ *Occasionally* is spelled with two *c*'s and one *s*.

▶ How many ='s should there be in this equation?

▶ Ashley had three *and*'s in one sentence.

8. **Use an apostrophe to replace omitted letters or numbers in a contraction.**

▶ They don't know when they'll be called back to work. [*do not; they will*]

▶ Terry can't go until tomorrow. [*cannot*]

▶ It's his turn. [*It is*]

▶ The class of '89 is planning a reunion. [*1989*]

Note: Do not confuse *it's* with the possessive pronoun *its*, which does not require an apostrophe: "The cat lost its catnip mouse." (*Its*, like *his* and *hers*, is in the possessive case.)

2e. Dash (—)

Dashes, parentheses, and brackets share a basic function: to set off information from the rest of the sentence. But these marks of punctuation differ in effect.

Dashes emphasize material whereas parentheses de-emphasize. Brackets are generally used to enclose clarifying information in direct quotations.

The dash is informal punctuation that indicates an interruption of a sentence. A dash can signal a break in thought or provide special emphasis. Often used in pairs, dashes are bold and dramatic—as long as they are used sparingly. (If your keyboard lacks a dash, use two hyphens without spacing.)

1. **Use a dash or a pair of dashes to emphasize an appositive or other explanatory material.**

   ▶ "Soon members of the PMAC—referred to as the Derg—were dispatching their 'enemies' without trials."

   ▶ "There was not—and never had been—a Communist Party in Ethiopia: the country was linked to the West and dependent on free-world aid."

   ▶ "Soon he realized that his one hope was to make contact with two notorious smugglers who might guide him out—an idea fraught with risk."

   ▶ "He had to do this—regardless of the consequences."

   Note: The preceding examples of dashes are taken from "Escape from Ethiopia," by Trevor Armbrister.

2. **For clarity, use a dash or a pair of dashes to set off nonrestrictive (nonessential) elements containing commas.**

   ▶ The Kincaid triplets—Jane, Janice, and Jeanette—enrolled in Miss Hickman's first-grade class.

3. **Use a dash or a pair of dashes to set off interrupters or to indicate a pause.**

   ▶ Sarah has twenty—yes, twenty—Angora cats!

   ▶ That cat is a nuisance—just a big, fat freeloader.

2f. Parentheses ( )

You might think of the parenthesis as a whisper whereas the dash is more like a shout. For a discussion of the basic functions and different effects of parentheses and dashes, see the first paragraph of section 2e in this handbook.

1. **Use parentheses to enclose (and de-emphasize) nonessential material.**

   ▶ The United States two-cent piece (issued in 1864) was the first coin with the motto "In God We Trust."

2. **Use parentheses to enclose explanations or definitions.**

   ▶ According to the National Association of Insurance Commissioners (NAIC), faked car accidents and phony insurance claims have been increasing.

▶ The NAIC says that the increase in fraud claims is partly the result of no-fault auto insurance (requires insurers to pay up to $250,000, regardless of the cause).

▶ Semicolons have only two basic uses (see section 2b).

3. **In some documentation styles, use parentheses to enclose reference information such as page numbers or dates.**

▶ In *The Laughter Prescription,* Dr. Lawrence J. Peter advises making "yourself the target of your own quips" (146).

(For more information on documentation styles, see chapters 28 and 29.)

4. **Occasionally an entire sentence or more is enclosed in parentheses as a kind of aside.**

▶ "In a Pullman berth, a man can truly be alone with himself. (The nearest approach to this condition is to be found in a hotel bedroom, but a hotel room can be mighty depressing sometimes, it stands so still.)"

Note: The preceding sentence is from E. B. White, "Progress and Change."

2g. Brackets [ ]

1. **Use brackets to insert explanatory material in a quotation:**

▶ E. B. White wrote: "In a Pullman berth [a curtained bunk on a sleeping car of a train], a man can truly be alone with himself. . . ."

▶ Euripides wrote: "This is courage in a [person]: to bear unflinchingly what heaven sends." The original passage says "man." It was updated to avoid sexism.

2. **For clarity, use brackets instead of parentheses to enclose material already within parentheses.**

▶ We should be sure to give Emanuel Foose (and his brother Emilio [1812–1882] as well) credit for his role in founding the institute.

(For more on using brackets in quoted material, see chapter 29.)

2h. Hyphen (-)

www.mhhe.com/dietsch
To learn more about hyphen use, go to:
Editing>Hyphen

1. **Use a hyphen to divide a word at the end of a line.**

At least one syllable of three or more letters should be before the division: *con-sequently.*

2. **Use a hyphen in spelled-out compound numbers from twenty-one through ninety-nine.**

3. **Use a hyphen in spelled-out fractions.**

▶ one-fourth

▶ two-thirds

▶ five-eighths

▶ four and one-third

4. **Use a hyphen between two or more words used together as a modifier before a noun (unless the first word ends in *ly*).**

    ▶ thought-provoking speech

    ▶ problem-solving quiz

    ▶ rosy-cheeked baby

    ▶ lightly salted peanuts

    ▶ all-out effort

    ▶ on-the-job training

    ▶ up-to-date data

    ▶ highly rated programs

    Exception: Do not hyphenate when such modifiers do not precede the noun they modify.

    ▶ The quiz was about problem solving.

    ▶ The baby was rosy cheeked.

    ▶ Training was conducted on the job.

    ▶ The data were up to date.

5. *Rule of Suspension:* **Use suspended hyphens (hyphens followed by a space or by punctuation and a space) in a series of compounds having the same main elements.**

    ▶ Ann organized her essay in most- to least-important order.

    ▶ The first- and second-grade students no longer have a recess.

    ▶ Our local preschool accepts two-, three-, and four-year-old children.

    ▶ Nineteenth- and twentieth-century American literature can provide insight into the emancipation of women.

6. **Use a hyphen with certain prefixes.**

    These include *ex-* and *self-* with the exceptions of *selfless* and *selfsame*. There is no hard-and-fast rule about other prefixes such as *anti-, co-, pre-, pro-, re-,* and *well-.* Check an up-to-date dictionary, and if given a choice, be consistent.

    ▶ anti-intellectual

    ▶ co-owner

    ▶ ex-president

    ▶ pre-election

    ▶ self-denial

    ▶ well-being

    Note: Always use a hyphen when the word to be prefixed begins with a capital as in *pro-American, non-British,* or *mid-July.*

7. **Use a hyphen to avoid doubling a letter and to avoid confusion.**

    ▶ semi-invalid [avoids *semiinvalid*]

    ▶ re-enlist [avoids *reenlist*]

    ▶ re-form [avoids confusion with *reform*]

2i. Slash (/)

1. **In certain situations, such as highly informal writing or technical papers, use a slash to replace *or*, which is ordinarily required to show alternatives.**

    ▶ all ready/already   ▶ radio/television   ▶ to/too/two

    Note: Many readers object to the use of *and/or*. Often *and* or *or* is sufficient.

2. **Use a slash to separate elements in certain expressions.**

    ▶ Dates: 1998/99   ▶ Fractions: 1/4

    ▶ Places: Dallas/Fort Worth

3. **Use slashes (with a space on each side of the slash) in prose to indicate divisions between lines of poetry.**

    ▶ Shakespeare writes: "Like as the waves make towards the pebbled shore, / So do our minutes hasten to their end. . . ."

    (See "Preparing an Analysis of a Poem," chapter 22.)

2j. Quotation Marks (" ")

www.mhhe.com/dietsch
For additional information on quotation marks, go to: Editing>Quotation Marks

Although quotation marks have more than one use, they usually indicate the beginning and end of someone's exact words. Dialogue requires quotation marks. Citations require quotation marks (see chapter 29). Quotation marks may also be used to indicate words used in special ways. Titles of short written works or parts of works are enclosed with quotation marks.

1. **Use quotation marks in dialogue to enclose the exact words of a speaker.**

    ▶ Phoebe called, "Sparky, bring that shoe back here!"

    ▶ "Come on, Sparky," she cajoled, "bring the shoe back, and I'll give you some Teeny Bits."

2. **Use quotation marks to enclose short direct quotations.**

    Short is defined differently in different documentation styles. The most commonly used style in English, that of the Modern Language Association (MLA), defines *short* as four lines or less. (Long quotations are indented. For more on quoting sources, see chapter 29.)

    ▶ In *The Conduct of Life,* Emerson wrote as follows: "The art of conversation, or the qualification for a good companion, is a certain self-control, which now holds the subject, now lets it go, with a respect for the emergencies of the moment."

3. **Use quotation marks to enclose the titles of parts of books and periodicals.**

    Because this rule is often confused, here is an informal guideline that will help you remember the principle: Underline (italicize) the title or name of a whole item; use quotation marks around the title of a part. The lists below indicate how the guideline applies:

Underline "Whole" Items	Use Quotation Marks for "Parts"
book title	chapter or story title
songbook title	song title
poetry book title	poem title
title of a very long poem (e.g., *Paradise Lost*)	
name of a newspaper	comic, article, or feature title
name of a magazine	article, feature, or story title
pamphlet title	speech, short report
name of a plane, ship, or train	
title of a film, painting, record album, television or radio program	title of an episode of a radio or television series

Finally, a writer does not underline or use quotation marks with his or her own title at the beginning of a work. (See also section 2k on italics [underlining].)

4.   Use single quotation marks to enclose a quotation within a quotation.

If a quotation occurs within a quotation already marked with double quotation marks, enclose the inside quotation in single quotation marks. This will sometimes result in three quotation marks at the end of the quotation.

▶ "You must have read Eiseley's 'The Real Secret of Piltdown,'" Bill's friend observed.

Note: In ordinary American usage, the only exceptions to the use of double quotation marks for main, or outside, quotations are long quotations (block quotations), which are not placed within quotation marks because they are indented. (See chapter 29.)

5.   Traditionally, quotation marks were used to enclose words discussed as words. However, many writers now prefer italics for this purpose (see also section 2k, "Italics").

▶ "Computer" is derived from the Latin verb *computare*.

6.   Use quotation marks to enclose words used in a special or ironic sense.

▶ What chain of events caused the sinking of an "unsinkable" ship such as the *Titanic?*

Note: Do not use quotation marks for emphasis. The effect can be unintentionally ironic and humorous: Jordan Bailey, "President"; "I'm sure your 'wife' will enjoy the ring you bought at our store."

7.   Use other punctuation with quotation marks correctly.

Commas and periods always go *inside* closing quotation marks (except in one documentation situation). Colons and semicolons always go *outside* closing quotation marks. The rule for all other punctuation is that if the punctuation is part of the quotation, it goes inside, and if it is not part of the quotation, it goes outside.

▶ "Reading *Space Technology* gives me the insider's view," he says, adding, "It's like having all the top officials sitting in my office for a discussion."

▶ He said, "I will pay the full amount"; this certainly surprised us.

▶ She has two favorite "sports": eating and sleeping.

2k.   *Italics* (<u>Underlining</u>)

www.mhhe.com/dietsch
For more information about the use of italics, visit:
Editing>Italics

Italics is a typeface that slants to the right (*Moby Dick*). If your keyboard does not have italics, underline instead. Italics and underlining can indicate foreign words; special names of vehicles, vessels, or artworks; words used as words; and titles of long works. Since many foreign words have been adopted into English, check a dictionary to see whether or not they should be italicized. Direct quotations in another language are not italicized.

1.   Use italics (underlining) for titles of long works.

For a discussion of when to use italics and when to use quotation marks in titles, see section 2j.3 of this handbook. The treatment of titles differs from one documentation style to another. (For more information on titles of sources in research papers, see chapter 29.) Listed here are the most common kinds of works with italicized titles:

- **books:** *A Tale of Two Cities*
- *Exception:* Do not use italics (or underlining) for the names of sacred books: the Bible (or the Holy Bible), the New Testament, the Koran, and so forth.
- **long poems:** *Paradise Lost; The Iliad; The Wasteland*
- **newspapers and magazines:** the *New York Times; National Geographic*
- **pamphlets:** *Letters from an American Farmer*
- **vessels (planes, trains, ships, spacecraft):** the *Titanic;* the *Burlington Zephyr; Challenger*
- **plays:** *Hamlet; The Music Man*
- **comic strips:** *Doonesbury*
- **films and television and radio programs:** *Aladdin; The X-Files; A Prairie Home Companion*
- **albums and long musical works:** *Thriller;* Mahler's *Symphony No. 9*

- **paintings and sculpture:** da Vinci's *Mona Lisa;* Michelangelo's *David*
- **software:** *Windows XP; PageMaker 7.*

2.   **For clarity, use italics for words discussed as words, particularly when quotation marks are used in the same sentence for another purpose.**

▸ The word *boudoir* comes from an Old French verb, meaning "to pout or sulk."

3.   **Use italics for emphasis, but do so sparingly.**

▸ Trust me—take Route 315, *not* Route 23.

▸ What is the *evidence* for that position?

2l.   Ellipsis (. . .)

An ellipsis is a set of three spaced dots that indicate an omission. When an omission occurs at the beginning of a quotation, an ellipsis is *not* necessary; but an omission in the middle or at the end requires an ellipsis. To shorten a quotation, you can use an ellipsis as long as you do not distort the meaning. When omitting a word, phrase, sentence, or more, be guided by integrity: Is the result fair to the author? Is it grammatically correct?

Although the fifth edition of the *MLA Handbook* included the use of brackets to distinguish between your ellipses and the spaced periods that sometimes appear in works, the sixth edition of the *MLA Handbook* has reverted to the traditional use of ellipses, shown in earlier editions. Your instructor may decide to follow either style. The examples that follow reflect *traditional* usage. The first two are based on an excerpt from Linda Ryberg's "The Midwest Salutes Its Swedish Roots" in *Midwest Living* June 1996.

ORIGINAL

A harsh first winter on the windswept Illinois prairie in 1846 couldn't stop a tiny group of Swedish immigrants from prospering in the town they founded and named Bishop Hill. After all, they'd crossed the Atlantic, sailed the Great Lakes, and walked 160 miles southwest from Chicago to get there.

1.   **Use an ellipsis to show an omission in the middle of a quotation.**

▸ Tracing the history of an Illinois town, Linda Ryberg writes: "A harsh first winter . . . in 1846 couldn't stop a tiny group of Swedish immigrants from prospering in the town they founded and named Bishop Hill."

2.   **Use an ellipsis to show an omission at the end of a quotation.**

▸ Linda Ryberg, tracing the history of Bishop Hill, Illinois, explains that in 1846 a small band of Swedish settlers "crossed the Atlantic, sailed the Great Lakes, and walked 160 miles southwest from Chicago. . . ."

▸ Linda Ryberg, tracing the history of Bishop Hill, Illinois, explains that in 1846 a small band of Swedish settlers "crossed the Atlantic, sailed the Great Lakes, and walked 160 miles southwest from Chicago . . ." (40).

Note: Since there is no parenthetical reference in the first example, the sentence period is placed flush against the last word within the quotation marks. In the second example, however, the sentence period is placed after the parenthetical reference of this short quotation. (For information on using ellipses in long quotations, see chapter 29.)

3. **Use an entire line of ellipsis points to indicate omission of a line or more in quoted poetry.**

   ▶ William Wordsworth was a poet of the city as well as the countryside. While crossing Westminster Bridge, in London, he wrote:

   Earth has not anything to show more fair:
   Dull would he be of soul who could pass by
   A sight so touching in its majesty:
   . . . .
   Ne'er saw I, never felt, a calm so deep!

4. **Use an ellipsis to indicate a pause or hesitation, but use this device sparingly.**

   ▶ Don't swim in this water . . . unless you're fond of sharks.

2m. Period (.)

1. **Use a period at the end of statements, mild commands, and indirect questions.**

   ▶ The temperature in the cave is a constant 58 degrees.

   ▶ As you tour the cave, please stay on the marked trail.

   ▶ Many people have asked how the cave was first discovered.

2. **Use a period (or periods) with some abbreviations.**

   If an abbreviation comes at the end of a sentence, use only one period. (For more on abbreviations, see section 4 of this handbook.)

3. **Use a period as a decimal point in numbers.**

   ▶ 1.06   ▶ 0.910   ▶ $149.95

2n. Question Mark (?)

1. **Use a question mark at the end of a direct question or request.**

   ▶ Will you please pick up a roll of stamps on your way?

   ▶ A group of citizens discussed the question, "Does our town need a city manager instead of a mayor?"

2. **Use a question mark after each elliptical question in a series.**

    ▶ Should obscenity be controlled on the Internet? If so, by whom? How?

3. **Use a question mark in parentheses after an item that is of doubtful accuracy.**

    ▶ The tunnel from his cell, disguised by a huge poster, was started in 2001(?) but was discovered only after he had fled.

2o. Exclamation Point (!)

An exclamation point indicates strong emotion: pain, fear, surprise, indignation, or excitement. An exclamation point cannot bolster a weak statement or make an argument more convincing. Use exclamation points sparingly; otherwise, they lose their power.

1. **Use an exclamation point to add force to a command or expression of emotion.**

    ▶ "Ouch!"

    ▶ "Help!" Jimmy screamed. "The horse is standing on my foot."

    ▶ WATCH OUT! Deer Crossing

2p. Comma Splices and Fused (Run-on) Sentences

www.mhhe.com/dietsch

Want online coverage of fused sentences and comma splices? Go to:
Editing>Fused Sentences
Editing>Comma Splices

Beginning writers sometimes omit punctuation between clauses in a compound sentence. This error results in a *fused sentence*, sometimes called a *run-on sentence*. A related error is the *comma splice*, which occurs when two clauses are joined (spliced) with a comma. (See chapter 7 for more on compound sentences.)

1. **Punctuate sentences correctly to avoid comma splices.**

    Never use the comma alone to punctuate a long compound sentence. If you use a comma, you must also have a coordinating conjunction. Note, too, that a semicolon is required before a conjunctive adverb such as *however* or *therefore*.

    INCORRECT

    ▷ Terrariums are costly at a flower shop, they are inexpensive to make at home.

    ▷ Terrariums are costly at a flower shop, however, they are inexpensive to make at home.

    CORRECT

    ▶ Terrariums are costly at a flower shop, *but* they are inexpensive to make at home. [coordinating conjunction and a comma]

    ▶ Terrariums are costly at a flower shop; however, they are inexpensive to make at home. [semicolon]

2. **Punctuate sentences correctly to avoid fused (run-on) sentences.**

   INCORRECT

   ▸ The ordinance won wide support it was passed by a two-thirds vote.

   CORRECT

   ▸ The ordinance won wide support; it was passed by a two-thirds vote. [semicolon]

3. Capitalization

If you become lost in the thicket of capitalization, first consult an up-to-date dictionary. If you should find more than one way to capitalize, then let your audience be your guide. In other words, when you are writing for an employer, follow conventional business and technical usage. When writing a college research paper, follow the style your instructor recommends.

www.mhhe.com/dietsch
You'll find additional help regarding capitalization at: Editing>Capitalization

For example, leading dictionaries capitalize both "Roman numerals" and "Arabic numerals." But the *MLA Handbook for Writers of Research Papers,* 6th edition, and the APA *Publication Manual,* 5th edition, do not capitalize "roman numerals" or "arabic numerals."

Once you master the following standard rules of capitalization, you will be able to capitalize most words without consulting other sources.

1. **Capitalize the first word of a sentence.**

   ▸ The sentence above is an example; so is this one.

   Note: In most writing, capitalization of a sentence following a colon is optional, but be consistent. Some documentation styles specify whether such sentences should be capitalized, so if you are writing a research paper following a particular documentation style, see the appropriate guidelines. The Modern Language Association specifies that the second sentence is capitalized if it enunciates a rule or principle, but not if it simply elaborates on the first sentence.

2. **Capitalize proper nouns and trade names.**

   Capitalize the names of people; places; political, racial, and religious groups; institutions and organizations; sacred writings; brand and trade names; ships, planes, and trains; monuments; awards; and specific academic degrees and courses.

▸ Lily O'Neill	▸ the South
▸ the Dead Sea Scrolls	▸ Congress
▸ the Bible (or the Holy Bible)	▸ Calculus 101
▸ Twenty-first Street	▸ University of Michigan
▸ Colorado River	▸ Catholic, Protestant, Jewish

▸ the Koran

▸ Purina Cat Chow

▸ United States Post Office

▸ League of Women Voters

▸ the *Spirit of St. Louis*

▸ Master of English Education

Exceptions: Do not capitalize directions, ideologies, or philosophies (unless derived from the name of an individual—Marxism, for example).

▸ After Caleb left Philadelphia, he drove *south.*

▸ Ava is an *idealist.*

▸ Many Russians feel they were better off under *communism.*

3. **Capitalize proper adjectives and abbreviations.**

Capitalize adjectives and abbreviations derived from proper nouns.

▸ the French language

▸ Palestinian soldiers

▸ Cooper's hawk

▸ Appalachian quilt

▸ Japanese maple

▸ Boston terrier

▸ IRS

▸ UCLA

Note: There are exceptions: for example, *Venice* but *venetian blind, French door* but *french fry.* If in doubt, check a dictionary. See also section 4, "Abbreviations."

4. **Capitalize official and personal titles.**

Capitalize a title (or rank) immediately before the name of a person.

▸ Dr. Stephanie Winters

▸ Professor Celia Kincaid

▸ Justice Sandra Day O'Connor

▸ President Dwight Eisenhower

▸ General Colin Powell

▸ Reverend Jamison

▸ Mr. Jacob Turner

▸ Ms. Shannon Maguire

Exception: When no name is given, do *not* capitalize a title.

▸ The professor encouraged the class to share their opinions.

▸ The president of the United States visited flood victims.

5. **Capitalize titles of literary and other artistic works.**

Ordinarily, capitalize the first and last words as well as all major words in the title of a literary or artistic work.

▸ Last week Mason read the autobiography of William O. Douglas, *Go East, Young Man: The Early Years.*

▸ Erma J. Fisk's *The Peacocks of Baboquivari* is an unusual story of an elderly woman who lived alone for five months in the foothills of Arizona, recording and banding birds.

▶ At the Louvre, we saw Leonardo Da Vinci's *The Mona Lisa*.

Note: Rules for capitalizing titles of works differ from one documentation style to another. If you are writing a research paper and following a particular style, check the appropriate guidelines.

6. **Capitalize calendar items and historical periods.**

Capitalize months, special weeks, days, holidays, and historical periods.

▶ April	▶ New Year's Day
▶ Tuesday	▶ Right-to-Read Week
▶ Easter	▶ Middle Ages
▶ the Renaissance	▶ the Great Depression

Exceptions: Do not capitalize seasons or centuries.

▶ our spring break ▶ the twentieth century ▶ in the winter

7. **Capitalize events and documents.**

Capitalize wars, treaties, constitutions, and other important events and documents.

▶ World War II	▶ Treaty of Versailles
▶ World Series	▶ United States Constitution
▶ Rose Bowl game	▶ Magna Carta
▶ the Louisiana Purchase	▶ Battle of Gettysburg

Exceptions: Do not capitalize laws, theories, or hypotheses:

▶ nature's laws	▶ theory of relativity
▶ code of Hammurabi	▶ Mendelian principles

4. Abbreviations

When writing, avoid unnecessary abbreviations and use them appropriately. Use only conventional abbreviations that can be easily understood. Except for addresses and documentation, spell out the names of countries, states, and possessions in the United States. In desk dictionaries and many other reference sources, you will find a key to the abbreviations used, in either the front or the back of the publication. (For abbreviations used in MLA works-cited entries and in APA entries, see chapter 28.)

www.mhhe.com/dietsch
You'll find more help using abbreviations at:
Editing>Abbreviations

4a. Guidelines for Using Abbreviations

Abbreviation styles may differ significantly from one dictionary to another or from one documentation style to another. If you are writing a research paper and following a particular style, check the appropriate guidelines. *Generally, use abbreviations in a table and a list of works cited, but not in the text of a research paper.* If you do use an abbreviation in the text, be sure to define it. The examples that follow are based upon the *MLA Handbook for Writers of Research Papers,* 6th edition, by Joseph Gibaldi.

1. **Use no periods or spaces between abbreviations of most letters that are capitalized.**

FBI	IBM	MD	BA
PSAT	PhD	RN	AD
IRS	EST	DNA	BC

SOME EXCEPTIONS:

U.S.S.	Scott Felder, Jr.	Mr. Daley
N.P.	S.S.	
J. R. Smith	Ms. Jones	

2. **Use a period after each lowercase letter of most abbreviations that represent a word.**

p.m.	ed.	i.e.
a.m.	r.s.v.p.	e.g.
n.p.	p.p.a.	

THERE ARE MANY EXCEPTIONS:

2nd	mph	rpm

3. **Use a period after most abbreviations that end with lowercase letters.**

govt.	Eng.	wk.	Wed.	assn.
dept.	mkt.	mo.	Mar.	biog.
Mar.	obs.	yr.	fig.	introd.
adj.	arch.	ed.	def.	cont.

4b.   Common Abbreviations and Reference Terms

AD	*anno Domini* (in the year of the Lord). Precedes numerals (AD 16). Follows centuries (eighth century AD).
arch.	archaic
BC	before Christ. Follows numerals (23 BC).
c., ca.	*circa:* "about"; used with approximate dates
comp., comps.	compiled by, compiler(s)

Cong.	Congress
Cong. Rec.	Congressional Record
e.g.	*exempli gratia:* "for example"
et al.	*et alii:* "and others"
ex., exs.	example(s)
DA, DSI	Dissertation Abstracts, Dissertation Abstracts International
diss.	dissertation
doc.	document
H. Doc.	House of Representatives document
ibid.	*ibidem:* "in the same place"
i.e.	*id est:* "that is" (set off by commas)
ips	inches per second (refers to tape recordings)
LC	Library of Congress
ms., mss.	manuscript(s)
par.	paragraph
pref.	preface, preface by
pt.	part
rept., repts.	reported by, report(s)
rpt.	reprint, reprinted by
S. Doc.	Senate document
sec., sect.	section
sic	thus in the source (place in square brackets as an editorial note, otherwise in parentheses)
S. Rept.	Senate report
var.	variant

5.   Numbers

Roman numerals and two basic systems of arabic numbers—ordinary style and technical style—are explained here. Choose the style that is appropriate for your purpose, audience, and occasion. All three systems call for consistency and specify numerals (figures) in certain situations. General guidelines for the ordinary style and the technical style are also shown. (Dictionaries capitalize "Arabic" and "Roman" numerals, but the MLA and APA style do not. For research papers, do not capitalize these terms.)

www.mhhe.com/dietsch

If you want more coverage of using numbers in your writing, visit:
Editing>Numbers

5a. Roman Numerals

1. **When citing pages from a book with lowercase roman numerals, cite the number as written.**

    ▶ page xxvii

    ▶ pages xv–xxiii (range of pages)

2. **When the divisions of a play are written in roman numerals, you may cite as written unless your instructor prefers decimals (see section 5c.2).**

    ▶ King Lear III.i (Act 3, scene 1)

3. **Use uppercase roman numerals for the major divisions of a formal outline (see chapter 5) and after the names of persons in a series.**

    ▶ King Henry IV

    ▶ William A. Dixon III

5b. Ordinary Style of Arabic Numbers

When writing about a topic that requires few numbers, you may use ordinary style. Using this style, you spell out numbers written in two words or less. Use numerals, however, for numbers requiring three or more words.

- One or two words: ten million, four thousand, one hundred, sixty-five, ten, one-half
- Three or more words: 1,537; 101; 5½

Exceptions: Special uses such as in dates, time, addresses, and precise measurements require the use of numerals.

5c. Technical Style of Arabic Numbers

In technical style, numbers are usually written as numerals. If you write a report or paper that requires many numbers, use the technical style. This style is used to express statistical findings and describe scientific projects. For charts, figures, and tables, the technical style is required. Decimals are often used to express precise measurements, but decimals should not be used for data that is normally expressed in fractions.

1. **Express all numbers 10 and above as figures.**

    ▶ seven members   ▶ 10 officials

    Exceptions: Numbers preceding a unit of measurement, as shown below.

2. **Use figures for numbers that precede specific measurements.**

    ▶ 3 miles   ▶ 7 hours   ▶ 6 feet

    ▶ 28½ cubic inches (If the keyboard does not have a fraction key, add a hyphen.)

3. **Unless a unit of measurement is quite short, abbreviate it when preceded by a figure.**

   ▶ 150 hp (horsepower)   ▶ 125 ppm (parts per million)

   ▶ 65 mph (miles per hour)   ▶ 90 wpm (words per minute)

5d. General Guidelines for Ordinary Style and Technical Style of Arabic Numbers

1. **Begin sentences with spelled-out numbers.**

   Never use figures to begin a sentence. Either spell out the number or invert the sentence if the number is large.

   ▶ Seventy-five students were enrolled in CM 111 last quarter.

   ▶ Last quarter 250 students were enrolled in CM 110.

2. **Use numerals in pages and divisions of written works (also see section 5a.2).**

   ▶ page 33   ▶ lines 30–36   ▶ part 5   ▶ chapter 3

   ▶ Act 3   ▶ scene 1   ▶ King Lear 3.1

3. **Spell out round numbers (tens, hundreds, thousands, etc.), estimates, and approximations.**

   ▶ Experts estimate we have enough coal to last two hundred years.

   ▶ Our home cost about thirty thousand dollars to build in 1964.

   ▶ Over eight hundred persons were homeless in Columbus, Ohio, in October 2004.

4. **Use numerals to express decimals and other precise measurements.**

   ▶ 0.625

   ▶ The average age of our students is 27.5 years.

   ▶ The temperature was 98 degrees.

5. **Combine numerals and words to avoid very large figures with many zeros.**

   ▶ 25 million   ▶ 300 billion   ▶ 100 trillion

6. **Spell out the smaller number when two numbers immediately follow in a phrase.**

   ▶ 10 eight-inch planks   ▶ three 5-man crews

7. **If two numbers occur together, either spell out the smaller number or else recast the sentence to separate them.**

▸ In 2004, 3,532 students registered for fall quarter.

▸ In fall quarter 2004, there were 3,532 students registered.

8. **Use numbers correctly in addresses.**

Except for the house number *one*, express house numbers as numerals. If a street name is a number less than eleven, spell out the number. If the street name is number eleven or higher, use a hyphen preceded and followed by a space to separate the house number from the street number.

▸ One Blaine Avenue	▸ 9 Blaine Avenue
▸ 454 East Fifth Street	▸ 4310 - 12th Street

9. **Use numerals in dates and times of the day.**

▸ April 1936	▸ 15 March 2005
▸ March 15, 2005 (not March 15th)	
▸ the 1990s	▸ the 90s (or: the nineties)

▸ 1893-97 [Use a range of years in same century.]

▸ 1897-1907 [Write both years in full for two centuries].

▸ 15 BC	▸ AD 375

Exceptions:

▸ six o'clock [When the word *o'clock* is used, spell out the number.]

▸ the twentieth century

▸ nineteenth-century literature

10. **Use numerals with abbreviations or symbols.**

▸ 7 KB	▸ 10:30 a.m.	▸ $6
▸ 4 lbs.	▸ 125 rpm	▸ 32° centigrade

11. **For percentages, use the percent symbol or spell out percent as appropriate.**

In a sentence, spell out the word *percent* when preceded by a figure. Use the symbol for percent in charts and tables.

▸ 50 percent [in a sentence]	▸ 50% [in charts and tables]

12. **Ordinarily, use numerals for sums of money.**

▸ $1.38	▸ $454.06	▸ $1,564
▸ $5	▸ $10 [Zeros can be omitted for even amounts.]	

▶ eighty-nine cents [amounts less than one dollar in ordinary style]

▶ $0.89, 89¢, or 89 cents [technical style]

Special usage: In legal documents, spell out the sums of money and then write the figures in parentheses:

▶ I agree to pay a monthly rental fee of one hundred and ten dollars ($110).

13. **Be consistent in writing numbers in parallel construction. Write related numbers, such as items in a series, in the same style.**

- Ordinary style: Kaya bought five books, six pens, and two notebooks.
- Technical style: The owner hired a crew of 1 plumber, 4 carpenters, 8 laborers, 1 foreman, and 2 masons.

14. **If a small number is used in the same sentence with a larger number but in a different context, spell out the smaller number.**

▶ Those two technicians are operating machines that cost $105,000 each.

6. Spelling

6a. Spelling Tips

Many people feel inferior because they are poor spellers. They feel less intelligent than people who spell accurately. But not all very bright people are good spellers. For example one ninth-grader, a physician's daughter, was a brilliant student except for her spelling. Her essays were filled with misspelled words. Once, after she had corrected a theme, a word was misspelled in a different way. When asked why she hadn't used a dictionary, she replied, "Oh, I asked Dad." This example illustrates the need for spelling tip number one: *Use a dictionary; don't ask someone how to spell a word.*

The mystery of poor spelling has not been completely solved. But we do know that incorrect pronunciation sometimes leads to incorrect spelling. Students who mispronounce words frequently misspell those same words. The left list below contains some words that are commonly misspelled due to mispronunciation:

Incorrect	Correct
Artic	Arctic
congradulations	congratulations
discribe	describe
goverment	government
enviroment	environment
convience	convenience

www.mhhe.com/dietsch
For online spelling assistance, go to:
Editing>Spelling

secratary	secre*t*ary
wr*e*ck havoc	wr*ea*k havoc
pit*ch*ur	pi*c*ture
then (used in comparison)	th*a*n

If you are unsure of the spelling or pronunciation of a word, look it up in a dictionary. Then practice writing and saying the word correctly. One way is to keep a list of words that you misspell frequently and practice writing them. (Chances are there will be fewer than a dozen.) After you look up the correct spelling of each word on your list, write each one at least a dozen times. That practice will strengthen your mental image of the word.

6b. Association Aids to Improve Spelling

One way to improve spelling is to devise an association that will help you recall the correct spelling. For example, one student who had difficulty with the word *occasion* could not remember whether it had two *c*'s and one *s* or vice versa. She looked the word up several times until she devised this sentence: "Twenty-one is a special occasion." Twenty-one (21) reminded her that occasion had 2 *c*'s and 1 *s*. Listed below are some other associations to help you recall certain spellings.

▸ A *secretary* is a keeper of *secrets.* [An *e* follows the *r* in both words.]

▸ *Separate* has *a rat* in it. [An *a* follows the *p.*]

▸ *there, their, they're*

   there: Without the *t, there* becomes *here.* [Both words refer to location.]

   their: Without the *t, their* becomes *heir.* [Both words refer to ownership.]

   they're: This is a contraction of *they are.* [The apostrophe indicates that *a* has been omitted.]

▸ *principal and principle:* The following sentence should help you remember that *principal* refers to someone or something of importance: "The *principal* points of his speech were. . . ." On the other hand, *principle* refers to a code, law, or doctrine.

   • The *principal* of our school was a *pal* to the students.

   • The Tenth Commandment is a difficult *principle* to follow.

▸ *prejudice:* Just remember that *prejudice* means to *pre-judge* something.

▸ *stationery* and *stationary:*

   Remember that you write on an envelope. [Both *envelope* and *stationery* have *e*'s.]

   Something *stationary* stays in one place. [two *a*'s]

▸ *maneuver:* When you are riding a horse, the mane is in front of you. Just remember that the *mane* is before the *u.*

You may want to devise your own association aids for words that give you trouble.

6c. Other Spelling Aids

▶ **Only one English word ends in** *-sede: supersede.* **Only three words end in** *-ceed: exceed, proceed, succeed.* All other words of similar sound end in *-cede.*

▶ **Drop the final** *e* **in most words when the suffix begins with a vowel:** *chang(e)ing, hop(e)ing, purchas(e)able.*

▶ **Keep the final** *e* **when the suffix begins with a consonant:** *hopeful, vengeful, homeless.* In some instances, however, the *e* is kept: *changeable, knowledgeable, peaceable.* And some words have two spellings: *salable/ saleable, livable/liveable,* and others.

▶ *Pre* **means "before."** *Preschool:* before school

▶ *Per* **means "through, to, for, by each," or "by means of."** *Perceive:* to become aware of directly through any of the senses

▶ *Pro* **means "in favor of" or "acting as."** *Procapitalism:* in favor of capitalism or private ownership of production

Plurals of words ending in *y* are formed as follows:

▶ **When a consonant precedes the final** *y,* **change the** *y* **to** *i* **and add** *es:* *company/companies, lady/ladies, cherry/cherries.*

▶ **When a vowel precedes the** *y,* **keep the** *y* **and add** *s: monkeys, attorneys, byways.*

Exceptions: Plurals for proper names such as the *Berrys, Kellys,* or *Malinys.*

▶ **To form the plural of nouns ending in** *ch, s, sh, x,* **and** *z,* **add** *es: matches, gases, bushes, taxes, buzzes.* This rule also applies to the singular forms of verbs ending in these letters. (Just remember to use *es* for plurals that have the *z* sound.)

6d. Six Ways to Improve Spelling

Probably the biggest factor in any improvement is motivation. If you resolve to refine your spelling skill and follow a plan, you will become a better speller. Here are six techniques to aid you:

1. **Use a dictionary to check words if you are unsure of their spelling.** Carry a spelling checker or pocket dictionary and keep a desk dictionary in a convenient place at home. But remember that computer spelling checkers are limited in their helpfulness. (See "Glossary of Usage," pages H-50– H-57, for similar words that are commonly confused.)

2. **Pronounce words correctly.** If you leave out letters or syllables in pronun- ciation, you may leave them out when writing the word.

3. **Compile your own spelling list.** Review this daily for a few weeks. Look at each word. Then shut your eyes and see if you can spell it correctly.

4. **Write misspelled words correctly several times so that you can visualize their correct spelling in your mind.**

5. **Familiarize yourself with the memory association aids.** Then devise some aids of your own.

6. **As a last resort, if you cannot recognize misspelled words, ask someone to mark them. Then get out the dictionary and correct the spellings your-self. With practice, your spelling ability will improve, and you will be able to catch more of your errors.**

7. Glossary of Usage

Some words in the English language are commonly confused because they look or sound alike. Other words used in conversation are sometimes mistaken for standard usage. This glossary will help you select the appropriate word for your college and business writing. The recommendations here are based on usage listed in current dictionaries. For clarity, misspellings and other unaccepted variations are listed after the standard word.

a, an Use *a* before words starting with a consonant sound. Use *an* before words starting with a vowel sound.

- a bristlecone pine, a history, a quail, a sinkhole
- an aardvark, an egg, an infant, an honorable man

accept, except *Accept* means "to believe," "to approve," or "to take" (as take an offered gift). *Except* means "without" or "excluding."

- Can he *accept* constructive criticism?
- All the children *except* Jane are here.

access, excess The noun *access* is the "ability or right to enter, to use, or to approach." The verb *access* is used in a technological sense, as "to locate data." *Excess* means "too much" or "exceeding that which is normal and sufficient."

- It is impossible to gain direct *access* to the freeway from here.
- Lucinda can *access* those files easily.
- She stored the *excess* bread dough in the refrigerator.

adapt, adept, adopt *Adapt* means "to make suitable for a specific situation." *Adept* means "very skilled; proficient." *Adopt* means "to take up and use as one's own," as an idea, word, or the like. *Adopt* also refers to the process of child adoption.

- Do you think you can *adapt* the part to make it fit?
- Jeff is *adept* at programming.
- When customers complain, Sarah *adopts* the tactic of "A soft answer turneth away wrath."

adverse, averse *Adverse* means "harmful or unfavorable." *Averse* means "unwilling" or "disinclined."

- William has surmounted *adverse* circumstances before.
- Mike is *averse* to risk taking.

advice, advise *Advice* is a noun that means "a view, opinion, or judgment." *Advise* is a verb that means "to counsel," "to inform," or "to recommend."

- His *advice* was to look for another job.
- I really don't know what to *advise.*

affect, effect *Affect* is a verb meaning "to change" or "to influence." *Effect* is usually used as a noun to mean "result." As a verb *effect* means "to make" or "to implement."

- How will that *affect* your decision?
- What will be the *effect* of that decision?
- Can you *effect* an improvement in that procedure?

all ready, already *Already* refers to time, meaning "previously." *All ready* means "prepared" or "available for action."

- Did you *already* clock out?
- Are you *all ready* to leave?

all right *All right* means "satisfactory" or "proper." *Alright* is a common misspelling.

- It is *all right* to go in the kitchen; the floor is dry.

all together, altogether *All together* means "in a group." *Altogether* means "completely."

- The birds huddled *all together* to keep warm.
- Joe's answer was not *altogether* right.

allot, a lot *Allot* means "to parcel out" or "to give a certain portion." *A lot,* used to mean "a large extent, amount, or number," is informal. *Alot* is a common misspelling.

- The government *allots* only one per family.
- He has *a lot* of confidence.
- Jill's grandmother is *a lot* better.

allusion, delusion, illusion An *allusion* is "a reference" (often to a literary work). A *delusion* is a "mistaken idea." An *illusion* is "an erroneous perception of reality."

- He made an *allusion* to Hamlet.
- He suffers from the *delusion* that he is immortal.
- The ghost was an *illusion,* created with special lighting.

among, between Use *among* when referring to three or more units or people. Use *between* when referring to only two.

- Let's keep this secret *among* our family members.
- *Between* you and me, I like his beard.

amount, number *Amount* refers to a quantity or weight. *Number* refers to a numeral, unit, or indefinite quantity of items or individuals.

- The recipe called for a small *amount* of black pepper.
- The crowd *numbers* in the thousands.

an, a See *a, an.*

any, any other *Any* can mean "one, some, every," or "all." *Any other* is used in a comparison. Do not substitute *any* (by itself). The following examples are correct:

- Brian was faster than *any other* runner in his age group.
- You may select *any* of the top prizes.

anyone, any one *Anyone* is a pronoun that means "any person" or, in some instances, "everyone." *Any one* means "whichever one (just one) of a group." *Any one* can refer to a person or a thing.

- *Anyone* may come, not just members.
- *Any one* of the band members can carry the flag.

appraise, apprise *Appraise* means "to evaluate or estimate the value." *Apprise* means "to give notice to or inform."

- Will you *appraise* this emerald ring for me?
- Did you *apprise* the prisoner of his rights?

assure, ensure, insure *Assure* means "to inform positively." *Ensure* means "to make sure or certain." *Insure* means "to cover with insurance." *Insure* also means "to make certain, especially by taking precautions."

- I *assure* you that every precaution will be taken.
- Checking the map beforehand will *ensure* that you find the right road.
- Did you *insure* the contents of your house?

averse See *adverse, averse.*

awhile, a while *Awhile* is an adverb that means "a short time." *A while,* which consists of an article and a noun, means "a period of time." (The preposition *for* may be used with *a while.*)

- He stopped *awhile* to rest. (not *for awhile*)
- Don't rush off—stay for *a while.*

beside, besides *Beside* means "next to." *Besides* means "also."

- The scissors are lying *beside* my sewing basket.
- *Besides* my fishing equipment, I'm taking a picnic lunch.

between See *among, between.*

breath, breathe *Breath* is a noun; *breathe* is a verb. Both refer to inhalation and exhalation.

- The speech instructor advised taking a deep *breath* before starting to speak.
- *Breathe* deeply as you work out.

capital, capitol *Capital* refers to the "official place or city of government" or an "amount of money." *Capitol* refers to the "building that houses the official government offices."

- Denver is the *capital* of Colorado.
- We need more *capital* to fund the project.
- Sue visited the *capitol* building during her trip to the state *capital.*

censor, censure *Censor* is "to examine books, films, or other materials to remove or suppress what is considered objectionable." *Censure* is "to criticize severely or blame."

- The school board plans to *censor* books purchased for the school.
- The editorial *censured* a city council member for his failure to attend meetings regularly.

cite, sight, site *Cite* means "to quote." *Sight* refers to the ability to see or view. *Site* refers to location, as a building site.

- Can you *cite* his exact words?
- Can you *sight* Venus above the evening horizon?
- They selected a lovely wooded *site* for their new home.

complement, compliment *Complement* means "to complete or bring to perfection." *Compliment* means "to express praise."

- That floral arrangement *complements* your table setting.
- Brad *complimented* Cindy on her new shoes.

conscience, conscious *Conscience* is "the awareness of a moral or ethical aspect of one's conduct" and the desire "to prefer right over wrong." *Conscious* refers to "awareness of one's environment and existence."

- Jeannette returned the wallet to its owner to relieve her *conscience*.
- Is the patient *conscious* yet?

continual, continuous *Continual* means "recurring regularly or often." *Continuous* means "uninterrupted."

- Uncle Jake's *continual* complaining made our visit unpleasant.
- The flow of fresh air throughout the building is *continuous*.

council, counsel *Council* refers to a group of people who are delegated "to serve in an administrative, legislative, or advisory capacity." *Counsel*, as noun or verb, refers to advice.

- Anthony is a member of the town *council*.
- The admissions office *counsels* students.
- Lawyers charge for their *counsel*.

criteria, criterion A *criterion* is a "standard, rule, or test upon which a judgment or decision can be based." *Criteria* is the plural of *criterion*.

- She gave only one *criterion* for the job: a strong back.
- He stated six *criteria* for the upcoming performance evaluation.

delusion See *allusion, delusion, illusion.*

effect, affect See *affect, effect.*

emigrate, immigrate When people *emigrate*, they leave their homeland to reside elsewhere. When they *immigrate*, they enter a different country to reside.

- My paternal ancestors, five brothers, *emigrated* from Wales in the late 1700s.
- They *immigrated* to the United States and traveled to the territory that later became Ohio.

eminent, imminent *Eminent* means "of high rank, station, or quality." *Imminent* means "about to occur, impending."

- Today is the birthday of that *eminent* inventor Thomas A. Edison.
- Skating on thin ice poses an *imminent* danger.

enthusiastic *Enthusiastic,* meaning to have great excitement or interest, is standard usage. *Enthused* is used only colloquially.

- Cody was *enthusiastic* about traveling to the Rocky Mountains.

except See *accept, except.*

excess See *access, excess.*

explicit, implicit *Explicit* means "fully and clearly expressed; leaving nothing implied." *Implicit* means "implied or understood though not directly expressed."

- The doctor's directions were *explicit:* "Take one tablet with a full glass of water after meals."
- The company president has *implicit* trust in Sheila's judgment.

farther, further *Farther* refers to "physical distance" and *further* to a nonphysical dimension such as distance in time.

- We drove *farther* than usual the second day of our trip.
- If we go *further* back a few generations, we find other family members who also suffered from breast cancer.

fewer, less *Fewer* is used in comparisons to refer to "individual units, things that can be counted." *Less* is used in comparisons to mean a smaller amount or "a mass of measurable extent."

- *Fewer* people attended the state fair this year than last year.
- Opals cost much *less* than diamonds of the same size.

flaunt, flout *Flaunt* means "to parade or display ostentatiously." *Flout* means "to show contempt for" or "to scorn."

- Lorrie *flaunted* her new engagement ring.
- Timothy *flouted* the dress code.

further See *farther, further.*

get *Get* means "to receive" or "to bring." Avoid the many colloquial uses of *get* in college and business writing. (See a dictionary for other examples of colloquial usage.)

- Standard: Will you *get* a gallon of milk when you go out?
- Colloquial: I hope the frost doesn't *get* our garden.
- Colloquial: That really *gets* to me!

good, well *Good* is an adjective meaning "positive or desirable." *Well* is often used as an adverb to mean "satisfactorily or sufficiently" or "skillfully or proficiently." *Well* is also used as an adjective to mean "a satisfactory condition; right or proper."

- Jerry received *good* news this morning.
- Jeremy did *well* on his calculus exam.
- Henry is *well;* he has completely recovered from pneumonia.
- The project is going *well.*

hanged, hung People are *hanged.* Objects are *hung.*

- The convicted murderer was *hanged.*
- Derek *hung* the painting over the fireplace.

idea, ideal An *idea* is "a thought." An *ideal* is "a principle" or "a conception or model of something in its absolute perfection."

- Suddenly he had a delightful *idea.*
- Her *ideal* husband would be a wonderful father.
- Always be true to your *ideals.*

illusion See *allusion, delusion, illusion.*

implicit See *explicit, implicit.*

its, it's *Its* is the possessive form of *it. It's* is a contraction of *it is.*

- The dog has lost *its* collar.
- *It's* over seventy miles to the next town.

leave, let *Leave* means "to go out or away from." *Let* means "to permit or allow."

- Will you *leave* Jiffy at the kennel when you go to the lake?
- Please *let* me help you with those packages.

less See *fewer, less.*

let See *leave, let.*

loose, lose *Lose* is a verb meaning "to mislay." *Loose* is an adjective meaning "not tight" or "unconfined."

- Did you *lose* an earring?
- My watchband is too *loose.*
- An orangutan was *loose* in the park.

medium, media *Medium* is (1) an "intermediate course," the midpoint between two extremes; (2) a way that something is "transmitted or carried"; (3) "an agency by which something is accomplished or conveyed or transferred." *Media* is the plural of *medium* and takes a plural verb.

- The Internet is a *medium* that relays daily stock market reports.
- The *media* frequently refer to the escapades of the royal family.

moral, morale *Moral* is an adjective that refers to "judgment of the goodness or badness of human action and character." *Morale* is a noun that means "the state of the spirits of a person or group."

- The *moral* code of society seems to be changing.
- Employee *morale* is high at XYZ Company.

number See *amount, number.*

passed, past *Passed* is a verb that means "having moved on; proceeded." *Past* as an adverb means "beyond" and as a noun or adjective refers to time that is over. Do not write "*past* history" because all history is past.

- Jerry *passed* the bakery without stopping.

- Jerry drove *past* the bakery without stopping.
- Let's forget the *past* and look to the future.

patience, patients *Patience* is the ability to "bear pain, provocation, or annoyance with calmness." *Patients* refers to people who "receive medical attention, care, or treatment."

- *Patience* is a quality that is learned.
- The physician saw thirty-seven *patients* yesterday.

personal, personnel *Personal* refers to the private matters of an individual. *Personnel* refers to a group of people who work for an organization. (Note that *personnel* has two *n*'s and two *e*'s.)

- Please don't ask *personal* questions.
- Their *personnel* are very courteous.

precede, proceed *Precede* means "to go before." *Proceed* means "to go" or "to continue."

- The Rose Bowl game *precedes* the Orange Bowl game.
- Let's *proceed* with the meeting.

principal, principle See "Association Aids to Improve Spelling," page H-48.

quiet, quite *Quiet* means "free of noise." *Quite* means "very; entirely."

- Our dorm is rarely *quiet*.
- Your homemade apple pie is *quite* tasty.
- It is *quite* all right to park there.

quotation, quote *Quote* is a verb that means "to repeat or copy the words of [another]," usually citing the source. *Quotation* is a noun meaning "the act of quoting" or "a passage quoted."

- Do you plan to *quote* John F. Kennedy in your speech?
- A *quotation* from Winston Churchill might make an effective introduction.

real, really *Real* is an adjective meaning "genuine or authentic," "free of pretense or falsehood." (Avoid using *real* to mean "very.") *Really* is an adverb meaning "truly; genuinely."

- Her diamond is *real*.
- *Really*, I can't go with you.

regardless *Regardless* means "in spite of everything; anyway." *Irregardless* is redundant and nonstandard.

- Many people neglect to buckle their seat belts, *regardless* of the danger.

sight See *cite, sight, site*.

sometime, some time, sometimes *Sometime* means "an indefinite or unstated time." *Some time* refers to an amount of time. *Sometimes* means "occasionally."

- Stop in *sometime*.
- I haven't seen him for *some time*.
- *Sometimes* I feed the elephants at the city zoo.

stationary, stationery *Stationary* means "not moving" or "not capable of being moved." *Stationery* refers to writing materials.

- The tables in that restaurant are *stationary*.
- Would you like some monogrammed *stationery* for Christmas?

than, then *Than* is a conjunction indicating a comparison. *Then* is an adverb indicating time.

- Harrison likes pistachio ice cream better *than* chocolate.
- I will meet you *then*.

their, there, they're *Their* is the possessive form of *they*. *There* is an adverb that refers to place. (*There* can also be used in several other ways.) *They're* is a contraction of *they are*.

- *Their* cars are parked on the street.
- Do you see that ten-dollar bill lying *there* in the grass?
- *They're* the third couple from the left.

to, too, two *To* is a preposition meaning "toward," "in contact with," "in front of," or "constituting"; or it can be the sign of an infinitive. *Too* means "also" or "more than enough." *Two* is the whole number following *one*; a couple.

- I walked *to* the town square.
- *To* ensure you arrive safely, check the cable that is towing your glider.
- May I go, *too?*
- *Two* robins built a nest.

try to *Try to* means "to attempt." *Try and* is not generally accepted usage.

- *Try to* pull up the cap of the bottle after the arrows meet.

two See *to, too, two.*

which, who Use *which* when referring to an object or an animal. Use *who* when referring to a person. (For more information about usage, see section 1b.7 on pronouns.)

- The black horse, *which* is near the barn, belongs to Stanley.
- *Who* did you say is calling?

who, whom *Who* is in the subjective case, *whom* in the objective case.

- These are the men *who* you thought were responsible. [*who* were responsible]
- These are the men *whom* you chose for the job. [you chose *whom*]

who's, whose *Who's* is a contraction of *who is* or *who has*. *Whose* is the possessive form of *who*.

- *Who's* the best candidate for the position?
- *Whose* dalmatian is that?

your, you're *Your* is the possessive form of *you*. *You're* is the contraction of *you are*.

- Will you take *your* car?
- *You're* the winner of a trip to Tahiti.

Credits

Angelou, Maya. "Momma's Encounter" from *I Know Why the Caged Bird Sings* by Maya Angelou. Copyright © 1969 and renewed 1997 by Maya Angelou. Used by permission of Random House, Inc.

Baker, James T. "How Do We Find the Student in a World of Academic Gymnasts and Worker Ants?" from *The Chronicle of Higher Education,* 1982. Reprinted by permission of the author.

Baxter, Charles. "Scheherazade" from *A Relative Stranger* by Charles Baxter. Copyright © 1990 by Charles Baxter. Used by permission of W. W. Norton & Company, Inc.

Brown, Norman. "Mind Over Munchies." Copyright © 1992 by Norman Brown. Reprinted by permission.

Carter, Carol J. "Write Your Own Success Story" adapted from *Majoring in the Rest of Your Life* by Carol Carter. Copyright © 1990, 1995 by Carol Carter. Reprinted by permission of Carol Carter www.lifebound.com.

Carter, Stephen. "The Insufficiency of Honesty" from *Integrity* by Stephen Carter. Copyright © 1996 by Stephen L. Carter. Reprinted by permission of Basic Books, a member of Perseus Books, L.L.C.

Ciardi, John. "Dawn Watch" from *Manner of Speaking* by John Ciardi. Copyright © 1982 by John Ciardi. Reprinted by permission of the Ciardi Family Trust.

Cofer, Judith Ortiz. "The Myth of the Latin Woman: I Just Met A Girl Named Maria" from *The Latin Deli: Prose and Poetry* by Judith Ortiz Cofer. Copyright © 1993 by Judith Ortiz Cofer. Used by permission of the University of Georgia Press. All rights reserved.

Cullen, Countee. "Incident" by Countee Cullen. Copyright held by Amistad Research Center and administered by Thompson and Thompson, New York, NY.

Davis, Lisa. "Where Do We Stand?" by Lisa Davis. Copyright © 1990 *In Health®* Magazine. For subscriptions please call 1-800-274-2522.

Dickinson, Emily. First verse of "Success Is Counted Sweetest . . ." Reprinted by permission of the publishers and Trustees of Amherst College from *The Poems of Emily Dickinson*, Thomas H. Johnson, ed. Cambridge, MA: The Belknap Press of Harvard University Press, copyright © 1951, 1955, 1979 by the President and Fellows of Harvard College.

Dickinson, Emily. "I Never Hear the Word" reprinted by permission of the publishers and Trustees of Amherst College from *The Poems of Emily Dickinson*, Thomas H. Johnson, ed., Cambridge, Mass.: The Belknap Press of Harvard University Press, Copyright © 1951, 1955, 1979 by the President of Fellows of Harvard College.

Dunbar, Ian. "Fast Track to Perfection" as appeared in *Dog Fancy*, April 1999. Copyright © 1999 by Ian Dunbar. Reprinted by permission of the author.

Gage, Nicholas. "The Teacher Who Changed My Life" by Nicholas Gage. Reprinted by permission of Nicholas Gage.

Gibbons, Euell. "How to Cook a Carp" from *Stalking the Wild Asparagus* by Euell Gibbons. Copyright © 1962 by Euell Gibbons. Used by permission of Alan C. Hood & Company, Inc., P.O. Box 775 Chambersberg, PA 17201.

Gold, Matea and David Ferrell. "Going for Broke." *The Los Angeles Times*, 12/13/98. Copyright © 1998 Los Angeles Times. Reprinted by permission of Tribune Media Services.

Greenburg, Dan. "Sound and Fury." Copyright © by Dan Greenburg. Published in the United States by *Men's Health* Magazine. All rights reserved. Used with permission of Sheldon Folgelman Literary Agency.

Guiterman, Arthur. "On the Vanity of Earthly Greatness." Reprinted by permission of Louise H. Schlove.

Hegi, Ursula. "Doves," reprinted by permission of Simon & Schuster from *Hotel of the Saints* by Ursula Hegi. Copyright © 2001 by Ursula Hegi.

Henninger, Daniel. "Street-Fightin' Men Stomp the Quiet Virtues." *The Wall Street Journal*, December 3, 2004, p. A18. Copyright © 2004 Dow Jones, Inc. Reprinted by permission of *The Wall Street Journal* via Copyright Clearance Center.

Houston, Jean. "The Art of Acknowledgement" from *The Possible Human* by Jean Houston. Copyright © 1982 by Jean Houston. Used by permission of Jeremy P. Tarcher, a division of Penguin Putnam, Inc.

Hubbell, Sue. "Caterpillar Afternoon" from *A Country Year: Living the Questions* by Sue Hubbell. Copyright © 1983, 1984, 1985, 1986 by Sue Hubbell. Reprinted by permission of Houghton Mifflin Company. All rights reserved.

Joso. "The Barley Field." From *An Introduction to Haiku* by Harold G. Henderson. Copyright © 1958 by Harold G. Henderson. Used by permission of Doubleday, a division of Random House, Inc.

Jordan, Barbara. "Becoming Educated" from *A Self-Portrait*. Copyright © 1979 by Barbara Jordan. Reprinted by permission of the Wendy Weil Agency.

Kübler-Ross, Elisabeth. "The Emotional Quadrant," reprinted with the permission of Simon & Schuster, Inc. from *On Children and Death* by Elisabeth Kübler-Ross. Copyright © 1983 by Elisabeth Kübler-Ross, M.D.

Lee, Andrea. "Black and Well-To-Do" by Andrea Lee. *The New York Times*, 2/17/82. Copyright © 1982 by The New York Times Co. Reprinted by permission.

Levine, Dan. "Wal-Mart's Big City Blues" by Dan Levine reprinted from the November 24, 2003 issue of *The Nation*. For subscription information call 1-800-333-8536. Portions of each week's magazine can be accessed at http://www.thenation.com.

Lewis, C. S. "We Have No 'Right' to Happiness" from *God in the Docks* by C. S. Lewis copyright © C. S. Lewis Pte. Ltd. 1970. Extract reprinted by permission.

Lopate, Phillip. "A Nonsmoker With a Smoker" from *Against Joie de Vivre: Personal Essays* by Phillip Lopate. Copyright © 1989 by Phillip Lopate. Reprinted by permission of The Wendy Weil Agency, Inc.

MacLeish, Archibald. "Ars Poetica" from *Collected Poems 1917–1982* by Archibald MacLeish. Copyright © 1985 by The Estate of Archibald MacLeish. Reprinted by permission of Houghton Mifflin Company. All rights reserved.

Malanga, Steven. "The War on Wal-Mart." This article, reprinted from *The Wall Street Journal* (4/7/04) was adapted from the Spring 2004 issue of the Manhattan Institute's *City Journal* (www.city-journal.org) where Steven Malanga is a contributing editor.

Mannes, Marya. "How Do You Know It's Good?" from *Will It Sell?* by Marya Mannes. Copyright © 1962 by Marya Mannes, copyright renewed 1990.

Norman, Liane Ellison. "Pedestrian Students and High-Flying Squirrels." *Center Magazine*, 1978. Reprinted by permission of the Center for the Study of Democratic Institutions.

Raspberry, William. "The Handicap of Definition" from *Instilling Positive Images* by William Raspberry. Copyright © 1982 by The Washington Post Writer's Group. Reprinted with permission.

Raymond, David. "On Being 17, Bright, and Unable to Read." *The New York Times*, 4/25/76. Copyright © 1976 by The New York Times Co. Reprinted by permission.

Roiphe, Anne. "Why Marriages Fail" by Anne Roiphe. Reprinted by permission of International Creative Management, Inc. Copyright © 1983 by Anne Roiphe.

Rose, Robert. "For Welfare Parents, Scrimping Is Illegal" from *The Wall Street Journal*, 1990. Copyright © 1990 by Dow Jones & Co., Inc. Reproduced with permission of Dow Jones & Co. Inc. via Copyright Clearance Center.

Sachs, Andrea, "When the Lullaby Ends." Copyright © 1990 Time, Inc. Reprinted by permission.

Sakamoto, Nancy Masterson. "Conversational Ball-games" from *Polite Fictions: Why Japanese and Americans Seem Rude to Each Other* by Nancy Masterson Sakamoto. Reprinted by permission of Kinseido Publishing Co. Ltd.

Sandburg, Carl. "Grass" from *Cornhuskers* by Carl Sandburg. Copyright 1918 by Holt, Rinehart and Winston and renewed 1946 by Carl Sandburg. Reprinted by permission of Harcourt, Inc.

Sone, Monica. "The Stubborn Twig: My Double Dose of Schooling" from *Nisei Daughter* by Monica Sone. Copyright © 1953 by Monica Sone. Copyright renewed 1981 by Monica Sone. By permission of Little, Brown and Company (Inc.).

Sora, "The Barley Field." From *An Introduction to Haiku* by Harold G. Henderson. Copyright © 1958 by Harold G. Henderson. Used by permission of Doubleday, a division of Random House, Inc.

Sullivan, Andrew. "The Pursuit of Happiness: Four Revolutionary Words." Copyright © 2002 by Andrew Sullivan. Reprinted with the permission of the Wylie Agency, Inc.

Tan, Amy. "Mother Tongue." Copyright © 1990 by Amy Tan. First appeared in *The Threepenny Review*. Reprinted by permission of the author and the Sandra Dijkstra Literary Agency.

Tannen, Deborah. "Gender Gap in Cyberspace" from *Newsweek*, 4/16/94. Copyright © 1994 Newsweek, Inc. All rights reserved. Reprinted by permission.

Updike, John. "Still of Some Use" from *Trust Me* by John Updike. Copyright © 1987 by John Updike. Used by permission of Alfred A. Knopf, a division of Random House, Inc.

Vare, Ethlie and Greg Ptacek. Introduction from *Mothers of Invention* by Ethlie Ann Vare and Greg Ptacek. Copyright © 1987 by Ethlie Ann Vare and Greg Ptacek. Reprinted by permission of HarperCollins Publishers Inc.

Vest, Jason, Warren Cohen and Mike Tharp. "Road Rage," June 2, 1997. Copyright © 1997 U.S. News and World Report, L.P. Reprinted with permission.

Weiss, Phillip. "How to Get Out of a Locked Trunk" by Phillip Weiss. Copyright © 1992 by Harper's Magazine. All rights reserved. Reproduced from the 1992 issue by special permission.

Welty, Eudora. Reprinted by permission of the publisher from *One Writer's Beginnings* by Eudora Welty, pp. 73–75, Cambridge, Mass.: Harvard University Press, Copyright © 1983, 1984 by Eudora Welty.

Wilbur, Richard. Excerpt from "Clearness" in *Ceremony and Other Poems*. Copyright © 1955 and renewed 1978 by Richard Wilbur. Reprinted by permission of Harcourt, Inc.

Author-Title Index

Note: Student writers and works are indicated by an asterisk.*

Subject Index

INVITATION FOR SUBMISSIONS

Instructors are invited to submit student writing for possible publication in future editions of *Reasoning and Writing Well*. All submissions will be read and carefully considered. Entire papers, as well as sample paragraphs, introductions, and conclusions are welcome.

All submissions should be typed, double-spaced, and accompanied by the following information:

- Heading: Submission for future editions of *Reasoning and Writing Well*.
- The student writer's name, permanent street address, e-mail address, and telephone number
- The submitting instructor's name, school affiliation, telephone number, and e-mail address

Please send submissions to either the street or e-mail address below:

Betty Mattix Dietsch
c/o Joshua Feldman, McGraw-Hill English
Two Penn Plaza, 20th Floor
New York, NY 10121

<joshua_feldman@mcgraw-hill.com>